This is the first study in English of Altichiero, one of the most important painters of the later Italian trecento. Altichiero, a native of Verona, worked exclusively for the despotic rulers of Verona and Padua and their courtiers, translating their chivalric aspirations into fresco cycles of extraordinary beauty and originality and serving as the favourite artist of the proponents of the revival of classical learning at these courts. Altichiero, whose work is indebted to Giotto, worked in close collaboration with Petrarch, the greatest of early Italian humanists, and with his friends and followers in Padua. In addition to an informative catalogue and bibliography, the book also contains a wealth of illustrations in both colour and black and white, which bring the work and world of Altichiero to life.

John Richards is Lecturer in the History of Art at the University of Glasgow.

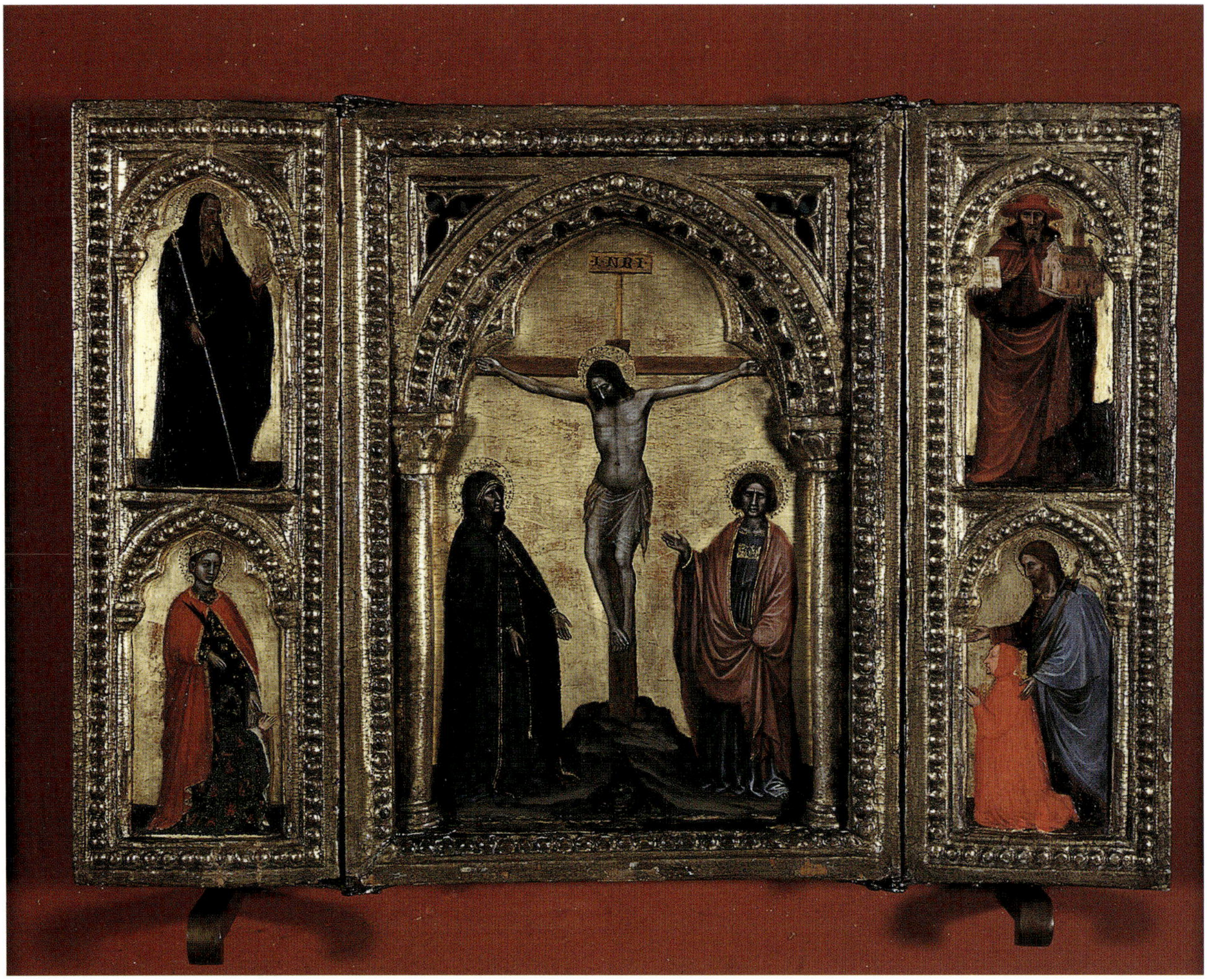

Altichiero: *Crucifixion* triptych. Virginia Museum of Fine Arts, Richmond, VA. The Arthur and Margaret Glasgow Fund.

ALTICHIERO

An artist and his patrons in the Italian trecento

John Richards

CAMBRIDGE
UNIVERSITY PRESS

PUBLISHED BY THE PRESS SYNDICATE OF THE UNIVERSITY OF CAMBRIDGE
The Pitt Building, Trumpington Street, Cambridge CB2 1RP, United Kingdom

CAMBRIDGE UNIVERSITY PRESS
The Edinburgh Building, Cambridge CB2 2RU, UK http://www.cup.cam.ac.uk
40 West 20th Street, New York, NY 10011–4211, USA http://www.cup.org
10 Stamford Road, Oakleigh, Melbourne 3166, Australia

First published 2000

Printed in the United Kingdom at the University Press, Cambridge

Typeset in Plantin 11/14 [SE]

A catalogue record for this book is available from the British Library

ISBN 0 521 35649 0 hardback

For R. B. R. and K. P. R.

Contents

Illustrations

DRAWINGS

COLOUR PLATES

FIGURES

PLATES

From page 267

All works by Altichiero unless otherwise stated

Photographic sources

Biblioteca Vaticana, Rome. Figs. 30–8
Bibliothèque Nationale, Paris. Pls. 35–8
British Museum, London. Pls. 3, 4 and 5
Centro Studi Antoniani, Padua. Pls. 39–43, 50b, 50c, 51b, 51c, 51d, 52–75
Giorgio Deganello, Padua I–VIII
Robert Gibbs. Figs. 81 and 83
Hessische Landes-und-Hochschul-Bibliothek, Darmstadt. Fig. 58. Pls. 21–32, 34
Istituto Centrale per il Catalogo e la Documentazione, Rome. Figs. 17 and 18
Kunsthistorisches Institut, Florence. Figs. 19–24, 52, 54
Museo Civico, Padua. Figs. 75–80. Pls. 33, 44, 46, 77–80, 82, 85–6, 88–93, 95–8, 101, 103, 105–9, 111, 113, 115, 117–19
P. Gerhard Ruf, Assisi. Fig. 26
Service Photographique de la Réunion des Musées Nationaux, Paris. Pls. 2, 15
Soprintendenza, Verona. Fig. 51, Pl. 17
Sotheby's, London. Pl. 1
Tommasoli, Verona. Pl. 16
Umberto Tomba, Verona. Pls. 6–14, 122
Virginia Museum of Fine Arts, Richmond, VA. Pls. 124–7

Preface

The fact that this is not only the first book on Altichiero in the English language, but one of only a handful of discussions of his work on any scale ever published in English, points to the extraordinary tenacity with which the Vasarian view of trecento art history has held sway outside Italy. Berenson's most entertaining – and misleading – book, *Homeless Paintings of the Renaissance*, in which the whole of the exuberantly inventive Bolognese school is dismissed in favour of the most bone-headed and slavish followers of Jacopo di Cione, is a representative sample. Berenson's own assessment of Altichiero in his general survey of Renaissance painting is generous but essentially misconceived, judging him from a position which awards him gold stars for supposedly Florentine virtues of plasticity and monumental form but which slaps his wrists for a northern inability to concentrate. Giotto, Berenson thinks, would never have allowed a *dog* at the Crucifixion. It is especially ironic that Altichiero's wider reputation should have been so long and so effectively stifled by a neo-Vasarian tradition rooted in the cult of Giotto maintained by men amongst whom and for whom Altichiero himself worked. To have revived and reinvented the principles of Giottesque painting for the later trecento, only to be relegated to footnote status in a history increasingly couched in terms of Florentine hegemony, is hard indeed.

Altichiero's name, never entirely forgotten by the antiquarians and civic historians of the Veneto, was revived in modern times by Italian and German scholars, stimulated by Ernest Förster's actions in freeing the frescoes of the Oratory of S. Giorgio in Padua from their coat of Napoleonic whitewash. In 1841 Förster produced a book on S. Giorgio; an Italian version by Pietro Selvatico followed in 1846. Selvatico later discussed the frescoes in his own 1869 guide to Padua, and it is on Förster's and Selvatico's work, together with Schubring's monograph of 1898 and the studies of Julius von Schlosser, that the modern recognition of Altichiero's importance is based. Scholars of more recent times have insisted on Altichiero's exceptional status amongst trecento painters – for Pietro Toesca he was second only to Giotto himself – and the 1960s saw monographs by Plinia Pettenella, Gian Lorenzo Mellini and Hanno Walter Kruft. Much of this material followed the lead of the nineteenth-century accounts in treating as the central issue the tradition, stemming from Savonarola in the mid-fifteenth century, that Altichiero collaborated with another artist, variously Avanzi or Avanzo. In 1963 and 1966 P. Antonio Sartori OFM Conv. published most of the available documentary evidence surrounding this question, together with much other valuable material. Since then Altichiero's artistic personality has come increasingly sharply into focus and the question of collaboration has been put in its proper place as an important, but secondary, issue.

I should say a word about the scope of this book. The corpus of Altichiero's work is easily defined and needs little in the way of protracted attributional wrangling. I have accordingly used the catalogue section as a convenient place for material relevant to the textual discussion, not as a location for further argument on any scale. Some readers might find the space devoted to two fresco cycles which no longer exist rather baffling. I can only emphasise a point which is made in greater detail in the relevant chapters, that these cycles on themes from the Antique, the Sala Grande in Verona and the Sala Virorum Illustrium in Padua, are of cardinal importance in the context of early Renaissance cultural history, and of fundamental significance in Altichiero's career; the most important things, I would argue, that he did. What they are, or what they were, can be discussed, so I think they should be discussed. To have omitted them, or to have alluded to them briefly, would have been to obscure any sense of Altichiero's career as a whole by failing to give proper consideration to the heart of his achievement. The two surviving Paduan cycles, splendid as they are, must at the time have taken second place to the frescoes in which Altichiero gave visual expression to the humanist pretensions of the Scaligeri and Carrara *signori*. The overriding purpose of this book is to emphasise not just Altichiero's extraordinary qualities as a painter, but his importance in a wider humanist context, as the first European artist to have served and articulated the needs of a Renaissance whose doors were previously all but closed to the visual arts.

Just over 600 years have passed since the deaths of Altichiero and his Paduan patron Bonifacio Lupi. Both were illustrious in their lifetimes, and their subsequent fame has not been commensurate with their virtues. If this book goes some way to redressing the balance, it will have succeeded. It is not too presumptuous, I think, to borrow some of the magnificent trecento rhetoric inscribed on Bonifacio's tomb and apply it to Altichiero too:

> QUO NON PRAESTANTIOR ALTER . . . GELIDUM LICET OSSA SEPULCRUM
> STRINGAT ET AETERNUM SUA VIVET FAMA PER AEVUM

(Please note that Latin and Italian sources are quoted throughout this book in the original, or in translation, according to the importance of the exact wording. In some cases, even where the text is translated, key words and phrases in the original language are given in parentheses.)

Acknowledgements

My thanks are due to many individuals and institutions. I am grateful for the financial assistance of the Scottish Education Department from 1982 to 1985, to the Whistler Fund for enabling me to begin my research in Italy in 1982, and to the Delmas Foundation for a generous travel grant in 1988. Research funds from the School of Art History of the University of St Andrews enabled me to complete the acquisition of my illustrations on an appropriately ample scale. I owe a great deal to the directors and staffs of the Vatican Library, the Biblioteca Capitolare and the Biblioteca Civica in Verona, the Biblioteca Civica in Padua, the Bibliothèque Nationale in Paris, the Hessische Landes-und-Hochschul-Bibliothek in Darmstadt, the Archivi di Stato in Verona and Padua, and to the staff of Glasgow University Library and the library of the Department of History of Art.

In Verona I received invaluable help from Sergio Marinelli of the Castelvecchio, who enabled me to study the soffit frescoes of the Sala Grande while they were in storage, from his successor Paola Marini, who helped me trace several elusive photographs, and from Pier-Paolo Brugnoli, who long ago shepherded me round normally inaccessible parts of the old Scaligeri palace complex. In Padua Father Livio Poloniato, former director of the Centro Studi Antoniani, has been unfailingly helpful on many occasions. His successor as director, Fr. Luciano Bertazzo, was equally supportive, and the Centro has been extraordinarily generous with its photographic archive. I am grateful to Fr. Claudio Gottardello for allowing me to take photographs inside the Santo, and to the staffs of all the photographic departments and museums from whom I have sought illustrative material.

I have had countless useful conversations with people who are too numerous to mention by name, but I should single out Robin Simon, the pioneer of Altichiero scholarship in the English-speaking world, whose article on the documents published by P. Antonio Sartori in the 1960s remains of seminal importance, and who has always been ready to share his thoughts on Altichiero. I learned more from two or three brief conversations with Professor Benjamin Kohl of Vassar College than from months of reading; I am especially grateful for his generous provision of access to unpublished drafts of his eagerly awaited book on Padua under the Carraresi. I first encountered Altichiero in the pages of John White's trecento volume in the Pelican series and a tribute to his enthusiastic recognition of Altichiero's status must find a place here. My more or less instantly acquired Altichiero fervour was disciplined and shaped in Robert Gibbs's trecento seminars at Glasgow University, a process which has endured in more informal circumstances ever since. I cannot imagine having had the confidence or the energy to keep myself going without Robert's tireless encouragement.

As I was writing, the news of Andrew Martindale's death shocked the whole world of Renaissance studies. Since my first meeting with him in 1989 he offered constant, pertinent, and active support for this project. I have included, more or less wholesale, a letter from him as a footnote to chapter 4. The summary it offers of a particular and rather tangled problem is characteristically both searching and elegant. It is typical, too, of the generosity of a great scholar that he remembered my interest in the MS under discussion and did something about it. I wish he could have read this book in its finished form.

That it ever reached such form is due to the extraordinary care and patience with which the editing, copy-editing and design teams at the Press have treated it. If they have sometimes felt that this book was older than the rocks among which it sits, I know how they feel and also how much I owe them.

I must finally express my gratitude to my wife Helena, for her support, for her forbearance in the face of an inexorable tide of paper, and for her tolerance of this long dead stranger with whose cause I seem to have been bound up for half a lifetime.

As this book goes to press work is continuing on a full-scale cleaning and restoration of Altichiero's two surviving fresco cycles in Padua. Times like this have their effects on the nerves of those who love the objects about which they write. It is my hope that the newly resplendent qualities of the S. Giacomo and S. Giorgio frescoes will go a long way towards restoring Altichiero to his true place in art history. The Paduans have an extraordinary wealth of trecento fresco painting of the highest quality in their care. The responsibility must feel as heavy as the rewards are great. I wish those in charge of the programme well.

I

ALTICHIERO DA VERONA

Altichiero's career as we know it begins with a commission so prestigious that it must either have established or confirmed him as the leading painter of Verona. The surviving fragments of the frescoes of the Sala Grande reveal an experienced master in full command of his art, well suited to the ambitious demands of his Scaligeri patrons. His very position as *de facto* court painter must, one would have thought, have been founded on a body of earlier work, some perhaps also for the Scaligeri. But of any such work there is no trace, and this in a city with a very large corpus of surviving trecento frescoes.

Various reasons may be brought forward to account for this apparently instantaneous rise to the top. Physical evidence of the distant past is, of course, frail and it tends to survive, at best, in fragmentary order; only one document is known which records Altichiero's presence in Verona in the second half of the 1360s, a period when we have every reason to think he lived there. Perhaps a sizeable body of work has been lost. Precious little survives from the large complex of interlocking palazzi which formed the Scaligeri residence in the centre of the city, and which must, like the much better documented palace of the Carraresi in Padua, have been decorated during the trecento. But perhaps there was never much by Altichiero in the first place. It is likely that he did not receive his training in Verona, and the simplest explanation may be that he had not worked there much either before landing the Sala Grande commission. One might expect, had he been there at this time, to find signs of the kind of impact of his style on the general level of painting in the 1360s that can be found abundantly in the 1380s and 1390s. Arguments *e silentio* are of course unsatisfactory, but in the case of Altichiero's early years silence is just about all there is to go on. This is in marked contrast with his well recorded years in Padua,[1] and, indeed with the wider field of painters' activities in Padua, for which city the documents have revealed the names of well over 100 artists active in the period 1330–1410.[2]

The one Veronese document bearing Altichiero's name tells us little enough.[3] It comes from the archives of the Dominican convent of S. Anastasia and records the transfer of a parcel of land in the Valpolicella in 1369. Altichiero appears as second

[1] The documents for Altichiero's Paduan years are printed in Sartori, 'Nota su Altichiero', pp. 17ff. and Sartori, 'La Cappella di S. Giacomo al Santo', pp. 39ff.

[2] See Sartori, 'La Cappella di S. Giacomo', pp. 57–79.

[3] Verona, Archivio di Stato Anastasia, Sec. XIV, doc. no. 39 (1369).

witness, after one Guarino, a baker. His presence signifies little; it certainly sheds no light on the date of the great Cavalli votive fresco which Altichiero painted in S. Anastasia; but the document does provide a few precious facts about him. The name of his father, already dead, was Ser Domenico, and the family home was in the parish known as Ferraboi ('de Ferabobus'). No indication of his father's profession is given. Ser Domenico, called *Magister* in a later Paduan document, may or may not have been a painter like his son and like his grandson Antonio, who followed his uncle Altichiero to Padua.[4]

The parish of Ferraboi[5] occupies a narrow strip running between the present Piazza Bra, site of the Roman amphitheatre, and the *corso*, once the Decumanus Maximus of Roman Verona and the main thoroughfare of the medieval city. The only street of any size in the parish is the present Via Carlo Cattaneo, site of the demolished Church of S. Donato alla Colomba; it must at least be likely that Altichiero's home and workshop were located somewhere along it. Whether he was born here, or even in Verona itself, is unclear. The belief, maintained in much of the older literature, that his birthplace was Zevio, a small town down the Adige from Verona, finds no documentary support; in Paduan records he is always Altichiero da Verona, never da Zevio. But the tradition is a persistent one and there is no particular reason for anyone to have associated him with Zevio unless there had been at some stage a record of such an origin. It is just possibly confirmed by the name of the wholly fictitious artist 'Sebeto', conjured up by Vasari[6] as a collaborator of Altichiero's in Padua, but conceivably a garbled misreading of Zevio in its Latin guise, perhaps seen by Vasari's source in a document or, more likely, as part of a signature.[7] Later uses almost certainly depend on Vasari.

Altichiero, an unusual but by no means unique name in the region, probably of Longobard origin, is broadly cognate with Alighieri. Any temptation to make something of the coincidence that Dante's descendants, headed by his son Pietro, a judge, were settled in Verona during the trecento should be resisted. There may, though, have been a professional relationship between Altichiero and this important family; Vasari says Altichiero worked for the 'Serenghi', that is the Serego-Alighieri,[8] at the end of his career, and the tomb in S. Anastasia of Giovanni Salerni,[9] Pietro di Dante's brother-in-law, was decorated by a close follower of Altichiero, perhaps a member of his workshop. That there was a family of Altichieri in Verona is revealed by a 1362 document drawn up by the notary 'Alticlerius . . . condam dni Belavi de Alticleriis de pontepe-

4 'ego mag. Antonius pictor, nepos q. Alticherii de Verona et nunc habitator Paduae'. Venetian document of 27 April 1402 (Verona, Archivio di Stato Cancelleria Inferiore, b.130), cited in Sartori, 'La Cappella di S. Giacomo', p. 61, no. 18. Sartori takes this to be the same as the Antonio di Pietro da Verona living in Padua in the 1390s, for whom see also Gloria, 'Monumenti', no. 1841. Simon, 'Altichiero Versus Avanzo', p. 261 n. 4, comments on the use by Antonio of his uncle's name in this manner, a use which suggests some professional connection between the two. The obvious inference is that Antonio was, at some stage, Altichiero's assistant.

5 See Lenotti, *Verona nei suoi Antichi Rioni*, pp. 30–1.

6 See Simon, 'Altichiero versus Avanzo', p. 265.

7 See *ibid.*, pp. 265–6 for a discussion of this.

8 See Scaralla, *Gli Alighieri di Verona*. Pietro was a judge in Verona from 1332 to 1362. For the Serego-Alighieri, see Cartolari, *Cenni sopra varie Famiglie Illustri di Verona*, pp. 66–8.

9 Cipolla, 'Ricerche Storiche intorno alla Chiesa di Santa Anastasia in Verona' discusses the chapel and tombs of this exiled family of Pistoiese Black Guelphs, for whom see Cartolari, *Cenni*, p. 64. Pietro di Dante Alighieri was married to Giovanni's sister Giacoba, who died in 1358.

tre'.[10] Whether Altichiero was related to them and actually bore the full name Altichiero Altichieri used by Berenson and others[11] can only be a matter for speculation.

We may, at least, know what he looked like. The presence of self-portraits in the works of trecento painters is more often than not the product of wishful thinking on the part of enthusiasts or tourist guides, but it would not be unexpected in the case of one who included so many portraits in his frescoes.[12] The prime candidate must be the dark figure on the extreme right of the *Funeral of St Lucy* in the Oratory of S. Giorgio in Padua (pl. 115), who is standing over the largely illegible inscription on the fictive frame (fig. 73). The apparently pointed association of this figure with the inscription and, by extension, its function as marking the completion of the task at hand may lend some weight to this identification. It bears no resemblance to the portrait bust set up much later in that mini-Pantheon of Veronese luminaries, the vestibule of the Biblioteca Civica.

If the S. Giorgio figure is a self-portrait, then Altichiero was certainly not an old man when he painted it. We know from a Mantuan document that he was dead by 1393,[13] but have no record of his date of birth. He can hardly have begun the Sala Grande frescoes in the mid 1360s as a total novice; a birth date no later than 1335–40 seems likely. This would allow him to have had first-hand contact with the later *Giotteschi*, and it would just about fit with the look of the S. Giorgio figure if we choose to consider it in this context. He would then have been in his late twenties when he began the Sala Grande, *satis iuvenis* in our terms perhaps, but no beginner.

The two signorial cities of Verona and Padua together furnish the major backdrop to any consideration of Altichiero's activity. All his surviving frescoes are located in one or the other, and it is clear that in both he worked more or less exclusively in the service of the highest levels of society: for the signori, and for the class immediately subject to them – the great courtiers, military commanders and administrators. All his surviving or known work was done for these people. He is a genuine example of that oft-mooted type, the court artist.

Both cities lie in the most fertile agricultural area of the Italian peninsula, fertile enough to support throughout the late thirteenth and the fourteenth centuries a cluster of city-states, restricted in size, but in character fully autonomous under the largely nominal overlordship of the emperor. The prestige and political influence of the more important signorial cities is probably more usefully compared with those of independent kingdoms like France or England than with even the largest cities within those realms. The courtiers of Visconti Milan or Scaligeri Verona, the latter occupying a territory no larger than an English county, may have felt entitled to view their English and

[10] This document concerned Petrarch's friend Rinaldo Cavalchini, the tutor of his son Giovanni. Ant. Arch. Veronesi, Esposti rot. 2959, 1362, Oct. 3, cited in Biadego, 'Per la Storia della Cultura Veronese nel XIV Secolo', pp. 619–21.

[11] Berenson, *Italian Painters of the Renaissance*, p. 1.

[12] Mardersteig, 'I Ritratti del Petrarca e dei suoi Amici di Padova' discusses Altichiero's portraits.

[13] Vattovani, 'Tomaso e Altichiero', p. 275 cites this document (Mantua, Archivio Capitolare, Perg. b.16, no. 2250), dated 10 April 1393 and referring to 'bonae memoriae magister Aldigherius magister de Verona'.

French counterparts as equals, and we know that the English crown at least regarded a daughter of Bernabo Visconti as something of a catch.[14]

The histories and cultures of the Veronese and Paduan *signorie* are inextricably intertwined. The closing decades of the thirteenth century found both cities, formerly *commune*, responding to the collapse of the despotic rule of the terrible Ezzelino III da Romano in 1259.[15] Their different reactions to Ezzelino's fall, the contrasting routes by which both came eventually to fall into the same pattern of government by relatively stable and enduring dynastic *signorie*, reveal much of the distinctive nature of the two cities.

Verona is neatly situated in a loop of the Adige, a river of considerable size and occasional snow-fed destructive power. Easily defensible because it requires only one main stretch of wall across the neck of the loop, the city is relatively compact, and although suburban developments on the far bank of the Adige existed in Roman and medieval times, the circuit of wall flung out to the north by CanGrande della Scala in anticipation of further settlement in this area never had the effect desired. Thus this hilly part of the city, beyond the older settlements along the riverbank, still has a semi-rural character.

The overall look of central Verona has probably altered very little since the fourteenth century. It has kept its major medieval churches for the most part, as well as the signorial *palazzi*. In this it has fared rather better than Padua, which has lost its Romanesque cathedral (though not the splendid baptistry) and the great Abbey of S. Giustina through sixteenth-century rebuilding, the Dominican S. Agostino, burial place of the Carraresi, in the early nineteenth century, as well as most of the profusely decorated Carrarese Palace (this last, wantonly, as recently as 1878). In Altichiero's time, as now, Verona's Roman past was everywhere visible. His own house, whatever its exact location, was only yards from major Roman structures like the Porta Borsari, the Arco dei Gavi and the amphitheatre.

Straddling major routes to the transalpine north via the upper Adige Valley and the Brenner Pass, Verona had for centuries developed close ties with that region. Veronese loyalty to the empire was more or less constant from the tenth century. The majority of Veronese bishops in the eleventh century were of German origin,[16] and German-speaking communities in the hills to the north of the city are still recorded in the fourteenth century.[17] The fidelity to the empire which is characteristic of Verona well into the period of Scaligeri rule probably had as much to do with the geography of trade routes – vital for a city less dependent on agriculture for its prosperity than on trade[18] – as with more abstract loyalties. The importance of this access to the north constantly colours

[14] F. Cognasso, *I Visconti*, p. 241.

[15] For Ezzelino and the collapse of his rule, see Hyde, *Padua in the Age of Dante*, and for Verona, Cipolla, *Compendio della Storia Politica di Verona*, pp. 98ff.

[16] See Ederle, *Dizionario Cronologico Bio-Bibliografico dei Vescovi di Verona*, pp. 31–5.

[17] E.g. Rovere di Velo (now Rovere Veronese), a settlement of German immigrants in the lower Lessine Alps, established in 1287. See Allen, *A History of Verona*, p. 116 and Rossini, 'Il Territorio e i suoi Problemi', p. 410.

[18] For the importance of trade and its effect on the social structure of Verona, see Rossini, 'La Città e i suoi Problemi' and 'La Signoria Scaligera', pp. 125–6.

Veronese history in the duecento and trecento:[19] in the number of official German translators maintained by the Veronese merchants' guild, in the German mercenaries and cavalry used by CanGrande I della Scala as his personal shock-troops, and by CanGrande II as a garrison to hold down the city in a period of crisis.[20] It can be seen in the very design of that nervous man's Castelvecchio, designed specifically to cover a rapid escape route to the north (and used as intended by Antonio, last of the Scaligeri lords, as the *signoria* crumbled around him in 1387), in the spread of Altichiero's influence up the Adige and into the Germanic lands, reaching as far as Vienna, in which city many of the dispossessed Scaligeri made their homes in the years following 1387.[21]

Ezzelino's fidelity (after an initial period of anti-imperialism) to the empire was probably, and accordingly, less irksome to the Veronese than to the Paduans, with their traditional Guelph sympathies. Indeed his rule, however harsh, seems to have provoked a less critical response generally in Verona, where it was supported by the rising mercantile class and where Ezzelino made at least a show of supporting the *popolo basso* against the party of the local nobility, than elsewhere.[22] Certainly the passage, during the years following Ezzelino's fall, to a *signoria* proper was considerably smoother than in Padua.

Neither of the future signorial families of Verona and Padua were at all obviously the grandest in their respective cities, or, on the face of it, the most likely to fill the vacuum left behind by Ezzelino. Though, according to the Paduan chronicler Da Nono, the Carraresi were not *echt* nobles in origin, they were by his time (*c.* 1318) treated as such.[23] But in the late duecento and early trecento they were seen as one of several equally powerful families, from which group they emerged supreme only after prolonged struggles. The Scaligeri were quite manifestly not nobles, a factor which helped rather than impeded their rise to signorial status.[24] Though in Ezzelino's time several of the leading Scaligeri had belonged to the party of the Montecchi, allied at one stage with Ezzelino against the local nobles' party led by the counts of San Bonifacio, it was not via open factional struggle that they came to power. The re-emergence of magnatial factionalism around 1260 occurred despite Mastino della Scala's attempts at reconciliation, and the events of the ensuing period, leading to the counts' expulsion in 1263 and the purging of their party, left Mastino, as champion of the *Popolo*, unscathed. In fact the power of the feudal lords had been largely curbed well before this time, with the restrictions written into the city statutes.

Descendant of lawyers and administrative officials, *podestà* in Ezzelino's last year, Mastino I della Scala, who is commonly counted as the first figure of the Scaligeri

[19] See Rossini, 'La Signoria Scaligera', p. 128 for the important German presence.

[20] After the abortive revolt of Fregnano della Scala in 1354, CanGrande II installed a large garrison of German knights in a house opposite the small church of S. Pietro Martire, which was given over to their worship and which still has heraldic and other frescoes dating from this period of German use. See Gerola, 'I Cavalieri Tedeschi ed i loro Ritratti e Stemmi dei Secoli XIV–XV in San Giorgetto di Verona'.

[21] Carrara, *Gli Scaligeri*, pp. 260–8 traces the fortunes of the exiled Scaligeri.

[22] See Larner, *Italy in the Age of Dante and Petrarch*, pp. 129–32.

[23] See Hyde, *Padua*, pp. 82–3.

[24] For the origins and early history of the Scaligeri, see Sancassani, 'Notizie Genealogiche degli Scaligeri di Verona: da Alberto I ad Antonio della Scala (1277–1387)'.

signoria, was at the same time never properly *signore* at all. His tenure of various offices after 1259, *capitano del popolo* in 1262 and *podestà della casa dei mercanti* in 1265, paved the way for his family's control of the city without overtly suggesting any dynastic ambitions at that stage. Despite this, by 1277, when Mastino's brother Alberto was appointed captain-general for life by the *concio*, the largest council of the citizens,[25] the *signoria* may be regarded as an established fact – and the powers given him with that title were accordingly sweeping.[26] The hereditary principle was established beyond doubt in 1293, when Alberto secured the election of his son Bartolomeo as *capitano del popolo*. The true basis of Scaligeri power lay in their control of the merchants' guild, for whom Alberto built the extant headquarters in the Piazza Erbe, and on their tenure, permanent from the time of Alboino della Scala (d. 1311), of the post of merchants' *podestà* (*podestà della casa dei mercanti*), for practical purposes the most important of the offices they held, since this guild had not only absolute priority over all the others but also the extraordinary and, for them, crucial property that its rulings immediately and automatically passed into law.[27]

The Scaligeri maintained the traditional links with the empire, adding to their internal titles an imperial vicariate in 1311.[28] The difference in character between this *signoria* (and others of its time) and that of Ezzelino is indicated by this care for legality. *De facto* Scaligeri rule may have been, but the family were concerned that it should be seen to be *de iure* as well. The process by which the *signoria* absorbed the communal institutions, where Ezzelino had simply ignored them,[29] tended, at least in its first phase, to integrate the *signoria* into the fabric of the city's life to an extent far greater than with Ezzelino, lord of many cities and committed to none. Running alongside this internal integration went another process by which the Scaligeri married into the wider signorial class of northern Italy. By 1350 they had contracted marriages with the Bonnacolsi (Mantua), the Gonzaga (Mantua after the Bonnacolsi), the da Correggio (Parma), the Visconti (Milan), the da Camino (Treviso) and the Carraresi (Padua). To strengthen the imperial bonds, Bartolomeo della Scala married the great-granddaughter of one emperor (Frederick II), and CanGrande II the daughter of another (Louis of Bavaria).[30]

[25] The new statutes of 1277 set out the structure of Veronese administration under the *podestà*. Below him came the thirteen *Anziani*, drawn from the guilds and the different quarters of the city. Below them was the Council of Eighty and below them the *concio*, representative of the whole population. In practice the *podestà*'s role was reduced to that of a Scaligeri functionary, and the *concio* had virtually no independent powers at all.

[26] For Alberto I, see Rossini, 'La Signoria Scaligera', pp. 168–94. He held the office of merchants' *podestà* for thirty-two years. His full title was Captain-General of the Gastaldi of the Arts and the People of Verona, with which went the right to govern according to his pleasure, make, alter or abolish statutes, make decrees with instant legal force, assert control over communal property, and confirm or quash judicial sentences.

[27] See Cipolla, *Compendio*, pp. 76–7 for the origins of this mercantile authority.

[28] Alboino and CanGrande I della Scala became imperial vicars under Henry VII on 7 March 1311, along with the ruling families of several other cities. CanGrande also received the vicariate of Vicenza in 1312 (Alboino died in November 1311).

[29] Ezzelino rose to power via existing institutions even if he ignored them once his position was secure. He was *podestà* of Verona in 1226. After his conversion to the imperial party he became vicar of the march of Treviso, and he governed his vast realm in turn from Verona, Padua and elsewhere.

[30] For Scaligeri marriages see Sancassani, 'Notizie 1277–1387'.

The passage of the Carraresi to power was less smooth.[31] For some decades following Ezzelino's fall, Padua was governed by a commune of militantly Guelph sympathies. During the early trecento, a time when Padua came increasingly under the shadow of Ghibelline Verona under the dynamic CanGrande I della Scala, and during which the commune began to disintegrate, several Paduan families jostled for position. In the event, and by virtue of having reached an accord with CanGrande, it was the Carraresi who took the first material step towards a *signoria* with the election of Giacomo da Carrara as *capitaneus et dominus generalis* in 1318. It took a further twenty years for his family to secure an independent hold on the city, years punctuated by war, and in which the Carraresi were forced to submit to Scaligeri control in order to maintain their own position. The final overthrow of Scaligeri power in Padua in 1337 left the now autonomous Carrarese city with two legacies which came to bear heavily on their later rule: a lingering resentment on the part of the new masters stemming from their time as creatures of the Scaligeri, and an uncomfortable debt to the Venetian republic, the real power behind their seizure of Padua. With the once Paduan-controlled territory of Vicenza securely in Veronese hands, and with the western boundary of the strong and expansive Scaligeri state less than twenty miles from the centre of Padua, the Paduan sphere of influence and potential expansion was restricted to the lands to the east and north-east of her: to the Venetian *terraferma* and the area around Treviso. This led by extension to dealings with larger powers to the north-east which also had interests in these regions, most notably the kingdom of Hungary, Padua's ally against Venice for many years.[32] This, combined with the already equivocal relationship between the young *signoria* and the ancient republic to which it owed its existence, eventually proved fatal for the Carraresi, just as the rise of the Visconti state to the west of Verona did for the Scaligeri. The period in which Altichiero worked for the two courts was precisely that in which the pressure from the Visconti west and the Venetian east came fully to bear on the smaller *signorie* in between. With hindsight his patrons appear as men bound to fail in an unequal struggle against stronger opponents, and their cities as doomed to absorption into larger political and territorial units. It should come as no particular surprise, though, that the moment of greatest cultural richness coincides precisely with this period of mounting tension and impending crisis.[33]

The nature of the class whose patronage supported this cultural vitality is probably peculiar to these north Italian signorial states. Certainly the speed with which a courtly class developed under the *signorie* sets it apart from its longer-established equivalents elsewhere. The rise of the ruling families from the ranks of their peers led to a situation in which families formerly – and recently – their social equals or superiors now served under them. The loyalty of these families was clearly vital, both in the interests of

[31] Hyde, *Padua*, pp. 252–82 gives a detailed account of this.

[32] See Norwich, *A History of Venice*, pp. 231ff. and Plant, 'Portraits and Politics in Padua'.

[33] Levi, *Francesco di Vannozzo e la Lirica nelle Corti Lombarde durante la seconda Metà del sec. XIV*, gives a full picture of the cultural vitality of the northern courts in the mid and late trecento.

day-to-day internal peace and for the long term continuation of the *signorie*. This was perhaps less of a problem in Verona, where the events of 1263 left only one indigenous family of the high nobility, the Malaspina, in the city during the trecento. The growth of a full signorial government was accompanied by the transformation of an executive class – those in positions of trust and responsibility under the *signore* – into a class of courtiers, a new nobility in effect, comprising men of markedly different origins. Thus men like Spinetta Malaspina and Bailardino Nogarola,[34] both dispossessed feudal lords, served in similar capacities and with similar status as members of landowning extra-Veronese families like the Castelbarco,[35] and with men of much humbler notarial and legal stock – men, that is, from the same background as the Scaligeri themselves. Such service tended to continue through succeeding generations of certain families. Great courtiers in Altichiero's time like Giacomo Cavalli, Guglielmo Bevilacqua and Antonio da Legnago were all following in their fathers' footsteps.[36] The Malaspina and Nogarola served the Scaligeri faithfully throughout the trecento until they were brutally purged in 1381;[37] in their continuity of service they were the most prestigious amongst many such families.

The nature of the courtier class is well illustrated in the pages of the fourteenth-century Paduan *Cronaca Carrarese*, which gives a very detailed picture of it in action. In 1372 Francesco da Carrara 'il Vecchio', *signore* of Padua, called a meeting of representatives from the ninety or so leading families of Padua to consider the terms of a proposed treaty with Venice. Listed by the *Cronaca* here[38] are those names which crop up time and time again, and interchangeably, throughout its account of this period in high military, administrative, or ambassadorial capacities. As a group they form the overwhelmingly largest concentration of power, wealth and artistic patronage under the *signore*. Here we find families such as Giusto de'Menabuoi's patrons the Conti,[39] the original comital family of the district, and the Camposanpiero,[40] once contenders for the *signoria*, with others originating from territories in the *contado* like the da Peraga and the da Vigonza (also patrons of Giusto),[41] and with new magnates like the Scrovegni and Macaruffi, these last of humble origin but also rivals of the Carraresi before their final success. Alongside these new magnates and older nobles are such as the Buzzacarini (Giusto again), reputedly descended from a baker – more recently and more certainly from legal specialists – and by the late trecento allied by marriage to the Carraresi, the Sanguinacci, originally doctors of medicine and moneylenders and possibly patrons of Altichiero,[42] the da Rio, for da Nono[43] once rustics and then doctors

[34] See Rossini, 'La Signoria Scaligera dopo CanGrande', p. 469, and for the two families in general, Cartolari, *Cenni*, pp. 35–8 and 45–6.

[35] For the Castelbarco, see their entry in the *Dizionario Biografico*.

[36] For the Bevilacqua and Cavalli, see Cartolari, *Cenni*, pp. 7–8 and 19 and the *Dizionario Biografico*. For Antonio da Legnago, see Biadego, 'Per la Storia'.

[37] Rossini, 'La Signoria Scaligera dopo CanGrande', pp. 720–1.

[38] Gatari, *Cronaca Carrarese*, p. 51.

[39] For Giusto and the Conti see Semenzato, *La Cappella del Beato Luca e Giusto de'Menabuoi nella Basilica di Sant'Antonio*.

[40] For these Paduan families see Hyde, *Padua in the Age of Dante*.

[41] For the da Vigonza see *ibid* and Gloria, *Monumenti*.

[42] The extant fresco tondo of the *Madonna and Child* by Altichiero probably came from the tomb of Ilario Sanguinacci in the Eremitani, part of which was moved from its original site in 1690. See Mellini, *Altichiero e Jacopo Avanzi*, p. 56.

[43] See Hyde, *Padua*, pp. 178–9.

and notaries, and the da Montagnone, former landed nobles who had declined and become holders of judicial posts.

The development away from a society formerly dominated by great landed families is indicated by the high profile of a family like the Dotti.[44] These were not of noble origin, rather they were essentially urban, with no power base in the *contado*, and had risen to a position of great standing under the Carraresi through the continuation of a long history of service as knights stretching well back into the communal period, a history culminating in the well-documented career of Francesco Dotto,[45] and a position indicated by the prominence of their family chapel in the church of the Eremitani, complete with a tomb painted by Altichiero (pls. 117 and 118).

The related flexibility of employment for a member of this class can be illustrated by the career of Simone Lupi, *marchese* of Soragna, a prominent member of this great Parmese family[46] who had settled in Padua. Socially of far higher original rank than the Carraresi, Simone is to be found in 1384 serving at one moment in his capacity as a great courtier – as an example of gentlemanly conduct and bearing to the young Francesco Novello da Carrara – and at the next as a military leader – captain-general of the Paduan armies – or in an administrative capacity as *podestà* of Carrarese Treviso. Such a pattern is echoed in the lives of large numbers of the leading figures of Verona and Padua, all Altichiero's non-signorial patrons included. The personal wealth of these men obviously varied (Simone Lupi, though his kinsmen Bonifacio and Raimondino built magnificent funerary chapels for themselves and had them decorated by Altichiero, was buried in a simple wall tomb in the Santo cloisters (fig. 1), already occupied by three members of his family[47]), as did the source of that wealth, but the character of the new courtiers and magnates is suggested by the documented involvement of men like Tomaso Pellegrini and Guglielmo Bevilacqua of Verona, great courtiers both, in the textile trade,[48] and by their ownership of warehouses and shops. Nor did the *signori* themselves disdain to involve themselves in trade, as we know from documents of Mastino II della Scala's time.[49]

A significant admixture of exiles from other courts and cities, especially in Padua, reflects the unstable political background of Lombardy and the Veneto at this time. In 1405, of the five families known to have employed Altichiero (Scaligeri, Cavalli, Lupi, Dotti, Carraresi), only the Dotti occupied anything like the same position they had in 1305, or were still wholly resident in their native city. It is symptomatic of the age that many of the more prominent members of what we might call Altichiero's families spent much of his lifetime engaged in trying to wipe each other out.[50]

[44] See *ibid.*, pp. 99–100, and Gloria, *Monumenti*.

[45] See Gatari, *Cronaca Carrarese* and Gloria, *Monumenti*.

[46] Gatari, *Cronaca Carrarese*, pp. 63, 71–2, 92, etc.

[47] See Gonzati, *La Basilica di S. Antonio di Padova*, vol. II, p. 42.

[48] Cipolla, 'Ricerche Storiche' cites documents showing that Guglielmo Bevilacqua traded in *panni* and that Tomaso Pellegrini opened a shop selling them.

[49] The Scaligeri owned properties on the corner block of the Piazza Erbe and the *corso*, with shops below and warehouses above. Perbellini, *Castelli Scaligeri*, pp. 34–40 gives a general account of their property in this area.

[50] That is, at various times: the Scaligeri fought against the Carraresi, the Cavalli against the Scaligeri, the Lupi against the Carraresi, Bonifacio Lupi's heir and nephew Ugolotto Biancardo against the Scaligeri, and so on.

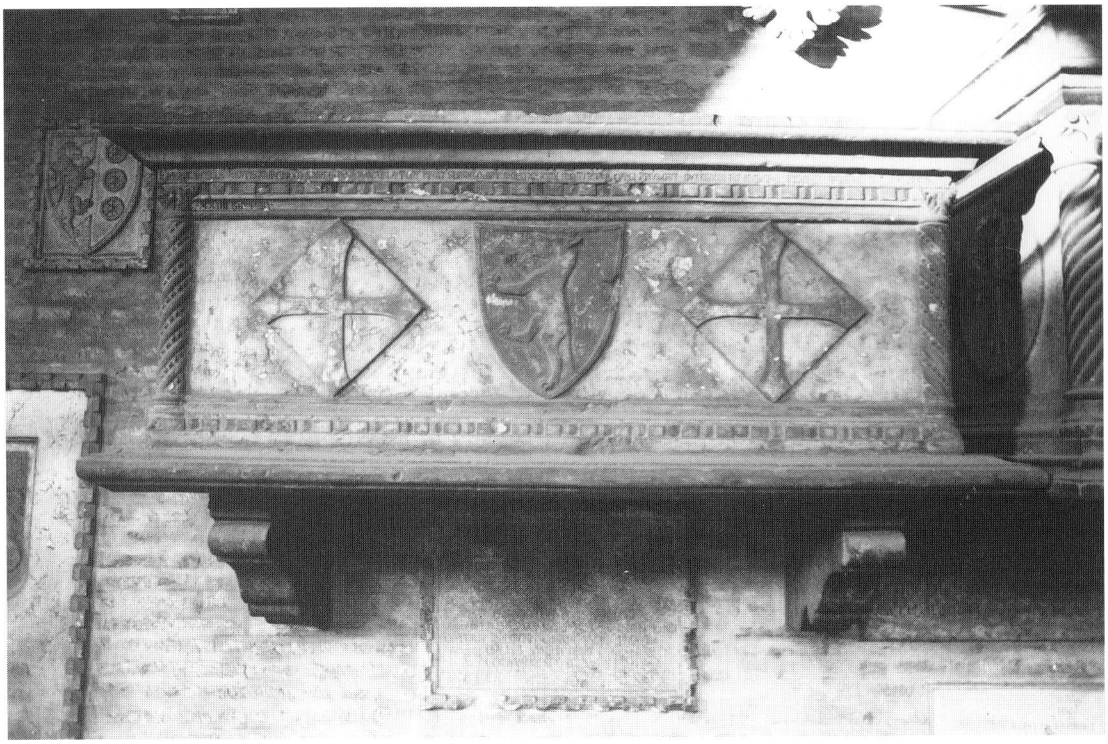

Fig. 1 Padua, Il Santo. Lupi tomb in cloister.

A further consequence of this instability, and of the sort of distances between cities which allowed an army to be placed on a neighbour's border in a matter of hours, was a habitually fluctuating state of tensions between adjacent powers expressed in numerous leagues and counter-leagues. The relationship between Verona and Padua was no exception to the norm. But the inherent antagonism between them, expressed in open warfare in the early and late trecento – eventually costing both *signorie* control of their respective cities – was temporarily abated during Altichiero's time. This island of good relations was chiefly based on the support given by Francesco da Carrara to the nascent rule of his nephew Cansignorio della Scala following the murder of CanGrande II in 1359.[51] The period of Cansignorio's rule (1359–75), though not without its tensions, still represents the peak of friendly interchange between the two *signorie*.

This accord, in which an element of rivalry at court level was only to be expected, was maintained after Cansignorio's death until that of his son Bartolomeo in 1381. It was reinforced by the marriage in 1377 of Francesco Novello da Carrara to Taddea d'Este, daughter of Verde della Scala and granddaughter of Taddea da Carrara and Mastino II della Scala, a union which further strengthened the family ties between the two *signorie*.

The kind of high-level contacts and exchanges between the two courts that surrounded such unions were supplemented by a constant, wider, and more varied stream of intercourse on many levels. Contact between the leading intellectuals at each court,

[51] Carrara, *Scaligeri*, pp. 201–2.

both directly and via such a seasoned envoy as Petrarch, and at a lower social level by a Villonesque figure like the poet Francesco di Vannozzo,[52] shuttling between the two courts throughout this period, is extensively recorded. The occasionally murky waters in which Francesco swam in both cities, made up of crowds of court officials, poets, teachers and notaries, were precisely those in which humanism was nurtured. Whatever the social gulf between a man like Francesco and someone like Antonio da Legnago, Cansignorio's chancellor, in this area at least a sense of common purpose and interests seems to have transcended other considerations. So Petrarch's young Veronese friend Gasparo Broaspini, shield painter's son, copyist and humanist, corresponded on more or less equal terms with mighty Paduan courtiers like Giovanni Dondi and the Florentine chancellor Coluccio Salutati.[53] This intellectual fervour constitutes a vital background to the dynamic development of both the range and quality of northern Italian painting which took place in the wake of Altichiero's achievement.

The context for this artistic upsurge in Verona must be traced back to the late thirteenth century and may be associated, to some extent, with the rise of the Scaligeri *signoria* itself. The introduction of Gothic architecture to this city, full even today of great Romanesque buildings, coincides with the arrival of the Mendicants, or, rather, with their final settlement at full strength on permanent sites, a process closely following the establishment of Scaligeri prominence.

In 1260 land was donated to the Dominicans (present in the city from *c.* 1220) which allowed them to build their Church of S. Pietro Martire (now S. Anastasia). The 1260s also saw the papal bull (1261, confirming one of 1257) turning the former Benedictine monastery church of S. Fermo Maggiore over to the Franciscans (present on another site from 1230), and the arrival of the Augustinian friars (1262).[54] All three orders received the support of the rising *signoria* in various forms. In 1324 the Servites, despite the opposition of the nearby Franciscans, began to build their Church of S. Maria della Scala on land directly donated by CanGrande I.

The churches built by these orders in Verona by no means conformed to a common pattern.[55] Both the Eremitani at S. Eufemia (from 1275, consecrated 1331) and the Franciscans at S. Fermo (*c.* 1312–20) reconstructed existing Romanesque churches, in both cases pretty thoroughly. They, like the Servites, built aisleless preaching halls (in the case of S. Fermo, replacing a three-aisled structure). The Dominicans, on the other hand, began (by 1292) a transepted basilica of considerable size and intentional grandeur, possibly in response to the close and early involvement of the Scaligeri, who had perhaps already envisaged S. Anastasia as the public church of their court.

S. Eufemia and S. Maria della Scala have been extensively rebuilt or damaged, and only S. Anastasia and S. Fermo give any reliable picture of the first Veronese Gothic style – or styles, since the two buildings reveal very different approaches to the design of

[52] See Levi, *Francesco di Vannozzo*, *passim*.

[53] See Garibotto, 'Un Amico del Petrarca (Gasparo Squaro dei Broaspini)' for Gasparo's career and friendships.

[54] Ederle, *Dizionario Cronologico*, pp. 45–7.

[55] For Mendicant architecture in Verona see Cuppini, 'L'Arte Gotica', pp. 225–38 and Dellwing, *Studien zur Baukunst der Bettelorden im Veneto*.

big preaching churches. S. Anastasia, large, measured, with vaulted nave and, for all the richness of its decoration, rather austere (figs. 40–3), has affinities with that classicising Gothic style peculiar, in various forms, to Italy, and with specific local styles like that of the Franciscan S. Lorenzo in Vicenza: for Dellwing, S. Lorenzo was the direct source of this church's design.[56] The adjacent S. Pietro Martire, also part of the Dominican complex and, unlike the larger church, begun and completed in the trecento, recalls Lombard styles.

S. Fermo, by contrast, enriches and enlivens a vast unbroken interior with a spectacular wooden roof *a carena*, typical of the region. The exterior (fig. 2) reveals the Veronese taste for the involved and picturesque silhouette, expressed in multiple gables, pinnacles and turrets, and for the articulation of basically planar wall surfaces by means of intricate decorative detail, using, typically, a mixture of juxtaposed brick and stone courses – simply on the facade and other main walls, but with increasing fantasy at cornice and gable levels.

Support for these building campaigns came from the Scaligeri themselves, and also from numbers of the wealthier citizens. Both the Franciscans and Dominicans benefited in particular from the patronage of one of the most prominent of CanGrande's courtiers, Guglielmo Castelbarco, whose canopied tomb over the entrance to the courtyard of the Dominican convent (fig. 40) set the fashion for the subsequent series of Scaligeri tombs, which show the development of Veronese Gothic style at its richest.

The majority of Scaligeri burials in the cemetery of S. Maria Antica, Ruskin's 'little field of sleep',[57] were in handsome sarcophagi of the type derived from Roman models, of which examples still survive in the city. But the tombs of CanGrande I (d.1329) and Mastino II (d.1351) (fig. 3), both completed in Mastino's time, take the design of Castelbarco's tomb several stages further, adding to it an equestrian figure. CanGrande's canopy employs the arch, gable and parapet of the Castelbarco tomb with only minor variants (though it is, of course, wall-mounted while the former is free-standing, the design only minimally reflects this – it almost has the look of a free-standing structure subsequently engulfed by a wall). The pyramid above this level is pitched steeper than on the earlier tomb, and the addition of crockets enlivens the silhouette. This process of embellishment gathers pace with Mastino's tomb, which is free-standing and square in section. The design is much more vertical, the gables and pyramid steeper, and the overall decoration of the canopy far busier, with figurative sculpture on the gables.

The development of Veronese Gothic towards a greater intricacy and complexity, in the hands of probably local sculptors[58] for the tombs of Castelbarco, CanGrande and Mastino II, reaches saturation point with the tomb of Cansignorio (d.1375), by the Milanese workshop of Bonino da Campione (figs. 4, 53).[59] Here elements which perfectly animate and balance Mastino's tomb are remixed to quite different effect. The now hexagonal free-standing base is swamped by a proliferation of cusped arches,

[56] Dellwing, pp. *Studien zur Baukunst der Bettelorden im Veneto*, 64–81.

[57] See Mellini, *Sculturi Veronesi del Trecento*, pp. 94ff.

[58] *Ibid.*

[59] See Cuppini, 'L'Arte Gotica', pp. 271–8.

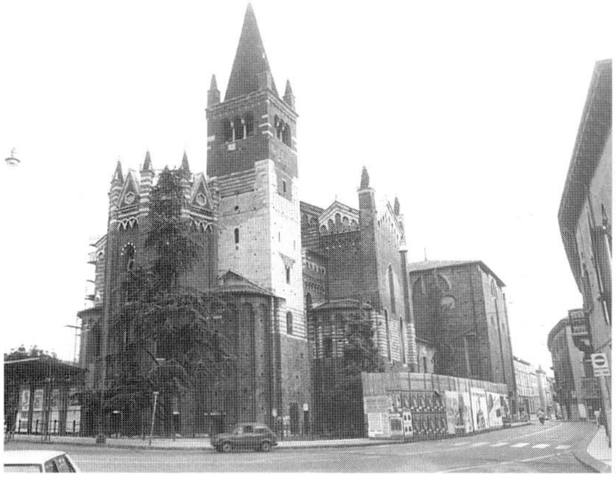

Fig. 2 Verona, S. Fermo Maggiore. Exterior from east.

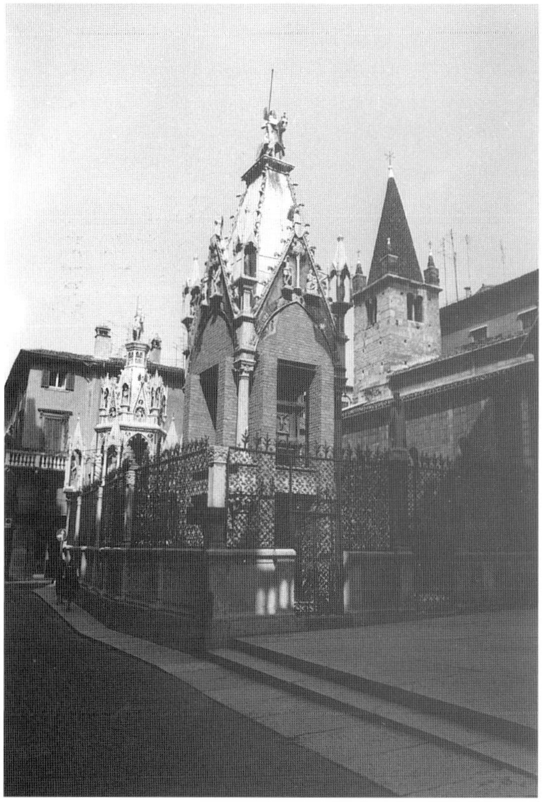

Fig. 3 Verona, S. Maria Antica, Scaligeri cemetery: tombs of Mastino II della Scala and Cansignorio della Scala.

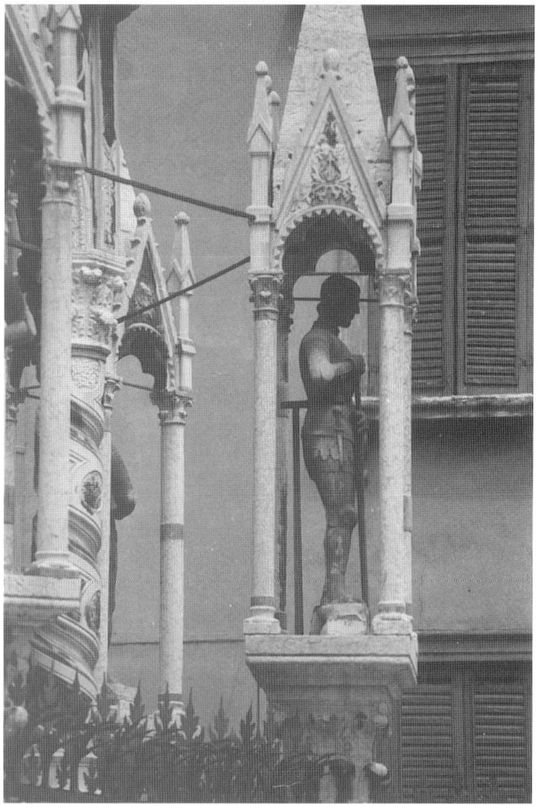

Fig. 4 Verona, S. Maria Antica. Tomb of Cansignorio della Scala (detail).

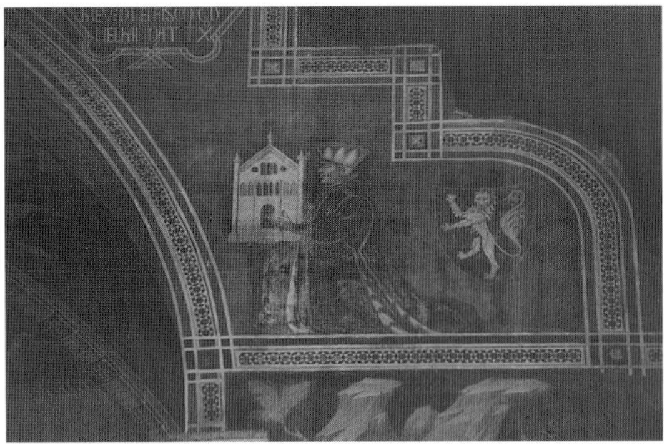

Fig. 5 Maestro del Redentore: *Portrait of Guglielmo Castelbarco.* Verona, S. Fermo Maggiore.

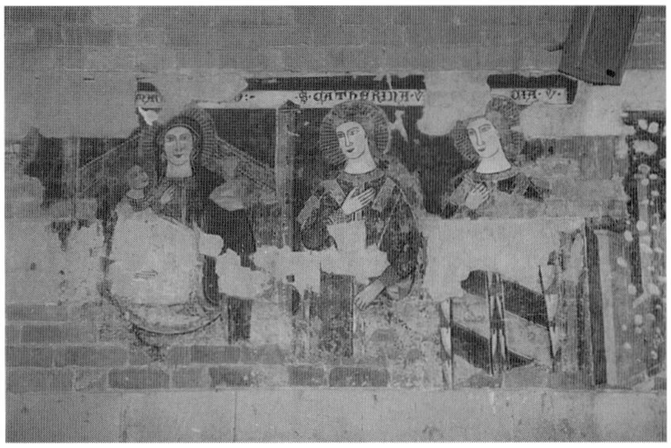

Fig. 6 Circle of Cicogna: *Madonna and Child, Sts. Catherine and Lucy*. Verona, S. Zeno Maggiore.

crocketed gables and pyramid, subsidiary canopies, figures and roundels, the whole ensemble further complicated by an extra ring of tabernacles and figures surrounding the base, and topped with an extremely elaborate plinth supporting the equestrian statue. This is a very rich brew indeed. Building though it clearly does on the style of its predecessors, Cansignorio's tomb ushers in the final stage of Veronese Gothic, restrained for the most part in Altichiero's version, but which flourishes in its full ripeness in the work of his followers, most startlingly in the sometimes extraordinarily massive and elaborate thrones, a taste for which marks Veronese images of the Madonna well into the quattrocento.

The arrival of a full trecento painting style in Verona seems to have taken place in the second decade of the century, the period of the first datable examples: the fresco over the tomb of Abbot Giuseppe della Scala (d.1313) of S. Zeno Maggiore, and the choir and triumphal arch frescoes of S. Fermo Maggiore, with large portraits of the prior Daniele Gusmerio, and the donor Guglielmo Castelbarco (painted 1319/20, fig. 5).[60] The association of the introduction of the new style with the patronage of men closely associated with the ruling family is probably significant, though this preference, if such it was, by no means banished the older style to the outer darkness as far as the majority of patrons were concerned. A large body of work of this kind exists in Verona and its district, grouped for convenience round the signed and dated work of Cicogna,[61] active until 1336.

This painter's four signed works are all outside Verona, but the style he represents cannot simply be dismissed as rustic or provincial, for attributable or cognate examples are also to be found in S. Zeno Maggiore[62] and the Palazze del Commune in Verona, and in the *castello* of Soave, an important stronghold in the *contado* and one of CanGrande's hunting lodges.[63] The fresco in S. Zeno (fig. 6), an *Enthroned Madonna*

[60] For the S. Zeno tomb fresco see Sandberg-Vavalà, *La Pittura Veronese del Trecento e del Primo Quatrocento*, pp. 43–4; for the S. Fermo scheme *ibid.*, pp. 44–52, Cuppini, 'Pitture del Trecento a Verona', pp. 75–83; and for both, Cuppini, 'L'Arte Gotica', pp. 286–300.

[61] For Cicogna, see Sandberg-Vavalà, *La Pittura Veronese*, pp. 26–32.

[62] *Ibid.*, pp. 33–9.

[63] For Scaligeri Soave, see Perbellini, *Castelli Scaligeri*, pp. 155–62.

and Child with Sts Lucy and Catherine (and fragments of two other saints), which relates to dated frescoes of 1322 in S. Nicola at Assenza di Bruzone, shows this style to have developed without any radical change out of the late Romanesque. If anything the linear and formulaic smiling faces, the minimal gestures, and the flat patterns of the drapery suffer by comparison with the more vigorous local art of the duecento, as a comparison between adjacent duecento and trecento frescoes of St Bartholomew in S. Giustina at Palazzolo sul Mincio demonstrates.[64]

A rather more assertive and eloquent version of this style is represented by the *Crucifixion* in the Sala di CanGrande in the castle keep at Soave, which generates a degree of pathos at least equal to that of the general run of Veronese trecento painters proper. The fragmentary *Chivalric Scene* to the right of the gate of the inner courtyard of the *castello* reminds us that, far from being just a backward phenomenon confined to rural backwaters in the early trecento, the style of these painters was put at the service of the sort of patronage associated with as self-consciously chivalric a court as CanGrande's. The Soave *Chivalric Scene*, for all that it is outside Verona itself, is still a product of Signorial patronage. Accounts of CanGrande's justly famous court[65] and related (and almost wholly conjectural) generalisations about the art of that court should be tempered in the light of such facts, for the quality of this work, even in perfect condition, must always have been modest.

The first securely dated example of a new style, the *Madonna and Child with Saint*s from the tomb of Abbot Giuseppe della Scala in the cloister of S. Zeno is scarcely in good enough condition for more than general conclusions to be drawn. The central mass of mother and child has a certain bulky insistence which relates it to contemporary developments in Padua and elsewhere in the region. The heavy facial modelling and the emphasis on the plastic qualities of the drapery proclaim a true trecento style, and there is some attempt at conveying a sense of emotional interplay between the figures. The sober forcefulness of this fresco is broadly characteristic of the ensuing first phase of the Veronese trecento style, best represented by the well-preserved S. Fermo fresco scheme of 1319/20, less so of later development towards the mid-century.

The first and severest style is extensively represented on the walls of both the Benedictine abbey church of S. Zeno and the Franciscan S. Fermo, with examples by all the distinct hands formerly fused into the so-called First S. Zeno Master. Madonnas are seated frontally on mainly wooden thrones, decorated with foliate detail or simple panelling, and with rounded or triangular gables and flat-topped pinnacles. In most cases the Child is contained within the Virgin's silhouette, either in a matching frontal pose or seated on one of her knees and blessing with his right hand. Facial modelling varies in strength. The two painters dominant in S. Zeno, Cuppini's 'Maestro della Presentazione' and 'Maestro di Corte Lepia',[66] model the face with a light shading on a very pale basic ground – often with some subtlety – which tends to enhance the rather remote and hieratic character of their frontally posed groups (fig. 7). The figure style

64 Rossini, 'Signoria Scaligera', figs. 33, 34.

65 E.g. Carrara, *Gli Scaligeri*, pp. 111ff.

66 Cuppini, 'L'Arte Gotica', pp. 294–5.

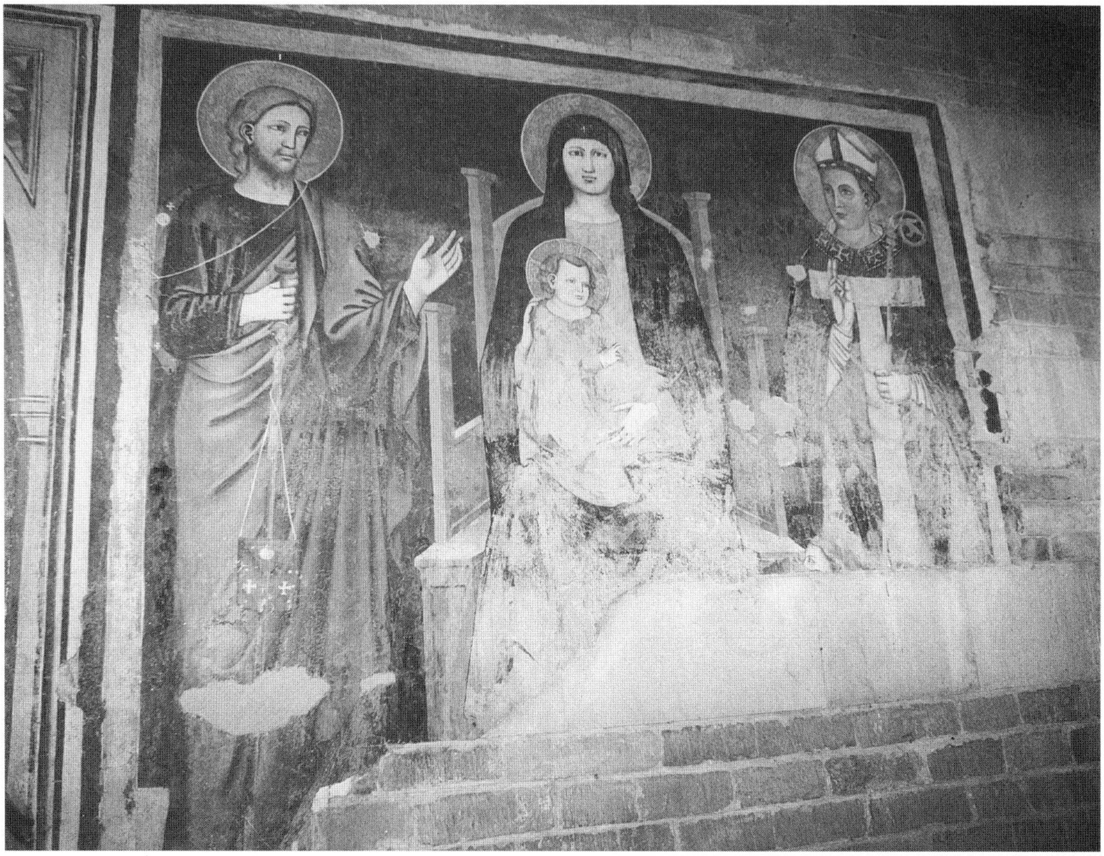

Fig. 7 Maestro di Corte Lepia: *Madonna and Child, Sts James and Zeno.* Verona, S. Zeno Maggiore.

generally develops a simplicity of outline and a certain massiveness, at its most imposing in the S. Zeno *Presentation*, and not without an appealing tenderness of facial expression at times, in the nearby *Pietà* (fig. 8) for instance.

The S. Fermo frescoes, by Cuppini's 'Maestro del Redentore',[67] exhibit a wider emotional and gestural range, a tauter and more plastic handling of drapery, and a more forceful facial modelling. The rather gauche intensity of the apsidal vault Standing Virgin to the left of the central Redeemer, or of the vault St Matthew, seems beyond the capabilities of the other masters in this group, as does the kneeling profile *Portrait of Guglielmo Castelbarco* (fig. 5), a memorable image. The vigorous style of this master, unfortunately represented in no narrative context, has been related to the relatively coherent style of Paduan painting in the wake of Giotto's activity there. Rasmo, for whom the painter of the two S. Fermo portraits (not, for him, the same hand as carried out the rest of the choir frescoes) is (un) 'certo Padovano',[68] connects him with the documented Nicolò da Padova, working in Trento in 1320, and probably the author of a frescoed *Madonna and Child* in the Church of S. Apollinare there. Nicolò, if the Trento

[67] *Ibid.*, pp. 291ff.

[68] Rasmo, in Grossato, ed., *Da Giotto a Mantegna*, p. 64.

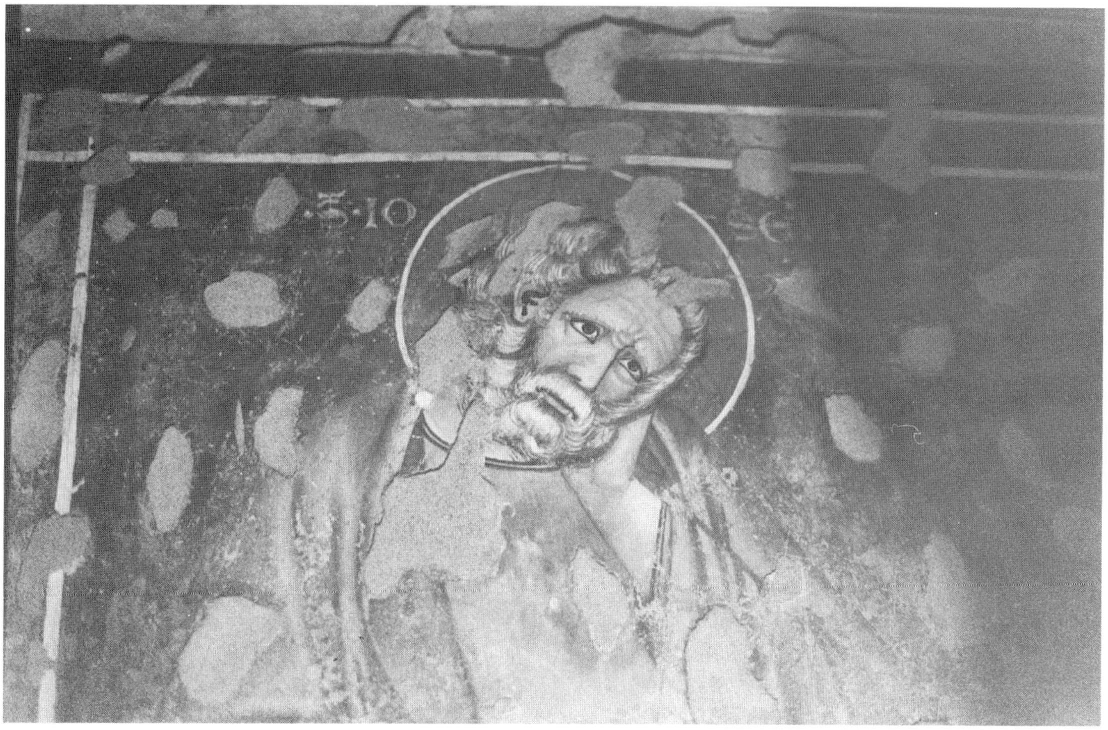

Fig. 8 Maestro della Presentazione: *Pietà* (detail). Verona, S. Zeno Maggiore.

attribution is correct, cannot be the author of any of the S. Fermo frescoes, which are of a quality beyond the powers of the S. Apollinare painter, but the Veronese frescoes do share certain characteristics with the Trento style, and with the styles of the probably Paduan author of a series of Enthroned Madonnas in the Church of the Eremitani in Padua (fig. 9) and a panel now in the Gallerie dell'Accademia in Ravenna:[69] energetic drapery modelling, massive heavy-jawed heads with very large eyes and fat lower eyelids, staring expressions where the pose is frontal, and a strong sense of the body pushing against the draperies. This art is hardly subtle, in fact one would imagine the painters to be virtually incapable of refinement or delicacy, but it has at least absorbed the assertive weightiness of the developing trecento style, if nothing else.

The S. Fermo painter may be a Paduan (as may the painter of the della Scala tomb in S. Zeno), but comparative material demonstrably Veronese does not exist for this period and it is impossible to be certain that this first Veronese style is not simply part of the wider birth of the trecento in north Italian painting, associated to some extent with Giotto's presence in the region, but not necessarily as directly dependent on his example as older accounts assumed.

The Franciscan narrative frescoes in the right transept of S. Fermo are by the fourth artist of this first group, the 'Maestro dell'Annunciazione', author of the eponymous

[69] These paintings are discussed by Lucco, ''Me Pinxit': Schede per un Catalogo del Museo Antoniano', pp. 245ff.

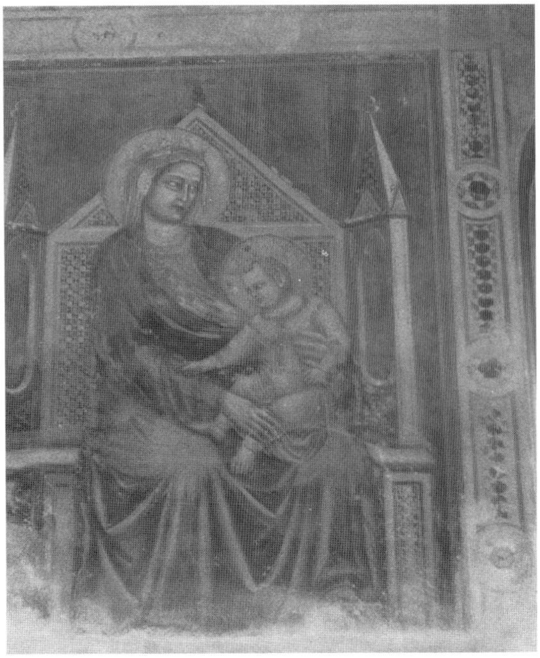

Fig. 9 Paduan (?) painter: *Madonna and Child*. Padua, Eremitani.

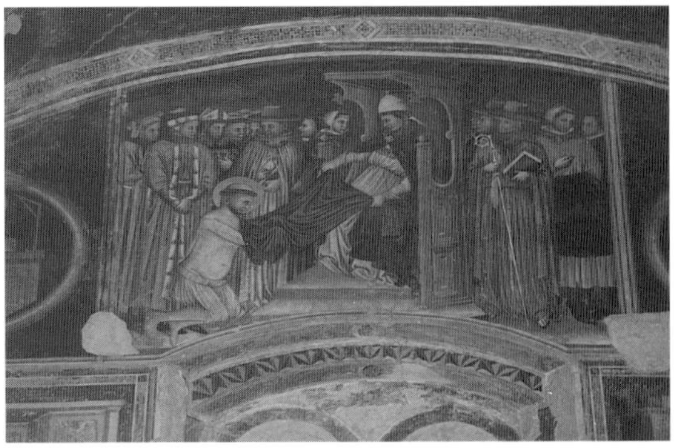

Fig. 10 Maestro dell'Annunciazione: *Confirmation of the Rule*. Verona, S. Fermo Maggiore.

fresco further down the nave. The multiplicity of parallel folds in his drapery, though reminiscent to some degree of the 'Maestro del Redentore', more immediately recalls the painting of Rimini, as do the faces and the collective interplay of glance and eye contact of his principal narrative scene (fig. 10). The intimate and touching emotional climate of this master's several frescoes in S. Fermo (there is no trace of him elsewhere in Verona) set him apart from his brusquer colleagues. The tone of his work anticipates that of Veronese painting towards the mid-century, though there is no reason to suppose he was himself working as late as that. The influence of Rimini at this time would accord with the known presence of Riminese painters in Padua in the 1320s.[70]

The period dominated by the masters of what should perhaps be called the first S. Zeno group can be pinned down by the few positive dates we have: 1319/20 for the Castelbarco scheme in S. Fermo; 1327 for the *Madonna and Child with Saints* over the tomb of Antonio Pelacani in the adjacent cloister. But, given the presence of a cognate style in S. Zeno as early as 1313, there is no reason why some of this work should not pre-date 1319 by several years.

Between this body of work and a later group centred on a dated fresco of 1354 in S. Anastasia the development of Veronese painting is uncertain, even though reasonably large quantities of it, mainly in fresco, survive. It is by no means certain that a straightforward development from the First to the Second S. Zeno Masters, or groups, represents an accurate picture of the period – it should at any rate be treated as a provisional reading of the situation in the absence of extensive documentation.

[70] Grossato, ed., *Da Giotto al Mantegna*, nos. 3–7.

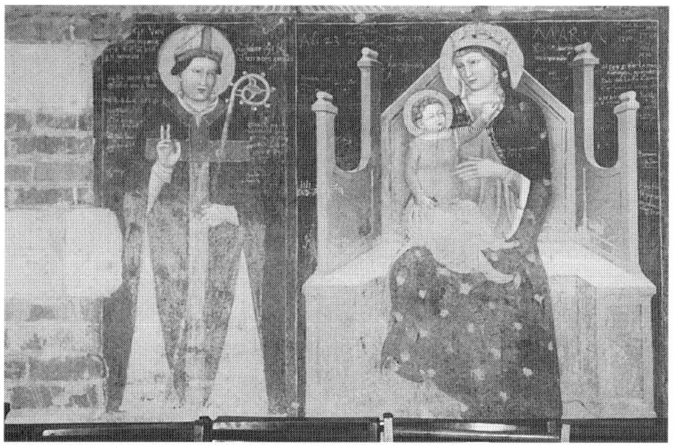

Fig. 11 Second S. Zeno Master: *Madonna and Child with S. Zeno*. Verona, S. Zeno Maggiore.

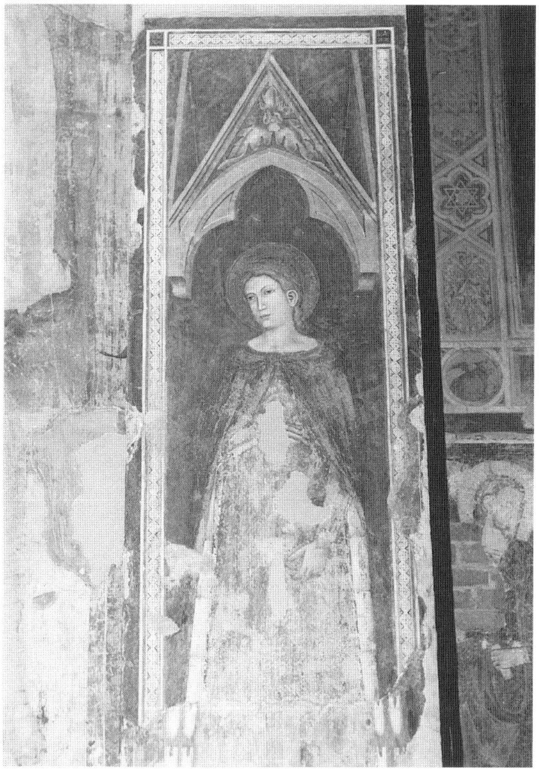

Fig. 12 Circle of Second S. Zeno Master: *St Catherine*. Verona, S. Zeno Maggiore.

Veronese painting in the period spanning this putative development, *c.*1320–50, settled into a productive but essentially repetitive phase, dominated to the exclusion of virtually all other subject matter by the production of small frescoes of the Madonna, sometimes with saints or donors. The prevalent style, common to a series of more or less capable hands within the orbit of the Second S. Zeno Master, develops without any detectable major break from that of the Maestro di Corte Lepia and the Maestro della Presentazione, both working in S. Zeno, where the greatest bulk of work in the second style is to be found.

Two examples of this in S. Zeno, perhaps the earliest of the group, a still frontally posed *Madonna* and a *St Anne with the Virgin*, preserve most of the salient features of the first style but animate the basic model with a more sympathetic eye contact with the spectator and a pinker and generally healthier facial colouring. In the general run of these masters' products (fig. 11), the frontal pose is abandoned in favour of a more relaxed posture for the Virgin, allowing for contact between mother and child. Facial expressions become more open and humane, radiating in the best quality work a certain sweetness and an undeniable charm which contrasts with the impenetrable inner life of the Maestro di Corte Lepia's blanched and inscrutable figures. The green-clad, curly haired child of some of the earlier frescoes becomes absolutely standard, as does the Virgin's drapery: red, under a blue mantle lined with miniver, tied across the breast but

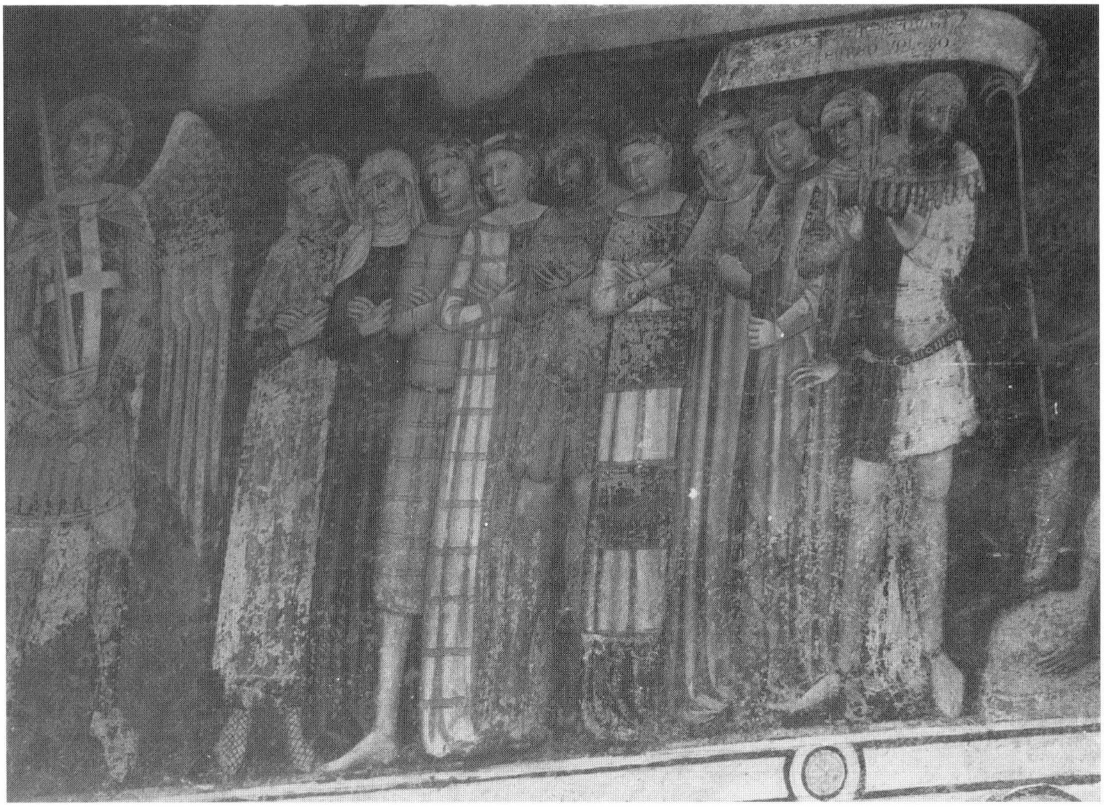

Fig. 13 Verona, S. Anastasia, *Last Judgement* (detail) The Damned.

hanging open down to the lap, and falling to the floor with a diagonal line exposing the right side of the undergarment – a pattern repeated just about identically in countless instances and seemingly by several different hands. The rather severe drapery style of the Maestro del Redentore gives way to a more elegant and refined Gothic rhythm, breaking into little waves and curls as the folds touch the ground, just as the rather bulky figure style of the earlier period is replaced by a more supple conception of the basic form. The advent of a more elegant Gothic sensibility, perhaps towards the mid-trecento, may be indicated by the presence of a cusped and gabled canopy on a fresco of *St. Catherine* in the upper church of S. Zeno (fig. 12), drawn with a grasp of perspective scarcely shown in the wooden thrones of the earlier painters. Perhaps such a taste filtered down from more exalted contexts like the Scaligeri tombs.

What may be identified as a more advanced and ambitious version of this style characterises a series of frescoes, mostly in S. Anastasia and S. Pietro Martire, all Madonnas except for a *St George and the Dragon* in S. Zeno and a *Last Judgement* in S. Anastasia. The *Last Judgement*[71] is as monotonously laid out as many of the S. Zeno frescoes, but reveals in its portrayal of the fashionably dressed Damned (fig. 13) a slightly greater degree of

[71] This fresco is discussed by Arslan, 'Una Tavola di Altichiero e un Affresco di Turone', pp. 105–6, and Cuppini, 'Alcune Pitture del Trecento a Verona', pp. 237–40.

characterisation, albeit at a very unexcited level. This is broadly comparable with the attempts evident in the 1354 *Madonna* and related frescoes to unite the figures into some kind of unified psychological relationship – they are, to an extent which largely eluded the earlier masters, all aware of one another. The limits of this advance are demonstrated by the S. Zeno *St George and the Dragon*. Here the princess reacts with the same tepid unconcern as the more phlegmatic of her cousins amongst the Damned of S. Anastasia.

It is probable that the painters of the second S. Zeno group satisfied the demands of the great majority of local patrons, the merchants and knights whose donor portraits cluster round the Madonna's feet in numerous frescoes, giving us an interesting visual record of the commissioning classes of the early and mid-trecento. But it seems likely that a demand existed in some circles, and especially perhaps at court level, for art of a quality and sophistication evidently beyond the majority of native workshops in the middle of the century. The Scaligeri-commissioned *Madonna of Humility* formerly on the now destroyed *tramezzo* of S. Anastasia, painted *c.* 1356 (the two donors included, with Sts Dominic and Peter Martyr, are probably CanGrande II and Elisabeth of Bavaria), is one of a series of Venetian works in Verona datable to the mid-century. These panels and frescoes, which have all been attributed, with varying degrees of credibility, to Lorenzo Veneziano,[72] brought the Veronese in contact with a level of refinement painfully lacking in most of the indigenous art of the city, just as the work of Bolognese painters in Verona and Vicenza[73] at much the same time may have shown up the essentially inanimate nature of local painting.

Even the dominant 'Veronese' painter of the 1350s, Turone,[74] was of Lombard origins. He received the Scaligeri commission for a new painting of the *Madonna delle Grazie* in S. Maria della Scala, centre of a local cult supported by the signorial family. Turone is the first painter of trecento Verona whose activity is known to any extent from documentary sources. His *œuvre*, based on the signed and dated SS Trinità polyptych of 1360 (figs. 14, 15), requires careful sifting, for it is clear that he spawned, and probably trained, a small host of followers. He seems to have run a large and productive shop, producing frescoes and manuscript paintings as well as panels. His achievement is not as impressive as those of his more adventurous contemporaries, Guariento, Giusto de'Menabuoi and Tomaso da Modena, but he invested Veronese painting with a quality and a range of invention it had mostly lacked up to this point.

The figures of the saints in the SS Trinità polyptych have a fully realised mass, and a weight that presses convincingly down on the ground. They stand or turn in a narrow but convincing spatial field. They react with intelligence and move with purpose. The emotional range is wide, within a Veronese context at least, from the implacable stare of the Father to the sweetness of the angels flanking the *Coronation of the Virgin*, and in the various moods of the saints. Handling is assured – the facial modelling combining delicacy with strength.

[72] Cuppini, 'Pitture' and 'Pitture II'.

[73] For Verona see Arcangeli, 'Affreschi Veronesi di Jacopino di Francesco'; for Vicenza, see Gibbs, 'Group of Bolognese Painters'.

[74] For Turone see Cuppini, 'Alcune Pitture', and 'L'Arte Gotica', pp. 300–10.

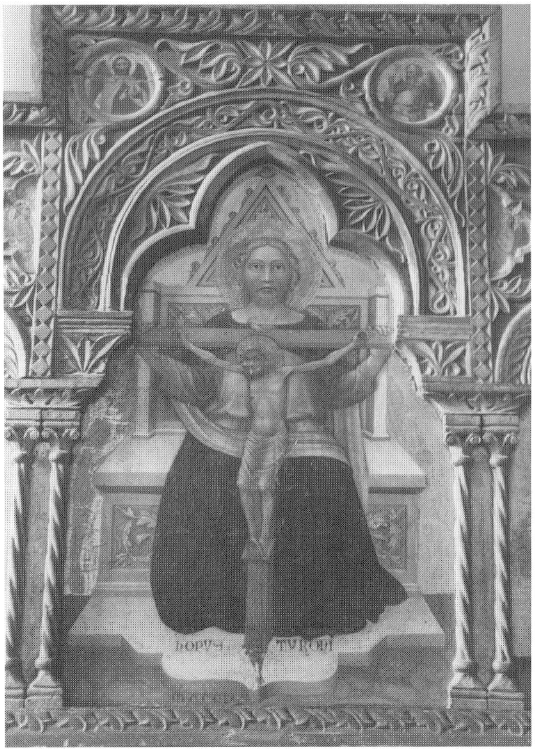

Fig. 14 Turone: SS.Trinità polyptych, *Trinity*. Verona, Castelvecchio.

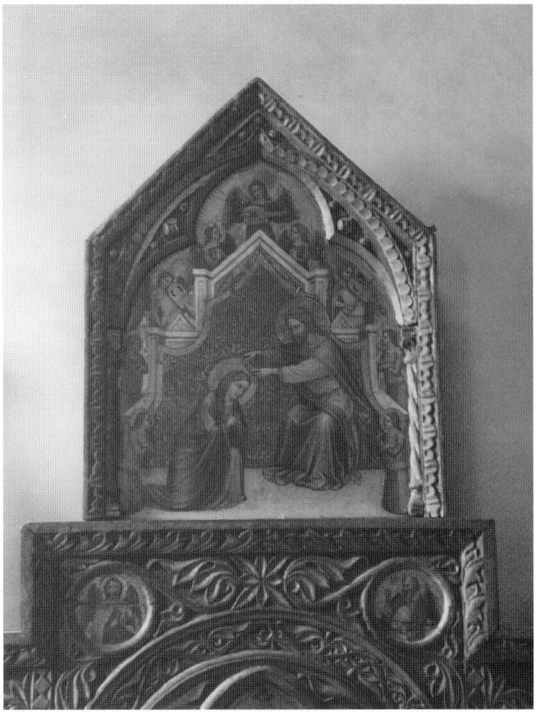

Fig. 15 Turone: SS.Trinità polyptych, *Coronation of the Virgin*. Verona, Castelvecchio.

With the *Crucifixion* fresco over the inside of the west door of S. Fermo (fig. 16), a secure attribution, Turone may have introduced to Verona the complex and crowded narrative format seen earlier in Tuscany, but here in the particular configuration most commonly used in the north, with the crowd broken into four blocks – two mounted and two standing, a pattern ultimately derived from Giottesque sources, and the basis for Altichiero's own versions. Several foreground figures here have the kind of massive cylindrical bulk associated with Tuscan painting at its most monumental, or with the work of Tuscan expatriates like Giusto, working in Lombardy and the Veneto from around 1348. In fact Turone's fresco is better organised and more convincingly proportioned than the Florentine master's own *Crucifixion* in the Paduan baptistry, or any of the native Lombard treatments of the subject. Like the SS Trinità polyptych, but on an expanded scale, the fresco features a diversity of incident, reaction, pose, and figure type beyond anything previously seen in Veronese painting. Turone's work here places Verona in some kind of relationship with contemporary developments in the wider field of the Po Valley.

The limitations of Veronese painting before Altichiero are clear. Rarely does it produce work of a quality comparable with that of even the lesser artists of Florence or Siena, and it is distinguished by none of the formal or iconographic adventurousness of a

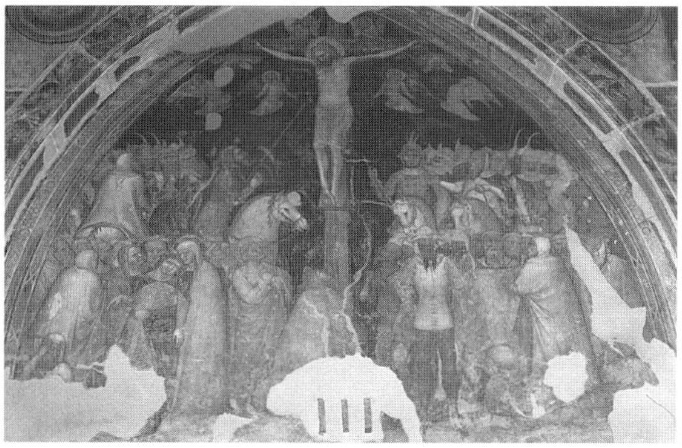

Fig. 16 Turone: *Crucifixion*. Verona, S. Fermo Maggiore.

smaller school like that of Rimini. Neither does it aspire to the emotional intensity of the native sculptors, of the author of the great *Crucifixion* group[75] now in the Castelvecchio for instance. Although the Veronese school is coherent and distinctive, and although it was generally dominant in Verona and its district, there is no sign of any extensive demand for it beyond this strictly local area until Altichiero and his followers set the standards for north Italian painting in the last quarter of the century. Attempts to identify earlier Veronese painting further afield – in the cathedral of Modena[76] for example – are unconvincing. The apparent lack of demand for Veronese art abroad is in marked contrast with the wider dissemination of Riminese, Bolognese, or even Paduan painting in the early trecento and during the career of the well-travelled Guariento,[77] and with the constant presence of Venetian painters throughout the north-east. How much the limitations of the local art and its innate conservatism are due to the perhaps equally limited scope of local demand can only now be guessed at, but it may have been a factor to some extent. The practice of buying in art of a better quality on the part of some patrons is significant in this context. Altichiero himself, for all his Veronese origins, may have been recently imported when he painted the Sala Grande.

Given the enormous numbers of surviving frescoes from the period *c.* 1320–60, the number of extant panels of certain Veronese authorship from the same period – three, including Turone's signed polyptych – seems significantly small,[78] for all that rates of attrition between different types of painting must vary enormously according to location and circumstance. Obviously every church had at least one altarpiece of some kind, though not necessarily a painted one. Stone altarpieces of local manufacture survive in Verona,[79] and the illustrator of one of the trecento choir-books of Verona Cathedral chose to depict one of these in his *Eucharist*,[80] perhaps reflecting Veronese taste.

The restricted range of demand for the fresco painter's skills must, again, given the surviving quantity, be reflected to some extent in the extant products. Apart from the

[75] See Mellini, *Scultori Veronesi*, pp. 19ff.

[76] For the trecento frescoes of the cathedral of Modena, see Gibbs, *Tomaso da Modena*, pp. 22–5 and figs. 6–14.

[77] D'Arcais, *Guariento*, gives a full account of Guariento's career.

[78] See Sandberg-Vavalà, *La Pittura Veronese*, pp. 108–12.

[79] E.g. the altarpiece in the crypt of S. Maria in Organo. See Mellini, *Scultori Veronesi*, pp. 106–8.

[80] Verona, Biblioteca Capitolare Cod. Cor. MLII, fo.145r. A fresco by Martino da Verona in the crypt of S. Zeno shows a similar altarpiece. See Cuppini, 'L'Arte Gotica', p. 313 and fig. 71.

early commissions in S. Fermo there are few narrative scenes, let alone full cycles,[81] to be seen in any of the many Veronese churches preserving Trecento frescoes. The local repertoire consists, for the most part, of Madonnas of one or two endlessly repeated types, and standing saints in various combinations, often painted over existing frescoes – frequently of the same subject and themselves at times probably dating from as recently as the early trecento. Presumably a rather small number of busy workshops devoted their energies to the production of such images, and a production line, encountering no pressing need for radical development, and accordingly sticking with tried and tested formulae, is what Veronese trecento painting most resembles.

Comparisons with Padua, on the face of it much richer in this respect, are inevitable, though they should probably be made with caution, given that patterns of survival are different. It is true that Altichiero's most extensive surviving work is in Padua, and that extant frescoes by him or his followers in Verona are, apparently, typically single scenes. Padua has kept many of its major trecento cycles: by Giotto, Guariento, Giusto, Altichiero and Jacopo da Verona, while retaining nothing like the quantity of more common-or-garden frescoes still to be seen all over Verona. Apart from cycles by Altichiero and Giusto and fragments of Giottesque painting in the chapterhouse and chevet, the Santo has little which corresponds with the much painted walls of S. Fermo in Verona.[82] But Verona in turn may have lost more than one narrative cycle by Altichiero, and the evidence is really too confused to allow us to make more than a tentative suggestion that Padua was inherently more fertile a source of patronage for an artist of Altichiero's scope than Verona.

The one thing that can be said with some certainty is that Altichiero's own art cannot be derived to any significant extent from the painting of the early Veronese trecento. It is not just that there is an enormous qualitative gulf between his work and everything else in Verona, for that would not in itself rule out a Veronese training, it is that there is simply nothing of Veronese painting reflected in his work at all. There are occasional affinities with Turone, but these almost certainly stem from Turone's independent contact with Lombard versions of that Tuscan monumentality which is the chief formative influence on Altichiero's own style.

It is, in fact, abundantly clear that Altichiero was either wholly trained within a Tuscan Giottesque milieu, or that he made a study of Giotto and his most advanced followers so profound that it eclipsed any previous training. Neither of these is likely to have taken place in Padua, though it may seem an obvious source given its proximity, for it is the work of the later Giotto, from the 'stretched' versions of Arena Chapel compositions and other frescoes by Giotto in the lower church of S. Francesco at Assisi to

[81] Apart from the Franciscan cycle in S. Fermo, there is a three-scene St Nicholas cycle in S. Zeno, by one of the second S. Zeno group, and a Passion cycle in SS Trinità. Family chapels with surviving trecento decoration typically contain numbers of single frescoes rather than whole-chapel schemes like those of the Lupi chapels in Padua. The usual caveats about patterns of survival must, of course, be made.

[82] See D'Arcais's discussions in Semenzato, *Le Pitture del Santo di Padova*.

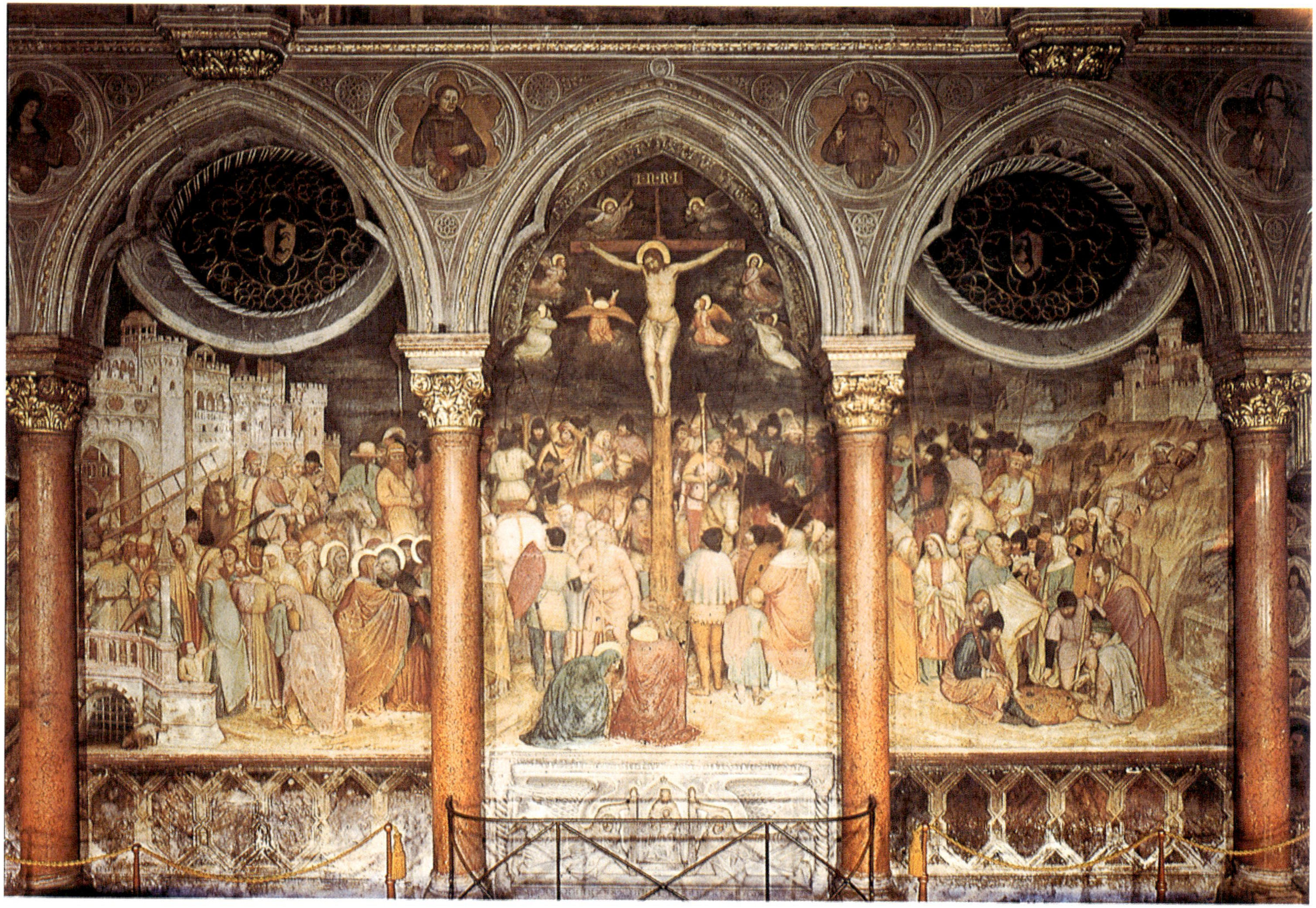

Plate 1 Altichiero: *Crucifixion.* Padua, Il Santo, Chapel of S. Giacomo.

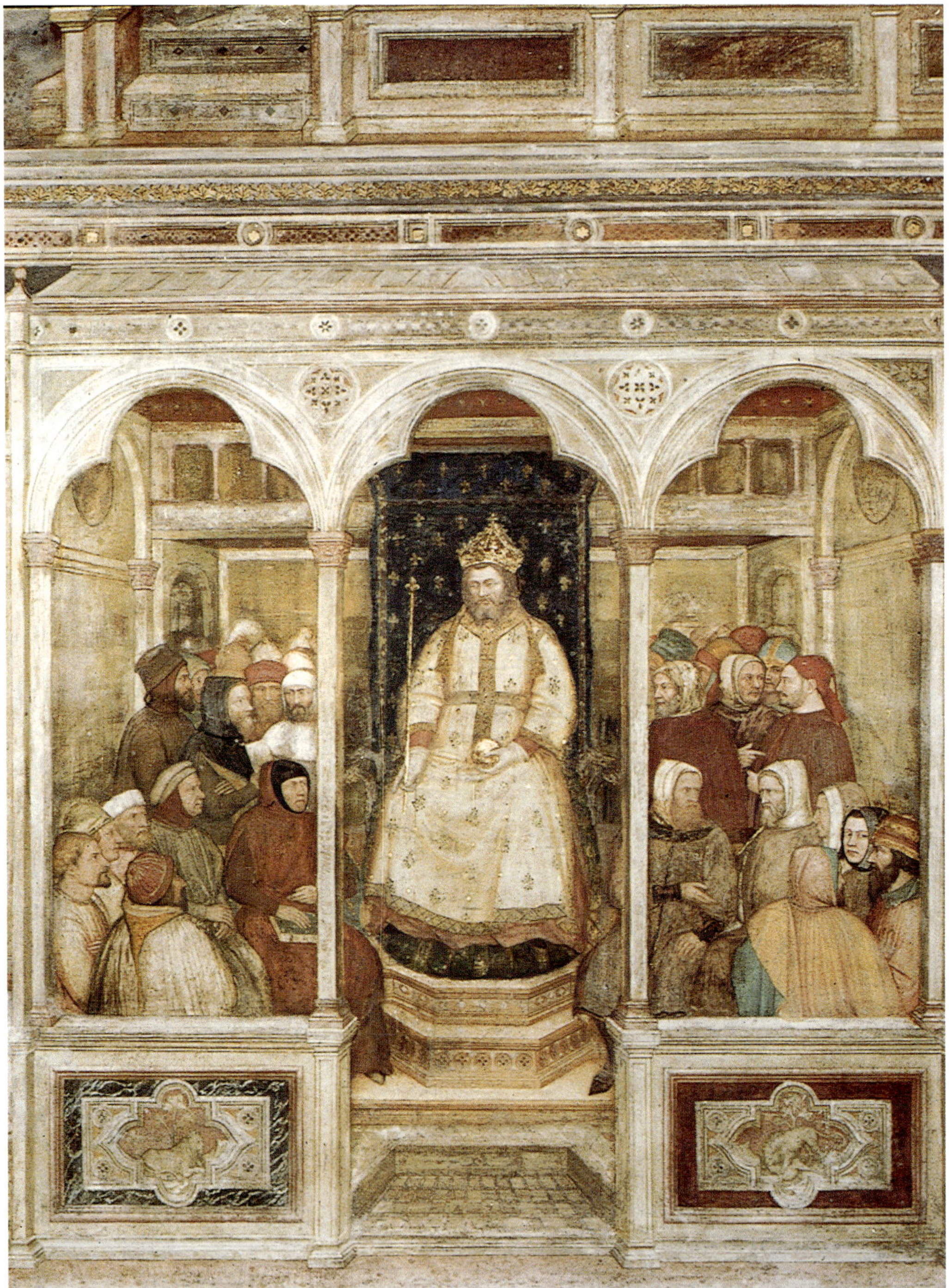

Plate II Altichiero: *Council of King Ramiro.* Padua, Il Santo, Chapel of S. Giacomo.

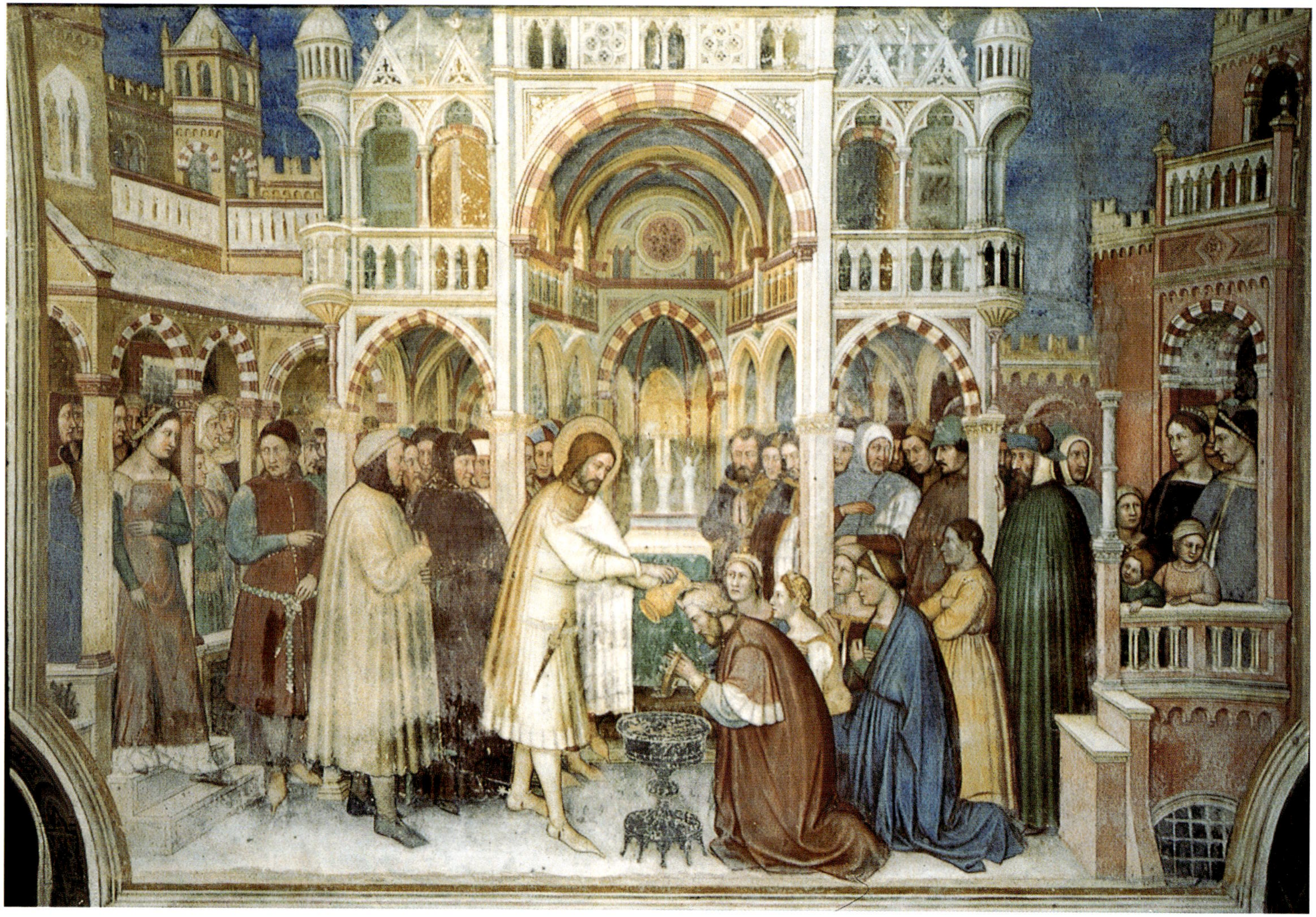

Plate III Altichiero: *St George baptising King Sevio and his court.* Padua, Oratory of S. Giorgio.

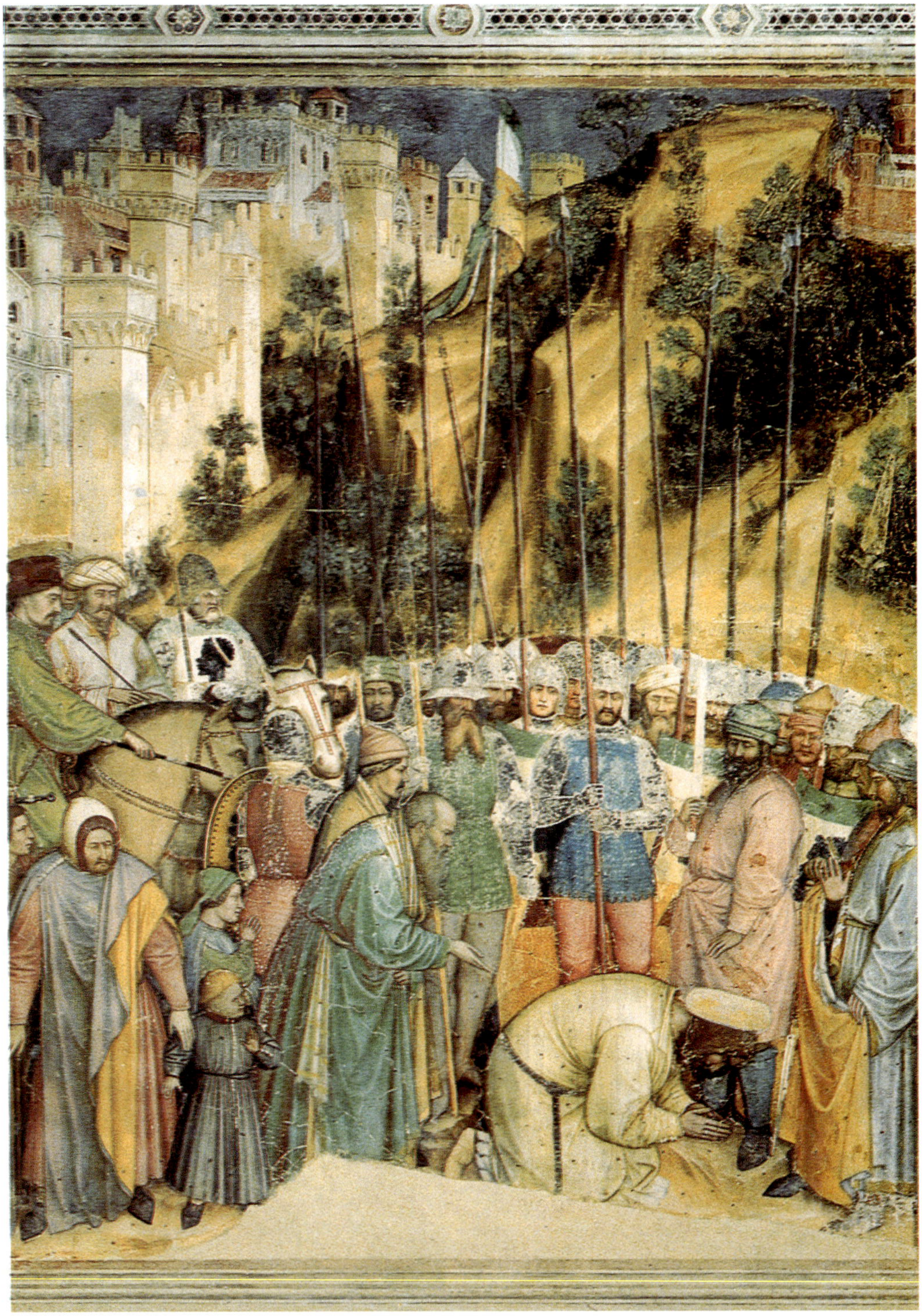

Plate IV Altichiero: *Beheading of St George*. Padua, Oratory of S. Giorgio.

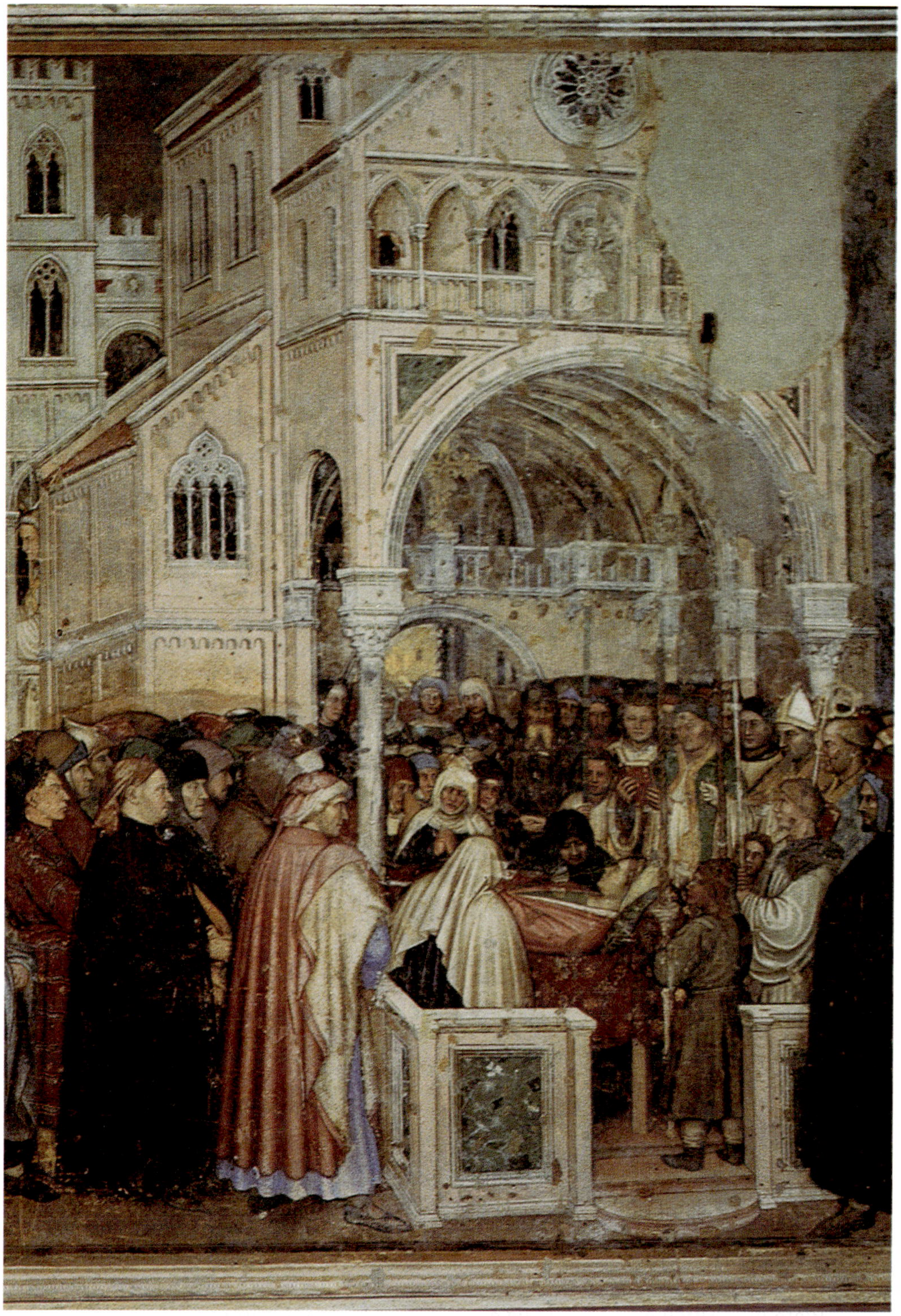

Plate v Altichiero: *Funeral of St Lucy.* Padua, Oratory of S. Giorgio.

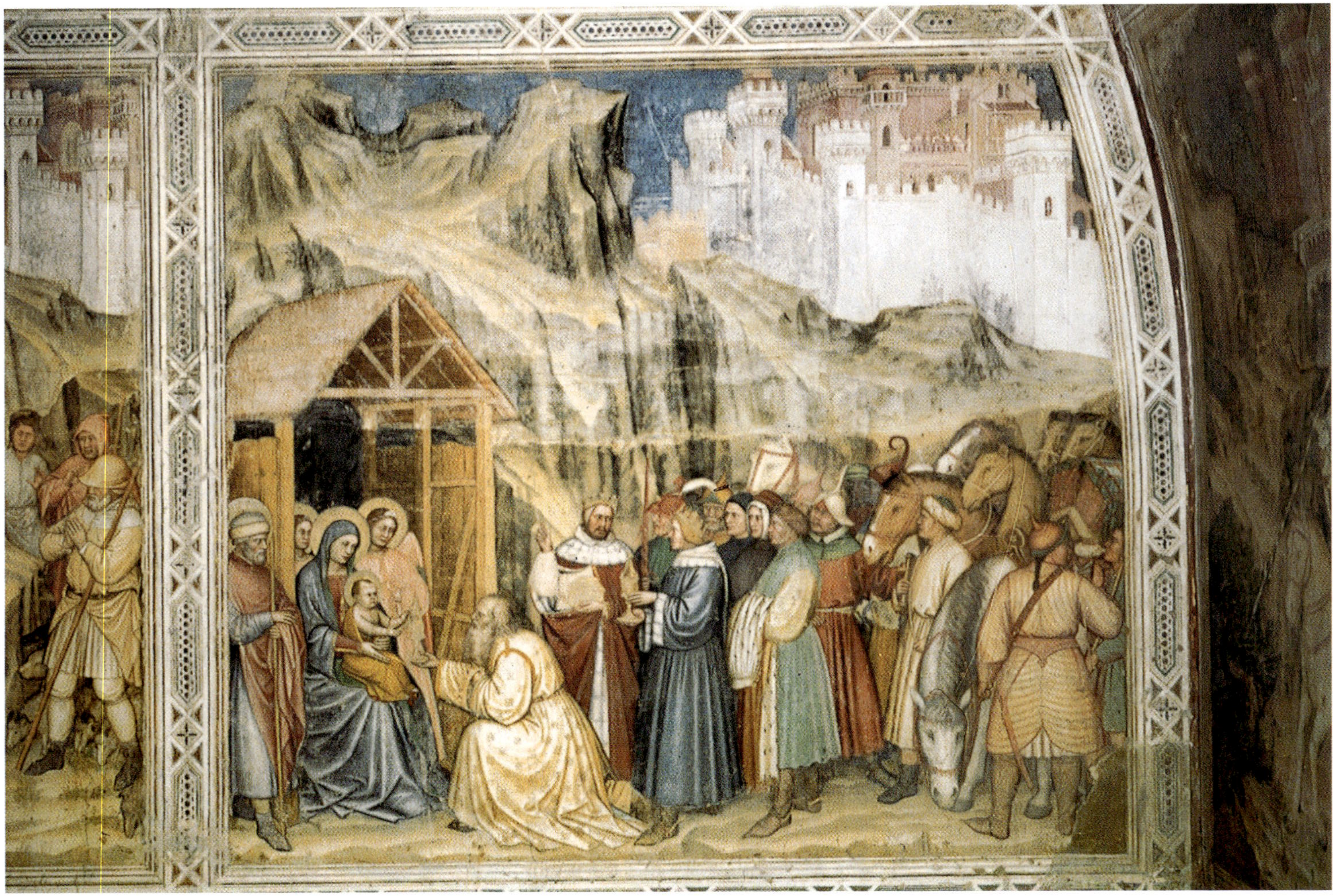

Plate VI Altichiero: *Adoration of the Magi*. Padua, Oratory of S. Giorgio.

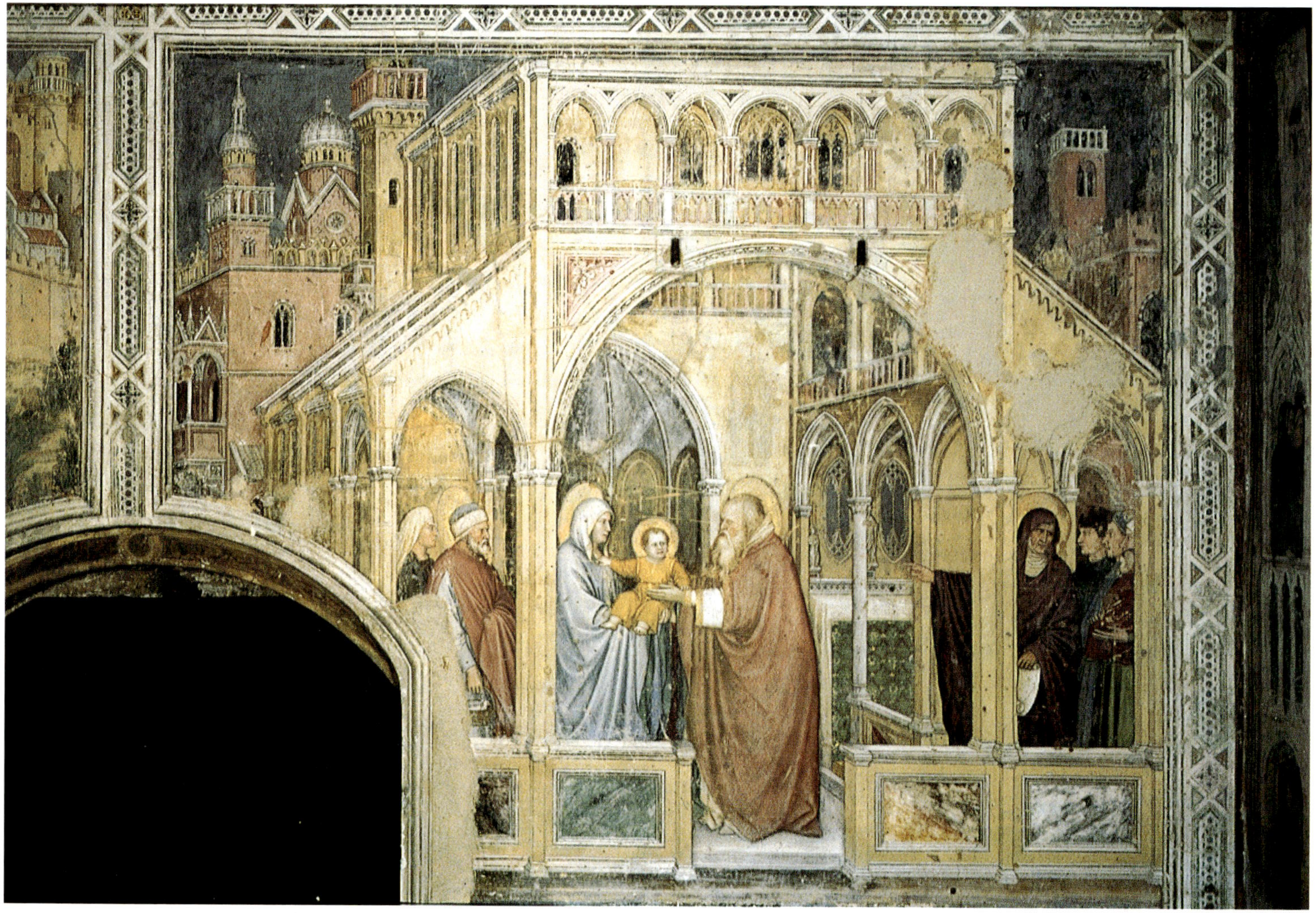

Plate VII Altichiero: *Presentation in the Temple*. Padua, Oratory of S. Giorgio.

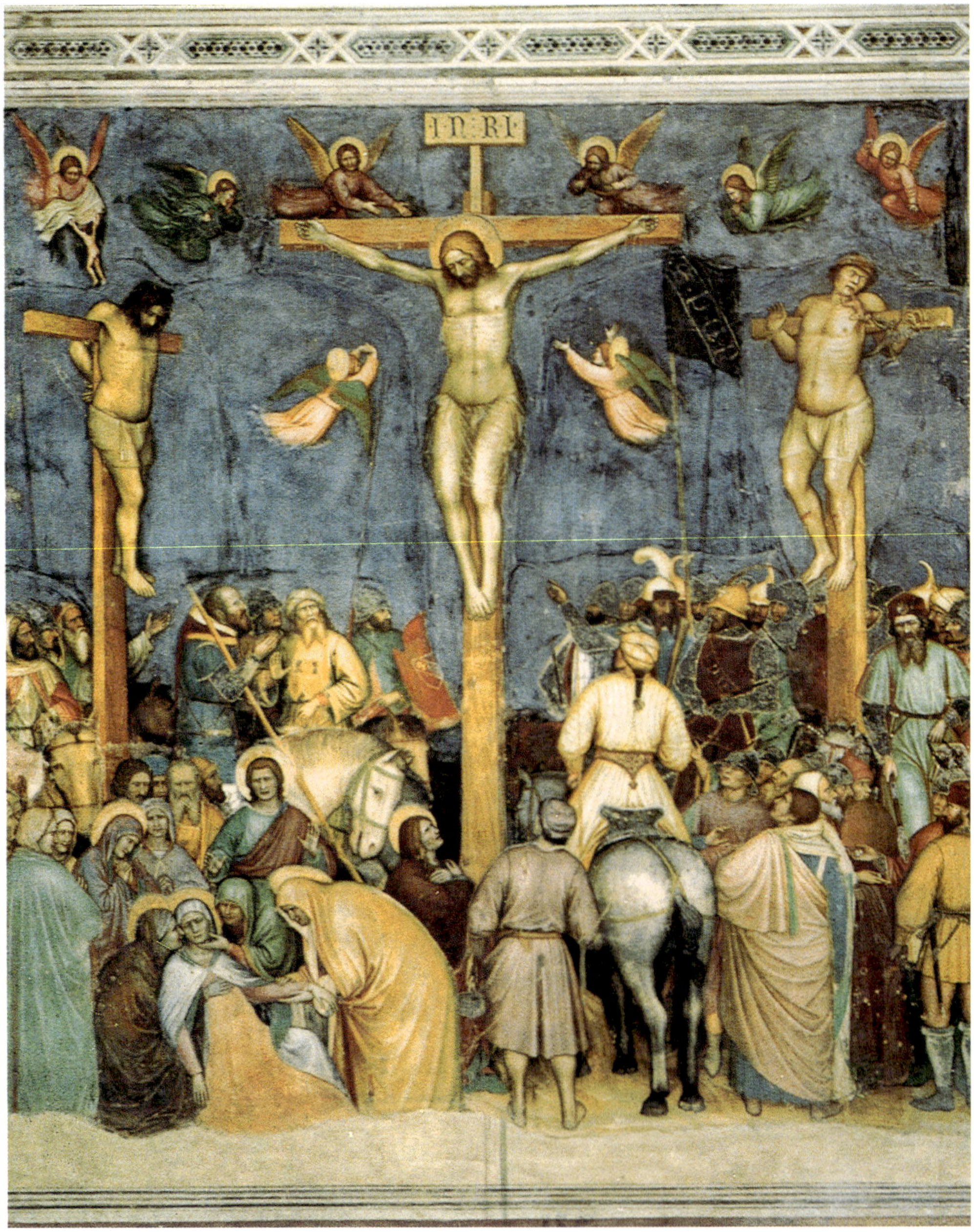

Plate VIII Altichiero: *Crucifixion.* Padua, Oratory of S. Giorgio.

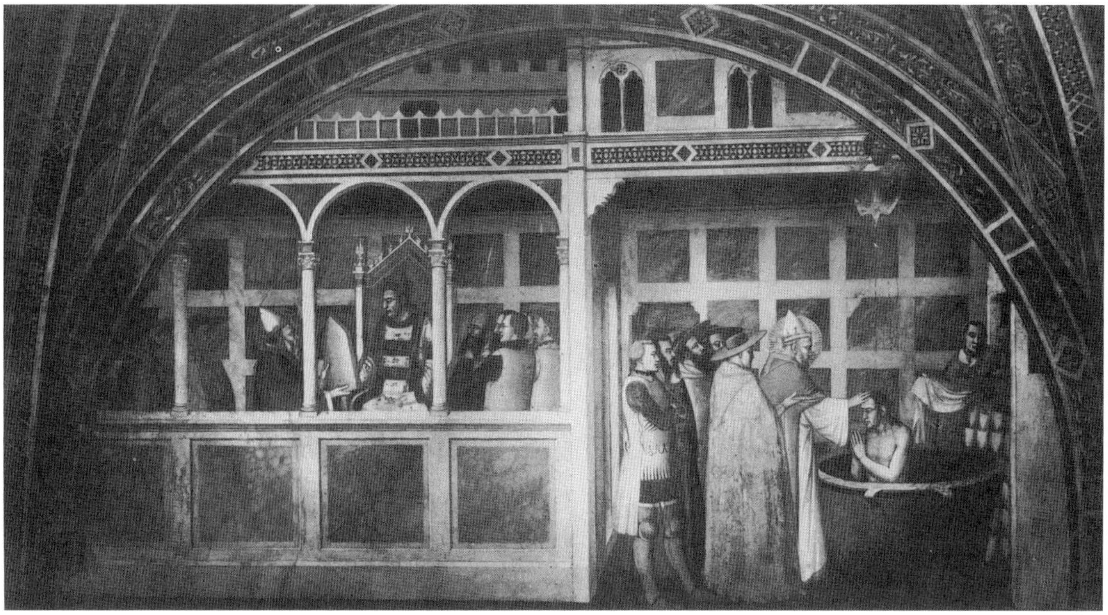

Fig. 17 Maso di Banco: *The Baptism of Constantine*, Florence, S. Croce, Bardi di Vernio Chapel.

the Bardi Chapel frescoes in S. Croce in Florence, which is reflected in Altichiero's work rather than the style of the Arena Chapel.

The extent of Altichiero's debt to the developed Giottesque style is easily demonstrated. The extraordinary clarity, realism and range of his use of spatial and architectural settings derives directly from Giottesque precedent, particularly from the line of three-bay architectural structures developed by Giotto in Assisi and the Bardi Chapel, and which were subjected to increasingly logical and rigorous refinements by the greatest of the *Giotteschi*, Maso di Banco (figs. 17, 18). The three-bay setting of *Ramiro's Council* (pl. 66) in the chapel of S. Giacomo in the Santo, and of *St George Baptising* (pl. 93) and the *Tortures of St Lucy* (pl. 113) in the Oratory of S. Giorgio are openly reminiscent of the *Presentation* and *Christ among the Doctors* in the lower church transept at Assisi (figs. 19, 20), Giotto's Bardi Chapel *Apparition at Arles*, and Maso's *St Sylvester Restoring a Bull to Life* (fig. 18) in the Bardi di Vernio Chapel in S. Croce, itself a sophisticated version of Giotto's composition. The five-bay backdrop to Altichiero's Cavalli votive fresco in S. Anastasia in Verona (pl. 16) is conceptually a development of the same idea. The controlled spatial recession, and the accuracy of architectural draughtsmanship which channel this space in Altichiero's work, ultimately derive – and via a clear line of descent – from Giotto, especially from the two Assisi transept frescoes, which represent the peak of his achievement in this respect.

Detailed aspects of Giottesque spatial control find echoes in more complex contexts throughout Altichiero's work. The kind of spatial imagination which conceives a three-dimensional object at the same time as the space containing it, and which calculates the changing relationship between the containing and the contained according to

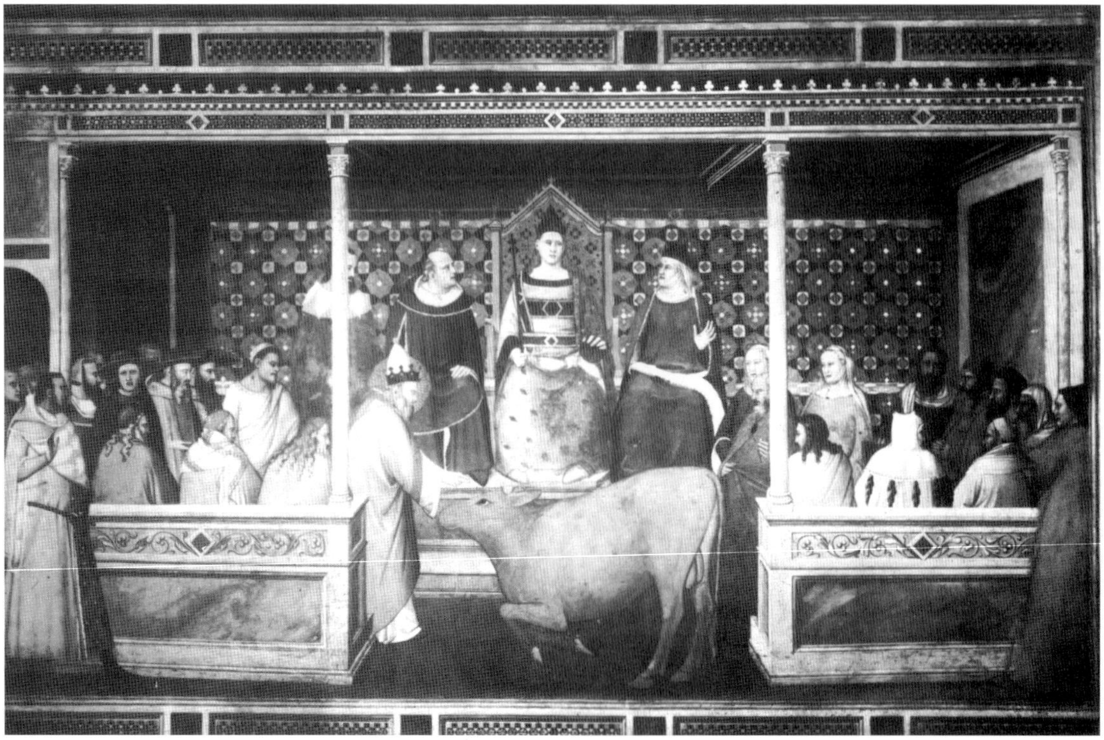

Fig. 18 Maso di Banco: *St Sylvester Restoring a Bull to Life*, Florence, S. Croce, Bardi di Vernio Chapel.

circumstance – seen first in Giotto's use of the temple structure in the *Joachim* sections of the Arena Chapel frescoes, is the ancestor of Altichiero's sophisticated treatment of the shed in the S. Giorgio *Nativity* and *Adoration* (pls. 78, 79). There the angle of view into the shed shifts slightly between the two scenes, a change echoed precisely, and to scale, if one may put it that way, in the crenellated city wall in the far distance, where the angle of recession between the two farthest towers has been adjusted to take account of the foreground shift.

In a similar fashion Altichiero's figure style, and especially the habitual blocks into which he groups his figures, reveal Giotto as the decisive model. The isocephalic disposition of figures across the composition in, for instance, *St George Baptising* recalls countless examples of Giottesque organisation – the Assisi *Presentation* for one – and the detailed design of a group like that of the crowd on the left of the *Funeral of St Lucy* in S. Giorgio (pls. 115, 116) owes much to groups like those in the Assisi Franciscan miracle frescoes (fig. 21), or the Berlin *Dormition* panel. Not only the ponderous gravity of the individual figures, but also the way the group is subdivided and at the same time animated by means of one or more figures looking back or at each other within the group, and the way in which the group (see the *Funeral of St Lucy* again) seems to process past the spectator – the figures on the left turned slightly towards him and those on the right slightly away – are derived from Giotto.

Of Giotto's Florentine followers it is clearly Maso di Banco who had the major impact on Altichiero. The S. Croce *Restoring a Bull to Life* is a composition which seems to have

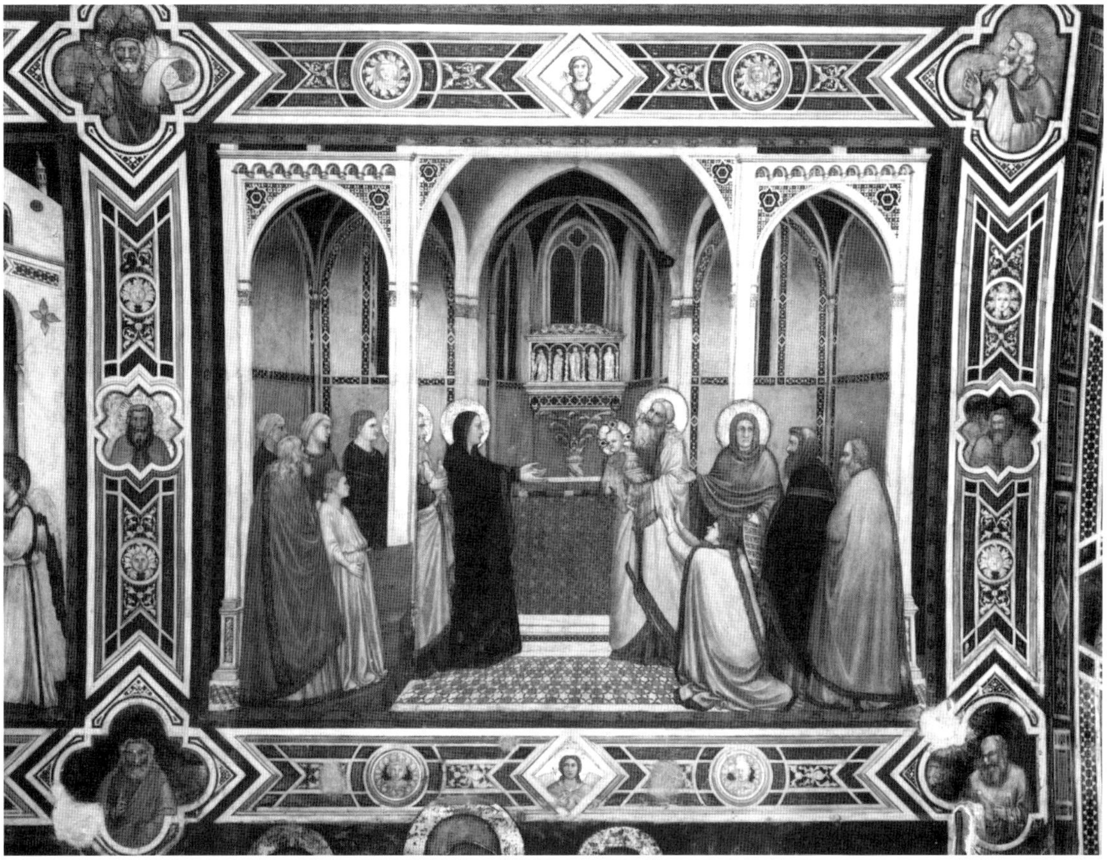

Fig. 19 Giotto: *Presentation in the Temple*. Assisi, S. Francesco, lower church.

particularly impressed him. Not only can its superb spatial clarity be sensed beneath many of Altichiero's own architectural inventions, even to the extent of minute adjustments to take into account the spectator's position (compare, e.g., the minimal recession of the upper cornice of the Temple in the S. Giorgio *Presentation* (pl. 82) with the subtly different receding angles of the containing frontal walls in Maso's fresco), but a section of it also appears as a direct quotation in *Ramiro's Council* and, apparently, in the form of the putative *Self-portrait* in S. Giorgio, standing, just like Maso's framing figure, on the far right and against the low wall (pl. 115). The fact that these quotations occur in particularly significant locations in each case – highlighting what is almost certainly the portrait of the patron in S. Giacomo, and the signature and possible self-portrait in S. Giorgio – is worth noting. In the case of S. Giacomo at least there is circumstantial evidence which suggests that the quotation was particularly appropriate in the context of the patron's personal history, but both instances more generally, and quite unequivocally, proclaim Altichiero's artistic patrimony. The low frontal wall seen in two of Maso's S. Croce frescoes, a device which frames the action, defines the foreground-middleground transition, and marks off a small shelf of space close to the picture plane, becomes a basic feature of Altichiero's organisational vocabulary, often further refined by the adoption of Maso's trick of placing standing figures at the sides of the frontal shelf to give a measurable character to this area outside the main space of the narrative.

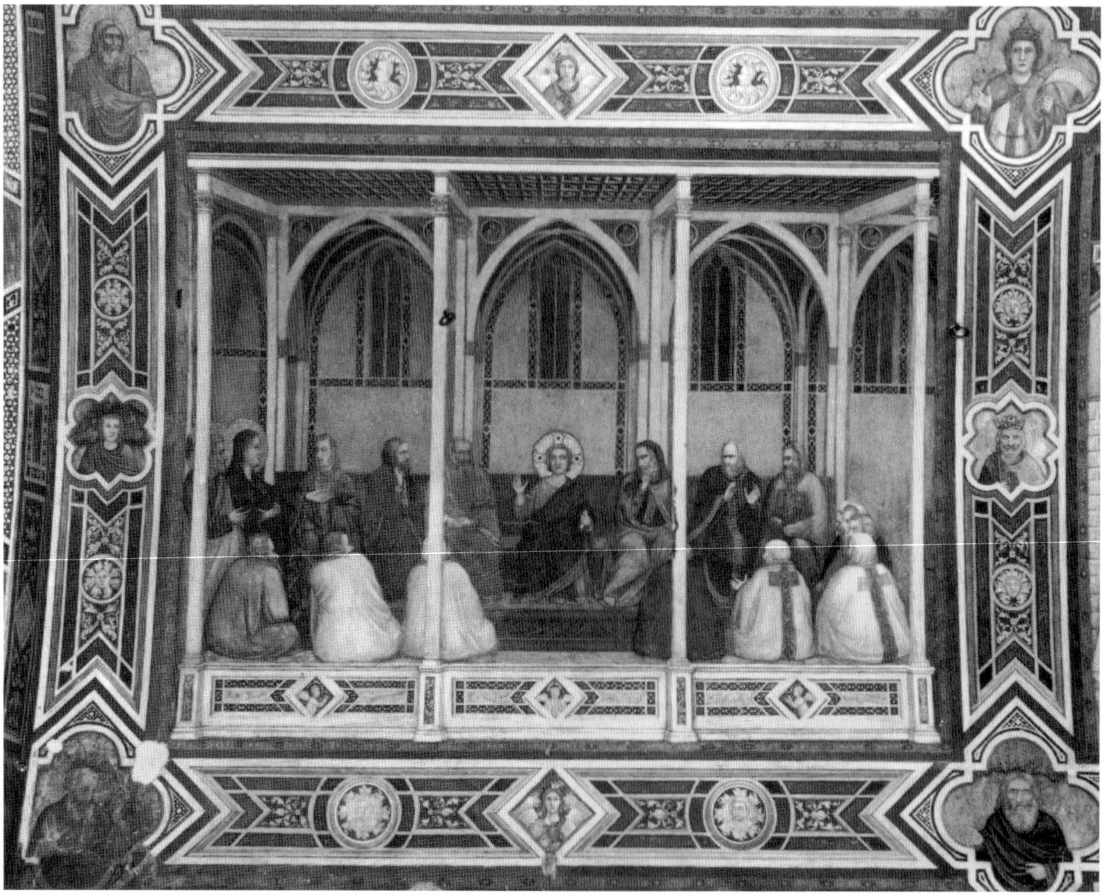

Fig. 20 Giotto: *Christ Among the Doctors*. Assisi, S. Francesco, lower church.

Altichiero must also have studied Maso's S. Croce *Baptism* (fig. 17). Maso here attempted to make rational sense of a scene which required him to combine interior and exterior settings in the same pictorial field. This evidently forms the basis for Altichiero's own delight in making intricate combinations of outside and inside in both Paduan cycles, and the 'telescoped' transition from lower to upper storey in the architecture of the *Baptism* is probably also a source for Altichiero's much more involved versions of the same idea.

Maso is a mysterious figure, and he stands at the head of a strand of development after Giotto which history has rather obscured. The famous 'Stefano' and 'Giottino' are still allowed to float freely in search of documented *œuvres*, but the situation has been clarified by the relatively recent reconstitution[83] of a small corpus of works attributable to the documented Puccio Capanna, working in Assisi in the early 1340s. Puccio's

[83] The key reconstitution of Puccio's *œuvre* under his own name and based on the documented 1341 fragment of a Madonna and Child from the Gate of S. Rufino in Assisi (Assisi, Pinacoteca no. 42) is in Scarpellini, 'Di Alcuni Pittori Giotteschi nella Città e nel Territorio di Assisi', pp. 242–62. See also Todini and Zanardi, *La Pinacoteca Communale di Assisi*, pp. 56–8 and Ragghianti, *Pittura tra Giotto e Pisanello*, pp. 49–63.

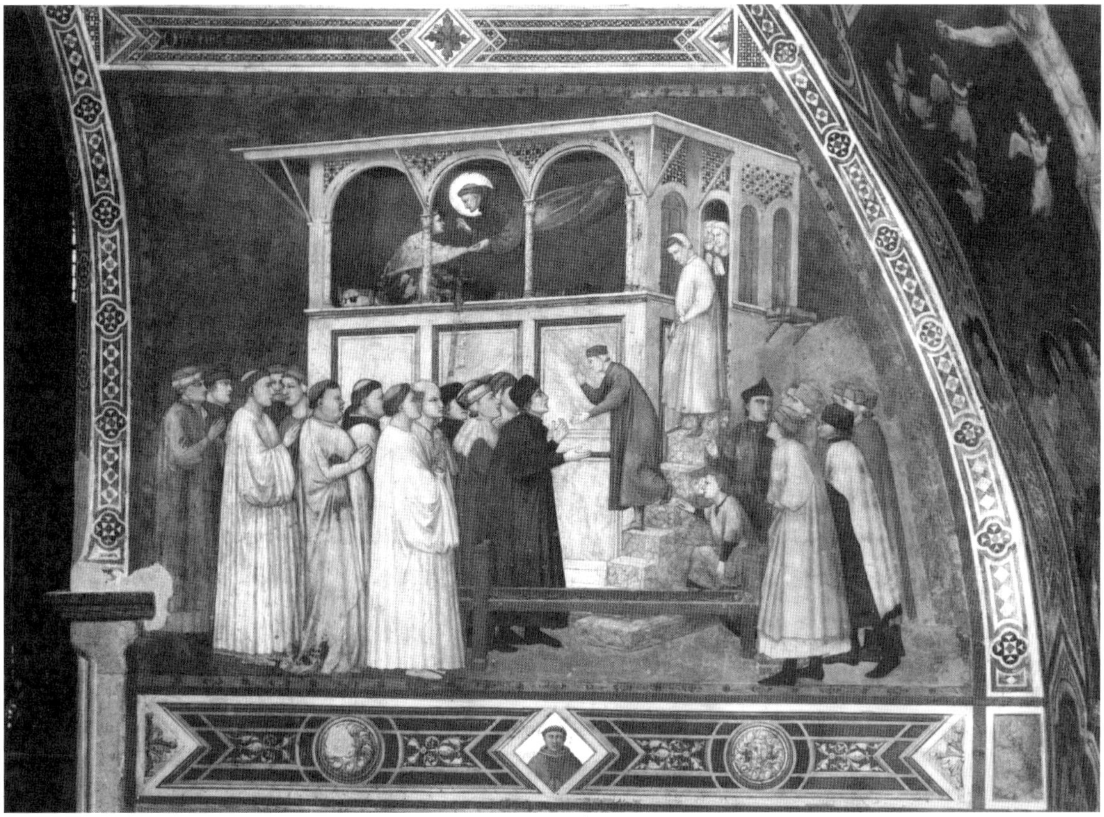

Fig. 21 Giotto workshop: *Raising of the Young Man of Suessa*. Assisi, S. Francesco, lower church.

works – a handful of frescoes in Assisi and a panel divided between Rome and North Carolina – have a significant role in any attempt to reconstruct Altichiero's early influences. It is worth noting that frescoes by Puccio have been identified in the past as either late works by Maso or early ones by Altichiero. Though these attributions are wrong, the stylistic connections they severally and perhaps unknowingly suggest are persuasive and illuminating.

Puccio shares Maso's interest in comprehensive spatial clarity, and though the only surviving examples of architectural settings by him are found in the restricted context of the small frescoes of the *Life of St Stanislaus* in the lower church at Assisi, they provide clear evidence of his place within the Giotto–Maso tradition. The laterally receding upper levels of the church in *St Stanislaus Raising the Dead* (fig. 23) is clearly a version of Maso's idea and its combination of oblique and frontal-foreshortened patterns is echoed in Altichiero's work. The church interior which forms the setting for the *Martyrdom of St Stanislaus* (fig. 24), a miracle of measured spatial recession given the awkwardly curved surface on which the artist had to work, could have been a model for something like the basilical backdrop to Altichiero's *Baptism of King Sevio* in S. Giorgio, and it is fair to assume that we have lost architectural settings by Puccio on a much grander scale.

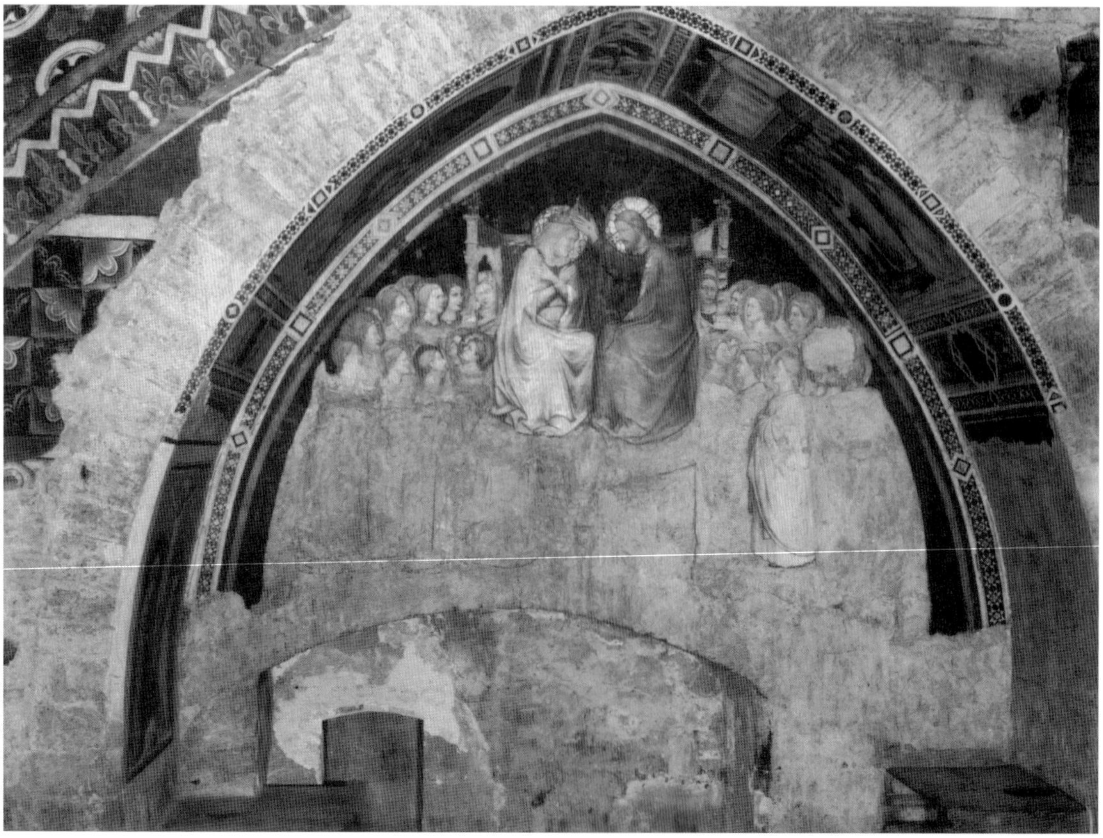

Fig. 22 Puccio Capanna: *Coronation of the Virgin*. Assisi, S. Francesco, lower church.

The grandeur of Maso's figure style is echoed in Puccio's work too. A figure like the standing saint in a pink cloak on the left of the *Crucifixion* in the chapterhouse of S. Francesco in Assisi (fig. 26) has the monumental weight of Maso, though the drapery eschews the simplicity of Maso's style in favour of a more complex and ruffled surface. Puccio shares, however, Maso's taste for modelling the form with a rather light palette, avoiding over-heavy chiaroscuro, a preference which is characteristic of Altichiero too. The effect in all three painters is to combine a quasi-architectural monumentality and power in the figures with extreme visual clarity and legibility.

Altichiero's reflections of Puccio suggest a relationship closer than that of a common debt to Maso. A direct comparison between the St John of Puccio's *Crucifixion* (fig. 27) from the Oratory of S. Rufinuccio in Assisi (now in the Museo di S. Rufino) and the equivalent figure in Altichiero's S. Giorgio *Crucifixion* (pls. VIII, 86) in Padua suggests that Altichiero was using a basic model of the saint derived from Puccio's example. The square post-box mouth, the slit eyes, the sharply contracted eyebrows, are common to both versions, as are the basic shape of the face and the way the hair is curved across the forehead. The general design of Puccio's St John, monumental, even classical, in conception, with thin, highly expressive hands and a general air of psychological intensity, finds echoes throughout Altichiero's work. The peeping angels of the Cavalli votive

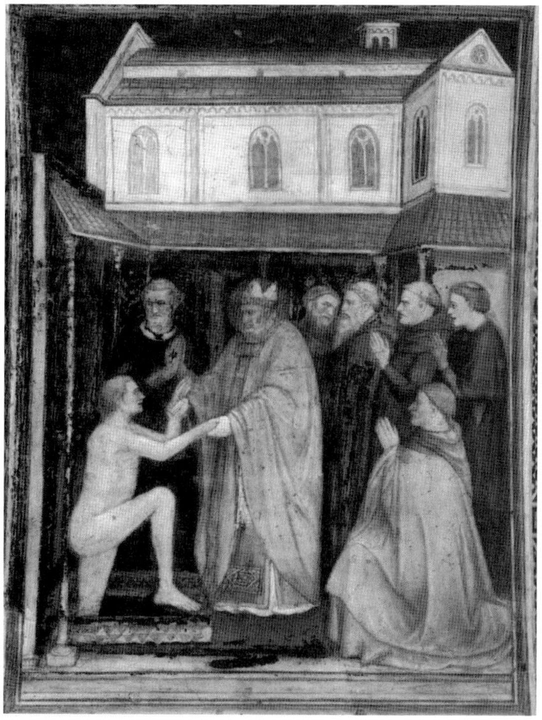

Fig. 23 Puccio Capanna: *St Stanislaus Raising the Dead.* Assisi, S. Francesco, lower church.

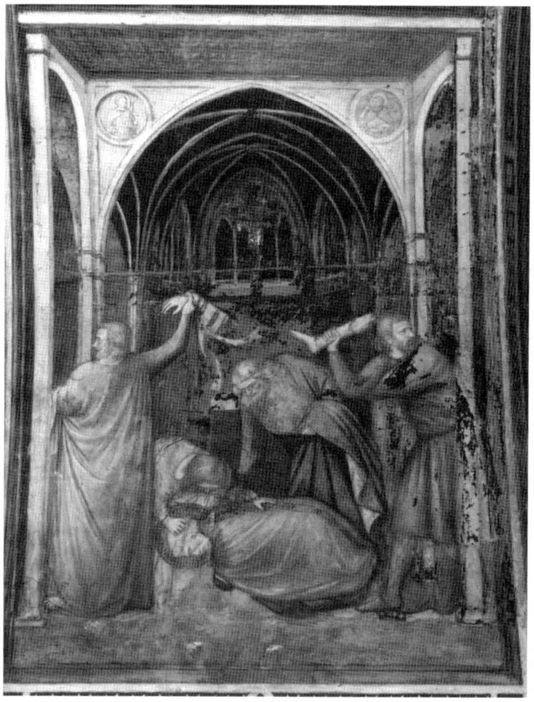

Fig. 24 Puccio Capanna: *Martyrdom of St Stanislaus.* Assisi, S. Francesco, lower church.

fresco are extremely reminiscent of those in Puccio's lower church *Coronation of the Virgin* (fig. 22). The exceptional delicacy of modelling found in the better preserved parts of Altichiero's frescoes also recalls Puccio. The quality of Puccio's touch, with a continuously modulating shaping of the surface, darkening to a wonderfully refined *sfumato*, can best be seen in the Christ-child of the detached fresco fragment of 1341 in the Pinacoteca at Assisi (fig. 25) or some of the arch soffit saints framing the S. Francesco chapterhouse *Crucifixion.*

Close scrutiny of Puccio's *œuvre* increases the conviction that it is here that Altichiero's artistic roots must lie, along the Giotto–Maso–Puccio line of descent. His evidently profound study of Maso, his familiarity with the expansive compositions of Giotto and his workshop in the lower church at Assisi (on which it has been suggested the young Puccio cut his teeth[84]), and his close affinities with Puccio himself, all tend to confirm it. The precise circumstances of the connection remain obscure. The visual evidence suggests a master–pupil relationship. Puccio is usually reckoned to have been active up to about 1350, Maso himself was probably alive until 1347,[85] and Taddeo Gaddi could have provided first-hand contact with the Giottesque tradition until as late as 1366. But Taddeo Gaddi's art finds few echoes in Altichiero's, and the specifically

84 Todini and Zanardi, *La Pinacoteca di Assisi*, p. 56.

85 For Maso's activity see Offner, 'Four Panels, a Fresco, and a Problem'.

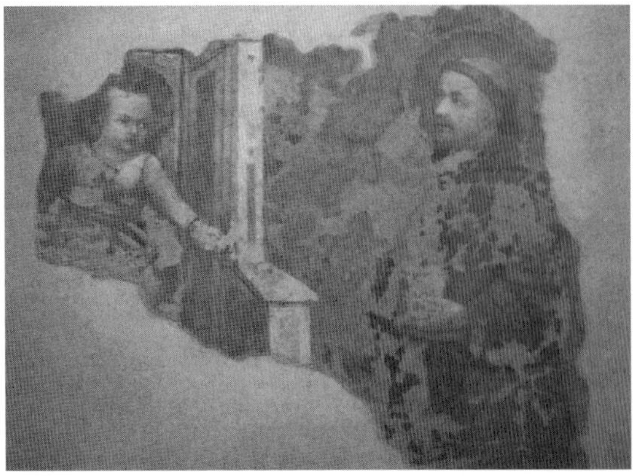

Fig. 25 Puccio Capanna: *Madonna and Child with St Francis* (fragment). Assisi, Pinacoteca.

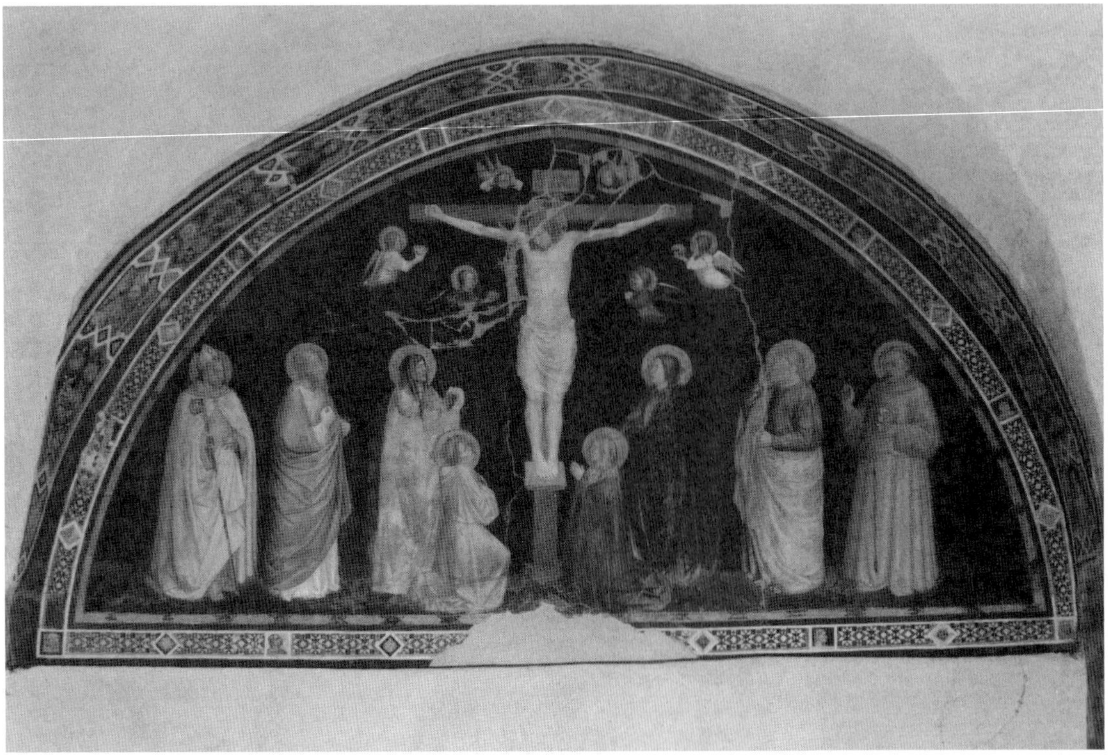

Fig. 26 Puccio Capanna: *Crucifixion*. Assisi, S. Francesco, former chapterhouse.

Assisian elements seem so marked that we must, again, return to the Puccian interpretation of the Giotto–Maso line as the most likely source for the formation of Altichiero's style.

Giotto's art was well known in the north, of course – he may have worked in Verona itself[86] – and the influence of his work in Padua was more or less constant during the trecento. Though it is not Giotto's Paduan work (as we know it today) which lies at the roots of Altichiero's style, it is worth asking if there may have been any other north

[86] Cuppini, 'L'Arte Gotica', p. 288.

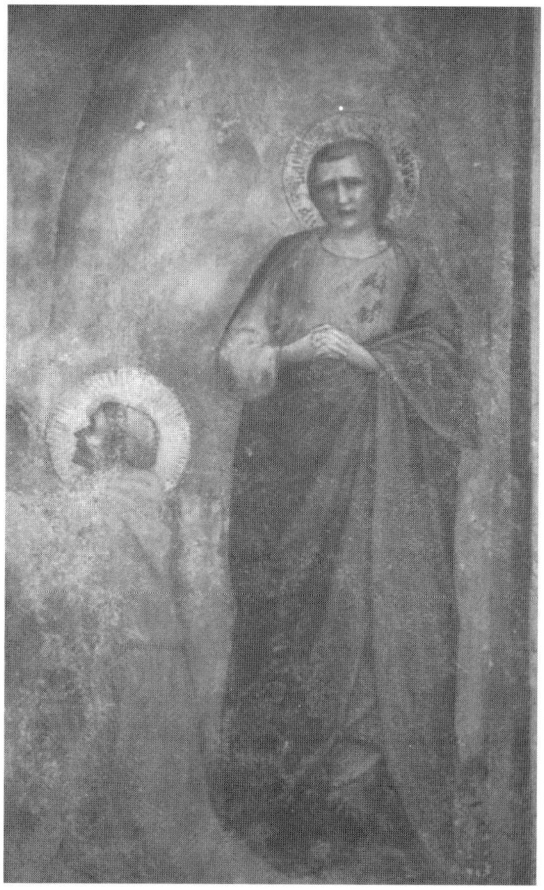

Fig. 27 Puccio Capanna: *Crucifixion* (detail). Assisi, Museo di S. Rufino.

Italian source contributing to his development. The nearly ruined *Crucifixion* fresco in S. Gottardo in Milan[87] does reveal that a developed version of Giotto's style was available closer to hand than Florence or Assisi. The painter of these magnificent fragments reveals himself as one of the most considerable artists of the early northern trecento. The columnar grandeur of his figure style and the clearly structured realism of his faces are broadly analogous with the Tuscan and Umbrian styles already considered. Not much more can be said about this great *anonimo*, given the condition of his one surviving work, and no specific connection with Altichiero need be made, but his work does at least tell us that north Italian painters had access to examples of this quality without having to travel too far.

The S. Gottardo Master furnishes a convenient starting point for a brief discussion of Altichiero's development in the wider context of north Italian painting from about 1340, after the time, that is, when the initial influence of Giotto had been assimilated. While it is true that Verona itself seems to offer little which helps us understand the formative processes of Altichiero's style, a look at the stylistic trends general to the Po Valley as a whole suggests that we can usefully place him in the regional context, and

[87] Matalon and Mazzini, *Affreschi del Tre e Quattrocento in Lombardia*, pp. 35–6.

particularly against the background of painting in Lombardy from *c.* 1350.[88] It is here, to the west of Verona, that we find signs of a widespread and positive response to Giotto's example. The painters of Lombardy clearly studied Giotto with some attention, an observation supported on general stylistic grounds but also by the evidence of direct borrowings on the part of most of the important masters working after 1350. Thus the group on the right of the Arena Chapel *Flagellation* appears with minor alterations in the *Kiss of Judas* in the nave of the abbey of Viboldone, in the frescoes of the Oratory of S. Caterina at Solaro, and in the *Crucifixion* in the Oratory of S. Stefano at Lentate. The impact of a Florentine artist like Giusto de'Menabuoi, himself working at Viboldone as early as 1349,[89] may have contributed to a renewal of interest in post-Giottesque forms of expression some decades after the initial injection of Tuscan monumentality to the Po Valley. There are no grounds for seeing any particular influence of Lombard styles on Altichiero – after the 1360s the influence may have been the other way round. Neither can a case be made for any decisive influence of Giusto himself. Beyond a shared interest in coherent architectural space, Altichiero has little in common with Giovanni da Milano, a Lombard working in Florence, whose name sometimes floats round discussions of Altichiero's origins.[90]

Connections between Altichiero and the painters of Lombardy, including Giusto, have the character of parallel trends rather than direct influence. The same can be said of his relationship with Guariento di Arpo, the major figure in Padua until 1370. Guariento obviously drank from some of the same sources as Altichiero, but the older man's style is fundamentally different. There are signs in Altichiero's Paduan work that he was impressed by Guariento, as well as by his Venetian pupil Nicoletto Semitecolo, but that was a response of his maturity, not of his apprenticeship. It belongs to a later stage in his development, when Altichiero already had behind him the major Veronese works which established him as Guariento's successor as the most sought after painter of the eastern Po Valley.

88 For Lombard painting in the trecento see *ibid., passim.*

89 Delaney, 'Giusto de'Menabuoi in Lombardy' gives a full account of Giusto's activity in Lombardy. For Viboldone, see particularly pp. 22–6.

90 E.g. Ragghianti, *Pittura tra Giotto e Pisanello*, pp. 49–63.

2

THE SALA GRANDE IN VERONA

Della Scala rule in Verona falls into three main phases: the acquisition and consolidation of power under Mastino I and Alberto; the period of maximum territorial expansion under CanGrande I (1311–29) and Mastino II (1329–51), when the Scaligeri domain was extended to the edge of the Venetian lagoon in the east and to the south as far as Lucca; and finally the period of retrenchment within the original borders of the Veronese district, a process already under way in Mastino's time. This last phase, punctuated by fratricidal struggles amongst the Scaligeri themselves and occasional bouts of more widespread bloodletting, may be said to have begun on the night of 13 December 1359, when the teenage Cansignorio della Scala encountered his older brother CanGrande II near the Church of S. Eufemia, quarrelled with him and killed him.[1] Cansignorio, fearful perhaps of retribution at the hands of the German knights employed to protect his brother, fled to Padua; but with the encouragement of his uncle Francesco da Carrara he quickly returned and established himself as absolute ruler. Cansignorio firmly excluded his older brother Paolo Alboino from power, as CanGrande had done, and later imprisoned him. On his deathbed, in 1375, Cansignorio, looking to protect the succession of his two illegitimate sons, sent orders for the wretched Paolo to be killed, so ending his rule much as he had begun it. Cansignorio, sickly – he was only thirty-six when he died – pious and rich,[2] really seems to have had no taste for the bellicose lifestyle of his illustrious forebears, and his famous remark that, given the choice, he would ask for nothing more than to spend his time and money on building projects – 'un dolce impoverire' as he called it[3] – is borne out by an impressive legacy of structures of all kinds in Verona and its subject territories. His status as the last really substantial ruler of the della Scala dynasty probably rests more securely on this – he was beyond question the greatest patron of the arts his family produced – than any figure he may have cut on the wider political stage, where he was easily outshone by real *aficionados* of the game like Bernabò Visconti.

[1] Carrara, *Gli Scaligeri*, p. 201, and Rossini, 'La Signoria Scaligera dopo CanGrande', p. 700.

[2] See Rossini, 'La Signoria Scaligera dopo CanGrande', pp. 701–15 for Cansignorio's rule.

[3] Biancolini, *Cronica della Città di Verona descritta da Pier Zagata, colla Continuazione di Jacopo Rizzoni*, vol. 1, p. 95. Saraina, *Le Historie e Fatti de' Veronesi*, who gives an extensive account of Cansignorio's building programme based on a wide range of sources, ascribes to him, p. 52v, the remark that 'il fabricare era un dolce impoverire' and that if he were a private citizen he would ask for nothing more than to spend his time and money building, 'credendo con quello beneficiare le posteri'.

We know a great deal about Cansignorio's buildings and other projects, of which many survive, but the greatest pictorial monument of his time, Altichiero's frescoes of the Jewish Wars of Titus and Vespasian, are lost, and even their precise location was a mystery until Mellini's discovery of surviving borders and other fragments of the cycle in the late 1950s.[4] The prestige of this fresco cycle makes its mark pretty consistently throughout the period between its execution and the publication of Vasari's second life of Altichiero, inserted with other material in his life of Carpaccio, in 1568. Vasari was able to refer to a clear tradition for these frescoes, which were evidently well known in the fifteenth century, and his account is correspondingly lucid. That there was one pre-eminently splendid painted hall in the former Scaligeri palace, the residence of the Venetian *podestà* during the quattrocento, is clear from a number of references. A document of July 1427[5] is drawn up 'super sala magna depicta existente supra viridarium palacii residentie Domini Potestatis', and one of July 1431[6] 'super sala magna depicta Palacii residentie Domini Potestatis'. In his *Fioretto* of 1477, Francesco Corna describes 'una sala per certano / tutta depinta con magne figure / a le istorie de Tito Vespisiano; / et e si rica d'oro de de penture / con le figure tante naturale, / che tutta Italia non ha un'altra tale',[7] and in his *Itinerario* of 1483 Marin Sanuto mentions as one of the principal sights of Verona the palace 'dil podestà, magnifico, con la salla pynta excelente'.[8] The wording of these references makes it clear that the hall was unique and could not be confused with any other apartment of the palace complex.

Vasari's attribution of the cycle to Altichiero, together with a much fuller account of the frescoes themselves, is made in the later edition of the *Vite*, building on the 1550 edition's note that amongst other fine work done by Altichiero in Verona was 'la sala del palazzo del Podestà'. In 1568 Vasari says:

> There was in the same city of Verona Altichiero da Zevio, who was the friend (*famigliarissimo*) of the della Scala Signori, and who, besides many other works, painted the great hall of their palace, where the Podestà now lives, making there the War of Jerusalem, as it is written about by Josephus: in which work Altichiero showed great spirit and judgement, distributing one history over every side of the walls of that hall (*da ogni banda una storia*), with only one ornament which encircled it right round, on which ornament, as if to finish it off, he placed a row of medallions (*partimento di medaglie*), in which it is believed that there are portraits from life of many distinguished men of those times, and in particular many of the della Scala Signori: but because the truth about this is not known, I will say no more. I must say that Altichiero showed in this work that he had intelligence (*ingegno*), judgement and invention, having taken into consideration everything to do with a war of importance. Beyond that, the colour is very well preserved. And amongst many portraits of great men and literary figures, there is seen one of Messer Francesco Petrarca.[9]

This is far less confused a text than the later part of Vasari's account of Altichiero's career, and in virtually all respects it can be supported by corroborative evidence of one kind or another. It is the last account from which it can be inferred that the painted hall was still extant in its original form. In 1718 Dal Pozzo remarked that because of altera-

4 Mellini, 'La "Sala Grande" di Altichiero e Jacopo d'Avanzo'.

5 Sandri, *I Palazzi Scaligeri di S. Maria Antica*, p. 10.

6 *Ibid.*

7 Corna, *Fioretto de le Antiche Croniche de Verona*, stanza 135.

8 Sanuto, *Itinerario per le Terraferma Veneziana*, p. 97.

9 Vasari, *Le Vite*, vol. III, p. 633.

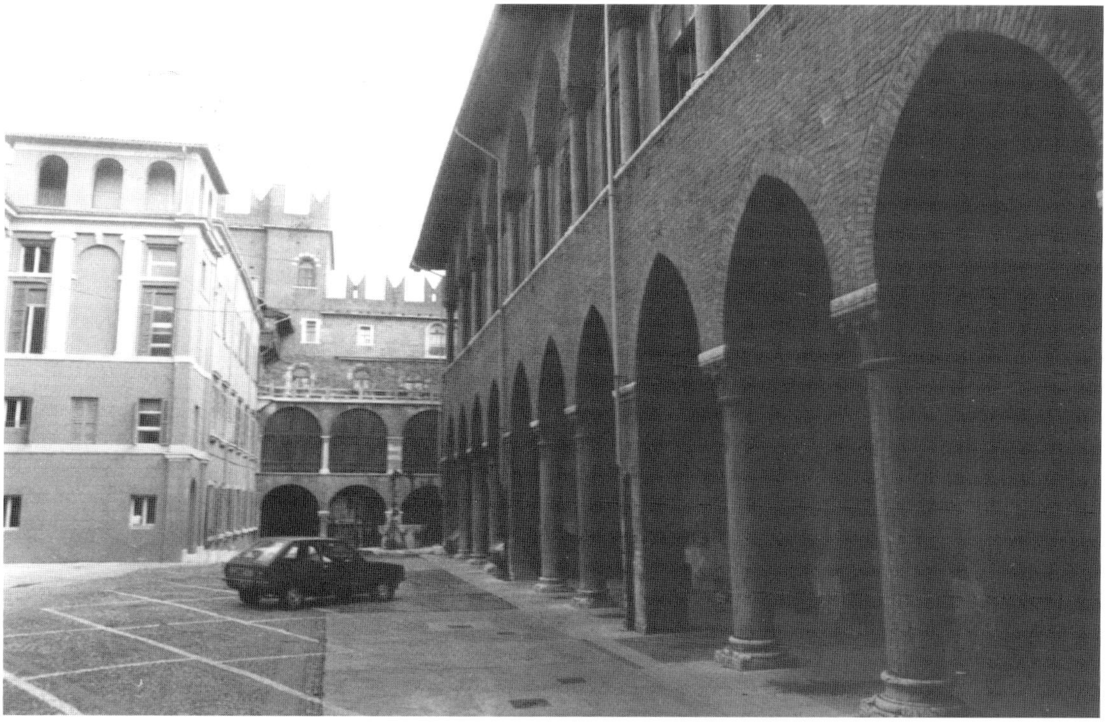

Fig. 28 Verona. Cansignorio's loggia.

tions to the hall the frescoes could no longer be seen.[10] From this point, and after further remodellings of the fabric of the building, the memory of the Josephus frescoes was obscured. In 1895 Julius von Schlosser[11] discussed the work as reported by Vasari, but it was still possible for Gerola in 1909[12] to dismiss the Veronese palace decoration altogether, believing that Vasari had simply muddled the two cities in which Altichiero worked, together with their respective *signori*, and transferred elements of the Paduan Sala Virorum Illustrium to Verona.

The precise location of the great painted hall remained unclear throughout the nineteenth-century campaign to restore the Scaligeri palace complex to something like its trecento form. Matters were only clarified in the late 1950s by Mellini's discovery of a series of imperial portrait busts painted in fresco (pls. 6–14) on the soffits of the upper-storey arches of a large structure running between the south block of CanGrande's palace and the *corso* (figs. 28, 29). These busts, enclosed within a fictive moulded border of a clear trecento pattern, closely resemble equivalent examples found in Altichiero's surviving frescoes in Padua. Investigation of the interior of the upper storey, evidently once an open loggia, but now given a false ceiling and divided into a corridor and offices, revealed areas of what were clearly once extensive frescoed surfaces, together with a border fragment of recognisable Altichieresque type. On the basis of

10 'Di queste Pitture hoggi per l'alteratione delle fabriche non se ne vede vestigio alcuno' – Dal Pozzo, cited by Mellini, 'Sala Grande', p. 319.

11 Schlosser, *L'Arte di Corte nel Secolo Decimoquarto*, pp. 55–6.

12 Gerola, cited by Mellini, 'Sala Grande', p. 334.

these discoveries Mellini published in 1958 his identification of this structure as the Salla Pynta' of the early sources, Vasari's Sala Grande.

The building identified by Mellini is a two-storey brick construction of considerable size, with an arcade along the north east side at both levels, open at ground level, but partly blocked and glazed on the upper storey. The north-east side of the building juts out beyond the line of CanGrande's palace, to which it is attached, and into an open space formed by the interior courtyard of that palace and a further area running up to the edge of the *corso*. The Gothic style of this building distinguishes it from the surrounding palace structures, typically massive and round-arched, scarcely different in essence from the Romanesque Palazzo del Commune. It was clearly added to the main body of CanGrande's palace at a later date. Suggestions that this might have happened as late as the fifteenth century[13] can be disregarded in the light of the presence of fresco fragments of unarguably trecento date.

None of the early sources give a date for the Sala Grande, and Vasari does not specify which of the Scaligeri was Altichiero's patron. But he does state that Altichiero's work for the family preceded his years in Padua, which began at some time in the early 1370s, and we know that he was resident in Verona in 1369; all of which suggests that his activity there must fall within the period of Cansignorio's rule. We know, too, that Cansignorio began a major reconstruction and enlargement of the palace complex in 1364 'cum cameris et ornamentis',[14] during the course of which he extended the wings of CanGrande's palace in the direction of the *corso*, and there is no reason to doubt that the Sala Grande was built as part of this programme, replacing an earlier and necessarily smaller hall, presumably in response to the same expansion of court ceremonial that prompted Francesco da Carrara, a few years later, to replace his original hall, the Sala Thebana, with the much larger Sala Virorum Illustrium.[15]

The building of a more or less self-contained loggia on such a scale is unusual. Other palaces had loggias, but they were usually incorporated within the body of a larger building, often as part of some quasi-claustral arrangement. The main arcade of this Veronese loggia faces north-east, admitting (together with the single arch of the south-east wall) early morning sunshine, but providing constant shade throughout the rest of the day. The pointed arches of the loggia distinguish it from earlier examples in the region, like the round-arched (lower storey) and trabeated (upper storey) patterns of many castles in the Veronese district, and the fully trabeated loggias of the Carrarese Palace in Padua.

The original internal condition of the building cannot be reconstructed with absolute certainty, but it seems to have consisted of a single great hall on the first floor, with the ground floor probably divided as now into separate rooms, with only a narrow passage behind the arcade open to the elements.[16] The soffits of the lower arcade are decorated

13 Sandri, *Palazzi Scaligeri*, p. 23.

14 Paride da Cerea, *Chronicon Veronense*, vol. 658.

15 For the Sala Virorum Illustrium see Mommsen, 'Petrarch and the Decoration of the Sala Virorum Illustrium in Padua'. Gasparotto, 'La Reggia dei da Carrara' puts it in the context of all the other known apartments of the Carrarese Palace.

16 The beams running across the external corridor of the lower storey of the loggia appear to be old, and not to have been tampered with.

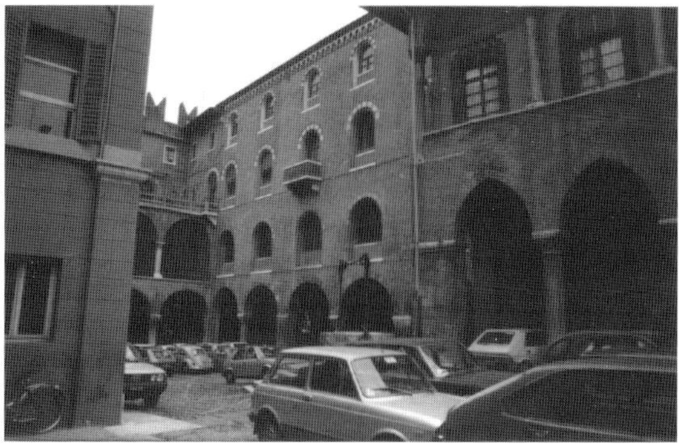

Fig. 29 Verona. Cansignorio's loggia(r.).

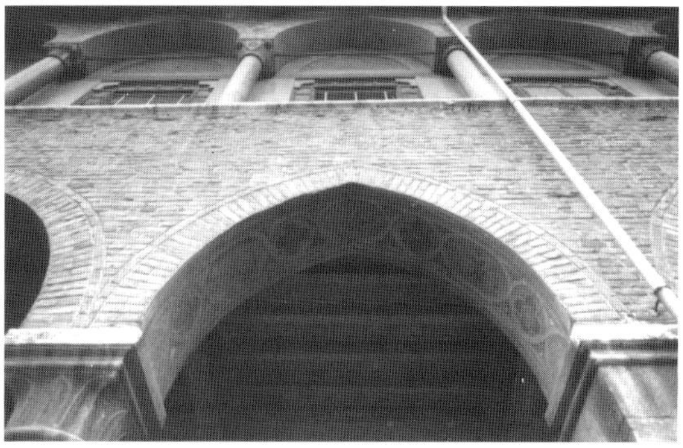

Fig. 30 Verona. Cansignorio's loggia, detail of ground floor arcade.

in exactly the same way as those of the upper storey, except that the polyfoils are blind (fig. 30). These may have been added at some stage to match the imperial soffits above, and the paintwork looks too good to be of trecento date. But they may have been extensively repainted like the imperial border, and it cannot be ruled out that this was the original disposition of the borders, with busts above, marking the most important area, and abstract motifs below. The first floor is presently entered from the end of the wing of CanGrande's former palace, extended by Cansignorio, but it is not certain that this was the only original means of access. The long back wall seems not to have been broken by any windows or doors, and the same goes for the short north-west wall giving on to the *corso*. The arcaded wall gives on to an open space which was probably then a garden, perhaps created with the loggia as an integrated project. The present wall and fence dividing the space from the street are not original, though they must have replaced an older barrier of some kind.

The decoration of the Sala Grande can be reconstructed to some degree on the basis of Vasari's account and the surviving fragments. It seems to have consisted of three main elements: the narrative frescoes mentioned by Vasari and Corna, probably undivided into separate scenes, a prominent border ('ornamento') running right round the hall above the narratives and containing portraits of notable contemporary figures, and the partly extant decoration of the window soffits containing fictive stone profile busts of Roman emperors. To these can be added a fourth element, mentioned in a later section of Vasari's text: 'due trionfi bellisimi' painted, 'similmente a fresco', 'sotto le sopradette pitture'.[17]

Of the frescoes based on the *Jewish War* of Josephus there remain inside the Sala Grande nothing more than a few patches of what Mellini identified as a landscape,[18] together with fragments of border decoration. The long back wall of the loggia, which must have carried the bulk of the fresco cycle, seems to have been almost completely resurfaced in

[17] Vasari, *Le Vite*, vol. III, p. 634.

[18] Mellini, *Altichiero e Jacopo Avanzi*, p. 33.

the course of past alterations, and nothing short of a full-scale archaeological survey is likely to reveal anything more of its original condition. The area available for frescoes was considerable, around 265 m^2 for the long back wall, with another 65 m^2 on the short north-west wall, as well as a certain amount on the entrance wall.[19] Vasari's account suggests that the cycle concentrated on the combat sections of Josephus's text, which only dominates the latter half of the book, and Corna's description makes it clear that, as one would expect, the figure of Titus was prominently featured.

This gives us no sense of the look of the frescoes. For that we must turn to a series of drawings, mostly done in the fifteenth century, when the Sala Grande seems to have been frequently observed and admired, not least, according to Vasari, by Mantegna. The drawings are not particularly coherent as a group, and their relationship with the lost frescoes needs to be examined with considerable caution, but some of them, whose connections with Altichiero's surviving work is clear enough, do seem to shed invaluable light on the Sala Grande cycle.

Of the seven drawings which comprise this group (labelled A–G for convenience) the first (pl. 1), formerly in the Bertini Collection in Prato, is the most significant in that it has an explicit link with the lost frescoes in the form of an inscription, in a fifteenth-century hand, on the sheet to which the drawing (evidently cut from a larger sheet) is attached. This reads: 'di maestro Altichiero qual dipinse la sala del podestà'. The drawing shows part of a city wall with a gate reached by a small bridge, across which a party of cavalry has just passed, and at the near end of which a skirmish is taking place. The architectural background is manifestly related to those of Altichiero's Paduan frescoes (e.g. the S. Giacomo *Crucifixion*, the first and second scenes from the St George cycle in the Oratory of S. Giorgio), and the general design of the drawing accords in every detail with equivalent passages in the fresco cycles in Padua. The style of the composition is so clearly related to Altichiero's known work that there would be no difficulty in seeing this drawing as a record of something of his even without the inscription. Given the inscription, there is no reason to doubt that this is indeed a record of a part of the Sala Grande cycle.

Another copyist seems to have been impressed by this same part of the cycle, for a drawing (B) in the Louvre (pl. 2) reproduces the same incident, as well as other material, probably drawn from the same cycle, but piled up in an incoherent heap which scarcely reflects Altichiero's known methods of handling large-scale narrative. Rather than an imitation of Trajanic relief style, as Plant[20] suggests, this should probably be seen as a sort of fantastic compilation of details, each of which has, on its own terms, Altichieresque traits. The existence of this second copy reinforces the assumption that some shared model lies behind the drawings.

A drawing in the British Museum, a chalk and wash *Camp Scene* (C, pl. 3) probably

[19] For the dimensions of the hall see catalogue entry below. They, and the proportions drawn from them, are based on the drawing printed in Mellini, *ibid.*, pl. 19–20, and measurements of the exterior made by the author. Accurate measurement of the interior is presently impossible given the division of the structure and the difficulty of access to it (as the seat of the *Prefettura*).

[20] Plant, 'Portraits and Politics', p. 417.

of early quattrocento date, resembles the receding landscape of the *Battle of Clavigo* in the Chapel of S. Giacomo in Padua (pl. 69), and the way the knots of figures are disposed across the scene, as well as the actual design of the figures themselves, also recall equivalent passages in Altichiero's known work, though the details of costume and armour clearly point to the drawing's post-trecento origins. Such features might be ascribed to the more or less unconscious modernisation of some contemporary of Pisanello's or Gentile's, but this drawing's connection with the Sala Grande, often claimed, is not certain. The scene depicted can be matched with book 3 of Josephus's text, which describes fighting on the shores of Lake Gennesaret, but not so specifically that any firm argument can be developed on this basis.

A rather more precise connection of this kind seems to be provided in the case of drawing D, a group of studies in the Lugt collection (reproduced by Mellini 1965, fig. 46). This shows several groups of soldiers in fourteenth-century armour and dress: three in repose, the men just standing in conversation, and two in violent action. Also included are a single figure of a man pulling on his breeches and a rather incongruous study of a bird. The standing and fighting figures are reminiscent of groups in both Paduan cycles, and the five-studded shields are of the type commonly carried by Altichiero's soldiers. The small group on the left, which shows a soldier apparently being disembowelled after the removal of his armour, bits of which lie strewn around him, brings to mind Josephus's graphic description[21] of the incident in which Syrians and Arabs rip open the stomachs of refugees, believing them to have swallowed their gold coins for safe-keeping, part of the lengthy description of the siege of Jerusalem and all its attendant horrors, the central matter of Josephus's account and, presumably, of the frescoes.

Related in subject matter, costume and armour types, and figure style to parts of C and D is a drawing of four soldiers with a scaling ladder, now in Oxford (Corpus Christi College). Like A, and unlike the rest of this group, this (E) is drawn on parchment. It is also rather more decisively finished and more fully modelled than D, for instance, or than the breezily drawn and rather sketchy C. The general design of the figures here shares with these two an affinity with the background figures of the *Battle of Clavigo* which goes beyond that merely attributable to the similar subject matter. Characteristic of the figures in all three drawings and the Paduan fresco is a virtuosity shown in the many variations on complicated twisting and bending postures – figures looking upwards, exerting strain, moving the top and bottom halves of the body in different directions, all contrasted with standing figures in repose, a juxtaposition wholly characteristic of Altichiero.

A pair of drawings in the British Museum, recto and verso of the same sheet, completes this series. The recto side (F, pl. 4) shows various scenes of fighting in a camp, with, at the bottom right, a group of soldiers erecting a tent. The cavalry battle at the top is particularly reminiscent of *Clavigo* in detail. This drawing may represent one of the skirmishes following Jewish sorties against the Roman camp, described by

[21] Josephus, *The Jewish War* v. 548. Mellini, *Altichiero e Jacopo Avanzi*, p. 34 also makes this suggestion.

Josephus, perhaps the very one led by Josephus himself which resulted in his capture and the subsequent interview with Vespasian, one of the most famous incidents of the book.[22]

That incident comes to mind again when one looks at the verso of this sheet (G, pl. 5), which shows an enthroned emperor receiving a supplicant. Attempts to relate G to one of the lost scenes painted by Pisanello in the Doge's Palace in Venice (e.g. *Otto's Supplication Before Barbarossa*[23]) fail on the grounds that this is manifestly a trecento composition, both in overall conception and in the details of figure style and dress. The specifically Altichieresque provenance of the composition is quite clear; the groups of standing figures on either side of the scene precisely resemble such groups in the S. Giacomo frescoes (*Ramiro's Council*, pl. 66) and in the lives of all three saints depicted in the Oratory of S. Giorgio. The use of the opened-up but convincingly scaled interior is wholly characteristic, as is the bringing in of the left-hand group through an opening. The affinities extend to minor touches like the lively foreground dogs. The seated figure, close in many ways to King Ramiro in the Council scene in S. Giacomo, is strictly speaking anachronistic if intended as a portrait of Vespasian, not yet emperor at the time of Josephus's capture, merely commander of Nero's armies in Judea. The importance of the conversation between Vespasian and Josephus lies, of course, in the latter's prophecy that Vespasian was himself destined to become emperor. For the seated figure in the drawing, crowned, and surmounted with an eagle, such a prophecy would seem somewhat redundant. The setting of this scene, clearly within a palace, is also inappropriate for the incident described by Josephus, which took place on the field of battle following the fall of Jotopata. These reservations do not necessarily rule out a connection between these drawings and the lost frescoes. They have strong, even overwhelming, affinities with Altichiero's work and they show scenes of battle and imperial power. The Court scene may not represent the interview with Vespasian at all, and it is perhaps significantly close to a detail in a fifteenth-century illustrated Josephus[24] showing, not Vespasian, but Nero in his court, on the same page as a representation of Josephus's capture, with Nero a crowned and bearded figure, enthroned and surrounded by courtiers.

Each of these seven drawings has at least some claim to be considered as a possible record of the lost Josephus frescoes. A and parts of B have very strong claims in this context. The two parchment drawings, A and E, may have been made quite close to the time of the frescoes' execution, but even those which were probably not, like C, still preserve something of Altichiero's manner. All more or less go with what, on the evidence of extant work, we would expect such a work from Altichiero's hand to look like, though obviously none is large enough to enable even the most sketchy reconstruction of the

22 Josephus, *The Jewish War* III. 204ff.

23 Popham and Pouncey, *Italian Drawings in the Department of Prints and Drawings in the British Museum. The Fourteenth and Fifteenth Centuries*, pp. 189–90. The parapet of the background building has a Venetian look to it, but it has close cousins in Altichiero's S. Giorgio frescoes in Padua.

24 Reproduced on the cover of the 1981 Penguin Classics edition of the *Jewish War*.

entire cycle to be attempted. It can be assumed that in the Paduan *Battle of Clavigo* we have an abbreviated version of the sort of composition originally laid out across the long wall of Cansignorio's loggia – and if the relevance of G is accepted, with just such a switching from interior to exterior scenes as characterises the *Ramiro* scenes in the chapel of S. Giacomo.

A little more can be usefully said on the subject of the overall disposition of the frescoes, using Vasari's text and the extant fabric of the building. The proportions of the upper hall are remarkably harmonious. The ground plan is a double golden section rectangle; the elevation of the south-west wall a triple golden section rectangle; and those of the short walls both root-two rectangles.[25] The height of the arcade on the north-east side precludes any extensive painting of narrative on the open side of the loggia, though we can assume that some such border system as survived on the window soffits also framed the arches internally, a supposition confirmed by Mellini's discovery of border fragments in this area, including a largely intact six-pointed star.[26] This necessarily qualifies Vasari's statement that Altichiero painted his narrative 'distributing one scene over the walls of that hall on every side (nelle facce di quella sala da ogni banda)'. The impression that he or his source[27] intended to give must have been that the narrative continued without a break round all the available wall space, that is, something over half the south-east, the whole of the south-west, and the whole of the north-west walls. Surviving fragments indicate that the bottom level of the upper border ran along the walls some way below the line of the lower parts of the roof brackets, leaving a band of considerable width for the 'partimento di medaglie'. The presence of a dado must be assumed. It is unlikely that dado and upper border between them used up more than half the overall height of the wall, but, given the proportions of the walls, the available space for the narrative can hardly have been other than extremely long for its width, even if the narrative band was pushed further towards the floor than is the case with Ambrogio Lorenzetti's *Effects of Good Government* in Siena. Ambrogio's fresco probably gives some sort of an idea of the overall look of the Sala Grande cycle in large-scale terms – it goes well enough with Vasari's description for analogies of a very loose kind to be suggested. Altichiero's detailed treatment of his pictorial field can only be the subject of speculation. Even the largest scenes of S. Giacomo give no real indication of his likely response to the ribbon-like space available to him in Cansignorio's loggia. He may have broken it into strips and 'chapters' like those of Guariento's Old Testament frescoes in the Carrarese Chapel in Padua (fig. 46),[28] but, given his usual concern for

25 See n. 19 above.

26 For Mellini, *Altichiero e Jacopo Avanzi*, p. 33, this star furnished 'testimonianza iconologica inconfutabile' of the Jewish subject matter of the fragmentary frescoes, an overstatement of the case given the presence of similar stars in other works by Altichiero.

27 It is not clear whether Vasari had actually seen the frescoes. He visited Verona at the end of 1541, but afterwards mentioned only the antiquities he had seen there. His declared source for the early history of Veronese painting, Fra Marco de'Medici, is not regarded as the last word in reliability by modern scholarship – see Cuppini, 'L'Arte Gotica', p. 311 – but Vasari had another and perhaps more visually alert source for Verona in the form of his Veronese assistant Giovanni Caroto. The description of the Sala Grande smacks of first-hand visual experience, though not necessarily Vasari's. See Rubin, *Giorgio Vasari*, pp. 129 and 196.

28 D'Arcais, *Guariento*, pl. 64.

spatial continuity and unity it is perhaps more likely that he let the action unfold in a more or less continuous flow, treating the subject as one vast field of action in a single pictorial field, like Lippo Vanni's fresco of the *Battle of Val di Chiana* in the Palazzo Pubblico in Siena,[29] only on a vaster scale. One can only try to imagine the overall effect, splendidly coloured, picked out in gold, 'con le figure tante naturale'.

The only part of the Sala Grande cycle to survive in anything like presentable form is the series of imperial busts formerly (they have been removed for safety) on the soffits of the main arcade. The eleven arches of the north-east wall have, or had, four busts each, alternately facing left and right. Attribution of these profile portraits to Altichiero can be made on the basis of abundant comparative material from the Paduan cycle, most obviously with the imperial profiles in S. Giorgio (pl. 85) and, less conspicuously, S. Giacomo. A direct comparison between the *Maximus* of the Sala Grande (pl. 11) and the right-hand head in S. Giorgio makes the validity of the attribution absolutely clear. Other comparisons confirm it: between the bust of *Caracalla* (pl. 8) and the supposed profile portrait of Bonifacio Lupi in the Council scene of S. Giacomo (pl. 68); between the bust of *Maximus* and the 'Arab' in the left bay of the S. Giacomo *Crucifixion* (pl. 42); between the Veronese *Gordian I* (pl. 12) and both the Gabriel of the S. Giacomo *Annunciation* and the St Catherine of the Dotto tomb *Coronation* in the Eremitani in Padua (pl. 118); and between the *Balbinus* (pl. 13) of the Sala Grande and the right-hand angel of the S. Giacomo *Resurrection* (pl. 74). In addition, the younger faces of the Sala Grande soffits (*Balbinus, Gordian*) resemble the rather masculine type extensively used by Altichiero in Padua for female saints (e.g. Sts Catherine and Lucy in their frescoes in S. Giorgio, pls. 105–16).

The soffit border is painted in a rich grisaille, with a range of warm sandy yellows and greens and a dark blue infill to the central sexfoils of the main lozenges, a colour scheme which sets off the cold and lapidary tonality of the busts themselves, not merely grisaille profiles but quite specifically fictive stone busts. The drawing of those heads which are still in good condition (*Caracalla, Balbinus, Faustina*) (pls. 8, 13, 10) is firm and incisive, if anything rather more so than the heads in S. Giorgio. The quality allows an attribution to Altichiero himself, for all that this is just a border. It is, however, a rather exceptional border, and in any case the quality of many of the upper-border busts of saints in S. Giorgio indicates his personal intervention in a comparable instance. The removal of the soffit frescoes revealed a series of remarkable sinopie,[30] not preparatory drawings for the border but free sketches, including several of buildings (perhaps related to the main frescoes inside), and a number of imperial profiles, at least one of which is so monstrous in character as to suggest a rather sardonic view of the job in hand. The same could be said for one or two issues of Roman imperial coinage, presumably made with no such intent, and the Paduan imitators of these coins in the later trecento seem to have accepted even the grosser specimens of imperial physiognamy as viable models for

[29] Carli, *La Pittura Senese del Trecento*, pl. 266.

[30] These are presently held in the Museo degli Affreschi attached to the site of 'Juliet's Tomb'.

signorial medals – objects one would imagine even less likely to display conscious satirical overtones.[31]

The surrounding border is painted as if in high relief and lit from the north-east. A pair of fictive stepped-up roll mouldings articulates the surface of each soffit, crossing over scissor-fashion to form the near-circles containing the quatrefoils, and the longer foliate lozenges in between. The overall effect, compounded by the ogee of the central foliate element in the long lozenges, is powerfully rhythmic and rather more curvilinear than the highly organised geometric structures of Altichiero's later borders. The individual foliate elements within the lozenges are assertively plastic in conception, fleshy even. The intricacy of Gothic polyfoils, cusps, multicusps and elaborately pierced infills which characterise the borders of S. Giorgio were either not yet a part of Altichiero's ornamental repertoire, or consciously eschewed in this instance. In the local context, compared for instance with the simple borders of the painters of S. Zeno and S. Fermo, this 'architectural' border stands out, and it must be related to the richer Gothic style characteristic of the products of court and court-related patronage. Such a style only fully penetrates the Veronese vernacular towards the end of the century.

A handful of the soffit busts were identified[32] after their rediscovery on the basis of inscriptions written in white round the edge of the quatrefoil lobes (for a full discussion of the identification of the portraits, and the texts of the inscriptions see the catalogue entry below). Subsequent restoration has revealed that a great deal of this writing has been repainted, as a comparison of the busts in their present state with the plates published by Mellini in 1959 and 1965 will show. But what survives of the trecento inscriptions suggests that the repainted sections followed the originals faithfully, and that identifications made on the basis of repainted inscriptions now lost are mostly reliable. In the initial surveys of the busts a number of erroneous identifications were made and one or two of the inscriptions were incorrectly read. The sequence of the busts, a matter of some importance, as will emerge, was never discussed. But the early accounts recognised, without discussing the full implications, that the frescoed busts, clearly derived in general terms from Roman coin portraits, could be rather more precisely connected with the marginal drawings, themselves based on coins to some extent, of the *Historia Imperialis* (hereafter *HI*) written by the Veronese cleric Giovanni de Matoci 'il Mansionario' (d.1337).[33]

Fifteen of the original forty-four busts can be identified with some certainty on the basis of their inscriptions, or by inscription and affinities with either coin portraits or those of the *HI*: *Hadrian* (arch 2, bust 1), *Geta* (2/2), *Sabina* (2/4), *Caracalla* (3/1), *Faustina Senior* (4/1), *Severus Alexander* (4/2), *Maximinus* (4/3), *Maximus* (4/4), *Gordian I* (5/1), *Pupienus* (5/3), *Balbinus* (5/4), *Philip I* (6/2), *Aurelian* (8/4), *Tacitus* (9/1) and *Carus* (9/4).

[31] Though Fox, *Roman Coins and How to Collect Them*, pp. 103–4 believes some coins were designed with satirical intent.

[32] Mellini, 'Sala Grande', pp. 323–6.

[33] Mellini, *Altichiero e Jacopo Avanzi*, pp. 30–1. Schmitt, 'Zur Wiederbelebung der Antike im Trecento', pp. 190ff. In his first discussion of the frescoes ('Sala Grande') Mellini had not yet recognised the manuscript source.

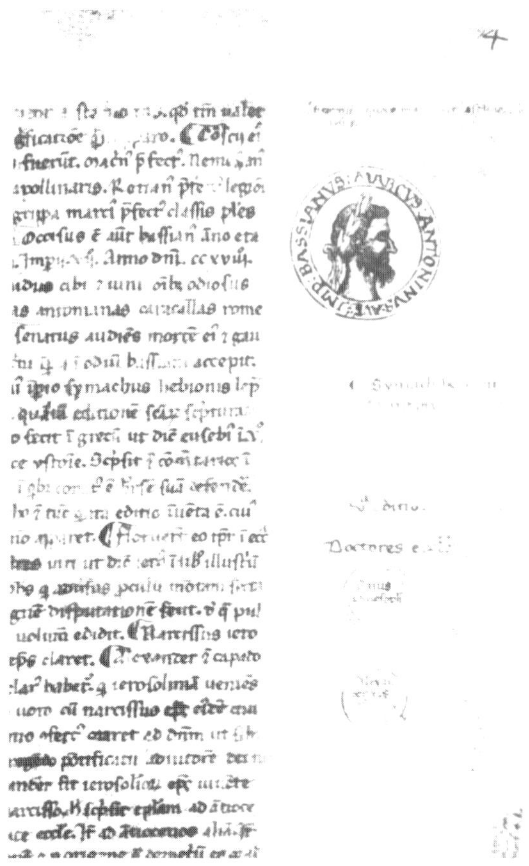

Fig. 31 *Caracalla.* From Giovanni de Matoci, *Historia Imperialis*, fo. 4r.

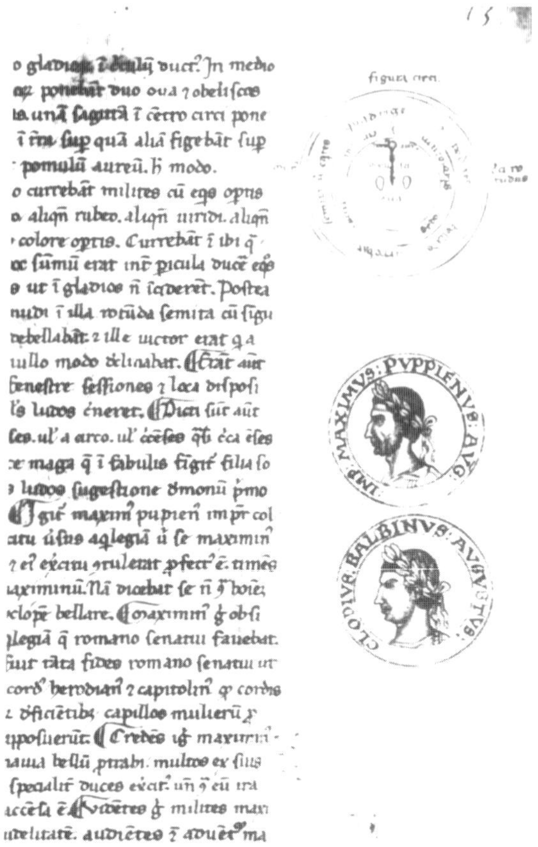

Fig. 32 *Balbinus and Pupienus.* From Giovanni de Matoci, *Historia Imperialis*, fo. 13r.

Giovanni di Costantino de Matoci[34] (doc.1306–37), notary, canon, and then sacristan of Verona Cathedral, one of four *mansionarii*, a post from which he takes his nickname, wrote his history of the Roman Empire, or more precisely, of the Roman emperors, between *c.* 1306 and 1320. His original intention was to cover the entire list of emperors from Augustus to Henry VII, but none of the three surviving manuscripts of the work gets beyond the ninth century. Of these manuscripts, that in the Vatican Library (Vat. Chigi. I. vii. 259) is autograph,[35] with marginal emendations and additions by the author, and probably a fair copy. It is illustrated throughout with marginal roundels containing profile portraits of the emperors – and occasionally empresses – under dis-

[34] For Giovanni 'Il Mansionario' see Simeoni, 'La Famiglia di Giovanni Mansionario Autore delle Historie Imperiales'; Adami, 'Per la Biografia di Giovanni Mansionario'; Avesani, 'Il Preumanesimo Veronese', pp. 119ff.; Carrara, 'Gli Scrittori Latini dell'Età Scaligera', pp. 35–8; Weiss, *The Dawn of Humanism in Italy*, p. 13; Weiss, *Dawn of Humanism*, 'La Cultura Preumanistica Veronese e Vicentina del Tempo di Dante'; Weiss, *Dawn of Humanism*, 'The Study of Ancient Numismatics During the Renaissance (1313–1517)', p. 178; Weiss, *Dawn of Humanism*, 'Ausonius in the Fourteenth Century', pp. 68–9.

[35] Weiss, 'Ausonius', p. 68, n. 8.

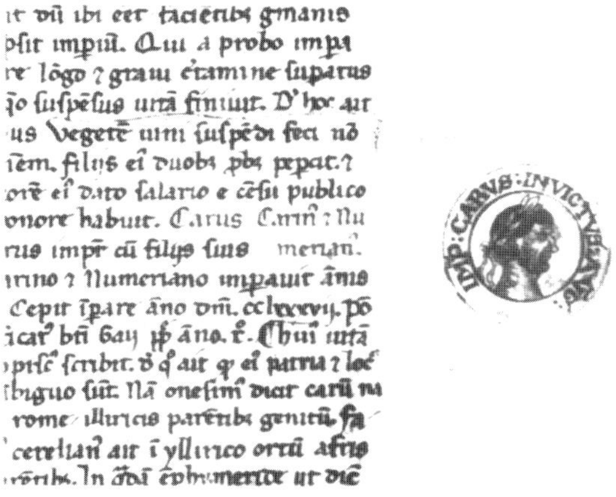

Fig. 33 *Carus*. From Giovanni de Matoci, *Historia Imperialis*, fo. 29r.

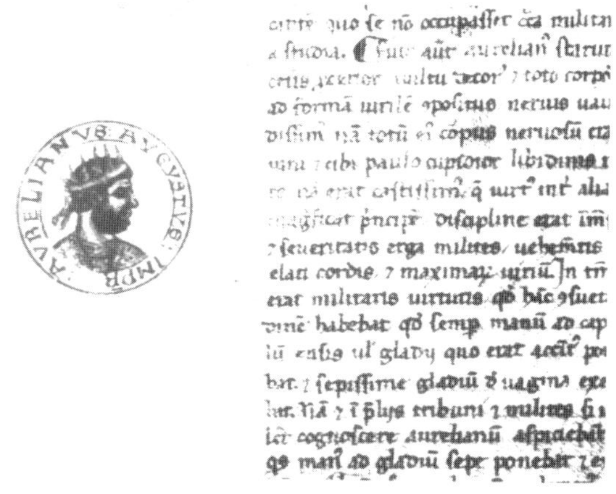

Fig. 34 *Aurelian*. From Giovanni de Matoci, *Historia Imperialis*, fo. 24v.

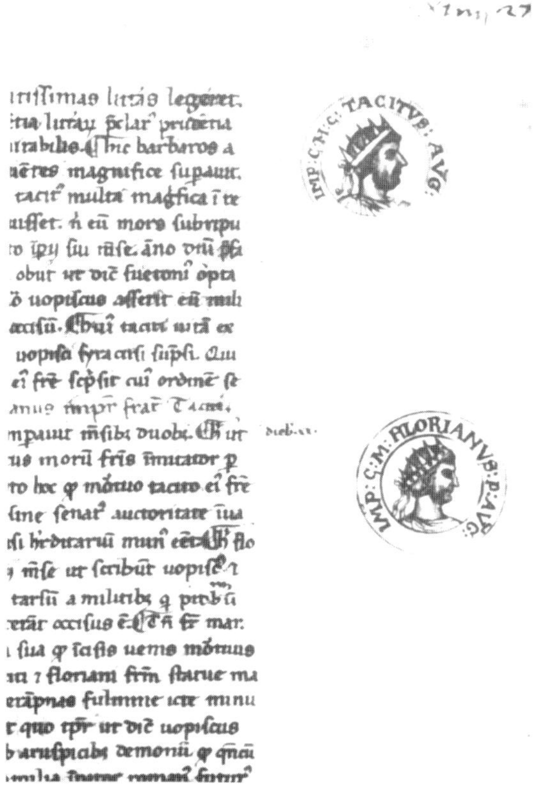

Fig. 35 *Tacitus and Florianus*. From Giovanni de Matoci, *Historia Imperialis*, fo. 27r.

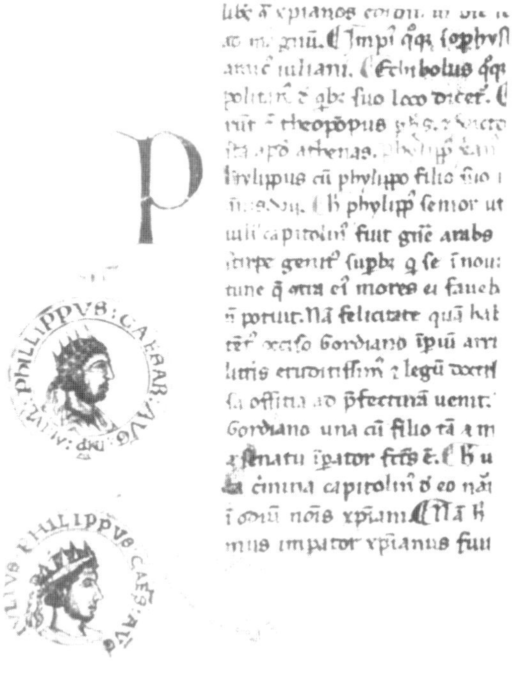

Fig. 36 *Philip I and Philip II*. From Giovanni de Matoci, *Historia Imperialis*, fo. 15v.

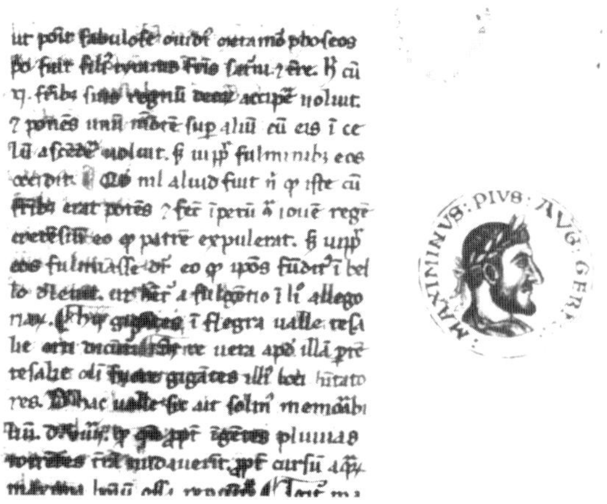

Fig. 37 *Maximinus*. From Giovanni de Matoci, *Historia Imperialis*, fo. 10v.

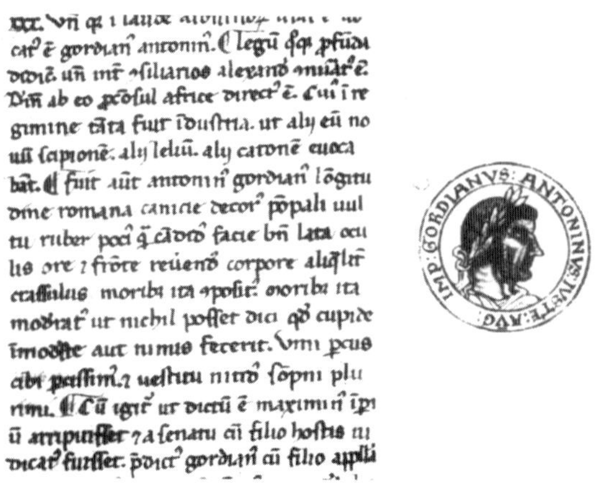

Fig. 38 *Gordian I*. From Giovanni de Matoci, *Historia Imperialis*, fo. 12r.

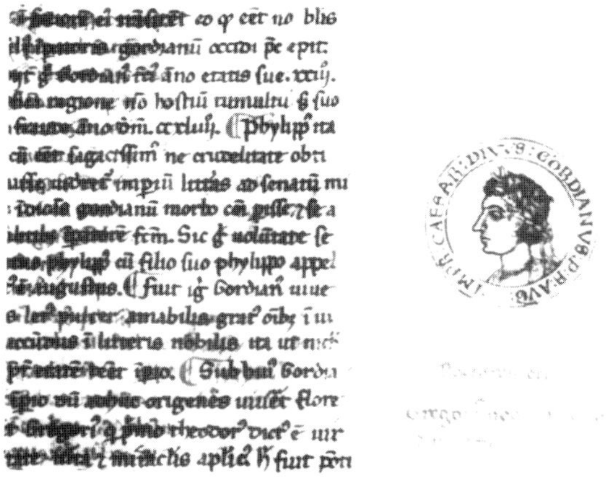

Fig. 39 *Gordian III*. From Giovanni de Matoci, *Historia Imperialis*, fo. 14r.

cussion, with smaller roundels containing the names of prominent Christians of the era, and with ground plans of important Roman buildings: the Colosseum, a theatre, the Circus Maximus. The text as we have it today, with folios clearly missing from both ends, extends from the reign of Septimius Severus to that of Louis the Pious.

The manuscript now in the Biblioteca Capitolare in Verona (cod. CCIV) – where much of it was presumably written – is probably a scribe's copy. It too has roundels of both kinds and the plans, but the main roundels, though drawn in throughout, are without portraits, and, except for the first thirteen folios, without the inscriptions which identify all the portraits of the Vatican manuscript. This text breaks off at Charlemagne.[36]

[36] In most respects the Verona text is tidier than the Vatican autograph; it was almost certainly being prepared at the same time, and under Giovanni's supervision. I am grateful to Robert Gibbs for his assessment of the relationship between the two MSS. Any conclusions drawn here are, of course, entirely mine.

The third copy of the *HI*, in the Biblioteca Vallicelliana in Rome (MS. D 13), is not autograph, has no illustrations, but does contain in addition part of a work evidently conceived in tandem with the *HI*, a history of all the popes, the *Gesta Pontificum.*[37]

The quality of the drawings in the Vatican copy is variable, though rather more refined than photographs suggest, as is the degree of characterisation. In the earlier part of the manuscript the drawing is supplemented by the use of a brown wash. In one instance the portrait (Probus, fo. 28r) is picked out with touches of blue for the helmet and gold for the armour and laurel wreath. That the portraits depend on Roman coins, a relationship which, on the face of it, seems obvious, is only true for a proportion of the roundels. Broadly speaking, the later the emperor the less certain it is that a coin has been consulted. In detail this is sometimes rather hard to determine, but the *HI* drawings of the Vatican copy can be broken into two broad groups: the sequence from Septimius Severus to Constantine, where the majority are either based on coins or on a coin type close to the original; and the sequence from Constantine II to Louis the Pious, where it is clear that Giovanni had either never seen, or was not impressed by, the coinage of the Byzantine Empire, basing his portraits instead on the profile style of the early empire. This, however anachronistic in terms of numismatic style, does serve his purpose of emphasising the continuity of the medieval empire from that founded by Augustus.

Altichiero's dependence on this (or another lost copy of the *HI*, also with illustrations), rather than on coins themselves (at least in the majority of cases) is easily demonstrated. Giovanni's drawing of Caracalla (fo. 4r, fig. 31) is quite distinctive, and not close to the coinage, except in picking up the gathering of the beard into separate ringlets under the chin. Otherwise, the face, with its long beard, partially recalls the coin profiles of the earlier Marcus Aurelius, whose portrait is one of those lost from the Vatican manuscript. Altichiero's fresco of *Caracalla*, identifiable from the partly surviving inscription, is clearly copied from this drawing, for it follows the idiosyncrasies of the manuscript, for which there are no other sources – certainly not the coinage itself.

The fresco of *Balbinus*, which has its inscription largely intact, is anomalously labelled CLODIVS BALBINVS AVGVSTVS. The name *Clodius* belongs instead to Balbinus' co-emperor Pupienus (Clodius Maximus Pupienus), raised to the Purple with Balbinus (D. Caelius Balbinus) for a brief period from April 238. None of the coins, obviously, make the mistake of transferring this name, but on fo. 13r of the Vatican manuscript of the *HI* (fig. 32) the roundel of Balbinus, next to that of Pupienus, is labelled, just as on the fresco, CLODIVS BALBINVS AVGVSTVS. Even in humanist Verona it is scarcely conceivable that Altichiero could have independently hit on the source of Giovanni's mistake (the *Historia Augusta*[38]), and the dependence of his frescoes on the *HI* can be regarded as absolutely certain. Where they are, or were, legible, Altichiero's inscriptions invariably follow Giovanni's, which are very largely of his own invention and not mere copies of the coinage.

Enough of Altichiero's imperial portraits survive for it to be clear that the heads were

[37] And breaks off during the reign of Justin II.

[38] *Scriptores Historiae Augustae*, Gordiani Tres. X. 1 and XXII. 1.

laid out in chronological sequence. The best preserved section, arches 4, 5 and 6, follows the sequence laid out in the *HI* from Severus Alexander to Philip I, with only one missing portrait, which should be that of Gordian II. Other sections, where survivals are more sporadic, still suggest the sequence. Thus a series of nine unidentifiable (on the basis of any of the categories mentioned above) busts stretches from *Philip I* (6/2) to the next identifiable bust, *Aurelian* (8/4), just as one would expect. And from *Aurelian* the sequence goes: *Tacitus* – two gaps – *Carus* – again, exactly in accordance with the known sequence. Extending this forward to the last available space on the northernmost window arch brings the list to Licinius, last pagan emperor of Rome, and a quite logical place to bring the series to a close.

That Altichiero followed the *HI* rather than some other source containing the historical succession of emperors is clear from his inclusion, as in the *HI*, of occasional female portraits like *Sabina* and *Faustina*. Such figures were selected according to Giovanni's purposes and are not self-selecting like the emperors themselves. The fact of Altichiero's reliance on the manuscript source for his sequence makes it all the more odd that *Faustina* appears quite anachronistically in the fourth arch, just before *Severus Alexander* and well past *Caracalla*, all of which is chronological nonsense. Deviation from the *HI* sequence such as occurs in the second arch, where *Sabina* comes after *Geta* and not with *Hadrian*, her husband, may be accounted for on the grounds that it was thought proper for *Hadrian* and *Sabina* to face each other across the arch. But such a consideration hardly justifies the inclusion of *Faustina* in the fourth arch rather than much earlier in the sequence.

In fact *Faustina* could not be fitted into the arcade sequence as it was discovered – her portrait would have to come before the first arch. The north-east wall soffit sequence must have begun with Lucius Verus, well into the succession as laid out in the *HI*, and it seems highly unlikely that this was the case. The *HI* succession itself has to be reconstructed by collating the Vatican and Verona manuscripts. The Verona manuscript has inscribed roundels from Julius Caesar (though the text actually starts with Augustus) up to Lucius Verus. Thereafter they are totally blank. The Vatican copy begins with Septimius Severus. There is thus a gap of indeterminate length (in terms of roundels). The existence of a fresco of *Faustina* so obviously based on her coin portraits allows us to suppose the existence of a roundel of her (lost from the Vatican manuscript and never inscribed or drawn in the Veronese), and we must assume that the emperors Commodus, Pertinax and Didius Julianus were represented. The pretenders Clodius Albinus and Pescennius Niger, though both issued coins, were almost certainly not represented. If we assume that the fresco sequence following *Caracalla* filled the three available spaces with *Macrinus* (the fresco broadly resembles Macrinus's coin portraits), Diadumenus and Elagabalus, the *HI* sequence, and that, for all that the sequence would not be entirely right, Septimius Severus can be put in the blank space (2/3) following *Geta*, then room has to be found (if the fresco sequence began, like the *HI*, with Julius Caesar) for twenty portraits at the beginning of the succession. Given that the frescoes do to a large extent follow the sequence of the *HI*, and that the whole border is manifestly based on it, it would be odd if the fresco series began with anyone but Julius, and even odder if a design showing such a developed taste for the Antique excluded the majority of the famous Twelve Caesars.

One possible solution suggests itself. If the single window of the short south-east wall, facing CanGrande's palace, originally had quatrefoils with busts instead of the blanks it has today, then with arch 1, a further eight heads are accounted for, leaving twelve. The arcade of the north east wall has eleven arches, and therefore twelve spandrel fields. The disposition of the coherent and accepted group of the Twelve Caesars on either the interior or exterior spandrels of the arcade, with the rest of the sequence following on on the soffits, seems a wholly plausible hypothesis, giving, as it does, special emphasis to the Suetonian group. The placing of painted busts in such a position accords with Altichiero's practice in Padua and, for that matter, with then extant Roman decorative ensembles which Altichiero or his humanist associates could have seen for themselves.[39] Intellectually and visually this seems the most promising hypothesis.

If two conditions are allowed – that the south-east window had portraits like the rest of the upper-floor windows; and that the two pretenders were excluded from the roundels of the *HI* and therefore from the frescoes – then the layout of the imperial busts can be reconstructed as follows: it followed the *HI* sequence from Julius Caesar to Licinius, with only minor deviations and no omissions, and it gave special prominence to the first Twelve Caesars on the spandrels. The acceptance of neither condition seems to me to involve special pleading. Indeed, it is arguably much more likely that they should have obtained than that the sequence should have been so arbitrarily laid out as it must have been if they did not.

One of the more fascinating aspects of this imperial sequence lies in the opportunity it provides for a comparison to be made between the different literary and artistic approaches to a source stemming from the Antique, and at a very early stage in the development of a *rapprochement* between writers and artists in this field. Altichiero's approach to his task is informed by a more consistent sense of classical style than the artist of the *HI* drawings. This man, no mean draughtsman on his own terms, follows the available coin portraits closely, while Giovanni adopts a much more liberal approach to the construction of inscriptions based on his reading of the many textual sources, a process leading him at times into error, at others to quite sensible clarifications and emendations. Altichiero in turn follows the given inscriptions of the *HI* slavishly, only deviating from the text to the extent of expanding the odd abbreviated AVG to the full AVGVSTVS if space allowed.

His attitude to the drawings, by contrast, is as free as Giovanni's was to the coin inscriptions. The frescoes reveal an independence in regard to the visual source which reflects a process of intentional critical analysis on Altichiero's part. Basic artistic instinct probably accounts for deviations such as those of the frescoes of *Carus* and *Caracalla*, in which Altichiero has added draped shoulders in instances where the

[39] E.g. the revetment of the temple of Junius Bassus, drawn by Sangallo and surviving as S. Andrea in Catabarbara until the seventeenth century. See Krautheimer, *Rome. Profile of a City, 312–1308*, pl. 33.

drawing (figs. 33, 31) had simply left a long bare neck. Where the *HI* leaves a head uncovered, Altichiero provides it with a laurel wreath, while usually following his source when it furnishes a radiate instead of laureate head (*Aurelian* (fig. 34), *Tacitus* (fig. 35), but not *Philip I and Philip II* (fig. 36)).

The frescoes of *Sabina* and *Faustina*, of which empresses the *HI* drawings are no longer extant, resemble their coins so closely that we can assume a clear chain of descent from the original portraits, through the *HI* and down to Altichiero. The rest of the frescoes, however, show a marked idealisation of the facial features as compared with the *HI* portraits. The fresco of *Caracalla* has a nobility lacking in the rather ill-humoured and craggy manuscript profile. *Severus Alexander*, though damaged like Geta, is still visibly more youthful and open-faced than the drawing, resembling in fact the group of young imperial fresco heads (*Balbinus*, *Gordian*) more than the drawing. With *Maximinus*, Altichiero restores to the likeness something of the obstinate and rather quirky nobility which characterises the coin portraits and the surviving portrait busts, without in the process actually recording the actual appearance of the originals, as the drawing does. Clearly, though intent on improving his material, Altichiero did so here without consulting any numismatic source, but rather on the basis of his own existing repertoire of facial types.

This process of reinvention is very marked in the subsequent fresco of Maximinus' son *Maximus Caesar*, where the bland and curiously prim *HI* likeness is replaced by a head of great character, rather excessive, in fact, from a purely historical point of view. In the case of *Gordian I,* Altichiero's probable dislike of a rather unattractive *HI* drawing (which correctly attempts to show the age of this ancient man, fig. 38) leads him to substitute, quite anachronistically, the face of a handsome youth, the youngest looking, in fact, of all the surviving fresco heads, close to the coin portraits of Gordian III – closer indeed than to the drawing of the last of the Gordians. Giovanni, to judge from his *Gordian I*, had no coin available, and his artist must have had to base his drawing on verbal clues alone. Perhaps in this case Altichiero did consult a coin, choosing, or having chosen for him, a Gordian, but the wrong one.

That the coins themselves did to some extent come into Altichiero's reckoning is suggested by the next pair of identifiable frescoes, *Pupienus* and *Balbinus*. It is clear that Giovanni de Matoci had no access to the coinage of the joint reign (which lasted only three months and cannot have produced any great number of coins). His drawings neither resemble the highly individualised coin portraits of the two emperors, nor do they preserve the marked distinction between the two faces, a refinement well within his capabilities where other contexts required such distinctions to be made. The scrawny type which serves for both men in the *HI* is no more reflected in Altichiero's versions than it reflects the coin portraits. But the frescoes do maintain the distinction between the faces shown on the coins, and also, allowing for the process of idealisation seen throughout the series, reflect them individually. The coins of Balbinus show a powerful, usually clean-shaven face, with a rather short hooked nose. Those of Pupienus feature a longer face with a considerable beard. The frescoes show what can quite reasonably be seen as the face of the Balbinus coins stripped of some of its fat (the amount of which in any case varies from issue to issue), and the fragment of a longer, long-bearded head (identifiable from the inscription as Pupienus). There seems every reason here to believe that Altichiero used as his models the coins themselves. The fit between the pair of frescoes and the pair of coins, given that the *HI* offered no assistance, is too good to be explained as coincidence.

The fresco which, from its position in the sequence, can be taken for *Gordian III* is missing the front of the face, but what survives seems to reflect the youth of the *HI* drawing (fig. 39). The headgear of *Philip I*, radiate in the *HI*, is replaced in the fresco by the more common laurel wreath, but the fresco seems to follow the drawing's rather receding forehead and the continuous profile line of nose and brow. The bust of *Aurelian*, damaged down the facial profile, is crowned, as in the *HI*, and preserves something of the drawing's air of bad temper. That of *Tacitus* also reflects the character of the drawing, while eliminating, as do all the frescoes, anything tending towards caricature. With the last identifiable fresco, the damaged *Carus*, Altichiero has followed, though not to such a marked extent, the procedure he adopted with *Maximus* and *Gordian I* – complete rejection of the drawing. The fresco portrait, a cross between those of *Aurelian* and *Maximus*, has little in common with the crabby features of Giovanni's drawing.

Altichiero's imperial border, then, was based exclusively on the *Historia Imperialis* for its inscriptions, and for the choice of personalities depicted too (figures like Sabina and Faustina being optional in this context). The heads themselves were based generally on the example of the *HI* drawings, but with independent inventions by Altichiero in many instances, drawn usually from his own stock, but on occasions probably from original coin portraits. The marginal drawings of the *HI*, variable in quality and based primarily on the need to illustrate Giovanni's often lurid delineation of later imperial excesses, can have offered little in the way of stylistic help. They served as a starting point and a framework. The fresco heads are largely of Altichiero's devising, more idealised than the drawings, often more so than the coin portraits themselves, while at the same time preserving the idea of a set of individuals quite as distinct. They show Altichiero developing, in trecento Gothic terms, an authentically classicising style in response to classical material. It would be too sweeping to suggest that the great shift in emphasis away from a 'medieval' approach to the Antique – not primarily looking to match *all'antica* style with the appropriate subject matter to a 'Renaissance' concern with just such a correspondence – occurs here, but it must be accepted that Altichiero's emperors are extremely significant in this context. They may have been forgotten in recent centuries, but the proliferation of later versions all over the buildings immediately adjacent to Cansignorio's loggia shows that the Veronese at least must have taken notice.[40]

The imperial busts of the window soffits must not be confused with the 'partimento di medaglie' mentioned by Vasari, which is clearly to be understood as a feature of the

[40] E.g. on the facade of the Loggia del Consiglio in the Piazza dei Signori and the adjacent arch into the Via Fogge.

interior of the hall. His description of this element of the decoration is unambiguous. It was placed above, 'quasi per fine', the single ornamental border running right round the main frescoes. The wording suggests that it was, to an extent, separate from that border. And in the medallions of this upper band were portraits 'di naturale' of 'molti uomini segnalati di que'tempi, ed in particolare molti di que'signori della Scala'.

The basic type of this border can be imagined on the basis of the upper border of the Oratory of S. Giorgio in Padua, where a broad band containing polylobes with busts of saints rests on fictive consoles which also separate it from the upper border of the narrative frescoes. Though in that instance designed for a barrel-vaulted structure, there is no difficulty involved in seeing how such a border would accommodate a ceiling with beams and brackets like that of the Sala Grande. Once again the example of the Sala dei Nove in Siena may be used to suggest the general look of such an arrangement; it has just such a border above the narratives, punctuated by the real consoles which support the beams.

The content of this border merits consideration, given that it was obviously striking enough, though, again, merely a decorative adjunct to the main material, for Vasari or his source to draw particular attention to it. Julius von Schlosser[41] connected with it a series of profile portraits in Florence and Vienna, identifying them as copies of the medallion portraits of members of the della Scala family mentioned by Vasari. The men represented are CanGrande I, Mastino II, CanGrande II and Cansignorio – the successive *signori* from 1311 to 1375. The quality and style of these probably distant copies precludes conclusive judgments, but the dress style seems to be that of the trecento, and it is known that others in the collection of Paolo Giovio, to whom these portraits once belonged, were drawn from frescoes.

A far more comprehensive list of those portrayed in the medallion border may be available if a connection can be established between the border and the nineteen short biographical sketches of the *Epigrammata* by the Scaligeri chancellor Antonio da Legnago. Only one manuscript of this work is known, that included in a vast compendium of material compiled in Mantua around 1400 by Ramo Ramedelli (Biblioteca Vaticana Lat. 3134). This brief text (MS cit. fos. 92r–93r), the sections of which are between six and twenty-four lines long, is headed:

> Epigrammata quorundam nobilium dominorum magnificorum regum et principum tunc temporis extantium vel de proximo defunctorum, eorum probitates operationes et gesta brevi compendio declarantia, composita per egregium et facendum virum Antonium Gai de consilio Dominorum de la Scala.

There follow epigrams on: Francesco da Carrara; Cardinal Albornoz; Edward, Prince of Wales; Galeotto Malatesta; Castruccio Castracani; King Louis of Hungary; Mastino della Scala; Charles, Duke of Calabria; King John of Bohemia; Ugolino Gonzaga; Cansignorio della Scala; Duke Otto of Brunswick; Uguccione da Faggiuola; Paganino Bizzozzero; Romeo de'Pepoli; Charles of Calabria (again, a longer paragraph); Ezzelino da Romano; Henry VII; and CanGrande della Scala.

This obscure work is not dated, beyond the obvious *terminus ante quem* of Antonio da

[41] Schlosser, *L'Arte di Corte*, pp. 55–6.

Legnago's death in 1384, but Avesani, who first published it in connection with the Sala Grande,[42] infers from the plural *Dominorum* of the title that it must have been written during the joint rule of Cansignorio's sons Bartolommeo and Antonio (1375–81). Antonio served as chancellor under Cansignorio, Antonio and Bartolommeo, and finally Antonio alone.[43]

The scope of the *Epigrammata*'s subject matter relates them to a type of composition common in the Middle Ages and amongst early humanists: the collection of a series of lives of *uomini illustri*. The work's scale, however, is in marked contrast with other examples of the genre, which all tend to encyclopaedic length. So brief is it that some special reason for its composition must be sought. Avesani's identification of the portraits of the Sala Grande as this special circumstance is based on the evidence of the text, which in one instance suggests that it was to be read in conjunction with a visual image,[44] and in another that the paragraphs were intended to fit some extratextual order[45] (they obviously do not follow any chronological order); on the basic similarity between the contents of the work as given in the introductory title and the subject of the medallion border as described by Vasari; and presumably, though he does not say so, on the otherwise inexplicable brevity of the work. Aware of a probable date for the Sala Grande frescoes some years earlier than his preferred date for the *Epigrammata*, Avesani sought to resolve this anomaly by suggesting that the medallions were painted after the main frescoes, after, in fact, Altichiero had left Verona.[46]

That the medallions could have been added in this way is extremely unlikely. It is virtually unthinkable that the upper borders of a fresco field would be painted after the lower narratives were completed, and inconceivable that the medallions would have been deliberately left, as Avesani implies, to be filled in as and when required. There is, in fact, no need to postulate such an unlikely course of events. It is perfectly easy to accept the *Epigrammata* as a little guide to the portraits rather than the text on which they were based, easier in fact. They would thus have been written after the frescoes were painted – which is exactly what happened in Padua, with the Carrarese commission of a compendium of Petrarch's *De Viris Illustribus* to be used as a guide to the frescoes of the Sala Virorum Illustrium.[47] It is perhaps significant in this context that the wording of the title page suggests this summary aspect 'eorum probitates operationes et gesta brevi compendio declarantia'. If the epigrams are connected with the frescoes, this seems the most likely form such a connection (Avesani makes no comment on the exact nature of any connection) could have taken. The length of some of the paragraphs, the unevenness of those lengths, and the wording of the texts, slipping at times

42 Avesani, 'Preumanesimo Veronese', pp. 132ff.

43 For Antonio da Legnago's life and career, see Biadego, 'Cultura Veronese', and for his work, Avesani, 'Preumanesimo Veronese', pp. 131–6 and Riva, 'Il Trecento Volgare', pp. 120ff.

44 'Eximia non sine reverentia Canis Grandis primi contemplanda est effigies.' Vat. Lat. 3134 fo. 93r (CanGrande I), cited by Avesani, 'Preumanesimo Veronese', p. 133.

45 'Hinc enim ingenioli mei, illinc vero augustissimi loci parvitas . . . calamum . . . proposito anstinere coegit' (Henry VII), cited by Avesani, 'Preumanesimo Veronese', p. 133p.

46 *Ibid.*, p. 134.

47 For the *Compendium* of the *De Viris Illustribus* see Mommsen, 'Sala Virorum Illustrium', p. 106 and Pellegrin, 'Manuscrits de Pétrarque en France', pp. 374–5.

into the first person, rules out the possibility that they simply record inscriptions written on the frescoes themselves.

Not too much should be read into the *Dominorum* of the title either. The wording of the title makes it clear that it is not by Antonio himself. The use of the word *tunc* makes no sense unless the title was written after Antonio's time, probably by Ramo, looking back from a later date. The epigrams are of men *then* alive or recently dead – in Antonio da Legnago's lifetime. It follows therefore that the *Dominorum* must also be Ramo's choice of expression, not Antonio's. The use of 1375, the year of Cansignorio's death, as a *terminus post quem* is consequently ruled out. Ramo, looking back, knew Antonio had served, in effect, three successive Scaligeri administrations and used the plural accordingly. But it has no bearing on the date of the original composition, now only limited by the *terminus ante* of 1384. Antonio was probably born *c.* 1335–40 and was therefore in his forties at the time of his death. Entering Scaligeri service while very young, he became chancellor in 1369. There is no reason why the *Epigrammata* could not have been written at any time from the mid 1360s.

More significant than the title is the list of those included in the text. Several of the names are exactly what one would expect in a Veronese – and a Scaligeri – context; most obviously the three Scaligeri *signori*, matching Vasari's account and coinciding with von Schlosser's portraits except for the exclusion of CanGrande II, an omission which may itself tell us something. Verona's pro-imperial leanings are reflected in the inclusion of the great Tuscan Ghibellines, Uguccione and Castruccio, the former of whom is buried in Verona, Henry VII, allied to CanGrande I and the original source of the Scaligeri imperial vicariate, and Ezzelino, precursor of the Ghibelline Scaligeri *signoria*. Others would figure on any list of prominent figures of the middle decades of the fourteenth century: the Black Prince; John of Bohemia; Louis of Hungary; Cardinal Albornoz (united with Cansignorio, Francesco da Carrara and others in the anti-Visconti league of 1362–8). The inclusion of Cansignorio's uncle, Francesco da Carrara tends to suggest a date for the compilation of this list no later than 1381, when relations between Francesco and the fratricidal Antonio della Scala became extremely strained. The distinction accorded to Francesco, architect and promoter of Cansignorio's rule, of heading this group of *uomini illustri* also points to a date in Cansignorio's lifetime for the gathering of this material together. The evidence of Cansignorio's own epigram, implicitly posthumous, suggests that the text of the epigrams as we have it now must have been written after 1375.

Romeo de'Pepoli, Galeotto Malatesta and Ugolino Gonzaga are presumably included as famous members of other signorial families (Ugolino's first wife was Verde della Scala, Cansignorio's sister). The inclusion of Charles of Calabria, *signore* of Florence in 1325 and a principal opponent of CanGrande's Ghibelline allies in Tuscany again suggests a compilation date in Cansignorio's time, on the grounds of the kinship between Charles and Cansignorio's wife Agnese da Durazzo. Agnese left Verona on Cansignorio's death, and neither of his sons (not by Agnese) had any reason to pay particular attention to a long-dead, if notable, member of the house of Anjou, as Cansignorio clearly did.

Paganino Bizzozzero of Milan, podestà of Bergamo, Vercelli and then of Parma for Luchino Visconti, is probably the least-known figure on this list, only remembered for his friendship with Petrarch (which is not mentioned in Antonio da Legnago's text). Duke Otto of Brunswick, ally of the Green Count of Savoy, regent in the minority of the sons of John II Paleologus Marquis of Montferrat, *de facto signore* of Asti, fourth husband of Queen Joanna of Naples, is now most famous for his less than resolute behaviour in a duel with the Duke of Lancaster in 1351, but his lifetime of military service for the marquis, for King Jean le Bon, for the Angevins, and finally for the house of Durazzo, marks him out as an exceptional man of action. Otto led one of the armies of the anti-Visconti league of 1368, in alliance with Charles IV, then harrying the Veronese district in tandem with Bernabo Visconti. Cansignorio hurriedly, and typically, disengaged himself from this conflict and made peace with the league. It seems at least likely that Otto's inclusion in Antonio's list is to be associated with this period. Otto's original status as an opponent is not necessarily relevant in this context, and in any case he and Cansignorio were on the same side after 1368. The anti-Visconti context seems to seep into the text of the *Epigrammata*, which, pointedly (we may feel) omitting to give him his own epigram, nevertheless mentions Bernabo Visconti's name in four of the epigrams,[48] remarkable in a work which contains only four other references to men not included in the list (Philip of France, Edward III of England, Pope Urban V and Charles IV).

The nature of the texts themselves tends to confirm the idea that they were not intended to stand alone. The epigrams cannot be described as brief lives, potted biographies, for they disseminate little concrete information. The sections on men best known in Verona – the three Scaligeri, Henry VII, Francesco da Carrara – are largely devoted to a list of moral qualities, the respective subject's best claim to fame. Thus the passage on Cansignorio passes from a brief and rather conventionally pious list of his qualities to a mention of his relationships with Charles IV and Urban V. Of actual biographical detail there is nothing. The epigrams of men longer dead and not of local provenance are furnished with at least a nugget of factual background, but in each case this seems intended only as support to the main purpose of establishing the exemplary status of the subject. This feature of the epigrams, that they give only a generalised summary where the subject is presumed to be well known in Verona but are more informative where he is not, giving just enough in each case for the reader to get his bearings, is very strongly suggestive of a role for the text that is less than fully autonomous. As it stands it simply has no evident purpose – it is not, on the face of it, much of a read for courtiers who could be expected to wade through the *Entrée d'Espagne* or (for the more seriously inclined) the *De Viris Illustribus*.

Neither is there any reason to suppose that the *Epigrammata* is a reduction of a now lost literary text, in the manner of Petrarch's Compendium of his own *De Viris*. The discrepancy between the likely combination of the list (before 1375) and the likely writing

[48] Bernabo is mentioned in the sections on Galeotto Malatesta, Ugolino Gonzaga, Cansignorio della Scala and Uguccione da Faggiuola.

of the text (between 1375 and 1381, or at the latest, 1384), in conjunction with the other factors mentioned, points to the text as having a supporting role to something already existing. That they were conceived as a small guide to the portrait gallery of the Sala Grande border seems a strong possibility, if not an absolute certainty.

The Louvre *Triumph* drawing and Jacopo Avanzi

One further drawing may be added to the list already discussed (pl. 15). The style of composition and figures suggests the proximity of this *Triumph* to the most Altichieresque of those previously considered, and the presence of such a subject in the Sala Grande is supported by the concluding part of Vasari's account:

> Jacopo Avanzi, a Bolognese painter, was engaged on the works in this hall at the same time as Altichiero; and under the aforementioned pictures he painted, also in fresco, two most beautiful Triumphs, done with such skill and good style that Girolamo Campagnuola states that Mantegna praised them as most rare painting.[49]

Here we encounter for the first time the issue which has so dominated past discussions of Altichiero's work. Vasari's remarks immediately precede his account of Altichiero's Paduan frescoes, in which he is heavily dependent on a new set of sources, some of which are demonstrably misleading.[50] The chief problem posed by this passage lies in the disentangling of Vasari's relationship with his sources for the *Triumphs* of the Sala Grande. If he is relying, as the subsequent nod in its direction suggests, on the notoriously misleading lost letter of Girolamo Campagnola to Leonico Tomeo (*c.* 1510), the source of so much muddle in his account of Altichiero's Paduan work, then the very existence of the *Triumphs*, let alone their authorship, should be treated with some suspicion. The primary source for the story of Altichiero's collaboration with Jacopo Avanzi is Savonarola,[51] who restricted it to the Chapel of S. Giacomo in Padua. The spread of the story of Avanzi's intervention in other areas of Altichiero's work seems to be Campagnola's doing. On the basis of their Paduan track record, there is little obligation to believe anything Campagnola or Vasari – when he is using Campagnola – have to say on the subject, were it not for the fact that the Louvre drawing seems to confirm both parts of Vasari's story.

The drawing shows part of a triumphal procession of two laureate figures in a cart or chariot passing beneath a large temple inscribed 'Templum Iovis' and about to enter a gateway or arch. The iconography closely fits the description given by Josephus[52] of the double triumph of Titus and Vespasian; it seems to record the passage where the procession approaches the Temple of Jupiter on the Capitol. This is, of course, exactly the kind of *Triumph* one would expect in this context, perhaps as the culmination of the whole fresco cycle.

49 Vasari, *Le Vite*, p. 634.

50 See Simon, 'Altichiero Versus Avanzo', pp. 263 and 266–7.

51 Savonarola, *Libellus*, p. 44.

52 Josephus, *Jewish War* VII.

The drawing deviates from Josephus's text in one particular only, in showing Vespasian and Titus together in the one chariot (Josephus: 'behind them [the spoils of Victory] drove Vespasian first with Titus behind him'). But we know from Petrarch's references to the event that a medieval tradition for this famous event had Vespasian and Titus enjoying their triumph 'in a single chariot, a sight never seen before', as Petrarch described the event in a letter (*Fam.* XIII. 1), (and in similar terms in book 2 of the *Africa*). If this tradition (the source is Orosius) was fixed in the mind of the Veronese humanists in control of the Sala Grande's iconography then the deviation from Josephus's text is of little consequence.

The Louvre drawing leaves several aspects of the *Triumphs* unresolved. There were, Vasari says, two. Since the drawing seems to record the triumph of both Vespasian and Titus in the one composition, what was the other? Or did Fra Marco express himself in such a way that Vasari took him to mean two separate scenes when what he actually described was a double triumph? The drawing looks as though it reproduces only a slice of a wider composition, as one might expect the original to have been. Vasari's description of their location is unclear. Mellini took 'sotto le sopradette pitture' to mean that the *Triumphs* were on the walls of the storey below the loggia. The precise meaning of such directions in early source is notoriously difficult to determine. On balance it would seem more likely Vasari meant that they were below the other frescoes *in the same room*, if it were not so difficult to imagine how this arrangement might be, not just on the basis of the (completely hypothetical) reconstruction of the Sala Grande given above but on that of known decorative practice. The *Triumphs* are unlikely to have been painted at dado level, where they could not be protected from damage and where they could hardly be well seen. They could have been painted below the main frescoes but above the dado, thus conforming to a layout something like that used by Guariento in the chapel of the Carrara palace in Padua. But this contradicts Vasari's account of the main frescoes and their disposition in the room.

Given the clear dependence, albeit mostly at one remove, of the soffit frescoes on an antique visual source, it may be asked to what extent this version depends on authentic Roman triumph iconography and style. It is clear that artists of the thirteenth and fourteenth centuries did on occasion draw on such sources. The illustrator of the thirteenth-century *Liber Ystoriarum Romanorum*[53] clearly based his version of the *Triumph of Julius Caesar* (fo. 90v) on a Roman pattern for such a scene related to that employed on the Arch of Titus, in which the triumphal figure is accompanied by a figure of Victory, crowning him, both riding in the same chariot. This is embellished with carved ornament and drawn by four horses. Similarly, the drawing of the *Triumph of Marius* in a trecento Sallust[54] adapts with little variation the format of the *Triumph of Augustus* on the reverse of a coin.

Drawing H, with its full spatial field and agitated crowd, is clearly a trecento scene rather than a faithful copy of an antique original. It shares, however, several features with a triumph format represented by the panel from a lost monument of Marcus

[53] Hamburg, Staats-und-Univ. Bibl. MS 151, illustrated in Schmitt, 'Zur Wiederbelebung', pl. 76.

[54] Fermo, Bibl. Comunale MS 81, fo. 157v, illustrated in Schmitt, 'Zur Wiederbelebung', pl. 75.

Aurelius (in the Palazzo dei Conservatori in Rome – other panels were used on the attic of the Arch of Constantine). Both processions pass in front of a large building, a temple in the case of the panel, a two-storeyed structure with a loggia on the upper floor in that of the drawing; both are heading towards an archway on the right; and both feature musicians playing long trumpets. But the specific form of the Roman chariot, retained in the MSS mentioned above, is abandoned in the drawing, which places its triumphal figures in a kind of canopied cart. The number of wheels cannot be counted, but the implied length of the cart suggests four, as with those depicted in similar contexts in the Darmstadt Petrarch, and partly based on the frescoes of the Sala Virorum Illustrium in Padua (pls. 21–32). Neither can the number of horses pulling the cart in drawing H be easily determined. Only two can clearly be made out, but a third mane is visible to the right of the rider holding a baton over his shoulder, and two more rumps just to the left of him. These are unaccountable if not attached to the chariot. The horses as a group scarcely resemble Roman depictions of the quadriga – especially when one of the draught horses carries a rider – but the number at least seems to be in accordance with authentic triumphal iconography and practice.

Also in accordance are the two figures in the chariot. Both carry the sceptre and wear the laurel wreath proper to the *triumphator*. The figure of the crowning Victory is missing, though perhaps she was originally included in that part of the composition lost in this evidently cropped version.

The presence of other elements of the Roman triumph is rather harder to detect. No sacrificial oxen can be seen, but it is at least possible that the mounted figure already noted, with a baton over his shoulder, is meant for a lictor. The trumpeters are present, as are, probably, the principal captives traditionally paraded on their way to execution at the Clivus Capitolinus. Several of the figures on foot in the mid foreground of the drawing, just on the near side of the chariot, seem to have their wrists bound, and one of the riders on the extreme left of the drawing apparently has his hands tied behind his back. The abrupt cropping at this point, and the rather sketchy nature of the drawing as a whole, preclude absolute certainty, but in conjunction with the other points mentioned, these features suggest a considered attempt to reproduce the known features of a Roman triumphal procession with some fidelity. The nature of this attempt, which reproduces, point by point, the list of elements required, but without in most cases drawing on antique visual representations of them (unlike the manuscripts), suggests the use of a literary source.

The exact way in which this drawing might reflect one, or both, of the lost *Triumphs* of the Sala Grande finally eludes certain definition. Even a cursory comparison between the drawing and any number of the frescoes of the Oratory of S. Giorgio in Padua confirms its general affinities with Altichiero's documented work. While the architectural details of the two-storeyed building behind the triumphal procession seems to have been treated to a quattrocento modernisation by the copyist, the other structures, and particularly the way they are used to frame the narrative, are entirely characteristic.

The same can be said for many details of the composition. The group of men restraining playful children in the left foreground, the mounted group behind them, the figures watching from balconies, all are abundantly echoed in both the Paduan cycles. For all his tinkering with architectural details, this copyist seems to have produced a faithful and careful reproduction of a composition by Altichiero. No one who knows his style well could fail to see recollections of it in every part of this drawing.

The very fidelity of the copyist to his original brings us back to Vasari's attribution of the *Triumphs* to Jacopo Avanzi of Bologna rather than Altichiero. The major locus of the Altichiero–Avanzi collaboration problem is the Chapel of S. Giacomo in Padua (see chapter 5 below), but it confronts us here too, if only at one remove. Jacopo Avanzi's artistic personality has been brought much more sharply into focus in recent years;[55] his work at Mezzarrata, in the upper parts of the chapel of S. Giacomo, in the illustrations of the Chester-Beatty *Thebaid*, forms a coherent whole. He is an artist of considerable importance, as the Malatesta provenance of his signed *Crucifixion* panel in the Colonna Collection in Rome suggests.[56] Comparison with Altichiero reveals his more excitable nature. In Padua and in the pages of the *Thebaid* he uses compositions close in general terms to Altichiero's, but he populates them with a hurly-burly crowd of sometimes explosively restless figures. He is nowhere more typical of his native city's art than in his intense interest in the exact appearance and mechanical implications of the human or equine figure in motion, preferably violent, or in attitudes of extreme tension. In this he is at several removes from Altichiero's usual *gravitas*.

If the Louvre *Triumph* does record some part of the Sala Grande frescoes, then Vasari's assertion of Avanzi's presence must be treated with greater respect. Parts of the drawing are as reminiscent of his known style as others are of Altichiero's. The right foreground, with leaping dog and outstretched, straining horse, are particularly close to equivalents in the *Thebaid* and the battle fresco recently revealed at Montefiore. In the light of this rather paradoxical feature of the drawing, it is surely significant that a similar blending of styles within a fundamentally common idiom can be detected in some of the other drawings discussed, especially since this is often the case precisely where the echoes of Altichiero's style are strongest. The foreground horsemen of drawing A and some of the figures of drawing D appear to reflect the agitated Avanzi style; just as C, the recto of D, and other parts of A, a drawing with a very old tradition of its Altichieresque origin, reflect Altichiero.

The discussion of a later drawing whose connections with the Sala Grande cannot be proved, however likely it may seem, is not the place to attack the whole issue of any possible collaboration between Altichiero and what we might call the newly restored Avanzi. But it must at least be recorded here that the evidence, tenuous though it is, suggests just such a mixture as we would expect in the case of two formidable artists, with distinct personalities, but who share certain stylistic characteristics and are, perhaps, used to working with one another. The evidence of Altichiero's having worked in tandem with another artist – and the same artist – recurs in the material associated with the Sala Virorum Illustrium and in the first phase of the decoration of the Chapel

[55] See Benati, *Jacopo Avanzi nel Rinnovamento della Pittura Padana del secondo '300*.

[56] Reproduced by Mellini, *Altichiero e Jacopo Avanzi*, pl. 314.

of S. Giacomo. We may be picking up traces of an important and constant feature of Altichiero's professional life throughout the 1360s and the 1370s.

The Sala Grande in context

Josephus was an important writer for the later Middle Ages. Since the loss of the Latin Kingdom of Jerusalem in 1244 his work constituted one of the principal sources of knowledge of the Holy Land, increasingly so throughout the period during which it was inaccessible.[57] For humanists like Petrarch and his Veronese friend Guglielmo Da Pastrengo the chief value of Josephus lay in the *Antiquitates Judaicae* rather than the *Bellum Judaicum*; it was on the *Antiquitates Judaicae* that Petrarch chiefly drew for the patriarchal sections of the first, 'All Ages' version of his *De Viris Illustribus*. This was compiled in the years following his closest association with the Veronese circle and his intensive researches in the Chapter Library in Verona. Rather earlier in the trecento, Josephus's work had been the object of extensive study and imitation by Giovanni de Matoci's contemporary, the Scaligeri chancellor Benzo d'Alessandria.[58]

The character of the *Bellum Judaicum* (hereafter *BJ*), and its medieval role, were rather different. Despite having been written at first in Aramaic by a Jew, and then translated by the author into Greek, the *BJ* is essentially a Roman history. Written in Rome, with access to official Roman archives, including the military reports compiled by Vespasian and Titus, submitted to these two before public circulation and receiving their *imprimatur* – and by an imperial pensioner who had adopted the name Flavius – it is hardly surprising that this should be the case. As such, the material of Josephus's book had by the fourteenth century been co-opted into one of the three great 'matters' of epic chivalric poetry; the matter of Rome. Of the three, this underwent the greatest growth in popularity during the later Middle Ages. Although the preliminary impetus for this growth probably stems from the schools of twelfth-century France,[59] interest in the material on the part of a chivalric audience was not based on the antiquarian or scholarly aspects of the classical past so much as on its contemporary relevance for a military and courtly class. Later treatises, with no humanist pretensions, insisted particularly on the exemplary role of Roman material in chivalric contexts, an insistence which, albeit accidentally, approached a position close to the kind of didactic and exemplary use of classical material favoured by later humanists. The extent to which strictly non-humanist chivalric concerns gave unintentional support to the emerging humanism of the Italian cities must have been considerable. The grey area which for many, including probably the majority of princes and knights, lay between Romance proper and History proper contained for the most critical humanists, with Petrarch at their head, a clear boundary – in theory at least. Both Petrarch and Boccaccio openly derided the treatment of Roman history as just another matter of Romance,[60] but in this they were in a minority, probably even amongst humanists. In fact, and despite the markedly

[57] Feldman, *Josephus and Modern Scholarship*, p. 853.

[58] See De Nolhac, *Pétrarque et l'Humanisme*, vol. II, pp. 152–6 and Feldman, *Josephus*, p. 865.

[59] Keen, *Chivalry*, pp. 107ff.

[60] Petrarch, *Fam.* I. 2; and, for Boccaccio, Keen, *Chivalry*, p. 192.

more secular flavour of the chivalric temper once it began to draw on classical material, it was still within a largely religious framework that the matter of the *BJ* was adopted by late medieval courtly and chivalric circles.

Ever since the pioneering Latin translations by the author of the version known as the *Hegesippus* in the fourth century, and by Cassiodorus in the sixth, the thrust of Josephus's narrative, with the storming and sacking of Jerusalem in AD 70 at its centre, had been bent to Christian, and eventually to crusading purpose. Feldman comments that the intention of the *Hegesippus*, which draws on other Roman histories too, was primarily 'religious, to prove that the war was a divine punishment inflicted upon the Jews',[61] a reinterpretation involving not so much a rewriting of Josephus's text as a reorientation of material already there, but without Christian overtones.

This adaptation of the *BJ* came during the course of the early and later Middle Ages to stand as the central point of the book for these periods. The prime example of what we must probably call the legend of the sacking of Jerusalem, as it develops in the later Middle Ages, is in the tenth-century appendix to the apocryphal *Acts of Pilate*, in which we read that Titus (described as King of Bordeaux!) was cured of a cancer when he heard of the death of the prophet Emanuel and exclaimed: 'I would have slain these Jews with my own hand for destroying my Lord'.[62] There follows the assertion that Titus, by now a Christian convert, 'sent for Vespasian to come with all his forces, and he came with 5000 men, and said: "What do you want me for?" "To destroy the enemies of Jesus."' The story concludes, after much more in this vein, with an account of Josephus's prophecy to Vespasian that he would become emperor which is more soberly based on Josephus's own account. A more compact version of the same is found in the Arthurian material of the *Queste del Saint Graal* (*c.* 1225), which says that 'it was this deed (the Crucifixion) that led Vespasian, on learning the truth about the prophet they had betrayed, to seize their land and crush their nation under foot'.[63] This penetration of the matter of Rome into Grail material was matched by instances of the same process, but in reverse, as it were. The thirteenth-century French *Roman de l'Estoire dou Graal*, or *Joseph d'Aramathie*, includes the story of the rescue of the aged Joseph of Arimathea, custodian of the Grail, by Vespasian – converted to Christianity having undergone a miraculous cure via contact with the Sudarium of St Veronica.[64] The dominant interest in the Jerusalemic material continued to be French throughout the thirteenth century, under the umbrella of royal patronage, and it culminated in the fourteenth-century epic chanson *Le Livre Titus et Vespasianus.*[65]

For Dante it was Titus who 'con l'aiuto / del sommo rege, vendico le fora / ond'usci'l sangue per Giuda venduto'[66] and for the men of the fourteenth century Titus had become, in effect, a crusader. The account given by 'Mandeville' is succinct, based in parts on Josephus, but clearly drawing on the Christian reinterpretation: 'For Titus, son of Vespasian, who was Emperor of Rome, laid siege to Jerusalem to destroy the Jews

[61] Feldman, *Josephus*, p. 42.

[62] James, *The Apocryphal New Testament*, pp. 159ff.

[63] Matarasso, *The Quest of the Holy Grail*, p. 64.

[64] *Encyclopaedia Judaica*, vol. XV, pp. 1168–71; 'Titus, Flavius Vespasianus'.

[65] *Ibid.*

[66] Dante, *Purgatorio* XXI, 82.

because they put Christ to death without the assent and leave of the Emperor.'[67] Mandeville's *Travels* began to circulate in Europe from about 1356, achieving enormous popularity, and its version of Josephus's material, with Titus now the completely transformed *miles Christi*, can be taken as that generally accepted in the period during which the frescoes of the Sala Grande were planned and executed. It is perhaps important to stress that this quite unhistorical interpretation of the material was thus far unchallenged even by as critical a student of classical texts as Petrarch, who, in the letter already cited (*Fam.* XIII. 1), proclaimed that Vespasian and Titus 'achieved a glorious vengeance for Christ and the acclaimed Triumph over Jerusalem', though he noticeably avoids any commitment to the idea that this was their conscious intention.

Since the loss of the Holy Land, interest in crusading and in the history and possible future of crusading enterprises tended to take on the quality of ideal aspirations rather than concrete proposal. The actual history of late crusading is for the most part a sorry one. Always present as at least a background noise, and with the development of the mythological material mentioned above an essential part of the idealogical baggage of a ruler or knight with any chivalric pretences, late medieval crusade fever still underwent periodical revivals, sometimes with practical intent.[68] Just such a revival – undoubtedly the most important of the fourteenth century – coincides with the suggested date for the Josephus frescocs in Verona.

Since well before his accession to the throne of Cyprus in 1359, Peter I de Lusignan had promoted the idea of a new crusade with some vigour, founding by 1347 the multinational Order of the Sword, which was devoted to the crusading ideal.[69] On his accession, Peter moved to give this ideal concrete form. With the support of two successive popes (Innocent VI and Urban V) Peter's plans rapidly took shape.

The history of the successful but bloody crusade against Alexandria and its bathetic aftermath is well known and was subject to at least mixed responses even at the time. But the original enthusiasm for the enterprise was genuine, as was the rejoicing at the initial success of the venture. Whatever the actual behaviour of some of the forces which followed the king to Egypt, his intentions and those of his advisors and of his princely backers were true to the ideal. The taking of Alexandria was no mere substitute for a real crusade against Jerusalem, it was a necessary preliminary step. The ideology of this crusade was to be taken at face value.

The impact of the venture once it was mooted on the signorial courts of north Italy was extremely forceful.[70] When Peter arrived in Venice at the end of 1361 to begin his trip across the Veneto and Lombardy seeking support, he was met and feted by envoys from the Estensi and the Carraresi, bringing gifts and pledging support. While the various *signorie* vied with each other in the ostentation of their welcome, Cansignorio trumped them all by receiving Peter first in Vicenza and then in Verona itself in January 1362, welcoming him in both cities with lavish hospitality. The extent of any concrete

[67] Mandeville, *The Travels of Sir John Mandeville*, p. 81.

[68] Atiya, *The Crusade in the Later Middle Ages*, pp. 319ff.

[69] For Peter's crusade see *ibid.* and Jorga, 'Philippe de Mezières et la Croisade au XIVe Siècle'.

[70] See Jorga, 'Philippe de Mezières', pp. 148ff. and Verci, *Storia della Marca Trivigiana e Veronese*, pp. 38ff.

help given is difficult to gauge, but Cansignorio was both extremely wealthy and extremely pious, and the seriousness of his interest in crusading is emphasised by his known support for successive enterprises in the years following the Alexandrian crusade.[71] He cultivated good relations (in this matter at least) with Urban V, who in June 1364 sent him a letter of recommendation on behalf of Thomas Beauchamp, Earl of Warwick, who, with a large party, had taken the Cross and was travelling through northern Italy on his way to the Holy Land. Two years later Cansignorio also lent assistance to the crusade of Amedeo VI of Savoy (1366/7).[72] The continuing high profile accorded to these various manifestations of late crusading zeal at the Veronese court is reflected in the lament written by one of the court poets, Nicolo degli Scacchi, on the death of King Peter in 1369. The power of the cult – if that is not too strong a word – of this 'athleta Christi' is recorded in this poem, in which the death of the king – 'suprema voce de cortesia' – is perceived as a blow to all Christendom and a comfort to the heathen.[73]

The significance of Cansignorio's personal enthusiasm for the crusading revival of the 1360s in the context of the Sala Grande is clear. Peter, titular King of Jerusalem as well as of Cyprus, visited Verona early in 1362. His army sailed from Venice in June 1365, and on from Rhodes in October. Alexandria was taken on October 10th. These dates coincide exactly with the period when it is recorded that Cansignorio began to rebuild and redecorate the Scaligeri palaces; and the overall contents of the frescoes of the Sala Grande as we understand them are in complete accord with the prevailing concerns of the period 1362 to 1369. If they were projected and commissioned in 1364, the date of the initiation of the building programme, they would coincide with the period at which it can be supposed that crusading fervour at court was at its peak.

In the context of traditionally Ghibelline Verona, and of a *signoria* with its imperial vicariate recently restored, it is significant that 'Mandeville' presents as a basis for the criminal character of the Crucifixion that it was a flouting of imperial authority. There existed within the crusading tradition an imperial strand, which followed the efforts of Vespasian and Titus with the crusading enterprise of Charlemagne, of Barbarossa, and of Frederick II. That the first was only legendary, the second a disaster, and the third, if technically successful, spiritually inglorious, scarcely affects the sense of an imperial crusading tradition spanning the period from the Roman to the Holy Roman Empire. The suggested date also coincides with a period in which high hopes were entertained in Italy, not least amongst humanists like Petrarch, of the effective presence of the emperor once more as a living force for good and for unity in the Italian peninsula. Coluccio Salutati's excited reaction on seeing Charles IV – 'now at last ours' – in Rome in 1369 is probably representative[74] (though Petrarch, the most ardent promoter of the *renovatio imperii*, was curiously silent on the subject, in spite of his long personal

[71] Jorga, 'Philippe de Mezières', pp. 205–6; Atiya, *Crusade*, p. 339.
[72] Cox, *The Green Count of Savoy*, pp. 204ff.
[73] Riva, 'Il Trecento Volgare', pp. 125–6.
[74] Ullman, *The Humanism of Coluccio Salutati*, p. 78.

campaign to persuade the emperor into Italy once more, and in spite of his meetings with Charles in the north at the beginning of his descent).[75]

To these factors can be added the internal circumstances of Verona during the same years, which are of equal relevance. The period *c.* 1362 to 1366 is that in which Cansignorio made his signorial mark with the greatest force.[76] The policies he adopted in the early 1360s must be seen against the background of immediate Veronese history, and as a deliberate exercise designed to reverse, publicly at least, many of the trends which had culminated in the later years of the rule of his brother CanGrande II, a period of profound crisis for the Scaligeri *signoria*, in which their hold on Verona became extremely insecure, only being maintained by mercenaries from the Germanic north, and in which their formerly splendid reputation abroad, amongst enemies and friends alike, as one of the great Italian courts, was almost wholly erased.

Intelligent and imaginative though some of his policies were, the latter part of CanGrande II's reign came to be one of the least stable periods in the history of Scaligeri Verona. The insurrection of Fregnano Della Scala, which took place in 1354, when CanGrande was out of the city, and which was put down with the greatest force on his return, changed CanGrande's character to a considerable degree; he seems in fact to have gone quite mad for a while. It certainly altered the character of his rule. He built himself the castle of San Martino in Aquario (now known as the Castelvecchio[77]) well away from the central palaces hitherto occupied by his family and lived there, with only his closest familiars, for the rest of his life. Court life, in anything like the sense in which it had flourished under CanGrande I and Mastino II, more or less ceased to exist, a reaction perhaps to the brilliant Fregnano's former dominance of court life. All pensions to scholars were cancelled and even the nominal consultation of councils representing the wider interests of the Veronese *commune* ceased. The rest of CanGrande's family, including his wife, lived on in the old central palaces, deprived of all but the means necessary for a modest and private lifestyle.[78] The design of CanGrande's new castle is symptomatic of the change which had taken place. Straddling the old inner ring of the city walls close to the Adige, it places the residential block – which is, in comparison with the average set of palatial apartments, rather small – outside the wall, with a larger garrison block on the city side. Between the two blocks an ingenious set of walls and passages further protects the signorial rooms and the quick access to the north provided by a new bridge over the Adige. The visible point of the castle is that it defends itself, not against the outside world, but

[75] See Bayley, 'Petrarch, Charles IV and the Renovatio Imperii' for this aspect of Petrarch's thought. Bayley is too dismissive of the emperor, who had to contend with political realities which never came into the idealist Petrarch's calculations. See pp. 335–6 for Petrarch's silence in 1368.

[76] For the history of this period see Allen, *Verona*, pp. 288–305; Carrara, *Gli Scaligeri*, pp. 191–211; Cipolla, *Compendio*, pp. 153ff.; Rossini, 'La Signoria dopo CanGrande', pp. 655ff.; and Saraina, *Historie e Fatti*, pp. 46ff.

[77] For the design and building of the Castelvecchio see Perbellini, *Castelli Scaligeri*, pp. 40–5.

[78] 'Eius autem mater cum ceteris filiis murabatus in antiquis Palatis ipsorum de la Scala, sitis ad plateam sed satis obscure' – Azario, *Liber Gestorum in Lombardia*, col. 420. See also Allen, *Verona*, pp. 296–7.

against the city. The contrast with the design and disposition of the previous Scaligeri residences is marked.

It would be an exaggeration to say that Cansignorio reversed all of these trends, or that he successfully tackled the root causes of a crisis which, though his brother had brought it to a head, was already a feature of their father's rule and a direct consequence of his ambitious policies, but there is little doubt that his assumption of power was greeted with relief. And while access to the *signore* never again came to be as open as it had been in CanGrande I's time, the emphasis did shift from CanGrande II's fortress mentality back towards at least the outward forms of a *signoria* whose concerns were allied with those of the city and not in opposition to them.

Of this realignment Cansignorio's new building policy was symptomatic, concentrating once more on the Quartiere della Chiavica, dominated by Scaligeri property, in which, from the fall of Ezzelino Da Romano, they had systematically created a central complex in which their palaces, no longer heavily defensible fortresses, were developed in a continuum with the buildings housing the centres of communal and mercantile organisation. The building programme of the 1360s marked a return to earlier family policy in its mingling of civic and signorial interests. So while Cansignorio embarked on a process of revamping the family palaces, he also began a series of projects designed to benefit the wider community: the bringing of piped water to the heart of the city[79] and the building of a splendid fountain incorporating classical spoils in the Piazza Erbe, serviced by the new supply, the construction of a clock tower at the north-west end of the Piazza, a new bridge, the Ponte delle Navi, and granaries and warehouses to store supplies as an insurance against bad harvests.[80] In the other major towns of the Scaligeri state and in the smaller towns and villages of the *contado*, Cansignorio's building activity was similarly prodigious.

Hand in hand with this activity went a public revival of court life. The early 1360s were marked by a series of great spectaculars which served to restore the Scaligeri court's wider prestige: the proxy marriage of Cansignorio's sister Verde to Nicolo II D'Este in Verona in 1362, to which representatives of all the major powers of the Veneto and Lombardy were invited, the reception of Peter of Cyprus earlier in the same year, and Cansignorio's own marriage in 1363 to Agnese da Durazzo, followed by a fifteen-day *curia* of a magnificence never seen before in Verona,[81] even in the time of CanGrande I. In the wake of this followed the building programme, which essentially served two related purposes: to re-establish a sense of the mutually beneficial relationship between *signoria* and city cultivated, at least on the level of propaganda, by the early Scaligeri; and to clothe the revived *signoria* in the trappings of a great court.

The decoration of the Sala Grande by Altichiero must be seen as a central, probably *the* central, act of artistic patronage associated with this revival. It reflects a Scaligeri humanist revival too, after a long period (corresponding roughly to the rules of

[79] For which see Saraina, *Historie e Fatti*, p. 53v.

[80] Allen, *Verona*, pp. 303–4.

[81] Saraina, *Historie e Fatti*, pp. 51r and 51v.

Cansignorio's father and brother) during which the humanist studies so vigorously and centrally pursued in Verona during the early trecento had become detached from the centre of civic life and had become a feature of the private lives of various citizens rather than of their public standing.

The humanist tradition in Verona had long antecedents, based principally on the unrivalled collection of early manuscripts held in the cathedral chapter library, but it burst into the fullest life in the early trecento, particularly under CanGrande I.[82] The radically different political positions of the two cities kept a certain distance between the Veronese humanists and their Paduan contemporaries, but interchange there was, and mutual respect, and a certain community of purpose. The work of the Veronese reflects a Ghibelline and signorial background just as the work of Mussato in Padua reflects that of a city which felt itself threatened by such ideologies.[83] Working under however well disposed a despotism the Veronese tended to apply their studies to questions of political and governmental propriety and theory less strenuously than the Paduans. The Veronese tended to concentrate on textual study, with a certain archaeological bent, and it was as a repository of texts, and of competent textual analysts, that Verona maintained its attraction for other humanists during the mid-century and after.

The humanism of the early Veronese trecento nevertheless made its mark at signorial level: witness the importance in this context of Cangrande's chancellor Benzo d'Alessandria,[84] himself a keen student of Josephus and the application of a style and concept of history based on Livy and Sallust to contemporary (Scaligeri) history by the Vicentine Ferreto Ferreti.[85] The work of the chief humanists in Verona in the first thirty or so years of the trecento, Giovanni de Matoci, Benzo, the anonymous author of the *Flores Moralium Auctoritatem*,[86] reflects the political and cultural vigour of CanGrande's court and of the broadly expansionist role of the Scaligeri state at this time.

The less central role played by humanism in the difficult mid-century is best represented by the position of the leading Veronese humanist of that period, Guglielmo da Pastrengo.[87] In the early years of his life Guglielmo served the Scaligeri administration in several important capacities: as ambassador to Venice in 1323, as judge and *podestà*'s vicar in Vicenza from 1324 to 1325, as one of the *sapientes* of the Veronese council in 1333 (in which he sat alongside Pietro Alighieri) and twice as special ambassador for Mastino II to the papal court in Avignon, where he met Petrarch. From *c.* 1339 he effectively retired from public life and devoted himself entirely to scholarship. It is

[82] The principal accounts of Veronese humanism as a whole are to be found in Avesani, 'Preumanesimo Veronese'; Carrara, 'Gli Scrittori Latini'; and Weiss, 'La Cultura Preumanistica'.

[83] Hyde, *Padua*, pp. 283–310 and Guido Billanovich, 'Il Preumanesimo Padovano' offer full accounts of Paduan humanism in the early trecento.

[84] For whom see Berrigan, 'Benzo d'Alessandria and the Cities of Northern Italy'.

[85] For Ferreti see Gargan, 'Il Preumanesimo a Vicenza, Treviso e Venezia', pp. 143–6 and Carrara, 'Gli Scrittori Latini', pp. 27–32.

[86] For the *Flores* see Avesani, 'Preumanesimo Veronese', pp. 121–2 and Carrara, 'Gli Scrittori Latini', pp. 38–42.

[87] Avena, 'Guglielmo da Pastrengo e gli Inizi dell'Umanesimo in Verona' is the principal account of Guglielmo's life. His work is discussed by Avesani, 'Preumanesimo Veronese', pp. 126–30 and Carrara, 'Gli Scrittori Latini', pp. 54ff. The *Liber de viris illustribus* and *De originibus rerum* were published together as the *De origine rerum libellus* by Scipione and Michelangelo Biondo in Venice in 1547 and, with Marzagaia's history, are the only major works of the indigenous Veronese group to have been published.

symptomatic of the situation of the Veronese humanists at this time that Petrarch's relationship with them was largely a private concern, not, as was the case with his relationship with the Paduans, associated with court connections. Petrarch's two chief intellectual friendships at this time, with Guglielmo and with Rinaldo Cavalchini, bypassed the court altogether. The only material connection between Veronese humanism and the court during this period consisted of Rinaldo's employment to write the Latin epitaphs for the tombs of CanGrande I and Mastino II.[88] Petrarch's own relationship with the Scaligeri at this time was exclusively formal, and there seems to have been no interest on either side in having him as a court ornament, a role for which he was eagerly sought by other *signorie* and to which, whatever he might have said on the subject, he was by no means averse.

Symptomatic of Cansignorio's policies of revival is the extent to which the intellectual centres of Verona came once more to be concentrated within the court and within the administration. Antonio da Legnago, author of the *Epigrammata* and an important letter on the subject of the ruins of Rome, served as chancellor and later on the council of regency for Cansignorio's sons. He and Marzagaia,[89] the boys' tutor, were responsible for grooming them for power on the basis of a comprehensive humanist education, and together with the judge Leonardo da Quinto,[90] Cansignorio's city surveyor and witness both to his accession and to his will, Gasparo Broaspini,[91] and, until 1362, Guglielmo and Rinaldo, they made up a group as impressive as that of the early trecento and amongst whom, one must assume, was nurtured the project for a great fresco cycle from the Antique at the centre of Cansignorio's new court.

The renewal of interest in the 1360s in Giovanni de Matoci's *Historia Imperialis*, which was evidently laid aside unfinished in 1320, and, judging by the discrepancies between the three known manuscripts, in some textual disarray, is less remarkable in the light of a demonstrable continuity of interest in the work through the following two generations of Veronese humanists. It is known that Guglielmo da Pastrengo studied the *HI* – a comment on the book survives in Guglielmo's hand – and that he based parts of his own work on it.[92] The manuscript now in the Biblioteca Capitolare in Verona is annotated

[88] Carrara, 'Gli Scrittori Latini', pp. 61–6. See also Biadego, 'Per la Storia della Cultura Veronese'.

[89] For Marzagaia see Avesani, 'Preumanesimo Veronese', pp. 137–8 and Carrara, 'Gli Scrittori Latini', pp. 73–8. His *De Modernis Gestis* and the three *Opusculi* were published by Cipolla, *Antiche Chronache Veronesi,* and constitute a vital source of information on the later years of Scaligeri rule.

[90] For Leonardo see Cipolla, *Notizie intorno a Leonardo da Quinto Giudice e Letterato Veronese del Secolo XIV* and Carrara, 'Gli Scrittori Latini', pp. 16–21. Marzagaia gives an account of him in the *De Modernis Gestis*, see Cipolla, *Antiche Chronache*, vol. 1, p. 87. Leonardo lived, like Guglielmo da Pastrengo, in the contrada della Pigna, close to the Capitolare. Sentences passed by Leonardo as a judge are documented from 1364. Marzagaia records his fame as an astrologer.

[91] See Garibotto, 'Un'Amico del Petrarca' and Carrara, 'Gli Scrittori Latini', pp. 67–9. Gasparo Squaro dei Broaspini is the exception amongst the humanists of the later Veronese trecento in that he had no exalted position at court, nor, probably, any great wealth. He worked for a time as Petrarch's copyist, though his family trade was painting ('Squaro', i.e. *scudaio*, suggests heraldic painting) – and it is as 'Gaspar Pictor q. dni. Petri' that he is styled in a document of 1364. He seems to have owned a collection of Cicero's letters and was regarded as a valuable source of old MSS. He was highly thought of by Petrarch and Coluccio Salutati, corresponded with both, and with Giovanni Dondi in Padua.

[92] Carrara, 'Gli Scrittori Latini', p. 19.

by Leonardo Da Quinto.[93] The probability is that this volume was one of the books taken by Leonardo to Venice in 1386 to protect them from what he feared was the impending collapse of Scaligeri rule. The Vatican manuscript, on which the frescoes are based (unless another illustrated copy is lost), is most likely still to have been in the chapter library, to which Giovanni de Matoci bequeathed all his books.[94] How the second copy might have come into Leonardo da Quinto's own hands (if it did – the annotation does not imply ownership, though the removal to Venice would) is unclear. (It is recorded, though, that the Scaligeri tended to treat the contents of the library as though it were their personal property.[95]) Possibly Guglielmo had somehow obtained the less elaborate copy, which had in turn been acquired by Leonardo following Guglielmo's death in 1362. Given that the soffit frescoes are demonstrably based on the *HI* and that someone as close to Cansignorio as Leonardo had studied the work in great detail, it would be extraordinary if the two factors were not connected. It must be regarded as highly probable that Leonardo da Quinto played some role in devising the contents and scope of the decoration of the Sala Grande.

The availability of the *Historia Imperialis* having been accounted for, some comment is required on its application to the Sala Grande scheme. It is worth remarking, in passing, that the use of the illustrations of a text in a setting which otherwise ignores this text altogether, which draws in fact on a completely different book, is rather unusual. The overall design of the Sala Grande's pictorial content, drawing on different sources and types of source to construct a coherent assembly, suggests both careful and sophisticated planning, and a clear iconographic purpose.

Antique material and Antique style

Widespread medieval exposure to antique coins and to related gems followed largely in the wake of the Crusades and proliferated after the sack of Constantinople in 1204, from when 'antique precious stones poured into the West in incalculable profusion'.[96] Motifs based on such examples began to feature in a wide range of contexts. The actual imitation of Roman coins by later medieval Italian mints was restricted to the Augustales and half-Augustales of Frederick II, and the fidelity with which a slightly later series of seals of prominent churchmen, many closely associated with the papacy,

[93] Verona, Biblioteca Capitolare cod. CCIV, fo. 32r, beside a list of Giovanni de Matoci's sources: 'Hos omnes suprascriptos libros ego Leonardus iudex de Quinto de Verona habeo, qui sunt elegantissimo stilo.' The source of the story that Leonardo took his books to Venice for safety when he went to pawn Samaritana da Polenta's jewels on behalf of the beleaguered Antonio della Scala is Marzagaia. See Avesani, 'Il Preumanesimo Veronese', pp. 134–5. For Cipolla, 'Leonardo da Quinto', amongst the books taken to Venice was 'indubitamente' the present Capitolare MS of the *HI*. Once Visconti rule in Verona was established, Leonardo returned to Verona from Venice (where he had gone to live when the Scaligeri finally fell) and died in 1392.

[94] 'Item relinquo sacrario predicto omnes libros meos qui sunt in secrestia ecclesie maioris verone', Verona, Arch. Cap. A.C.62 m.3 n. 9, cited by Simeoni, 'La Famiglia', p. 75. Perhaps not all his books were kept there. Giovanni owned at least two houses in his own right.

[95] Avesani, 'Preumanesimo Veronese', p. 135 ascribes this to the inability of Bishop Pietro della Scala (1350–87) to defend the library's resources against other members of his family.

[96] Wentzel, 'Portraits *a l'Antique* on French Mediaeval Gems and Seals', p. 342.

reflects them[97] probably signifies a conscious attempt to reclaim this iconography from too exclusive an association with the Hohenstaufen. It is in fact solely in these ecclesiastical contexts that equally faithful early copies of coin style and iconography were made. Only with the seals of the Malatesta of Rimini from the early trecento was coin imitation fully absorbed by a signorial culture. By the fourteenth century it is probable that for most educated people the profile bust was the antique motif *par excellence*, and that however varied the context, it was to the classical past that use of the motif inescapably and recognisably referred. Coin-based seals varied widely in the strictness of their imitation. The early church seals follow the Augustales in the extent of their fidelity to the source, as do certain of the Malatesta seals. For these the exact detail of the antique model is deemed worthy of imitation. For the majority of other seals the imitation is less close, only the use of the profile bust indicating the antique source.

The extent of Giovanni de Matoci's familiarity with Roman imperial coinage suggests that he was able to draw on the resources of a considerable collection. Though evidence exists of individual coin collections from as early as the Carolingian period,[98] that used by Giovanni – of which there is no other record – seems to have been both the first systematic example, and one of the most comprehensive of its kind, much larger than the collections of Petrarch and Boccaccio,[99] and, presumably, than that of the antiquary Oliviero Forzetta.[100] It was, seemingly, not a complete collection though, and whoever controlled Altichiero's access to the source material was evidently able to provide him with coins not known to or used by Giovanni (Balbinus and Pupienus, for instance). The importance of this apparently thoroughgoing antiquarianism so early in the history of the Renaissance is undeniable. But the proto-Renaissance element in Giovanni's use (and possible assembly) of the collection should not be overemphasised. Giovanni found and used a source for the actual appearance of his subjects on a par with those literary sources on which he drew for their characters and actions. The coins were of practical use to him more, I would suggest, than they were classical talismans in the sense such relics had for later generations of humanists. His attitude anticipates in some respects that of Petrarch, for whom the ruins and surviving artefacts of Rome were more interesting as reminders or pointers to the lost culture than as objects in their own right. Real enthusiasm for the objects themselves as objects was, we know, occasionally displayed by artists in the trecento (and by private collectors like Forzetta), but only later became central to literary humanism. Petrarch and Boccaccio both used coins as Giovanni had done, as portraits. In one instance at least Petrarch shows that the talismanic status of the coins of Rome had begun to penetrate fourteenth-century humanism: in his presentation of

97 Wentzel, 'Mittelalterliche Gemmen in den Sammlungen Italiens' traces the development of the coin profile in an Italian context throughout the thirteenth and fourteenth centuries.

98 E.g. the collection of Theodulf, Bishop of Orleans from before 798. See Wolff, *The Awakening of Europe*, pp. 42–3.

99 For Boccaccio (and Petrarch) see Weiss, 'Ancient Numismatics', p.179.

100 Gargan, *Cultura e Arte nel Veneto al Tempo di Petrarca*, pp. 34–65 discusses Forzetta's collection in depth. There are also useful summaries in *ibid.*, 'Oliviero Forzetta e la Diffusione dei Testi Classici nel Veneto al Tempo di Petrarca', pp. 73ff. and *ibid.*, 'Il Preumanesimo', pp. 168–70, both of which also deal with his equally interesting collection of MSS.

a selection to Charles IV in 1354.[101] Here the coins are expected to do more than just record the emperors' features; they stand for the empire and its virtues in a rather more active, significant and exemplary way. They have, in this context, some moral force attached to them. The ideology of Petrarch's approach is radically different from that of Giovanni de Matoci, who wrote his history very much from the position of a churchman, as the ubiquitous lists of martyrdoms suffered in each reign suggest. The evidence of the coins was secondary to his main purpose.[102] The frescoes of the 1360s, on the other hand, do have a special quality of reverence towards the look of the Antique, signs of an intention to create a true *all'antica* style, a consequence, it may be suggested, of the artist's interest as well as that of the patron and his agents.

Altichiero's frescoes, even at one remove, are not in the strict sense imitations of Roman coins at all. They are related to the adaptations of coin profiles in monumental contexts characteristic of thirteenth-century France more than to seal or coin copies in Italy. The frescoes are fictive stone profiles in a fictive moulded architectural border, *trompe l'œil* versions of a real architectural element like the coin-based spandrel heads of Rheims.[103] In their original setting, if the present reading of the sources is right, they must have been read in conjunction with the portraits of recent and living *uomini illustri* on the internal border of the Sala Grande, which were painted 'di naturale' and therefore presumably not in grisaille like the soffit heads. The two sets would embody a structure of analogies between antiquity and modern times, while preserving at the same time a differential between the rulers of the old Roman Empire (stone busts *all'antica*) and contemporary *uomini illustri* (naturalistic portraits). The parallelism of this concept, which sheds a significant light on the apparent closing of the imperial sequence just before Constantine, was a regular feature in such contexts. The two sets act as a frame round the central matter of the Sala Grande, the moment at which the old pagan empire acted, willy-nilly to be sure, on behalf of Christendom. In the chivalric context this reinforces the central role of the matter of Rome in providing forebears and examples. The ancestry of the old empire was made visible and explicit, but with a proper regard for historical distance and perspective, a distance which, embodied in the lapidary status of the busts, restricts their individual roles as exemplary *uomini illustri*, a role for which, as individuals, many of them were clearly unsuited – and recognised as such by the trecento (certainly by anyone familiar with the text of the *Historia Imperialis*, which reproduces much of the racy gossip contained in the *Historia Augusta*). They

[101] Discussions of this event are in Bayley, 'Petrarch and the "Renovatio Imperii"', p. 331 and Weiss, 'Ancient Numismatics', pp. 177–8. Petrarch accompanied the gift with 'an exhortation to follow the example of such illustrious predecessors'. Petrarch's actual words were 'ecce inquam Caesar, quibus successisti, ecce quos imitari studeas'.

[102] Weiss is wrong, though, to claim that Petrarch 'was the first who considered the imperial coinage of Rome as a "portrait gallery"', 'Ancient Numismatics', p. 177. In this, if not in the moralising sense, Giovanni de Matoci has precedence, and the revival of this attitude in Verona in the later trecento may well be a native phenomenon, not based on any assumed Petrarchan example. It is of course entirely possible that Petrarch discussed such matters with his Veronese friends before Altichiero's time.

[103] Panofsky, *Renaissance and Renascences in Western Art*, pp. 58–9 places the Rheims heads in a tradition of the 'lapidary magnification of classical gems or coins', a tradition which, he points out, was closely associated with the rise of the Gothic style of the north and not in 'what may be called the home ground of the proto-Renaissance movement (South France and Italy)'.

figure instead as a set. They stand for the old empire in its entirety (again, supposing the present reconstruction to be correct), as an accomplished historical fact.

The soffits are probably the first large scale, public and systematic set of portraits of men of the distant classical past in late medieval times which exhibits a cognate sense both of the correct historical appearance of such men, and of an artistic style historically appropriate to them. The main frescoes, if we read the evidence correctly, still exhibited that eschewal of the 'unity of classical form and classical content'[104] characteristic of Italian art until the quattrocento. This has, as Panofsky has pointed out, its positive side.[105] Only when the sense of continuity between the classical past and the medieval present was lost did the 'correct' recreation of classical style become necessary when referring to classical material. For the courtiers of Cansignorio's Verona the classical past, however remote, was still part of the same historical continuum to which they themselves and their history belonged. Only perhaps in certain areas of Petrarch's thought or in that of circles close to him at this time was there formulated any clear sense of an absolute divorce between two ages – for him the lost age of light and the present age of darkness – and, as the history of the Sala Virorum Illustrium shows, even for him the question of stylistic and iconographic coherence in the representation of classical material was probably of little consequence.

The two parts of the Sala Grande scheme which draw on the Antique illustrate what may be seen as different phases of the transition from a medieval to a Renaissance approach to the Antique. Hauser's dismissal of 'the thesis that the Middle Ages never became aware of their distance from classical antiquity and always considered themselves its direct heirs'[106] is partly supported, but also revealed as something of a *non sequitur*, by the present context, for the Sala Grande scheme both insists on the distance from antiquity *and* at the same time on the role of Titus and Vespasian as ancestors of contemporary chivalric and crusading princes and knights (in the main frescoes). The scheme as a whole, unusual in drawing on two distinct sources, is doubly so in that the two parts which relate to the Antique do so in different ways, the narratives being, in this light, more conventionally medieval, the soffits more prophetic of a fully integrated Renaissance culture.

How does the evident celebration of the empire stand in relation to the development of humanism? Accounts of the rise of humanism in quattrocento Florence tend to associate the development of true 'civic' humanism with a bias towards the Roman Republic rather than with a (for them) medieval adherence to the empire.[107] The concept of empire which I suggest was embodied in the Josephus frescoes is essentially that held by the whole of medieval culture up to and including Dante: that it was

[104] Panofsky and Saxl, 'Classical Mythology in Medieval Art', pp. 268ff.

[105] Panofsky, *Renaissance and Renascences*, pp. 110–13.

[106] Hauser, *The Social History of Art*, vol. 1, p. 139.

[107] See Baron, *The Crisis of the Early Renaissance*, and the critiques by Robey, 'P. P. Vergerio the Elder: Republicanism and Civic Values in the Work of an Early Humanist' and Seigel, 'Civic Humanism or Ciceronian Rhetoric? The Culture of Petrarch and Bruni'.

divinely ordained and served a transcendental purpose. It has been held that Petrarch, especially in his earlier work and in the *Africa*, jettisoned this view.[108] His preference for the republic at this time is a fact, but the attack in his epic[109] is directed not at the Roman Empire as such (as the description of the campaigns and triumph of Titus and Vespasian shows), but rather at the, for him, usurpation of it in later times by Franks and Germans; and the position he adopted in his later years, embodied in the massive life of Caesar (whom he had earlier criticised) written for the *DVI* in its final form, is no longer recognisably anti-imperial at all.

Attitudes to the empire in the various centres of humanism obviously varied according to the political tradition of each city. The position of men of Guelph Florence, threatened throughout the trecento by the expansionist policies of both the Scaligeri and Visconti imperial vicars was clearly going to differ from that of the courtiers of Ghibelline Verona. A perfectly coherent theory of the superior benefits of signorial rule in a humanist context was developed by the Carrarese chancellor Giovanni Conversino on the basis of a reading of Roman history.[110] Giovanni's contention that scholarship and humanism flourished under the northern *signori*, as under Augustus, because of, not despite, the despotic form of government (with the Roman Empire giving it historical pedigree and legitimacy), was doubtless a convenient stance for a citizen of such a state to adopt. But no more so than, *mutatis mutandis*, for his Florentine equivalent. Descriptions of Cansignorio's renovative policy for Verona – sometimes called 'La Marmorina' at this time – tend to bring Augustus to mind, and Augustus was clearly the model for Giovanni Conversino's portrayal of Francesco da Carrara, Cansignorio's mentor, as the archetypal enlightened humanist prince. Cansignorio's decision to decorate his palace with frescoes based on themes from the Antique must in some degree be based on the example of his uncle, whose palace was by the 1360s liberally decorated with such subjects, and whose family already had a long and public association with the greatest humanist of the trecento. In the new climate of Cansignorio's court, the long estrangement between Petrarch and the Scaligeri must have been a matter of profound regret, and in a milieu where a visit from Petrarch was something to boast about, it must have caused the Scaligeri no little loss of face. Cansignorio, possibly at Guglielmo da Pastrengo's suggestion, restored Giovanni di Petrarca to his Veronese canonry and thus removed the declared cause of Petrarch's refusal to visit Verona after 1354. This olive branch seems to have been effective – Petrarch almost certainly visited Verona once more in 1368[111] – and it was perhaps augmented, or commemorated, by the portrait of the poet which Vasari mentions as a feature of the Sala Grande, but of which we have no other certain record.

The importance of the Sala Grande, whose glories can be very dimly glimpsed from the surviving fragments and other records, for Altichiero's career was almost certainly immense. Probably it made his name. For all that any reconstruction of the lost frescoes

108 Seigel, 'Civic Humanism', p. 5.

109 Petrarch, *Africa* II. 348–64.

110 For Giovanni Conversino see Baron, *Crisis*, pp. 109–20.

111 Wilkins, *Petrarch's Later Years*, pp. 144 and 157–8.

must be speculative and imprecise, his own contribution was clearly more than that of a mere executant. The imperial heads show an approach to the iconography and style of the Antique which is, for its time, impressively systematic, looking always for a genuinely classicising style even if it involves going against the guidelines of the immediate source. The border has an importance quite out of proportion to its nominally secondary role, and the extraordinary interweaving of different layers of material throughout the cycle suggests an artist working in the closest possible collaboration with the patron and his advisors. Vasari's term for Altichiero's relationship with the Scaligeri – 'famigliarissimo' – defies translation, but it confirms that we are in the presence of an artist uniquely, in this context, alert to his patron's needs and in accord with the prevailing concerns of the signorial imagination. The distance between art at this level and the work of the honest craftsmen who covered the walls of S. Zeno is immense.

3

THE CAVALLI VOTIVE FRESCO

If the historiography of trecento painting had been guided less by patriotic or programmatic agendas and more by a recognition of absolute quality, the fresco Altichiero painted for the family of Giacomo Cavalli (pls. 16–20), one of Cansignorio's most illustrious courtiers and soldiers, would long ago have been ranked with its close neighbour for over 500 years, Pisanello's *St George and the Princess*. It is perhaps the greatest of all trecento votive frescoes, and gives us a far more concrete idea of the allure of Altichiero's early style than the *disjecta membra* of the Sala Grande can ever do. It is in many ways his most sheerly beautiful and poetic creation, its unparalleled glamour and refinement perfectly complementing the precocious *all'antica* revelations of Cansignorio's frescoes and unforgettably enshrining the self-mythologising imagination of the courtier's world. No wonder the Paduans were soon so eager for his services.

The Cavalli fresco,[1] high on the south wall of the family's chapel in S. Anastasia (figs. 44, 47), shows three male donors, all wearing emblazoned surcoats, and each with a helmet, either slung across the back or placed on the ground, sporting the horse's head of the family arms. The precise identity of the knights, presented by Sts George, Martin and James the Great, remains to be established, as does the date. The fresco is most likely to have been painted between the completion of the Sala Grande and the beginning of Altichiero's work in Padua in the mid 1370s. Though there is no documentary evidence certainly associated with the commission – for the 1369 document cannot be used in this way[2] – and no surviving signature or date, the circumstantial evidence suggests it must have been painted before 1375 at the very latest, which makes perfect sense in terms of Altichiero's stylistic development too. If Altichiero's major role in the decoration of the Sala Virorum Illustrium is accepted, it is also reasonable to assume he was in some sort of contact with the promoters of the scheme by 1374 or 1375,[3] though he need not, at that stage, have been living in Padua. Once he was actually at work on the Petrarch frescoes his residence there can be taken for granted. He may already, espe-

[1] The principal previous accounts are Mellini, *Altichiero e Jacopo Avanzi*, pp. 38–40, Kruft, *Altichiero und Avanzo*, pp. 127–30, and Pettenella, *Altichiero*, pp. 52–5.

[2] S. Verona, Archivio di Stato Anastasia, Sec. XIV, doc. no. 39 (1369).

[3] Mommsen, 'Sala Virorum Illustrium' gives a chronological window for the *SVI* of 1367–1379, but his preference for a pre-1370 beginning for the scheme is based on an unacceptable attribution of the extant Petrarch portrait to Guariento (d.1370). Simon, 'Altichiero Versus Avanzo', p. 270 suggests a date 'during the 1370s some time up until 1376'. The date of the Sala Virorum Illustrium is discussed in chapter 4, below.

cially perhaps after the death of Cansignorio della Scala in October 1375, have envisaged Padua as his centre of operations for some years ahead. Though he was never, as far as we know, accorded Paduan citizenship, he seems to have joined the Paduan painters' guild in 1382[4] and was still there in 1384. The Cavalli fresco must, then, have been painted either before *c.* 1374/5 or after 1384. The argument for the earlier period is, as has already been suggested, the more persuasive, especially in the light of all the available background evidence for Cavalli patronage in Verona.

The present S. Anastasia was the second church built by the Veronese Dominicans, replacing the much smaller S. Maria Mater Domini, erected outside the city walls within a few years of the order's arrival, consecrated in 1238, and found by *c.* 1260 to be wholly inadequate.[5] The land within the city on which the new church and convent were to be built came to the Dominicans as a donation of bishop-elect Manfredo in 1260. Confirmed by Bishop Bartolomeo della Scala in 1281, this donation included, as well as various houses and gardens, the two churches of S. Remigio and S. Anastasia, the latter dating from the ninth century or earlier.[6]

There almost certainly existed by the time of the confirmation an intention to build a church in honour of the Veronese Dominican, St Peter Martyr, canonised within a year of his murder in 1252 and co-patron saint of Verona with St Zeno.[7] Funding for the project came initially from the sale of S. Maria Mater Domini in 1268, and afterwards from a variety of sources, including donations and legacies from major Veronese families, with the Scaligeri, engaged from 1260 onwards in establishing their *signoria*, well to the fore. Additional purchases of existing properties are recorded in the late 1270s, but it was not until the Dominican Bishop Pietro della Scala's[8] donation of the land now forming the piazza in front of the church in 1292 (fig. 40) that the concrete existence of the new structure appears in documents. The appointment in 1290 of a Dominican bishop probably gave a decisive impetus to the work.

All the evidence suggests that the Scaligeri themselves played an important role in the

4 Simon, 'Altichiero Versus Avanzo', p. 261 and his source, Moschini, *Dell'Origine e delle Vicende della Pittura in Padova*, p. 9.

5 Origins and early histories of both convent and church are in Cipolla, 'Ricerche Storiche', and Dellwing, *Studien zur Baukunst der Bettelorden im Veneto*, pp. 64–81.

6 The site of the old church is marked by, and possibly some of the fabric retained in, the present Chapel of Crocefisso just to the west of the south transept. See Dellwing, *Studien*, p. 64 and Cappelletti, *La Basilica di S. Anastasia*, p. 33. The only two pillar frescoes in S. Anastasia are on the columns flanking this chapel and facing across the aisle towards it, so the area may have been especially venerated. The vault decoration of the bay of the south aisle off which the chapel opens is older than that of the other bays or any other vault decoration west of the crossing. It belongs stylistically with the eastern chapel borders.

7 The Veronese have shown a marked reluctance to accept a church dedicated to Peter. The new church seems to have reverted, even in official usage, to the older (and present) dedication at least by 1424, when the small church of S. Giorgetto was turned over to the lay confraternity of S. Pietro Martire and rededicated to that saint. But this second dedication also failed to stick, and the little church is still, to the Veronese, S. Giorgetto. Perhaps the memory of Peter's persecution of the local *patarini* lingered on.

8 Not, as used to be thought, one of the Veronese della Scala, but a member of a family of the same name from Bergamo. See Sancassani, 'Notizie 1277–1387', p. 332. There were five bishops of the Veronese Scaligeri between 1252 and 1387, four of whom were *naturali* of men in the main signorial line. See Ederle, *Dizionario Cronologico*, pp. 51–9.

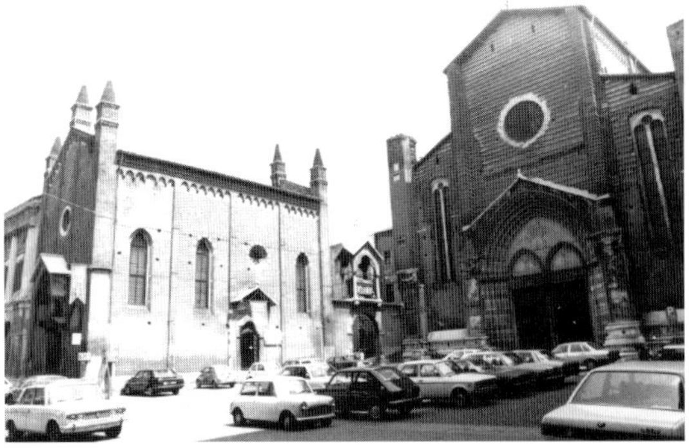

Fig. 40 Verona. Piazza S. Anastasia, *left* S. Pietro Martire ('S. Giorgetto') *right* S. Anastasia.

funding of the new church in these early years, support which is recorded by the two della Scala *stemmi* over the entrance arch of the *cappella maggiore*, itself, in Cappelletti's view,[9] due wholly to Scaligeri donations, and which is further indicated by the terms of Alberto I della Scala's will, in which money is left which was specifically destined for the needs of the Dominican building campaign.[10]

During the period following Alberto's death in 1301 the major patronage of his family was largely devoted to other orders. But the Dominicans found a new and generous patron in the person of the remarkable Guglielmo da Castelbarco, subject of the S. Fermo portrait and one of CanGrande's closest and most influential supporters.[11] His support may be regarded in some senses as Scaligeri patronage by proxy. The Castelbarco were prominent amongst that class of ancient families now allied to the Scaligeri. Though great feudal lords in their own right and the possessors of many estates and castles in the Val d'Adige and Trentino, from which they maintained uneasy and often stormy relations with both the bishops of Trento and the counts of Tyrol, they evidently lacked the power base from which to establish any sort of quasi-signorial rule on any significant scale.[12] Several of the most able members of the family became high-ranking administrative and military servants of the expanding Scaligeri *signoria*. Guglielmo himself was *podestà* of Verona in 1285, and as late as 1318, when he must have been in his seventies at least, he was still riding with CanGrande's armies beneath the walls of Padua.

Guglielmo's patronage was by no means confined to Verona.[13] He supported the renovation of Rovereto and donated handsomely to the Franciscans there. He financed the building of the south aisle of the cathedral at Trento, which church he later enriched by a legacy for the construction of a chapel after his death. In Verona, as well as funding the Dominican building programme from 1307 to 1310 and again from 1317 to 1319, he assisted the Franciscans substantially from 1310, being instrumental in implementing

[9] Cappelletti, *S. Anastasia*, p. 40.

[10] For Alberto's will see Cipolla, 'Ricerche Storiche'. It was witnessed by Bishop Tebaldo and the Dominican prior, Nicolo de Musso. Alberto had previously established his piety by burning the 166 Patarini rounded up in 1276 by Mastino I but only imprisoned by him. See Cipolla, *Compendio*, p. 107.

[11] For Castelbarco see his entry in the *Dizionario Biografico*, vol. XXI.

[12] Rossini, 'La Signoria Scaligera', pp. 193–4.

[13] For Guglielmo's patronage see the *Dizionario Biografico*, vol. XXI, p. 573.

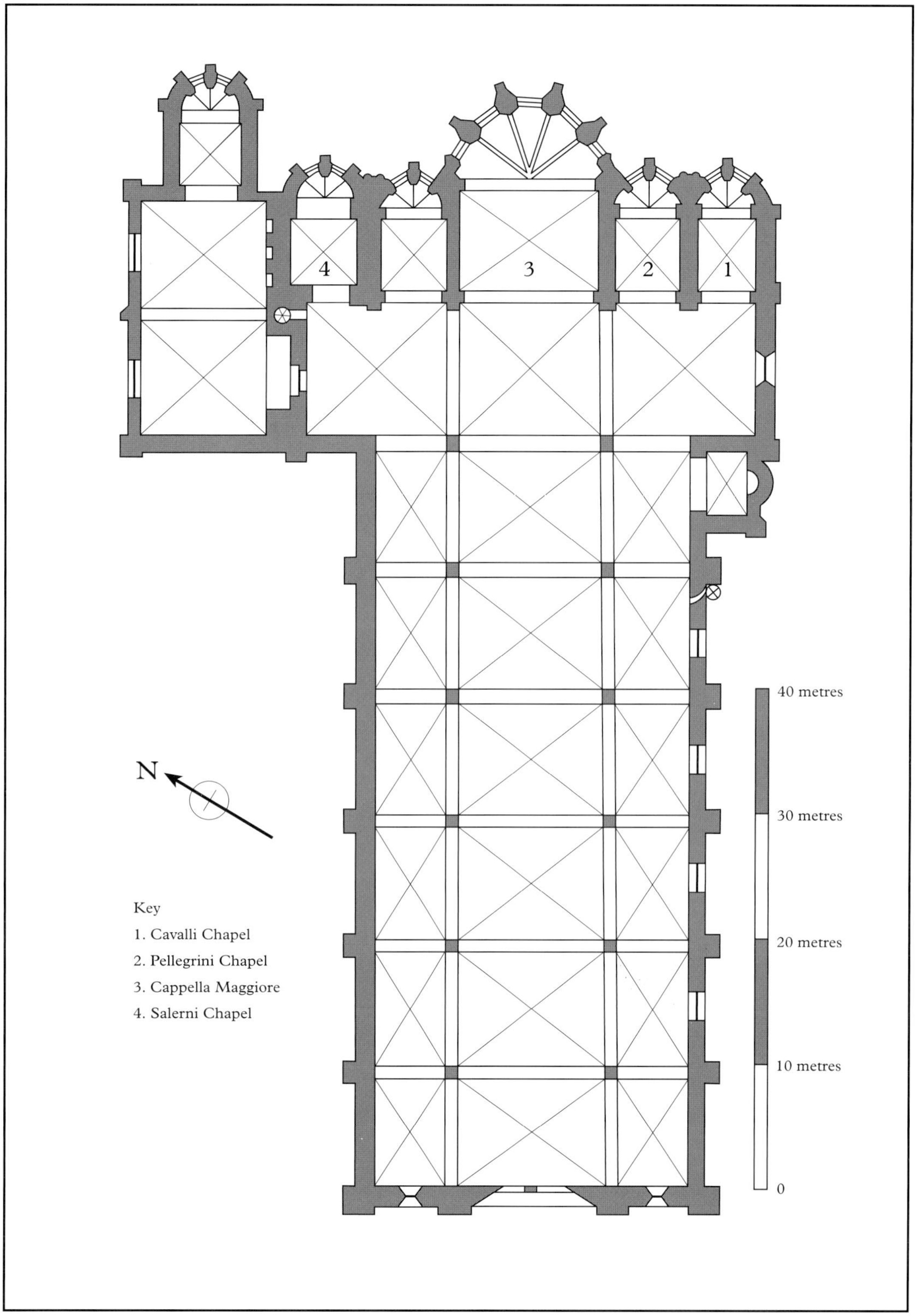

Drawing I Verona, S. Anastasia. Ground plan.

the long-standing and long-disregarded papal decree by which they gained possession of S. Fermo Maggiore.[14] His generosity is commemorated in that church with the splendid portrait on the presbytery arch,[15] but he chose the Dominican house for his tomb. Inside S. Anastasia his support is marked by the decoration of the first two pairs of nave columns from the east with the Lion Rampant of his family. It is probable that by the time of Castelbarco's death in 1320 the whole eastern half of the new church – the five chapels, transepts, crossing and the first bay of the nave – was complete (fig. 41), and that the western half of the building, not in fact finished until the fifteenth century, was well under way.[16] Certainly the facade had risen high enough by the 1320s for the sculptor of Castelbarco's tomb to decorate the architrave above the main portal with an impressive Passion cycle.

Both the site and design of S. Anastasia testify to the importance with which the new church was regarded in Verona. Standing at the head of the *corso*, it also lay on the principal route between the central Piazza Erbe and the cathedral, with access to the northern gate of the city and through it to the Ponte Pietra and the settlements north of the Adige. It also lay conveniently close to the rapidly expanding area of the signorial palaces clustered round S. Maria Antica (fig. 42). The 1292 donation, providing for what was in the context of a crowded medieval city a spacious piazza in front of the church, may have been made with public and ceremonial use of the church in mind.

Some such consideration may have been in the mind of the designers and donors of S. Anastasia too. In scale and in the grandeur of its conception S. Anastasia surpasses its apparent model, S. Lorenzo in Vicenza, especially in the far greater scale and prominence given to the east end, with its five chapels and spacious transepts.[17] The imposing character with which such an ample eastern section invests S. Anastasia is matched, and in terms of scale alone surpassed, by S. Nicolo in Treviso. But S. Nicolo curtails the full processional power of a big six-bay nave by having the main entrance on the north, while S. Anastasia has a full double portal at the west end of the nave, and had the western exterior been completed would no doubt have faced the piazza and the *corso* with a facade at least as imposing as that of S. Fermo.[18] The apparent stylistic and conceptual isolation of S. Anastasia is only local to Verona, for the design belongs to a recognisable class of Dominican churches in the Veneto, in which region the order consistently opted for basilical designs on a grand scale for the larger cities.

Early in the trecento, probably as soon as they were completed, the eastern chapels of the new church were being used for the burial of important men, particularly those

[14] For the decree of 1257 see Ederle, *Dizionario Cronologico*, p. 45. Only in 1312 was the issue finally resolved 'grazie all'intervento di Enrico VII e dello stesso CanGrande della Scala verosimilmente sollecitati dal C(astelbarco)', *Dizionario Biografico*, vol. XXI, p. 573.

[15] Cuppini, 'L'Arte Gotica', p. 292 argues that this is the image of Guglielmo's father Azzone, in whose memory Guglielmo supported the church. But whatever the arguments, the portrait *looks* like the tomb effigy of Guglielmo, which is pungently characterised.

[16] Cipolla, 'Ricerche Storiche' and Dellwing, *Studien*, p. 65.

[17] For S. Lorenzo and S. Nicolo see Dellwing, *Studien*, pp. 45–59 and 82–97. S. Lorenzo has only a five-bay nave with three eastern chapels, and the transepts only project by an extra half-aisle's width.

[18] *Ibid.*, pp. 68–72 for the west front of S. Anastasia and its relationship with the completed facade of S. Fermo.

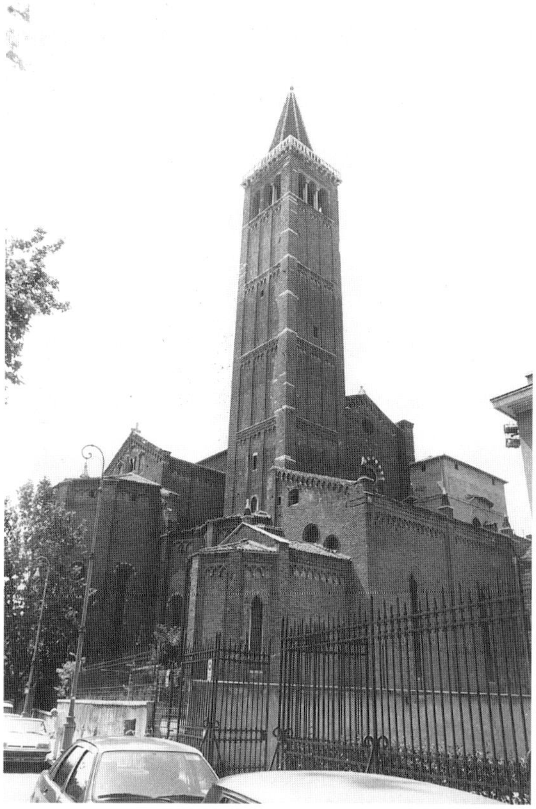

Fig. 41 Verona, S. Anastasia. Exterior from North.

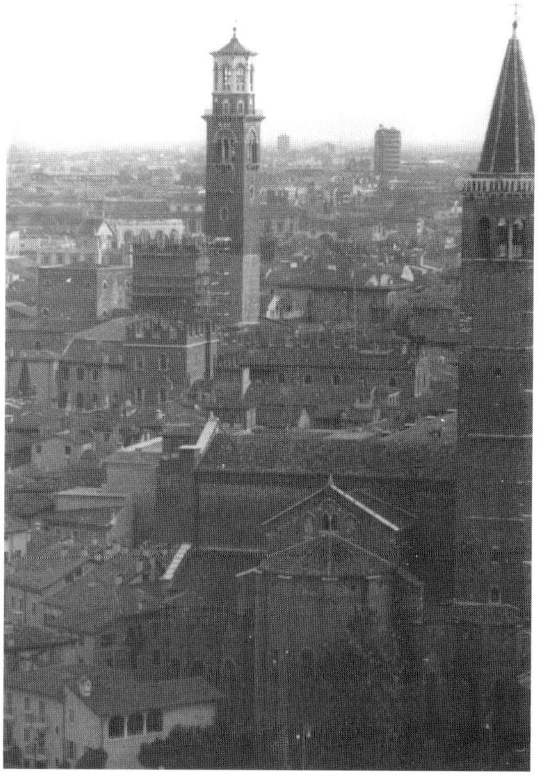

Fig. 42 Verona. S. Anastasia, Scaligeri palaces and Torre dei Lamberti.

associated with Scaligeri interests. Prominent amongst these were Walram of Luxembourg, brother of the Emperor Henry VII, and CanGrande's ally the great Tuscan Ghibelline Uguccione della Faggiuola (possibly one of the figures represented in the Sala Grande). The Cappella Maggiore in particular, possibly because burial rights there were treated as a Scaligeri preserve, seems to have been used for the tombs of the major German knights on whom CanGrande was increasingly reliant – there exists a list of the numerous *Teutonici* buried in this area in the early trecento.[19] Towards the mid-century, and especially after the revolt of Fregnano della Scala in 1354, this function was transferred to the adjacent church of S. Giorgetto, which was then given over to the devotions and burials of these men, who were quartered in a Scaligeri house on the south-east side of the piazza, and many of whose votive frescoes and heraldic devices can still be seen in the little church.[20]

The original decoration of S. Anastasia was essentially simple. That it can now be seen best in the Cavalli Chapel is largely due to an extremely thorough post-war restoration which has not only removed the majority of the trecento frescoes superimposed

[19] For these burials see Rossini, 'La Signoria Scaligera', p. 227. The list is Verona, Archivio di Stato S. Anastasia, Reg. 68.

[20] See Gerola, 'I Cavalieri Tedeschi'.

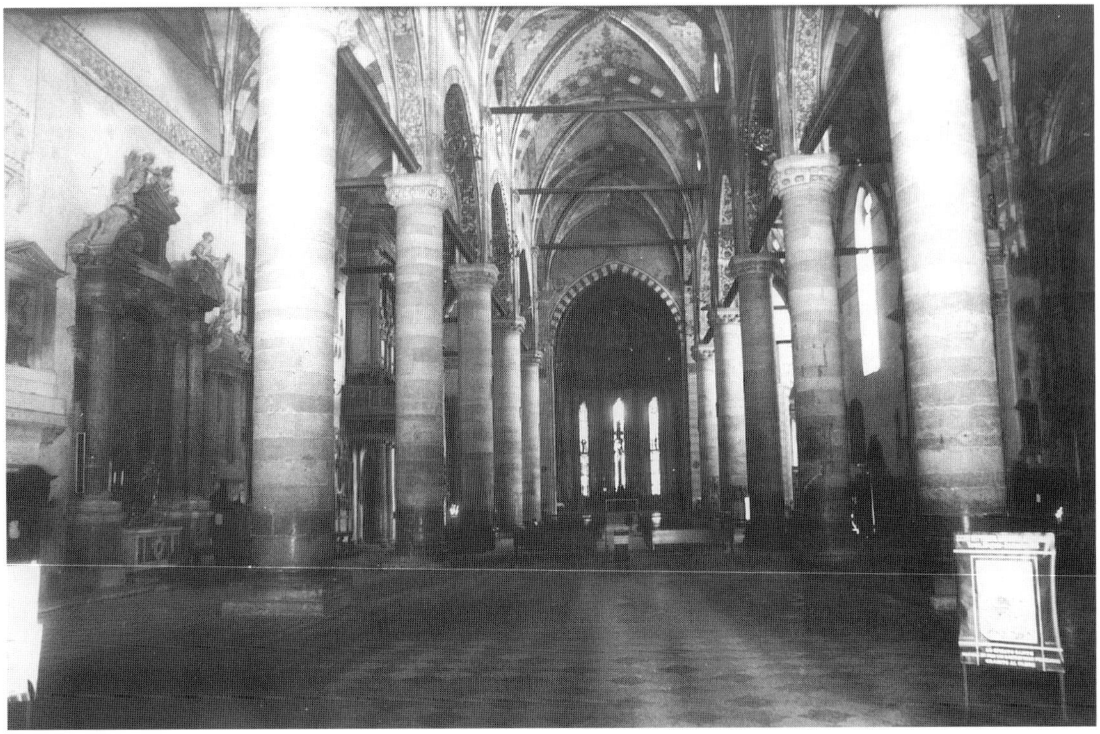

Fig. 43 Verona, S. Anastasia. Interior to east.

on the early scheme but left bare the putlog holes. The first decorative phase after the completion of the eastern chapels[21] and the transepts consisted of a double red and green foliate band and a series of roundels with a kinked border and enclosing a crisply plastic star motif composed of contrasting light and dark wedges. The apse lunettes also have these roundels, while the larger lunettes above the main side walls are empty, at least as they stand today. The vaults are decorated with a related foliate scrolling in the cells and a vigorous chevron band framing the ribs. Though the vault has lost about half its original paint surface, the overall scheme in the Cavalli Chapel is legible enough.

High on the external wall of the entrance arch of the chapel (fig. 46) is a fragment of a similar border. This evidently ran across the face of the two chapels of each branch of the transept. The border type was probably common to the whole eastern area.[22] Extensive stretches survive in the Cappella Maggiore, partly overlaid by a later fresco, and flat foliation of the same kind is used in the piscina niche below this fresco. A fragment of similar design also survives on the wall behind the tomb of Giovanni Salerni in the Salerni Chapel, northernmost of the eastern group. The vault decoration of this chapel, though related to that used in the Cavalli Chapel, is a degree less refined in design (and closer to late duecento styles), and it may be that the chapel vaults were frescoed in sequence from north to south.

21 For the eastern chapels and their dedications and families see Cappelletti, *S. Anastasia*, pp. 35–44.

22 And to S. Giorgetto, where a similar foliate band shows through on the north wall, partly overlaid by later trecento frescoes.

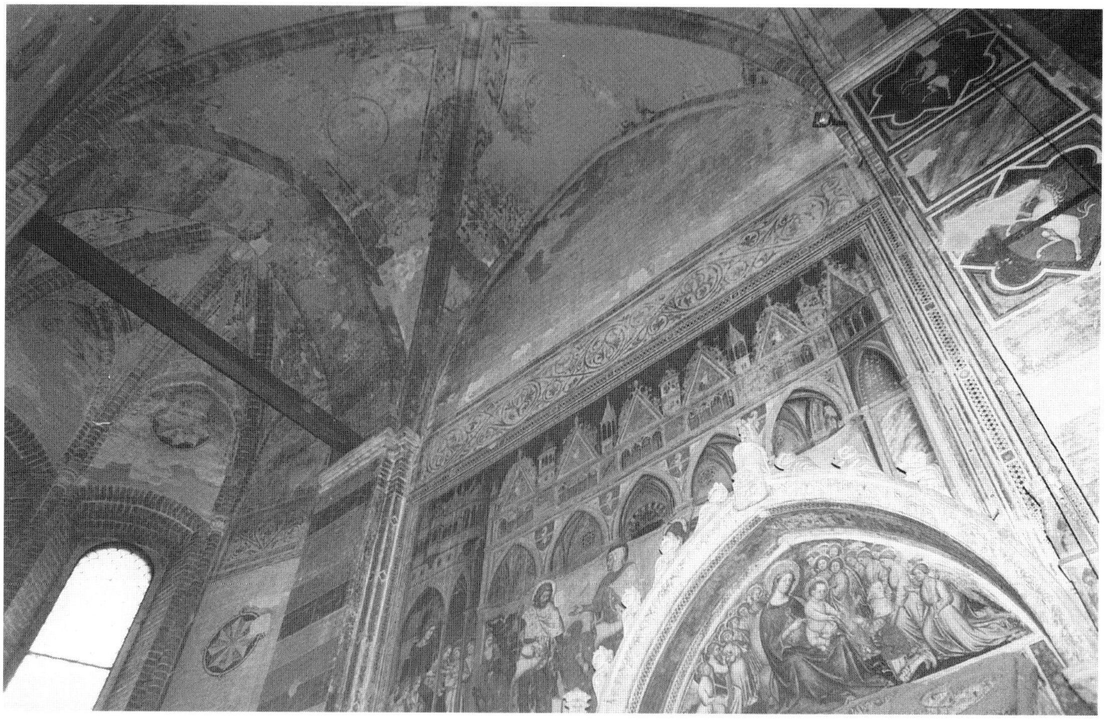

Fig. 44 Verona, S. Anastasia. South wall of Cavalli Chapel.

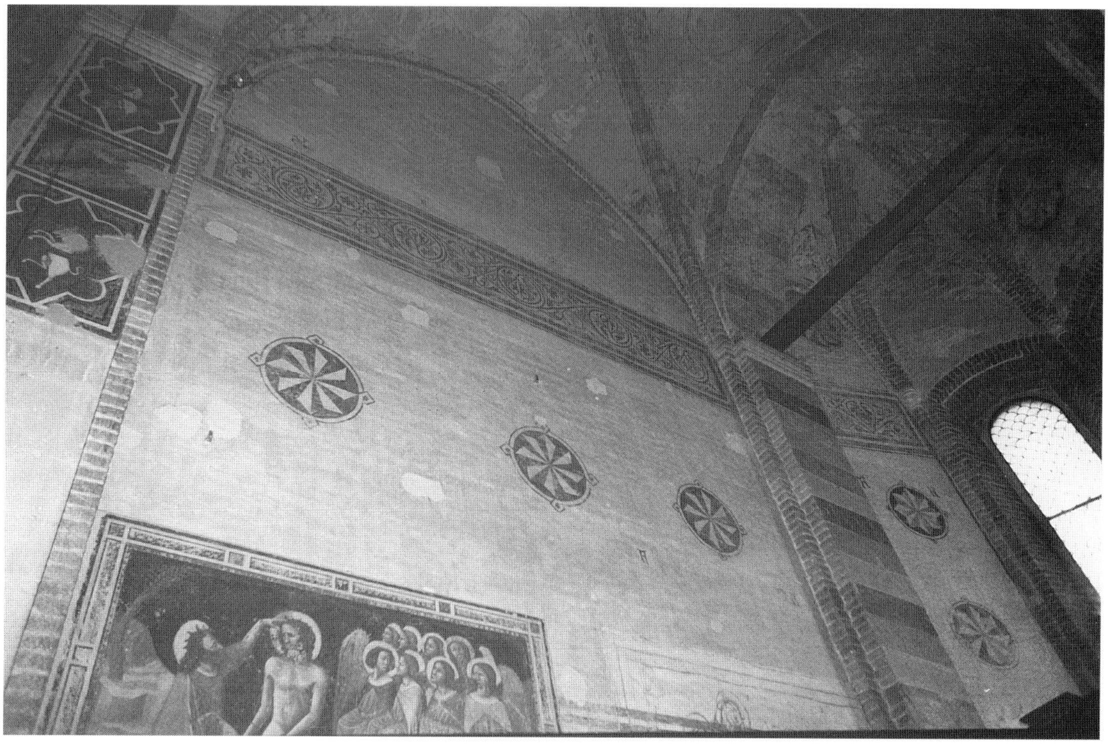

Fig. 45 Verona, S. Anastasia. North wall of Cavalli Chapel.

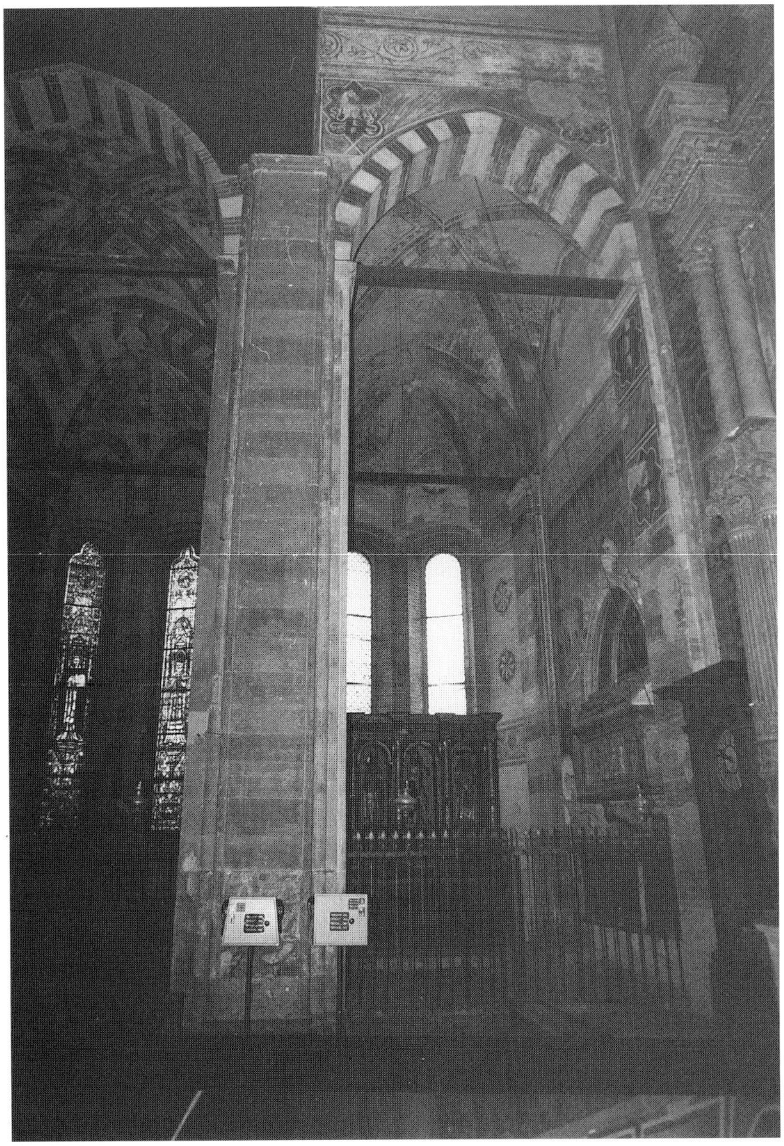

Fig. 46 Verona, S. Anastasia. Cavalli Chapel from transept.

This whole scheme, lively enough but wholly subordinate to the architecture, is in marked contrast with the decoration of the eastern arm of the Franciscan S. Fermo in Castelbarco's time, the cradle, as far as can now be determined, of Veronese trecento painting.[23] The work of the painters of S. Fermo in the second and third decades of the century finds no equivalent in S. Anastasia, where we find no figurative painting until late in the period dominated by the painters of the second S. Zeno group,[24] that is, towards and after the mid-century. For perhaps the first twenty-five years from completion, the finished parts of S. Anastasia were left free of that rash of small votive frescoes

[23] See Sandberg-Vavalà, *La Pittura Veronese*, pp. 44–52 and pp. 55–6, and Pettenella, *Altichiero*, pp. 17–18.

[24] See Sandberg-Vavalà, *La Pittura Veronese*, pp. 70–99 and pp. 88–92 in particular.

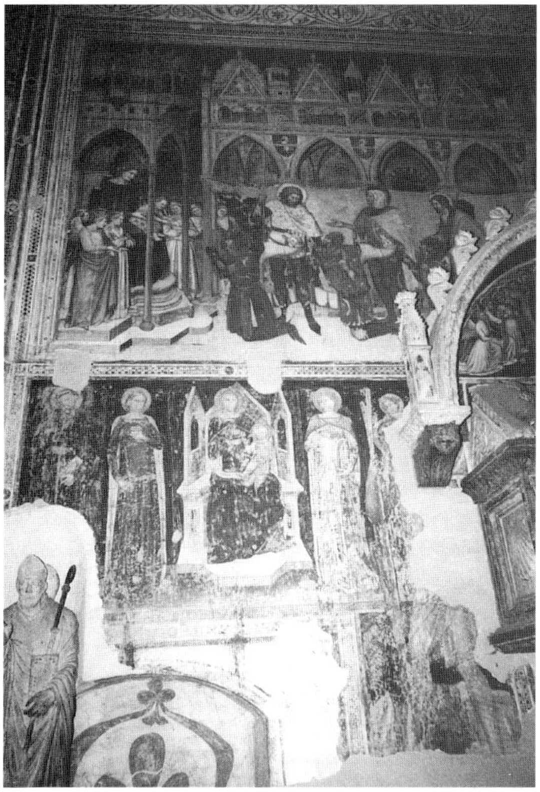

Fig. 47 Verona, S. Anastasia. South wall of Cavalli Chapel.

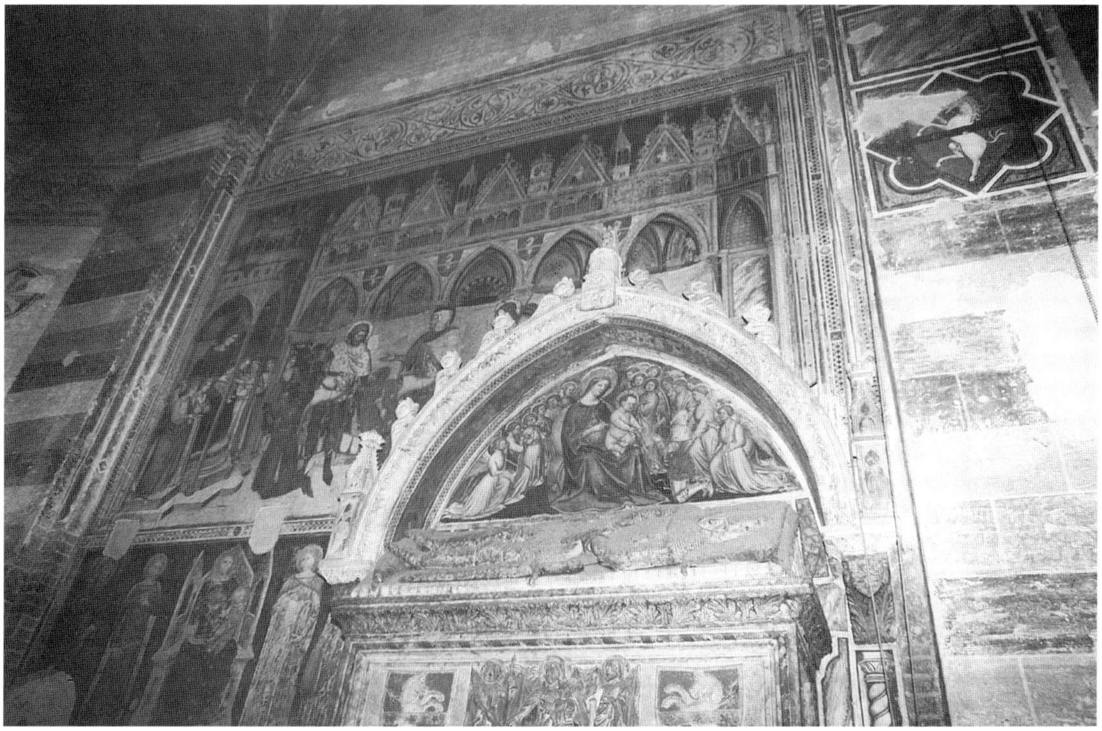

Fig. 48 Verona, S. Anastasia. South wall of Cavalli Chapel with tomb of Federigo Cavalli.

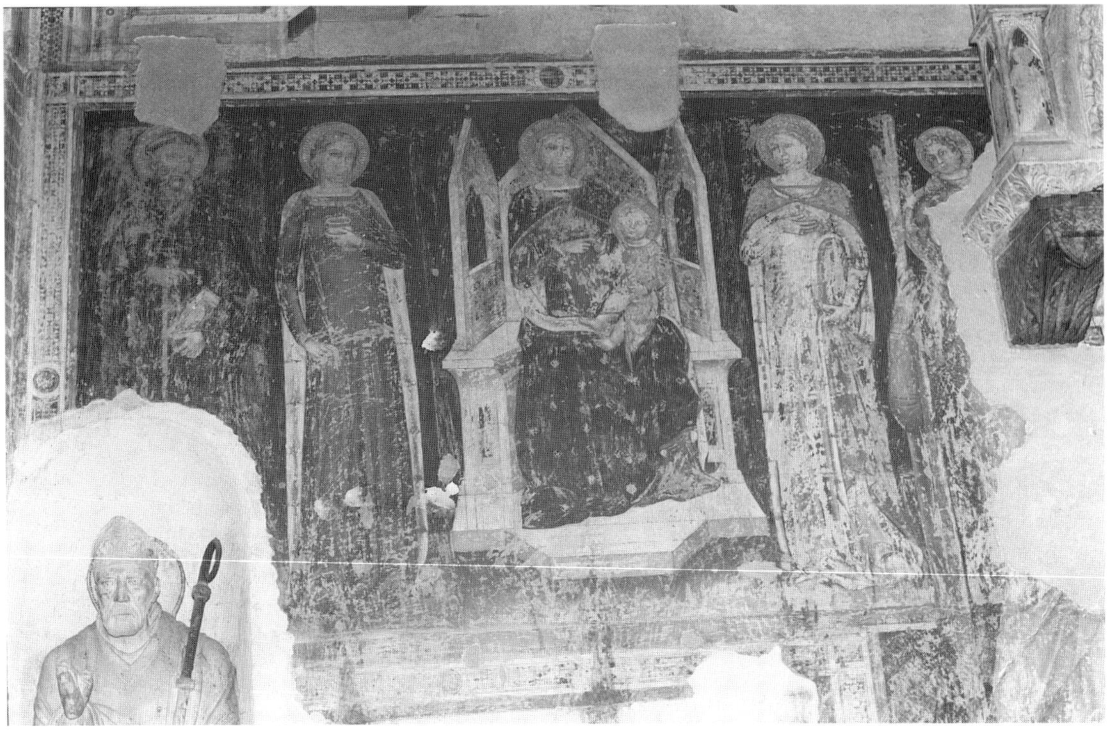

Fig. 49 Verona, S. Anastasia. *Madonna and Child with Saints*. S. Anastasia Master: *S. Geminiano*.

which covered the walls of all the other churches of Verona. What happened to alter the situation from *c.* 1345 to 1350, from which time S. Anastasia fell more or less into line with the rest of the city, is unclear. Perhaps the Black Death released funds and demands which could not be resisted.[25] The disposition of figurative frescoes in S. Anastasia is markedly more disciplined and less chaotic than elsewhere – the tops of adjacent frescoes follow a common line, and groups of frescoes tend to form loose but coherent bands.

The eastern chapels were probably completed by 1320 at the latest. The Cavalli Chapel preserves the earliest concrete indication of a dedication in the statue of *S. Geminiano* (fig. 49), which is still in the chapel, though no longer in what may be assumed to have been its original position on the altar. This may be attributed to the circle of the so-called 'Anastasia Master', author of a number of free-standing works now held in the Castelvecchio. A date in line with the first phase of sculptural activity in the church (*c.* 1320 for the Castelbarco tomb and the portal Passion Sequence) seems about right.[26]

[25] The Black Death made a considerable impact on Verona. The population was reduced from *c.* 35,000 to 40,000 before 1348 to *c.* 15,000 by the end of the century, with no increase until after 1425. For this and other effects see Herlihy, 'Mapping Households in Medieval Italy' and 'The Population of Verona in the first Century of Venetian Rule'.

[26] The attempt by Mellini, *Sculturi Veronesi*, p. 13 to date it before 1300 on the grounds of an entirely unconvincing affinity with the figure of *S. Zeno* in S. Zeno Maggiore is surely misguided.

The dates of the chapels' first adoption by specific families is unclear. In none of the transept chapels is there any tomb which can definitely be attached to the respective family and to a date before 1380. But the Cavalli Chapel again gives the best indication. High on the outer side of the entrance wall are two Cavalli *stemmi*, with four more on the sides of the arch itself lower down – two each side. These last four, much repainted by later generations of Cavalli in Mellini's view,[27] are inscribed within a polylobe consisting of a flat white strip and two simple roll mouldings. This is clearly a much more primitive system than anything used by Altichiero, to whom Mellini attributes them, and the frames of the probably contemporary *stemmi* above the arch, with a simple strip and a single moulding, are of a type used as part of the S. Fermo presbytery scheme of *c.* 1320 and in another scheme in SS Trinità in Verona, though neither of these latter examples has even the simple moulded element of the Cavalli *stemmi*. But there is no reason why the Cavalli *stemmi* should be much later than these – they certainly pre-date Altichiero's work in the chapel by decades – and the inference must be that the chapel was adopted by the Cavalli almost from the moment of its completion, and that all the frescoes added in the later trecento were Cavalli commissions.

These frescoes are part of a larger body of work in S. Anastasia by painters within the orbit of the Second S. Zeno Master. In addition to the Cavalli Chapel frescoes, this includes two sets of Standing Saints on the sides of the entrance to the Salerni Chapel, an important votive fresco within the chapel, a standing saint under a Cosmatesque canopy flanking the entrance to the Lavagnoli Chapel, and a *Madonna Lactans with Two Saints* on the first nave column from the crossing on the south side.

Within the Cavalli Chapel were three substantial frescoes: a *Madonna and Four Saints* still *in situ* on the south wall below Altichiero's fresco (fig. 49), a *Madonna della Misericordia with Two Saints*, and a *Man of Sorrows with Four Saints*. These last two have been removed,[28] as have a number of smaller frescoes described while *in situ* by Corso, who listed no fewer than twelve different trecento frescoes here,[29] of which only five remain in the chapel, and only four are still attached to the wall. Given this state of affairs, and the rather imprecise descriptions of the chapel in its pre-restoration condition by both Corso and Sandberg-Vavalà, reconstruction of the mid-trecento campaign is not easy. The relatively coherent disposition of the large frescoes on the side walls and the smaller ones of the apse in a continuous and regular band round the wall, which is the layout described by Sandberg-Vavalà,[30] suggests a single campaign suited to the available space rather than the longer-term additive process characteristic of other family chapels in Verona and Padua. It must be assumed that it was the presence of this pre-existing layer of frescoes which necessitated the elevation of Altichiero's fresco to

[27] Mellini, *Altichiero e Jacopo Avanzi*, p. 40.

[28] They are presently stored in S. Giorgetto.

[29] Corso, 'La Cappella Cavalli in S. Anastasia Verona'. As well as the frescoes discussed in this chapter, Corso listed the following: a *Miracle of S. Eligio* attributable to Martino da Verona; a *St Christopher* (perhaps that attached to the south wall *Madonna*); figures of *St Bartholomew* and *St Valentine* flanking the entrance arch, attributed to Martino; and an *Apostle* with kneeling donor. His descriptions are inaccurate; he described non-existent saints in Martino's tomb lunette, referred to the *Madonna della Misericordia* as a *Madonna and Child*, and placed the figure of *S. Geminiano* on the *left* wall. But there is no reason to discount the overall picture he gives of the chapel's contents.

[30] Sandberg-Vavalà, *La Pittura Veronese*, pp. 88 and 90.

the upper part of the south wall, a position which can never have been terribly advantageous even before alterations to the lower wall further obscured the fresco from the viewpoint of the spectator standing in the chapel.

The three big frescoes share with each other and with the *Magdalen* in the apse the same type of Cosmatesque border as the Salerni Chapel votive fresco, but without the inner double moulding of the Salerni frame. Only in S. Anastasia are such comparatively sophisticated (if old-fashioned in a wider context) borders found in the work of the second S. Zeno group, which elsewhere uses the simplest of flat red bands, occasionally elaborated by the addition of an inner white strip with or without an inner moulded profile. For this reason, and because of an affinity with the dated votive fresco of 1354 in S. Giorgetto,[31] it would seem reasonable to accept Sandberg-Vavalà's date for these frescoes of *c.* 1350. The Salerni fresco is, if anything rather more sophisticated than the 1354 *Madonna*, and this must represent the last phase of the Second S. Zeno Master's – or Masters' – work before the impact of Turone, felt in S. Giorgetto and here in the Cappella Maggiore's *Last Judgement*, from *c.* 1356 onwards.[32] The greater complexity of throne construction, together with that fresco's marginally more advanced unity of action, all combine to suggest a date towards the mid 1350s for this campaign.

Work in the Cavalli Chapel was contemporary with the first series of frescoes in S. Giorgetto commissioned by CanGrande II's German captains, and with what seems to have been a renewal of signorial interest in S. Anastasia. This is marked by the *Madonna of Humility* painted by Lorenzo Veneziano,[33] almost certainly for CanGrande II, and probably executed at the same time as his great *Crucifix* now in S. Zeno, but which, with its Dominican donor, must have come from S. Anastasia.[34] To judge from the size and splendour of the painting, it may have been the chief Crucifix of the Dominican church, hung over the *tramezzo*, or *pontile*, on which the *Madonna of Humility* was originally situated. This double commission from Lorenzo may have marked a phase in the building of the church beyond that achieved in 1320. Perhaps only by 1355/6 was the construction of the western part of the nave at a stage where the *pontile* could be fully finished and decorated.

Associated with this burst of activity after 1350 are a number of frescoes of probably Bolognese origin,[35] including a *Baptism of Christ*, recorded in early accounts of the Cavalli Chapel and still there, though now detached. With the Turonesque *Last Judgement* in the Cappella Maggiore, the mid-trecento campaigns in S. Anastasia seem to have come to a halt. The next major period of activity took place in the 1380s and 1390s, heavily under Altichiero's influence.

[31] *Ibid.*, fig. 27.

[32] For this fresco see Arslan, 'Una Tavola di Altichiero', and the rejection of the attribution to Turone by Cuppini, 'Alcune Pitture', pp. 237–43.

[33] See Cuppini, 'Pitture II', pp. 243–4 for the *Madonna del Rosario*. When the *pontile* was dismantled the fresco was transferred to canvas and moved to the newly built Chapel of Rosario (1585–96). See also Cappelletti, *S. Anastasia*, pp. 49–50.

[34] Presumably at the time of the Dominican convent's suppression (19 March 1807). The convent became the property of the Veronese *commune* and the church was put to parochial use. See Cappelletti, *S. Anastasia*, p. 14.

[35] Arcangeli, 'Affreschi Veronesi' discusses the Bolognese frescoes of S. Anastasia.

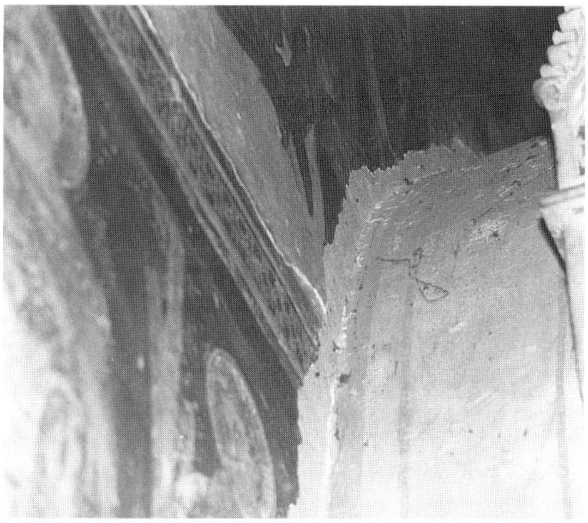

Fig. 50 Verona, S. Anastasia. Detail of south wall of Cavalli Chapel and tomb of Federigo Cavalli.

The present condition of the Cavalli Chapel's south wall (figs. 44, 48) is problematic. Four distinct phases of trecento decoration lie beside, and in places on top of, one another and though the broad sequence is clear, the exact pattern of the sequence is not – and has been obscured by later restorations and what one might call de-restorations of various kinds.

That Altichiero's fresco postdates the Madonna of the lower part of the wall is obvious on stylistic grounds, and is confirmed by a clearly visible overlap of the respective plasters, with Altichiero's the upper and later layer (fig. 50). The condition of the boundary between the two is itself puzzling. The high position of Altichiero's fresco was presumably chosen with a view to preserving the decoration of the lower wall. The possibility that it was designed to accommodate the arched tomb below can be ruled out, for it is clear that Altichiero's plaster was broken by the insertion of the arch at a later date. A strip of bare wall surface is visible above the tomb, running over the top of the arch, and the edge of the upper fresco surface – Altichiero's – has been cut, leaving a jagged edge. Together with the accompanying truncation and partial eclipse of the third donor of Altichiero's fresco, this excludes any possibility that the tomb arch and the upper fresco formed part of an integrated scheme, though the location of the tomb so far to the right of the north wall was probably in response to some obligation to minimise the damage to Altichiero's fresco. The apparently empty area on the right of the fresco may, I think, have contained at least one other figure kneeling behind the third knight, below the fourth arch of the arcade within the painting, and which was all but destroyed by the tomb arch.

Federigo Cavalli, the occupant of the tomb, died in 1390,[36] as the inscription on the

[36] Federigo di Nicolo Cavalli, elected captain by popular vote in June 1390 during a pro-Scaligeri uprising against Visconti rule, and killed in September after the rising failed. The inscription gives the date of his death as the seventh of that month. He must have been held captive, as the decisive reassertion of Visconti authority by Ugolotto Biancardo (nephew and heir of Altichiero's patron in Padua, Bonifacio Lupi) was during the night of 25/6 June (and was accompanied by the savagery for which Ugolotto was famous all over northern Italy). For this see Carrara,

sarcophagus records, thus giving a *terminus ante quem* for Altichiero's fresco. No equivalent factor exists to provide such a precise *terminus post quem*, beyond the likely date of the lower-wall Madonna, and further arguments for Altichiero's date must rest on historical and stylistic evidence. But the condition of the Cavalli fresco and the wall on which it is situated have more to tell which may clarify the original sequence of events.

The curious condition of the lower edge of Altichiero's fresco has only been fully exposed by restoration of the south wall. In old photographs (i.e. those universally used in all previously published accounts of the fresco,[37] see pl. 17) there runs along the remaining lower edge a simple double light-coloured strip, possibly intended to represent a length of moulding, and lying just above the outer red strip of the Cosmatesque upper border of the lower-wall Madonna. But restoration, which has stripped from this latter fresco both the extensive repainting visible in Sandberg-Vavalà's plate[38] and the later white border round the niche housing the statue of *S. Geminiano*, shows that Altichiero's fresco has lost its lower border altogether. And so the double white strip was evidently added at some later date to disguise the fact that, as a raking light reveals, Altichiero's plaster here too has been abruptly cut. As it stands, there is now no lower border of any kind attached to his fresco (fig. 50).

It is unlikely that Altichiero simply left the upper border of the lower fresco to serve as his own lower border. Even had he done so he would have left the sort of smoothed-down edge commonly seen when frescoes of different periods jostle together. The rudely cut edge is inconceivable as a planned resolution of the boundary, and since even in its truncated state his plaster impinges on the lower Madonna's border, it is probable that something of Altichiero's has been removed.

Confirmation of this can be found by looking at the outer side borders of the Cavalli fresco. On either side, beyond the main outer Cosmatesque element of Altichiero's fictive inlaid and moulded border, on both sides of the first step of the flanking pilasters, is an additional decorative strip of diamond and lattice work. This is not found elsewhere in the chapel and must be part of his border. At the top of this strip on each side the border is neatly closed just below the level of the upper band of the original foliate chapel decoration. The lower end of the left-hand strip (the right is now obscured by the tomb at its lowest level) has by contrast been as crudely chopped off as has the lower border, and at the level of that border, leaving – if this end echoed the top – some inches of the strip and the closing white line missing. Clearly this truncation was intended to tidy up this area and bring the outer border into line with the rest of Altichiero's fresco in its present state. But the implication must again be of a missing area. The top left corner of fig. 49 shows also how the main star Cosmati strip of the fresco border within

footnote 36 (*cont.*)
Gli Scaligeri, pp. 252–3, and, for Federigo's tomb, Corso, 'La Cappella Cavalli'. The erection of the tomb may have preceded or postdated Federigo's death. The prominent scallop shells on the flanks of the sarcophagus might suggest that the tomb was intended for someone with a particular devotion to St James, like Giacomo Cavalli. But the kneeling knight on the tomb front is actually presented by St George, with St James only in attendance, so it can probably be ruled out that this was a tomb intended for Giacomo and used instead for Federigo.

[37] E.g. Mellini, *Altichiero e Jacopo Avanzi*, figs. 52 and 53, Pettenella, *Altichiero*, fig. 43 and the colour plate in Magagnato, *Arte e Civiltà del Medioevo Veronese*.

[38] Sandberg-Vavalà, *La Pittura Veronese*, fig. 32.

this outer strip has itself been interrupted, and also that it was never intended to line up with the side border of the lower-wall Madonna, all of which further suggests that Altichiero cannot have made use of any part of the existing upper border of the older fresco.

The nature of the lost lower border can only be guessed at. Inspection of the lower left internal corner of the fresco suggests that the inner moulded elements of the border 'rested' on the ground plane of the pictorial space (as they do in a 1396 imitation of the Cavalli fresco in S. Zeno[39]), with presumably only the Cosmati band turning the corner and running along the bottom to complete the frame. Even so, this must have eclipsed the upper border of the older fresco. This Madonna was damaged to some extent when Federigo Cavalli's tomb was erected, and the St Christopher severely mutilated at the same time. Whatever the nature of Altichiero's solution to the border between the older frescoes and his own, it probably only lasted for a few years. The St Christopher at least can hardly have been presentable after 1390 and may have been covered over. The Madonna too was possibly whitewashed then, or at some other stage, probably before the niche for S. Geminiano was cut in the sixteenth century,[40] damaging the original piscina niche in the process.

How and when Altichiero's lower border was lost is also unclear. Perhaps it too was abraded or damaged as early as 1390, and removed as being unsightly whenever the lower Madonna was revealed and repainted.[41] Possibly with it were lost the names of the donors, painted to match those of the saints still visible above,[42] either on the border or just above it, against the ground plane, as they are in the votive fresco in the Oratory of S. Giorgio in Padua (pl. 95).[43]

In common with many leading north Italian families, the Cavalli were ultimately of Germanic stock, but they were well established in Verona during the pre-Scaligeri era.[44] From early in the trecento they aligned themselves closely with signorial policy and held high office, both civil and military, under successive Scaligeri rulers. Federigo I Cavalli (grandfather of the Federigo in the wall tomb) was knighted by CanGrande on the occasion of the Veronese conquest of Padua in 1328, was *podestà* of Vicenza and later Padua, and served as governor of the castle of Saline in 1336. He held the office of captain-general under Mastino II and was evidently on familiar terms with him. He was dead by 1362. It is most likely that it was during Federigo's time as head of the family that the chapel in S. Anastasia was appropriated to Cavalli use.

[39] The Votive Fresco of Abbot Capelli on the south wall of the upper church, dated 1397 and attributed by Cuppini, 'L'Arte Gotica', p. 330 to Ranuccio Arvari.

[40] This must have been done when the present altarpiece, with elements by Liberale da Verona, was erected.

[41] Perhaps it was done in 1390 to correct the asymmetry produced by having lost the lower border on the right. The apparent continuity of the chopped edge along the bottom and over the top of the tomb is suggestive of only one phase of mutilation.

[42] The saints' names are written on the abaci of the arcade columns just above each saint's head. James's is less legible than the others.

[43] There are no inscriptions for the saints in the Paduan fresco.

[44] Chief sources for the Cavalli are: Corso, 'La Cappella Cavalli'; Orti-Manara, *Di Alcuni Antichi Veronesi Guerrieri che Fiorirono ai Tempi Scaligeri*; Cartolari, *Cenni*; and for Giacomo Cavalli, his entry in the *Dizionario Biografico*.

This tradition of service was inherited by Federigo's sons from his marriage to Anna Lamberti (from one of the oldest great Veronese families, builders of the Torre dei Lamberti). Of Pietro little is known, though he is probably the same as the Pietro Cavalli documented as a canon of Verona Cathedral at the same time as Petrarch's son Giovanni. Nicolo, too, had been a non-ordained canon, but pursued an administrative career, holding the prestigious and strategically vital post of *podestà* of Scaligeri Vicenza for twelve years from 1361, leaving office 'con plauso di tutti' in 1373.[45] Giacomo Cavalli was one of the most celebrated military captains of the period. Appointed while still apparently very young as Cansignorio della Scala's ambassador in the formation of the fifth anti-Visconti league in 1362, he served in the same year as captain-general of the Veronese armies against Bernabo Visconti, and throughout the 1360s and early 1370s led Cansignorio's forces in various campaigns, winning for himself a reputation as 'huomo saggio, e nel mestiero dell'armi espertissimo'.[46]

Giacomo's service was rewarded by a marital alliance with the Scaligeri. Probably in the mid 1360s he married Costanza della Scala, a descendant of the former *signore*, Bartolomeo I. The decade 1365–75 represents the zenith of his and his family's standing in Scaligeri Verona. After Cansignorio's death in 1375 this standing was undermined and the close accord breached under circumstances which are unclear, and Giacomo, together with others of the family, left Verona. After a brief period serving the Gonzaga, Giacomo entered service with the Venetian Republic, leading sections of their army in the war of Chioggia and once again securing a high reputation. Already in 1376 documents show he had lost one of his brothers in Venetian service (probably Pietro, since we know he died in Crete[47]). In the same year the *Cronaca Carrarese* records that a young son of Giacomo was leading a contingent of Venetian troops under his father's overall command, and that a nephew was captured by the Austrians in the same engagement.[48]

The evidence suggests that the events of 1375/6 led to the estrangement of the whole Cavalli family, and that all three brothers left Verona together at that time. Relations deteriorated to the extent that Bartolomeo and Antonio della Scala sent assassins in 1376 to try and kill Giacomo at Feltre,[49] and though banning orders against him and confiscation of the family goods were rescinded by treaty in 1378, Giacomo never returned to Verona, dying, by then a Venetian citizen and a member of the Consiglio Maggiore, in Venice in 1384.[50] The remaining years of the century show the family to be widely scattered, some still in Venetian service, returning to Veronese life only with the absorption of Verona into the Venetian state, some in Visconti service, and some living in Brescia.[51] The fragmentation is shown by the events of 1390 when Federigo di

45 Conforto da Costoza, *Frammenti di Storia Vicentina (AA.1371–1387)*, part 1, p. 6.

46 Saraina, *Historie e Fatti*, p. 50v.

47 Venetian document of 17 December 1376: 'Quod pro bono exempio aliorum considerato laudabili portamento Capitanei nostri generalis terre et quod perdidit fratrem suum in servitio nostro.' Conforto da Costoza, *Frammenti*, appendix 2, p. 50.

48 Gatari, *Cronaca Carrarese*, p. 144.

49 Conforto da Costoza, *Frammenti*, appendix 3, pp. 51–2.

50 His tomb is in the Dominican SS. Giovanni e Paolo. For the tomb see Wolters, *La Scultura Veneziana Gotica*, cat. no. 134.

51 Giacomo Cavalli's sons Corrado and Nicolo, together with (Giacomo's brother) Nicolo's son Giovanni appear in

Nicolo Cavalli, occupant of the tomb on the north wall of the family chapel, led an unsuccessful rising against Visconti rule in Verona, dying in the attempt (either at the hand of, or at the hand of troops commanded by, Ugolotto Biancardo, nephew and heir of Altichiero's Paduan patron Bonifacio Lupi). At this time both Cavallino and Federigo's brother Giorgio were in Visconti service. For a short time in 1378 Giacomo Cavalli himself had been seconded by the Venetians to Bernabo Visconti.[52] Evidently the family was effectively dispossessed and exiled after 1375, and its members had to find work where they could, even if this meant brothers fighting on opposite sides.

Before leaving Verona the three Cavalli brothers, Giacomo, Pietro and Nicolo, made in 1375 a donation to the family chapel[53] – 'pro dote altaris Sancti Geminiani'. In past discussions of the Cavalli fresco this donation has been used to reinforce the identification of the kneeling donor knights as the three sons of Federigo I Cavalli. Only Sartori has challenged this,[54] substituting Giorgio and Cavallino for Pietro and Nicolo, while remaining in agreement with the identification of the third knight, presented by St James, as Giacomo Cavalli. In fact the donation, which makes no mention of a painting, cannot be specifically linked with the fresco, and cannot therefore be used, as Kruft uses it,[55] as a *terminus post quem* for the painting's execution.

Nor can it be proved beyond all doubt that the third knight is Giacomo Cavalli. But it seems very likely. Though the presence of his name saint is not itself conclusive, the connection between donor and presenting saint here seems particularly and pointedly intimate, and given that Giacomo held the rank or title of Cavaliere di S. Iacopo,[56] suggesting a special devotion on his part, the balance of probability must be strongly in favour of this identification. And such an identification would suggest 1375 as a *terminus ante quem*, for it is hard to believe that a votive fresco associated with Giacomo

a Paduan document of 1390, all 'nunc hab. in Alino territ. Brix.' (Brescia), from where they appoint a procurator in Padua (Francesco Turchetto, a Lupi associate). Gloria, *Monumenti*, no. 1747. Nicolo di Giacomo later served the Venetians in 1404 (Gatari, *Cronaca Carrarese*, p. 547) with Antonio Cavalli. In 1411 he was *capitano* of Soave, where he built a still extant house and where he made his will in 1431. His cousin Giorgio Cavalli was military captain of Antonio della Scala in 1387, and served as *consigliere* to the Emperor Wenceslas, who in 1387 invested Giorgio with the fief of Sant'Orso in the Vicentino (doc. published by Verci, *Storia*, lib. 19, p. 178). In 1389 Giorgio was in Zurich on Visconti business, where he recognised the fugitive Francesco Novello da Carrara at an inn (Gatari, *Cronaca Carrarese*, p. 390). Giorgio, still hoping for a Scaligeri revival, died in Sant'Orso in 1416. Cavallino Cavalli was also in Visconti service in 1391. In 1381 he appears amongst those present at the signing of the Treaty of Turin (Verci, *Storia*, doc. no. 1759). The Antonio Cavalli mentioned above figures in no published source except the *Cronaca Carrarese*, but he appears in a number of unpublished Veronese documents of the early quattrocento (Verona, Archivio di Stato arch. priv. CAVALLI 1427), when various sources (e.g. Guarino Veronese, *Epistolario*) show that a fair number of the Cavalli once more made their homes in Verona. Guarino, writing in 1421, mentions a Pietro Cavalli as one of those who formally handed Verona over to the Venetians in 1405 (Guarino, *Epistolario*, C. 242). This cannot be Giacomo's brother, but a lost letter of Guarino's to Lodovico di Sambonifacio shows that Giacomo Cavalli was still remembered and admired in Verona many years after his death.

52 Conforto da Costoza, *Frammenti*, pp. 52–3.

53 'Ex donatione nobilium virorum et dominorum Jacob; Nicolay et Petri ab Equis et hec donatio facta est pro dote altaris Sancti Geminiani', from the *Liber Possessionum Conventus 1420*, Archivio di S. Anastasia, A.Arch. Ver., p. 65 under '*De Yebeto'*. Published and discussed by Cipolla, 'Ricerche Storiche', 1916, pp. 115–25.

54 Sartori, 'La Cappella di S. Giacomo', p. 278 identifies the first knight as Giorgio because of the presence of St George, and the second as Cavallino because of the extra horse on his shield. Neither argument is persuasive, especially in the light of the other factors discussed here.

55 Kruft, *Altichiero und Avanzo*, p. 127.

56 Cartolari, *Cenni*, p. 19.

Cavalli would be projected for the Scaligeri court church after the events of 1375 and 1376.

All previous accounts assume that the fresco as we see it today has the full complement of figures originally provided. The intrusion of Federigo Cavalli's tomb has masked what would otherwise stand out: the unusual extent of apparently empty space on the right. In fact photographs taken from scaffolding reveal what looks like the crown of a fourth head below the fourth arch and behind St James. The height is just right for another kneeling figure, as is its lateral position. Since the fragmentary head seems to be without either mail or plate, and lacks its own presenting saint, it can be assumed that it was either a woman or (less likely) a youth. Given its position, it must be in the train of the third knight, attached to his devotional act – ushered in with him as it were, which tends to point to him as the chief promoter of the fresco. A number of Lombard votive frescoes, to which Altichiero's format is related,[57] have a sometimes extensive group of women and children bringing up the rear. The existence of such a group here, lost when the tomb was erected, is hypothetical, but it would make sense of the chosen format.

The general acceptance of the identification of the three knights as the three Cavalli brothers has left unremarked what seems to be a rather careful set of distinctions established between the donor figures. The knight here identified as Giacomo Cavalli is clearly the central figure. He is, in the first place, literally so. The central arch of the background arcade and the prominent opening below it both serve to emphasise him, as does his location along a vertical axis marking the focus of the perspectival field. His presenting saint, unlike the others, actually lays hands – both hands – on him, stooping slightly to do so. And this knight may have had his wife at least – Costanza della Scala, if this is indeed Giacomo – accompanying him. Compared with him – what can be seen of him – and Sts George and Martin, the first two donor knights, especially the first, seem to dress like men from a different age. Military styles of dress in the period following the experimental 1340s and 1350s settled into the comparative uniformity of the so-called Camail and Jupon period, where the loose knee-length surcoat was transformed into the skin-tight and almost invariably very short jupon, as worn here by St George and, apparently, the third knight.[58] The surcoat of the first knight in particular (pl. 18) seems pointedly archaic in this context. The length of his surcoat obscures much of his suit of armour, but what can be made out seems not to be plate, or the studded-and-splinted work of the second knight (pl. 19) but rather *cuir-bouilli*, with perhaps plate elbow pieces, rather old-fashioned in this company.[59]

[57] E.g. those of the oratory at Mocchirolo, now in the Brera, Milan, and of the Oratory of S. Stefano at Lentate. See Montel, *Gli Affreschi Gotici Lombardi*, vol. II, fig. 1, and Matalon and Mazzini, *Affreschi in Lombardia*, pl. 41.

[58] For the development of armour in this period see Ashdown, *British and Continental Arms and Armour*, chapters 9 and 10.

[59] Ashdown shows isolated examples of the retention of older styles in England, e.g. *cuir-bouilli*, generally forgotten after 1360, on the brass of Sir William Cheyne (*ibid.*, p. 157 and fig. 197); and studded-and-splinted work on the lost brass of Sir Miles Stapleton (d.1364; *ibid.*, p. 189 and fig. 235). As Ashdown points out, at this time the wearing of such armour is the mark of personal eccentricity. However, and to make the point that though armour was far less nationally peculiar than other forms of dress, time

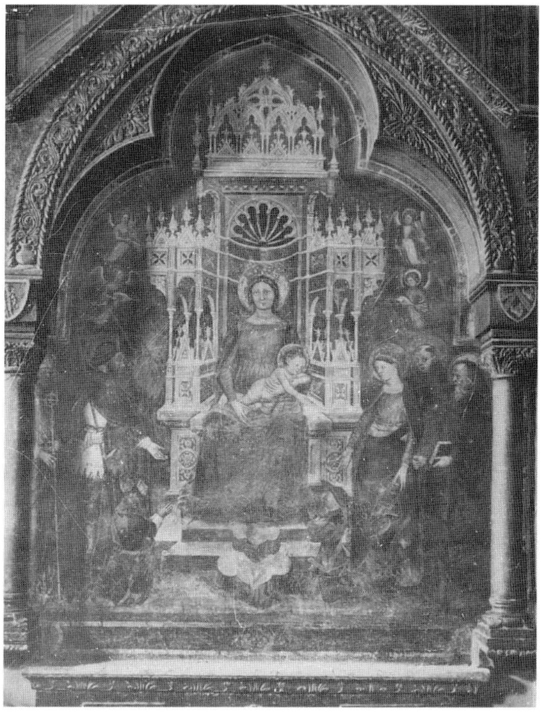

Fig. 51 Verona, S. Anastasia. Pellegrini Chapel, Martino da Verona: *Madonna and Child with Saints and Donors* (Bevilacqua tomb).

Too much should not be made of the actual details of the armour, for we know that workshop memories of archaic styles were very short, but there does seem to be some attempt here to suggest a differential between the donors – rather against the grain of normal donor iconography, which tends to stress the solidity of peer groups. The nature of this differential is hard to interpret with any confidence. The particular layout of this fresco suggests that the first knight has in some sense gone before. He is no longer being presented; St George has turned his attentions to the second knight, and the first knight is already in the Divine presence. One possible inference, that this knight was already dead when the fresco was painted, would explain his old-fashioned appearance. Perhaps he is meant for Giacomo Cavalli's father, or grandfather.[60] In the Oratory of S. Giorgio Altichiero paints Rolandino Lupi, father of the donor and sole member of the oldest of three generations of Lupi knights shown in the votive fresco there (pl. 95), with a more old-fashioned and longer surcoat than the tight model worn by all the other knights (less old-fashioned, though, than the first Cavalli knight's). And next door to the Cavalli Chapel the Bevilacqua tomb fresco (fig. 51), by Altichiero's follower

lapses and variations must be allowed for, one of the mounted figures in Altichiero's S. Giacomo *Crucifixion* sports studded arm pieces. At *c.* 1376–9 this must limit the extent of the Cavalli knights' wearing of it as evidence for an early date. The other evidence still suggests a date before 1375/6.

[60] Precise dating of deliberate representations of old-fashioned dress and armour is often problematic. See Kent, 'Monumental Brasses – A New Classification of Military Effigies', p. 78 for the brasses of Sir Robert and Sir Thomas Swynborne at Little Horkesley in Essex. Figures of father and son, both done in the son's time, show that they 'are in fact designed to point a contrast. If one may attempt to read the mind of the designer, I should suggest that he was merely conscious of the fact that "in those days they wore an aventail and different elbows and pauldrons, &c." His memory, or the obsolete patterns at his disposal, did not go back beyond the last series but one, type 9 (col. 1402–6), and the result was an effigy that had no resemblance to those his workshop was producing in 1391.'

Martino da Verona, expresses what is also an apparent generation gap between donors in this way.[61]

However one interprets the apparent distinctions in the fresco, it seems certain that the first two knights cannot represent, as Sartori thought, Cavalli of a generation younger than Giacomo himself.[62] If the dress of the first knight looks archaic in *c.* 1370–5, it would be extraordinarily so on a man flourishing in the 1390s and into the following century.

The Cavalli fresco confirms the essentially Florentine formal roots of Altichiero's style.[63] The loggia before which the saints stand is conceptually a development of the three-bay architectural setting of the later Giotto and his followers. The range of colours used for architecture here – grey/violet for the throne canopy, greens and reds for parts of the loggia – is rather more typically northern in character. The use of architecture is more modest than in some of the Paduan frescoes. The action is not contained in the full sense, but the fur-trimmed curtain hanging along the arcade at capital level shows a characteristic suppression of too deep a penetration into a space which is nevertheless quite explicitly there. The reality of the hidden space behind the curtain is reinforced by the glimpses of string course and vault springers on the back wall of the arcade, and more playfully by the angel peeping out from behind on the left.

Such assurance in the conception of fictive architecture is on a par with that of the late Paduan frescoes, but there are touches of awkwardness in the execution of such ideas absent in Padua. The area of the steps below the Madonna's throne, and the foot of the throne itself, is an uncomfortable passage. The recession of the various ascending elements is not really convincing by the standards of equivalent areas in S. Giorgio, and the spatial relationships have consequently gone awry. The drawing of the column base nearest the spectator suggests that it is either too close to the panelling of the throne steps behind it, or, worse, that it is hovering slightly above the ground. The drawing of the arch above the throne front, out of which the Child reaches, is also insecure. Such infelicities are minor and might reflect the work of assistants, though given the primacy of architectural painting in Altichiero's work I doubt he would have delegated the design and laying out of such complex details. They suggest an earlier date, if

[61] The isolated donor on the left of this fresco wears a long and apparently baggy surcoat of a style at odds with the flared and dagged jupons of the two facing donors. The tomb is without inscription, but all three donors are clearly marked with the *demi-vol* of the Bevilacqua. Since the tomb has both Bevilacqua and Pellegrini arms on it, it may be that this tomb points to the close association between Guglielmo Bevilacqua and Tomaso Pellegrini. It may be Guglielmo's tomb. The Bevilacqua previously (and afterwards) used the small church of SS Teuteria e Tosca for their tombs. I know of no intermarriage between the families in this period, but the existence of a Pellegrina Bevilacqua (see Guarino, *Epistolario*, col. 188) in the early years of the following century suggests such a connection at some stage, or at least a particularly close bond between the families. The tomb can be dated to *c.* 1395–1400. Guglielmo died in 1397. His grandsons Ernesto and Onofrio (b.1395 and 1401) were pupils of Guarino (*ibid.*, col. 191).

[62] Giacomo and Nicolo both surface in the early 1360s, but while the job of leading troops can be entrusted to a very young man, the *podesteria* of Vicenza, a key post in Scaligeri strategy, is hardly likely to have gone to an inexperienced youth, even if there were no statutory bar on a *podestà* under the age of thirty. So Nicolo, at least, was probably older than Giacomo, whose youth is commented on in the sources.

[63] See chapter 1 above.

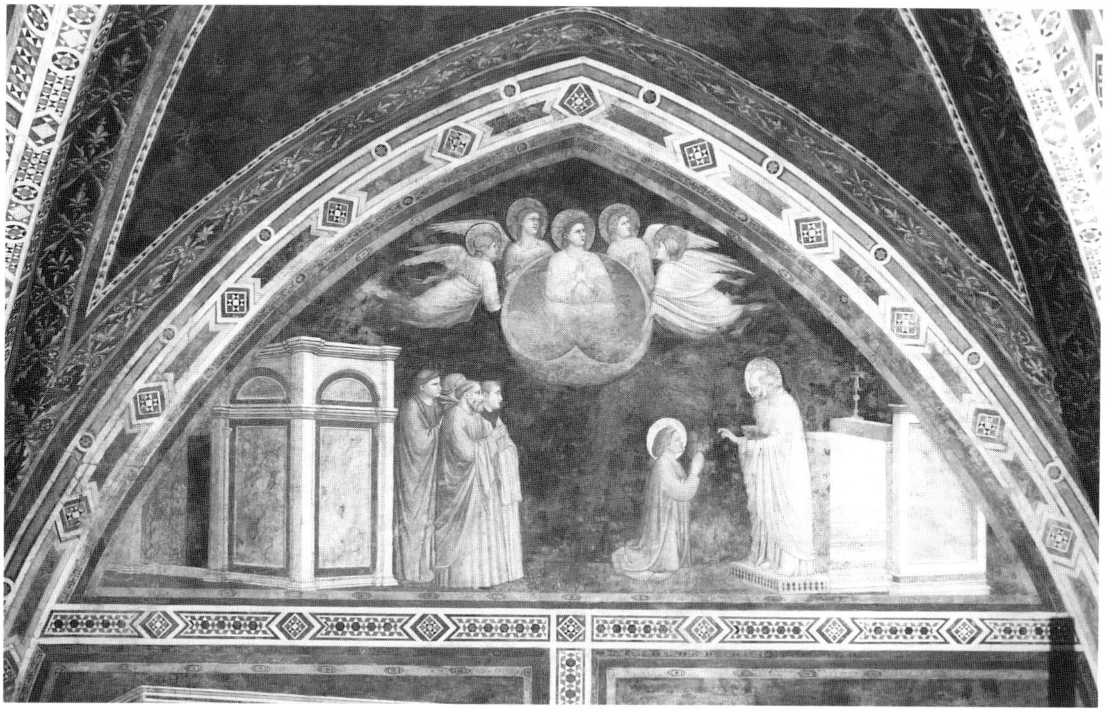

Fig. 52 Giotto workshop: *Communion and Ascension of St Mary Magdelen*. Assisi, S. Francesco, Magdalen Chapel.

only because it is hard to imagine such uncertainties as coming after S. Giorgio. The use for the loggia and (more significantly, for the use of the loggia as processional backdrop virtually necessitates the choice of spatial system) for the throne and baldacchino (which could have been set obliquely) of the frontal-foreshortened system, to which Altichiero adhered until what are probably the latest frescoes of S. Giorgio, also supports a pre-Paduan date.[64]

The figure style shows equally strong Tuscan tendencies. The type of the profile angels is related to many examples within the broad Giottesque field, and the left-hand group is one of many variants which Altichiero made of the compact, largely self-contained figure group found widely in Giotto's and Maso's work in Florence and in the lower church of S. Francesco at Assisi. This particular example recalls the left-hand group of the lunette fresco of the *Magdalen's Communion and Ascension* in the Magdalen Chapel in Assisi (fig. 52).

The Madonna departs from the Veronese norm in being bareheaded except for a very light transparent veil descending from the rolled hair at the back of her neck. Her lateral position is without Veronese precedent, and virtually without local imitation in this period. The modelling of her face is a degree softer than in any of the equivalent exam-

64 The architecture is painted as if lit from two directions. To the left of the centre line the chapel window is taken as the source. To the right it is the west window of the transept. A secondary light source catches the arcade vaults on the right, located in the arched opening behind the curtain on the extreme right.

ples in S. Giorgio and is closer perhaps to some of the female saints in S. Giacomo. Without exaggerating the extent of the change, it is broadly true that Altichiero's conception of the female figure, Mary included, tends increasingly towards the heroic in S. Giorgio, with an accompanying growth in the monumentality of the figure and a rather more lapidary, less veiled, approach to flesh modelling than in S. Giacomo. The Cavalli Madonna relates more to the first Paduan cycle's naturalism than to the grander and more sculptural style of S. Giorgio. In this quasi-regal context she is accessible and humane rather than a figure of power. Similarly, the Child's gesture is more openly and humanly welcoming to the donors than that of his equivalent in S. Giorgio, benign enough there, but more authoritative and markedly less childlike.

The Cavalli Christ-child is himself unrelated to earlier Veronese examples. Nor does he particularly recall anything directly by Giotto or his workshop. There is a distinct affinity, though, with his equivalent in Puccio Capanna's fragmentary *Madonna and Child*, now in the Pinacoteca Comunale in Assisi (fig. 25).[65] The shape of the head, the hairline, the shading of dark inclined eyebrows towards the nose, the suggestion of a pointed chin poking through the fat gathered into a soft roll under the jawline, all are analogous, as is the soft *sfumato* of the modelling.

St George is of the same physical type Altichiero used for him in S. Giacomo (one of the busts above the choir stall) and the Dotto tomb *Coronation* (pl. 118) – hair light, a sort of ginger-red, cut to leave the back of the neck bare, and a light beard of the same colour. In S. Giorgio we find these characteristics transferred to St Martin in the votive fresco, with St George there looking more like Altichiero's usual image of St James, and dressed in the full knight's costume of the late trecento: tight, short, and elaborately dagged jupon, full plate armour, horizontal decorated baldric, and a short cape of the chlamys type, open to one side. The Dotto St George is almost identically dressed, as is the half-length figure in S. Giacomo – what one can see of him. The Cavalli figure is apparently without full armour, wears a simpler and thinner slung sword belt, and has round his shoulders instead of the side-opening cape a luxurious cloak of ermine-lined white material decorated with gold clusters. His jupon is quite plain. Though spear and sword proclaim his knightly status, he is seen here in courtly rather than military guise.

The tone is maintained in the figure of St Martin, dressed in the civilian costume of a knight at court (compare his more overtly martial self on Cansignorio's tomb, fig. 53): fur-lined hood with liripipe, tight buttoned surcoat, hose, and a splendid – and undivided – cloak.

St James – the surviving two-thirds of him – generally resembles his Paduan counterparts but, like the Madonna, is here conceived as a rather gentler creature. The equivalent figures in the votive fresco of S. Giacomo (pl. 72) and, to an even greater degree that of the Dotto tomb (pl. 118), are developed with a more imposing physical bulk. The Dotto figure, head in near profile, drapery ranged in massive sculptural folds, is so like the most monumental figures of S. Giorgio that it must surely date from late in the Paduan years. If the overall progress of Altichiero's work towards a greater severity and

[65] See Scarpellini, 'Alcuni Pittori Giotteschi', pp. 211–70, fig. 250.

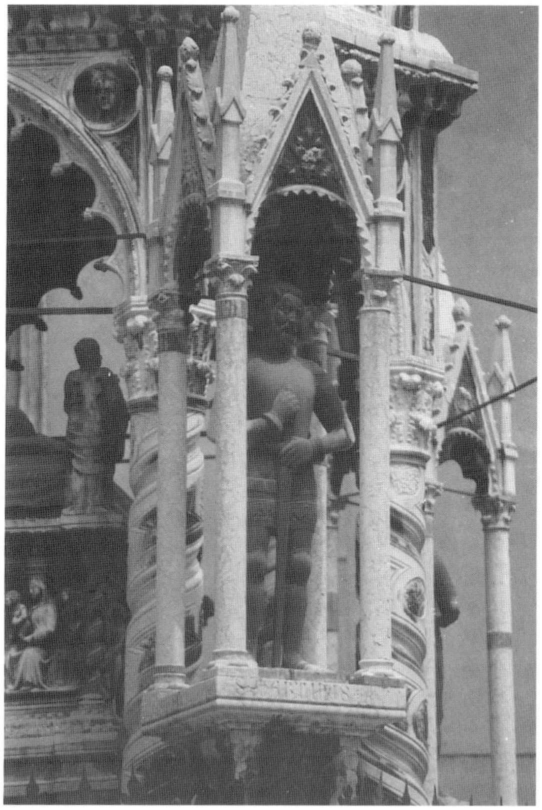

Fig. 53 Verona, S. Maria Antica. Tomb of Cansignorio della Scala (detail): St Martin.

monumentality is accepted, then the Cavalli St James must belong earlier in the sequence than any of the Paduan examples.

A further connection between the fresco and the Chapel of S. Giacomo in Padua has been seen in a supposed reflection, or anticipation, of the five-bay facade of that chapel in the loggia of the Veronese fresco. Sweeping inferences can be drawn from that likeness if it is accepted: either that it proves a date for the fresco after the Paduan years (if it reflects the chapel) or that Altichiero had some hand in designing the chapel himself (if it anticipates it). Mellini discusses possible meetings between Altichiero and the architect of S. Giacomo, Andriolo de'Santi, in Verona, where Andriolo had indeed worked around 1360.[66] But leaving aside the basic improbability of a painter's having usurped an architect's work, and the fact that we have Andriolo's very specific contract for the Paduan chapel, the premise that there is some particular connection between the two designs is in any case unfounded. Both have five bays, but this is hardly conclusive. The presumed original appearance of the Paduan chapel's upper level may have resembled that of the Cavalli loggia, but only to the extent that they shared a common enough pattern. The Cavalli building has close local parallels at hand in the shape of the gable and pinnacle layout of the later Scaligeri tombs and the upper levels of the

[66] Mellini, *Altichiero e Jacopo Avanzi*, p. 44.

eastern exterior of S. Fermo (fig. 2).[67] It is, if anything, more like these than it is like S. Giacomo.

Mellini's analogy with the loggia built by Cansignorio and decorated by Altichiero is similarly unconvincing, beyond the point at which similar settings for basically similar courtly ceremonies may generally resemble one another. The structure in the Cavalli fresco reflects a whole set of interrelated Gothic patterns for wall elevations, loggias and cloisters, without actually drawing on any particular one. It is a one-off, developed for the particular occasion.

The fresco is the most overtly courtly of Altichiero's surviving works. It enshrines more single-mindedly than any of the Paduan frescoes the spirit of *cortesia* much vaunted in early trecento Verona and in the other courts of the north, a spirit for which CanGrande's court was the most renowned in its time, and which was probably no more than a memory during the rule of Cansignorio's brother in the years up to 1359. With the chapels, frescoes and tombs commissioned by Giacomo Cavalli, Tomaso Pellegrini, Guglielmo Bevilacqua (probably) and Leonardo da Quinto,[68] the greatest and closest of Cansignorio's intimates, S. Anastasia took on something of the aspect of a court Pantheon. In the wake of this came a burst of artistic activity, first by Altichiero himself, and then by a series of painters working well into the quattrocento and all in varying degrees dependent on Altichiero's example. Between them these men and the sculptors working with them made of the church the monument to Cansignorio's court it remains today.

Altichiero here reinvented the local votive tradition in the light both of courtly and regal imagery, and of Giottesque narrative realism. Where the early Veronese painters treated saints and donors simply as further elements to be added to the basic, static and wholly standardised Madonna formula as required, here the participants share in a particular and fully realised narrative event. The immediate iconographic source for a lateral and processional votive presentation is to be found in images of the Adoration of the Magi, a scene which itself underwent a process of regalisation and the acquisition of genre elements (the latter at least as early as Nicola Pisano's Siena Cathedral pulpit). The conceptual dependence of Altichiero's fresco on something like Giotto's *Adoration* in the lower church at Assisi (fig. 54) is clear. The baldachin over the throne here, which turns into a house at the top, must be derived from examples such as Mary's house in the Assisi fresco. Also borrowed from Adoration iconography are the angels attendant on Mary's throne – the two peering either side of the pillar and through the curtain derive from motifs widely found in trecento tomb sculpture – and from the angels looking through the throne arms of many enthroned Madonnas and Coronations, the posture of the presenting Saints in this lateral context, recalling the gesture and position of the guiding angel (often complete with staff) in early examples,[69] and the Child's gesture, not blessing but receiving. Nor can one rule out a deliberate equation between

[67] Magagnato, *Arte e Civiltà*, p. 74 suggests the same connection.

[68] In the small courtyard to the left of the facade.

[69] E.g. Schiller, *Iconography of Christian Art*, vol. 1, figs. 268, 269, 270.

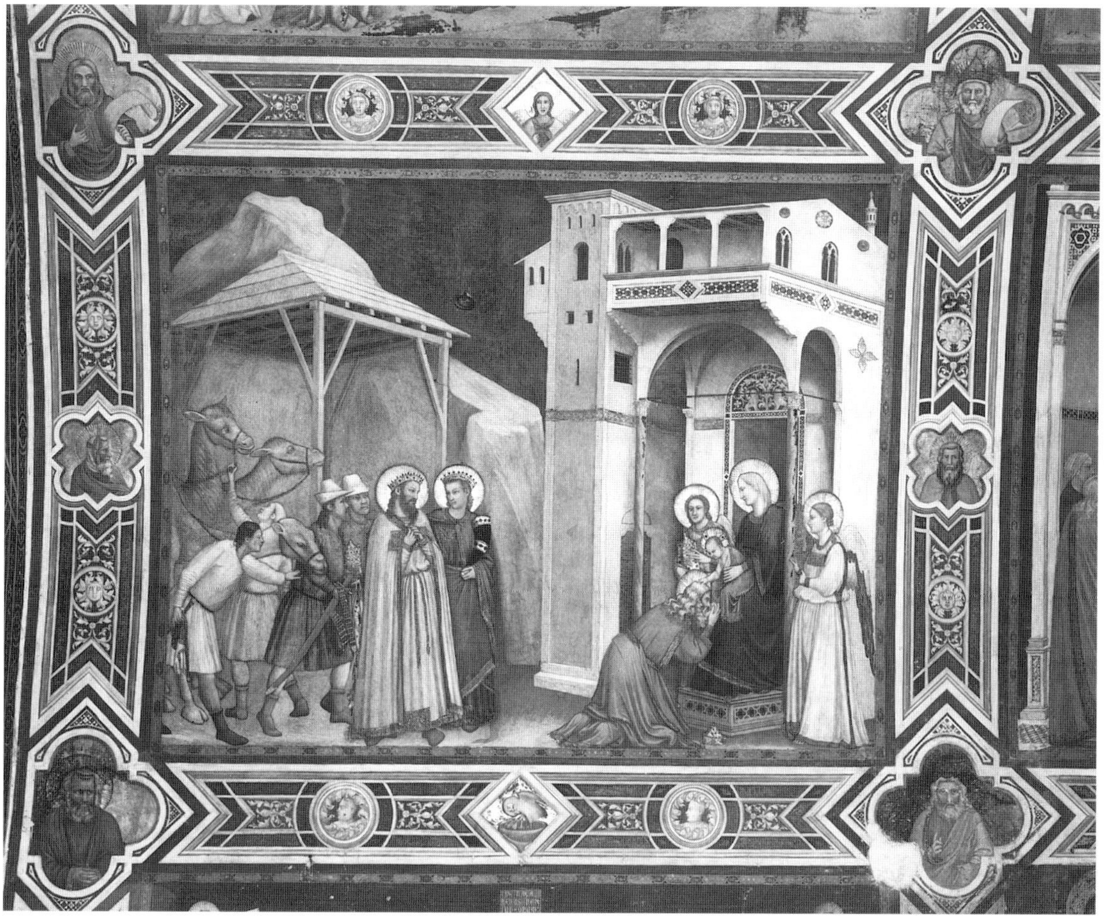

Fig. 54 Giotto: *Adoration of the Magi*. Assisi, S. Francesco, lower church.

the disposition of the three principal donors and that usual for the Magi, with the oldest first.

The shared iconography is particularly apt in a courtly context, since many of the accretions to the basic Adoration model were themselves adapted from court ceremonial,[70] most notably the kneeling position of the Magi and the attendants round the Madonna. Altichiero is hardly likely to have made a detailed study of early Adoration iconography. His source for the imagery of court life was closer to home and to his patrons' experience. As court painter to Cansignorio, for such we can surely call him, he must have been familiar enough with the ceremonies for the housing of which the Sala Grande had been designed. He could have made the visual and analogical connections himself, including perhaps that between the processional Adoration format and its ultimate visual source, antique triumph iconography,[71] which he had adapted for the *Trionfi* of the Sala Grande and which can still be felt as a background to analogous scenes in the two Paduan chapels. In the climate of the extensive embellishment of the

[70] *Ibid.*, vol. I, pp. 102, 103, 111 and pp. 100–14.

[71] *Ibid.*, vol. I, p. 100.

Magi, their claimed status as 'ancestors' of many families, or as patrons of confraternities, and of their enhanced regality, the equations with this subject – obvious to any contemporary – cannot have been less than enormously flattering to the Cavalli, even if no specific metaphor was intended.

The specific combination of court and Adoration iconography, here blended with no discernible distinction, represents an approach to the votive format which relates it to the mural of Edward III of England and his sons formerly in St Stephen's Chapel in the Palace of Westminster, painted as recently as *c.* 1360. The English painting, whose regal overtones are naturally quite overt, clearly separates the donors, who appear in niches below the *Adoration*, from the Magi, where Altichiero suggests a process of partial elision between the two groups (the Magi are, of course, only implicitly referred to in the Cavalli fresco), but the intended resonances are the same. The use in each case of an elaborate arcaded background (at Westminster apparently related to the real architecture of the chapel), as well as the shared iconographic elements already mentioned, confirms both paintings as part of the mainstream of European court art.

The narrative scope of the fresco, in which real and distinct individuals are presented by saints who are on one level at least their fellow courtiers, serves as a prelude to the Paduan cycles, in which such individuals witness the lives and deaths of Christ and his saints. The derivation from the donors included at the foot of the cross, say, is clear. But the great conceptual leap from donor to participant is Altichiero's alone and could perhaps only have been made in a signorial court at this period.

The exceptional status of the Cavalli fresco is emphasised by the fact that although most of the painting of late trecento Verona is derived from Altichieresque models – much of it was done by men probably trained in his workshop – there is almost no response to the full reinvention of the votive genre. The challenge was taken up only, as far as we can now tell, by the not over-abundantly gifted painter of Abbot Cappelli's votive fresco in S. Zeno Maggiore, who copied without understanding, and by Altichiero himself in the votive fresco in S. Giorgio in Padua. The prevailing Veronese response was to a more modest, frontal, pattern of Altichiero's, that now represented in his work only by the S. Giacomo votive fresco in the Santo in Padua, but of which there must once have been examples in Verona.[72] Five tomb frescoes in S. Anastasia reflect this pattern. Though the sequence of these frescoes from *c.* 1380 to the late 1390s shows a move away from the chunky figure style characteristic of work immediately based on Altichiero's towards something closer to International Gothic, all retain the basic Altichieresque format (fig. 51).[73] Such frescoes can be found extensively throughout

72 Altichiero's frontal enthroned Madonna-type derives, via Lombard examples like Giusto's 1349 votive *Madonna* in the Abbey of S. Pietro at Viboldone, from the Florentine *Madonna* with architectural throne. The expansion of this single element from architectural setting to full blown architecture is perhaps a typically northern response to a Tuscan idea used more modestly by its originators. The simple wooden thrones of the early trecento Veronese masters are no more influential here than the slightly more advanced thrones of the mid-century, for all that these latter (e.g. the thrones of the second S. Zeno group in S. Anastasia) attempt to come to grips with the concept of the architectural throne.

73 For these tombs see Cipolla, 'Ricerche Storiche', 1914, and Sandberg-Vavalà, *La Pittura Veronese*, p. 201.

Verona and in regions subject to its influence. From the 1380s some such composition became *de rigeur* either for the tomb fresco of a wealthy patron or as one of the last series of Veronese wall Madonnas, with or without donors.

The Cavalli fresco stands in relation to the general run of such frescoes rather as Cansignorio's tomb does to the extensive series of late trecento tombs, which in scale and complexity it surpasses, reflecting an altogether higher plane of ambition. Just as the tomb is a clear response to the work done under Cansignorio's father Mastino II, which elevated the cemetery of S. Maria Antica from a mere burial ground to a great heraldic and chivalric image of Scaligeri ideals, rather than to local norms, so Altichiero's fresco responds to the immediate climate of courtly *renovatio* rather than to established Veronese tradition. Just as the Josephus cycle must have shown the humanists of the Veneto that here was an artist uniquely suited to the visual expression of their concerns, so the Cavalli fresco must have drawn to Altichiero the attention of the Carrarese princes of Padua and their courtiers, many of whom were intimately connected with the humanists. Altichiero now stood on the verge of more than a decade's work for these men: princes, courtiers and humanists alike, work which would place Padua in the vanguard of Italian art.

4

THE SALA VIRORUM ILLUSTRIUM AND THE MANUSCRIPTS OF THE *DE VIRIS ILLUSTRIBUS*

The Sala Grande must have ensured that Altichiero's name was well known in Padua well before he began work there in the 1370s. Situated in so public a space, the frescoes would be seen by the courtiers, ambassadors and other visitors attending the Scaligeri court. Even if Petrarch himself had not seen them, reports would surely have filtered back to his friends in Carrarese Padua, where he had been in residence since 1367. Paduan awareness of the existence so close at hand of a painter of the highest quality, well versed in the art of representing Antiquity, may even have been instrumental in crystallising the intention to add a major visual component to the existing project for the completion of Petrarch's last prose work.

Since his final arrival in Padua Petrarch, seizing what he probably felt was the last chance to deliver a definitive expression of the central idea of his intellectual life – the enduring value of Antiquity as a repository of the kind of virtues so manifestly lacking in war-torn and factional fourteenth-century Italy – had been engaged on the completion of his great work of historical biography, the *De Viris Illustribus* (hereafter *DVI*).[1] In Padua and at Arquà, his country retreat nearby, he had found not only the peace in which to work on this vast book but also the active and interested support of Francesco da Carrara, son of his lamented friend Jacopo II da Carrara (*Signore,* 1345–50, fig. 79). He had also found in the Paduan notary Lombardo della Seta (pl. 67) the perfect amanuensis and secretary. In this secure and supportive environment Petrarch worked on the final version of his text. At some stage Francesco da Carrara conceived a plan to translate the *DVI* into visual terms, in the shape of the Sala Virorum Illustrium,[2] the latest and most ambitious of the many lavishly decorated rooms of the Carrarese Palace. Both projects proceeded in tandem until Petrarch's death in 1374, and continued afterwards under the supervision of Lombardo, and with full signorial backing.

The greater part of the frescoes of the Sala Virorum Illustrium were lost in a catastrophic fire in the early sixteenth century, but the fragmentary portrait of Petrarch

[1] The major studies are: Martellotti, *Petrarca – De Viris Illustribus*, especially the introduction; Wilkins, *Petrarch's Later Years*, pp. 283–302; Kohl, 'Petrarch's Prefaces to *De Viris Illustribus*', with translations of both and illuminating discussion; and Mommsen, 'Sala Virorum Illustrium', who treats the *DVI* in relation to the frescoes.

[2] The most important modern account of the Sala Virorum Illustrium itself is Mommsen, 'Sala Virorum Illustrium'. See also Simon, 'Altichiero Versus Avanzo', pp. 266–71.

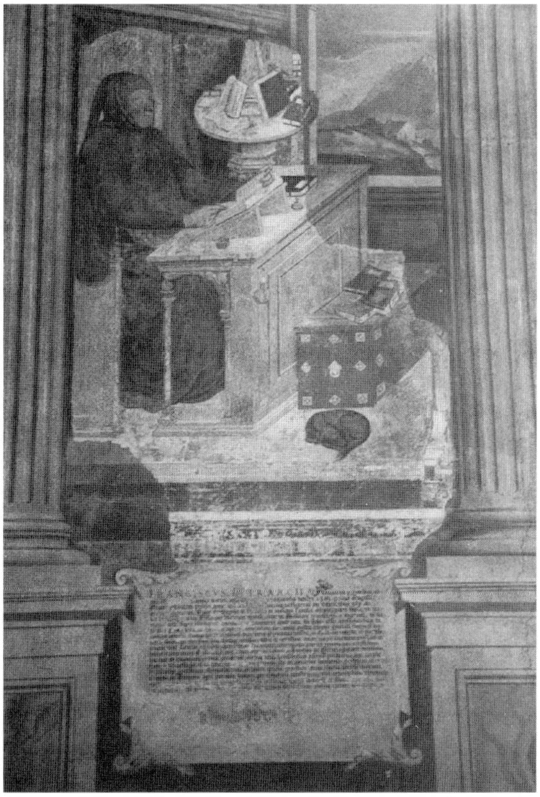

Fig. 55 Altichiero: *Petrarch in his Study*. Padua, Sala dei Giganti.

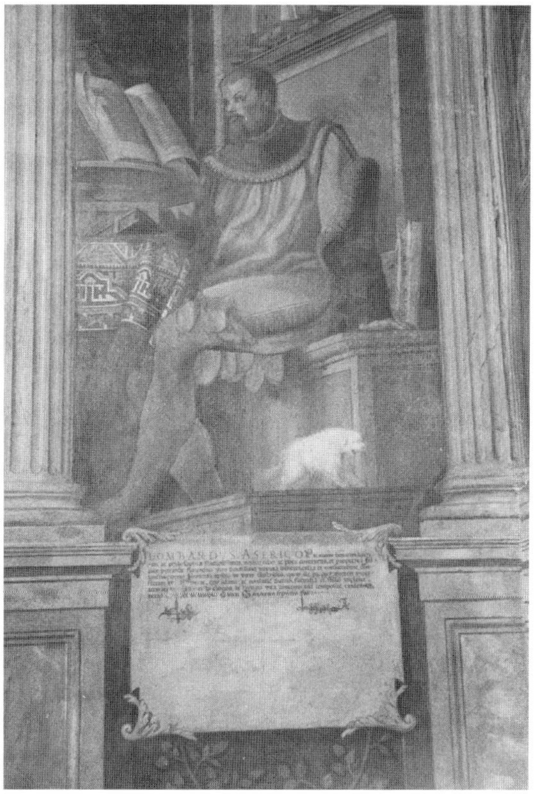

Fig. 56 Domenico Campagnola and Stefano dell'Arzere: *Lombardo della Seta*. Padua, Sala dei Giganti.

himself which survived (pl. 33, fig. 55) and was retained when the hall was repainted as the Sala dei Giganti in 1540, together with putative copies and various other kinds of circumstantial evidence, confirms a long-standing literary tradition that Altichiero was wholly or partly responsible for the frescoes. His association with this venture so soon after working on the Sala Grande is unlikely to have been coincidental, and it is at least likely that Cansignorio was prevailed upon to 'lend' Altichiero to his uncle specifically for this project. Perhaps Petrarch himself had some say in this, if he had seen the Sala Grande in 1368, and especially if Altichiero had indeed painted a portrait of him. This portrait, if it existed, was the first of several; our knowledge of Petrarch's appearance owes more to Altichiero than to any other source.

The *De Viris Illustribus* is a virtual archetype of a text more talked about than read. For those of Petrarch's admirers – and they must constitute the majority – who still regard his scholarly productions as a lamentable waste of time on the part of the author of the *Rime*, the *DVI* is just the kind of thing they view with the greatest regret. Petrarch himself may have regarded it as the most important thing he ever did. On and off he spent over thirty years trying to complete it. Work on it first occupied him from around 1337, when he conceived the idea of extracting exemplary biographical material from

Livy[3] and other sources, until his death, when it was still unfinished. Throughout the intervening years the shape and scope of the book changed several times, expanding in the 1350s to encyclopaedic dimensions (the so-called 'All-Ages' version, treating lives from Adam to Julius Caesar). In 1367, resuming work on the text at Francesco da Carrara's behest, Petrarch returned to the more restricted and classical format originally envisaged in 1337, but slightly expanding it to include non-Romans like Alexander and Hannibal. This final version seems to have been in line with the wishes of both poet and patron.[4]

We know for certain that Francesco da Carrara had suggested using the *DVI* as the basis for a major fresco cycle during Petrarch's lifetime, for he asked Petrarch to put together an abbreviated version of the book, the *Compendium*, for use as a little guide[5] to the frescoes. Petrarch duly began work on this, which must have held him up on his work on the full text, but he had only written fourteen of the thirty-six brief lives by the time of his death, and the rest, like the unwritten twelve lives of the main text, were written by Lombardo della Seta (working, presumably, on the basis of material already assembled by Petrarch). The request for the *Compendium* only establishes that the Sala Virorum Illustrium was being planned by 1374; it furnishes no conclusive proof that the frescoes were actually begun by this date, though they may well have been under way before Petrarch's death.

Once Lombardo had completed the two versions of the *DVI*, he wrote them out in fine presentation copies for Francesco da Carrara. These manuscripts of the main text, the *Epitome*, and the short text, the *Compendium*,[6] were finished in January 1379 and December 1380 respectively. Both have headpieces by Altichiero – a monochrome *Triumph of Fame* in the *Epitome* (pl. 36) and an allegorical scene of the *Bull of Padua Pushing the Lion of Venice into the Sea* in the *Compendium* (pl. 38). It is clear from a reference to them in the last biography written by Lombardo for the *Epitome*, that of Trajan, that the frescoes of the Sala Virorum Illustrium were also finished by this time.[7] Altichiero's involvement in the double project probably lasted from the initiation of the fresco scheme before 1374 until 1380, when he painted the *Compendium*'s headpiece. The main work on the frescoes, though, is likely to have been completed before he began work in the chapel of S. Giacomo in 1377, so a date window of *c.* 1374 to 1377 for

[3] For Petrarch's interest in Livy see Giuseppe Billanovich, 'Petrarch and the Textual Tradition of Livy'. Especially significant in this context is the central role played by Petrarch and his friends in tidying and disseminating Livy's work. Billanovich stresses the crucial importance of this early period of Petrarch's life, with his purchases of books in Rome and his discussions with fellow enthusiasts in Avignon, joint centre, with Verona, of textual discoveries and restorations.

[4] 'I am ready to turn my pen to that which you have requested namely to Romulus, founder of the city of Rome' – short preface, translated by Kohl, 'Petrarch's Prefaces', p. 144. This emphasis may also stem from the older tradition of Padua's foundation by Antenor and the related claims of the early Paduan writers that 'Padua is worthy to be called a second Rome' – Hyde, *Padua*, p. 298 – a common enough conceit, not perhaps convincing to Petrarch, but attractive to the Paduan *signoria*.

[5] Mommsen, 'Sala Virorum Illustrium', p. 106.

[6] The presentation copy of the *Epitome* is Paris, Bibliothèque Nationale, MS Lat. 6069F, and that of the *Compendium* is Paris, Bibliothèque Nationale MS Lat. 6069G.

[7] 'Just as you have placed Trajan among the others in the extreme corner of your beautiful hall, so I, in this work, set out to treat him as the last one.' Mommsen, 'Sala Virorum Illustrium', p. 99.

the Petrarch frescoes seems most likely. An earlier date for their initiation cannot be ruled out, though, which would allow for Altichiero's having had direct contact with Petrarch.

Attempts to convert this possibility into certainty are unpersuasive. Theodor Mommsen argued that the frescoes were begun before 1370 on the grounds that both Buoninsegni's *Florentine History* for that date and a letter from Lombardo to Petrarch, probably written in 1370, supposedly attach the death of the Florentine soldier and Paduan resident Manno Donati to the Sala Virorum Illustrium, the former by (apparently) saying Manno had his portrait painted in it, the latter by asking Petrarch to sanction Manno's inclusion amongst the heroes of the *DVI*. This argument can be dismissed. It is now known that Manno did not die until at least 1374, so no weight can be placed on Buoninsegni's testimony. In fact this testimony does not even say what Mommsen takes it to, for it does not actually mention the Sala at all. No more does Lombardo – it is the *DVI*, the text, which is at issue, not the frescoes.[8]

Evidence of direct contact between Altichiero and Petrarch (which will be discussed below), cited by Wilkins[9] as proof that the frescoes were begun before 1374, is no more conclusive. All it suggests is some form of dialogue at the planning stage.

The attribution[10] by the author of one of the early descriptions of the Sala Virorum Illustrium, Marcantonio Michiel, of parts of the scheme to Guariento, who died in 1370, carries no weight at all in this context. There are no valid reasons to accept Michiel's attribution, which is reflected in none of the other early sources, the surviving fragments, or in any of the putative copies of the frescoes . If Guariento has any role in this, it is perhaps to suggest a date *after* 1370. As court painter to the Carraresi, and having already worked in their palace,[11] one might expect him to have secured this prestigious commission were he still alive, especially in the wake of his great Venetian commission for the Paradise fresco in the Doge's palace. The appearance of Altichiero and of Giusto de'Menabuoi as the leading painters of Padua in the 1370s, carving up the court commissions between them, was probably in response to the market niche left by Guariento's death.

The hall which was turned into the Sala Virorum Illustrium runs on an east-west axis overlooking the northern courtyard of the Carrarese Palace. It is lit by windows in the shorter east and west walls. The west wall faces the main entrance to the courtyard from the piazza beyond. The overall layout of the Sala Virorum Illustrium in its trecento condition was carefully and plausibly reconstructed by Mommsen.[12] He argued that the

[8] Buoninsegni's text reads: 'the lord had Manno's portrait painted in a hall amongst the other men famous for their feats of arms' – Buoninsegni p. 548, quoted in *ibid.*, p. 98. Lombardo's letter asks for Manno to be included in the *DVI*: 'hunc s(cilicet) te intra opus illustrium inserere rogo' – Wilkins, 'Petrarch and Manno Donati', p. 388.

[9] 'This probability carries with it the probability that the decoration of the hall was begun, at least, within the years 1368–1369', Wilkins, *Petrarch's Last Years*, p. 301. Petrarch's house in Arquà was under construction in 1369. The poet returned to Padua from a visit to Pavia in the summer of 1369 and first lived in his new country home from the beginning of 1370. *Ibid.*, pp. 170ff.

[10] Michiel, quoted in Simon, 'Altichiero Versus Avanzo', p. 267.

[11] See D'Arcais, *Guariento*, p. 82.

[12] Mommsen, 'Sala Virorum Illustrium', pp. 105–6.

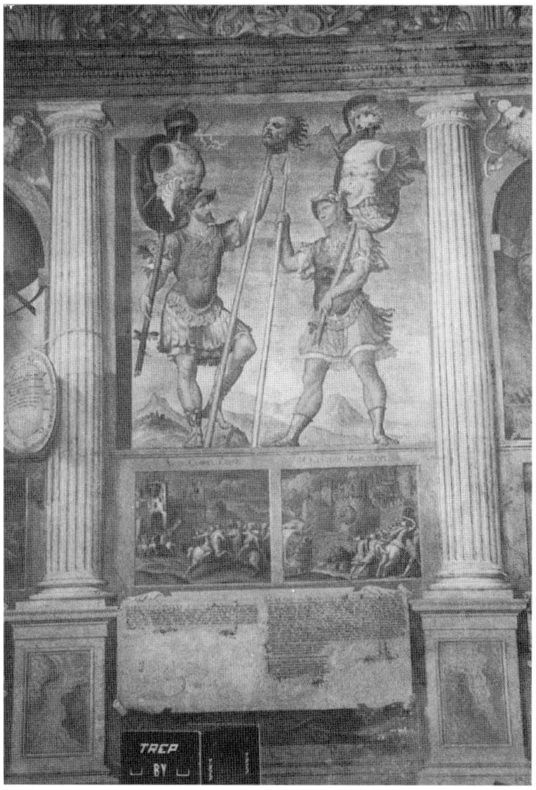

Fig. 57 Domenico Campagnola and Stefano dell'Arzere: *A. Cornelius Cossus & M. Claudius Marcellus*. Padua, Sala dei Giganti.

shape of the hall makes it virtually certain that the thirty-six heroes of the *DVI* must simply have been divided into two sections, one for each of the long walls of the hall, eighteen figures on each side (the cinquecento frescoes of the Sala dei Giganti follow such a pattern, with twenty figures on each long wall). Each section seems to have been divided into three, with the main standing figure, probably in full colour, above a representative scene from his biography, probably in grisaille, and an identifying inscription below – an arrangement at least circumstantially confirmed by the adoption of such a scheme in the post-fire fresco cycle (fig. 57). Mommsen ruled out any suggestion that the brief lives of the *Compendium* were actually painted on the walls of the hall, and though his argument that they are too long to be thus used[13] is undermined by the considerable length of some of the sixteenth-century *tituli* painted in the hall, he is surely right. The implication of Lombardo della Seta's note on completing the *DVI* is clear: 'I know that you (i.e. Francesco da Carrara) . . . are eagerly waiting . . . so that you can learn briefly and in the right order about the deeds of your famous heroes.'[14] The figures, scenes, and names were up on the wall, but without further biographical detail of any kind.

The two earliest descriptions of the Sala Virorum Illustrium (that such was its normal title we know from documents of the 1380s[15]) are strikingly different, but both confirm

[13] *Ibid.*, p. 106.

[14] *Ibid.*, p. 99.

[15] See Gasparotto, 'La Reggia', p. 104.

the association of Altichiero's name with the frescoes. Michele Savonarola's *Libellus* of 1447 follows 'what is very clearly an eyewitness account'[16] of the hall, both with regard to its position and importance within the palace, and to the subject matter and quality of the frescoes, with an unequivocal attribution:

Stantque due amplissime et picturis ornatissime sale ad latera horum situate, quarum prima Thebarum nuncapatur, altera Imperatorum nominatur prima maior atque gloriosior, in qua Romani imperatore miris cum figuris cumque triumphis, auro optimoque cum colore depicti sunt. Quos gloriose manus illustrium pictorum Octaviano et Alticherii configurarunt.[17]

A century later Michiel, in his *Notizie*, is far less secure:

Nella sala di Giganti, segondo al Campagnola, Jacomo Davanzo dipinse a man mancha la captivita di Giugurta, et triompho di Mario. Guariento Padovano li XII Cesari a man dextra e li lor fatti. Segondo Andrea Rizzo vi dipinsero Altichiero et Octaviano Bressano. Ivi sono ritratti el Petrarcha et Lombardo, i quali credo dessero l'argomento di quella Pittura.[18]

As Robin Simon showed,[19] the tradition in which Savonarola (who has evidently seen the frescoes) is confirmed by Andrea Riccio is always to be preferred to that of Michiel where he follows Campagnola, who, even if he had seen the frescoes, does not seem to have known what he was looking at. In Michiel's text only the existence of portraits of Petrarch and Lombardo comes across as a first-hand observation, and Michiel is clearly less than certain about their relevance to the other frescoes, whose subject matter in Campagnola's version is indeed hard to connect specifically with Petrarch. Michiel's confusion here, as elsewhere, is obvious, and we should perhaps be grateful that he felt unable to choose between his sources, for he obviously inclines to place more weight on Campagnola. Savonarola, of course, knew the hall before the fire of *c.* 1500, as Riccio (born in Padua *c.* 1470) must have done. Though Campagnola was also a Paduan and probably old enough by 1500 to have seen the trecento frescoes, the incoherence and inaccuracy of his account (if Michiel correctly represents it) suggests that he had not. Perhaps he only ever saw them after the fire, but before the repaint of 1539, in which case he was making valiant but uninformed guesses[20] (this might explain his relative certainty about the portraits, since Petrarch's at least survived the fire) – and Riccio's testimony indicates that an accurate tradition was available at the time.

The other possibility (suggested by Mommsen[21]) is that Michiel misinterpreted Campagnola, as he did in the case of Savonarola's word 'Imperatores' for instance, which either Campagnola and Michiel, or Michiel alone, misinterpret as meaning 'Emperors' instead of 'Generals'. It is hard to believe that Campagnola would have made such an error if he had himself seen the frescoes before the fire, for the *tituli* would have left no literate spectator in any doubt as to the predominantly republican nature of the heroes depicted on the walls of the Sala.

Elsewhere in the early literature we find Riccio correcting Campagnola, and where he

16 Simon, 'Altichiero Versus Avanzo', p. 267.

17 Savonarola, *Libellus de Magnificis Ornamentis Regies Civitatis Padue*, p. 49.

18 Michiel, *Notizie di Opere di Disegno*, p. 30.

19 See Simon, 'Altichiero Versus Avanzo', pp. 261ff.

20 Except that Campagnola (in Michiel's testimony) is quite as confused by the intact frescoes in the Oratory of S. Giorgio.

21 For this see Mommsen, 'Sala Virorum Illustrium', p. 101 and Simon, 'Altichiero Versus Avanzo', p. 267.

is pointedly specific (for example when, following Michiel's quotation of Campagnola's attribution of the Oratory of S. Giorgio frescoes to 'Iacomo Davanzo e . . . Altichiero Veronese' we find Riccio's statement that '*solo* Altichiero vi dipingesse'[22]) he is supported by documentary and stylistic evidence. We need not seriously doubt, then, the authenticity and reliability of the tradition attributing the Sala Virorum Illustrium frescoes, at least in part, to Altichiero. 'Ottaviano', of whom we know nothing, is a problem, but Riccio's testimony should be given credence, especially when it adds specific detail – 'Bressano' – to Savonarola's account.[23]

These arguments might seem to boil down in the end to a choice between sources, an unsatisfactory exercise where even the best of them must be treated with considerable caution. But the attribution of the lost frescoes substantially to Altichiero is powerfully supported by the visual evidence. The extant *Portrait of Petrarch* (for which see below) is clearly his, as are the manuscript paintings in the central volumes associated with the project. These volumes form a small part of an extraordinary outpouring of Petrarch manuscripts issued from what can only be described as a factory for the production of reliable texts of Petrarch's works set up by Lombardo della Seta in the years following the poet's death. The more important of these manuscripts were intended for circulation amongst humanists or for inclusion in signorial libraries. At the outer edges of this enterprise, though, lay a demand for rather more approachable texts than the rather forbidding *DVI* in its original Latin. Petrarch's friend Donato degli Albanzani[24] took on the responsibility of making the *DVI* accessible to those who wanted to explore this last great product of Petrarch's pen but felt balked by so much Latin. One of the earliest manuscripts of Donato's Italian translation is profusely illustrated, and these illustrations, which have clear Altichieresque traits, may record – to an extent which needs careful determination – the lost narrative frescoes of the Sala Virorum Illustrium.

Donato's translation was made in 1397, and was of a text which included Lombardo's additions, but lacked all of the supplementary material Lombardo provided when he knew the text was destined for a humanist readership.[25] This is simply a reader's text, giving no indication (as the great manuscripts now in Paris do) of the break between Petrarch's and Lombardo's sections. For the scribe of this text, as for the reader, the book is simply the 'Liber di messer Francesco Petrarca intitolato de viris illustribus'. The Darmstadt manuscript, clearly a luxury volume, has a full colour frontispiece portrait of Petrarch in his study (pl. 34) facing the first page of text, which has a headpiece

[22] Michiel, *Notizie*, p. 6, quoted in Simon, 'Altichiero Versus Avanzo', p. 263.

[23] Another Brescian painter, Bertolino di Giacomo, is documented in Padua in 1383 – see Sartori, 'La Cappella di S. Giacomo', p. 327, no. 28. The *podestà* of Padua from 1371 to 1373 was the Brescian Federigo Lavellongo. He died in Carrarese service, and his fine tomb (now cleaned), with a rather English-looking 'weeper' arcade and an interesting fresco of a *Madonna of Humility*, is in the passage to the cloister of the Santo adjacent to the Chapel of S. Giacomo. A *podestà* from another city tended to bring or attract many of his fellow citizens to the town in which he held his office during the period of that office. See Levi, *Francesco di Vannozzo*, pp. 56–7 for an example of this.

[24] For Donato see Jannaco, 'Donato Casentinense Volgarizzatore del Petrarca'; Martellotti, *Petrarca*, p. LI; and his entry in the *Dizionario Biografico*.

[25] A description and list of *incipits* and *explicits* of this MS are given in Sottili, 'Codici del Petrarca nella Germania Occ.1', pp. 458–60.

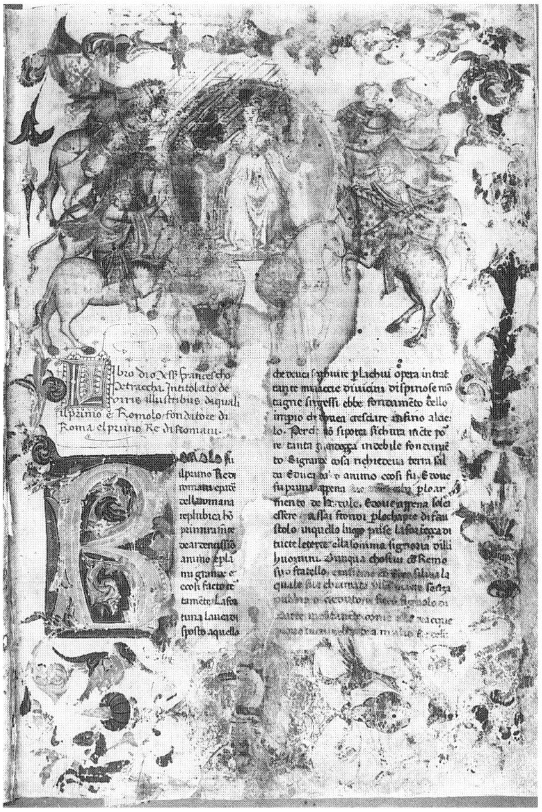

Fig. 58 Petrarch (trans. Donato degli Albanzani), *De Viris Illustribus*: *Triumph of Fame*. Darmstadt, Hessische Landes-und-Hochschul-Bibliothek, cod. 101, fo. 2r.

of the *Triumph of Fame* (fig. 58) above the first two half-columns, which are themselves decorated with a rather coarse version of the Bolognese-derived borders common to all the manuscripts associated with the Paduan Petrarch industry. Seven of the biographies have figurated initials illustrating the subject of the particular section.

At the foot of twenty-four of the manuscript's 245 pages are found oblong narrative scenes in grisaille (pls. 21–32), relieved only by touches of gold for crowns, and of red for blood. These scenes are not distributed at all evenly throughout, though every page has a space left at the bottom. The earliest scenes (e.g. fos. 3v and 4r) have a double pen-line border filled in with yellow wash, perhaps in imitation of the fictive moulded border of a fresco, but in the later scenes this is replaced by a single drawn line.

The Darmstadt codex was first published in 1895 by Julius von Schlosser,[26] who connected it with Padua because he recognised the crest of the Paduan Papafava family at the foot of fo. 2r, and specifically with the Sala Virorum Illustrium on the basis of the striking similarity between the full-page portrait of Petrarch on fo. 1v and the surviving fresco in the Sala dei Giganti. Von Schlosser also suggested that the *bas-de-page* scenes in the manuscript might record the narrative scenes placed below each figure in the trecento decoration of the hall. He also argued that the *Triumph of Fame* on fo. 2r, the same subject as the headpieces of two of the early Carrarese manuscripts of the Latin text,

26 See Schlosser, 'Ein Veronisches Bilderbuch und die Hofische Kunst des XIV Jahrhunderts', pp. 61–5, whose identification of the crest is shared by Sottili, 'Codici del Petrarca', p. 460.

might record a fresco of this subject formerly (though mentioned by no early source) in the Sala Virorum Illustrium.

The validity of von Schlosser's belief that the grisailles of Darmstadt cod. 101 'give us an approximate idea as to what the (lost) frescoes . . . looked like'[27] was supported by Mommsen on the basis of three points. His first point, that the miniatures are closely responsive in detail to particular emphases of Petrarch's text, is hardly conclusive. All it indicates is attention to the text on the part of the illustrator of the manuscript. It may, but it need not, support his argument. His second point is more particular and rather more convincing. Noting that 'it seems curious that the illuminator did not choose to depict the actual killing of Remus by Romulus, although this dramatic climax of the quarrel has always been one of the best known facts of Roman history',[28] he suggests that this is as a result of Petrarch's deliberate downplaying of the incident in the *Epitome* of the *DVI* (in which Romulus' role is not mentioned) and its total exclusion from the *Compendium*. Mommsen concludes that 'the assumption seems warranted that . . . he suggested to the artists of the Paduan hall that they omit the fratricide. . .'[29] and that 'this instance, then, would seem to support the statement made by Marcantonio Michiel that "Petrarch supplied the subject-matter of these pictures"'.[30] While, on the face of it, this looks like little more than a variant of his first point, there is a significant difference here. While it is true that a strict reading of the *Epitome* would have offered an, as it were, negative source for the Romulus–Remus fight, so that were he totally ignorant of all other sources he might have excluded the fratricide, it must be more probable that anyone who knew to any extent what he was looking at reading in the text that 'Remus was killed'[31] would normally have shown Romulus as responsible. It is scarcely credible that the painter would simply have been handed a text and told to produce frescoes on that basis, unless the painter himself were known to be literate and well versed in the stories. If this were the case the result is the same as if the painter's interpretation of the text was controlled by someone else familiar with the Roman material of the *DVI* – the exclusion of the fratricide was a deliberate decision in line with Petrarch's own views. The point is generally persuasive, though, again, it is not as absolutely binding as Mommsen supposed, for this care to observe Petrarch's wishes need not involve the Sala Virorum Illustrium at all. If the Darmstadt illustrations were independently conceived for the manuscript, with no reference at all to any pre-existing frescoes, the result could be exactly the same as long as someone associated with it (Donato himself comes to mind) was steeped in the Petrarchan versions of Livy's histories. In the light of the other evidence tying the miniatures to the frescoes, though, Mommsen's point is generally convincing.

Much the same can be said of Mommsen's third point. The accurate and quite specific presence in several of the grisailles of various ancient Roman monuments has long been recognised.[32] We find the Janus Quadrifons in fos. 4r, 4v and 8r (pls. 22b,

[27] Schlosser, quoted in Mommsen, 'Sala Virorum Illustrium', p. 107.

[28] Mommsen, 'Sala Virorum Illustrium', p. 109.

[29] *Ibid.*

[30] *Ibid.*

[31] *Ibid.*

[32] *Ibid.*, pp. 110–11.

23a, 25a), the Vatican Obelisk in fos. 4v, 8r and 11r (pls. 23a, 25a, 26b), the Castel Sant'Angelo and Colosseum in fo. 4v (pl. 23a), the Pantheon and one of the columns in fo. 11r (pl. 26b), a column again in fo. 19r (pl. 28b) as well as the church of S. Nicolo in Carcere, incorporating Antique remains which the miniature shows with a degree of accuracy strongly suggesting first-hand knowledge of the building itself.

On balance, and bearing in mind the other factors which tend to tie the manuscript to the lost frescoes, this is a persuasive argument, and details like the inclusion of a domeless representation of the Colosseum, flying in the face of the popular Roman mytho-topography of the time, do suggest a quasi-archaeological control of the iconography more likely to have been Petrarch's than anyone else's. But other possibilities should at least be aired. Petrarch was never really as interested in the look of Roman buildings as he was in their historical resonances. What one might call a proto-romantic view of the ruins as being inherently worthy of study is more to be associated with men like Antonio da Legnago in Verona or with Petrarch's Paduan friend Giovanni Dondi dall'Orologio, who made a trip to Rome in order to study the battered fragments of Roman grandeur.[33] Nor can it be ruled out that the evident familiarity with S. Nicolo in Carcere shown on fo. 19r might reflect Altichiero's own direct experience of Rome. It is at least arguable (and it will be argued) that Altichiero had direct contact with at least one of the major surviving monuments of Roman antiquity, contact only obtainable in person. Whether or not this is so, Petrarch remains the most likely source for the relatively accurate versions of the buildings seen in the miniatures – we know he was a capable draughtsman – but it is an indication of the intensity of interest in the Antique in Padua and Verona that such a variety of options should even be available for consideration at this date.

If the miniatures of Darmstadt cod. 101 do, then, refer back to the frescoes of the Sala Virorum Illustrium, what, and how much can they tell us of Altichiero's role in the original project? While the scale of the grisailles makes comparisons with Altichiero's surviving frescoes difficult, individual figures and groups of figures do suggest connections. Groups of standing soldiers like those found in many of the miniatures (e.g., fos. 2v, 7v, 14r, 15r, 18r and 22r; pls. 21a, 24b, 27a, 27b, 28a, 30b) clearly resemble the standing figures of the *Execution of St Catherine* or the courtiers of the *Baptism of King Sevio* in S. Giorgio (pls. 108, 93). The standing figure on the right of fo. 14r (*T. Manlius Torquatus and the Tribune Pomponius*) is plainly a reversal of the figure standing in the left foreground of the *Battle of Clavigo* in S. Giacomo (pl. 69), even down to the style of the hat (of course, if the miniature is a reflection of a Sala fresco, it is the S. Giacomo figure which has been reversed).

Similarly, the mounted groups of fos. 6v, 51v and 53r, articulated by means of one head turning back to confront the profiles of the majority with a full face, are directly reminiscent of Altichiero's characteristic treatment of such passages (e.g. in the *Crucifixions* of S. Giacomo and S. Giorgio, pls. 42–4, 86), and of his crowd articulation

[33] For Giovanni Dondi and the art of antiquity see Krautheimer, *Lorenzo Ghiberti*, pp. 296ff. and Panofsky, *Renaissance and Renascences*, pp. 208–10.

in general. And while the small scale prevents the sort of convincing location of figures within architecture which is so marked a feature of Altichiero's naturalism, one can see a connection between fo. 8r (pl. 25a), in which the expulsion of Tarquin takes place within a space surrounded by buildings, and the background of the *Battle of Clavigo*, in which a similar compression of relative scales produces the same effect.

Further particulars which point to Altichiero's as the designing mind are: a general stiffness in the depiction of violent action, a marked feature of the more exuberant frescoes of S. Giorgio, and a highly characteristic use of turning or departing figures at the edge of the pictorial field. One might compare fo. 11r (*Camillus Expelling the Gauls from Rome*, pl. 26b) with the Oriental in green and salmon-pink in *St George on the Wheel* in S. Giorgio (pl. 98), and with equivalent figures on the right-hand edges of the *Fall of the Idols* and *St Catherine on the Wheel*, also in S. Giorgio. The tendency of the action in the battle scenes (e.g. fo. 19v, the *Battle Between the Armies of Darius and Alexander* pl. 29a) to spill off the edge of the pictorial field is reminiscent of the *Battle of Clavigo*.

The analysis of costume might establish whether, and how much, these drawings of *c.* 1400 (they must at least postdate 1397, the date of the translation) were based on frescoes of *c.* 1370–5. One might expect a later artist, albeit unconsciously, to update older models, just as some of the copyists of the Sala Grande frescoes seem to have done. In fact there seems little discrepancy between the costumes of the miniatures and those of Altichiero's surviving frescoes from the 1370s and 1380s, though details of armour, often an unfailing guide to date, are hard to determine on this scale. Having said that, there seems no reason to date the dress styles of the manuscript markedly later than those familiar from Altichiero's frescoes, with which they have so many other affinities.

It may be argued that these correspondences simply point to the illustrator's having been trained in an Altichieresque style or against the background of a period in which such an idiom was dominant in Padua. While this is not inherently improbable, it fits rather uneasily as an explanation for this particular set of similarities. The *style* of the Darmstadt artist, taking into account the obvious difficulties of comparison, is not especially reminiscent of Altichiero. It does not, for instance, recall him in the way that the coloured headpiece – another *Triumph of Fame* – of one of the Carrarese manuscripts of the Latin *DVI* (pl. 37) does. This headpiece is, to my mind, patently not autograph Altichiero. It is, equally, quite clearly by someone steeped in Altichiero's style down to the last facial expression. The Darmstadt miniatures have their own rather brisk style, related in recent studies[34] to a Bolognese rather than Paduan manner, with faces for the most part unlike Altichiero's. They recall Altichiero precisely on the level of large-scale invention and design, exactly what one would expect of a not particularly inventive artist following a great and overwhelming model.

Even if some connection between the miniatures of the Darmstadt *DVI* and the lost frescoes, and Altichiero's authorship of those frescoes, are broadly accepted, there is still a considerable area of doubt as to how the manuscript reflects the actual appear-

[34] See Benati, *Jacopo Avanzi nel Rinnovamento della Pittura Padana del Secolo '300*, pp. 79–83. Benati sees the hand of Jacopo di Paolo in the Darmstadt miniatures, which he believes are direct records of the frescoes of the Sala Virorum Illustrium, parts of which he attributes, on the basis of Jacopo di Paolo's copies, to Jacopo Avanzi.

ance of the frescoes. There is, most crucially, a major numerical obstacle to seeing the grisailles in simple terms as small copies of twenty-four of the thirty-six lost narratives. Unless we have badly misunderstood the format of the Sala Virorum Illustrium, there can only have been room for one monochrome narrative below each figure (as in the present scheme, where the narrative serves as a kind of predella). There can hardly have been room for as many as five, but in the manuscript we have five full scenes for Romulus,[35] another five for Alexander, two apiece for Tullius Hostilius and Camillus, one and a part of one for Hannibal, and less than one for Horatius Cocles and Cincinnatus, who have to share one miniature between them. Had the manuscript simply followed the frescoes, we would expect just one scene per hero, perhaps at the head of each biography. The provision of a miniature for each page would have been an extraordinarily ambitious project given the length of some of the lives.[36]

A further difficulty arises if we bear in mind the twin factors which seem to tie this material together: the evidence of Petrarch's intervention, and the affinities with Altichiero's extant work. For if, of the two sets of five miniatures, *one* stood out per set which met both criteria, one could point with some confidence to that as the record of the Sala Virorum Illustrium fresco and see the rest as inventions of the Darmstadt artist specifically for the new context. But the material simply refuses to conform to this pattern. In the case of the five Romulus scenes, it is the last, the *Building of the Walls and the Quarrel Between Romulus and Remus* (fo. 4v, pl. 23a) which, for the reasons advanced above, records Petrarch's supervision. But the *Killing of Amulius* (fo. 4r) shows a specific Roman monument (another of Mommsen's criteria), and the first scene of all, showing King Amulius and his courtiers (fo. 2v, pl. 21a), has by far the clearest reference to Altichiero of all the Romulus illustrations in the group on the left.

That it was intended for every biography to be illustrated by at least one central scene is demonstrated by the miniature on fo. 8v (pl. 25b), in which both Horatius Cocles and Cincinnatus have the most memorable episodes of their lives jammed awkwardly into one space. This conflation was necessitated by the brevity of the two biographies, which allowed only one page bottom for the two men. The consequent sacrifice of unity and tidiness suggests an overriding wish to include some 'canonical' scene for each hero of the text. This does, perhaps, point to the thirty-six frescoes of the Sala Virorum Illustrium. The two scenes included here (*Cocles and the Tiber Bridge* and the *Recall of Cincinnatus*), at such inconvenience, are certainly those one would expect to have been chosen. The next and facing page after fo. 8v begins the biography of Camillus only half way down the second text column, but the *bas-de-page* is occupied by an illustration of his Triumph. Camillus' life continues until fo. 14r, and of the nine available spaces only one other, on fo. 11r, has a miniature (*Camillus Expelling the Gauls from Rome*). As the *Triumph* is placed, out of chronological order, at the beginning of the biography (and its location there, when there were other places available and necessitating the untidiness of fo. 8v, suggests some imperative that *this* scene had to stand at the beginning), and

35 Probably six originally – the foot of fo. 5 has been cut out.

36 The life of Scipio covers fos. 51v–79r, that of Caesar fos. 83v–179v.

bearing in mind the Triumphs mentioned by Savonarola, this seems an obvious candidate for a fresco-derived scene.

But other parts of the codex tend to confound such arguments. If these principles applied, then one would expect some important scene, perhaps his Triumph, to stand at the head of the extraordinarily long life of Scipio, in Petrarch's eyes probably the most important hero of the *DVI* and central to its purpose.[37] Yet the first page of his biography (fo. 51v – the Scipio text begins in the second column) has a miniature of the joint *Triumph of Claudius Nero and Livius Salinator* (pl. 31b), and only on fo. 53r, after two blank spaces, do we find the *Triumph of Scipio* (pl. 32a). There is no particular obstacle to seeing this as a likely fresco subject, but if it is, then ought it not to be placed at the very beginning, as with Camillus' Triumph (pl. 26a), or in its culminating position at the end? So, although it is probably safe to say that the manuscript preserves the appearance of the Sala Virorum Illustrium frescoes to some degree, the extent to which the example of the hall was allowed to dictate the layout of the manuscript under discussion is less than might be thought. The illustration of the manuscript is clearly unfinished, but enough was carried out to give a clear picture of the enterprise as a whole. In parts of the manuscript the illustrator worked consistently through a biography, drawing on page after page, as in the case of the life of Romulus, where the first five spaces are all filled. And this is just where the diffusion of the influence of Altichiero and of the other factors tying the miniatures to the Sala makes itself felt. Exactly the same diffusion characterises the five Alexander scenes (pls. 28b–30b). The one thing that simply cannot be said of the grisailles of Darmstadt cod. 101 is that they are copies of two-thirds of the lost frescoes of the Sala. They show the sort of influences one would expect if the frescoes were an iconographic source to some extent, but not in the way one would expect if the Sala material were transmitted directly to the makers of the manuscript. The most obvious conclusion must be that the Darmstadt artist, clearly not a member of the Altichiero circle himself, but equally clearly (all the more so for that very reason) working on the basis of some Altichieresque model, must have drawn on some intermediary source with its own connections with the Sala frescoes.

The nature of such a source is not hard to imagine. Donato degli Albanzani's translation of the *DVI* into the vernacular is believed to have been made on the occasion of the marriage in 1397 between Nicolo d'Este and Gigliola da Carrara (Francesco Il Vecchio's granddaughter), possibly in tandem with Donato's translation of Boccaccio's *De Claris Mulieribus* (this for the bride, perhaps, with the *DVI* going to the groom). A presentation copy of Donato's text must have been given on this occasion. Neither this copy nor Donato's first autograph is known to survive. A good early text (1398) is known,[38] but it has no illustrations. It is at least feasible that any presentation copy, as befits a signorial marriage, would have been more than averagely sumptuous, and probably illustrated. The nature of the Darmstadt codex – ambitious in scope but of slightly less than top quality – together with its provenance in the Papafava family, a branch of

37 See Bernardo, *Petrarch, Scipio and the Africa*, especially pp. 11–20 for Scipio in the *DVI*.

38 See Jannaco, 'Donato Casentinense', pp. 189–90.

the Carraresi, suggests that it may have been based on such a previous manuscript, which possibly had a full set of illustrations.

The presence of illustrations in the Darmstadt codex may, in any case, have been an afterthought. They fill a cramped space at the foot of the page, which leaves no room for a gap between the last line of the text and the top of the miniature; some examples cling very precariously indeed to the *bas-de-page*. The appearance of the basic 39-line page is perfectly well balanced, better balanced in fact, without the illustration. The later addition of illustrations to a manuscript which has already been laid out and written would explain things like the log-jam of the Horatius Cocles/Cincinnatus illustration, the duplication of illustrative material already included in the figurative initials, and the puzzling distribution of the main illustrations throughout the book. None of these features suggests much in the way of forward planning. Perhaps the Papafava owner of this manuscript asked for it to be upgraded at a later stage in its production, something at least circumstantially suggested by another peculiarity of its layout (see below). Such a history sits perfectly well with the suggestion that the Darmstadt illustrations must reflect the Sala Virorum Illustrium frescoes from a distance.[39]

Other hypotheses may be advanced. None offers more than a partial account of the exact way in which the Sala frescoes might have influenced the Darmstadt artist in the way they seem to have done, accumulating other Altichieresque material along the way. My feeling, though, is that it is easier to see how this might have happened via a prestigious manuscript of top quality, perhaps the product of signorial patronage, by artists closer to Altichiero himself than our illustrator (and we know such artists were to be found in Padua at this time), under Donato's supervision, than in the rather confused Darmstadt manuscript.

The portrait of Petrarch

The factor linking the Darmstadt manuscript with the Sala Virorum Illustrium frescoes which has always been regarded as decisive is the use of the surviving *Portrait of Petrarch* as the model for the full-page portrait facing the first page of Donato's text. This portrait (pl. 34) is immediately striking for its quality, which is superior to that of the other illustrations of the manuscript, clearly by different hands, and it is very closely based on the fresco. Even here, though, all is not straightforward.

What survives of the trecento fresco portrait of Petrarch is easily visible as a distinct L-shaped patch of the original plaster incorporated into the cinquecento setting (fig. 55, pl. 33). The untidiness of the border between the two areas suggests that everything was done to retain as much of the original as possible. Presumably the portrait had by 1500 acquired iconic status. So, while the sixteenth-century painter tidied up the joins by recreating in his part the upper right corners of the desk and the chest in front of it, and by adding the lost tip of the bookstand on Petrarch's desk, he also left, just to the right of the stand, what can be seen from the miniature to be the left-hand edge of a pile of

[39] For the relationship between the Papafava and the Carraresi see Hyde, *Padua*, pp. 82–4. For the initials, see n. 47, below.

books sitting in a wall cupboard, a cupboard replaced in the new painting by the mountainous view seen through a window.

It can be seen from the fragment of panelling still surviving behind Petrarch's head in the fresco that the sharply converging perspective of the miniature accurately reproduces that of the original, distinctly at odds with the perspectival scheme of the cinquecento surroundings. That the *Portrait of Lombardo della Seta* on the other side of the window (fig. 56) is a complete repaint, retaining nothing of the trecento original, is evident from its total adherence to the new perspective, and from the increased size and more forward location of the figure. The original presumably matched the *Portrait of Petrarch* in its recession from the frontal plane. Both were probably framed by the sort of border which encloses the miniature, an arched set of fictive panels with inset (and now badly abraded) foliate strips and roundels. The fictive three-dimensionality of this, drawn by the miniaturist as if seen from the right – as the fresco is most easily seen – may well record the original rather exactly. The confused border area surviving at the foot of the trecento patch on the wall is too indistinct to be very helpful in this context, but the border in the Darmstadt portrait has every appearance of being a fresco border translated into miniature terms.

Where features are repeated, and allowing for the obvious difficulties of comparison, the very badly smoked and damaged colours of the fresco reflect those of the miniature – the brick pink of the undersleeve and hood, the rather cold dark brown of the robe, the green and red of the books, and the warm orange brown of the furniture. But nothing now visible on the wall of the Sala dei Giganti matches the range and delicacy of colour in the miniature – the clear apple and rather darker greens of books and border, the dark blue of the window, the slate blue between the joists, the sparkling light blue for the convex mirror (or lens) on the table, the reds of the border roundels, and the clear yellow of the spandrel panels in the frame. Viewed as a whole, this impressive range of mostly clear and light colours is inescapably reminiscent of a fresco painter's palette, and quite specifically of Altichiero's own in S. Giorgio. The affinities are very distinctive.[40]

The poor condition of the fresco extends to the facial features of the portrait. While the basic structure corresponds with that of the Darmstadt miniature and with Altichiero's other images of Petrarch, the imperious glare which characterises the fresco in its present state is probably a consequence of its rather battered condition. Some sense of an inner life is retained – the figure has a powerful presence *in situ* – but the clear and alert gaze of the miniature (rather youthful in appearance) accords better with the sharp intelligence of the profile grisaille in the presentation copy of the latin *DVI* (pl. 35), with which it shares rosy cheeks, and with the calm and benign portrait in the *Baptism of King Sevio* in S. Giorgio. The youthfulness of the Darmstadt portrait may

[40] Other details confirm the very high quality of this miniature. The drawing of the smaller architectural elements, many of which are very complex, is absolutely assured and is again reminiscent of equivalent passages in the Oratory of S. Giorgio. The atmospheric feel of the page is heightened by the coloured shading of the back wall and the floor round the back of the desk and chest, done in a warm brown hatching which gives a rich depth to the darker end of the colour range.

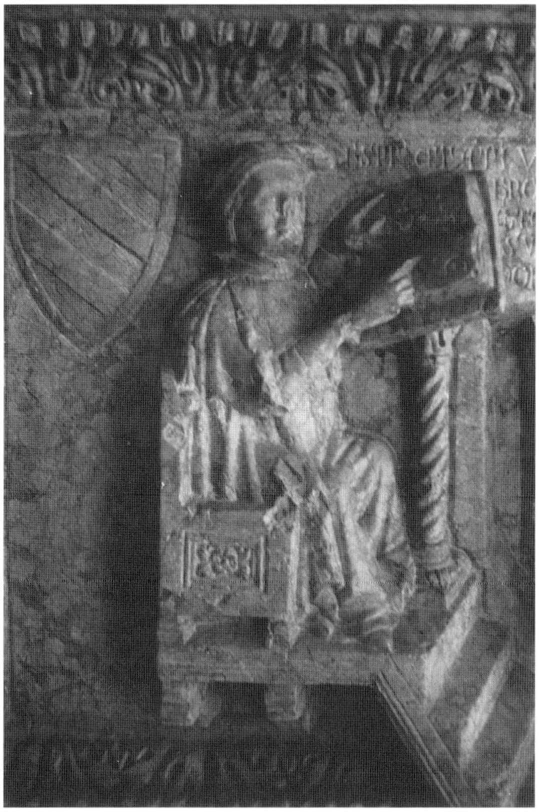

Fig. 59 Verona, S. Fermo Maggiore. Tomb of Antonio Pelacani (detail).

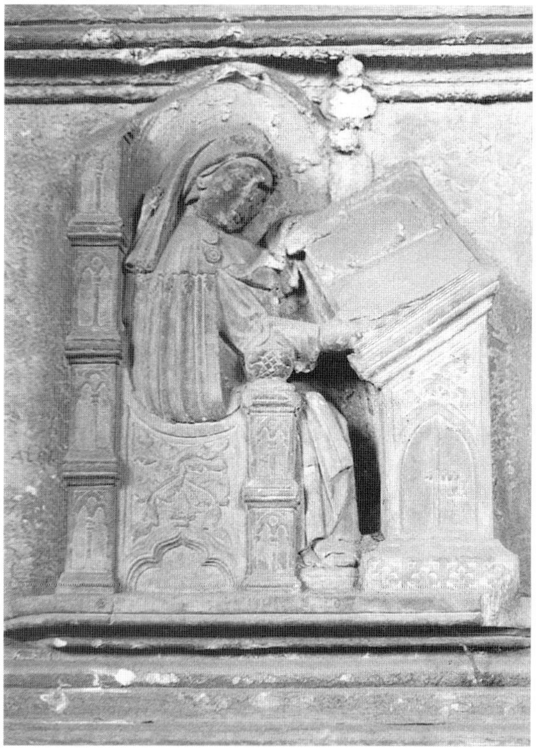

Fig. 60 Padua, Il Santo, cloister. Tomb of Nicolo da Monselice (detail).

result from a process of idealisation as direct memory of the man Francesco Petrarca was overtaken by a veneration for 'Petrarca'.

While the *Portrait of Lombardo* preserves nothing of the trecento original except, presumably, the general concept, the nature of the two portraits as a pair is open to reconstruction. Though in some respects the iconography of the Petrarch reflects that of Doctors' tombs, ubiquitous throughout Bologna, Verona and Padua (figs. 59, 60),[41] and the glance is evidently directed across the wall towards Lombardo, it is less likely that Lombardo was portrayed in a subordinate or learning role than that his portrait and its setting simply mirrored Petrarch's. A stylistically cognate arrangement can be seen in the Altichieresque Martino da Verona's pulpit frescoes in S. Fermo Maggiore in Verona, where four pairs of seated scholar-saints face one another across the pulpit and its canopy (figs. 61–3). Possibly the two portraits of the Sala Virorum Illustrium exhibited a subtler relationship, with Lombardo paying attention rather than being actually taught, rather as the Dominicans of Tomaso da Modena's scheme in the chapterhouse of S. Nicolò in Treviso had their independent scholarly activities centred on the (now

[41] For Bologna see Grandi, *I Monumenti dei Dottori e la Scultura a Bologna 1267–1348*. Examples of different variants of the type can be found in Verona in the cloisters of S. Fermo Maggiore and on the facade of S. Pietro Martire, and in Padua in the first cloister of the Santo.

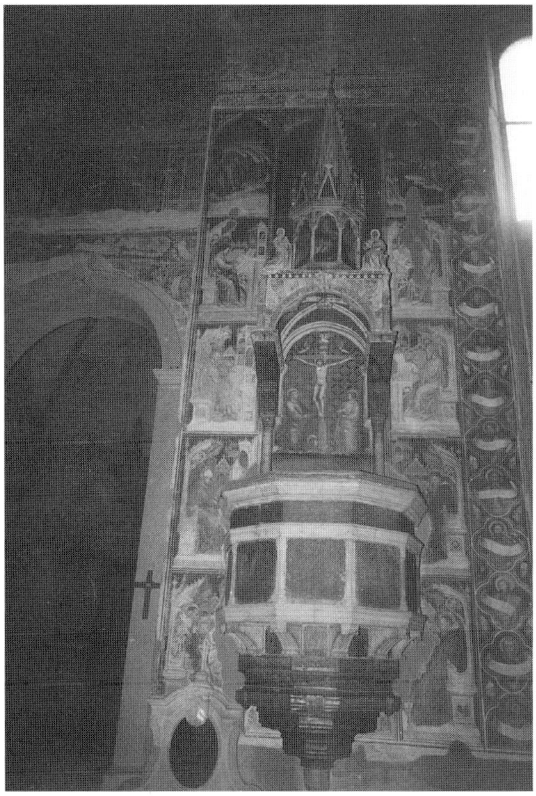

Fig. 61 Verona, S. Fermo Maggiore. Pulpit with frescoes by Martino da Verona.

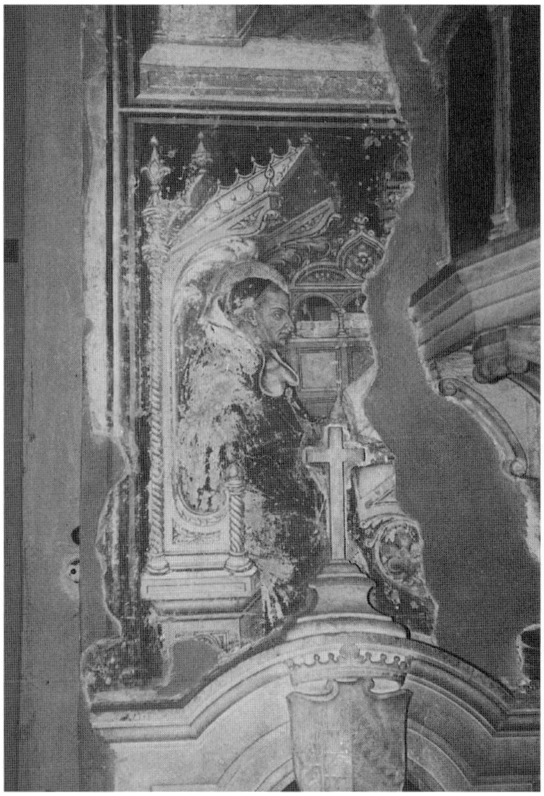

Fig. 62 Martino da Verona: S. Fermo pulpit frescoes (detail).

lost) group of Dominican saints on the east wall, without being overtly directed by them.[42]

There is no valid reason why a portrait of Lombardo should have been painted in the Sala Virorum Illustrium until his assumption of the leading role in the project, and since the portraits were obviously conceived as a pair, this must apply to the Petrarch as well. But they need not have been painted as late, say, as 1379/80, when Lombardo had completed the literary side of the enterprise. While the inclusion of such portraits might have met with Petrarch's disapproval while he lived, even if Lombardo was in effective control on the site before 1374 (with Petrarch in Arquà most of the time), there is no obstacle to seeing them as having been painted at any time between Petrarch's death and before the completion of the presentation texts, which imply the frescoes are finished, for Lombardo's role would have been clear before this, and a signorial request might have come while the painters of the main frescoes were still available. The pair of portraits is likely to have been meant to record the culmination of the long artistic and literary enterprise (perhaps this was made explicit in an inscription, or a pair of inscriptions – hence the otherwise baffled Michiel's informed remarks regarding Petrarch's

42 See Gibbs, *L'Occhio di Tomaso*, pp. 57–92.

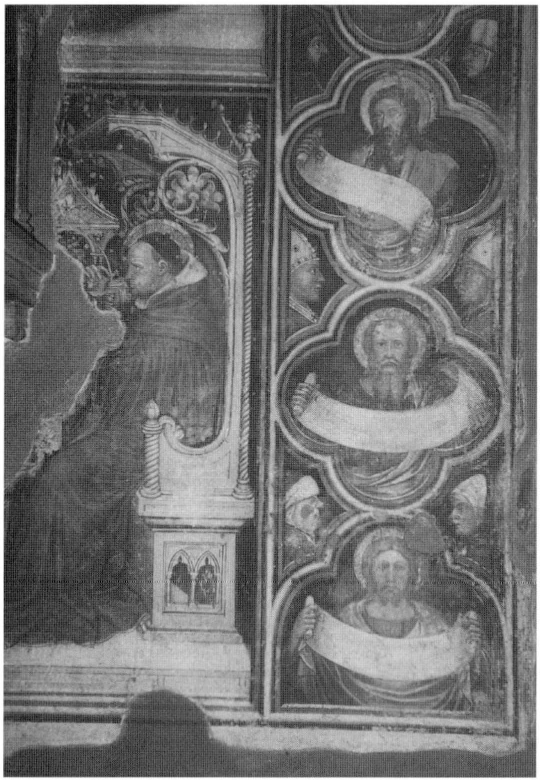

Fig. 63 Martino da Verona: S. Fermo pulpit frescoes (detail).

role). But, as with so many tombs and epitaphs, the record need not necessarily have been made *after* the event it marks. While the portraits, jammed into rather awkward spaces between the window and the corners of the hall, do look somewhat like afterthoughts, they probably only postdate Petrarch's disappearance from the scene.

The iconography of the portraits, which is probably of Lombardo's choosing, derives from that commonly associated with images of the Doctors of the Church, principally Jerome, and the Evangelists. The aptness of this iconography for a representation of Petrarch, scholar and the object of scholars' veneration, needs no underlining.[43] The version used in the Sala Virorum Illustrium and recorded in the Darmstadt miniature shares with Tomaso's frescoes of 1351–2 in Treviso, and with the slightly later *St Jerome* on a nave column of S. Nicolo there,[44] a magpie's interest in the tools and other minutiae of the scholar's trade, but goes beyond these (with their different concerns) towards a complete recreation of the scholastic environment, towards, indeed, a 'portrait' of his study quite as significant as that of the scholar himself.[45] Such a concern with the depiction of the figure in a full and rationally described setting is wholly characteristic of Altichiero, and there need be no hesitation in ascribing to him at least the invention and design of this portrait, in both versions.

[43] *Ibid.*, for other adaptations of the Doctor iconography.

[44] *Ibid.*, pl. XXII, and Coletti, *L'Arte di Tomaso da Modena*, figs. 50–2.

[45] See Meiss, 'French and Italian Variations on an Early Fifteenth-century Theme: St Jerome in his Study', p. 158.

The inclusion in Darmstadt cod. 101 of such a conclusive indicator of links between the manuscript, the frescoes, and Altichiero's known work would seem on the face of it to reinforce the rather ill-defined connections suggested by study of the *bas-de-page* illustrations. But the status of the portrait on fo. 1v as an integral part of the manuscript *ab initio* is doubtful. It is extraneous to the gathering sequence, and the sheet on which it was painted appears to have been considerably larger in its original state than those of the rest of the manuscript. The portrait folio has been noticeably cropped at some stage – on the left by as much as half the width of the border (assuming there to have been no outer framing element here beyond the main strip of which we see part at the bottom), and by rather less at top and bottom. Furthermore, the right-hand border is jammed very tightly into the spine, to the extent that one cannot see it except curving round very sharply when the volume is held open. Yet, while the facing fo. 2r, which is in very poor condition, may have lost a small fraction at each edge, examination of the rest of the folios shows no sign of cropping at all, certainly nothing of the severity experienced by fo. 1v.

All of this suggests that the manuscript portrait was originally larger than the rest of the volume, that it originated elsewhere, was cropped to make it fit in with the rest of the folios, and that it was bound in with it later, perhaps at the same time as the *bas-de-page* illustrations were added. The desire of those responsible for this, whoever and whenever they were, to include so clear a reference to the fresco still allows us to take the portrait's presence as corroboration of the manuscript's connection with the Sala Virorum Illustrium, for these two blocks of material were evidently seen to belong together by someone, and someone who went to some pains to preserve the connection. If it is argued that this someone merely wanted a portrait of Petrarch to stand at the beginning of his copy of a book by Petrarch and only coincidentally picked one explicitly linked with the Sala, one would have to reply that it is possible, but that, given the rest of the loose but undeniable connections, this is putting something of a strain on mere coincidence.

There is little more that scrutiny of Darmstadt cod. 101 can tell us of the lost frescoes. It is, for instance, virtually impossible to estimate the extent to which the actual look of the frescoes has filtered through to the manuscript illustrations. The rather simple foreground spatial fields of the miniatures may result from the restricted space available in the book, rather than from the precedent of the Sala Virorum Illustrium. Neither the predella-like nature of the manuscript scenes, nor the relief-like development of the action from side to side would be out of place standing below a single figure, but the present scheme, physically enlarged though it probably is, shows how detailed and complex even such a 'predella' can be on such a scale. It is possible to imagine that the format of the Darmstadt scenes might have been reduced from fuller narratives, though the illustrations of a manuscript of Statius's *Thebaid* in the Chester-Beatty Library,[46]

[46] Mellini, *Altichiero e Jacopo Avanzi*, figs. 318–29. It is unlikely, in my view, that the Chester-Beatty miniatures directly reflect the lost frescoes of the Sala Thebana in the Carrarese Palace. These were evidently painted by 1347, too early to be direct models for drawings so clearly reflecting styles contemporary with Altichiero's work in Padua. There may have been some looser connection. See Gasparotto, 'La Reggia', pp. 95–6 and n. 75.

which inhabits the same stylistic world as much of this material, shows that complex narratives can be effective on a small scale. On the other hand, the discrepancy in scale between the heroes and the figures in the narratives below may not have been as great as between the present *giganti* and the figures in theirs, in which case the simplicity of the miniatures may reflect original designs intended to be legible from some distance (which the complex narratives of the cinquecento scheme are not).

Of the main frescoes, the heroes of the *DVI* themselves, we have absolutely no visual record, for, as Mommsen established, the seven figured initials of the Darmstadt manuscript cannot reflect them.[47] But fo. 54r, the last grisaille in the manuscript, shows three standing figures – Scipio, Masinissa, and Hannibal – in a row (pl. 32b). Here perhaps we have some indication as to what the standing figures of the Sala Virorum Illustrium looked like.[48]

The headpieces of the *DVI* manuscripts

Altichiero's contribution to the Petrarchan project was not limited to his work in the Sala Virorum Illustrium. Three of the most important manuscripts of the *DVI*, two of the *Epitome* and one of the *Compendium* are headed by miniatures from his hand, or by his workshop. These manuscripts,[49] originally all Carrarese possessions, are Lombardo's presentation copy of the *Epitome* of the *DVI* (BN MS Lat. 6069F), his presentation copy of the *Compendium* (BN MS Lat. 6069G), and a copy of a different version of the full text (BN MS Lat. 6069I). The prominence in two of these (6069F and 6069I), as well as in the Darmstadt manuscript, of a headpiece which ostensibly refers to a quite different work of Petrarch's, the *Trionfo della Fama*, invites comment and has in the past been subject to various explanations, none entirely satisfactory.

All three manuscripts were taken to Pavia as part of the wholesale abduction of the Carrarese library carried out after the Visconti seizure of Padua in 1388. BN Lat. 6069F, which has had Visconti arms painted over those of Francesco da Carrara, is the presentation copy of Lombardo's definitive text of the Latin *DVI*, in his own hand, and completed on 25 January 1379. The volume includes Petrarch's short preface dedicating the book to Francesco da Carrara, Lombardo's additions to Petrarch's biographies, and his (Lombardo's) explanatory notes and introductions. The verso of the fly leaf has the fine grisaille portrait of Petrarch in profile (pl. 35), with touches of colour added on the face – a drawing of exceptional quality securely attributable to Altichiero himself. The facing fo. 1r has a monochrome *Triumph of Fame* (pl. 36) as headpiece above the rubricated title and the beginning of the text of the preface. On fo. 142r, which follows

[47] See Mommsen, 'Sala Virorum Illustrium', p. 110. It is one of the minor oddities of the MS that some of the figure initials show the very scenes portrayed below them in the grisailles. Thus the initial of fo. 8v for Horatius Cocles shows him with his bridge, as in the adjacent narrative, and fo. 9r shows Camillus in his chariot, as below.

[48] Given that Taddeo di Bartolo may have worked in Padua, and in response to a signorial request, there may be some general reflections of the Sala Virorum Illustrium figures in his equivalents in the Palazzo Pubblico in Siena. See Sartori, 'La Cappella di S. Giacomo', p. 342, for Taddeo in Padua.

[49] Both MSS are described in Pellegrin, 'Manuscrits de Pétrarque en France', pp. 373–4 and 376–7, and in Martellotti, *Petrarca*, pp. xv–xvii and xxiv–xxvi.

the *explicit* of the life of Julius Caesar, Lombardo's note of the date and place of Petrarch's death, and his overall note marking the end of Petrarch's portion of the finished work, is a large word square, inscribed within a gold border, on the 25-letter text INCLITO FRANCESCO DE CARARIA, which can be read in all directions from the central letter I, picked out in gold. Above the square are the two words CLARISSIMO DUCI . . . and an erased third word (both Francesco il Vecchio and Francesco Novello da Carrara were dukes by courtesy of the Emperor Charles IV). The rest of this page is blank. Given the location of this feature between Petrarch's and Lombardo's sections of the text, it is probably intended to mark Francesco il Vecchio's continuing support and interest after Petrarch's death. Possibly the rather odd blank space was left for a portrait of the patron (or even, matching the Sala Virorum Illustrium, of Lombardo), for some reason never executed, to match that of Petrarch on the fly leaf. At all events, the whole character of this manuscript is testimony to the exceptional importance attached by all parties to the various aspects of the enterprise, and to its signorial support. Francesco da Carrara's determination that his name should for all time be associated with Petrarch's last great work is very clear.

The other ex-Carrarese volume of the *DVI* (6069I) is a slightly larger volume,[50] written in a more commonplace hand. It is a radically different text, incorporating material from the *DVI* in its earlier incarnations, beginning with the older and longer preface written by Petrarch when he was still working on the 'All-Ages' version of the book, the early lives of which are included here. The text omits all Lombardo's additions to the final format and ends with the life of Julius Caesar. Fo. 1r has another *Triumph of Fame* (pl. 37), similar to that of 6069F, with monochrome figures, but with colour added on the sky and vegetation. The figured initial below has a coloured portrait of Petrarch. The three *stemmi* inscribed within polylobes at the foot of fo. 1r have been scratched out, but the two outer ones can still be identified as the red *carri* of Carrara, and there need be no doubt that this volume also belonged to Francesco da Carrara. This volume is clearly not, as has sometimes been assumed, merely a duplicate of Lombardo's fine copy. It is a variant text, a complementary volume to the definitive Carrara-promoted text so beautifully presented in 6069F.

The relationship between the two Triumph headpieces and that of Darmstadt cod. 101, and the meaning and origins of this apparently anomalous iconography is of considerable importance in the context of Altichiero's standing within humanist circles, and demands careful consideration. In the years immediately following Petrarch's death Lombardo, in between bouts of splenetic correspondence with the humanists of Florence, who were anxious to know what had become of Petrarch's major unfinished works like the *DVI* and the *Africa*, was engaged in sorting Petrarch's literary remains, of which he had charge, and releasing various texts in decent versions.[51] It is clear that he

[50] BN Lat. 6069F measures 320 mm × 230 mm, BN Lat. 6069I, 360 mm x 250 mm.

[51] The terms of Petrarch's will, for which see Mommsen, *Petrarch's Testament*, pp. 197–235, leave it unclear what was to happen to his papers. Giuseppe Billanovich, *Petrarca Letterato 1. Lo Scrittoio del Petrarca*, p. 298 believes most of his books went straight into the Carrarese library even before the canon's house used by Petrarch in Padua was vacated by his family. It is clear, though, that in practice Lombardo controlled access to the papers, a fact which

lavished nothing like the attention on the text of the variant edition of the *DVI* contained in 6069I which he devoted to 6069F or to another copy he prepared for Coluccio Salutati in Florence (Vat. Ottoboni Lat. 1883).[52] Nor did he ensure that only the best and most recent texts were available, as he always did when the particular volume was of importance. Volume 6069I uses unrevised, corrupt, and occasionally incoherent, texts of various parts of the *DVI*.[53] It is clear that Lombardo was only concerned in this case to make the older version available in a decent *volume*, without wasting any time on textual niceties. What probably happened is that Francesco da Carrara, who had presumably discussed the genesis and history of the *DVI* with Petrarch (the two men had developed a close friendship), asked for a copy of the older version to go with his copy of the final text. The point is important because it makes it almost certain that 6069I, with the coloured headpiece, was completed after 6069F. It is scarcely conceivable that either Lombardo or Francesco da Carrara would have given priority to the variant until the up-to-date *Epitome* was in Francesco's hands.

This relationship between the manuscripts is reflected in that between the two headpieces. Though both show very clear traits of Altichieresque design, only the monochrome version of 6069F can be attributed to Altichiero himself. It exhibits a high standard of draughtsmanship – markedly superior, for instance, to that of the Darmstadt grisailles. The similarities between the composition and that of *St George on the Wheel* in S. Giorgio (pl. 98), noted by Mellini and Kruft,[54] are clear. The crowd on the right of the *Triumph*, though mounted, is echoed very precisely in the equivalent part of the fresco. The opposition in the front plane of figures turning fully away from others and fully towards the spectator is a feature common to both compositions, as is the marked swaying away of the crowd from the central action. The grouping and tilting of heads in the *Triumph* can be matched in the fresco, and the same goes for the figures with raised arms common to the miniature and to many of Altichiero's frescoes, including both Paduan *Crucifixions*. The extent to which Fame's chariot is felt to be arriving towards the front from a plane distinctly beyond that of the crowd rather than simply above it is typical of the inherently spatial nature of Altichiero's designs.

Comparison of a figure like Fame herself in the monochrome *Triumph*, one of Altichiero's most common female types and here drawn with a characteristic refinement of facial expression, with the equivalent in the coloured headpiece shows the latter's relative weakness of draughtsmanship. Fame is markedly coarser in 6069I, and the sense of an articulated body beneath the draperies is much less obvious. Most direct comparisons reinforce the weaknesses of the coloured version. The ensemble of Fame's chariot in 6069I, already despatialised by the surrounding mandorla, is both flatter in

alarmed the Florentines a great deal. For the exchange of letters between Padua and Florence see Bernardo, *Petrarch, Scipio and the Africa*, pp. 172–5.

52 See Martellotti, *Petrarca*, p. l and pp. lxviff.

53 The other early MS of this version, Vat. Lat. 1986, has the early lives from Adam to Hercules, but lacks the long preface of BN Lat. 6069I, to which it is in some ways related. It also omits Lombardo's additions. See Simpson, 'A New Codex of Petrarch's "De Viris Illustribus"', and Martellotti, *Petrarca*, pp. xxvi–xxviii. Simpson establishes that this MS was not copied from BN 6069I and that 'it is more probable that both were copied from a third manuscript in which the common errors existed' – p. 269.

54 Mellini, *Altichiero e Jacopo Avanzi*, p. 37. Kruft, *Altichiero und Avanzo*, p. 138 mentions the *Crucifixions* in this context.

itself, and, in effect if not in intention, set above, not behind, the crowd. While odd figures in the coloured *Triumph* clearly reproduce those of 6069F, as a set this part of the second *Triumph* is clearly a separate invention, not a straightforward copy. It is as clearly based on recognisable Altichieresque patterns, and several faces closely resemble examples seen in crowds in the surviving Paduan frescoes. The drawing of the mounted figures has its own refined quality, delicate and courtly at its best, where the monochrome hand is sharp and forceful.

The condition of the coloured headpiece is problematic. The figures have been touched up with white highlights, but even so they tend to get lost against the strong opaque blue of the sky. Where this blue meets the drawn figures the edges are often clumsily negotiated (particularly in the sky, where the *spiritelli* blow their trumpets) and it must be probable that this thick and rather coarse layer of colour was added as an afterthought. The drawing itself can be attributed to a member of Altichiero's workshop – a capable one – happier with the more gracious aspects of the shop style than with the monumental and spatial.

The inclusion of the two Triumphs in these manuscripts of the *DVI*, and of another in the Italian text volume in Darmstadt, which is visually very different and shows no signs whatever of Altichiero's influence, has been regarded as problematic ever since Julius von Schlosser gathered this material together. The traditional line, in brief, has been that since the three Triumphs neither belong, or seem to belong, in manuscripts of the *DVI*, nor even reflect at all closely the text of Petrarch's own poem the *Trionfo della Fama*, they must have been adapted from another context and be based on another source. This other source was identified by Dorothy Shorr[55] as Boccaccio's *Amorosa Visione*, a poem of 1342, in which the description of Fame's arrival has been credibly shown by Creighton Gilbert[56] to depend on a lost fresco by Giotto of *Vanagloria*, painted in the Milanese palace of Azzo Visconti in 1335. Gilbert develops from this an argument that the three manuscript Triumphs also depend on the fresco by Giotto (which was destroyed during rebuilding work in 1362) as does Boccaccio's poem, though via lost intermediaries. This idea is the only serious alternative as yet offered to the traditional belief that the headpieces reflected a fresco of the *Triumph of Fame* supposedly attached in some way to the Sala Virorum Illustrium.[57]

The relationship between Boccaccio's text and the miniatures is crucial, so I give the relevant passage in full. Boccaccio is describing a mural painting of 'terrestrial fame in the form of a lady':

> infra gran gente
> Donna pareva li leggiadra e pura.
> Tutti li soprastava veramenta
> Di ricche pietre coronata e d'oro,
> Nell'aspetto magnanima e possente:

[55] See Shorr, 'Some Notes on the Iconography of Petrarch's *Triumph of Fame*'.

[56] Gilbert, 'The Fresco by Giotto in Milan'.

[57] Discussions of the putative *Triumph* fresco are found in Schlosser, 'Ein Veronisches Bilderbuch', pp. 190ff; Mommsen, 'Sala Virorum Illustrium', p. 107; and Simon, 'Altichiero Versus Avanzo', p. 269.

Ardita sopra un carro tra costoro
Grande e trionfal lieta sedea,
Ornato tutto di frondi d'alloro,
Mirando questa gente: in man tenea
Una spada tagliente, con la quale
Che'l mondo minacciasse mi parea.
Il suo vestire a guisa imperiale
Era, e teneva nella man sinestra
Un pomo d'oro; e'n trono alle reale
Vidi sedeva, e della sua man destra
Due cavalli eran che cio petto forte
Traeano il carro tra la gente alpestra.
E intra l'altre cose, che iscorte
Quivi furon da me intorno a questa
Sovrana donna, nemica di morte,
Nel magnanimo aspetto fu, ch'a sesta
Un cerchio so movea grande e ritondo
Da pie passando a lei sopra la testa.
Ne credo che sia cosa in tutto'l mondo,
Villa, paese dimestico o strano,
Che non paresse dentro da quel tondo,
Era sopra costei, e non invano,
Scritto un verso, che dicea leggendo:
Io son la Gloria del popolo mondano.[58]

Shorr prefaces her translation of this passage with the remark that 'a study of the three headpieces shows the iconographic development of the Triumph of Fame'.[59] The familiar images of the *Triumph of Fame* in Florentine painting of the quattrocento are close to Boccaccio's text, much more so than the two headpieces of the Latin *DVI*. The Darmstadt *Triumph* of *c.* 1400 (fig. 58) is much closer to the Florentine cassone versions, and Shorr's remark crucially obscures the fact that such development, in the series of *DVI* headpieces under discussion, is *towards* Boccaccio, not proceeding from him. What must be the first of the three, that of BN Lat. 6069F, lacks the laurel leaves covering the chariot, the sword, the apple in Fame's left hand, the throne, the circle and the verse. Here Fame in her chariot simply advances into the crowd, which parts to receive her, while she tosses laurel wreaths to it. The coloured headpiece of BN Lat. 6069I adds a mandorla (which may represent the 'cerchia') and the word GLORIA written twice. Both these Carrarese headpieces contain elements foreign to Boccaccio's text: the wings on the figure of Fame, the four trumpeters with winged trumpets, and the laurel wreaths distributed by Fame. These elements the Darmstadt headpiece (for Gilbert the closest of the three to his Ur-*Triumph*) omits, and it incorporates the 'cerchia' proper, together with the throne, though it rather absurdly leaves out the chariot while retaining the two horses provided by the text to pull it. As Shorr points out, this last miniature also shows much more emphatically than the others the eagerness of the crowd to touch the goddess.

Gilbert, who notes both the anti-chronological dependence of the headpieces on Boccaccio's text and the accompanying qualitative decline, accounts for this 'apparent

[58] Quoted in Shorr, 'Triumph of Fame', pp. 103–4, n. 6. [59] *Ibid.*, p. 103.

paradox'[60] by relating these two aspects. The reason, in his view, why the first headpiece (BN Lat. 6069F) is the furthest from the source is precisely because it was the work of the most inventive artist, just as the work of the least capable, the author of the Darmstadt *Triumph*, adds nothing of his own (and, as his omission of the chariot shows, has some difficulty with what is given him in the source). Gilbert's argument is that the immediate visual prototype, probably located in Petrarch's (lost) autograph and preserved in Lombardo's own copy (also lost – and conjectural), probably reflected the lost fresco in Milan more closely than do the two Carrarese examples now in Paris.

Gilbert's argument depends in part on there being enough common material in the three headpieces for the nature of the shared source to be inferred from each of them individually, or from any two in combination. So he stresses the point that although the headpiece of BN Lat. 6069F seems at first not to reflect at all the singling out of six principal heroes in Giotto's fresco, of which we have a detailed eye-witness account, as it must if the link is to be at all credibly maintained by this example alone, 'when we look more closely, we can find them plainly'[61] which to my mind is considerably overstated. Even less in the headpiece of BN Lat. 6069I can such a memory of six highlighted figures be found. In fact the figures singled out in the most obvious way here, by having already received laurel crowns, add up to nine.

There is no reason to insist on a complete separation of Altichiero's *Triumph* altogether from the Ur-*Triumph*, which Gilbert established beyond reasonable doubt as being by Giotto and as being reflected by Boccaccio, but it is necessary to establish the chain of relationships in the immediate Paduan context more exactly. This involves equating anomalies in this part of his overall argument with parallel discrepancies in his (equally stimulating) attempt to establish why this Triumph material should be so pointedly and persistently connected with the texts of the *DVI*, the fundamental question.

Gilbert suggests that Petrarch, living in Milan in 1353, at a time when he was at work on the 'All-Ages' *DVI*, saw the fresco of *Vanagloria* by Giotto, of whom he was a warm admirer, shortly before its destruction, recognised in it parallels with his own work at the time (the fresco celebrated only military heroes) and, finding analogies between the loss of such a 'memorial of talent' and his own lifelong concern with the destruction of the truly excellent, later made these associations concrete by having a miniature based on the lost fresco painted for his own celebration of 'illustrious men . . . who achieved *gloriam* for their deeds'.[62] The perpetuation of the Triumph composition in later, posthumous, copies of the *DVI* follows on from this rather obviously, via Lombardo, who knew Petrarch's wishes.

This argument is unconvincing for several reasons. In the first place Petrarch never anywhere mentions the fresco of *Vanagloria*. As Mommsen pointed out, omission was as much a part of Petrarch's critical arsenal as direct attack. Thus as significant as his recommendation (to a Milanese) in the *Itinerarium Syriacum* to visit the Royal Chapel

60 Gilbert, 'Giotto in Milan', p. 60.

61 *Ibid.*, p. 61.

62 *Ibid.*, p. 56.

in Naples and see 'great memorials of (Giotto's) hand and talent'[63] – the frescoes on biblical subjects – is his failure to mention the secular frescoes of the *Nine Worthies* in the Castelnuovo there (which he must himself have seen). Simple omission may not be significant, but consideration of the known contents of Azzo Visconti's fresco (see below) suggests that Petrarch, far from seeing it as any kind of a parallel with his current or long-term ideas, would have viewed it with marked disapproval. This would explain his failure to mention it and, more significantly, his positive praise of Galeazzo Visconti's building projects, which necessitated the loss of the *Vanagloria*. This praise, rather than being a sign of Petrarch's 'immense egocentricity',[64] would simply mean that he was indifferent to the fresco's fate. It is very unlikely that Petrarch would have rated the survival of one fresco, even by Giotto, above his deepest and longest-held convictions, convictions which, I would argue, would have prevented him from finding anything to admire in the programme of the *Vanagloria* as it is described in Flamma's *Opusculum*.

The section for the year 1335 in Flamma's text describes Azzo's fresco in some detail, together with its location in a 'magna salla gloriosa nimis, ubi est depicta vanagloria subi . . . ubi depicti sunt illustres principes'.[65] These 'principes' are identified as Aeneas, Attila, Hector, Hercules, Charlemagne and Azzo himself. In addition to these are mentioned unnamed 'plures alii'. The specified six make sense as a set of warriors each representative of his 'nation' (taking Aeneas here as a Roman[66]). The conclusion to be drawn from the fresco, as Gilbert suggests, was that Azzo stood in relation to his 'nation' as did the others to theirs. Such equations between signorial patrons and figures from the historical and legendary past are fairly typical of such schemes – the Sala Grande amongst others. But we can be virtually certain Petrarch would never have stomached this particular set of equations. In the first place it celebrated two heroes we can be sure he would never have considered as illustrious by his definition: Attila and Charlemagne. Petrarch's attitude to Charlemagne – rare for his time – was wholly dismissive. He called him 'King Charles whom, by the cognomen of "the great", barbarous peoples dare to raise to the level of Pompey and Alexander.' By the same token Attila, acceptable in courtly circles as a hero of chivalric romances, is unlikely to have

[63] *Ibid.*, p. 55.

[64] Gilbert's argument, *ibid.*, p. 56, that Petrarch's silence on the subject of this destruction was due to his wish to avoid saying anything detrimental about Galeazzo Visconti is not unlikely as such, but it assumes there to have been some exceptional need for Petrarch to remain silent. My point is that in all probability no such reason existed.

[65] Flamma, 15–17, quoted in *ibid.*, p. 52. The lacuna is in Flamma's text, which leaves a gap for the addition of the missing words. The late Professor Andrew Martindale examined the MS and communicated his observations to me in a letter of 18/8/94:

> The scribe left a lot of other gaps in his writing, mostly (and very clearly) dates, numbers, ages, etc. I assume that they were never filled in in the *urtext*. This omission is, however, an odd one. I think the space represents what the scribe thought he would need when he finally perfected his 'copy'. Consequently, although it may be a gap in his original, it seems more likely to be something he couldn't read. 'Subi' is a curious truncation, since . . . there is not very much it could be enlarged into except SUBIECTA. In that case, it would have to be AD something; and that 'something' has to contain in its script up to *c.* 25 minims to fill the line. Perhaps DIVINAM GLORIAM?

[66] See Gilbert, 'Giotto in Milan', p. 54.

survived the far more critical scrutiny of Petrarch's historical intelligence or his inveterate Romanism.[67]

Secondly, even if Azzo were as well regarded by Petrarch as Francesco da Carrara came to be, it is very doubtful that he would have approved of his being equated with men with real claims to be illustrious, like Hercules and Hector. He steadfastly refused to make such equations in his work, deeming none of his contemporaries worthy, or even capable of becoming worthy, of such comparisons. Such easy equations are against the whole thrust of the *DVI*, whose function was not to establish analogies between the men of antiquity and modern princes, but to underline the absolute gulf that lay between them. The matter of Azzo Visconti's fresco must have struck him as, at best, muddled and ignorant, and in all probability as actively harmful and, as he was so fond of saying, 'barbarous'. Any connection between Petrarch and the specific material of the lost fresco must have been antithetical, and the attachment of the *Triumph of Fame* to the *DVI* on these grounds must be ruled out.

No more persuasive is the traditional suggestion that there was a fresco of this subject in the Sala Virorum Illustrium. There is no mention of such a composition, and our knowledge of the decorations of the Carrarese Palace is unusually full[68] (and it is hard to see where it could have been if it was attached in any way to the Sala[69]). In any case the presence of such a fresco would still leave the problem of why apparently disparate material should be associated in the first place.

One obvious point, which is never made, is that, according to the evidence as we actually find it, the *Triumph of Fame* surfaces in conjunction with the *DVI* only *after* Petrarch's death, and that we would do better to look for the answer to this question in the circles dominated by Lombardo and Francesco da Carrara, with Altichiero translating their wishes into visual terms. How is it that Lombardo or Francesco da Carrara,

[67] See Mommsen, *Petrarch's Testament*, p. 120. The reference to Charlemagne is in *Fam*. I, 4: 'Carolum regem quem magni cognomine equare Pompeio et Alexandro audent'. Petrarch's opinion of the Medieval Empire and its claims to continuity from ancient Rome is correspondingly dismissive – see *ibid*., pp. 121ff. Mommsen also comments that: 'men like Attila or Charlemagne . . . certainly did not qualify . . . as *Viri Illustres*, but they were men whose power was the gift of *fortuna* and not of *virtus*'. Of the nine heroes of Naples (Solomon, Samson, Alexander, Hector, Aeneas, Achilles, Paris, Hercules, Caesar) and their wives, Mommsen comments: 'if any conclusion at all can be drawn . . . it may be that Petrarch considered that selection of heroes to be completely arbitrary and therefore hardly worth noticing; in other instances as well, in order to show his rejection of matters alien to him, Petrarch simply passed over them in silence', *ibid*., p. 116. It may be that for Petrarch not only must such men be fully worthy of such treatment (some of those in Naples would qualify), but they must also form a set with a correspondingly focused meaning. Such criteria clearly exclude Azzo Visconti's fresco. Petrarch's opinions of the leaders of his own time were generally acerbic:

> I thank those contemporary princes who free me from this labour [i.e. writing about them in the *DVI*], for they contribute material not for history but for satire. And though I realise that some of them have recently become famous because of military victories, these occurred because of good fortune or the inertia of the enemy, so that the success was not at all a question of military valour or true glory.

from the long preface, translated by Kohl, 'Petrarch's Prefaces', pp. 138–9. This is the most succinct statement of Petrarch's distinction between the genuinely illustrious and the merely lucky.

[68] For which see below.

[69] Mommsen, 'Sala Virorum Illustrium', p. 107 lends his backing to the theory of a Triumph fresco. Wilkins, *Petrarch's Later Years*, p. 300, n. 31 and Gilbert, 'Giotto in Milan', pp. 59–60, n. 94 reject Mommsen's arguments on the grounds that there is nowhere for the fresco to have been.

or both, felt the *Triumph* to be appropriate to the *DVI*? Both men are likely, I think, to have seen the completion of the joint *DVI*–Sala project, of which the fine copy of the *Epitome* was in a sense the keystone, as a monument to the dead poet and to their association with him. The survival of the memory and achievements of greatness through Fame – 'Sovrana donna, nemica di morte' as Boccaccio puts it – was always a major concern of Petrarch's, never more so than in his last years. Such a concern rather movingly informs the short preface to the *DVI* and it is obviously central to the *Trionfo della Fama*, which he left unfinished. My argument, against the trend of the recent literature, is simply that the *Triumph* headpieces *do* in fact have a connection with that poem, and that the subject matter of the *Triumph* in turn can be shown to have immediate relevance to the *DVI*.

Petrarch's view on Fame, Glory and Virtue was that they were all interconnected. In the *Secretum* we find that 'glory is like a shadow of virtue . . . whoever achieves true glory must also have acquired virtue'[70] and that a proper concern (i.e. one that involves the acquisition of virtue) with earthly glory is appropriate in this life, not to be dismissed by inappropriate comparisons with the greater glory of afterlife. In canzone no. 119 he develops this idea, with Glory and Virtue as sisters – a concern with the former inevitably leads to a knowledge of the latter. The poet becomes a follower of Gloria, the younger sister – 'una donna più bella assai ch'l sole, / E più lucente' – who grants him a vision of Virtue. Finally he receives a laurel crown.

Petrarch developed, as Mommsen pointed out, a concept of *virtus* markedly more secular than Dante's, for instance. His *virtus* is not, to be sure, synonymous with the amoral *virtù* which might be possessed in abundance by any successful *signore*, but it incorporates the concepts of capability and will central to that concept. Thus 'a truly "illustrious" man, who by his own choice is possessed of *virtus*, is able to shape his own destiny, as well as being the maker of history'.[71] The *Treatise on Good Government* which Petrarch wrote for Francesco da Carrara reconciles pagan and Christian concepts of virtue in this context and confirms the point that a ruler's legitimate concern with earthly fame is not displeasing to God.

The relevance of all these interconnected strands of Petrarch's thought to the didactic function of the *DVI*, with its concentration on the achievements of men of action in dealing with affairs of state is clear. The exemplary nature of the *DVI* and its extension the Sala Virorum Illustrium ('nothing is found except what leads to virtues or to the contrary of virtues'[72]) may be viewed against the background of the more detailed

[70] Petrarch, *Secretum*, book III, quoted in Bernardo, *Petrarch, Scipio and the Africa*, p. 55. See also Bishop, *Petrarch and his World*, pp. 211–12.

[71] Mommsen, *Petrarch's Testament*, p. 195.

[72] Kohl, 'Petrarch's Prefaces', p. 143. Petrarch's concept of history, set out here in the short preface to the *DVI* of *c.* 1370, is substantially based on that set forth by Livy himself in the *Ab Urbe Condita* ('in that record you can find for yourself and your country both examples and warnings; fine things to take as models, base things, rotten through and through, to avoid', Livy, *Ab Urbe Condita*, vol. I, p. 34). Petrarch's view of the uses and importance of historical study reverberates throughout the later Renaissance. Directly dependent on it is Salutati's view: 'I am glad that you have loved especially the historians, whose task it is to hand down the memory of past deeds to posterity, so that we by imitation of the example of kings, nations and illustrious men may exceed or equal the virtues of our forerunners . . . since the knowledge of things past warns princes, teaches peoples and instructs

advice contained within the *Treatise*, dedicated to a man who has within him 'a tiny spark that can be increased by fanning and will eventually burst into flame', who is 'such a true friend of virtue', who 'wants to be a good ruler'.[73]

Early in the *Trionfo della Fama* Gloria appears described in terms which develop the 'sister' theme of the canzone, as a stellar goddess behind whom stands a greater power. She is, in effect, Venus:

> quando, mirando intorno su per l'erba,
> vidi da l'altra parte giugner quella
> che trae l'uom del sepolcro e'n vita il serba.
> Quale in sul giorno un'amorosa stella
> suol venir d'oriente innanzi al sole
> ch s'accompagna volentier con ella

The goddess is accompanied:

> Da man destra, ove gli occhi in prima porsi,
> la bella donna avea Cesare e Scipio,
> ma quel più presso a gran pena m'accorsi:
> L'un di vertute, e non d'Amor mancipio,
> L'altro d'entrambi; e poi mi fu mostrata
> dopo sì gloriosa e bel principio
> gente di ferro e di valore armata[74]

and the 'gente di ferro e di valore armata' are identified throughout the ensuing first section of the poem. The list, though much longer, duplicates to an extent that of the *DVI*. The singling out of Julius Caesar and Scipio is significant. By this stage in his life these two men had become Petrarch's most constant points of comparison when dealing with men of action, each possessed of contrasting and complementary virtues, and each receiving in the *DVI* a biography massively longer than the rest, biographies both subjected to a process of revision and amplification more intensive than anything Petrarch lavished on any other part of the book. In Petrarch's final estimate these two men were the most exceptional figures of antiquity and they constituted the ultimate standards against which all contemporary princes were judged.[75]

The monochrome *Triumph of Fame* does not explicitly reflect this aspect of the poem, but it does share with it the sudden arrival of the goddess (and the headpiece of 6069I shows the beams of light mentioned by Petrarch and not by Boccaccio), together with the 'gente di ferro'.[76] It can be argued that the headpiece of 6069F fits the opening of

footnote 72 (*cont.*)
individuals on conduct' (Salutati, *Epistolario* II. 290, trans. Whitfield, *Petrarch and the Renascence*, p. 101). The line of influence passes via Enea Silvio Piccolomini – 'Where letters cease darkness covers the land; and a Prince who cannot read the lessons of history is a helpless prey of flattery and intrigue' – *ibid.*, p. 110 and down to Macchiavelli's *Discorsi*.

[73] Kohl and Witt, *Earthly Republic*, p. 40.

[74] Petrarch, *Trionfo della Fama*, 7–12 and 22–8.

[75] See Bernardo, *Petrarch, Scipio and the Africa*, *passim* but especially pp. 73ff.

[76] Neither the distribution of laurel wreaths nor the chariot are mentioned by Petrarch. But they would probably have been taken for granted – in this non-descriptive context – as traditional props of a triumph. The significance of the laurel for Petrarch himself needs no underlining: 'from Scipio to Caesar to Robert (of Naples), as from Homer to Ennius to Petrarch, it is the "fragrant . . . incorruptible . . . and sacred" laurel whose verdure recalls both the drama of the Caesars and that of Apollo, and whose "immortality . . . symbolizes the immortality of fame sought through warfare or through genius" that will forever continue to decorate the forehead of friends of true virtue and learning', *ibid.*, p. 207, quoting from Bruère, 'Lucan and Petrarch's *Africa*', p. 83.

the *Trionfo*, albeit loosely, better than it does the *Amorosa Visione*, which has, as Petrarch's poem does not, a set of explicit pointers to visual imagery, by means of which we can be certain whether or not any given picture does reproduce the poem. In other words, the Petrarch is just the sort of text which an image would be expected to fit loosely, for it offers little that is visually explicit, whereas the Boccaccio is a text so explicit that the extent to which an image follows it can be judged rather easily (hence perhaps the eagerness with which the mainstream iconographic tradition for the *Triumph of Fame* came to reach for Boccaccio/Giotto).

The entirely different headpiece of the presentation volume of the *Compendium* of the *DVI* can safely be attributed to Altichiero himself. This miniature (pl. 38), on the verso of the fly leaf of BN Lat. 6069G, shows the Carrarese Bull pushing the Lion of St Mark into the sea, a reference to the long-running Paduan–Venetian conflict which rumbled on throughout Altichiero's years in Padua. Here indeed there is a poor fit between the headpiece and the text following it. In addition to the qualities noted by Simon ('the handling ranges from the finely detailed . . . to the extraordinarily free with all the appearance of a watercolour'[77]) there is a powerful sense of atmosphere, authentically wet and marshy, often lost in reproduction, but convincingly conveyed in the miniature by the same kind of tonal shading and blending seen in the best preserved of Altichiero's frescoes. This little allegory, with its border 'of a type used in fresco',[78] may reflect a lost large-scale version somewhere in the Carrarese Palace, but it is more likely to have been done for this specific context alone. The date of its execution, given the completion date of Lombardo's writing out of the text – 9 December 1380 – coincides so exactly with the Paduan conquest of Venetian Chioggia in the early autumn and winter of the same year,[79] a victory which for a time seemed to presage the complete expulsion of the Venetians from the mainland, that we can hardly doubt that this miniature expressly commemorates the event. The ship carries a pile of what looks like salt, a major object of dispute between the two powers. The setting, reed-fringed and complete with wading bird, recalls the landscape of the Po Delta, through which the Paduans had been fighting for some months.

It seems clear that Altichiero's role in the Paduan Petrarch project was central, at least on the visual side. The evidence confirms his association with the lost frescoes of the Sala Virorum Illustrium, and he is undoubtedly the author of the *Portrait of Petrarch* which survives. The headpieces of the key manuscripts of the project, as well as the profile portrait of BN Lat. 6069F, can be attributed to him or to his workshop. We see him once again developing new iconographies and transforming existing ones, perhaps in collaboration with the greatest humanist of the fourteenth century. The evidence of Altichiero's four surviving portraits of Petrarch leave little doubt that he must have taken the poet's likeness in the flesh, and it must at least be likely that contact between

77 Simon, 'Altichiero Versus Avanzo', p. 268, n.

78 *Ibid.* The border has alternating lozenges in yellow and a cool mid-green punctuated by rosettes in a light brick-pink, and is surrounded by a flat red strip reminiscent of fresco borders in Verona and Padua.

79 See, i.e., Gatari, *Cronaca Carrarese*, pp. 162ff. for this campaign.

them involved discussions at the planning stage of the Sala, perhaps via Lombardo della Seta.

The Sala Virorum Illustrium was the grandest of the many painted rooms of the Carrarese Palace and, as Savonarola's account shows, its exceptional importance was recognised during the quattrocento. For most of the people who saw it it must have seemed a fitting climax to the whole series of palace apartments decorated with themes from the Antique, the Sala Thebana, the Camera Neronis, the Camera Camilli, the Camera Herculis and the rest.[80] But it is important to contrast the Sala Virorum Illustrium with these, just as Petrarch's purposeful, scrupulous and essentially didactic classicism must be contrasted with the 'chivalric' interpretation of Roman history with which he was so impatient. In the majority of palace schemes, including most of those devoted to collections of 'illustrious' men (and occasionally women), of which the Carrarese Palace had its share, as well as those treating historical or mythical material (a distinction blurred for most people, if not for Petrarch), broad flattering equations were made between the deeds of great figures of the past and those of the *signore*, his family, or his contemporaries. The exclusion policy to which Petrarch adhered, with its firm insistence that no contemporary prince could validly be equated with the heroes of antiquity, makes the opposite point. The majority of such schemes, including the Sala Grande, conferred status or suggested lines of ancestry. They did not instruct, or persuade, let alone admonish by example. Precedents for such a view of history existed locally, associated with the fierce Guelph humanism of the pre-Carrarese Paduan commune, but in Petrarch's time this attitude had largely vanished, though it was beginning to flourish in the republican context of Florence. Altichiero's role in developing the iconography of the specifically Petrarchan view of history must be seen, in this wider context of the *rapprochement* between the visual arts and what has been called the 'civic humanism' of Petrarch and his followers, to be as central as his position in the narrower context of the Sala Virorum Illustrium.

80 See Gasparotto, 'La Reggia' and 'Gli Ultimi Affreschi', and Gasparotto's source Gloria, *Documenti inediti intorno al Petrarca*. These rooms are also discussed in Schmitt, 'Zur Wiederbelebung', pp. 170ff.

5

THE CHAPEL OF S. GIACOMO

Like all cities, Padua fostered the cults of its tutelary saints. The city long enjoyed the protection of its patrons Sts Prosdocimo, first Bishop of Padua, his successor Daniele, and Giustina, an early Christian martyr. The great abbey dedicated to St Giustina also houses a major relic of St Luke the Evangelist,[1] whose cult, surprisingly perhaps, the Paduans never promoted with anything like the intensity of Venetian identification with St Mark. Instead, from the early thirteenth century Padua's destiny became inextricably linked with the reputation of a Franciscan preacher from Lisbon who lived rather briefly in Padua but died in Paduan territory and was buried in the Franciscan church only recently established in the city. St Anthony of Padua, as he became in 1232, the year after his death, was a preacher of formidable power who already enjoyed a considerable reputation, and his cult grew enormously following his canonisation. The number of pilgrims wishing to visit his tomb soon put unmanageable pressures on the modest church of S. Maria Mater Domini which housed it, and by 1238 or even earlier the necessity of building a larger church was recognised and had been translated into a concrete plan.[2]

From this date until the early fourteenth century the Paduans gradually raised round the shrine of St Anthony one of the most astonishing buildings of medieval Europe. The original plan seems to have been for a large aisleless preaching church like the upper church of S. Francesco at Assisi, incorporating the existing structure as a lateral chapel. This plan was successively enlarged and elaborated with the addition of a second transept to the west of the original one and nave aisles (these by 1263), a fully fledged chevet with nine radial chapels (by 1290), and, most spectacularly, a covering of domes laid out on a Latin cross plan (by *c.* 1330). This ever-expanding design necessitated sending the body of the saint on an extended tour of the building as each section was finished: from the old church to the centre of the new one in 1263, probably to the chevet in 1310,[3] and finally to its present resting place in the northern arm of the larger, western,

[1] Wolters, *La Scultura Veneziana Gotica*, vol. I, pp. 151–2 discusses the tomb of St Luke. For the cults of saints in Padua see Marcianò, *Padova 1399*.

[2] For the construction of the Santo, see Lorenzoni, *L'Edificio del Santo di Padova*, pp. 17–30, and the contribution by Salvatori, 'Costruzione della Basilica dall'Origine al Secolo XIV', in *ibid.*, pp. 31–81.

[3] Lorenzoni, *L'Edificio*, pp. 24–30 discusses the translation question.

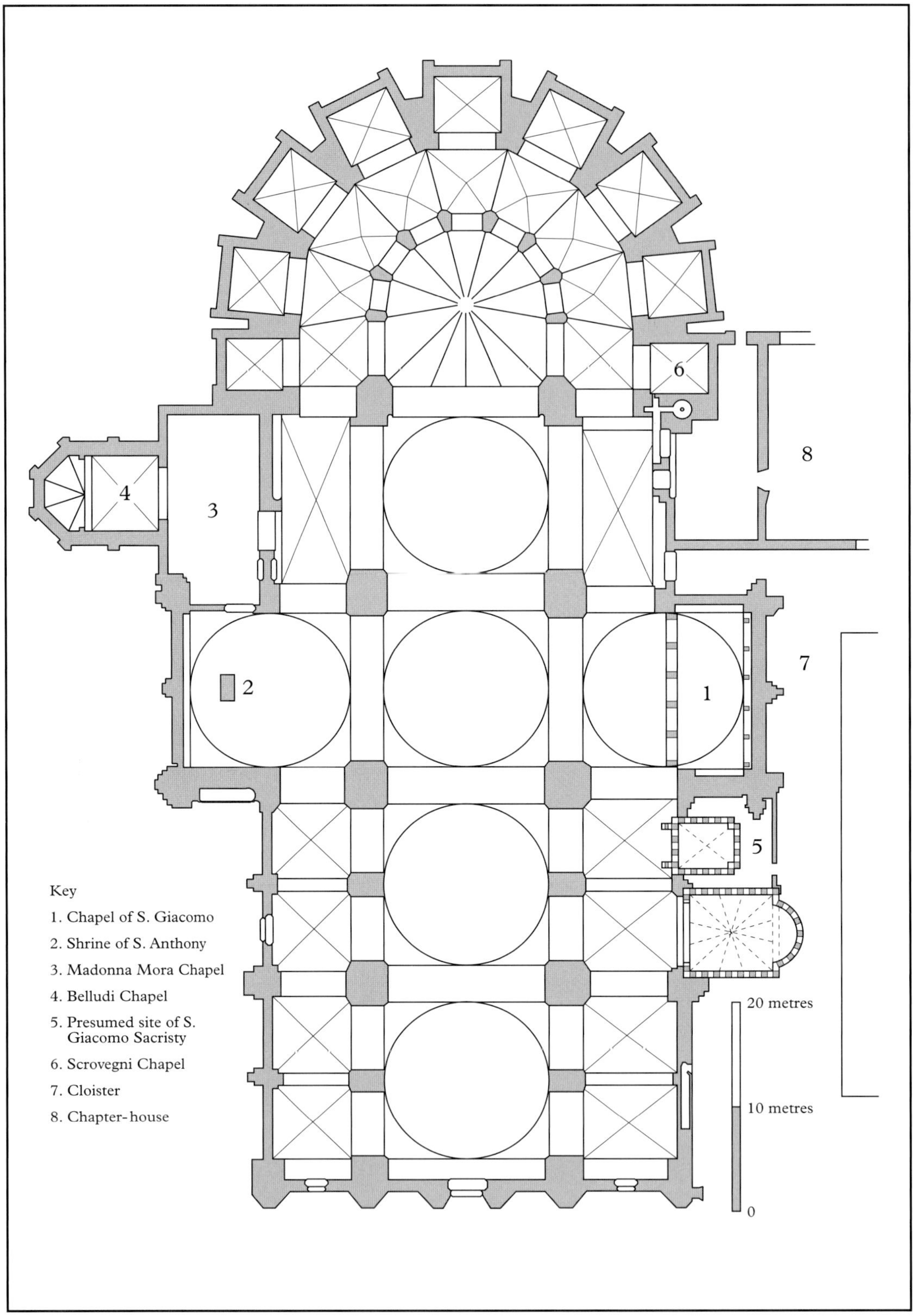

Drawing II Padua, Basilica del Santo. Ground plan.

transept in 1350, a translation made with great ceremony and witnessed by, amongst others, Petrarch.[4]

Stylistically the Santo presents a supremely confident, and often quite surprising, amalgamation of several architectural traditions, combining the brickwork and western screen facades of Lombardy and Emilia with Angevin Gothic in certain aspects of the interior, and most obviously with a Venetian model for the domes. But the restless external jostling of the domes, raised on high brick drums and interspersed with minarets and towers, is quite unlike S. Marco in effect. Partial glimpses of it from the surrounding streets are never less than intriguing. The Santo is powerful, even truculent, in character, and it is certainly unique. These assertive characteristics may reflect the close involvement of the Paduan commune in the funding of the building campaign. St Anthony, in his lifetime and posthumously, was closely associated with resistance to Ezzelino da Romano[5] and with the cause of Paduan self-determination, and the extraordinary prestige of the Santo is reflected in a design which the Paduans made sure no one who had seen it would forget. In various forms it haunts the architecture of the frescoes Altichiero painted within its own precincts, often greatly transformed, but quoted quite recognisably in the votive fresco in S. Giacomo (domes), the *Fall of the Idols* (domes again), in *St Catherine Refusing to Worship Pagan Idols* (a compressed version of the whole building) and the *Funeral of St Lucy* (facade), all in S. Giorgio (pls. 101, 105, 115).

One of the advantages of the greatly enlarged size of the new basilica, from the point of view of the friars and citizens alike, was that it allowed plenty of scope for the wealthier citizens to mark their association with the saint, in life, by means of donations for the fabric or its decoration, and in death, by means of burial 'apud locum Sancti Antonii Confessoris'. Types of patronage varied according to taste and pocket,[6] and the range of options was helpfully wide. A simple votive fresco, or a lamp or other item of furnishing to be placed near the shrine came relatively cheap. The really wealthy families built more substantial tombs, either in one of the nine radial chapels or elsewhere in the church. In both cases the proximity to the body of St Anthony was the essential factor, and this is stressed in the many surviving documents recording such acts of patronage. Enrico Scrovegni, for example, gave money in 1300 for the building fund,[7] and his family also held one of the ambulatory chapels. This still retains fragments of a fresco scheme by Giotto's workshop.[8] The crowding of tombs round the shrine produced its

[4] Petrarch mentions this event in *Fam.* IX, 13: 'hodierno die minoris corpus Antonii ingenti populi devotione transvexit . . . cui translationi ego interfui'. His presence is discussed by Cortese, 'Il Petrarca e le Traslazioni di Sant'Antonio di Padova', pp. 315ff. and Lorenzoni, *L'Edificio*, pp. 23–4. The argument for a 1310 translation into the chevet, allowing the construction of the domes above the transept and giving some reason for the construction of the ambulatory – arguably superfluous with the shrine in the transept – is persuasive.

[5] For Paduan views of Ezzelino da Romano see Hyde, *Padua*.

[6] Marangon and Bellinati, 'La Basilica del Santo nei Documenti d'Archivio e Storico-Letterati dalle Origini al 1405', pp. 195ff., give extracts of numerous documents recording patronage of various kinds in the Santo.

[7] *Ibid.*, p. 213.

[8] See D'Arcais, 'Presenza di Giotto al Santo', pp. 3–13 for Giotto's work in the Santo, especially pp. 5–7 for the former Scrovegni Chapel of S. Caterina (afterwards of S. Angela) and its fragmentary trecento frescoes, of which she gives two illustrations (pls. 1 and 2).

own problems, something illustrated by the donor of 1310 who arranged for a new tomb to be erected near that already occupied by other members of his family, but had to specify that no one but himself should ever lie in this new tomb except his wife 'si ibidem sepeliri voluerit'.[9] Simone Lupi's crowded tomb – four adults in a single sarcophagus (fig. 1) – is another case in point.[10] A more dignified opportunity for family patronage was provided by the new chapel of the Madonna Mora, created out of the surviving fabric of S. Maria Mater Domini, venerated as the original site of St Anthony's tomb and situated immediately next to the new location of the shrine. In 1364 this was renovated by the Negri family, who, in a mixture of piety and family pride entirely characteristic of this kind of patronage, placed the family coat of arms prominently outside as well as inside the chapel.[11]

Patronage of this sort commonly furnished opportunities for painters, and the Santo still contains a number of frescoed tombs of fine quality.[12] But all these tombs and chapels, however splendid, are overshadowed by the Chapel of S. Giacomo, begun in 1372, with architecture and sculpture by Andriolo de'Santi of Venice[13] and frescoes largely by Altichiero (pls. 39–41). This, which fills the whole of the lower part of the southern arm of the west transept, is one of the most elaborate and splendid of all European funerary chapels, a peak of Italian Gothic art, and further testimony to the exceptional levels of patronage emanating from the north Italian courts in the later trecento.

The man responsible for this chapel was neither a king nor a *signore*, not a member of the signorial family, nor even a native of Padua. Bonifacio Lupi, marchese of Soragna, Parmese exile, sometime mercenary and all-purpose courtier to the Carraresi (pl. 68), was nevertheless one of the most remarkable men of his time.[14] It is obvious that he and his wife Caterina de'Francesi were extremely rich. What also stands out is the extraordinary status he must have enjoyed to have been allowed to build a chapel so dominant and ostentatious and on such an exceptional site. It is clear from the position of his chapel that it was intended to mirror that of St Anthony himself, facing it across the transept. Indeed the contract for the Chapel of S. Giacomo makes this mimicry quite explicit (for example, the tabernacles on the outside of the new chapel are to be 'come

[9] Marangon and Bellinati, 'La Basilica del Santo nei Documenti', p. 216.

[10] For this tomb see Gonzati, *La Basilica di S. Antonio di Padova*, vol. II, pp. 42–4.

[11] For Negri patronage and the Madonna Mora Chapel see Ganguzza Billanovich, 'La Cappella della Madonna Mora e dell'Arca in un Nuovo Documento del XIV Secolo', and Marangon and Bellinati, 'La Basilica del Santo nei Documenti', p. 225 (Oct. 29 1364) and p. 226 (Apr. 23 1371).

[12] Three nearby tombs testify to this: those of Federico Lavellongo (d.1373) and Nicolò and Bonzanello da Vigonza (*c.* 1380), with frescoes by Giusto de'Menabuoi, in the passage from the church to the cloister, and that of Gerardo, Alberto and Giovanni Bolparo (*c.* 1382) in the passage from the Magnolia Cloister to the Novices' Cloister. The Lavellongo tomb has a *Madonna of Humility* in her apocalyptic guise in the lunette. The artist, not Altichiero, as Sartori, 'La Cappella di S. Giacomo', p. 279 suggested, seems nevertheless to have studied his work. The Bolparo tomb frescoes, in poor condition, also show signs of Altichiero's influence in the lunette *Coronation of the Virgin*. Bonzanello da Vigonza, a leading Carrarese captain, was also a friend of Petrarch's, and the poet left him horses in his will – see Selvatico, *Guida di Padova*, p. 104, n. 32.

[13] The text of Bonifacio's contract with Andriolo de'Santi is given by Sartori, 'Nota su Altichiero', pp. 311–14.

[14] For a general sketch of Bonifacio Lupi's life see *ibid.*, pp. 321–2.

fue mostrato ne la deta capella dipincta').[15] The present chapel of St Anthony is a largely sixteenth-century creation,[16] but its original Gothic format, with frescoes by Stefano da Ferrara,[17] and an arcade whose columns now support the portico of the Servite church in Padua, is evidently reflected, perhaps rather closely, in the design of Bonifacio's chapel. The coupling of the chapels confirms what had always been latent since St Antony's shrine was placed in the transept rather than the chevet, a lateral, north–south axis as important as the usual one from west to east.

Bonifacio's family suffered in a rather extreme form the unstable and itinerant fate of many magnatial families in signorial north Italy,[18] more so even than the Cavalli. To judge from the numbers of the Lupi who are documented as living in Padua in the later fourteenth century, the family had collectively adopted this city as their second home. But there is also evidence that they never abandoned their desire to return to their ancestral lands at Soragna and resume their part in the civic life of Parma, where they had for so long been powerful.

Men of the Lupi family are recorded in Parma in the important communal offices of *podestà*, consul, or rector from as early as 1182, in common with members of the other great Parmese families – the Rossi, the Pallavicini, and the da Correggio. All of these names reverberate consistently through the history of north Italy during the thirteenth and fourteenth centuries. The earliest Lupi *podestà* of Parma was Guido I in 1202, from whom the Paduan Lupi were descended. Guido married into the Rossi (as his ancestors had into the Pallavicini), and the association between the Lupi and the Rossi survived into the trecento. The commemoration of this association is one of the functions of Bonifacio Lupi's chapel, which contains, as well as his own tomb, those of four male members of the Rossi family, all of whom had died many years before and were now splendidly rehoused. In 1347 the Emperor Charles IV gave a charter confirming the Lupi as marchesi of Soragna, but this merely confirmed an existing fief – they were using the title in the thirteenth century, and the chronicler Fra Salimbene habitually refers to them as 'Marchiones Lupi'.[19]

Soragna is situated between Parma and Cremona, a little to the north of Fidenza, and it seems to have been well suited as a power base and a defensible retreat.[20] The frequency with which it was attacked, destroyed, and rebuilt well into the trecento tends to confirm its value in this respect. The Lupi must have used Soragna as a fall-back

[15] *Ibid*, p. 313, no. 16.

[16] See Alvarez, 'La Basilica del Santo nei Restauri e Ampliamenti dal Quattrocento al Tardo Barocco', pp. 110–11, and Selvatico, *Guida di Padova*, pp. 69–74.

[17] The original fresco decoration of the Chapel of St Anthony was paid for by the notary Francesco Salgeri. The document of 5 March 1350 recording this is published by Marangon and Bellinati, 'La Basilica del Santo nei Documenti', p. 224. The frescoes, scenes from the life of St Anthony, were first attributed to Stefano da Ferrara by Savonarola – 'Estque prima (capella) Antonio nostro suis cum pictis miraculis manu Stephanu ferrariensis dedicata', quoted by Ragghianti, *Pittura tra Giotto e Pisanello*, p. 93. This attribution, followed by Michiel and Vasari, who also attributed to Stefano a Madonna on one of the nave piers of the Santo, is also discussed by D'Arcais, 'Presenza di Giotto al Santo', p. 13.

[18] See Pezzana, *Storia della Città di Parma*, vol. 1, for the Lupi in Parma. See also the *Chronicon Parmense*. Most north Italian chronicles have at least occasional references to the Lupi.

[19] See Pezzana, *Storia della Città di Parma*, vol. 1, p. 62.

[20] For Soragna see Schumann, *Authority and the Commune, Parma 833–1133*, pp. 61–4.

position when their position in Parma itself became too unstable, as it did whenever the Ghibelline interest triumphed there. As leading Guelphs, like the da Correggio and the Rossi, the Lupi sustained the Parmese opposition to Frederick II following the election of Pope Innocent IV in 1243. They were expelled in 1245, re-entered in 1247, and were again expelled in 1250 by victorious Ghibellines from Cremona (from which city the Lupi themselves may have originated). This pattern repeated itself in various forms more or less incessantly for the next century. From 1331 the Lupi supported John of Luxembourg in his ephemeral control of Parma, and several of them, with various of the Rossi, fought for John at the Battle of San Felice in 1332, against a Veronese/Milanese coalition. After this victory John's son, the future Charles IV, knighted Marsiglio, Pietro and Andreasso Rossi and Raimondino Lupi on the field of battle. Marsiglio and Pietro are buried in the Chapel of S. Giacomo, and Raimondino Lupi was Altichiero's second major Lupi patron in Padua. After becoming emperor Charles IV maintained warm relations[21] with the Lupi, lasting until his death, and he frequently supported them, on paper at least, in their attempts to regain their castle and estates of Soragna.

These were finally lost, not for once as a result of the habitual Parmese infighting, but during the course of the seemingly inexorable rise of Visconti power in Lombardy. When Luchino Visconti took control of Parma in September 1346 the fate of the Lupi as permanent exiles was virtually sealed, and their considerable contribution (for good or ill) to trecento history from now on took place outside their native lands. Luchino systematically broke the power of the Parmese nobility, stripped them of their estates, and all the charters secured from Charles IV could not alter the reality of the situation. In 1350 Bonifacio Lupi and his father Ugolotto were granted a safe-conduct allowing them access to Parma, with Visconti permission. But on Ugolotto's death in 1351 Bonifacio was forced to swear allegiance to the Visconti, renounce the titles and rights invested in the imperial diploma of 1347, and offer financial security against breaking this promise.[22] After initially making efforts to comply, Bonifacio evidently decided enough was enough. In 1354 Charles IV again obliged him with a declaration that the promise sought by the Visconti was unjust and non-binding, but by this time Bonifacio may have resigned himself to exile.

He could be assured, at least, of a warm welcome in Padua. His father had served under the city's *podestà* in 1346, and his sister Donella is recorded as living there in the same year, along with other Parmese like Andrea Rossi and Bartolomeo Piacentini, a man of great standing in Carrarese Padua with whom Bonifacio was closely associated for the rest of his life. Bonifacio's path was presumably also smoothed by the memory of the exertions of his uncles Pietro, Marsiglio and Rolando Rossi during the anti-Scaligeri campaign which finally won Padua for the Carraresi in 1336/7.[24] Bonifacio was

21 See Pezzana, *Storia della Città di Parma*, vol. 1, pp. 24, 27, 33–4, 37, 39, 77–8, 82, 83–84.

22 *Ibid.*, p. 24. The document survives in the archives from Soragna as Arch. Sor. A. III. 29 (23 May 1350).

23 *Ibid.*, p. 34.

24 The role of the Rossi in wresting Padua from the Scaligeri, especially the heroics of Pietro Rossi, who died in the assault on Monselice on 7 August 1337, features in many chronicles. See , e.g., Gatari, *Cronaca Carrarese*, p. 18; Azarii, *Liber Gestorum in Lombardia*, pp. 169–70; the *Chronicon Estense*, etc. Marsilio Rossi's death a week later, of 'fatiche di guerra', is mentioned by Giovanni Villani, *Cronica*, p. 139.

Drawing III Genealogy of persons buried in the Chapel of S. Giacomo.
(* indicates burial in the chapel)

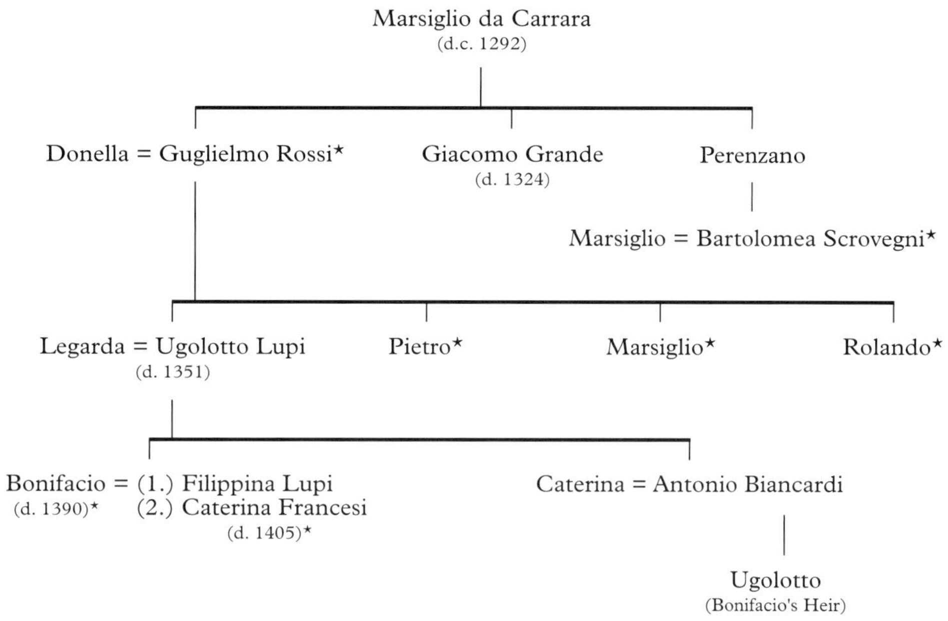

Drawing IV Genealogy of the Lupi family in Padua.
(* indicates inclusion in S. Giorgio votive fresco)

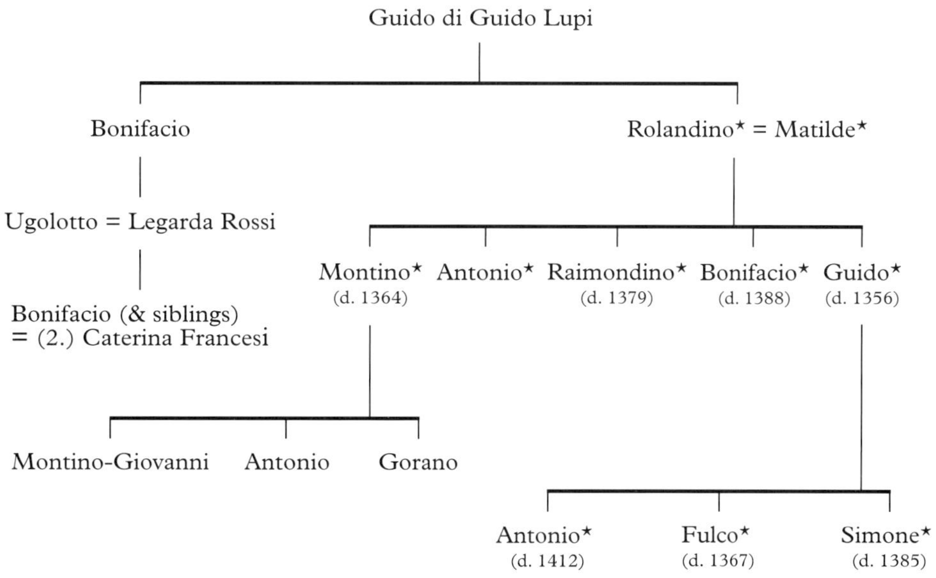

directly related to the signorial family via his grandfather Guglielmo Rossi's marriage to Donella da Carrara, a tie which meant that he had, as well as a Carrarese grandmother, a Carrarese great uncle too; Giacomo Grande da Carrara, *dominus generalis* from 1318 to 1319 (fig. 75). The same network of intermarriages meant that he was also related to another of the founders of the Carrarese *signoria*; Marsiglio da Carrara, *signore* from 1328 to 1338 (fig. 76), and to Marsiglio's first wife, Bartolomea degli Scrovegni. Bartolomea, who was the sister of Giotto's patron Enrico Scrovegni, is also buried in Bonifacio's chapel.

The next phase of Bonifacio's life is rather confused. He served Charles IV in various ways – letters from Charles refer to him in 1355 as 'consiliarium et familiarem nostrum dilectum',[25] a title Bonifacio used in later documents of his own – and travelled with the emperor during his journey through Italy in that year. Such was Bonifacio's standing with Charles that Florentine ambassadors sent to Pisa to talk with the emperor were told to consult Bonifacio first, as he was known to be in his confidence. He seems to have impressed them, for after Charles's return to Bohemia he entered Florentine service, becoming in 1362 captain-general of the Florentine armies during the war against Pisa, during the prosecution of which he was unflagging and resourceful. The chroniclers praise him unstintingly (though the Florentine authorities treated him with characteristic unevenness), and Matteo Villani, who mentions him often, gives a brief but invaluable sketch of his character, describing him as 'uomo d'onesta vita e di vergogna pauroso . . . quasi solitario e di poche parole, ma di gran cuore, e di buono e savio consiglio, e maestro di guerra'.[26] This last accolade was borne out in 1364, at the Battle of Cascina, when only the joint vigilance of Bonifacio and Petrarch's friend Manno Donati averted total catastrophe and allowed the eventual victory. It is one of the curiosities of the history of art that had Bonifacio's name not survived as Altichiero's patron, he would still have achieved (albeit anonymous) celebrity as one of the muscular heroes of Michelangelo's great design for the Palazzo Vecchio fresco.

Bonifacio's Florentine service brought him some recognition – he was granted Florentine citizenship in 1369[27] – but he was refused permission to be buried in Florence Cathedral. As Fiocco remarked,[28] Florence's loss was Padua's gain, and though Florence enjoyed Bonifacio's patronage in the form of his hospital of S. Giovanni Battista in the Via San Gallo,[29] built from 1376, he opted for burial in the Santo.

The Santo was, for Bonifacio, an obvious choice. Several members of his family were already buried there, and his own predilection for the Franciscans is well documented.

[25] *Acta Inedita: Charles IV*, p. 83. In 1366 Charles IV appointed Bonifacio 'consigliere, segretario, famigliare, domestico e commensale . . . e dell'Impero coll'assegnamento di sei cavalli e di altrettanti serventi' in a document from the archives of Soragna cited by Pezzana, *Storia della Città di Parma*, vol. I, p. 78.

[26] Matteo Villani, *Cronica*, vol. v, p. 165.

[27] Decree of 23 Jan. 1369. See Pezzana, *Storia della Città di Parma*, vol. I, p. 78. The Battle of Cascina is described by Filippo Villani, *Cronica*, book XI, ch. 96.

[28] Fiocco, '"Storia e Storie" della Cappella di S. Giacomo al Santo', p. 265.

[29] For the hospital of S. Giovanni Battista in Florence see W. and E. Paatz, *Die Kirchen von Florenz*, vol. I, pp. 395–405, and Cenci, 'Bonifacio Lupi di Soragna e i Frati Minori', p. 91. Sartori, 'Nota su Altichiero', pp. 323–4 publishes documents relevant to the hospital.

The Lupi oratory in their castle at Soragna, where Bonifacio's father was buried, was dedicated to S. Croce, and Bonifacio's Florentine hospital had connections with the friars of S. Croce in that city. Bonifacio also made handsome donations to the Clarisse in Padua and seems to have attributed his recovery from a near-fatal dose of malaria to the intercession of the Beata Elena Enselmini of Padua,[30] whose cult was maintained by the Paduan Clarisse. The later part of his life, after the 1360s, increasingly came to be centred on Padua, though he was frequently absent for periods of various length. From 1364 or thereabouts he appears with increasing regularity in documents which suggest he frequented the Carrarese Palace,[31] and from 1366 or earlier he lived in a house in the parish of S. Fermo, close to the city wall by the Pontemolino, the northern city gate. He also had a country residence in the Eugenean hills at Mandria. Bonifacio lived in Padua with his second wife Caterina Francesi di Staggia,[32] whom he presumably met in Tuscany, but neither with her nor his first wife, a Lupi cousin – Filippina di Ubertino Lupi – did he have children. In 1363 comes the first documentary mention of his chosen heir, his nephew Ugolotto Biancardo, whose exploits in Visconti service later made his name a byword for ferocity throughout the Po Valley.[33]

Bonifacio's Paduan career is well recorded and he seems to have served the Carraresi faithfully, as ambassador to Hungary in 1372, to Leopold of Austria in 1383, and in various military actions, until 1388, when he sided with the invading Visconti. The exasperation provoked by the increasingly desperate actions of Francesco il Vecchio da Carrara as he fought to hold on to power may have proved too much for Bonifacio, as it seems to have done for large numbers of previously loyal Carrarese courtiers, and in June 1390, when Francesco Novello da Carrara sent word to Bonifacio to open a hole in the wall near his house to let his army in, Bonifacio refused, in a reply of great dignity, to betray his new master GianGaleazzo Visconti.[34] This is ironic, given his family

[30] See Bordin, 'I Frati del Santo e i Monasteri Femminili di Padova e del Veneto', pp. 422–3 for the cult of Beata Elena Enselmini; see Fiocco, '"Storia e Storie"', p. 266 and Sartori, 'La Cappella di S. Giacomo', p. 274 for Caterina's offerings to the Beata Elena on behalf of her sick husband. The source for this story is Bartolomeo da Pisa: 'Sancta Helena de Padua, quae fuit monialis in monasterio exteriori de Arcello, . . . quondam nobilem marchionem de Lupis de Parma, dominum Bonifatium, in articulo mortis positum, emisso voto ab eius uxore pro eo, ad sanitatem perfectam deduxit' – *De Conformitate,* vol. IV, p. 238, quoted by Sartori, 'La Cappella di S. Giacomo'.

[31] ASP *Notarile* vol. 407 contains dozens of documents to do with Bonifacio and other Lupi drawn up by Bonifacio's usual notary, Andrea Codagnelli of Parma. Many others can be found in Gloria, *Monumenti.*

[32] For Caterina see Sartori, 'La Cappella di S. Giacomo', pp. 276–7.

[33] Pezzana, *Storia della Città di Parma*, vol. I, pp. 72–3. Ugolotto's later career is subjected to scathing commentary by the Scaligeri tutor Marzagaia in his *De Modernis Gestis*, published in Cipolla, *Antiche Chronache*, pp. 1–338. References to Ugolotto occur on pp. 122–4 and 240.

[34] 'Io non fuy may traditore; e mentre io fuy al servixio de la caxa da Carara fuy lialle a loro, e così intendo de eser a la caxa di Visconti, e specialmente d'il Conte di Vertù', Gatari, *Cronaca Carrarese*, p. 418. Cenci, 'Bonifacio Lupi', p. 94 notes that Bonifacio was not listed amongst those Visconti supporters who took refuge in the castle at the south-west corner of the city when the Carrarese army took control. The pages of the *Cronaca* preceding this describe Bonifacio's actions during the period of Visconti rule. Francesco Novello's presumed fury at Bonifacio's reaction to his note was probably in proportion to Bonifacio's previous reputation for loyalty: Novello himself praised him in extravagant terms during the final crisis of 1388, just preceding the Visconti invasion, calling him 'cavaliere de gran nominanza . . . liale e antico . . . come suo padre'. On 24 November 1388 Bonifacio was appointed his lieutenant by the fleeing Novello. By December Bonifacio had been elected captain-general of the *popolo* in Visconti Padua.

history since 1346, but GianGaleazzo's powers of wooing were not the least of his gifts, and by this stage anything may have seemed preferable to the Carraresi again. In the event Francesco Novello's army took the city fairly easily without Bonifacio's help, and Bonifacio abruptly vanished from the records. The inference is clear enough. No vengeance was exacted against his corpse, however,[35] and he was buried in the tomb prepared for him in the Chapel of S. Giacomo (pl. 48).

The site chosen by Bonifacio for his chapel, at a time when his disillusionment with the Carraresi lay many years ahead, may to some extent have suggested itself. This part of the Santo already contained an altar dedicated to St Michael,[36] though it is not clear if the south transept arm already functioned as a quasi-independent chapel. It probably also housed the original tombs of the four Rossi, as well as that of Bartolomea degli Scrovegni, the front of whose early trecento sarcophagus[37] Bonifacio set into the wall of his chapel below Altichiero's *Crucifixion* (pl. 40). It is possible that Bartolomea was originally buried in the nearby Scrovegni Chapel, but this seems less likely, for there would then have been no particular reason for her to be moved at all, and it would have been rather unusual to transfer her from the ambulatory to the transept for no other reason than to stress Bonifacio's kinship with her. These previous interments probably directed Bonifacio's attention to this part of the church as one particularly associated with his family, though its very prominence must have made it desirable for a patron determined to make his mark in the most lavish fashion. The already existing tomb of other members of the Lupi family lies close at hand, attached to the cloister side of the chapel's south wall.

Bonifacio's intentions for his chapel, set out in his contract with Andriolo de'Santi of 12 February 1372, involved a more far-reaching transformation of the existing structure of the Santo than in the case of any other family chapel there.[38] The fitting out of the ambulatory chapels, or even of the Madonna Mora Chapel, involved nothing more than the embellishment of a pre-existing space. Bonifacio's plan was for a virtually autonomous and extremely elaborate structure, complete with its own vaults, to be slotted into the right transept. This was, again, presumably in line with what had already happened in the case of the chapel containing the shrine of St Anthony. The effect in each case

[35] For Francesco Novello da Carrara's refusal to allow the body of Lombardo della Seta burial in Padua, see Simon, 'Altichiero Versus Avanzo', p. 270 and Mommsen, 'Sala Virorum Illustrium', p. 100.

[36] For the dedication of altars in the Santo and the significance of this in a Franciscan context see Poppi, *Liturgia, Pietà e Ministeri*, p. 37.

[37] For Bartolomea's sarcophagus see Wolters, *Scultura Veneziana Gotica*, vol. I, pp. 159–60. Wolters believes she was initially buried in this part of the building, which contained an altar dedicated to St Michael, first mentioned in 1293. See Marangon and Bellinati, 'La Basilica del Santo nei Documenti', p. 209 (29 Aug. 1293). Bartolomea di Rinaldo degli Scrovegni was the sister of Enrico Scrovegni of Arena chapel fame. She died in 1333. Gonzati, *La Basilica di S Antonio*, vol. II, p. 35 speculates that she was murdered by her husband Marsilio II da Carrara to allow his marriage to Beatrice da Correggio.

[38] The chapel of the B. Luca Belludi, built by Naimerio and Manfredino Conti, with frescoes by Giusto de'Menabuoi, was added to the flank of the Madonna Mora Chapel and consecrated in 1383. It involved no rebuilding of extant structures except to the extent of a hole being knocked through the north wall of the Madonna Mora Chapel. See Marangon and Bellinati, 'La Basilica del Santo nei Documenti', p. 227 for the relevant documents.

was to transform the basic appearance of the transept by giving prominence to the lower levels of what is actually an extremely tall space, a transformation emphasised by the alignment of the front walls of each chapel with the back wall of the nave aisles. This masking of the full scale of the transept was reinforced when the facade cornice of the chapel was raised at the end of the quattrocento.[39]

The chapel faces the main body of the church with an arcade of five cusped arches with foliate capitals, and a twisted cord moulding above the arches and along the lower cornice (pl. 39). Above this are five tabernacles with figures of saints and a row of gables. The tops of the gables must originally have been more ornately finished than they were left after the cornice was raised. The background structure in the Cavalli fresco (pl. 16) gives a general indication of what the original state may have been, with crockets and finials elaborating the presently rather bare gables. The basic chromatic layout of the architecture is dominated by contrasting red and white stone (red and white are the heraldic colours of Padua), with gilded areas on the tabernacles, the mouldings and the heraldic devices on the arcade spandrels and gables.

The interior is spanned by three bays of rib vaulting (pl. 51a), of which the central bay is rather wider. Lunettes below the vaults carry the first eight scenes of a cycle of the Life of St James round all four walls, a cycle completed on the middle section of the east wall. The south wall echoes the five-arched design of the entrance. Each of the outer bays of the back wall houses a wall tomb, extremely richly carved and gilded (pls. 47, 48), and the short sides have wooden stalls, with carved and painted stone canopies. The lower part of the south wall has a three-bay fresco of the *Crucifixion* (pls. 40–6), flanked in the lunettes above the tombs by a *Pietà* and a *Resurrection* (pls. 73, 74). The vaults and inner arcade spandrels have painted busts of assorted saints.

The chronology of the chapel's construction and decoration are relatively easily charted via the surviving records of the payments made for various stages of the work. The main constructional scaffolding was taken down in March 1377, at the same time as five mats were provided 'per lo dipinctore'.[40] Another kind of scaffold seems to have been erected following this, and we may assume this was for the painting of the chapel. Some time after May 1379 Altichiero was paid the considerable sum of 792 ducats for his work here and in the now lost sacristy – 'per ogni raxon ch'aveva a fare cum messer Bonifacio cussì nel dipingere la capella de san Iacomo como per la sacrestia'.[41] To place this sum in context, Sartori cited the payment of 244 ducats made in 1441 to Giovanni Storlato for his frescoes in the Chapel of S. Luca in the Abbey of S. Giustina. To provide a more immediate context one might compare it with the payment of 6 ducats for each of the carved capitals of S. Giacomo itself or that of 2 ducats, 12 soldi and 2 pennies for the

[39] See Sartori, 'La Cappella di S. Giacomo', pp. 294–6.

[40] 'Ancora per spese fate del mese di marzo, per fare abasare l'armamento de la capella, magisterio e chiodi, e per store V per lo dipinctore, ducati II soldi XII denari VI' – Sartori, 'Nota su Altichiero', p. 320, no. 32. This payment is discussed by Simon, 'Altichiero Versus Avanzo', p. 253.

[41] 'Ancora dado al maestro Altichiero, per ogni raxon ch'aveva a fare cum messer Bonifacio cussì nel dipingere la cappella de san Iacomo como per la sacrestia, como appare nel libro de la cappella, ducati settecentononanta-dui ducati DCC.LXXXXII' – Sartori, 'Nota su Altichiero', p. 320, no. 37.

considerable operation of demolishing and removing the builders' scaffolding. The sculptor Rinaldino da Francia, who made the figures for the altar, was paid just over 196 ducats, and the missal for use in the chapel cost 42.[42]

The documents record the fact that Bonifacio gathered together all the material to do with the chapel's endowment and construction and bound it into a volume, the 'libro de la cappella' mentioned in the record of Altichiero's payment. This volume, along with a similar one made later for the Oratory of S. Giorgio, is lost, and with it, presumably, Altichiero's own contract. This loss is particularly vexing, for although the chapel is generally well documented this applies less to Altichiero's participation in the scheme, and it leaves open a number of questions about his work here which have tended to dominate past accounts of the frescoes. The most pressing question revolves around the nature and extent of Altichiero's supposed collaboration with another painter, variously 'Avanzo' or 'Avanzi', for which there is a long, if grievously confused, literary tradition. The historical and documentary arguments provoked by this tradition have tended to dominate discussions of the chapel to a degree which has probably proved harmful to Altichiero's reputation, leaving him with a dubious standing as one element of a classic art-historical 'problem'. Discussions of his work have tended to treat the collaboration issue as all-important. Recent, and fundamentally sympathetic, attempts to place the focus back on Altichiero as a whole have tended to throw up their own excesses, and far too much work of different kinds – the *Madonna Verona* in the Piazza Erbe in Verona,[43] the architectural backgrounds of Giusto de'Menabuoi's frescoes in Padua,[44] frescoes and panels of all kinds, have been attributed to him, as if to make up for earlier injustices. The attributional view of S. Giacomo adopted here, and based on quite clear stylistic distinctions, can be summarised briefly. Altichiero painted the whole of the lower part of the chapel below the cornice, as well as three of the St James lunettes and the roundels and transverse arch figures of the western vault bay. The rest, five lunettes and two bays of the vault, are by another hand.

One aspect of a pan-Alticherian approach to S. Giacomo is relevant here. Mellini, Sartori and Alvarez all discuss the possibility that Altichiero himself may have designed the Chapel of S. Giacomo, leaving the execution merely to Andriolo and his shop. Sartori is quite definite in his attribution, though his grounds are hardly conclusive.[45] He argues that, left to his own devices, Andriolo de'Santi would have designed for the chapel a high altar like that of the Madonna Mora Chapel,[46] which would, of course, have blocked the central bay of the *Crucifixion* just as the sixteenth-century altar tomb of S. Felice did until it was demolished in the 1960s.[47] All this suggests – and we know the altar was originally raised on two steps only – is consultation between the various parties before the final details were decided upon. Sartori's other point, that the setting

42 *Ibid.*, p. 316, and for the (lost) missal, described in an inventory of 1420, p. 317.

43 Mellini, 'Disegni di Altichiero e della sua Scuola, 1', p. 22. Cuppini, 'L'Arte Gotica', p. 272 attributes the ensemble to Bonino da Campione.

44 Ragghianti, *Pittura tra Giotto e Pisanello*, pp. 28–31.

45 Sartori, 'Nota su Altichiero', p. 299.

46 For the altar of the Madonna Mora Chapel see Wolters, *Scultura Veneziana Gotica*, vol. 1, pp. 209–10.

47 Alvarez, 'L'Architettura e l'Arredo dela Cappella di S. Giacomo ora detta di S. Felice al Santo' discusses the altars of SS Giacomo/Felice, with good illustrations of the chapel before and after the alterations.

was 'evidemente ideata per la decorazione', hardly proves anything. In an enterprise of this sort the correlation of fresco and architecture is hardly going to be left to chance, and his remark also constitutes a case of putting the cart before the horse, of considering the decoration of a chapel as a determinant of that structure rather than, as must normally be the case, something which is strictly secondary to the building itself.

The possibility of some input by the painter need not be dismissed altogether. The design of the south wall (pls. 40–1) certainly suggests that the remarkable decoration intended for this part of the chapel was taken into consideration. There is, of course, abundant trecento precedent for the interest of painters in architecture: one need only think of the successive involvement of Giotto, Orcagna and Andrea Bonaiuti in the development of Florence Cathedral, and Altichiero's work reveals the most sophisticated architectural imagination of any fourteenth-century painter. But the evidence specific enough to allow for an outright dismissal of Andriolo as chief designer of the chapel simply does not exist. Affinities between S. Giacomo and Veronese models either by, or known to, Altichiero are too general. The juxtaposition of gables and tabernacles common to the chapel, the Cavalli fresco, and the tomb of Mastino della Scala are part of the lingua franca of trecento chivalric Gothic and are peculiar neither to Altichiero nor to Verona generally. Contrasts with the sober Gothic styles of the Santo fabric as a whole simply reflect changes in taste from the thirteenth to the late fourteenth century. Alvarez points to the presence 'nell'una e nell'altra costruzione [i.e. the Cavalli backdrop and the Chapel of S. Giacomo] l'unico attico',[48] which is not even strictly accurate, and to the similar way in which columns stand against flanking piers at the sides of each example. Again, neither of these points is persuasive enough to suggest anything more than a common architectural culture, though, equally, there is no reason to suppose that Altichiero could not have designed such a structure if neccessary. He would seem, on the evidence of his frescoes here and in the neighbouring Oratory of S. Giorgio, to have been exceptionally well equipped to do so.

Function and iconography

The function of Bonifacio's chapel seems to have undergone at least one revision during the course of its construction. If Cenci is right in his assertion that Bonifacio was refused burial in Florence as late as 1377,[49] he must have had no settled intention to be buried in S. Giacomo at the time of the contract of 1372, which makes no mention of any tombs. From a strictly practical point of view the chapel must originally have been meant simply as a chantry for use after his death and as his personal chapel for use when he was in Padua. But in 1376, the same year in which Bonifacio settled with the Franciscans the broad details of the arrangements to be made after his death for the funding and celebrating of thrice-daily masses for him, there is a record of payment made to Andriolo and a 'maestro Zoane' (Giovanni) for work on the tombs ('per l'overa

[48] Alvarez, 'L'Architettura e l'Arredo', p. 136.
[49] Cenci, 'Bonifacio Lupi', p. 91.
[50] Sartori, 'Nota su Altichiero', p. 319, no. 27.

de le arche').[51] These were, perhaps, planned from the beginning, despite their exclusion from the initial contract with Andriolo, even if Bonifacio's precise intentions for them were not at that stage fully resolved. They were evidently begun in 1374. There is no documented suggestion that Bonifacio intended S. Giacomo to be the funerary chapel of all the Lupi in Padua, or even a memorial chapel to them, as was the case with Raimondino Lupi's S. Giorgio. But the chapel is very large – much larger than any of the ambulatory chapels, and it must be likely that it was used by the family as a whole, especially since the prominent inclusion of the tombs of the Rossi and Bonifacio's Scrovegni/Carrarese kinswoman give a broad dynastic aspect to the whole enterprise.

The paired sarcophagi of S. Giacomo have an immediate local precedent in the form of Andriolo de'Santi's earlier pair of matching Carrarese tombs erected in the Dominican church of S. Agostino (now in the Eremitani).[52] Their existence furnishes an obvious reason for Bonifacio's choice of Andriolo to build his chapel, and it says something for Bonifacio's standing that he was able to employ the men who were, in effect, the Carrarese court sculptor and the Scaligeri (and now Carrarese) court painter respectively. Bonifacio had first intended that masses should only be said in his chapel after his death, but from 1384 he arranged for daily masses to begin during his lifetime, and he brought forward the endowment arrangements to cover this.[53] These arrangements are recorded on a stone set into the west wall of the chapel. The stone beneath Bonifacio's tomb, marking it as his, was only placed there in 1389, the year before his death.

The broader purpose of S. Giacomo is complex and its iconography correspondingly, and exceptionally, rich. One of its primary memorial functions was to mark the association of Bonifacio with the centres of political power in Padua. The ostentatious reinterment of Pietro and the other Rossi emphasises Bonifacio's kinship with the architects of the emergent Carrarese *signoria*, and the prominent inclusion of Bartolomea degli Scrovegni's tomb marks his own kinship with the Carraresi. Bonifacio's identity with the Carrarese cause, his close social and political ties with them – of which there is abundant documentary and historical evidence – is also seemingly alluded to in the frescoes. The *Council of King Ramiro* on the east wall (pls. 66–8) contains what can be regarded with varying degrees of certainty as portraits not only of Bonifacio and his wife Caterina, who may be compared with their portraits in the votive fresco on the west wall, but of Petrarch, Lombardo della Seta, and, according to tradition, others of the Carrarese court, including Francesco il Vecchio da Carrara and his son Francesco Novello.[54] Petrarch is easily recognisable on the basis of Altichiero's

51 The payment is for work beginning in November 1374 and ending in March 1376.

52 For the Carrarese tombs in S. Agostino see Wolters, *Scultura Veneziana Gotica*, vol. 1, pp. 168–9.

53 Sartori, 'La Cappella di S. Giacomo', pp. 305–6, document of 29 Sept. 1384, discussed by Simon, 'Altichiero Versus Avanzo', p. 257.

54 The portraits in S. Giacomo are discussed by Mardersteig, 'I Ritratti del Petrarca e dei suoi Amici di Padova', and, rather more cautiously, Plant, 'Portraits and Politics in Padua'. Both accept the identification of the two Carraresi in the *Council* scene. Mardersteig remarks that identification of the Lupi is made difficult by lack of certified comparative material. But Bonifacio is, of course, depicted in the votive fresco. He is also thought to be the kneeling donor presented by St Francis on an altarpiece by the Master of S. Verdiana (Paris, Musée Nationale, Campana collection) which originates from Bonifacio's hospital in Florence, for which see Boskovits, *Pittura Fiorentina alla Vigilia del Rinascimento*, pl. 108 and p. 105.

other portraits of him, and his companion here, the same as in the S. Giorgio *St George Baptising King Sevio and his Court* (pl. 93), may be identified on contextual grounds as Lombardo, linchpin of the Paduan Petrarch industry and a personality naturally paired with Petrarch, as we know from the Sala Virorum Illustrium. Lombardo drew up the initial contract for the building of S. Giacomo, and aspects of its design were based on architectural elements in the house he shared with his brother Domenico,[55] who shared control of the building project with Corradino Lupi and Caterina de'Francesi. Lombardo's friendship with Bonifacio is well documented.[56] The presence of the two Carraresi has always been assumed on the grounds that, given the general context, it would be surprising were they not here. The older and younger bearded men in the left wing of the Council scene are probably them – the same two appear very prominently in the fresco of *St Lucy Before Judge Pascasio* in S. Giorgio (pl. 109), and the older man closely resembles the one medal of Francesco il Vecchio not based on Roman coin portraits.[57] Bonifacio had every right to place himself in close juxtaposition with Petrarch, whom he knew,[58] and his circle, and his inclusion of the Carraresi themselves is rather obviously explained – and equally well justified.

Other aspects of Bonifacio's career find expression in the iconography of Altichiero's frescoes. His portrait in the Council scene is exceptionally interesting (pl. 68). In profile, heavily bearded, wearing a hat with the motto AMOR (echoing the MEMOR used by Francesco da Carrara[59]) on it, and visually singled out in what seems a very pointed manner, Bonifacio is located in that part of Altichiero's fresco which most openly quotes from Maso di Banco's *St Sylvester Restoring a Bull to Life* in S. Croce in Florence (fig. 18). When we remember Bonifacio's long-standing connections with Florence, and specifically with the Franciscans of S. Croce, the allusion seems peculiarly pointed. S. Croce was a church of great significance, albeit for different reasons, for both artist and patron, a community of feeling overtly recorded here.

Such references to Tuscan, and particularly Florentine art, though explicable in terms of both Altichiero's and Bonifacio's careers, can also be seen in the wider context of relationships between Padua and Florence. These took several forms. Politically the two cities had a close relationship during the period of Altichiero's work in Padua, with Florence on at least one occasion threatening direct intervention against Venice on behalf of Padua. This alliance reflects a whole range of contacts on commercial and cultural levels which bound the two cities together. The dominant painters of Padua in the 1370s and 1380s, Giusto and Altichiero, were Florentine and (indirectly) Florentine-trained respectively. The cult of the greatest of Florentine trecento painters was, as we

[55] 'Ancora per fatura e lavoratura de V archi . . . i quali deno essere volti sopra le sopradette colone da la parte de nanci de la deta capella, e deno essere a soace e cornixe seguitando quel modo ch'è in certi volti che sono in uno bancho il quale è nela stacone di Domenicho e di Lombardo a mano drita a l'entrata' – Sartori, 'Nota su Altichiero', p. 312, no. 9.

[56] See Billanovich and Pellegrin, 'Una nuova Lettera di Lombardo della Seta e la prima Fortuna delle Opere del Petrarca', pp. 228–9.

[57] Grossato, *Da Giotto al Mantegna*, p. 210, no. 133. The authenticity of this medal has been doubted.

[58] See Wilkins, 'Petrarch and Giacomo de'Rossi'.

[59] I owe this analogy to Professor B. Kohl of Vassar College, in a paper read at the art historians' conference in Edinburgh in 1984. See also Levi, *Francesco di Vannozzo e la Lirica relle Corti Lombarde durante la seconda Metà del sec. XIV*, p. 68.

shall see, maintained in Padua as nowhere else, not least in humanist circles with their own active links with Florence. The majority of literary figures in the Carrarese court, or inhabiting its outer, and shadier, fringes were of Tuscan origins, and the Florentines maintained their own identity – as a *nazione* – in Padua. None of this can be adduced to account for the conscious Tuscanisms of the S. Giacomo frescoes, but it furnishes a solid cultural background for the homage to Florence which forms part of the complex web woven by Bonifacio and Altichiero.[60]

The specifically Franciscan aspect of Bonifacio's devotion is, not surprisingly, underlined throughout the chapel. The four most prominent of the saints in large cusped polyfoils on the spandrels of the arcade, those on the south wall, facing the body of the church, are all Franciscan (Sts Clare, Francis, Anthony and Louis). The area of wall below Bonifacio's tomb has a fresco of a *trompe l'œil* niche, and beside it, in a smaller niche, kneels a figure in a Franciscan habit (pl. 49), in an attitude of prayer and with his eyes towards the adjacent *Crucifixion*. In almost every respect this figure has the aspect of a donor portrait (in scale he matches the foreground figures of the *Crucifixion*). The inference must be that this is a clean-shaven Bonifacio – and the figure does not appear to have the tonsure. There is no record of his belonging to the lay Franciscan order, but he may nevertheless have been buried in a Franciscan habit. This would not be surprising given his devotion – and generosity – to the order, and there are parallel cases, such as the tomb of Ostasio da Polente, *signore* of Ravenna from 1390 to 1396, whose tomb in S. Francesco in Ravenna sports a stone effigy also wearing the habit. The position of Bonifacio's niche, close to the tomb of Christ in the adjacent *Crucifixion*, evokes the niches commonly built into major shrines to allow close physical access to the relic.

Though the Franciscan figure goes perfectly well with the figure style of Altichiero's other frescoes in the chapel, it is possible that it was added as an afterthought. The whole area below Bonifacio's tomb is rather untidy, and there is an oddly asymmetrical relationship with the equivalent wall under the Rossi tomb. Deliberate asymmetries may be discounted, as between the polyfoil shapes framing images of the Virtues and the heraldic devices, or, obviously, between the supporting lions of the Rossi and the wolves of the Lupi sarcophagi. The sarcophagi themselves are subtly different, though adhering to a common overall design. The foliate carving of the upper cornice of the main chest is of a different design in each case, and the same goes for the decoration round the coat of arms on the lid of each tomb. Perhaps Andriolo and Giovanni carved one apiece.

The wall below each tomb has a fictive niche containing a tomb or altar (pls. 40–1), flanked at the Rossi end of the wall by blind panels, and under the Lupi tomb by one blind panel and the niche with kneeling donor. But the two main niches are of different widths, which seems unnecessary – the kneeling figure would fit just as well if the main

[60] See Levi, *Francesco di Vanozzo*, especially pp. 76ff. for Florentines in Padua. In practice, cultural and commercial interchange between the two cities may often have involved the same individuals, men like Andrea da Firenze, manufacturer of fustian in Padua in 1371, and probable author of an allegorical canzone – *Móvesi il Carro co'la vesta bianca* – on the wars in Lombardy.

niche of the Lupi tomb were as wide as that of the Rossi. The intervening area between the figure niche and the tomb niche is filled with a pair of doubled fictive columns 'supporting' the main brackets of the tomb chest above (the Rossi brackets rest on carved lion masks). These have extraordinarily spindly proportions and are not very well drawn, and it seems unlikely that Altichiero, whose fictive architecture always 'works', could have regarded these as adequate imaginary supports for a heavy tomb. The fretted strip which now functions each side as a kind of impost, looks peculiarly pointless – a decorative border used as a structural element, in effect. Perhaps the whole area below the tomb brackets was altered when the stone was installed, at a time when Altichiero was no longer resident in Padua. It is hard to connect him with the insignificant and illogical colonnettes, though the adjacent figure, credibly filling – overflowing from – his niche, looks absolutely right.

The specific reasons for Bonifacio's devotion to St James the Great are unknown. There is no record of Bonifacio or Caterina having actually made the pilgrimage to Compostella (as St Francis did), but the erection and decoration of this chapel dedicated to the Apostle may be seen as a kind of vicarious pilgrimage to the shrine, a reading supported by the apparent inclusion of Bonifacio and his wife as pilgrims in the seventh lunette of the St James cycle, following the body of the saint as the bulls draw it to Queen Lupa's palace (pl. 62). It is probably, then, no accident that the chapel was begun in 1372, a year in which the feast day of St James fell on a Sunday. In 1122 Pope Callixtus II had decreed that every year in which this happened was to be regarded as a Compostellan Holy Year. In such years particular merit is attached to those who make their devotions to St James.[61]

The cult of St James the Great fuelled the development of Santiago da Compostella into one of the major pilgrimage sites of medieval Europe. A visit to his shrine ranked with those made to Rome or the Holy Land, and after the loss of Jerusalem, Compostella naturally took on even greater importance. At the same time the original stories of St James in Spain were subjected to amplifications and embellishments rather like those undergone by the history of Titus and the sack of Jerusalem. The legends of St James were transformed and absorbed into the stuff of the chivalric and crusading imagination of the later Middle Ages, and the martial aspect of the Compostellan cult remained potent until long afterwards – the Armada sailed under St James's protection, and Don John of Austria laid the banner of Lepanto at the Apostle's shrine. This aspect was embodied in the energetic figure of St James *Matamoro*, visionary ally of Charlemagne at Pamplona, and of King Ramiro I at the Battle of Clavigo in 843, where the Apostle, mounted on a white horse, personally slaughtered 70,000 Moors. The iconography of the militant Apostle is featured in the Chapel of S. Giacomo, though in a rather unusual form.

The basic choice of scenes from the life of St James is very distinctive. The bulk of the cycle, of which the first eight scenes (pls. 52–64) are drawn from the *Legenda Aurea* of

[61] Hartley, *The Story of Santiago da Compostella*, p. 51.

[62] *Ibid.*, pp. 18–72.

Jacobus de Voragine, is devoted not to episodes from the Apostle's lifetime but to a series of miraculous events which took place after his execution, events which form the basis of the medieval cult of Santiago. The emphasis on this posthumous material steers the iconography towards the specifically Spanish aspects of the legend, and to the chivalric and crusading histories associated with them, and it leads up to the climactic scenes on the east wall in which various strands of material drawn from sources other than Jacobus de Voragine are interwoven. The miraculous intervention at Clavigo is thus preceded by various other instances of posthumous miracles effected by St James. The unusual emphasis of this cycle has been attributed to Bonifacio's desire, on the grounds of a nearly shared name, to underline the person of Queen Lupa, at first hostile to the saint and to Christianity, then converted, and finally seen rededicating her palace as a church.[63] What is rather more certain is that the iconography and location of some of the lunette scenes were carefully chosen in order to establish parallels with the larger scenes below. Thus the Dispute scene (pl. 52), its iconography broadly derived from that commonly used for images of Christ among the Doctors, is placed above the Council scene (pl. 66), which has similar ancestry – and in this case a very specific formal derivation from the Giottesque tradition for the Doctors. On the south wall the location of the *Execution of St James* (pl. 56) in the large central lunette above the *Crucifixion* establishes an obvious parallel, a point perhaps intentionally emphasised by the similarity of architectural setting in the frescoes. The overall planning of the south wall is extremely precise and active. A condensed Passion cycle at the lower level – *Annunciation*, *Crucifixion*, *Pietà* and *Resurrection* – has above it scenes of baptism, martyrdom, and burial in a ministry with close echoes of Christ's own. The two halves of the Annunciation, placed in the spandrels at the extreme left and right of the wall, tie the two ends together and emphasise the transition from the dead Christ of the Rossi tomb to the resurrected Christ above Bonifacio's.

The most remarkable iconography of this cycle is found on the east wall of the chapel. Here, under the first scene of the St James cycle, are grouped its three last scenes (pls. 65–71), in a striking arrangement whereby all three, *Ramiro's Dream*, the *Council of King Ramiro*, and the *Battle of Clavigo* share the same pictorial field. It has long been recognised that there is something in the iconography of this part of the St James cycle which is apparently at variance with the available sources.[64] The story of Ramiro's nocturnal vision of St James, his description of that vision in council, and the ensuing battle, is well known in several versions. The story appears in the eleventh-century Compostellan *Codex Callistinus*, which contains a great deal of material of different kinds to do with the cult of St James. As well as homilies and excerpts from the Church Fathers, the Codex has a section (bk. II) on the miracles of St James and another (bk. L) on the Spanish activity of Charlemagne. The basic material is also found in the twelfth-century *Historia Compostellana* of Archbishop Gelmirez and the thirteenth-century *Historia de Rebus Hispaniae* of Bishop Ximenius of Toledo.[65] But the story

63 Kruft, *Altichiero und Avanzo*, p. 17.

64 Plant, 'Portraits and Politics', pp. 418–19.

65 Hartley, *Santiago*, pp. 52–5, and Plant, 'Portraits and Politics', pp. 417–19.

derived from the *Codex Callistinus* is quite explicit about the events of the Battle of Clavigo, at which the saint appeared on a white horse and killed huge numbers of Moors. Altichiero's fresco instead shows the Apostle, not on horseback, causing the walls of the city in the background to collapse. This iconography, with the king kneeling as he watches the miracle (pl. 69), is traditionally associated not with Ramiro's victory at Clavigo but with Charlemagne at Pamplona, a story widely available in the Veneto in the *Entrée d'Espagne*, an epic poem of local origin.[66] Cuenod, who first pointed out the discrepancy,[67] suggested that the frescoes had simply been wrongly identified and should be interpreted instead as showing Charlemagne's vision and the Battle of Pamplona. Kruft[68] pointed out that this reading then leaves a problem with the Council scene, which does not belong to the Charlemagne material, and it is widely agreed that, despite the discrepancies, the original reading is correct. As Plant remarks, one of the planks of Cuenod's argument was the prominence in the battle fresco of the fleur-de-lys, which she associated with Charlemagne. But there was a far more immediate context for this in Padua in the 1370s, and especially for Bonifacio Lupi.

The inscription beneath Bonifacio's tomb (the text is given in the catalogue entry for S. Giacomo) is typical of the period in its lack of reticence (he accorded the same treatment to his Rossi forebears, complete with a sprinkling of fashionable classical allusions), though rather longer than most. It is very informative concerning Bonifacio's intentions and those aspects of his career he wished to emphasise and preserve. In addition to the expected outline of his own status and claims to fame, it underlines Bonifacio's links with the emperor, and it makes a pointed and perhaps less expected reference to Bonifacio's standing with the King of Hungary. The Paduan–Hungarian alliance has already made an appearance in the context of Altichiero's career, and we have seen him developing an allegorical iconography to express Padua's hostility to Venice. The three foci of Paduan politics from the early 1350s – close connections with Florence, hostility to Venice and military alliance with Hungary – all had a very powerful influence on the course of Bonifacio's life, and they all find expression in S. Giacomo.

The conflict between Venice and the Paduan–Hungarian alliance dated back as far as 1353 and hinged on the disputed territories of Istria and Dalmatia, then held by Venice, and claimed by King Louis of Hungary.[69] In 1356 Louis invaded the Friuli and besieged Treviso. This first campaign was generally successful and led to the Venetian abandonment of Dalmatia, ratified in a treaty of 1358. Louis's interests were primarily in the Venetian lands on the west side of the Adriatic, while Francesco da Carrara's eyes were on the Venetian *terrafirma* towards the lagoon and up to Treviso in the north. In 1360 he was rewarded for his support when Louis ceded to him Feltre, Cividale and Belluno.

[66] For the *Entrée d'Espagne* see Limentani, 'L'Epica in "Lengue de France": L'Entrée d'Espagne e Niccolo da Verona', pp. 338–68.

[67] Cuenod, 'Les Apparitions de Saint Jacques et deux Fresques d'Altichiero', p. 293.

[68] Kruft, *Altichiero und Avanzo*, p. 39.

[69] For the war between Venice and the Paduan–Hungarian alliance see Gatari, *Cronaca Carrarese*, pp. 36ff. A good modern account is given by Norwich, *A History of Venice*, pp. 230–68.

A second phase of the war broke out from 1369, with Padua securing firm promises of Florentine support in the event of any Venetian attack on her territory. Bonifacio's part in this new campaign was central to Paduan policy, and his good offices must have played a major role in Paduan dealings with Florence, as well as with the Pisans, whose ambassador was involved in the incessant diplomatic cross-trading that absorbed as much of the participants' energies as the usually sporadic and inconclusive military actions of this protracted and ultimately fruitless (from a Paduan point of view) quarrel. In May 1372 he went to Hungary with Checco da Lion and the Hungarian ambassador, returning in July with a body of Hungarian troops under his command. He may have visited Verona with the Hungarian envoys sent by Francesco da Carrara to Cansignorio della Scala[70] and seen the Sala Grande, which is where one would expect ambassadors to have been received. In August Bonifacio went to Bologna and then on to Tuscany to collect the famous English mercenary force, the White Company, whose services the Carraresi had engaged. In December 1372 the Venetians suffered a major defeat, and the captured banner of St Mark was taken ceremoniously to the tomb of St Anthony.

The *Cronaca Carrarese* shows Bonifacio throughout this phase of the war in close contact with Hungary – with Louis himself and with Stephen of Transylvania, Louis's nephew and his commander in the Veneto. It has been generally accepted since Gerola's crucial paper of 1929[71] that the figure of King Ramiro in the Council and Battle scenes of S. Giacomo can be identified with King Louis of Hungary, and that the lilies which are so prominent on the cloth behind the king in the *Council*, and on his surcoat in the *Battle of Clavigo*, are those of the house of Anjou. In addition, it has been established that the facial features of Altichiero's Ramiro accord very closely with those of three images of Louis from Hungarian sources.[72] The adaptation of the basic Ramiro iconography so that elements proper to that of Charlemagne infiltrate it is easily explained. For everyone except Petrarch, Charlemagne was still a figure of heroic stature, as the *Entrée d'Espagne* demonstrates, and his relevance in this Spanish context is obvious. The Paladins were, for the men of the trecento, the very archetypes of Christian knighthood, a point underlined on a domestic level by the popularity of the name Rolando (or Orlando or Rolandino) amongst the Lupi and the Rossi. That the Paduans themselves saw analogies between Charlemagne and Louis is established quite explicitly in the *Cronaca Carrarese*.[73]

Altichiero's overt dependence in the Council fresco on the design and iconography of Maso's *St Sylvester Restoring a Bull to Life* in S. Croce (fig. 18) takes on yet another layer of significance in this context. That this particular choice of model was apt for both Altichiero and Bonifacio is clear enough, and the suitability of a design originally developed for a scene of disputation or debate is obvious. But it has not, as far as I know, been pointed out how very closely the central figure of Altichiero's *Council* is based on that of Maso's fresco – Constantine. The addition of this extra element to the agglomeration of types present in this part of the Paduan fresco cycle seems quite deliberate – and it is,

70 Gatari, *Cronaca Carrarese*, p. 61, 11 July 1372.
71 Gerola, 'L'Effigie di Luigi il Grande d'Ungheria in un Affresco a Padova', pp. 17–20.
72 Plant, 'Portraits and Politics', p. 412.
73 Gatari, *Cronaca Carrarese*, p. 238.

of course, entirely suitable in a context tracing the actions of one Christian ruler back to those of an earlier predecessor. The hieratic frontality of Ramiro accords, of course, with an iconography commonly used in the depiction of figures of authority,[74] descending in this case from an image of Christ the Teacher. But the way he sits, the way the cloth pulls bulkily across his knees, the overall shape of him, as well as more standard shared attributes like the orb and sceptre and the peaked crown, all suggest a direct use of Maso's image of the first Christian emperor. Casual, or even habitual, visitors to the chapel are unlikely to have picked up this additional reference, but it is not impossible that Altichiero and Bonifacio intended it.

Louis's claims to be in some sense the successor of both Ramiro and Charlemagne – Christian monarchs fighting the infidel, a claim always perhaps slightly awkward with a Venetian opponent, were obligingly supported by events immediately contemporary with the decoration of S. Giacomo. Louis's victory against the Turks at Marienzell in 1378 has been cited in this context,[75] but equally relevant was the receipt by Francesco da Carrara in 1377 of a letter from Louis announcing his victory over the heathen Radano of Bulgaria.[76] The historical sanction thus given to the iconography of this part of the S. Giacomo cycle, in which the chivalric legends of St James merge with those of Charlemagne and take on the colouring of a contemporary campaign by Charlemagne's successor, must have been welcome, especially given the mostly rather inconclusive and scrappy course of the immediate struggle as the 1370s drew to their close. For Bonifacio, close associate of that other great borrower of Charlemagne's clothes, Charles IV, the extra glory accruing to that strong sense of his own honour of which his tomb inscription speaks must have been most gratifying. Very shortly after the completion of the frescoes, history once more seemed to smile on the heroes of the S. Giacomo frescoes, with the Carrarese capture of Chioggia, the event probably marked by the headpiece of BN Lat. 6069G (pl. 38). The dashing of this hope at the hands of a Venetian army led by none other than the exiled Giacomo Cavalli, counter-attacking in the winter of 1379/80, cannot detract from the extraordinary historical aptness of the *Ramiro* frescoes, presaged by 'crusading' victories won by the Hungarian king and immediately followed by a decisive crushing of Venice by the forces of the alliance. The timing of the completion of Bonifacio's new chapel, to all intents finished in 1379, facing the tomb of St Anthony, now adorned with the captured banner of St Mark, could hardly have been better arranged.

The general iconography and preoccupations of the S. Giacomo frescoes are, up to a point, typical of their time and of the prevailing signorial ideology. The crusading themes, the chivalric material, the interpenetration of contemporary life with that of a historical or mythical past, all these are common elements which had already shaped the course of Altichiero's career. On the other hand the density and sophistication of the S. Giacomo mixture has few parallels, and it can be argued, without at all implying that they were 'friends', that behind this (and not for the first time if Vasari is to be

[74] See Plant, 'Portraits and Politics', p. 413, n. 35.
[75] *Ibid.*, p. 419, for Marienzell.
[76] Gatari, *Cronaca Carrarese*, p. 145.

believed) lies an unusually close relationship between Altichiero and his patron. Their common experience is recorded in the Council scene, which underlines the central role of Petrarch in recent Paduan culture and history, and the complementary role of Carrarese Padua itself in the promotion of Petrarch's view of history's role. The S. Giacomo *Council*, in this light, is another gloss (like the *Triumph of Fame*) on the great Petrarchan project which was being brought to completion even as Altichiero worked on the frescoes of Bonifacio's chapel. It is, of course, overwhelmingly likely that Altichiero had had personal dealings with Petrarch. He must at any rate, as has already been argued, have seen him, and he certainly knew Lombardo della Seta. He had worked with these men and he had worked for the Carrarese court. If he did not go to Verona in 1368 Bonifacio probably first encountered Altichiero and his work while the painter was working on the Sala Virorum Illustrium. The prestige of this commission alone would have been enough to draw Altichiero to Bonifacio's attention – and so regular an *habitué* of the court can hardly fail to have been familiar with it – but in the light of Bonifacio's own relations with the men controlling this new emblem of the Paduan humanist tradition (Petrarch and his family, Lombardo, Checco da Lion, Francesco da Carrara himself), we may assume some familiarity with Altichiero's work on Bonifacio's part, and a clear grasp of the regard in which he was held in these circles. Once again, the east wall of S. Giacomo must be seen as a memorial to a dense network of associations shared by both the artist and his patron. The inclusion of Petrarch may have had an additional and rather less exalted significance in reinforcing Padua's 'possession' of the great humanist, whom the Venetians, promising much, failed to keep. Cocking a snook of this kind at Venice may have seemed, to the Carrarese court in the 1370s – and they will still have felt the smart of Francesco Novello's forced apology to the Most Serene Republic in 1373, in Petrarch's presence – irresistible. These aspects of S. Giacomo are virtually without parallel in the trecento and anticipate developments in artist–patron relations not usually regarded as at all common until the later Renaissance.

This extraordinary monument to a cultural phenomenon intended to mark Padua as the humanist capital of Europe is closely associated with Altichiero's precocity in another commonly remarked aspect of Renaissance culture – the cult of the individual, as recorded in portraits. Even for a marquis, Bonifacio is accorded an extraordinarily high profile in his chapel, if all the suggested portraits of him are accepted. The same may be said in the case of his wife, Caterina de'Francesi, and in a late medieval context this is, if anything, even more remarkable. Caterina's rather distinctive face appears in the votive fresco (pl. 72), in the Council next to Bonifacio (pl. 68), and with him in *Wild Bulls take the Body of St James to Queen Lupa's Palace* (pl. 62). The chapel originally contained a fourth portrait of her, on her fine tombstone, now set in the wall of the cloister passage to the east of the chapel.[77] This is arguably the most extensive, certainly the most concentrated, body of portraiture of one non-royal woman since antiquity.[78]

[77] For Caterina's tomb see Wolters, *Scultura Veneziana Gotica*, vol. 1, pp. 230–1 and fig. 559.

[78] Kohl, as per n. 59 above.

Caterina, chateleine of Staggia, was clearly a woman used to responsibility. Bonifacio entrusted to her the day-to-day, month-to-month, running of the building of the chapel, and the open, direct glance which she directs out of the Council scene speaks of both intelligence and confidence. The contrast with the 'closed' profile of Bonifacio – 'uomo di poche parole', and who never, in any of the putative portraits here, looks out of the pictorial space – is very striking.

The network of family and court associations displayed in S. Giacomo was evidently extensive, but the key to much of it has long ago died with the personalities involved. The precise weighting of the chapel – towards the court or towards the family – cannot be assessed in the absence of grounds for identifying most of the obvious portraits. A mixture of some kind is the safest assumption. It is clear, at any rate, that the multiple images of the donors stood at the centre of a much larger number of what, to judge from the sharply characterised and distinctive features and the clear deviation from Altichiero's basic repertoire of facial types, may be regarded with some certainty as portraits. The Council scene and the *Crucifixion* in particular are full of them, and in this respect too the Chapel of S. Giacomo has no surviving trecento precedent.[79] Beyond the handful of figures one may attempt to identify with reasonable confidence there is only speculation. The plump-featured and badly shaved man in profile above Bonifacio in the Council is accorded considerable prominence by his position and the pointing gesture of the man next to him.[80] Five or so years on, and carrying a corresponding extra layer of fat, the same man appears in S. Giorgio, in the *Funeral of St Lucy* (pls. 68, 115). His prominent inclusion in the frescoes of both chapels which contain the most portraits obviously indicates his importance for Bonifacio (whose control of the S. Giorgio project coincided with the period during which the oratory was decorated). The sharp-featured and stylishly bearded man on the bottom left of the Council appears again carrying the king's sword in the *Battle of Clavigo* (pls. 66,69), a position suggesting some particular and close connection with the king. The same goes for the ermine-caped older bearded figure holding Ramiro's helmet (pl. 70). Both of these figures seem to be portraits, and their position so close to the king suggests they must be men of some standing in this context. It may be worth mentioning that Simone and Antonio Lupi served as captain-general and vice-captain respectively during the Venetian campaign, and we might at least expect to find them here somewhere.

Perhaps we should expect to find Bonifacio here too. Fiocco and Sartori[81] identify as Bonifacio the bearded soldier standing at the centre of the *Battle*, holding a large shield (pl. 70) – the same figure, in their view, as the man looking up at the cross, with his back

[79] Individual portraits *qua* portraits are known from the earlier trecento – Simone Martini's of Petrarch's Laura is the best known – and many images of donors are probably portraits to some degree. Nardo di Cione's Strozzi chapel frescoes in S. Maria Novella in Florence contain a number of what have been taken as portraits, including those of Petrarch and Boccaccio, the latter of which may actually be an image from life. We know also that Petrarch had his likeness taken on a couple of occasions. But the systematic packing of narrative with portraits of the patron, his family, and his contemporaries which is so characteristic of the two Lupi chapels is a clear instance of the breaking of new ground.

[80] Mardersteig, 'I Ritratti', p. 270, identifies this figure as Bonifacio's brother, Giovanni Lupi.

[81] Fiocco, 'La Rivincità di Altichiero', p. 287; Sartori, 'Nota su Altichiero', p. 303.

turned, in the *Crucifixion* (pl. 43). Given the rather large number of heavily bearded knights who populate Altichiero's frescoes, these cannot be regarded as the only candidates, and in any case the figure mentioned is surely a man-at-arms rather than a knight, let alone a marquis. The imposing figure in red in the *Battle*, riding to the centre and carrying a marshall's baton, is clearly a person of substance, as is the similar mounted figure in the *Crucifixion*, sporting an ermine-trimmed bottle-green cloak and drawing his companion's attention to the cross. Even without their bascinets these figures, even where they can be distinguished from stock types, tend to resemble one another – the full beard was evidently *de rigeur* in these circles. As a group these men illustrate the absolute necessity of heraldic identification under martial conditions.

All the various strands of meaning in the S. Giacomo Chapel fan out from its overall function as a memorial to Bonifacio and to the Lupi name in the adopted Paduan context. The Wolf Rampant of the family crest is abundantly visible – on the facade, on Bonifacio's tomb, and on the shield of the foreground soldier of the *Battle of Clavigo*.[82] The frescoes give extended visual expression to the claims embodied in the text of Bonifacio's inscription. The scale of Bonifacio's patronage in Florence and Padua is remarkable, especially for a private citizen. The splendour of his Santo chapel, underlining his pedigree and dynastic connections, may be interpreted in the light of his position. There is something rather poignant about this man, in exile from his native lands and without issue, entrusting his fame to plaster and stone in the absence of a living tradition, perhaps compensating for the lack of it. It is probably a mercy that Bonifacio never lived to experience the odium in which his chosen heir came to be held, and it is an extraordinary coincidence that even as his own chapel was nearing completion he became involved in the decoration of Raimondino Lupi's Oratory of S. Giorgio, another extravagant monument built by a man in whom the dynastic line of the family had failed.

The decoration of the chapel

The exceptional qualities of Bonifacio's chapel are matched by Altichiero's contribution to it. His frescoes here represent a climax of trecento art, marking a new stage in the painterly conquest of the visible world. His work in S. Giacomo looks back to the past – consciously so – but it is at the same time profoundly innovative. The ancestral spirit of Giotto and the heroic age of Tuscan painting breathes through these narratives, but their naturalism is of an inclusiveness and sweep never attempted in Giotto's time or by any of his direct followers, and quite beyond the capabilities or ambitions of the increasingly academic and moribund art of Florence itself towards the end of the trecento. The controlling principles of Altichiero's art are laid out here with supreme clarity, and, for the first time in his surviving work, on an appropriately large scale.

These principles, the illusionistic creation of space, the related use of highly devel-

[82] The beast depicted on the shield could be taken for a lion, but it is much more like the rather thick-necked Lupi wolf than the shaggy lion of the Rossi tomb.

oped fictive architecture, the controlling use of figure groups derived, via Giottesque sources, from the relief style of Roman antiquity, all confront the spectator as he enters the chapel and encounters the great *Crucifixion*, one of the supreme *tours de force* of trecento painting. The illusion of the space in which the *Crucifixion* is set as a real space beyond the rear arcade is carefully worked out. This is achieved by architectural analogy, via the use of matching arcades for the entrance and *Crucifixion* walls, as well as by the use of an unusually low dado, allowing for a continuity between chapel floor and landscape ground-plane, and an eschewal of conventional borders round the fresco, which is framed only by the real arcade. This is the grandest of Altichiero's many versions of the three-bay setting, and in its systematic elimination of any framing element other than that provided by the actual architecture of the chapel it is his most far-reaching. The conception of the painted wall as a transparent window, unimpeded by any border which might draw the spectator's attention back to the wall as a flat surface, receives here its definitive trecento statement. The idea was always latent in the progressive spatial styles of Tuscany and Umbria, but it was left to Altichiero's supremely logical, clarifying, and synthesising imagination to draw the necessary conclusions and put them into practice.

A similarly radical illusionism is at work in the Ramiro scenes on the east wall (pls. 65–71), where the pictorial border is reduced to an absolute minimum and the lower border of the tripartite group is conceived as if it were a stone cornice running along the wall above the stall canopies, as part of the real architectural framework of the chapel. This reading is given further point by Altichiero's treatment of the real corner pier in the north-east corner as part of Ramiro's bedroom, complete with exiting servant (pl. 65). No painted border whatever impedes the transition between the east wall and the corner pier at this point.

The chapel's illusionism is carefully and centrally focused. The *Crucifixion* and the Ramiro wall are designed to be seen from a shared optimum viewpoint, just in front of the altar (pl. 40). From this spot the illusion of the *Crucifixion* landscape's recession into deep space is at its most persuasive, and it is from here that the perspectival structure of the architectural box sheltering *Ramiro's Council* makes most sense. It is from here, too, that the *trompe l'œil* niches flanking the *Crucifixion* line up with the tombs above them and with the orthogonals of the main fresco (pls. 40–1). This motif seems to be derived from the 'side-chapels' of the Arena Chapel sanctuary arch.

Other less prominent examples of illusionism are adjusted to take account of the spectator's progress round the interior of the chapel. The fictive double-skin polyfoil above the west wall endowment stone adjusts its two layers to be seen from the standpoint of someone reading the inscription below.[83] The south face of the re-entrant pier in the north-east corner gives an alternative set of fictive adjuncts to the architecture of

[83] This particular type of illusionistic motif has a Tuscan pedigree. Its most celebrated use is in Taddeo Gaddi's Baroncelli Chapel frescoes in S. Croce in Florence. Sartori, 'La Cappella di S. Giacomo', p. 278 identifies Taddeo as Altichiero's master. There are no particular stylistic reasons for accepting this, but Altichiero was clearly familiar with S. Croce.

Ramiro's Dream for the benefit of a spectator standing closer to the wall than to the altar. Such examples have abundant precedents in early trecento Tuscan art, but there is little from that period to compare with the sophistication of Altichiero's practice in this area. Such a *tour de force* as even so insignificant a part of the chapel as the north-east corner pier, photographs of which can leave one in genuine doubt as to where the fictive takes over from the real, shows how far Altichiero was in advance of his predecessors in the blending of real and imaginary worlds.

The centrepiece of the chapel's decoration is the *Crucifixion*, one of the peaks of trecento art, arguably the finest single fresco of the later fourteenth century. The epic naturalism of this great scene must give at least some idea of the qualities which drew so much attention to the lost Josephus frescoes in Verona. What is so remarkable is not so much the extent of this vast crowd, for it has precedents, but the discipline with which it is controlled and which sets it in a space whose depth is suggested, but never allowed to become a distraction. The concentration on the central focus of the scene is achieved in several ways. A three-bay wall might on the face of it seem to cry out for the inclusion of the thieves' crosses, but these, which would have effectively broken the fresco into three Crucifixions side by side, are passed over, in contrast with the later version in S. Giorgio (pl. 86), where the single field allows Altichiero to organise the three crosses in a centralised and unified group. For all the multiplicity of incident, the architecture of the crowd is strictly controlled. Slow, rising, diagonals lead from the bridge on the left, via the mounted figures, to the cross, and, on the right, from the game of dice up to the centre in much the same way, binding the two wings to the centre. The cross is framed by two prominent mounted men marked out by their active gestures, and it is located in space by a loose circle of standing figures round the base, viewing it from all sides. Other elements, like the parallel ladder and spear of the left bay, return the eye to the centre to compensate for the movement of the group leaving the scene across the bridge. Another, looser, kind of compositional chain may be traced from the lapping dog of the lower left corner, through the child which has observed it but turned back towards the centre, through its mother's gaze towards the cross, along the line of heads of the grieving women and up to the cross itself. Such subtle compositional links abound; it would be tedious to draw attention to them all.

The overall shape of the crowd is a broadly symmetrical triangular mound with a truncated and flattened top, where the horizon of heads acts as a marked spatial brake. Behind the broad design lies the ghost of the four-section Crucifixion format commonly employed since Giotto's time, but expanded and disguised. The large-scale grouping is subjected at local level to a vast range of variations of position and attitude. The area in the middle bay, to the left of the cross, contains a large number of figures (and horses), none of whose heads is at the same angle or degree of tilt as any other, and none of whose bodies stand in exactly the same plane. This virtuosity of figure drawing, reminiscent of the nearly contemporary drawing of the *Triumph of Fame* in BN Lat. 6069F, effectively leavens the mass, though, again, without detracting from the controlled quality of the overall design. Also present, in a shadowy form, are versions of the self-contained, isocephalic, figure group, so important to the quasi-architectural compositions of Altichiero's models. But here these groups, which dominate the more compact frescoes of S. Giorgio, are integrated with the whole crowd, each subgroup more or less inextricably compounded with its neighbours. The extent of Altichiero's transformation of the given format can be gauged by comparing the S. Giacomo fresco with Turone's S. Fermo *Crucifixion* (fig. 16), a version much more conventionally bound by the four-part division of the crowd inherited from early trecento Florentine sources.

The whole tripartite scene is framed by architectural and landscape repoussoirs. The buildings on the left and right are carefully placed, close to the window frames, but not eclipsed at any point by them. The city gate to the left and the rocky landscape to the right, as well as putting visual limits to the scene, at the same time serve to hint at undeclared spatial extensions beyond the confines of the three bays. Figures leave the scene on the left and enter from the right. The architectural repoussoirs at the lower level – bridge and tomb – similarly suggest areas beyond the limits of the given pictorial field as well as signifying the immediate past and immediate future of the particular narrative being illustrated. The location of the crowd in the receding space is established by the shelf of bare ground stretching from the dado to the main mass of figures, and the spatial reality of this shelf in turn is fixed in each bay by some element placed forward from the crowd – the bridge and weeping woman on the left, the women at the foot of the cross in the centre, the gamblers on the right. To the left and right of the whole scene the lower edge of the main body of the crowd recedes away and upwards in a soft curve. At the same time the rising line of the flanking buildings towards the outer spandrels of the arcade, together with the corresponding tendency of the bridge and gaming group in the side bays to pull the attention down to the lower corners, combine to give the total composition a kind of bowed shape which drags the gaze to the centre. These adjustments, which take account of the expected viewing position towards the centre of the chapel, are typical of an empirical and very alert approach to perspective which looks back again to Maso's frescoes in S. Croce. The slight angling of the foreground wall which is the closest part of the little bridge to the spectator, is typical of a whole series of smaller adjustments, and one which yet again points to Altichiero's profound study of Maso's *St Sylvester Restoring a Bull to Life* (fig. 18).

The panoramic and inclusive spatial grasp of the S. Giacomo *Crucifixion* is matched by its narrative and descriptive contents. The fresco contains 113 figures, including those seen only in part, and excluding Christ and the eight attendant angels. The variety of attitude and posture have been remarked, and behind each of these different poses lies some convincing narrative or emotional rationale – there is no empty virtuosity here. The actors in this vast drama take on a great variety of roles, from the mounted marshals and knights of the upper levels, to the more humble men-at-arms, down to the carpenters and artisans who are interrogated by passers-by (pl. 45) as they return to the city through a greatly embellished version of city gates well known to Altichiero, like those of the Ponte Pietra in Verona or the Paduan Pontemolino, yards from Bonifacio's house. With the exception of the mourning women, and a number of majestic bearded old men, who wear heavy cloaks and are probably meant for senior Jews, most of the figures wear contemporary dress, and the variety of carefully described different coloured and mi-partite stuffs, padded and quilted jackets, straw hats, coarsely and finely buttoned tunics – fashionably tight or loose and baggy – gives as comprehensive a picture of late fourteenth-century dress, and its social significance, as anything from the period. The exotic (from an Italian point of view) races are less abundant here than in S. Giorgio, though pigtails and turbans of various designs can be found, along with what seems to be an Arab (left bay), and one rather fierce black profile (right bay), regarded with some apprehension by his immediate neighbour. The Paduans had plenty of contact with the peoples of the East – the *Cronaca Carrarese* gives a description of the Turkish troops used against Padua by the Venetians in 1373[84] – but they do not seem to have impressed them with the intensity experienced by the inhabitants of Treviso when faced by the Hungarian hordes of Louis the Great in 1356,[85] perhaps because Padua itself was never besieged or realistically threatened with destruction by the Turks.

The military presence is, as is customary for a crowded Crucifixion, strongly in evidence here – appropriately too, given Bonifacio Lupi's career. The fresco preserves a great deal of very detailed observation of military hardware and costume, though much of the plate armour has suffered damage to the original metalled surfaces. Even so, the types of armour common in the 1370s are very clearly depicted, including an example of studded-and-splinted armour (central bay, upper left), something which might have been regarded as rather old-fashioned by this time, at least in an English context – and we know the impression made on Italian eyes by the constantly tested English equipment and methods of waging war.[86] The senior commanders here mostly wear full plate armour, with luxurious cloaks in some cases, and tight jupons. Their headgear varies from the full, closed, bascinet to the more common open-chinned and peaked helmet, worn in at least one case with a softer hat outside it. Some of the standing soldiers wear a short-sleeved quilted jacket over what may be a mixture of mail and plate. Others sport short and very fancy dagged and fretted jupons of a thin material. A wide variety of clasps and buckles is on show.

The prevailing emotional temper is grave, observant, attentive; anything remotely hysterical is firmly excluded. This is entirely characteristic of Altichiero's response to narrative, and it may be founded on direct exposure to Roman relief sculpture. The styles of early imperial and Flavian carving frequently make themselves felt through Altichiero's figure groups. This influence was partly transmitted via the Giottesque legacy, of which it formed a component part, but this is not perhaps enough, by itself, to account for the look of the great foreground friezes of S. Giacomo and S. Giorgio. While these, in Altichiero's time, undiscovered monuments of Augustan and Flavian art cannot be the direct sources for the group on the left of the S. Giacomo *Crucifixion*,

84 Gatari, *Cronaca Carrarese*, p. 113.

85 Gibbs, *Tomaso da Modena*, pp. 127 and 149–50.

86 See Temple-Leader and Marcotti, *Sir John Hawkwood*, pp. 39ff.

it is the style represented by the *Ara Pacis*, the *Ara Pietatis*, the Flavian reliefs from the Palazzo della Cancelleria in Rome or the great *Suovetaurilia Procession* in the Louvre which haunts Altichiero's Paduan frescoes. The juxtaposition of figures in closely adjacent planes, the articulation of groups by means of variously turned heads, the joining together of subgroups within the frieze by the use of great curves of drapery, all these recall imperial Roman style more precisely than if it had just been glimpsed through the filter of Giotto's interpretation of the same style. There is no great difficulty involved in seeing how Altichiero might have encountered such models – sarcophagi at least were plentiful all over Italy – and we may reasonably assume that, although the *Ara Pacis* and the others were not available, there may have been fragments now lost which artists could have seen. The evidence of the S. Giorgio *Crucifixion*, as well as that of the Darmstadt drawing of S. Nicolo in Carcere, suggests that Altichiero had visited Rome and seen these things for himself. Whatever the exact means of transmission, the spirit of first- and second-century relief sculpture is felt very strongly here, in the one city in Italy where we know such things were discussed (see chapter 6 below).

The extreme emotional agitation of Pictro Lorenzetti's Assisi *Crucifixion*, the menace of 'Barna's' version in S. Gimignano, or, closer to Altichiero's time, the explosively choreographed violence of Tomaso da Modena's *Massacre of St Ursula*, all stand at the opposite expressive pole from Altichiero's monumental *gravitas*. But the emotional core of Alticherian restraint lies very deep. The depth of sorrow in individual faces scattered throughout the crowd is profound, and the pinched, drained face of the Virgin, her body supported by her companion's arm, dragging a great sweep of drapery up with it, is unforgettable. More subtle reactions are charted too, like the whole range of different types and degrees of wonder, consternation and sheer bafflement displayed by various spectators close to the cross. Gestures expressive of the various reactions to the central event are typically reticent, but they are physically convincing and dramatically effective. The contrast, for instance, between the dignified and restrained gesture of the green-cloaked, plumed, commander on the right of the cross, a man supremely in control of himself, and the more overtly astonished response of the studded-and-splinted knight to the left, is very telling. Individual figures are of an extraordinary beauty – one might point to the white-robed young man in the right bay drawing his older companion's attention to the game of dice, and, where the dirt and damage are not too obtrusive, faces stand out which are modelled with a refinement hardly exceeded anywhere in the fourteenth century. The two bearded men to the left of the cross in the central bay stand out in this respect, or the old man just to the right of the column dividing the central and left bays. The drawing is incisive and supremely logical, but the handling is unmistakably painterly, and the modelling exhibits a wonderfully subtle control of a continously modulated surface. The long eyes of the young man in white distantly reflect some of Giotto's figures, but the general design more immediately suggests the art of the one Florentine contemporary whom Altichiero occasionally resembles, Nardo di Cione. The kind of head Altichiero is depicting here has affinities with a Nardo type seen, for instance, in the figure of St John the Evangelist in the panel of *Sts John the Evangelist, John the Baptist, and St James* of around 1365 in the National Gallery in London. But the typically Florentine primacy of preordained graphic decisions, of the smoothed-out, elegant line in Nardo's panel contrasts with the essentially painterly imagination revealed in Altichiero's figure. The differences are partly attributable to the contrasting media, but a comparison between Altichiero's work and any late trecento Florentine fresco makes the same point. The hard, metallic, surfaces of the figures in the frescoes of Spinello Aretino or Agnolo Gaddi are in every way the antithesis of Altichiero's more atmospheric style, just as the jerky anecdotal approach to narrative characteristic of much Florentine art after Orcagna's time is worlds away from Altichiero's dramatic control.

The figure of Christ is modelled with similar qualities. The type used distantly recalls the designs of Turone and his school,[87] though far outstripping them in terms of technical accomplishment. Altichiero places the torso and legs of Christ more centrally and frontally than is the case with most of the versions by Giotto and his followers, avoiding the expressive swing of the body out to one side. The proportions of the body are more compact, without the exaggerated length of lower abdomen typical of the Veronese school. The frontality and the refinement of modelling suggest once again Altichiero's affinities with Puccio Capanna. The S. Giacomo Christ, though more wasp-waisted and less elongated than either, stands somewhere between Puccio's completely frontal and four-square Christ in the S. Francesco chapterhouse *Crucifixion* at Assisi (fig. 26) and the smaller version from S. Rufinuccio, where the legs hang more obliquely.

No less remarkable than the *Crucifixion* are the three Ramiro scenes combined on the east wall. The use of architecture here, as it is in the three lunettes painted by Altichiero (cat. 2, nos. 5, 7, and 8; pls. 59, 60, 62 and 63), is extraordinarily imaginative, containing and linking the three scenes, and placing them in a continuous and logical spatial setting. The bedroom and the council chamber interconnect by means of a door at the back of the council chamber (pl. 65), and access is given to both from the shallow plinth in front of the latter, with a flight of steps leading to the bedroom. The architectural detail, rather abraded in this part of the chapel, is imagined with absolute clarity and conviction and painted with great delicacy, from the extravagant scroll-work of Ramiro's bed and the dainty loggia above it to more obvious star turns like the vaguely classicising relief panels *en grisaille* on the frontal wall of the council chamber. The exceptional nature of the spatial box containing the Council scene has often been noticed. A typically Alticherian sleight-of-hand is at work, making the structure look as though it projects out of the wall, seeming closer to the spectator standing in the centre of the chapel than the adjacent steps, which are 'actually' nearer. The purpose of this adjustment, which is marked by one of those minimal but very precise touches which mark Altichiero's use of the architectural setting for narrative, the slight projection of the ball finials at the top of the council chamber over the upper border of the fresco, is clear enough. It underlines what may have been, for Bonifacio, the part of the ensemble which had the greatest personal significance.

[87] E.g. the *Trinity* on the SS Trinità polyptych; the west wall and north wall *Crucifixions* in S. Fermo in Verona; the *Crucifixion* in S. Pietro Martire in Verona; the detached *Crucifixion* fresco in the Castelvecchio.

The *Council* itself is a sober affair and the response of these assembled courtiers to what is, on the face of it, a dramatic enough announcement shares none of the agitation characteristic of many other adaptations of the basic iconography, in legal or didactic contexts. Many a student in a trecento law manuscript or condemned to an eternal lecture on his master's tombstone[88] reacts with more fervour to the exposition of a line of the *Digest* than do these grave, self-possessed courtiers to the news of promised apostolic succour against the heathen. This is likely to reflect to some extent the realities of the Paduan court, where life, under the persistent influence of humanist culture, was perhaps less boisterous than that of a more 'horsey' court like Estense Ferrara before Petrarch turned his attentions to it.[89] An Augustan seriousness of demeanour may have been a matter of form in Francesco il Vecchio's court – and an extremely guarded expression of emotion at all times was undoubtedly a wise course for men who lived in daily contact with rulers whose suspicions and caprices lay, inevitably, very close to however polished a surface. The nature of this surface varied, obviously, but the ultra-polite Giangaleazzo Visconti was quite as formidable and dangerous from the viewpoint of any associate as the more overtly irascible Bernabo. On the whole, though, the combined influences of humanist culture and their own longevity of power rendered the later trecento courts more and more refined and increasingly subject to their own developing traditions. Francesco da Carrara seems, in fact, to have been reasonably approachable, not placing social barriers between himself and his subjects – something Petrarch praised[90] – and cultivating genuine friendships with selected associates. The piety, probity, and silence which Villani and the tomb inscription tell us were characteristic of Bonifacio Lupi are reflected in this wider portrait of the Carrarese court – intimate and formal at the same time.

It is, of course, a very pointed and selected image of the court, one which stresses its humanist credentials, which puts a premium on its scholarly and literary side. The humanist emblems crowd round this part of the chapel: the prominent portraits of Petrarch, who died while the chapel was under construction, and of Lombardo, the imperial profile portrait on the corner pier, the multilayered imperial associations of the central figure, all embraced within a design making clear references to the tradition of the humanists' favourite artist, Giotto. At the time of the frescoes' execution Francesco da Carrara had quite recently taken possession of the *Madonna and Child* by Giotto which Petrarch bequeathed to him.[91] Perhaps this was in Altichiero's mind when he painted the rather Giottesque framed Madonna seen above the rear door of Ramiro's bedroom.

When these serious men ride out to war, their demeanour is unchanged. The sobriety and calm of the *Council* extends to the battlefield, dominated not by the frenzied

[88] See Grandi, *I Monumenti dei Dottori*, *passim*; Gibbs, *Tomaso da Modena*, pp. 50–86 and 'Images of Higher Education in Fourteenth-Century Bologna'. Several examples of the Doctor's Tomb type, with students, survive in Verona, e.g. on the facade of S. Pietro Martire and in the cloister of S. Fermo.

[89] See Levi, *Francesco di Vannozzo*, p. 109.

[90] Kohl and Witt, *Earthly Republic*, p. 39.

[91] See Mommsen, *Petrarch's Testament.*

agitation characteristic of other trecento battle scenes but by a solemn, awestruck, and, in terms of the narrative, entirely appropriate response to a miracle. Actual fighting is relegated to the distance and to the right-hand margin, where two tremendous warriors press home their assault. The figure of Ramiro/Louis holds centre stage here too and the action slows to a standstill round his kneeling figure. In its original condition the *Battle of Clavigo* must have had a greater immediate impact than it does in its present condition. Blazon abounds here, the flags wave in the distance, and the tents, jupons and harnesses still glow with colour. The horizon is raised high, allowing the spectator standing on the chapel floor to read the receding landscape. On the left a great phalanx of soldiers tails off into the distance behind the tents. Perspective and scale are determined empirically – the spatial recession is not consonant with that of the council chamber, and figures in the right-hand background are in scale neither with their surroundings nor with their equivalents on the left of the scene. This is a response to the demands of the setting, high on the wall, made in the interests of narrative clarity, and in practice the anomalies are not obtrusive. They stem from the general difficulties thrown up by attempts to reconcile early Renaissance spatial logic with the kind of complex architectural settings provided by an evolved Gothic style.

Altichiero's own architectural imagination comes to the fore in the three lunettes of the St James series for which he was responsible (pls. 59, 60, 62, 80). In the fifth and eighth scenes the architectural framework for the narrative is the dominant element in the composition. The eighth scene, in which Queen Lupa is baptised and rededicates her palace as a church, locks the narrative into a single architectural structure. The calculated asymmetries of detail, the firm frontal lock, the spatial sophistication of the background – with what may be a reference on the right to Giotto's temple structure in the early Joachim scenes of the Arena Chapel – all disguise the fact that this is, fundamentally, another version of the three-bay setting, but with a central blank panel. The transition from secular building on the left to church on the right within the compass of a single structure is subtly managed – a pitched roof, gable-end with tabernacle, campanile and pulpit replace the loggia and balcony of the building's previous incarnation. The continuity and logic of architectural vision are remarkable – the left side of the building is a view of the part of the palace already seen in the seventh scene, but from a different angle.

The chapel as a whole exhibits a remarkable fusion of architectural and pictorial concerns. Careful planning at every stage is implied by the happy combination of large- and small-scale architecture, and the fresco decoration is painted more or less consistently as if lit from the window in the west wall. The exceptional treatment of the south wall was surely envisaged from early on, and it would scarcely stretch credulity to suggest that the painter was involved in the planning process from early on, even if one resists the inference that he must have designed the chapel as a whole. If this were the case, then the man involved was surely, one might think, Altichiero. His authorship of the frescoes so far discussed is beyond doubt, and his is, in any reading, the dominant contribution to the decoration as a whole. The long-standing tradition, which takes various forms, that Altichiero collaborated with another artist here, or even that this other artist, 'Avanzo' or 'Avanzi', was substantially responsible for the frescoes of S. Giacomo would seem to have been comprehensively rebutted by the publication of the 1379 payment,[92] in which no other artist is mentioned, and in which there is no suggestion that Altichiero was completing work begun by another man – as Rinaldino da Francia had done in the case of the altar figures, a sharing of responsibility which the chapel accounts scrupulously record.[93] The most obviously prestigious and prominent parts of the chapel are by Altichiero and he was paid a very substantial sum for painting them. It is tempting in this light to adopt Sartori's line and simply ascribe the chapel's frescoes wholly to Altichiero and his workshop, with any stylistic fluctuations explicable in terms of the number of people likely to be involved in any extensive fresco decoration.

But such a view of the frescoes is in conflict with evidence of two kinds. The first is purely stylistic. It is perfectly clear that five of the upper lunettes of the Life of St James (pls. 52–8, 61), together with the Prophets of the east bay of the vault and the Saints and Prophets on the adjacent transverse arch are not by Altichiero, but by a different hand altogether. The differences are too great to be explicable as indicating an assistant executing Altichiero's designs; it is precisely on the level of design that the difference between the two styles is so clear.

The architecture of the five lunettes reveals a fundamentally different approach to that shown by Altichiero in the lower wall scenes of S. Giacomo, and throughout S. Giorgio, where there is no question but that he was responsible for all the frescoes. The containing structures of the first, second, and fourth St James scenes are developed with a picturesque but unsystematic use of space quite alien to Altichiero's practice. The cramped interior of Lupa's palace in the fourth scene, the spindly circular wings of the second scene, the flattened and trapezoid aisles of the basilical structure of the first scene reveal an architectural imagination which is certainly not to be written off, but which has no relation to the particular kind of logic characteristic of Altichiero's work. The occasional instance of an architectural motif which echoes Altichiero's repertoire just emphasises the discrepancy. The uncertain handling of the city gate and foreground wall in the *Execution of St James* may be compared with the supremely assured perspective of its equivalent in the *Crucifixion* immediately below. If it is argued that these uncertainties reflect the difficulties of projecting architecture in frescoes located high on a wall, one need only look at the fifth, seventh, and eighth lunettes to see a contrasting and wholly confident approach to the problem.

The figure style of the five lunettes is also quite distinctive. The figures listening to the dispute between St James and Filetus in the first scene of the St James cycle (pl. 53) are squat in proportions, harshly drawn, and pungently characterised, almost to the point of caricature at times. The old men in the left wing of the first scene, their hard, tight, curly hair drawn in meticulous detail, are worlds away from the monumental and

[92] See Simon, 'Altichiero Versus Avanzo', p. 252.

[93] 'Ancora dato a maestro Raynaldin, per lavorero dele figure . . . e per lavorero del pedestallo fatto per altro maestro'. Sartori, 'Nota su Altichiero', p. 320, no. 38.

painterly sages of the *Crucifixion*. The five lunettes abound in faces drawn from a highly flavoured repertoire allied to a narrative style as striking in its operatic vigour as it is unlike Altichiero's own, much calmer, approach. The contrast in styles can be seen in detail in the roundels and transverse arches of the vaults. Where Altichiero never seeks to register a particular expression by giving prominence to any single feature, conceiving his faces as whole structures, rather than an assembly of emphatic details, the Prophets of the eastern vault bay and the adjacent transverse arch exhibit just such an attention to additive detail, with every expressive nuance squeezed from a combination of flashing eyes, exaggeratedly long noses and fleshy, sensuous mouths. The modelling of Jeremiah from the eastern vault traces every crease of the skin, every sinew of the neck. By contrast, the modelling in the Doctors of the western vault (pls. 51c, 51d), or any of the foreground faces of the *Crucifixion*, is highly atmospheric, painted with a veiled quality and an understatement of modelling which relates to the style of the other hand, in trecento terms, rather as Giorgione's does to Mantegna's.

The presence of two distinct hands at work on a fresco scheme of this size can be read in various ways, and past accounts of the frescoes differ in their interpretations. The problem for those wanting to keep the lunettes, even admitting their distinct characteristics, within the overall orbit of Altichiero's shop, with the Lunette Master, to adopt Schubring's term for the moment, as an assistant-cum-partner, a quasi-independent hand sharing a commercial and professional identity with his master – a sort of Taddeo Gaddi to Altichiero's Giotto – is that it is clear from the evidence of the vaults that it was the 'assistant' who took precedence, who began the frescoes of S. Giacomo and that, whatever he was doing, he cannot have been working on the basis of an overall design by Altichiero. The border types and ornamental detail of the S. Giacomo vault area (pl. 51b) are quite unlike anything in Altichiero's earlier work in Verona or his other work in Padua, and the use of heavy pictorial frames for the lunettes is at odds with the approach seen in the lower part of the chapel. The decorations of the S. Giacomo vault ribs, the running borders of the cells, the prominent framing elements round the lunettes, simply do not fit into the known pattern of his border style, which is both consistent and distinctive; they do not even resemble the repertoire of his followers throughout the region. It follows, then, that this painter cannot have begun the chapel in any capacity as Altichiero's assistant.

Two alternatives remain. Either Altichiero had a collaborator, or he took over from another master for some reason. The nature of the east wall might seem to favour the second option. Study of the eastern lunette (pl. 52) reveals a quite distinct change in tonality between the greater part of the fresco and the plinth which runs along the bottom of the basilica framing the dispute between St James and Filetus. The break between *giornate* at this point is easily visible. The plinth makes virtual nonsense of the architecture resting on it, suggesting that the receding inner arches of the aisles, which on their own terms must be as deep as the forward arches are wide, are only as deep as the much shallower plinth. The plinth, locked to the picture plane and placed in a perspective at odds with that of the superstructure, can easily be related to Altichiero's architectural style, and the inference must be that he took over this fresco and completed it, imposing himself on it at the expense of the other painter's conception. Such disregard for another master's work hardly suggests amicable collaboration.

On the other hand, the layout of the upper part of the chapel, the way the frescoes are divided between the two hands, tends to make collaboration look the more likely option. The division here is: two vault bays and one transverse arch to Altichiero, one bay and one arch to the other painter, with the overall borders attributable to him too. The western vault bay, with roundels by Altichiero, is directly above lunettes on the north and south walls (cat. 2, nos. 23, 24 and 25) executed by the other hand. It is extremely unlikely, impossible even, that this part of the scheme, if it were left incomplete because of the first painter's death or departure, would have been left incomplete in the way suggested by the layout as it exists, with the vaults unfinished, and work on the lunettes well advanced. One would always expect the vaults to have been painted in their entirety before the frescoes on the walls below. The overall look of the area above the cornice, Altichiero's narratives and figures notwithstanding, is the responsibility of the lunette master, just as the lower part of the chapel is Altichiero's.

A combination of the two options may resolve this apparently conflicting evidence. In this reading the S. Giacomo frescoes would have been begun by Altichiero and the other master, with the latter taking the lead at this stage, until, for whatever reason, Altichiero took over sole responsibility for the work, completing the unfinished east lunettes and painting the whole of the chapel below the main cornice. The dominance of the other painter in the initial stages, the subordination of Altichiero's narratives to his overall scheme, borders and all, makes it very difficult to see the relationship between the two as one in which Altichiero took the guiding role at the beginning of this commission.

This reading is, on the face of it, in conflict with the surviving documentation of the chapel. The earliest references to painting in the payment lists are to a painter in the singular – 'lo dipinctore' – and there is no mention in Altichiero's final payment of his having finished work begun by someone else, as there is in the payment to Rinaldino da Francia. It is also true, as both Sartori and Simon point out,[94] that 792 ducats is an excessive payment for a mere 'finisher-off'. But this is in any case an inadequate description of his role in S. Giacomo as a whole, which could only be regarded as secondary right at the beginning of the work, under circumstances which are still unclear, and dominant after that. The evidence of the frescoes themselves points pretty clearly to initial collaboration followed by complete takeover.

The second body of evidence in conflict with a pan-Altichiero reading of the chapel comprises the literary and historical tradition of Altichiero's shared authorship of the frescoes. This tradition, an extension of that attached to the Sala Virorum Illustrium, and which as a whole needs to be viewed with extreme caution, springs from two passages in Savonarola's *Libellus*, one describing the glories of the Santo, the other listing the most important non-Paduan painters to have worked in Padua during the trecento.

[94] Sartori, 'La Cappella di S. Giacomo', p. 281; Simon, 'Altichiero Versus Avanzo', p. 256.

In the first passage Savonarola refers to the chapel of St Anthony, with its frescoes by Stefano da Ferrara and goes on: 'Altera vero marchionum Soranee humandis corporis concessa, que manibus Iacobi de Avantio gloriosissimis imaginibus depicta est.'[95] He does not specify that this is the chapel of S. Giacomo *inside* the Santo, as opposed to the Oratory of S. Giorgio just outside it, but in context, paired with the shrine chapel in the text, as in reality, there is no reason to doubt that it is S. Giacomo that Savonarola is discussing.

In the second passage Savonarola gives pride of place to Giotto, then: 'secundam sedem Jacopo Avantii Bononiensis dabimus, qui magnificorum Marchionum de Lupis admirandam Capellam veluti viventibus figuris ornavit. Tertiam vero Altichiero Veronensi.'[96] Once again, Savonarola fails to specify which Lupi chapel he means – and S. Giorgio actually is a chapel of the Lupi in the plural – though the continuity from the first passage suggests that he is still thinking of S. Giacomo.

Savonarola's initial remarks are more important, and demand more serious attention, than the rest of the tradition, which grows more and more confused and increasingly remote from the objects described in the hands of Michiel[97] (except where he refers to Riccio) and Vasari. It is noticeable that Savonarola makes his attribution, not to the vague 'Avanzo' of the later tradition, but very specifically to Jacopo Avanzi of Bologna. He was quite wrong, of course, to exclude Altichiero's name from the authorship of the S. Giacomo frescoes, but it is not difficult to explain how he might have made this mistake. It may be assumed that, during the course of his researches, Savonarola examined the volume in which Bonifacio gathered all the chapel's documentation together. If, for the sake of argument, this lost book contained an early contract for the painting of the chapel which mentioned a name other than Altichiero's, Savonarola would quite naturally look no further for the author of the frescoes, and thus exclude Altichiero, whose name appeared either later in the same contract or on another, later contract. There clearly was a tradition of Altichiero's having worked in the chapel, and his name must obviously have appeared in the 'libro de la capella', if not on the walls, as Sartori asserted,[98] for his part in the decoration is the one thing about which even Michiel (who had the benefit of having consulted with the very reliable Riccio, even if he did not always believe him) is reasonably certain. Savonarola's mistake casts no particular shadow over his assertion that Jacopo Avanzi worked in S. Giacomo. The reference is so specific that something must lie behind it. Savonarola's other two artists, Giotto and Altichiero, left considerable bodies of work in Padua and their names were presumably well known. There is, on the other hand, no reason to suppose that Savonarola would have even heard of Jacopo Avanzi if there were not something known to be his visible in Padua. Presumably he took Jacopo to be the author of all the S. Giacomo frescoes, a reasonable mistake under the circumstances.

So why is there absolutely no mention of Jacopo Avanzi, or any other painter but Altichiero, at the other end of the process, in the payment lists? One obvious inference

95 Savonarola, *Libellus*, p. 13.

96 *Ibid.*, p. 44.

97 For Michiel see Simon, 'Altichiero Versus Avanzo', pp. 263–4.

98 Sartori, 'La Cappella di S. Giacomo', p. 284.

is that there simply was no other painter involved, except in the usual capacity of assistant, in which case we would not expect to find him named. But the painter of the five lunettes and the vault decoration cannot, as we have seen, be so described. We have lost all but the architectural contracts for S. Giacomo, but we would expect payment to another artist to show up in some form in the surviving records, which chart every minute output of cash in meticulous detail. Even if the lunette master had suddenly died, payment to his heirs or representatives would surely have registered in some form. The only alternative inference which makes any sense must be that Altichiero and this other painter shared their practice in some way, so that, commercially speaking, they were regarded as one unit, in which case a payment made to Altichiero covered the expenses owing to the other painter (or his dependants). Medieval contracts are usually very precise on the subject of divided labour and apportioned salaries, but the record at issue here is not a precise legal instrument of that kind, merely a running account of expended cash made for the convenience of the patron. If, as the layout of the frescoes suggests, Altichiero completed the chapel by himself, then he, and not the other painter, was on the spot to receive payment. There would be no need to mention anyone else, for the payment would be, in terms of money actually handed over, to Altichiero alone. Nor would there be any need to specify that he had completed some other master's work. The Rinaldino entry was specific in this way because he had a commercial identity quite distinct from that of the other artists working on the chapel. The physical evidence of the upper part of the fresco scheme, looked at in conjunction with these other arguments, suggests that, with regard to the painting, and for these purposes, Altichiero did not.

By itself, this argument only goes so far. But the previously shadowy outline of Jacopo Avanzi's *œuvre*, complicated by the fact that there are two documented Bolognese painters of this name working at the same time as Altichiero, has been considerably stabilised in recent years,[99] and the more coherent view of his style allows for more definite comparisons to be made between his work and the five errant lunettes of S. Giacomo.

The key works round which Avanzi's *œuvre* has accumulated are the signed panel of the *Crucifixion* in the Galleria Colonna in Rome, and the fresco of the *Massacre of the Idolatrous Hebrews* from the extensive Mezzaratta cycle, now in the Pinacoteca in Bologna. Avanzi's signature was once legible on this,[100] one of three scenes of the Life of Moses. The affinities with the S. Giacomo lunettes are strong. The figure style is the same, and the facial types characteristic of lunettes 1, 2, 3, 4 and 6 (see cat. 2) – the sharp profiles, the beady eyes, the tendency to express attention, passion, alarm, and other emotions, in visual terms suggesting bad temper, match up quite precisely. The Mezzaratta fresco also shares with the S. Giacomo lunettes examples of exaggerated foreshortening, and a tendency to tilt the occasional head at an angle so acute that it looks like a parody of Altichiero's less neck-wrenching versions of the same feat of draughtsmanship. An excitable and expressive use of gesturing hands and active body

[99] For Jacopo Avanzi's career see Benati, *Jacopo Avanzi*.

[100] The signature was seen in 1909 by Baldani. See Ragghianti, *Pittura tra Giotto e Pisanello*, p. 46.

positions accompanies these traits in both cases. More detailed comparisons between individual figures confirm the affinities.

These stylistic characteristics are found in a number of other works, most notably the newly revealed and very impressive frescoes at Montefiore. Jacopo Avanzi was clearly an artist of considerable calibre, and this is borne out by the fact that both the Colonna panel, which bears their coat of arms, and the Montefiore frescoes, were Malatesta commissions. He seems, in fact, to have been rather specifically a court artist, working outside Bologna for much of his career, in contrast with the majority of Bolognese artists, who stayed in Bologna and supplied the buoyant domestic market.[101]

In this respect Aranzi's career has obvious parallels with Altichiero's, and it is highly significant in this context that instances or reflections of Avanzi's style, or of a style resembling it, turn up repeatedly in some sort of association with Altichiero. The drawings of various kinds which reflect Altichiero's work in the Sala Grande and the Sala Virorum Illustrium also reveal the occasional presence of a second artist whose work, allowing for the second- or even third-hand transmission of the originals, is recognisably like that of Jacopo Avanzi. The Paris drawing of the *Triumph of Vespasian and Titus*, generally Altichieresque in spirit, also contains figures very like those of the Montefiore *Battle Scene*. The foreground rider, leaning sharply forward in the saddle, is almost exactly the same as one of the Montefiore knights. The sense of strain, of slight exaggeration in the interests of expressive and narrative urgency, is also reminiscent of a figure like the celebrated rider in the sixth S. Giacomo lunette. This characteristic is not generally suggestive of Altichiero's style – compare the four-square horse and rider combination of *St George and the Dragon* in S. Giorgio (pl. 92). Comparison between the tumultuous Montefiore *Battle Scene* and Altichiero's *Battle of Clavigo* reproduces exactly the sort of contrast which exists between the five lunettes and the rest of the frescoes of S. Giacomo. The same un-Altichieresque traits can be detected in some of the Darmstadt grisailles, juxtaposed with figures and groups which are clearly related to his style, as well as in the Louvre Triumph drawing. The possibly Bolognese author of the Darmstadt narratives may, of course, be responsible for the intrusion of a Bolognese flavour in this way, but it is still possible to see through the handling of the drawings to an earlier stylistic division.

The precise nature and extent of Altichiero's relationship with Jacopo Avanzi would be very hard to determine on the basis of the S. Giacomo chapel alone. The possibility that he may have collaborated in some way with him on his major commissions of the 1360s and early 1370s stabilises the picture somewhat, even if it does little to clarify it. There is still some uncertainty as to which Jacopo Avanzi signed the Colonna panel, but there are, just to add to the confusion, factors in both cases which might explain why either of them would have abandoned the S. Giacomo frescoes.

The first and better documented of the two Bolognese Jacopos, Jacopo di Avanzo, is

[101] Even the widely travelled Vitale left a considerable body of work in Bologna. The prolific *œuvre* of a stay-at-home like Simone dei Crocefissi testifies to the fecundity of local demand.

recorded in Bologna in February 1375, and again on 23 June 1378, when he combined with various painters and tailors to produce items for the pallio, including a pair of painted gloves.[102] This is not, on the face of it, the sort of commission that would lure a painter away from as important and lucrative a job as S. Giacomo, but neither is there any reason to suppose that this was the commission which attracted him back to Bologna, even assuming he was in Padua in the first place. The point, of course, is that the dates allow him to have been in Padua in 1377/8, and that his presence in Bologna in June 1378 coincides roughly with the time when Altichiero seems to have taken on the responsibility for the S. Giacomo frescoes by himself. In the case of the other candidate, Jacopo di Pietro Avanzi, there may be an even better reason for this, for a Bolognese document of 20 January 1378 shows him to have recently died.[103]

Whichever of these men is the author of the five lunettes, he seems to have had some sort of association with Altichiero stretching as far back as the Sala Grande, though the nature of the evidence in the case of the two great humanist cycles is such that one must allow for the possibility that extraneous stylistic traits have infiltrated during the process of copying and regurgitation. Even so, the clear presence in all three cycles of trends recognisably akin to the Mezzaratta–Montefiore stylistic axis is unlikely to be accidental or coincidental. What we know of the Sala Grande and the Sala Virorum Illustrium suggests that Altichiero was the dominant painter there. The fact that he did not, apparently, start the S. Giacomo frescoes does not, as such, mean we have to see him as a junior partner. It would be easy to think up possible reasons why he might have allowed Jacopo to begin the chapel frescoes in the way he seems to have done. Altichiero may have still been at work on the Sala Virorum Illustrium, and we know that he was involved in the project as late as 1379 and 1380, albeit only to the extent of producing two small manuscript paintings. It may be that Altichiero and Avanzi had some kind of commercial association whereby they collaborated on big commissions and filled in for one another when necessary.[104] If there was some such arrangement it seems to have ceased, for whatever reason, when Altichiero took over S. Giacomo. His later work in Padua, the Dotto tomb frescoes and the Oratory of S. Giorgio, show no signs of any hand except those of Altichiero's assistants working to his designs. Perhaps Bonifacio wanted Altichiero alone, or perhaps Altichiero, sensing that his stock in Padua stood very high, simply ousted Jacopo, with a ruthlessness we might feel is reflected in the somewhat truculent completion of the eastern lunette. Whatever actually happened, it is clear that Altichiero's position in Padua was a strong one, and his association with Bonifacio Lupi was by no means ended when he completed the S. Giacomo frescoes in early 1379.

102 Filippini and Zucchini, *Miniatori e Pittori a Bologna*, p. 131.

103 *Ibid.*, p. 148.

104 There are various documented or known instances of co-operation between artists in the trecento. The collaboration between Agnolo Gaddi, Bartolomeo Bertezzo and Nicolo di Pietro Gerini gives a useful picture of the division of labour according to speciality, with Nicolo painting figures in fictive tabernacles pre-painted by the other artists (see Cole, *Agnolo Gaddi*, p. 87). Gerini also collaborated with Jacopo di Cione, designing Jacopo's S. Pier Maggiore altarpiece (London, National Gallery), for which see Offner and Steinweg, *A Corpus of Florentine Painting. The Fourteenth Century*, section 4, vol. III, *Jacopo di Cione*, pp. 31ff. Nicolo may also have designed other panels for Jacopo, but the precise footing of their arrangement to collaborate is unclear.

Clarification of the precise weighting of the relationship may be allowed by a study of a manuscript already mentioned, the Chester-Beatty *Thebaid*. This copy of Statius' epic poem, a favourite in chivalric circles because of its 'crusading' element, its family quarrels, its multiplicity of incident and its bellicose themes, has splendid and elaborate illustrations to each book of the poem, painted in grisaille, but with blue skies, green vegetation and touches of colour (these are all original, unlike the same colouring later applied to the second *Triumph of Fame* from Altichiero's workshop). The basic style here, energetic and highly characterised in its approach to narrative, is homogeneous, and it is clearly very closely related to the S. Giacomo lunettes and the other associated material. It is also abundantly clear that this artist has at some stage come into some sort of contact with Altichiero, for Altichieresque figure groups, seen through the very different eye of the manuscript painter, are found throughout, groups recalling the Florentine roots of Altichiero's style, roots quite at odds with the prevailing style of the miniatures. What we seem to have here are signs of an artist of a temperament and background quite different from Altichiero's absorbing elements of Altichiero's visual language. This can be seen in S. Giacomo too, in the *Execution of St James* (pl. 56). It must be emphasised again that this mixture cannot be interpreted as one artist working to another's designs and imposing a gloss of his own personality. The differences are fundamental, not superficial, but the borrowings are unmistakably there. And this traffic is all in one direction. There are no signs in any of the frescoes which must be by Altichiero himself in S. Giacomo, or in those of S. Giorgio, which are all his, of any reciprocal influence. There are, to reverse the situation of the *Thebaid*, no instances of an Altichieresque interpretation of elements borrowed from the energetic vocabulary seen in the five lunettes of S. Giacomo, or the Chester-Beatty manuscript. The lunette master and the painter of the *Thebaid*, whether or not they are the same, borrow from Altichiero. From them Altichiero takes nothing. Whatever the practical and commercial connections between Altichiero and Jacopo Avanzi, if he is the lunette master, it is clear that Altichiero took first place on the purely artistic level.

The extent of Altichiero's commitment to Padua, where he worked for at least another four or five years, is unclear.[105] Obviously he made the city his base, but the presence back in Scaligeri territory of two frescoes which must be attributed to his workshop and are to be dated during the Paduan years, indicate that he may have maintained some sort of practice there.

The first of these, an enthroned *Madonna and Child* from Sezzana di Valpantena,[106] reflects the Cavalli fresco in the concrete sense that the heads of the Virgin and Child reproduce, identically except for the change in respective levels, the heads of the Cavalli Child and the angel just to his right. So close is the resemblance that the same cartoon may have been used. But the pale tonality and light modelling of the Sezzana Virgin's face, which has none of the Cavalli *sfumato* and little of its physical substance, suggests

[105] Moschini, *Dell'Origine*, p. 9, and Simon, 'Altichiero Versus Avanzo', p. 261.

[106] Magagnato, *Arte e Civiltà*, p. 80. His fig. 92 is a full-page colour plate of the Sezzana Madonna.

shop work, as does the rather flat appearance of her torso beneath the decorated tunic. The modelling of the mantle, too, is clearly less forceful than the drapery style of the Cavalli fresco, though this may in part be due to paint loss. The throne is less massive than the nearest autograph example, that of the S. Giacomo votive fresco, and the spatial projection is clumsy and exaggerated in a way that recalls the cruder local tradition. The Gothic vocabulary of the throne is, however, entirely consistent with an attribution to a source close to Altichiero himself, and its closeness to basic Altichieresque patterns – the way it is close to them – suggests the work of an assistant rather than an imitator.

The Sezzana *Madonna* has considerable charm – it is more elegant and perhaps more appealing than many of the later efforts of Altichiero's followers in Verona. It was commissioned by Abbot Bartolomeo of Sezzana, and can therefore be dated to the decade between 1375 and 1385.

The second fresco, a partially ruined *Deposition*, was recently discovered in the north aisle of S. Lorenzo in Vicenza. Only the figure holding Christ's feet survives sufficiently intact for any judgment to be made, but she exhibits an unmistakable affinity with the style of S. Giacomo. The relationship between this figure, with its great mass of drapery swinging out from the arms, and the holy women of the S. Giacomo *Crucifixion* is quite clear. The tonality is also apparently similar, though neither fresco is in good enough condition for more than tentative comparisons to be made. Defects in the actual execution of the Vicenza fresco (e.g. the always tricky far side of a foreshortened face, here rather awkwardly negotiated) suggest, again, the hand of an assistant, but the general style is clearly that of the early Paduan frescoes.

Commissions of this kind, modest enough when set beside the great succession of Altichiero's Paduan fresco cycles in the Sala Virorum Illustrium, S. Giacomo and S. Giorgio, are just what one would expect to be entrusted to capable assistants working on the basis of a design drawn up by Altichiero himself. We have seen something similar happening in the case of the less prestigious *Triumph of Fame* headpiece. The significance of these delegations is easily overlooked, but it helps in the context of S. Giacomo to compare these examples from Altichiero's workshop with the 'Avanzi' lunettes there. The Sezzana and Vicenza frescoes, the headpiece of the variant version of the *De Viris Illustribus*, all 'look like' Altichiero's work in general terms, differing only on the level of actual handling. This is the exact relationship one would expect between workshop and autograph styles, and it contrasts very sharply with the relationship between Altichiero and the other hand – and mind – at work in S. Giacomo.

Charting Altichiero's career before S. Giacomo is a frustrating exercise, involving, as it does, the sometimes speculative reconstruction of lost works made on the basis of back-bearings taken from the extant later works. The dangers of excessive wisdom after the event are always at hand. With the frescoes of S. Giacomo we come to grips, at last, with material in sufficient abundance for firm judgments to be encouraged. Study of the frescoes allows us to place Altichiero's achievement thus far in some sort of perspective. On several distinct planes it must be accounted the most considerable of its time. The sheer technical standard, the purely 'artistic' aspect, is easily established. On every level, from that of large-scale organisation to the detailed modelling of the individual face, Altichiero reveals himself here as the supreme master of the later trecento, combining naturalistic inclusiveness with coherent formal control. Less immediately obvious, but just as exceptional, is the profoundly innovative character of his approach to iconography. His career up to this point, in the Cavalli fresco, the two humanist cycles and their offshoots, the S. Giacomo Ramiro scenes and *Crucifixion*, is consistently marked either by a thoroughgoing reinvention of established iconography, or by the development of entirely new iconographic material. The S. Giacomo *Crucifixion* continues the process of transformation first seen in the Cavalli votive fresco, admitting the contemporary world in all its variety, locating the central narrative of the Gospels within a portrait of an entire trecento culture. It is the supreme pictorial monument of its era, painted by an artist at the height of his powers, and, for all the splendours of his other work, Altichiero's greatest single achievement. Even if nothing else of his survived it would serve to give the lie to the old chestnut that Italian painting slumbered through the decades separating Giotto and Masaccio. In the light of this judgment it may seem surprising to claim that, in many ways, Altichiero's richest outpouring was still to come.

6

THE ORATORY OF S. GIORGIO

The Paduan oratory of S. Giorgio is the last of Altichiero's surviving major works. The frescoes he painted here between 1379 and 1384 constitute the most comprehensive example of his work still extant, and they show his style in its latest phase. The nature of this late style, in which Altichiero seems to have re-examined his Florentine roots, reflects the Paduan milieu in which he had by now been working for some years, a milieu in which the appreciation of Giotto's art had reached a level then unique in Italy – had begun, indeed, to take on the semi-legendary aspect which characterised it for the next 200 years. The oratory is also of particular interest as being the only surviving example of a complete painted interior from his hand. The questions of collaboration, or of accommodation to a complex architectural setting, do not arise here.

But its impact is more immediate than that. The effect on the spectator entering the building for the first time is stunning. The walls are filled almost to bursting point with a profusion of colour and incident. Facing the door is a large *Crucifixion* (pls. 85–6) which seems to float above the altar, with a *Coronation* (pl. 88) supported on fictive spiral columns above it. To the left and the right are narrative cycles of Sts George, Catherine and Lucy, and behind, on the entrance wall (pls. 76b, 77), an *Annunciation* and four scenes from the Infancy of Christ. Above, in the vaults float Evangelists, Doctors and Prophets. The big scenes of the side walls have an insistent power, a physicality, which is really startling. The actors in these scenes – seen at close quarters – impress with their dignity and their presence. Many scenes are crowded and the crowds – multicoloured in their dress – react either with an extraordinary stillness or with a corporate agitation. They inhabit a detailed and apparently real world, contained within a range of architectural settings unequalled in the period, but a world of Gothic beauty and perfection which is also ideal in character, a transfigured synthesis of the courtly world in which the patron of the chapel, like Bonifacio, a soldier, moved.

The whole tenor of the frescoes is directed towards the soldier's imagination. Suffering and death are taken as a matter of course by the martyrs of the side-wall scenes. Hardship is borne with stoic gravity – by St Lucy, calm throughout her ordeals, classically dignified in her nudity (pl. 113), or by St George, both princely and sacerdotal as he administers the Sacrament of Baptism (pl. 93), almost graceful while tortured on the wheel (pl. 98), and a figure of rock-like and impervious strength at his end (pl. 103). The *Crucifixion* is witnessed by a group of high-ranking soldiers, men like

Raimondino Lupi, who react with all the required feelings of awe and moment, but with a restraint, a lack of ostentation which bespeaks the trained courtier as well as the hardened warrior, who has seen it all before.

The painted and precisely imagined world inhabited by these figures is both their own, seen *sub specie aeternitatis* as it were, and that of the saints and martyrs who live and die in the narratives and who profusely inhabit the borders and vaults of the oratory. It is also, as we shall see, the world of scholars, poets, and humanists. The coherence of this ideal portrait as well as its beauty – a beauty which has fared rather better than that of S. Giacomo – place it among the very greatest examples of total figurative decorative schemes. It belongs not only in an obvious line of descent from the Arena Chapel, but in its intentions, its location of a real world in a transfiguring and transcendent context, it must also belong – as we see it – in the company of more exalted and in a strict sense higher-ranking ensembles like Justinian's mosaics in Ravenna. Within Altichiero's *œuvre* it takes up the idealisation of the concretely real which we first saw in the Cavalli fresco but here spreads it out to embrace and include a whole range of experience.

Our knowledge of the circumstances under which the oratory was built and decorated is fairly extensive.[1] The chronology, though uncertain in some details, is broadly clear. But the lack of a number of key documents, most crucially the original contracts for both the building itself and (as with S. Giacomo) for the decoration, leaves a number of detailed and rather important questions hanging in mid-air. We know considerably less about the patron, Raimondino Lupi, than we do about his celebrated kinsman Bonifacio. Raimondino's recorded life runs a rather shadowy and intermittent course through the narratives of the chroniclers of north and central Italy.[2] He is at times dimly visible as part of the historical web of the mid-trecento, but exhibits nothing comparable with the high profile of Bonifacio Lupi or Giacomo Cavalli. No fulsome accounts of his gifts survive, and no contemporary potted biographies of the kind that help us flesh out the bare historical bones of Bonifacio or Giacomo. There are, all the same, reasons for supposing that this is rather more a feature of the imperfect transmission of information across 600 years than a reflection of any authentic obscurity surrounding the man in his lifetime. What little evidence we do have suggests that Raimondino was a figure of considerable importance (the Carraresi certainly thought so[3]), as, for that matter, does the size and prominence of his funerary chapel and the quality of its decoration.

The oratory (fig. 64) stands on ground formerly used as the cemetery of the Santo, a few yards from the west facade of the basilica. It faces north-north-west, and today forms part of a small row of buildings, including the later Scuola del Santo, with its fres-

1 The documentary evidence for S. Giorgio is discussed by Sartori, 'Nota su Altichiero' and 'La Cappella di S. Giacomo', and Simon, 'Altichiero Versus Avanzo', pp. 258–66.

2 For Raimondino's life see (i.e.) Matteo Villani, *Cronica*, vol. II, p. 47; *Chronicon Parmense*, pp. 220ff; *Chronicon Estense*, p.123; Pietro Azarii, *Liber Gestorum*; Pezzana, *Storia della Città di Parma*, vol. I.

3 His settlement in Padua was supported and possibly suggested by Francesco da Carrara. Raimondino had for many years been commander of the Mantuan armies. See Pezzana, *Storia della Città di Parma*, vol. I, p. 114.

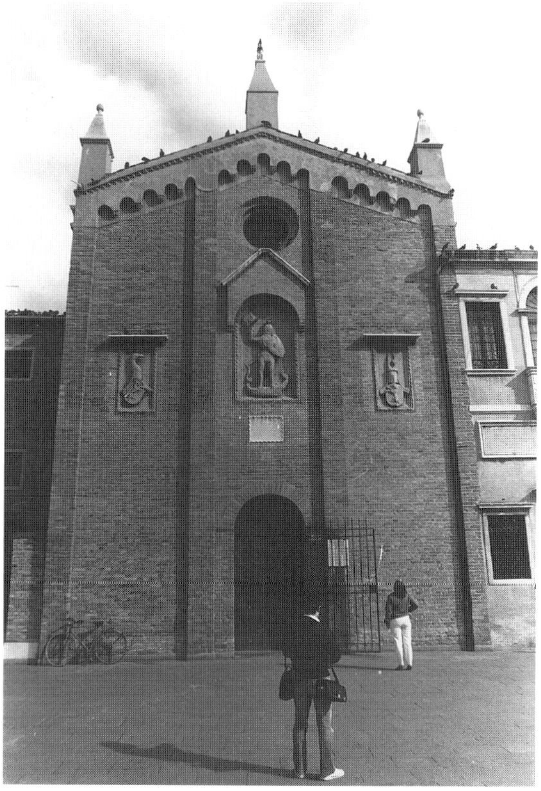

Fig. 64 Padua, Oratory of S. Giorgio. Facade.

coes by the young Titian, all more or less aligned with the Via Luca Belludi, the main street leading from the Piazza del Santo to the Prato delle Valle. The area contained in the angle of this row with the Santo's facade once housed the tombs of many of the major Paduan families of the late medieval period. Most have now been cleared away, including those attached to the facade and sides of the main basilica. Only the tomb of Rolando da Piazzola (d.1323), testimony to the precocity of Paduan humanist interests,[4] and Donatello's monument to Gattamelata, continue, with the oratory itself, to mark the original nature of what is now one of Padua's principal piazzas.

The structure of the oratory is plain. The simple brick facade, pierced by a central door and a single round window under the gable, is decorated with a central relief of St George under a simple gabled canopy, and two flanking heraldic reliefs.[5] Four pilaster strips articulate the facade wall, and the gable, raised on a course of archlets, carries three chunky pinnacles. This unexceptional design hardly stands out amongst the small churches of the Veneto and Lombardy. It is less ornate than that of the Arena Chapel, a broadly comparable (and seventy years older) building, or of another church dedicated

[4] Rolando da Piazzola's tomb of *c.* 1310 combines a sarcophagus of antique Roman format, with, in the gable above the containing arch, a Roman funerary stele recut to represent Sts Francis and Clare. Rolando, for whom see Hyde, *Padua*, was one of the most aggressively anti-Ghibelline figures of the humanist group in the later stages of the Paduan commune.

[5] These have been replaced by copies. The originals are displayed in the Santo cloisters.

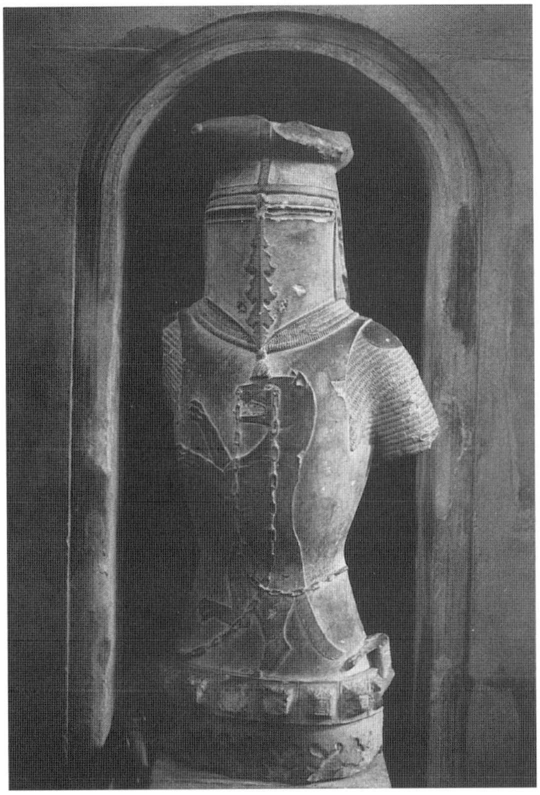

Fig. 65 Padua, Oratory of S. Giorgio. Fragment of tomb of Raimondino Lupi.

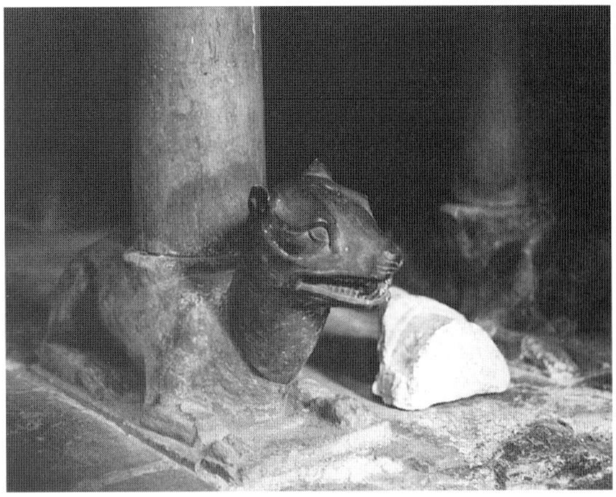

Fig. 66 Padua, Oratory of S. Giorgio. Wolf supporting tomb of Raimondino Lupi.

to St George and in the patronage of warriors, the rather larger S. Giorgetto (now S. Pietro Martire) in Verona (fig. 40), which could almost have been the model for Raimondino's oratory.

The internal design (pl. 76) is just as restrained. The barrel-vaulted room is lit by three lancet windows each side, by two more in the altar wall and by a roundel high up on each of the end walls. A wooden dado with benches (not original) runs all the way round the oratory,[6] broken only by the entrance, the altar, and by a small door in the left-hand wall (compass roughly east, liturgical north). The rest of the wall and vault surface was left absolutely plain and is entirely covered with Altichiero's frescoes.

We know from early sources[7] that the architectural simplicity of the oratory was orig-

[6] The original condition of the dado cannot be assessed, and the wall surface behind the present panels and benches, which replaced an older set described by Gonzati, *La Basilica di S. Antonio*, vol. II, p. 271, is rough plaster.

[7] The most important is Polidoro, *Le Religiose Memorie*, pp. 37ff. Polidoro wrote his description (given in full in the catalogue entry for S. Giorgio) in 1590, from memory, since Portenari, *Della Felicità di Padova*, pp. 487–8, writing in 1623, says the tomb was partly dismantled in 1582, with the canopy being removed (in the interests of visibility) and the ten statues placed round the walls of the oratory, recently adopted by the Goldsmiths' Guild. At this stage the sarcophagus itself was apparently still located in the original central position. Further damage to the remaining parts of the tomb was caused during the Napoleonic Wars, when the oratory was converted by the French army to a military prison. See Selvatico, *Guida di Padova*, pp. 22–3 and D'Arcais, 'La Decorazione della Cappella di San Giacomo', p. 46. Only one figure and a fragment of another survives of the sculptural ensemble.

inally offset by the extremely elaborate design of Raimondino Lupi's tomb, of which only the sarcophagus and a few sculptural fragments remain (figs. 65, 66), now moved against the side wall. This gabled and pinnacled tomb (later taken by many Paduans to be the tomb of some saint, something which no doubt contributed to its eventual destruction) stood in the centre of the building. The original effect may be reconstructed by imagining one of the Scaligeri tombs placed inside the Arena Chapel, the whole ensemble somewhat scaled down. We know from the surviving completion documents that Altichiero was contracted to paint the tomb as well as the walls.[8] It has, inevitably one might feel, given that we do not have the contracts, been suggested that he actually designed not only the tomb but the oratory itself. It seems likely at any rate that the building was expressly designed with frescoed walls in mind and it is hardly fanciful to imagine that Altichiero was at least consulted.[9]

The precise dates of the oratory's construction are unknown, but we know from the wording of a document of 3 May 1378,[10] in which the funding and endowments of the oratory are discussed and which confirms the original permission for the building, that the main fabric at least had been completed by this date. The date given on the exterior of the building, November 1377, may commemorate any one of several distinct stages in the oratory's planning or construction. Gonzati's belief that it marks the initiation of the building work is no more nor less likely than that it records the date of completion, or, as Simon suggests[11] (amongst other possibilities), the date of a crucial document to do with the process of endowment and construction.

Raimondino Lupi died on 30 November 1379, and the completion documents of 1384 reveal that Raimondino – 'dum vivebat' – had already made a contract with Altichiero for the decoration of the oratory and the tomb.[12] The day after Raimondino's death, 1 December, a document was drawn up[13] recording that other members of the Lupi family in Padua had, in accordance with Raimondino's wishes, taken over the supervision of the project for the oratory. The 1384 documents further reveal that it was specifically Bonifacio Lupi who took on the responsibility of supervising the carrying out of the contract made between Altichiero and Raimondino. This means that, in practice, Altichiero was once again working for Bonifacio, almost immediately after finishing his work in Bonifacio's own chapel.

The documents leave it unclear exactly when Altichiero began work on the oratory frescoes. He may have begun before Raimondino's death, but there is no justification

[8] 'Et etiam occaxione archae et ornamentorum, vel causa colorum quam auri, in qua archus corpus q.d. Raymondini praedicti tumulatum est' – Altichiero's completion document of 30 May 1384; Sartori, 'Nota su Altichiero', p. 306, no. II.

[9] Certain anomalies in the way the frescoes are laid out suggest less than complete unity of purpose between the builders of the oratory and the painter. The central window of the east wall, over the sarcophagus in its present position, is displaced to the right, so that the fresco on its left is wider than the one on its right, and the vertical border above does not meet the apex of the window arch at dead centre. The lack of integration between the upper border with busts and the alignments of the frescoes below is also curious. One might feel that were Altichiero responsible for the whole scheme, building and all, such problems would never have arisen.

[10] Sartori, 'La Cappella di S. Giacomo', pp. 303–5.

[11] Simon, 'Altichiero Versus Avanzo', pp. 258–9.

[12] Sartori, 'Nota su Altichiero', p. 305.

[13] *Ibid.*, p. 308, no. VI (1 December 1379).

for supposing, with Sartori, that the frescoes of the altar wall had been completed by 30 November 1379.[14] Altichiero had been paid for his work in S. Giacomo probably on or shortly before 3 May 1379, and it is most likely to have been between May and November of that year that he began at least preliminary work on the oratory (though the contract could have been drawn up before May, with the work timed to begin only once the S. Giacomo frescoes were finished).

It seems likely that the tomb, which would have been built after the main fabric of the oratory, was ready to receive the patron's body by this date, for the document of 1 December mentions that Raimondino had already been buried 'in eadem capella'[15] – with what seems rather exceptional urgency, given the season. Probably it had not yet been decorated, for it is more likely that the tomb would have been left till last, rather than risk all the slops of fresco painting falling on it in a fully decorated state while the vault and walls were being painted. It could, of course, have been covered, but the most likely chronology is that the decoration of the oratory followed the pattern of its building: walls first and tomb second. The period allowed by the documents for the painting to have been done, 1379–84, seems rather excessive, given that S. Giacomo, a more intricate job, probably only took two years (1377–9). The wall surface to be covered in S. Giorgio is greater, but not by so much that an additional three years' work would be needed. Though the completion documents of 1384 do not indicate how recently Altichiero had finished his work, there is no reason to suppose a gap of any great length between completion and the legal notification of the fact. Perhaps the tomb had not, in fact, been finished by the time of Raimondino's death.[16] If this were the case, that he had been quickly buried in a temporary grave to await completion of the tomb, then the additional period needed to build the tomb – probably after the walls were decorated, for the same reasons given above – would partly explain the length of time the job seems to have taken. But there is no evidence of this, or of any other exceptional circumstance. Neither, in my view, are there any grounds for supposing that the oratory frescoes were carried out in two distinct campaigns, with a break in between. Perhaps the intricacy of Altichiero's architectural detail (of which there is far more here than in the S. Giacomo frescoes) made for slow progress. Perhaps, also, he liked to do rather more of the work himself than was normal in a workshop system. The patron, after all, was dead and buried, and so beyond any displays of impatience. If the frescoes were in any sense carried out under the eyes of the Paduan humanist coterie, as I think we may at least suggest was the case, then ordinary imperatives of speed and all attendant claims of value-for-money and so on may have been somewhat relaxed.

Raimondino Lupi

Raimondino and Bonifacio Lupi, not brothers, as has often been claimed, were men of different generations. They were descended from the two most important members of

[14] *Ibid.*, p. 297. See also Simon, 'Altichiero Versus Avanzo', p. 258 for a dismissal of Sartori's argument.

[15] Sartori, 'Nota su Altichiero', p. 308.

[16] Raimondino's burial in the tomb, as opposed to the oratory generally, is only mentioned for the first time in 1384. See n.8 above.

the Lupi family in the early trecento, the brothers Bonifacio (our Bonifacio's grandfather) and Rolandino (Raimondino's father). This pair appear in the chronicles of the times as *de facto* heads of the Lupi clan. They were jointly exiled from Parma in 1305, during one of the incessant outbreaks of party strife in that unstable city. Their association was echoed by that of their sons Ugolotto (Bonifacio's father) and Raimondino, who seem to have inherited from their fathers the role of joint family heads. It was these two who, in 1347, secured (or rather resecured) from Charles IV the Lupi title to the march of Soragna. Following Ugolotto's death in 1351 Bonifacio seems to have stepped into his shoes as joint clan chief with Raimondino.

As was common for a man in his position, Raimondino had to earn his keep as a soldier. A basic and understandable anti-Visconti bias characterises his career in this field, taking various forms. On St Catherine's Day 1332 he too fought in the Luxembourg cause at the Battle of San Felice and received his knighthood from the young Charles of Luxembourg.[17] Raimondino's early service for the house of Luxembourg shaped much of the remaining course of his life, and like Bonifacio he retained close links with the Emperor Charles IV, as he became, throughout the following four decades.

Also influential in shaping the course of his later life was Raimondino's early service with the Carraresi, scions of whom fought alongside him at San Felice, and in their cause, as in 1337, when, with Rolandino Rossi and Ubertino da Carrara, he fought against forces of the Scaligeri at Montecchio. This was the same campaign in which Pietro Rossi died and which finally secured Padua for the Carraresi. So Raimondino stood in much the same position *vis-à-vis* the Carraresi as the Rossi brothers, re-entombed in Bonifacio Lupi's chapel, and his decision – perhaps in response to a Carrarese invitation[18] – to spend his last years in Padua was probably determined by the welcome he may have expected on the strength of his part in the early history of the Carrarese *signoria*.

Between his early and late connections with the Carraresi, Raimondino moved restlessly from engagement to engagement. In 1344 he shared Obizzo d'Este's defeat at the hands of the Visconti. In 1350, following up the imperial diploma of 1347, Raimondino was invested by the emperor with various fiefs and appointed his 'consigliere e segretario'.[19] In 1351, possibly at the emperor's request, he entered service with the Florentines, with some success, as Matteo Villani records.[20] In 1354 Raimondino was nominated by Charles IV as his *procuratore* to contract an alliance against the Visconti, with full powers to determine all aspects of the league as he saw fit. A number of letters from Charles to Raimondino survive from the year 1355.[21] In 1356 and 1357 Raimondino once more took the field against the Visconti, this time at the head of the Gonzaga armies. He seems to have been captured and almost immediately released. Imperial support continued through the 1360s, with a renewal of the 1350 Soragna

[17] For the Battle of San Felice and Raimondino's part in it, see the *Chronicon Parmense*, pp. 220–1 and *Chronicon Estense*, fasc. II, p. 100.

[18] See n.3 above.

[19] Pezzana, *Storia della Città di Parma*, vol. I, p. 78.

[20] Matteo Villani, *Cronica*, vol. II, p. 47.

[21] *Acta Inedita: Charles IV*, nos. 42, 48, 49.

investiture in 1364, confirmation of his imperial appointments in 1366, and an appointment as imperial vicar of Pisa and Lucca in 1367. In 1370 Raimondino was named as party to the peace treaty between the Visconti and the opposing league. He seems then to have gone to live in Mantua, where in 1372 he made a will, as a Mantuan citizen, founding and endowing a Hospital of Sts Lucy and Catherine so that 'in perpetuum infirmi peregrini senes orphani et aliae miserabiles personae, quae non habent unde vivere, in dicto hospitale recipiantur alantur procurentur et nutriantur'.[22] The endowment arrangements were made with the *Clarisse* of Mantua.

At some stage between this date and 1376 Raimondino decided to live in Padua, of which city he was made a citizen on 16 April of the latter year.[23] The decree reveals that Raimondino, who was accorded all the privileges of a native, lived in the parish of S. Giacomo di Pontemolino, which is close to where Bonifacio lived. We know also that the Carraresi had sold him some land. This land he later sold to his nephew Simone, who lived nearby. Raimondino's decision to build an oratory in Padua presumably dates from some time after his arrival in the city.

The purpose of Raimondino's oratory was twofold, as we learn from the inscription on the exterior of the building:

> Orathorium hoc sub auspiciis Beati Georgii Ubi chondentis est sepulcrum pro eius Parentumque ac fratrum et nepotum indelenda memoria Miles Egregius Raimundinus de Lupis . . . edifecit . . .

The funerary function was provided for by the free-standing tomb. Only Raimondino's body lies in the tomb[24] and there is no other record of any intention that other family members living in Padua should be buried in the oratory. Raimondino evidently had no wife (at this stage in his life at any rate) to share his tomb.

The memorial aspect of the building, specified in the inscription, was expressed in two forms: in the ten kneeling figures in the votive fresco on the left wall (pls. 95–6), each with an identifying inscription, and in the ten carved effigies originally attached to the upper levels of the tomb, now all gone except for parts of two knights (fig. 65), but also all formerly identified by inscriptions. These were recorded by the early sources, two of which, Polidoro (1590) and Portenari (1623), also give extremely detailed descriptions of the tomb itself.[25]

The votive fresco, which required of Altichiero an expansion of the customary votive format beyond even that of the Cavalli fresco, breaks the kneeling figures of the Lupi, each presented by a saint, into two groups. Closest to the throne and some way ahead of the main body are Rolandino and Matilda Lupi, Raimondino's parents and the progenitors of this particular branch of the family. The second group, all armoured

[22] Sartori, 'Nota su Altichiero', p. 310.

[23] See n.3 above. Raimondino was granted all the priviliges of a native of Padua. In 1376 he sold to Simone Lupi, who lived in the same parish, some land previously sold to him by the Carraresi.

[24] The tomb was opened in the eighteenth century and was found to contain one body 'coperto ancora d'alcuni cenci, anche reliquie della lunga toga nera che dovea ricoprirlo': Selvatico's introduction to Förster, *I Dipinti nella Cappella di S. Giorgio*, p. 15.

[25] See n.7 above.

knights, are individually identified as, from right to left: Raimondino's brothers Montino, Guido, Bonifacio and Antonio; his nephews Antonio, Simone and Fulgo; and, bringing up the rear, Raimondino himself, presented by St George. The dynastic character of the commemoration (the oratory was later known in Padua as the chapel 'de' Lupi') is reinforced by the wording of the inscriptions recorded under the tomb statues of these same ten people, which identify them in relation to Rolandino – 'Dna Mathilda eius coniux . . . Guido Marchio Soraneae, Filius . . . Dnus Simon Marchio Soraneae, Miles, Nepus . . . Dnus Raimondinus Marchio Soraneae, Filius' – rather than to Raimondino. The specific restriction to direct descendants of Rolandino and Matilda, made clear by the external and internal inscriptions, excludes the idea that the Bonifacio who appears in the votive scene is the same Bonifacio as the patron of S. Giacomo. The inscription on the tomb ran 'Bonifacius Marchio Soraneae, Filius'. He is, in other words, Bonifacio di Rolandino and not Bonifacio di Ugolotto,[26] who took over the oratory project, and with whose own chapel's function the oratory has so much in common.

The general scheme and iconography of the frescoes in the oratory can be assumed to be of Raimondino's choosing – they were presumably specified in the contract. The choice of the three saints whose lives are the subjects of the side-wall frescoes – St George on the left (east), Sts Catherine and Lucy on the right (west) – are unexceptional: St George as the patron saint of soldiers, and the two Virgin Martyrs to whom Raimondino had already dedicated his Mantuan hospital. Raimondino's devotion to St Catherine may stem from his early success at San Felice on St Catherine's Day 1332. The frescoes of the end walls, framing, as it were, the martyrs' lives of the side walls – an *Annunciation* and four scenes from the Early Life of Christ on the entrance wall, a *Crucifixion* and a *Coronation of the Virgin* above on the altar wall – again offer no surprises. A small host of saints and angels in the window splays, and the Doctors, Evangelists and Prophets of the vault complete the ensemble. The overall iconographic design of the oratory echoes that of S. Giacomo: a compressed Christological cycle in association with a martyr cycle (or here three cycles). The obvious parallels, which were reflected rather specifically in the layout of the altar wall in S. Giacomo, hardly need to be stressed.

The decoration of the oratory

S. Giorgio was made for painting, and the design of the fresco decoration must have presented nothing like the problems of S. Giacomo. Whatever the nature of Altichiero's role in the early stages of Bonifacio's chapel decoration, here he was clearly in sole charge from the start. The unity of the oratory's decoration can still be appreciated despite the alterations to the lower level of the interior. Specks of paint still adhering to the fragments of tomb sculpture suggest that the polychromy of the tomb matched the

[26] For the two Bonifacios see Pezzana, *Storia della Città di Parma*, vol. I, p. 99.

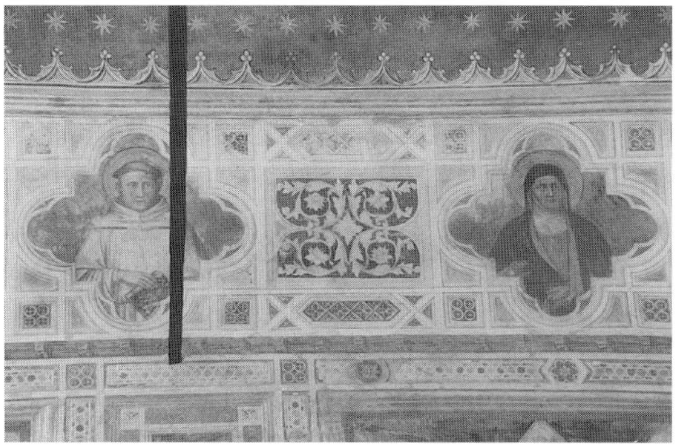

Fig. 67 Padua, Oratory of S. Giorgio. Upper border (detail).

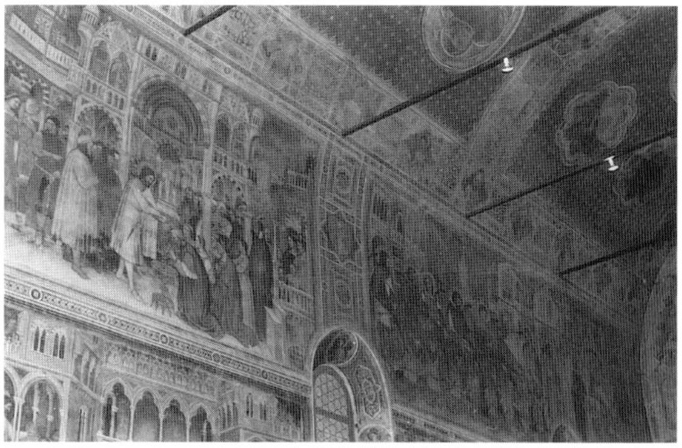

Fig. 68 Padua, Oratory of S. Giorgio. Upper part of east wall.

wall paintings for brightness of colour. And the faded but still clearly visible fictive arcades painted on the front and sides of the altar, as well as the painted borders of the small door in the east wall, make it clear that the exuberant architectural fictions of the narratives found echoes in the decoration of the other furnishings of the oratory.

The system of framing and border elements which imposes a structure on the plain walls of the building is rich in detail and laid out in a descending order of complexity, starting from the extremely ornate and rich moulded and interlaced polylobe border which separates the vault from the walls and rests on a line of small fictive corbels above the upper level of narrative borders (figs. 67, 68). This wide band, whose polylobes contain half-length busts of saints, also crosses the vault and divides it into three sections, devoted respectively to busts of Doctors, Evangelists and Prophets, enclosed within cusped roundels, ovals or octofoils (most of these are badly damaged). The upper and outer edges of the border are closed by a running band of double cusps in pink placed against the blue of the starred vault. Cusped banding of this kind is characteristic of much of the work of Altichiero's shop and followers during the next two decades.

From the upper banding wide borders of a different design descend to the apex of each window. These contain shields with the Wolf Rampant of the Lupi and octofoils enclosing a sort of blind rose window, adjusted to be seen *di sotto in su* and implying a drum-shaped space in the thickness of the wall, another throwback to Tuscan models like Taddeo Gaddi's vault roundels in the western bay of the Baroncelli Chapel.

Two patterns for the decoration of the window splays are alternated round the building, one with large roundels cusped into sexfoils and grisaille foliate lozenges (fig. 69), and the other with double-cusped quatrefoils with saints or elaborate six-pointed stars (fig. 70), very like that surviving in the Sala Grande. The quatrefoils are separated by simpler grisaille lozenges.

Framing the entrance wall Infancy cycle and separating the upper and lower frescoes of the side walls are borders of delicate lattice-work, gathered into lozenges on the entrance wall and punctuated by small roundels and inscribed hexagons on the side walls. The immediate framing elements of the narratives combine flat and rolled fictive

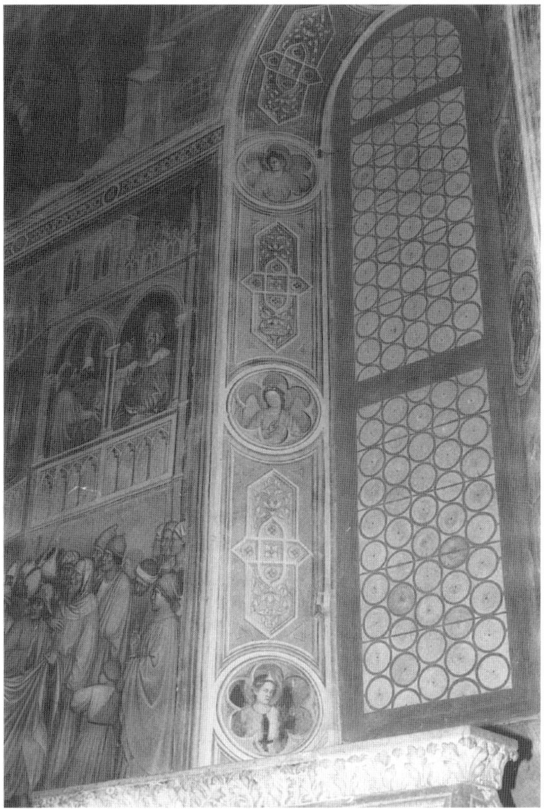

Fig. 69 Padua, Oratory of S. Giorgio. East-wall window splay.

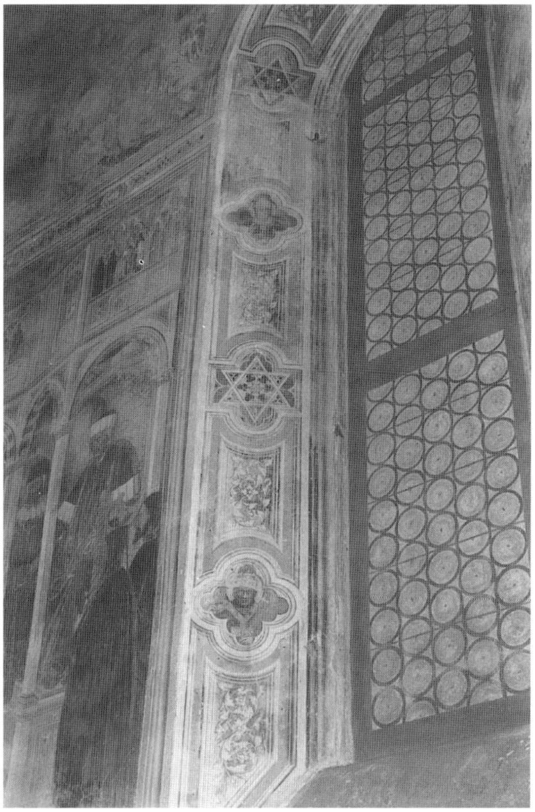

Fig. 70 Padua, Oratory of S. Giorgio. West-wall window splay.

mouldings similar to those of the main border and window polylobes and lozenges. A flat yellow strip between the border and the pictorial space of the main frescoes fulfils the same separating function as the red strip used by Giotto in the Arena Chapel.

Though related in much of its larger organisational tendencies, the details of this, the only large-scale border ensemble we can be certain is wholly of Altichiero's invention, reveals a thoroughgoing Gothic decorative vocabulary, in marked contrast with the more classical design of Giotto's borders. The simple geometry of the Arena Chapel vault roundels and wall quatrefoils, the related systems of Taddeo and Maso, give way to a controlled profusion of mouldings, cusps, fretted and pierced panels, all based around a system of various kinds of flat white lattice-work, which in its least elaborate form (e.g. in the margins of the heraldic borders above the windows, or framing the Infancy cycle) replaces the Cosmatesque strips of Giotto and the Giotteschi. The filigree effect is lighter, less 'Roman', and throughout the oratory the richness of ornament is leavened by the delicacy of the detailed design and execution. The predominant colour scheme of Altichiero's borders is lighter than that common to Giotto's school, and the choice of grisaille for the foliate lozenges of the windows (and grisaille on a dark ground for the vault border) further lightens the effect (compare the rich colours of the

Arena Chapel foliate panels). Contrasts as bold as those between Giotto's moulded elements and the dark infills of his border panels are rejected – the white strip is instead placed against various tones of the ubiquitous brick-pink, the apple-green of the heraldic borders, or the grey-blue of the vault and window polylobes. Forceful contrast between the 'architectural' elements of the fresco scheme and the narratives, though characteristic of the circles in which Altichiero learned his trade, is played down in the interests of a total harmonic unity, based, as one immediately sees on entering the building, on a lighter blue than Giotto used, rather powdery in character, and a warm pink, colours dominant in border and narratives alike, and which variously determine the overall look of the oratory, according to the time of day and the outside lighting conditions.

The Gothic language of the oratory border scheme is a specifically north Italian element in Altichiero's artistic complexion, something reflecting the prevailing tastes of his native city, and which makes a distinctive setting for the otherwise Tuscanising tendencies of his art. The combination in the oratory frescoes of the local Gothic language at its most refined and the monumental vocabulary of Giottesque narrative painting at its (in Altichiero's output) most controlled and severe is not the least fascinating aspect of this late phase of his art.

The architectural style of the buildings depicted within the narrative frescoes, and especially in the martyrs' lives on the side walls, amplifies the Gothic character of the containing and controlling structures of S. Giorgio, already established on one level by the borders. The fantastic variety and quality of Altichiero's architectural invention and the clarity with which he develops narrative within elaborate architectural settings recalls the great masters of the early trecento but surpasses them in the profusion of detail and the complexity of the basic structures. The actual style – or styles – of the fictive architecture seem to draw on various sources. The basilical structure in *St George Baptising* (pl. 93) suggests aspects of S. Anastasia in Verona, and other Veronese traits are reflected in the profusion of gables and pinnacles in several frescoes, the swallow-tail crenellations of the St Catherine cycle, and the several instances of red-and-white arch voussoirs. The various but related designs of the Scaligeri tombs may lie behind the wall-mounted structure to the left of the votive fresco (pl. 95), and the dainty Gothic canopies of *St George Condemned to Drink Poison* (pl. 97) and the *Tortures of St Lucy* (pl. 113).

Elaborate Gothic structures of a smaller type are reflected too, as in the votive fresco, whose wall-mounted tabernacle is reminiscent of a number of such structures surviving in Verona (e.g. the rather weathered votive tabernacle attributed to Giovanni di Rigino at S. Pietro Incarnario (fig. 71) or the one formerly situated near the Roman Amphitheatre). The detailed design of Altichiero's tabernacle, with its rising gables, is daintier than the two Veronese examples, which have emphatic flat cornices, but the basic format is very close, and the reference to these particular instances of micro-architecture in this votive context seems appropriate. The specific forms of the crenellated gables with crowned chimneys seen in the *Fall of the Idols* and *Miracle of St Lucy and the Bulls* (pls. 101, 111) seem to pick up late trecento building

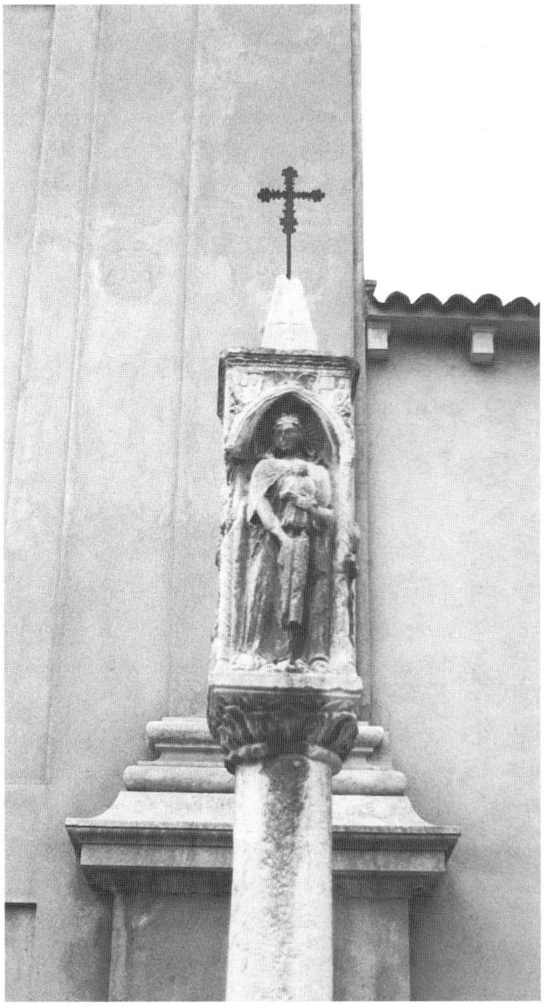

Fig. 71 Attributed to Giovanni di Rigino. Votive pillar. Verona, S. Pietro Incarnario.

styles characteristic of the region round Vicenza (i.e. in Scaligeri territory), as Mellini suggested.[27]

What seem to be locally Paduan aspects appear in several instances. Versions of the Santo itself can be seen in the first St Catherine scene (pl. 105) and in the extreme top right of the *Fall of the Idols* (pl. 102), combined there with a gable-and-pinnacle canopy which looks back to S. Fermo in Verona (fig. 2). The trabeated loggia on the left of the *Fall* may reflect the eastern courtyard of the Carrarese Palace, parts of which still survive. The flavour of much of the less showy architecture broadly recalls styles common to Lombardy and the Veneto, but a recognisably Venetian strain is visible in many details of window openings, and especially in the forms of the cresting which runs along the top of buildings in the fourth, fifth and sixth St George scenes and the penultimate and (just visible on the left) last St Lucy scenes (the existence of such cresting in known work by Altichiero makes it easier to accept the architectural details of Josephus

[27] Mellini, *Altichiero e Jacopo Avanzi*, pp. 74–5 and figs. 291–3.

drawing G (pl. 5) as his, rather than the invention of a later copyist with knowledge of Venetian styles – the Venetian influence is still clear in both cases).

The several external views of walled hill towns reflect a host of such places which dot the foothills to the north of the plain between Verona and Padua. Soave and Marostica are the most spectacular extant examples, and both had recently been upgraded and rebuilt by Cansignorio della Scala. The style of Altichiero's walls and towers reflects them (and, to be sure, fortress and wall styles generally), and he may have been familiar with the work of the Veronese military engineer/architects dominant in this field in the late trecento (and kept abundantly in work by Cansignorio) – may even have known some of them personally, like the Veronese military architect Ognibene, or his son Nicolò, employed by the Carraresi at this time to advise on the Paduan fortifications.[28]

The designer of Raimondino's tomb is unknown, and affinities between what we know of its design and the Veronese Gothic style of the Scaligeri tombs might suggest that 'Altichiero Architetto' has been at work again. But the completion documents, which mention the painting of the tomb by Altichiero, say nothing of its construction. The style of the surviving tomb chest is very close to that of the wall tombs of S. Giacomo and the most likely reading is that elements of Andriolo de Santi's workshop were responsible for the S. Giorgio tomb shortly after the completion of S. Giacomo.[29] It is not impossible, though, that Altichiero might have furnished a rough design for the tomb. It is at least worth consideration in view of the fact that obvious Veronese models exist for both the oratory itself and the tomb.

The basic features of the tomb are recorded in the detailed accounts given by Polidoro and Portenari and it can be reconstructed up to a point (see the not wholly convincing version by Vicinelli which Mellini publishes[30]). But the crucial details of moulding profiles and so on, all the real determinants of precise attribution, are of course lost. The tomb may have been the work of Rinaldino da Francia, evidently associated in some way with Andriolo de Santi's workshop, and resident in Padua in 1379, when he was paid for the five figures of the altar in S. Giacomo. Rinaldino's exposure to Lombard Gothic styles might account for any resemblance between the S. Giorgio tomb and Bonino da Campione's tomb of Cansignorio della Scala in Verona. But affinities between extant tombs and sketchy reconstructions cannot be pursued very far, and the tomb is just as likely to have been the work of the Giovanni, who was paid with Andriolo in 1379 for the tombs of S. Giacomo. The coarser carving of Raimondino Lupi's sarcophagus could well reflect the work of such an assistant of Andriolo's, and he has as valid a previous connection with the Lupi as Rinaldino.

Whatever the precise relationship between the author of Raimondino's tomb and Altichiero, and whatever the detailed affinities between the architectural styles of the tomb and the frescoes, one can assume that the oratory in its original and finished state offered to the spectator a rich set of correspondences between real and fictive architecture, and, on the physical level, an ever-changing view of the fictive through the real

[28] Ognibene da Verona lived in Padua in 1378. His son Nicolò was Francesco da Carrara's engineer. See Gatari, *Cronaca Carrarese*, p. 137, n.

[29] See Wolters, *La Scultura Veneziana Gotica*, vol. 1, pp. 210–11, cat. 132.

[30] Mellini, *Altichiero e Jacopo Avanzi*, fig. 157.

structures of the tomb. The correspondence between the two areas, made explicit on one level by the presence of the same ten figures prominently displayed on the tomb and in the votive fresco, must have been picked up and echoed throughout the ensemble right down the scale of decorative detail.

The roots of the architectural mode which dominates the S. Giorgio frescoes, and the extent of which surpasses any previous trecento painting, are various. The conceptual basis is derived from the Tuscan and Umbrian styles which underpin Altichiero's art throughout. But a local Paduan tradition also existed, and though it is probable, given the style of the Cavalli fresco, that Altichiero's development of the role of fictive architecture as a spatial, empirical and narrative device took place independently, it can hardly be coincidental that it was in Padua that this aspect of his art was seen at its most dazzling and mature. Two of the S. Giorgio frescoes seem to reflect this tradition so directly that we may interpret them as an overt critique.

The large basilical section which in two slightly varied forms dominates the *Presentation* (pl. 82) and the *Funeral of St Lucy* (pl. 115) seems to derive rather specifically from the equivalent structure in the background of the *Funeral of St Sebastian* (1367) by Guariento's Venetian follower Semitecolo, in the sacristy of Padua Cathedral. This panel develops its foreground action in front of a backdrop of two related structures, impressively realised in an empirical and conceptual sense. But a backdrop is what they remain, for all that the running of their top edges over the punched and tooled border thrusts them towards the spectator.

Semitecolo's buildings probably derive in turn from immediate models like the churches in several of Guariento's frescoes in the choir of the Eremitani, actually rather more ambitious in their containing function, but no more successful in solving the difficult problem of relating the receding apse of the interior to the main body. The moulding between the lower and upper part of both Semitecolo's apses dips with exactly the same exaggerated curve as Guariento's in the scene of *St Augustine Baptising*. Altichiero's handling of the equivalent passage is far more assured – the apses are consistently and logically continuous with the receding walls. The occasional lapses from perspectival coherence which characterise Guariento's and Semitecolo's work are absent from Altichiero's. The upper orthogonals of his buildings recede, in accordance with empirical observation, at a sharper angle than the lower, where Semitecolo, attempting the same passage, pushes them off at diverging angles. Neither Semitecolo's receding ceilings nor Guariento's vaults approach the scrupulous accuracy of the *Funeral of St Lucy* or any of the many and various feats of architectural design in S. Giorgio.

The key problem for the painters of the trecento, as their ability to represent space and the material objects either containing or contained within space grew, lay in the inherent conflict between the need to use fictive buildings as containing pictorial structures, the basis of trecento spatial conquest, and an increasing awareness that they could and should be represented as objects in space on the same terms as the figures. As early as Giotto's frescoes in the Arena Chapel we find the struggle to reconcile these aspects, and throughout the work of the more progressive of his followers the struggle is expressed in the form of various choices or compromises between the two basic systems for projecting architecture in pictorial space: the frontal-foreshortened and the oblique. The prevalence of the former system throughout the greater part of Altichiero's output, his adherence to the line developed through the Bardi chapels of Giotto and Maso rather than the Peruzzi/Baroncelli line, has already been stressed. In S. Giorgio he adapts this system with great brilliance to many different contexts, but in what are probably the last frescoes we find him abandoning it in favour of the oblique construction. In the *Presentation* a compromise between the two systems is developed which recalls the syntheses of Maso or Puccio Capanna. The base of the temple is securely and frontally locked parallel to the picture plane, but the upper moulding recedes slightly but unmistakably away to the right. This is consistent with an implied viewing point between the tomb in its original position and the door (another optimum viewing point is reflected in the design of the side wall frescoes at the other end of the oratory). And from the same spot the much sharper recession of the church in the *Funeral of St Lucy*, now a wholly oblique construction, is equally consistent. But since at the altar end of the oratory the concession to viewpoint was made still within the constraints of the frontal lock, this must represent a genuine shift in Altichiero's thinking. The shift is anticipated in the oblique settings of the shed in the *Nativity* and *Adoration* (pls. 78–9) and in the careful and minute adjustment of the view of the background city common to both to take account of the spectator's implied movement to the right as he passes from one to the other (an effect for which the ever-inventive Guariento may have provided a precedent), but neither case involves a clash with the requirements of front-plane interior narrative, the dominant type in S. Giorgio and for which the frontal system had always been Altichiero's first choice.

And yet, for all the apparent change of direction, the fundamental approach is the same. In all the oratory frescoes, including those in which landscape predominates, spatial penetration is severely curtailed. The narrative actions are thrust into the frontal plane, which is, as in S. Giacomo, continuous with the spectator's space. Where an area of sky, into which the orthogonals push, suggests a spatial depth beyond the narrative plane, a screen is placed to contain the action and discourage specific penetration (i.e. into a depicted rather than a suggested space). In a landscape setting Altichiero resorts to the delimiting crowd horizon he used previously in the S. Giacomo *Crucifixion*. In both cases the overriding concern is to maintain the primacy of the narrative, to keep the essential narrative area in focus and accessible.

Comparison with Altichiero's Tuscan contemporary Giusto de'Menabuoi, working in Padua at this time, helps define the degree of Altichiero's control. Giusto is arguably Altichiero's equal in terms of the representation of credible architectural space and architectural structures, and between them the two painters, following on from Guariento and Semitecolo, represent Padua's claim to a premier position in the development of late trecento painting. Were this development seen purely in terms of representational conquest, Giusto's ranking must be very high indeed. The spatial depth of some of the frescoes in the Chapel of B. Luca Belludi in the Santo is remarkable. The central fresco of the Life of Christ in the Paduan baptistry thrusts the background basilica (possibly a portrait of the old Romanesque Cathedral) into a daring and convincing depth which anticipates the recessive plunges of an artist like Uccello. But where Altichiero in using the oblique setting curbs the tendency of the eye to slip down the receding walls into space by clamping the background building of the *Funeral of St Lucy* to the picture plane frontally, Giusto allows the attention to shoot into the background, either to the basilica or to the area of blank sky between it and the building on the right. The diffusion of narrative content which is attendant on Giusto's determination to 'take depth by storm'[31] is in marked contrast with Altichiero's concern for presentational clarity and unity.

The interest in spatial conquest common in various forms to all the major painters working in Padua in the mid and late trecento is hard to account for with any certainty, though it belongs within the general tendency of north Italian art after *c.* 1340 to extend the empirical scope of painting beyond the point at which Florentine painting had, so to speak, got stuck. Guariento's interest in spatial problems must be associated with the specifically Giottesque strain in his complex bundle of roots and influences. The other artists in whom this progressive tendency was embodied were all non-Paduans, and, assuming Semitecolo's spatial style to have the same origins as Guariento's or to have come directly from him, the stylistic roots of the tendency are all based on earlier Tuscan models. But the stylistic origins are only half the story, and an interest in space can hardly be accounted an inherent or constant feature of north Italian art at this time, at least in the broad sense used above. The Veronese before Altichiero showed no interest in space at all, and hardly any after him. The work of Martino da Verona in Verona is as certainly based on Altichiero's example as that of Jacopo da Verona in Padua, but it is Jacopo who maintained the progressive flavour of Altichiero's style, where Martino, in some ways the abler painter, largely ignored it, setting the tone for the art of the late trecento in Verona, where selected aspects of Altichiero's art which tended towards International Gothic styles were consistently preferred to those which derived from the rationalism of early trecento Florence. The reflections of this art in Lombardy are only sporadic, and in nearby Venice scarcely evident at all. When Guariento secured the commission for the *Paradise* in the Doge's Palace in Venice, the result, magnificent though it must have been, was more in accordance with long-standing Venetian tastes and less 'advanced' than the immediately preceding work he did in the Eremitani in Padua (though comparisons are to an extent misleading, given the unique specification and setting of the *Paradise*).

There seems, then, to be a specifically Paduan element to this, and it can perhaps be associated with the nature of Paduan patronage at the highest level, that is, in the circles in which the court, the university, and the humanists mingled. This is, of course, precisely the circle of Altichiero's patrons. Its great monument was the Sala Virorum Illustrium, with all its various offshoots. The inference that this aspect of Paduan art was in some way connected with the recorded reverence for Giotto's work amongst the

[31] Panofsky, *Renaissance and Renascences*, p. 139.

very highest levels of Paduan social and intellectual life is hard to avoid. Suggestion of any specific links in this context between Altichiero and the Parmese Biagio Pelacani, author of the *Quaestiones Perspectivae* and teaching in Padua University from about 1382, must be regarded as purely speculative. But Biagio moved in the same circles as his fellow townsmen the Lupi,[32] and the parallel development in late trecento Padua of new perspectival theories and a taste for the progressively spatial in art must reflect areas of common cultural ground.

The specific literary source for Paduan interest in Giotto in the later trecento is the letter written in Padua in 1396 by the humanist Pier Paolo Vergerio comparing the use of Cicero as a suitable model for writers with a similar use of Giotto by painters. He says:

> Though Seneca considers one should not follow a single model but form a new style out of various models, I do not think this is so; one should have a single writer – and him the best – whom one imitates before all others, because the more one follows an inferior model and departs from the best, the worse one becomes. So one should do what the painters of our own age do, who though they may look with attention at famous paintings by other artists, yet follow the models of Giotto alone.[33]

Vergerio's use of such an analogy may have been conventional in humanist and rhetorical circles, but the reference to Giotto is too precise to be explained away as part of the post-Petrarchan baggage of late trecento literary humanism. If we doubt that Vergerio possessed either the eye to see by himself Giotto's influence in later work, or the vocabulary of concepts with which to understand such precise relationships between styles, then we must assume that he was reporting something he had heard. The substitution of 'we' for 'they' in the last sentence is all that is needed to turn it back into a verbal observation. Though Vergerio expands the extent of Giotto-worship by his use of the phrase 'the painters of our own age' (etatis nostre pictores) we may regard it as certain that it was a local painter who supplied him with this information.

Vergerio's testimony comes very late in the century – it must be roughly contemporary with the writing of Cennino Cennini's *Libro dell'Arte*. But we can trace a long pedigree for the reverence for Giotto's name in Padua. The fact of Petrarch's having famously bequeathed his *Madonna* by Giotto to Francesco Il Vecchio da Carrara in 1374, though significant in this context, is not as specifically revealing as the terms in which he couched the bequest, which precisely distinguish between a taste for Giotto characteristic of 'masters' and the dismissal of him by the ignorant.[34] We can assume the bequest to have been welcomed not only in terms of the personal regard between humanist and *signore* but because the terms implicitly include Francesco da Carrara amongst the discerning, a piece of flattery which, in the light of our knowledge of him, we need not regard as merely conventional. And in matters of taste, where the *signore* set an example, it would have been a foolish court which failed to follow it. So the inter-

32 For Biagio Pelacani's association with the Lupi circle see Gloria, *Monumenti*, no. 1652.

33 Quoted in Baxandall, *Giotto and the Orators*, pp. 43–4. For Vergerio see Robey, 'P. P. Vergerio'.

34 Mommsen, *Petrarch's Testament*, pp. 22ff. and 78ff.

est in Giotto in the courtly and humanist circles of Padua must be dated at least from the time of the writing of Petrarch's will, and probably from the beginning of his influence in Padua years before. Whether this taste was instrumental in bringing Altichiero to Padua, or whether he too was to some degree responsible for it, could only be established with any certainty if we had more native Paduan painting of the period 1350–75 in which to look for signs of his influence. It is probable on balance that he both benefited from the already existing taste and contributed to it. The coexistence in one small area of Italy at the same time of the only consistent literary worship of Giotto with the only body of painting based on Giottesque principles – though massively expanded and modernised – is unlikely to have been coincidental.

But here, as elsewhere, the silence of trecento sources when it comes to exact discussion of art impedes discussion. That Altichiero's art is based on Giotto's principles is easy to see now. But we simply do not know how painting was judged in 1380 and whether influence in the modern sense was a recognised feature of artistic style. Vergerio's famous remark hovers on the brink of such a recognition without actually completing the connection, for we cannot be certain that the Paduan painter(s) who talked to Vergerio drew from Giotto what we would like to believe they drew from him. To put it another way, the reverence for Giotto in Vergerio's time may have had the character of Cennino Cennini's admiration, that is, fundamentally non-stylistic, rather than what we may reasonably take to have been Altichiero's, that is, precisely and consciously stylistic in character. We may infer from his *work* that Altichiero himself knew very well how Giotto differed from, say, Orcagna or Vitale da Bologna, or Lorenzo Veneziano, and we might assume that if he was at all articulate he could have explained it, at least to another painter. But we dare not assume he could have made a literary humanist understand, and still less can we assume that the (unknown) and possibly less gifted painters to whom Vergerio talked shared a sufficiently developed common vocabulary for either to know what the other was on about. Had Cennino Cennini – in Padua in Vergerio's time – said to him something along the lines of the 'ancestral' passages in the *Libro*, it is probable that Vergerio's remark would have come out exactly as it did come out and that instead of an apparently exciting and precocious example of an artistic view shared by painters, humanists and princes we would have nothing more exciting than Cennino's reverence for Giotto as it stands.

At the same time, Petrarch's and Boccaccio's discrimination between those who know and the ignorant does seem to imply the existence of a vocabulary of looking which might distinguish between, say, the spatial rationalism of Altichiero and the hieratic art of mid-trecento Florence. That some notion of a set of criteria by which painting was to be judged on grounds other than those of the market is suggested by a remark made by Petrarch's follower Giovanni Conversino:

> 'When a painting is exhibited, the knowledgeable beholder expresses approval not so much of the purity and exquisite quality of the colours *as about the arrangement and the proportion of its parts*, and it is the ignorant man who is attracted simply by the colour . . .'[35] (My italics)

[35] Baxandall, *Giotto and the Orators*, p. 62.

This at least allows for a distinction between what is merely pretty, and what is visibly the product of the selecting and organising intelligence. The area of fourteenth-century thought out of which a developed apparatus for assessing the visual arts grew was essentially clustered round two concepts, both originally attached to Giotto: the painter's mimetic ability ('images formed by his brush agree so well with the lineaments of nature as to seem . . . to live and breathe'[36]), and his possession of 'ingenium', of sound judgment ('fuit sane Giottus'[37]). While it is too great an assumption to suggest that even the most alert humanists could 'read' Giotto's influence in Altichiero and see how he had expanded Giotto's discoveries in all directions, it is still straining coincidence too far to say that Altichiero's presence at dead centre of the circle in which such ideas were being mooted was accidental. It is not to be ruled out, and we too easily forget that all these figures were human beings like ourselves, that Altichiero simply *told* the Paduans how much he had studied the art of Giotto. If he had any inkling of the Paduan reverence for that master, letting this fact percolate through the circle of his potential patrons might have seemed an obvious step to take. He had, after all, a living to make, and he must have known his market.

S. Giorgio is, in many ways, the most Giottesque of Altichiero's works. The compositional and figure style of S. Giacomo seems to have marked the furthest extent of Altichiero's drive towards an epic naturalism, of which the great *Crucifixion* is the richest surviving example. The enormous expansion of narrative content, the great inclusive sweep of the invention, the evident intention to reproduce, as it were, a whole world, represents, at least in one sense, the furthest stage in Altichiero's progress beyond Giotto and the roots of his own style, without in any way violating (*pace* Berenson) the basic principles common to his and to Giotto's art. In some respects the frescoes of S. Giorgio continue this conquest of the phenomenal world: in the architectural realism of the settings, in the variety of racial types and costumes and in the evidently expanded role of portraiture in the narratives (for which see below). But at a more fundamental level, in the design of figure groups and individual figures, a more monumental, or perhaps architectural, principle is at work. While S. Giacomo and the Cavalli fresco clearly indicate the basis of Altichiero's style behind the expansive elements, the majority of the most direct reflections of a pure Giottesque style (excepting the quotations from Maso in S. Giacomo which may not be quite the same thing), or rather the most direct evidence of a grounding in that style, are to be found in S. Giorgio. The standing figure groups in the second, fourth, fifth and last St George scenes, in the last St Catherine scene, in the first and last St Lucy scenes, in the *Adoration*, *Presentation* and *Crucifixion* all bring to mind the classic groups of Giotto and Maso absolutely directly, in compositions which are taut and compressed.

Comparisons with S. Giacomo emphasise the severer control of the later frescoes. The bravura seas of heads and figures which mark the larger narratives of S. Giacomo – the *Crucifixion*, the *Battle of Clavigo*, the *Miracle of the Bulls* – each head turned at a

[36] Filippo Villani, quoted in *ibid.*, p. 70.

[37] *Ibid.*

different angle, in a different plane, from its neighbour, the complex interaction of gesture and glance through a large crowd, all the elements which articulate and enliven the larger masses of the S. Giacomo narratives, all this gives way to the more classical isocephaly of *St George Baptising*, *Drinking Poison*, *On the Wheel*, or his *Martyrdom*. The long chain of figures which marks the front plane of the S. Giacomo *Crucifixion* gives way to the compact and monumental type of the *Funeral of St Lucy*, complete with the archetypal Giottesque turn in from the wings to the centre. The shift is, of course, partly occasioned by the more compressed pictorial fields provided by S. Giorgio – a field like that of the S. Giacomo *Crucifixion* is always going to be something of a rarity – but comparison between the more directly comparable smaller frescoes of S. Giacomo and the S. Giorgio narratives confirms that a genuine stylistic shift has taken place.

The shift is reflected on the level of the individual figure. Nowhere in S. Giacomo can we find single standing figures as massive in conception as the Virgin or Simeon in the S. Giorgio *Presentation*, the extreme left-hand figure of the *Crucifixion* (pl. 86), or the toga-clad figure looking up at the cross to the right of the mounted Tartar in the same fresco. The drapery of these figures proclaims a more sculptural style – the folds are gathered in fewer, larger and straighter bunches and lines. The enhanced monumentality of the Holy Women in the *Crucifixion*, their increased power as single forms compared with their sisters in S. Giacomo, is clear, as is the greater architectural solidity and organisation of the group to which they belong.

The organisation of the *Crucifixion* as a whole is much tighter (in a narrower pictorial field) than that of the larger and earlier version, based on a series of interlocking triangles on the flat plane and on corresponding triangular groups on the receding spatial plane. In their different ways the *Crucifixions* of the two Paduan chapels may be accounted Altichiero's supreme compositional feats, and twin peaks of late trecento painting. The S. Giorgio *Crucifixion* contains individual figures as fine as anything he painted. Finest of all, perhaps, is the Good Thief, a study of the male nude *in extremis* which takes its place with the figure of the Bad Thief, St George on the Wheel, and Christ himself as part of one of the most impressive sets of male nudes in the fourteenth century, but which adds to the qualities displayed by all these figures a penetrating grasp of suffering and acceptance expressed in the deep *sfumato* of the face. The beautiful modelling of the torso suggests a level of attention on Altichiero's part not demonstrated to the same degree by the nude figure of St Lucy in her third scene, which may betray the hand of an assistant. The thieves occupy one *giornata* apiece, which suggests a considerable degree of facility.

The less expansive design of the S. Giorgio *Crucifixion* might at first seem to reflect a general aspect of the oratory frescoes, that they offer less in the way of the kind of iconographic innovations and renovations, of the redesigning of accepted scenes, which have been so marked a feature of Altichiero's work thus far. Up to a point this is true. The lives of the three saints are more orthodox in this respect than, say, the *Ramiro* scenes in S. Giacomo. This has little to do with Altichiero himself, and these frescoes are immensely distinguished and gripping on other levels. But elsewhere in the oratory we find the same process of re-examination that characterised the Cavalli fresco and the S. Giacomo *Crucifixion*. The votive fresco here (pls. 113, 114), which might at first glance be judged less successful than the S. Anastasia fresco, is actually an extraordinarily alert response to the virtually insurmountable problem of arranging nine more or less identical kneeling knights and one woman in a way that is neither dull nor confusing. As with the Cavalli fresco Altichiero here resorts to two basic mechanisms: the dramatic and the architectural. In dramatic terms the fresco expands the court-ritual aspect of the Cavalli scene, dividing the Lupi into a smaller and a larger group, divided by St James, who acts as a sort of major-domo, introducing, but at the same time holding back, the main body of knights. As with the Cavalli fresco, this may imply some distinction between the living and the dead, with Raimondino's parents already in the presence of the *Regina Coeli*.

The line of Lupi knights, differentiated from one another as far as is possible given the fraction of facial features visible under full bascinets, is also subtly articulated. None of them kneels in exactly the same position, or in the same plane, and the pure profile is eschewed in enough cases for the sense of a queue, a real danger here, to be avoided. This breaking up of the monotonous line is helped by the calculated irregularity of the line of presenting saints, who set up dialogues between themselves and with the knights.

All of this is set against a varied and complex architectural background which emphasises the narrative aspects of the scene, gathering to maximum density to mark the key figure of St James and to close the scene at both ends. The setting, which suggests a courtyard attached to a series of interconnected palatial structures, might be read as a stylistically idealised version of the Carrarese Palace, composed of just such a complex of open spaces and quasi-autonomous buildings.

This celestial architecture is echoed in another of the frescoes where Altichiero has expanded the traditional design, the *Coronation of the Virgin* (pls. 88–91), a common choice of scene for tombs at this time and visually very dominant here.[38] The huge throne, with its twin domes and fantastically intricate detail, was the kind of thing even the least gifted of Altichiero's followers could imitate to some extent, and echoes of it filter into all sorts of contexts during the last years of the century and beyond, often surviving in contexts where one would otherwise have no inkling of trecento influence.

An overall look at the altar wall (pls. 85, 88) shows Altichiero engaged in exactly the same kind of manipulation and blurring of the fictive and the real as in S. Giacomo. The arch which frames the *Coronation* is lifted up on fictive spiral columns (fig. 72), triumphs of *trompe l'œil*, which possibly echoed real spiral columns on the lost superstructure of the tomb. A fictive arcade also 'supports' the altar slab. At the centre of this ensemble is the *Crucifixion*, which, in contrast, appears to have no frame at all. The scene consequently floats free above the altar, as if seen through a great window, and the reality of the surrounding architecture, so positively asserted by the columns, is here negated. *In situ* the effect of the *Coronation*'s being set somehow within the building, an

[38] E.g. the Bolparo and da Vigonza tombs in the Santo and the tomb of Jacopo II da Carrara formerly in S. Agostino, now in the Eremitani, with a detached Coronation fresco by Guariento.

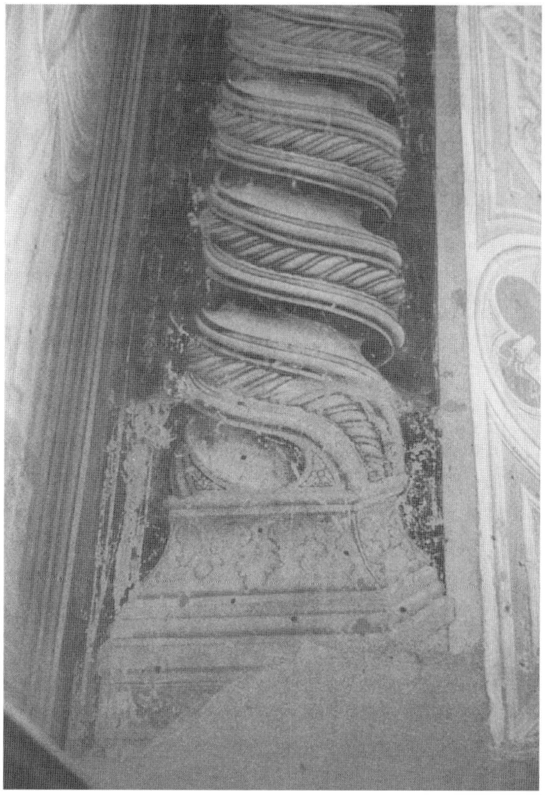

Fig. 72 Padua, Oratory of S. Giorgio. Altar wall: detail of spiral column.

effect emphasised by the kind of swooping perspective last seen in Ramiro's council chamber, whereas the *Crucifixion* takes place outside, is very striking.

The emotional tone of the S. Giorgio narratives corresponds with the formal severity. The great range of personal responses and moods which make the frescoes of S. Giacomo so rich in character studies is here subordinated to an all-embracing seriousness expressed by larger, slower and less expansive gestures, and by a gravity of mien and facial expression common to virtually every figure. The open grief of the S. Giacomo Holy Women, the sudden lurch forward of the figure catching the swooning Virgin, the clasped hands of the woman behind her, the weeping of the two foreground figures, the stricken facial expressions, give way to a less overtly expressive and more classical or stoical sense of the enormity of the occasion. The emotional force is undiminished, though – many of the faces round the Virgin exhibit a dignity in sorrow which is particularly haunting, and the chain of hands round the Virgin's arm and face is especially moving. The choice in this *Crucifixion* of the moment succeeding that shown in S. Giacomo – there the Virgin is in the act of swooning, here she is already on the ground – reflects the enhanced *gravitas* which is the abiding tone of S. Giorgio and the new preference for static poise rather than immediate narrative action. Perhaps the absence of Jacopo Avanzi led in some way to a clarification of Altichiero's style.

The narratives of the saints' lives are necessarily compressed in character, with four frescoes apiece for Sts Catherine and Lucy, and six (the votive fresco occupies a space as wide as two of the other frescoes) for St George. This gives the three brief cycles rather the character of allusions to the stories in the *Legenda Aurea*, and Altichiero pointedly ignores the extraordinary cataract of mutilation, recovery and dismemberment which constitutes St George's path to martyrdom,[39] just as he plays down the violence inherent in the scenes in which Sts George and Catherine are tortured on the wheel. Even their respective executions are dignified affairs. St Lucy is similarly dignified throughout her troubles, never more so than when exposed naked in a brothel in the third scene, displaying overt emotion only when about to be stabbed in the neck, a bathetic enough end one might think, given the imaginative catalogue of terrors she has already withstood by this stage. Here, as ever, witnesses are close at hand.

The least successful compositions of S. Giorgio are exactly those in which the narrative demands violent action, and in which the weighty tone of the late style shows itself not entirely suited to extravagant movement. The designs of the individual figures reacting to *St Catherine on the Wheel* (pl. 107) are all fine examples of complex draughtsmanship, but it can hardly be said that they add up to an entirely convincing portrayal of this explosive event. *Suddenness* of this kind, so suited to the abilities and temperaments of artists like Vitale or Tomaso or Jacopo Avanzi, is not really in the repertoire of Altichiero's late style, and a scene such as this fails to add up to more than the sum of its parts, greatly impressive though the parts are. The more restrained reaction to a similar event in *St George on the Wheel* (pl. 98) is more successful precisely because it registers the crowd's recoil in terms of the architectural poise of the figure groups, the right hand of which merely leans out and away from the vertical. The attempted effect is less exciting but the style is able to contain it better. More successful still are scenes in which the action is wholly invented in terms of the prevailing formal concerns, like the superbly composed *Execution of St George* (pl. 103), or the *Miracle of St Lucy and the Bulls* (pl. 111), in which the columnar immovability of the saint, established by a series of remarkable right-angled gestures, and contrasted with the strain exerted by the bulls, one of which is actually lifted off the ground, puts the essence of the architectural style at the service of the particular demands of the narrative.

A cognate restraint can be sensed in the *Fall of the Idols* (pls. 101–2). Where other trecento painters, including some within the broad Giottesque tradition, portray collapsing buildings with a whirlwind of shattering columns and flying bricks,[40] Altichiero, trading on the spectator's implicit trust in the workability of his architecture, gives an intricate structure poised on already impossibly tall columns which just begin to fracture, causing understandable consternation in those about to be crushed and in the alarmed but not immediately threatened witnesses opposite. The dramatic tension this generates is extremely powerful.

[39] Kaftal, *Iconography of the Saints in the Painting of North East Italy*, pp. 348–74.

[40] E.g. the *Earthquake at Ephesus* in S. Agostino, Rimini, reproduced by Volpe, *La Pittura Riminese del Trecento*, pls. 136–40.

The oratory in context

The return to stricter compositional principles after several years in Padua has been explained in the past as the result of a study of the Arena Chapel. This seems an insufficient explanation, at least in the sense of Altichiero's having made a private study of the Scrovegni frescoes. For a painter the whole basis of whose art ultimately derives from Giotto, and for a native of the immediate region, the Arena Chapel (well known, as we have seen, to artists of more distant regions of Lombardy in the mid-trecento) was hardly going to come as a surprise. And in any case Altichiero, whose interest in Giotto was concentrated on the late work and on the work of Giotto's younger followers, is unlikely to have been quite as impressed by a relatively early work like the Scrovegni frescoes, of which there is no direct sign in the frescoes of S. Giorgio, which instead abundantly reflect the lower church at Assisi and the chapels of S. Croce. The renewed interest in Giotto must be accounted for in a different way, and the apparent character of the oratory as some kind of 'copy' of the Arena Chapel should be seen in a wider context. The extent of Altichiero's personal need to re-inject Giotto into his own work in this way cannot be estimated. But the effect of the Giotto-worshipping humanist coterie of Padua, with whom we know for certain Altichiero more than any other artist was connected, must, as has already been suggested, have had its effect.

Other aspects of S. Giorgio may also reflect the impinging concerns of this group. Varying degrees of influence from the Antique have been suggested in earlier contexts and they register here too, beyond the obvious *all'antica* motif of the two imperial heads flanking the *Crucifixion*, by now a familiar trademark. It may, incidentally, have escaped notice, *re* these heads, that the interest in Roman coins in late Carrarese Padua which bore most famous fruit in the Carrarese medals,[41] has a clear local precedent in Altichiero's work in Verona some three decades earlier, and now in Padua itself, and that given his apparently central role as artist to the specifically humanist elements in both courts, it is at least likely that he himself transmitted this taste, or at least its modern visual expression, from Verona to Padua. The use of Giovanni de Matoci's *Historia* as a vague precedent for the Carrarese medals is insufficient as an explanation. But Altichiero's adaptation of the *Historia* was recent, presumably celebrated, and accessible to the right set of spectators.

It has already been suggested that Roman relief styles related to that of the *Ara Pacis* may lie behind figure groups like the foreground line of the left wing of the S. Giacomo *Crucifixion*. Precise identification of antique sources is impeded by the very nature of the tradition which Altichiero followed, where the ghost of early imperial Roman style seems to make itself felt in many contexts, but in which, either because it was itself experienced at second hand, or because it was thoroughly assimilated, it is hard to identify distinct borrowings. The classical flavour of many of the figure groups in S. Giorgio is as likely to be derived from the generally classical look inherited from the Florentines. But more direct borrowings from the Antique may be detected. The group standing at

[41] See Gorini, 'Iconografia Monetale', and Cessi, 'Monetazione e Medaglistica', in Grossato, *Da Giotto a Mantegna*, pp. 81–9.

the foot of the cross in the *Crucifixion* (pl. 86), looking up and with their backs turned, closely recalls Adlocutio scenes from both the Trajanic and Aurelian columns in which soldiers are addressed by their commander or emperor, and the figure immediately to the right of the cross, in the foreground, seems to come straight out of one of the columnar reliefs. The position and gesture of St John from the same fresco are both reminiscent of classical poses. One might, at a pinch, also see in the design of the man cutting the bull's throat in the first St Catherine scene (pl. 105)- one of Altichiero's most characteristic and emphatic uses of foreground space – the ghost of some Mithraic scene, or of some other example of antique sacrificial iconography.

The extent of the interest shown in and the knowledge of classical art shown by the literary humanists of the trecento is generally assumed to be limited. Artists, as we know for instance from the writings of the Paduan Giovanni Dondi, were stimulated by the example of antique sculpture,[42] but it has perhaps too easily been assumed that the division between artistic and literary enthusiasm, only, according to received opinion, reconciled in the Florentine quattrocento, prevented trecento humanists from taking a serious interest in the art of the Antique or regarding such an interest as a serious matter. But the observations of Dondi, characterised by Krautheimer as 'purblind'[43] and by Baxandall as 'bathetic'[44] really deserve no such summary dismissal. It is hardly fair to interpret, as Krautheimer does, the passages from his oft-quoted letter to Fra Guglielmo da Cremona as evidence that Dondi 'did not feel altogether at home with ancient art',[45] or that he regarded the sculptor whose enthusiasm he discusses as admiring 'beyond comprehension achievements of antiquity to which his own criteria did not apply'. Nor is there any reason to accuse him of sharing the 'new . . . incomprehension with which the learned looked upon those queer ducks who admired fragments of the ancient world for reasons other than their literary overtones'. The point, surely, of Dondi's letter is that he shows himself more or less fully capable of understanding the specifically aesthetic response to classical art expressed by his sculptor friend, a response which, in its setting up of the Antique as an example, recalls the exemplary status accorded Giotto in Padua in the same years and recorded in Vergerio's writings. Of the gap between literary, or 'learned' as Krautheimer rather invidiously calls it, humanist response and artistic interest there is no reason to doubt. The artists,

[42] I myself used to know a marble sculptor . . . famous among those whom Italy then had . . . More than once I heard him discuss the statues and sculptures he had seen in Rome with such admiration and veneration that in his discourse he seemed to be all beyond himself, so full of wonder was the subject . . . he talked a great deal about the excellence of these figures and praised their makers and acclaimed their genius beyond all measure. He used to conclude – I quote his own words – that if such sculptures had only the spark of life, they would be better than nature.

Giovanni Dondi, quoted in Krautheimer, *Lorenzo Ghiberti*, p. 296.

The letter is also discussed by Panofsky, *Renaissance and Renascences*, pp. 208–10. The wording of Dondi's letter is interesting. He says: 'if our modern artists look at them [i.e. antique sculptures] carefully they are stunned [*obstupescant*]', which closely parallels Petrarch's and Vergerio's terminology when discussing Giotto (Petrarch: 'cuius pulchritudinem ignorantes non intelligunt, *magistri autem artis stupent*'; Vergerio: 'faciendum est igitur *quod etatis nostre pictores* qui . . . solius tamen exemplaria sequuntur').

[43] Krautheimer, quoted in Panofsky, *Renaissance and Renascences*, p. 209, n.

[44] Baxandall, *Giotto and the Orators*, p. 52.

[45] Krautheimer, *Lorenzo Ghiberti*, p. 297.

responding in a more 'direct' spirit (to quote Krautheimer, who spoils it by equating 'direct' with 'naive') shared none of the growing nostalgia for the Antique characteristic of literary humanism and of the dawning Renaissance as a whole (a nostalgia 'born of estrangement as well as a sense of affinity'[46]). But Dondi evidently knew of this distinct approach to the Antique, and there is nothing in his remarks to indicate that he regarded it as queer or incomprehensible or naive. In fact he defines the precise and practical nature of the artistic response perfectly satisfactorily.

For the artists the assimilation of the full nostalgic vision had not yet happened. But it is at least possible in this most advanced intellectual climate, with which was associated a most unusual interest in art – unusual in that distinctions were made which were far more precisely discriminating than those between good work and bad work – that classical borrowings in art, in which the antique motifs were transposed into non-classical contexts, were nevertheless visible to the learned spectators. Overt references to the Antique like the imperial heads of S. Giorgio would obviously have presented no problems. It is not too much to suppose that during the course of Altichiero's long association with thc Paduan humanist circle, starting perhaps before Petrarch's death, such matters were discussed.

Members of this circle may be commemorated in some numbers here. The frescoes appear to contain more portraits than those of S. Giacomo, where they were confined to four scenes only. Applying the same criteria as there for isolating portraits from the mass of surrounding figures, convincing candidates can be identified (in addition to those of the votive fresco) in the second, fourth and fifth St George scenes (pls. 93, 97–8), the first, third and fourth St Lucy scenes (109, 113, 115–16), the *Adoration of the Magi* (pl. 79) and the *Crucifixion* (pl. 86). Borderline cases exist in the seventh St George scene and second St Lucy scenes (pls. 103, 111). The exclusion of the St Catherine cycle may not be significant. The crowds of the partly ruined first two scenes resemble those of other frescoes in which portraits do seem to be included, but their condition makes any distinctions impossible. Again excluding the votive fresco, the number of portraits in S. Giorgio add up to something between thirty and forty, depending on how strictly one applies the criteria. With the votive fresco the number may exceed fifty, an extraordinarily high count at any time and unprecedented in the trecento (though the Sala Grande may, as Vasari suggests, have teemed with portraits).

The starting point for any examination of the S. Giorgio portraiture must be the scene of *St George Baptising* (pl. 93), in which several of the figures identified in S. Giacomo appear once more.[47] Petrarch, securely identifiable on the basis of Altichiero's other portraits of him – a criterion we now take for granted, but astonishingly precocious in this context – is accompanied by the same distinctive figure as in S. Giacomo, who can be identified, on the basis of his association with Petrarch and with the Lupi, as Lombardo della Seta. The two faces squeezed between Lombardo and Petrarch may complete the repetition of the S. Giacomo portrait group, for they resemble the putative portraits of Francesco il Vecchio and Francesco Novello da Carrara close to

[46] *Ibid.*

[47] See Mardersteig, 'I Ritratti', *passim*.

Petrarch in the *Council of King Ramiro* (pls. 66–8) of the earlier chapel. The pairing of the older and younger Carraresi, not as certainly identifiable as Petrarch and Lombardo, may take on a more specific and pointed character in the scene of *St Lucy Before Judge Pascasio* (pl. 109). The identification of the two black-robed figures standing on the right of this fresco in what we may call the typical 'witness' position as the *signore* and his son, accepted by Mardersteig and others, rests only on their apparent resemblance to their portraits elsewhere in the two chapels, none of which can be other than circumstantially identified. The attention drawn to these two figures, though, with their sober clothes and their prominent position on the front plane of the scene means that we need not seriously doubt their status as portraits.

The left-hand portrait group of the *Baptism*, singled out by the pointing figure to the left of them, is matched by another, larger group to the right. Most of these standing men would seem to satisfy the criteria to some degree. Mardersteig's identification of them as members of the Lupi family,[48] though entirely conjectural, is not unconvincing – the layout of this court scene seeming to echo that of S. Giacomo – but his more specific naming of the two helmeted figures on either side of the outer column of the basilica (pl. 94), each sporting a commander's plume, as Raimondino Lupi himself and his brother Bonifacio di Rolandino cannot be sustained. There is simply no evidence. Raimondino's presence somewhere may be assumed, it would be odd if he were excluded. He is perhaps one of the captains in the *Crucifixion*, and it is at least worth noting that the prominent figure with the bifurcated beard in the *Baptism*, identified by Mardersteig as Bonifacio di Rolandino, seems to appear once more in the *Crucifixion*, gesturing to another bearded figure with a marshall's baton who seems, visually at least, to be the most important of the commanders' group.[49] This latter figure resembles, if anyone, Bonifacio di Ugolotto as we know him from S. Giacomo. Given the extent of his participation in the finishing of the oratory and the fact of his having placed his arms alongside Raimondino's on the exterior, we might expect him to be present. It is not inconceivable that the two mounted commanders are portraits of Raimondino and Bonifacio (di Ugolotto) Lupi. Their prominence suggests this, as does the visual relationship, which seems to emphasise a particular link between them – just such a link as might be felt appropriate as between the original patron of S. Giorgio and his executor. Neither can a pairing of Raimondino and Bonifacio's father Ugolotto be ruled out, given their close association during their lives.

This raises the broader question of the extent of Bonifacio's influence on the iconography and contents of S. Giorgio, probably substantially painted only after his assumption of responsibility for it, though, in my view, already determined on broad lines. The presence in the *Baptism* and elsewhere of elements of the Carrarese court, and specifically of the Carraresi themselves (if this is accepted), would be consistent with

[48] *Ibid.*, pl. xxv.

[49] This figure wears a jewelled pin on the front of his helmet, holding the plume in place, which somewhat resembles the *carri* of da Carrara. But the Carrarese crest is always red and of a quite recognisable pattern, to which this pin does not conform. A similar pin is worn by a young man standing in the right aisle of the church in the fresco of *St George Baptising*.

Raimondino's choice, given his connections with the Carraresi and their apparent role in bringing him to end his days in Padua. But the prominent inclusion of Petrarch and Lombardo, the former now dead for nearly a decade and the latter a close associate of Bonifacio Lupi, and neither of them, as far as we know, associated at all with Raimondino Lupi (living in Mantua during Petrarch's final years in Padua and Arquà), does tend to suggest some decisive role for Bonifacio in the choice of S. Giorgio's more detailed iconography. It seems to record once again Bonifacio's pride in his association both with the signorial family – not unusual in such a context and for such a man – and, more unusually, with the humanist circle supported by the *signore*. The repeated use of Petrarch's portrait as a kind of cultural emblem suggests an extraordinarily strong identification with that part of Paduan culture which responded most to Petrarch's example. Altichiero himself may have shared something of his patron's desire to record his association with the great man. The close-knit quality of this area of signorial/humanist culture, the extent to which courtiers, humanists and artists were more than ever before pursuing common and conscious goals is once more underlined. It is by no means unlikely that the body of portraiture in S. Giorgio amounts to a substantial group portrait of the humanist circle close to the Lupi and to the Carraresi themselves, and that it does so in a deliberate and programmatic sense.

It is perhaps worth reiterating at this point just how close Altichiero, on his own or via Bonifacio, stood to the central figures of north Italian humanism. His connections with Petrarch, whatever form they took, have been discussed. We know from the evidence of various exchanges of letters that Bonifacio Lupi and Petrarch had been friends,[50] and Bonifacio's friendship with Lombardo is well attested. It was Bonifacio's associate, and fellow traveller on the Hungarian mission of 1372, Checco da Lion, who underwrote the considerable expense of the production of the Petrarch texts by Lombardo's 'factory' in the years following the poet's death.[51] Bonifacio was also a friend of Petrarch's family in Padua, and of Ugolino Scrovegni, son of the founder of the Arena Chapel, husband of Bonifacio's cousin Luca Rossi and whose daughter Maddalena was the dedicatee of Lombardo's only independent literary work.[52] Another key figure in the Petrarch circle, Ottonello Descalzi, who mediated between the humanists at the Paduan and Mantuan courts, married Lombardo's niece Giovanna and was associated with Petrarch's son-in-law Francescuolo da Brossano; also with Simone Lupi, painted by Altichiero in the S. Giorgio votive scene.[53] In 1389 Lombardo, Ugolino and

[50] Evidence of Bonifacio Lupi's friendship with Petrarch is furnished by a three-way exchange of letters written in 1369 between Petrarch, Bonifacio and Philippe de Mézières, chancellor of King Peter of Cyprus, on the subject of the death of Bonifacio's kinsman Giacomo Rossi. For these letters see Wilkins, 'Petrarch and Giacomo de'Rossi'. Bonifacio may have met Petrarch as early as 1355, when he was in Charles IV's retinue on the emperor's journey through Italy, at which time Petrarch came to see Charles and accompanied him for part of the way. See Bayley, 'Petrarch, Charles IV, and the "Renovatio Imperii"', pp. 330ff. and Pezzana, *Storia della Città di Parma*, vol. 1, p. 39 for Bonifacio's role in this.

[51] The source for this fact is a letter written by Lombardo della Seta, discussed (with full Latin text) in Billanovich and Pellegrin, 'Una Nuova Lettera di Lombardo della Seta'; see especially p. 222.

[52] Gilbert, 'Giotto in Milan', p. 66.

[53] For Ottonello Descalzi see Zucchi, 'Ottonello Descalzi', and for his association with Bonifacio, Gloria, *Monumenti*, no. 1537 (AD 1382).

Bonifacio were all present in Bonifacio's house on the occasion of the legitimisation of Lombardo's son Pellegrino (named perhaps after Petrarch, 'peregrinus ubique'[54]). Bonifacio and Lombardo can both, in addition, be shown to have shared a friendship with Giovanni Dondi.[55] Pursuit of these connections through the abundant documentation is not difficult and it reinforces the tightly knit aspect of this group, the twin centres of whose social world seem to have been their connections with Francesco da Carrara and their shared memories of Petrarch. This may explain the high profile accorded to Petrarch in S. Giorgio, and the fact of Altichiero's portrait – another in what is, for the time, quite a long list by him – reminds us that Altichiero himself can be shown to have connections of one kind or another with most of these people, with – and the point is surely of great significance – *all* the key figures of the humanist circle at the Paduan court: Francesco da Carrara, promoter of the new *DVI* and the frescoes based on it; Petrarch himself; Lombardo; Checco, who paid for all the Petrarch manuscripts; and Bonifacio, who was tied to all these men in various ways. In the wake of what must have been a heightened sense of a very special elite in Padua comes the great rash of portraits which spreads across the walls of the oratory, most of whom will never now be identified, but whose features have been preserved in Altichiero's frescoes for more than six centuries.

They are not hard to spot. The five left-hand and two right-hand figures of *St George Condemned to Drink Poison* (pl. 97) are markedly individual in character, as is the portly man with chic haircut and elegantly pointed shoes on the left of *St George on the Wheel* (pl. 98). The Carrarese device of the negro's head prominently displayed on the breast of the old bearded captain in the *Execution of St George* (pls. 103–4) may mark him as a senior member of the family (the emblem is also displayed on the soldiers' shields). The group witnessing the *Miracle of St Lucy and the Bulls* (pl. 111) from the central gate are rather more individualised than the standard Altichiero types found in the rest of the fresco, and they figure as pious observers, in the role which seems to have been felt most appropriate for portraits. The figures on the extreme right of the *Tortures of St Lucy* (pl. 113), witnesses again rather than participants, similarly – perhaps more certainly – meet the criteria for portraits. The rather dour figure nearest the edge of the fresco closely resembles the man in the next fresco, the *Funeral of St Lucy*, fourth from the left in the front rank of what is the most prominent group of apparent portraits in the whole ensemble (pl. 116). The plump figure so expressly highlighted in the S. Giacomo Council scene reappears here, now even plumper. If the common identity of the two figures is accepted, the subject cannot be Giovanni Lupi, doctor of Decretals, canon of Padua Cathedral, and author of several learned works, as Mardersteig suggested,[56] for this man died in 1364 and is hardly likely to have got fatter between S. Giacomo and S.

[54] Billanovich and Pellegrin, 'Una nuova Lettera', pp. 230–1. The memorial function of Pellegrino's name was suggested to me by Professor B. Kohl.

[55] A letter from Giovanni Dondi to Lombardo mentions Bonifacio in terms which make their mutual affection clear: 'Cum dudum, amice, sentire di te condicionibusque tuis per certitudinem aliquid cuperem, contigit proximis diebus huc accessisse *nobilem militem tui meique communiter amatorem, dominum videlicet Bonifacium*' – Billanovich and Pellegrin, 'Una nuova Lettera', pp. 228–9.

[56] Mardersteig, 'I Ritratti', p. 270.

Giorgio. His prominence in each incarnation nevertheless suggests a degree of importance. There was, of course, as any study of the documentary evidence suggests, no shortage of Lupi in Padua,[57] nor of longstanding Parmese cronies of Bonifacio's. To his left stand two youths of different ages but clearly blood-relations if their features are anything to go by. The figure apparently repeated from the previous fresco is identified by Mardersteig as Giovanni Dondi dall'Orologio. Dondi was central to the intellectual circles who had known Petrarch, was the poet's close friend and legatee, and was also closely associated with the Lupi and the Carraresi themselves. As his account of the famous sculptor's passion for the Antique showed he had at least some connection with artistic circles, a connection at least tangentially confirmed by the documented association of the Dondi family with the Raini, one of the important artistic dynasties in Padua, originally Roman, and whose ranks also included important legal specialists. Dondi was no longer living in Padua while the oratory was being painted, having passed into service with Gian Galeazzo Visconti in Pavia in 1379/80. His inclusion would still be unsurprising, but this exact identification has no concrete evidence to sustain it.[58]

On the extreme right of this fresco, marking what may be the end of the painting campaign, his gaze directed not at the scene in which he appears but seemingly back along the west wall of the oratory, is another apparent portrait, the darkly clad figure discussed in chapter 1 (pl. 115). His isolation, and the way his foot pointedly rests on the moulding just above the now illegible signature of the chapel (fig. 73 – the signature is discussed in the catalogue entry for S. Giorgio), inevitably makes one wonder if this is not Altichiero himself. Nothing would prevent the acceptance of such a hypothesis – his costume is not that of a nobleman but only of a gentleman, a status Altichiero may have aspired to, and the relative youth of the face is only a problem if, like Mellini, one reads S. Giorgio as an old man's work.

The two young men between the Magi and the first servant in the entrance wall *Adoration* (pl. 79) are distinguished from the other figures by an almost photographic particularity which in turn suggests a family relationship between them. Establishing the presence of portraits in the *Crucifixion* is made harder than elsewhere by the preponderance in this fresco of a heavily bearded male type which is commonly seen in Altichiero's work in what are probably not portrait contexts, but which still seems on occasions to have recorded a distinct individual. Bonifacio Lupi himself is of this type. So while the major captains on the right seem to be signalled in a way that other contexts reserve for portraits, as does the praying mounted figure on the left, and the profile bearded head looking up just over the right (his right) shoulder of St John is a degree more particularised than the surrounding heads, they swim in a sea of such physical types which do seem to be merely standard repertoire figures.

As in S. Giacomo, the figures mostly wear modern dress. Where appropriate the major actors of the narratives wear the clothes of their modern equivalents, like the judges of the *St Lucy* scenes or the soldiers of the *Crucifixion*. Ermine-lined cloaks

[57] For the Lupi in Padua see Sartori, 'La Cappella di S. Giacomo', pp. 317ff.

[58] Mardersteig, 'I Ritratti', pl. XXVIII. For the Raini family see Gloria, *Monumenti* and Sartori, 'La Cappella di S. Giacomo', nos. 14, 22 and 59.

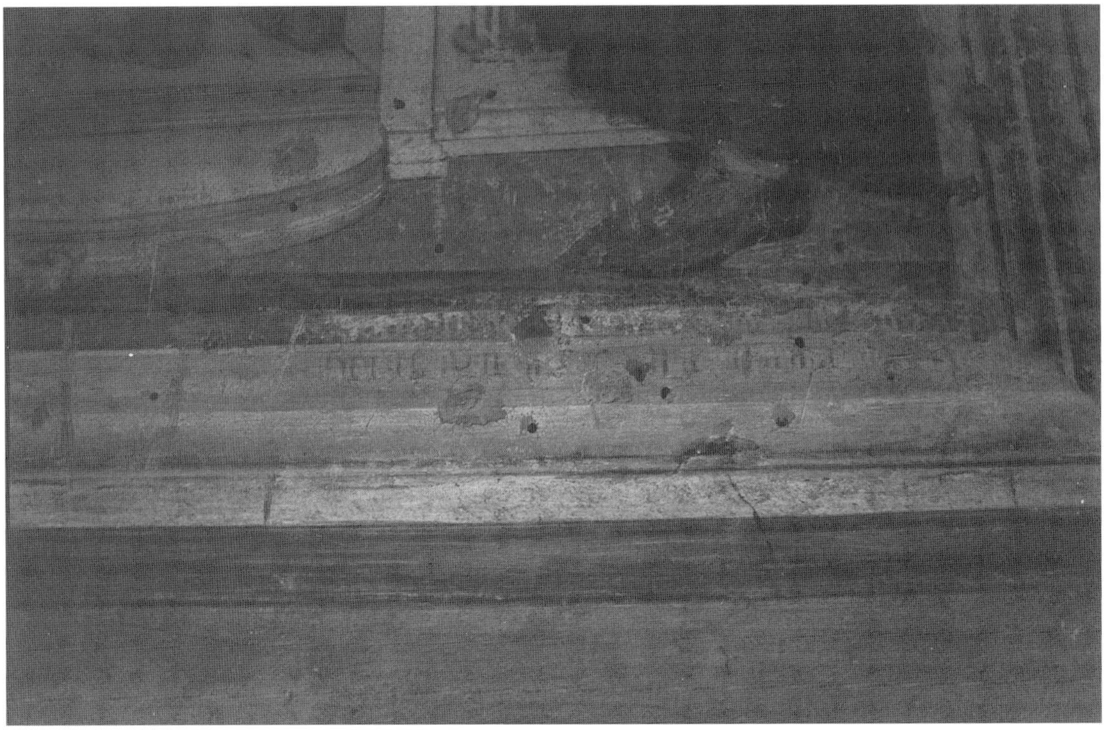

Fig. 73 Padua, Oratory of S. Giorgio. Signature on west wall.

proclaim the royal status of the Magi and of St Catherine. The vast range and variety of costume types in the frescoes, from the sumptuous dignity characteristic of the witnesses and portraits to the exotic dress of the many Asians included in the crowd scenes, give S. Giorgio a sartorial scope little short of encyclopaedic, and which is as important a feature of the continuing empirical expansion of the painted world as the fictive architecture. The better condition of the S. Giorgio frescoes enhances this aspect, for the colours, unlike those of S. Giacomo, are well preserved. This is of particular importance in the treatment of the great variety of stuffs and fabrics here, ranging from the curious quilted, padded and ribbed materials worn by the soldiers in the third *St Catherine* scene to the crimplene-like crêpe bunching on the child being led away from the *Execution of St George* (pl. 103), and the fancy striped stuff of the older youth in the *Funeral of St Lucy*. Great attention is paid to the detail of the possibly Lucchese fabric of the altar cloth in the *Presentation* (pl. 82) and the draped bier in the *Funeral of St Lucy*, and to the worked and tooled leather of the Tartar's belt and saddle in the *Crucifixion* (pl. 87). As a natural accompaniment to this expansive study of dress, a variety of hairstyles is on view. St Catherine, princess and philosopher, lets her hair flow in the simplest possible way until her executioners pin it up, while St Lucy (pl. 112) has a long plait wound up across her scalp, allowing the hair to fall in a soft swag at the back. But the men are the peacocks here, and pride of place must go to the modish bobbed cut affected by the imposing figure on the far left of *St George on the Wheel* (pl. 99), done for the occasion one might think.

All this is expressed in a colour scheme of great brilliance and unique character. Shot colours dominate some scenes – the *Execution of St George* for instance, with the mantle of the man leaving on the left, lilac shot with grey, the apple-green changing to red of the horseman above him, the light whitey-green with red shadows of the turbaned horseman next in line to him, or the sea-green and red of the majestic bending figure gesturing to the crouching saint. A related sea-green is found on the left of the *Crucifixion* together with the rich butter-yellow of the bending woman holding Mary's hand and the very unusual ash-blue/white of the Virgin's mantle. The standing judge in *St Lucy Before Judge Pascasio* (pl. 110) is dressed in a cloak of a distinctive cold iron-green with black shadows. The tonal sobriety of the group on the right-hand side of this fresco, the two judges and the two standing witnesses, contrasted with the lighter and warmer colours of the left-hand group may be an attempt to suggest the suppression of colour in the shade. Confirmation that Altichiero was interested in such areas of empirical expansion is provided by the *Tortures of St Lucy*, in which the man blowing on the fire with his bellows casts an unmistakable shadow on the wall behind him (pl. 114).

The peak of Altichiero's invention is perhaps reached in *St Catherine on the Wheel* (pl. 107), from the quilted tunic of the soldier on the extreme left – salmon-pink with apple-green shadows against the darker green of the sleeves, a reversal of the prevailing red/green pattern, through the extraordinary and here unique green (again, with red shadows) of the collapsing man in the centre, the citron-white of the pigtailed Tartar in the foreground, the citron/apple of the dress of the woman on the far right, with apple-green shadows, the semi-shining stuff of her child's tunic, the grey/pink shot fabric of the man behind the column to the left of the woman and child, to the brilliant electric-blue of the arm pointing down from the balcony to the miracle below. Such a colour scheme has no precedent and must be accounted Altichiero's own invention. The subtlety and range proclaim his painterly exuberance. The control which ensures none of these individual feats of tonal imagining stands out of the overall tonal and harmonic context proclaims the great organiser.

Other aspects of the frescoes may record the daily life and the visual world of the Paduan court. The administration of justice in the small cloister-like spaces of the first *St Lucy* or fourth *St George* frescoes (pls. 109, 97), the transactions recorded by benched notaries in the former, must have seemed a familiar scene to men like the Lupi, recorded in countless documents as witnessing judgments, major and minor, made in the courtyards and loggias of the Carrarese Palace. Altichiero's studies of the anxieties attendant on witnessing – or not being allowed to witness – such processes are wonderfully acute. The execution of capital sentences in rather more public and open spaces (*St George on the Wheel*, *St Catherine on the Wheel*), or beyond the city walls as in the *Executions* of the two saints (and as was Paduan practice for all but exceptional executions) would have been equally familiar occurrences. The prevalence in the narratives of large numbers of witnesses, a convenient location for the bulk of the apparent portraiture, also reflects an important element of daily life for this class, for anyone who reads any quantity of the surviving documents of the time could be forgiven for thinking that these men of power and influence spent most of their time witnessing each other's transactions in a more or less unending stream. Witnessing in a less narrowly legal sense, being present at important events, is also an inherent aspect of the courtier's life, and the semi-participatory presence in so many of the narratives of numbers of grandees marks this aspect of their daily experience. In this additional respect we may again interpret the frescoes of S. Giorgio as a portrait of the Paduan court.

But the depicted world is wider than this and includes men of different conditions and races. Most noticeable are the various exotics, more prevalent here than in S. Giacomo: Asians, Moslems, men of lands further to the East. The use of such figures, evidently observed from life, follows trecento practice in representing modern heathens as the pagans of the past. So a Tartar beheads St Catherine (pl. 108) and another presides over the *Execution of St George* (pl. 103), while a notary with marked Asian features records the process of justice administered to St Lucy (pl. 109). But the connotations are not all negative. The Magi (pl. 79) bring in their train another Tartar, a Mongol(?) and another Asian with a pigtail and a jacket of the quilted stuff worn by westerners in the St Catherine cycle. Altichiero's detailed fascination with men of the Asian races gives an exotic flavour to many passages in S. Giorgio.

The process by which the contemporary and the living are assumed as full individuals within the stories of long-dead martyrs, or witness the Crucifixion itself, relates to Altichiero's earlier reinvention of the role and status of donors in votive contexts and ultimately derives from it. The lack of curbs on the celebration of the individual, often interpreted as a proto-Renaissance concept, must also be understood as an integral feature of signorial societies, in sharp contrast with the republics of Venice and Florence where such vainglorious display on behalf of an individual was disliked and discouraged (witness Bonifacio Lupi's inability to get his way in Florence over the matter of his tomb) and where no amount of gratitude felt by the state for the service of a given individual could eradicate the basic mistrust of exceptional men, even of the idea of exceptional men within the body politic. Under a signorial government the sanctions against any individual accumulating a threatening degree of influence were drastic, immediate and potentially lethal. They were in consequence perhaps more effective as a deterrent, and allowed greater licence where there was a measure of trust. The perceived betrayal of such trust was a matter for more personal recrimination than characterised the reaction of a communal or republican government, as we see from the treatment by the Carraresi of Bonifacio Lupi and Lombardo della Seta (or rather his corpse) after 1388, and the brief disgrace of Checco da Lion as the *Cronaca Carrarese* records it.[59] In some respects – not the technically political or legalistic – the bonds between *signore* and courtier resembled those of king and noble within a feudal structure rather than those expected, say, of a citizen of Venice by his state. It is a crucial and sometimes forgotten aspect of the dawn of the Renaissance that two of its defining characteristics, two major

[59] For Checco's disgrace and pardon see Gatari, *Cronaca Carrarese*, p. 208. One of Checco's enemies in Padua was the poet Francesco di Vannozzo, who thoroughly relished Checco's brief fall from grace. For this glimpse of the tensions of court life see Levi, *Francesco di Vannozzo*, pp. 90–2.

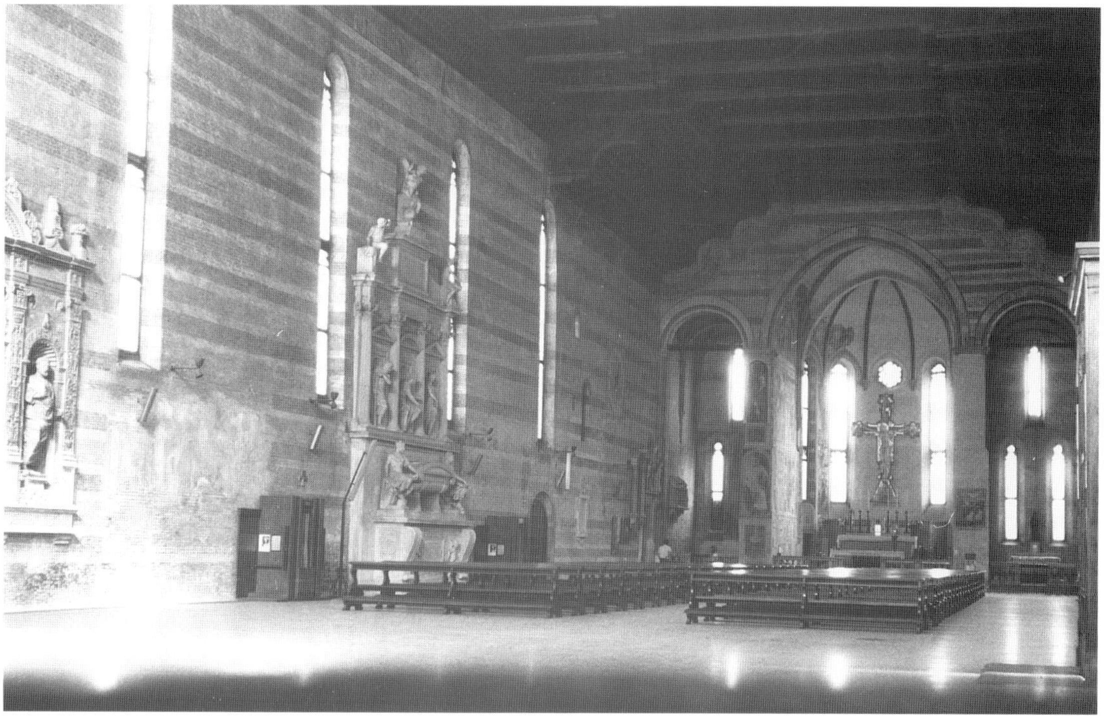

Fig. 74 Padua, Eremitani. Interior: Chapel of Sts Cosmas and Damien (to left of choir); Dotto Chapel (to right of choir).

buttresses of the edifice – humanism and individualism – were substantially the creations of despotic societies and not of so-called free republics, the dream cities of 'Civic Humanism'.

The real condition of the world reflected and recorded in Altichiero's frescoes, in its distinctly untransfigured sense, was, for most of the principals included within it, moving inexorably and rapidly towards catastrophe. The oratory frescoes have something of the immediacy of a group photograph, and in retrospect they have all the poignancy of such photographs taken on the eve of war or revolution. The world they record was essentially lost within four years of their completion. But it can never, in reality, have attained the perfect decorum and gravity with which Altichiero here enshrined it, or the ideal physical beauty of this, its finest monument.

Other work in Padua

One other important work by Altichiero, stylistically related to the S. Giorgio frescoes, survived in Padua until 1944, when the same bomb which destroyed Mantegna's Ovetari Chapel frescoes blew out the wall between this and the adjacent chapel of the Dotto family in the church of the Eremitani (fig. 74), annihilating Altichiero's frescoes (pls. 117–18) on the tomb set into that wall.[60] The tomb itself, a melancholy shadow of

[60] Bettini and Puppi, *La Chiesa degli Eremitani di Padova*, p. 48.

its former self, has been reconstructed. One tiny fragment of colour remains on the arch. The Dotto tomb iconography conformed to the general run of such painted tombs, with a *Coronation* set above the sarcophagus and busts of the Doctors and Evangelists on the arch soffit, but it had unusually large spandrels above, with an *Annunciation*, and grisaille figures of the Virtues like those of S. Giacomo set beside the tomb chest. The date of the tomb is unknown, but the insertion of a stone in the wall below, with an inscription relating to the death of Diamante Dotto in 1381,[61] suggests that it must have been decorated before this. Stylistic considerations suggest that it cannot have been done very much earlier, for the whole look of the two main scenes is redolent of S. Giorgio rather more than it is of S. Giacomo. The monumental sculptural weight of the figure of St James presenting one of the Dotto knights, his drapery falling in great measured folds, crisply outlined, is absolutely in line with the figure style of S. Giorgio. The same can be said for the architectural style of the *Coronation*'s throne and the house in which the *Annunziata* sits. Too much should not be made of this perhaps – we are not, after all, talking of work done at opposite ends of an artist's life when we contrast the two Lupi cycles. But a date for the Dotto frescoes which places them in the same period as S. Giorgio, no earlier than 1380, seems the most plausible.

There is no difficulty in seeing how Altichiero came to be working for the Dotti. Not only were they one of the leading families of Carrarese Padua,[62] they also had particularly close links with the circles in which the Lupi moved. The greatest member of the family at this time, Francesco di Paolo Dotto, whose recorded career[63] spans the last three decades of the trecento and part of the first decade of the quattrocento, fought in most of the same engagements as leading members of the Lupi and is documented in frequent association with men particularly close to Bonifacio, like Paganino da Sala, Francesco Turchetto, and Ugolino Scrovegni, as well as with Bonifacio himself. His wife Orsolina di Giovanni was a Parmese woman, and his nephew, also Francesco (di Antonio) had married a kinswoman of Bonifacio's, Costantina Rossi. Francesco, like Bonifacio, stayed in Padua to smooth over the transition from Carrarese to Visconti rule in 1388. He seems, however, to have fallen foul of the Visconti and was banished from Padua, luckily for him, we may think, given Bonifacio Lupi's presumed fate. Certainly he was welcomed back to Padua after the restoration of Carrarese power in 1390, took part in Francesco Il Vecchio's long-delayed funeral in 1393 (Francesco died in Visconti captivity in Monza), lived to see Padua handed over to the Venetians in 1406, and was eventually buried in the family tomb in the Eremitani.

[61] See Toesca, *Il Trecento*, p. 790, n. 319, who read the date as 1371. For a revised reading as 1381 see Arslan, 'Una Tavola di Altichiero', p. 105.

[62] For the Dotto family generally see Hyde, *Padua* (especially valuable for their origins), Gloria, *Monumenti*, and Gatari, *Cronaca Carrarese*.

[63] For Francesco di Paolo Dotto see Gatari, *Cronaca Carrarese* and Gloria, *Monumenti*, nos. 61, 117, 149, 228, 1463, 1558, 1566, 1569, 1629, 1652, 1656, 1671, 1681, 1693, 1791, 1857, 1885, 1888, 1894, 1907, 2169, 2171, 2176, 2180, 2234, 2246, 2249, 2275, 2304, 2306. Francesco's brother Antonio was killed in battle against the Venetians at Noale (*Cronaca Carrarese*, p. 159). Francesco lived in the *contrada* S. Andrea, though others of the family lived near the Eremitani. Francesco was *podestà* of Bologna in 1378, and of Florence in 1380 and 1395.

It is probable, though not certain, that the two knights presented by Sts George and James respectively in the *Coronation* fresco, were the two sons of Paolo Dotto – Francesco and Antonio (d.1379) – and it is probable too that the tomb, which had no effigy, was intended, like Simone Lupi's, for the general use of the family rather than for one person alone. It is not entirely clear from pre-war photographs of the Dotto tomb whether any other frescoes could be seen on the walls of the chapel. The corresponding chapel on the other side of the choir (discussed below) retains trecento frescoes of various type and date in a profusion which recalls the Cavalli Chapel in Verona before most of its frescoes were detached. The small chapels which lie along the south wall of the nave of the church seem to have been fully decorated in the fourteenth century, with fragmentary or ruined fresco cycles by Guariento and Giusto de'Menabuoi still visible on the walls. Guariento also covered the choir with frescoes, more than half of which were destroyed by the 1944 bombing.

Altichiero's own work in the Eremitani was evidently not restricted to that done for the Dotti. A tondo of the *Madonna and Child* (pl. 119) held in the sacristy may have come from the tomb of Ilario Sanguinacci (d.1381); originally placed over the door at the north end of the transept, it was moved to the adjacent chapel of Sts Cosmas and Damien, probably in 1690, almost wiping out a large and interesting votive fresco with a throne of extreme Gothic elaboration.[64] The Madonna, presumably cut from a larger composition when the tomb was moved (the child's attention is obviously directed towards something or someone outside the present limits of the tondo, the donor probably), is manifestly Altichiero's, as comparison with many of the female saints in the S. Giorgio borders (fig. 67), or with the Holy Women of the *Crucifixion* there (pl. 86) confirms. Though the connection with the date of the Sanguinacci tomb is circumstantial, a date of 1381 looks right. The original iconography of the Eremitani *Madonna*, which has no throne visible, must have been that in which the Virgin takes on her apocalyptic guise as the Woman Clothed in the Sun, a composition seen in full in the rather Altichieresque painting of Federigo Lavellongo's tomb of 1373 in the Santo.[65]

From this point we begin more and more to wander into the territory of 'scuola di' and 'seguace di', the great extent of which territory is evidence of the impact Altichiero's work had throughout the Veneto. It is almost impossible now to determine with any confidence whether the undeniably Altichieresque scenes of the lower interior walls of the Palazzo della Ragione, those less damaged by the great fire of 1420 which necessitated the repainting of most of the Salone, as the Paduans call it, can be connected with Altichiero himself.[66] Frescoes like the *Council of King Ramiro* clearly lie behind the design of the *Trial of Pietro d'Abano* in the Salone, just as the great enthroned *Coronation* presupposes his development of the elaborate Gothic throne in several contexts. Individual figures like the enthroned Virtues obviously have an affinity of some sort with Altichiero's style, but the level of damage and repair is clearly far too extensive for attri-

[64] Mellini, *Altichiero Versus Avanzo*, pp. 55–6.

[65] Sartori, 'La Cappella di S. Giacomo', p. 279.

[66] See Ragghianti, *Pittura tra Giotto e Pisanello*, pp. 44–8, 91–4 and figs. 95, 96 and 99.

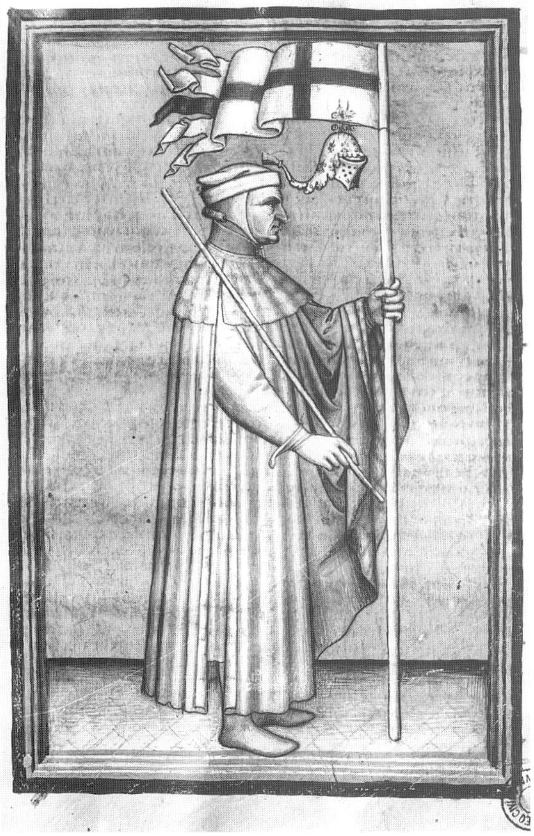

Fig. 75 *Giacomo I da Carrara.* From P. P. Vergerio, *De Principibus Carrariensibus.*

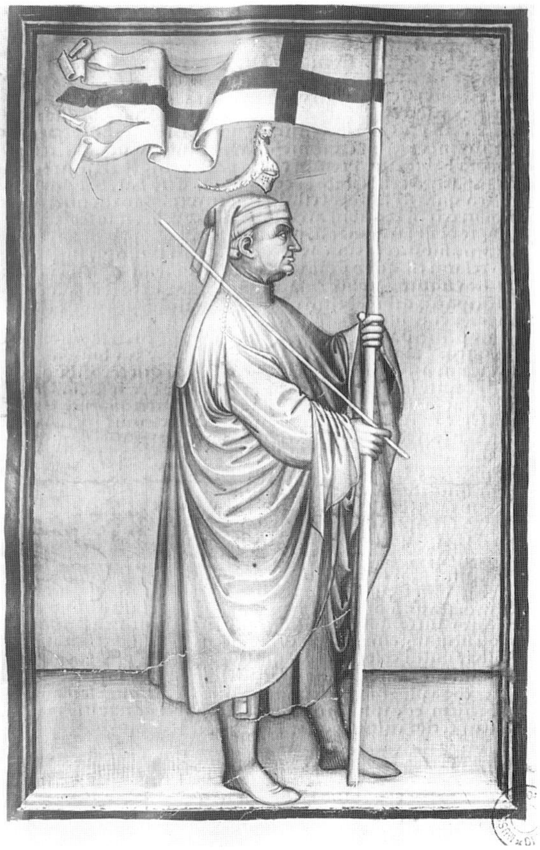

Fig. 76 *Marsiglio Maggiore da Carrara.* From P. P. Vergerio, *De Principibus Carrariensibus.*

butional comfort. All that can be said is that any commission to paint so extensively in the Salone, originally decorated by Giotto and the secular centre of Paduan civic life in most respects, is likely to have gone to the best artist or artists available, and that if in its present condition it still looks recognisably Altichieresque, that may be because under all the later accretions of paint lurk a whole series of frescoes by Altichiero himself.

One more hypothetical lost work remains to be discussed. Of all the various fresco cycles lost when the greater part of the Carrarese Palace, only a step from the Palazza della Ragione, was demolished, one alone can be mentioned with some confidence in this context, the so-called 'pozzetto' in which portraits of the Carrarese *signori* 'dipinte al naturale in terretta verde', as Michiel describes them,[67] greeted the visitor on his entry to the palace. These portraits are probably recorded in a series of full-length profile miniatures, *en grisaille*, in a manuscript of Pier-Paolo Vergerio's apologia for the Carraresi, the *Liber de Principibus Carrariensibus* (Padua, Museo Civico, MS B.P. 158). The design of these figures (figs. 75–80), their solidity, the way the near foot sometimes

[67] Michiel, *Notizie*, p. 79 quoted in Gasparotto, 'Gli Ultimi Affreschi', p. 37.

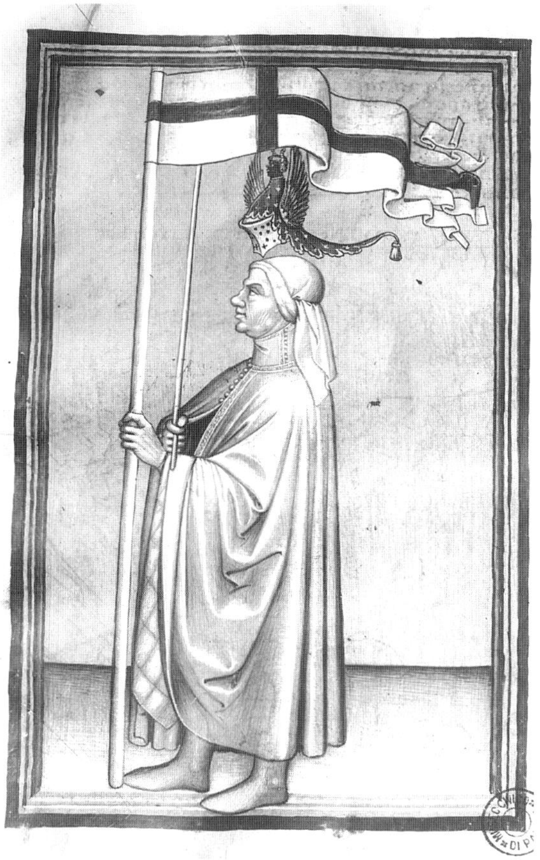

Fig. 77 *Ubertino da Carrara*. From P. P. Vergerio, *De Principibus Carrariensibus*.

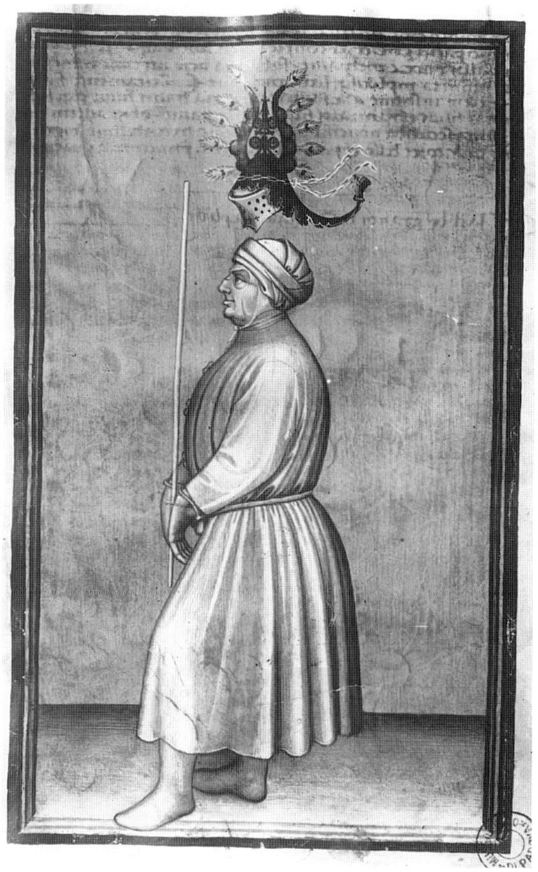

Fig. 78 *Nicolo da Carrara*. From P. P. Vergerio, *De Principibus Carrariensibus*.

moves assertively over the fictive stone frame, the way the figures inhabit a fully realised spatial field, all recalls Altichiero. Comparison between the portraits of Giacomo Grande (Bonifacio Lupi's great uncle; fig. 75) or Marsiglio da Carrara (fig. 76) and the mourners at the *Funeral of St Lucy* in S. Giorgio (pls. 115–16) makes this very clear. In addition the portraits *look*, in a way that is not easy to define, like frescoes. Whether or not Mellini's attribution of the miniatures themselves to Altichiero's presumed pupil Jacopo da Verona[68] is accepted, there is really no obstacle to seeing them, in a relationship of a kind which seems to recur throughout any discussion of Altichiero's career, as records of another lost fresco cycle.

[68] Mellini and Folena, *Bibbia Istoriata Padovana*, p. XXXIII.

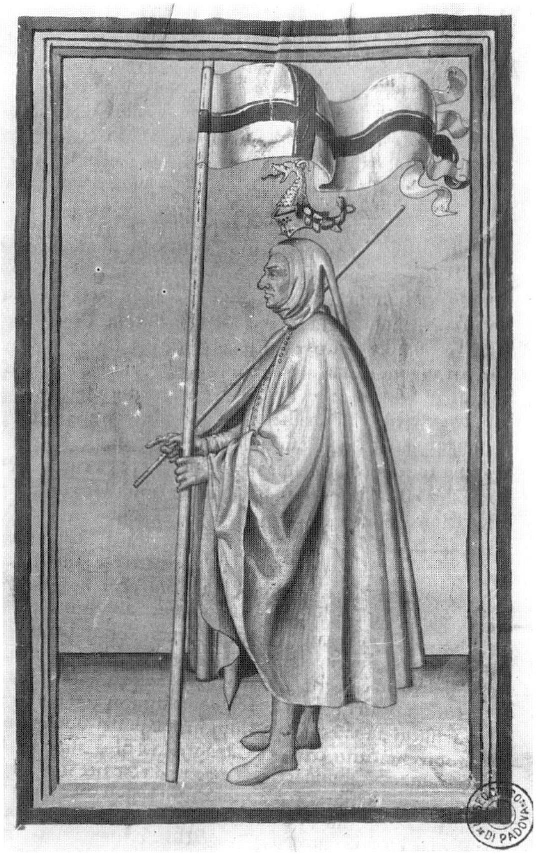

Fig. 79 *Jacopo II da Carrara*. From P. P. Vergerio, *De Principibus Carrariensibus*.

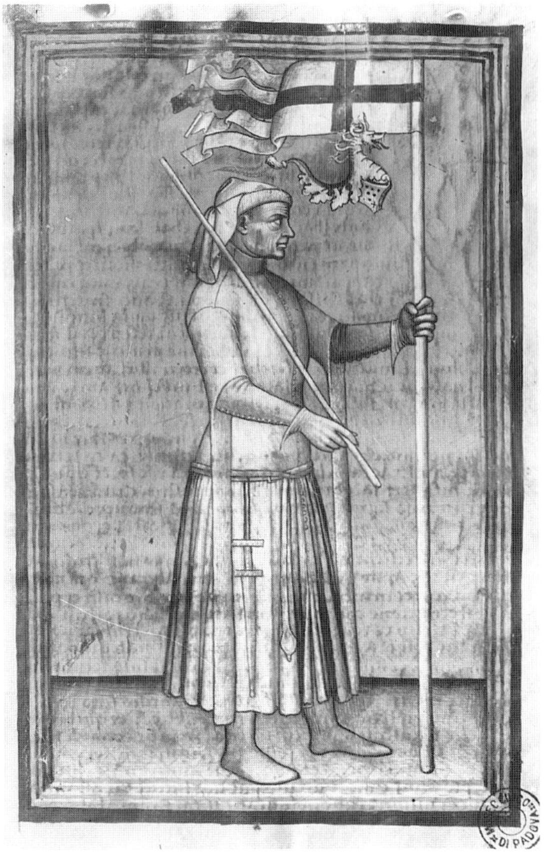

Fig. 80 *Jacopino da Carrara*. From P. P. Vergerio, *De Principibus Carrariensibus*.

7

LAST WORKS, FOLLOWERS AND IMITATORS; VERONA AND ELSEWHERE

Altichiero's career after 1384 is nearly as elusive as it is before 1364. Trying to follow it in terms of extant work is to find oneself picking over a series of undocumented works and more or less puzzling fragments. His base seems, though the evidence is hardly overwhelming, to have shifted once again to Verona. We cannot be sure how long after completing S. Giorgio he stayed on in Padua. On 29 September 1384 he was included in a list of four men nominated by Gianpaolo Pantagliati, a scholar of medicine and Veronese cleric, to accept on Gianpaolo's behalf any offices falling vacant in Verona Cathedral while Gianpaolo was in Padua.[1] But the document recording this was drawn up and witnessed not in Verona, but in the Carrarese Palace in Padua, and the men included on the list are named 'absentes tanquam praesentes', so there is no particular reason to suppose from this that Altichiero had yet returned to Verona. But it seems likely that he did go home at some stage after the completion of S. Giorgio, as Vasari says,[2] and that he ended his career in Verona.

Of the frescoes which Vasari says Altichiero painted (in collaboration, he says, with Jacopo Avanzi and 'Sebeto') for the Serego-Alighieri family in Verona, a pair of 'nozze', with 'molti ritratti', there is no trace. But a fresco of the *Crucifixion* (pl. 120) in S. Zeno Maggiore datable to the 1380s or later on the basis of a partly surviving inscription, tends to confirm his presence in Verona. The figure of Christ is virtually identical to that of S. Giorgio, and the four attendant saints, once allowance has been made for the poor condition of the painting, have affinities with the obvious comparative material in the Paduan frescoes.[3] Only the obsessively staring St John the Baptist betrays unmistakable shop intervention. The profile portrait of the donor is nicely characterised. The warm yellow of St Mary Magdalen's cloak and the rather sharp shot green of the Baptist's are colours familiar from S. Giorgio, as are the motifs used in the richly

[1] Sartori, 'Nota su Altichiero', pp. 306–7, no. III (ASP Notarile, vol. 36, col. 246).

[2] 'Dopo tornati tutti e tre questi maestri in Verona, dipinsero insieme, in casa de'conti Serenghi, un par di nozze, con molti ritratti ed abiti di que'tempi' – Vasari, *Le Vite*, vol. III, p. 634.

[3] Compare: St John the Baptist with the drapery of the toga-wearing figure in the S. Giorgio *Crucifixion*, the angels with those of S. Giorgio (see Sandberg-Vavalà, *La Pittura Veronese*, pp. 190–2), the Virgin with that of the S. Giacomo *Pietà* or the S. Giacomo stall canopy *St Veronica*, the Magdalen with many of the female figures of S. Giorgio (*St George Baptising*, for example).

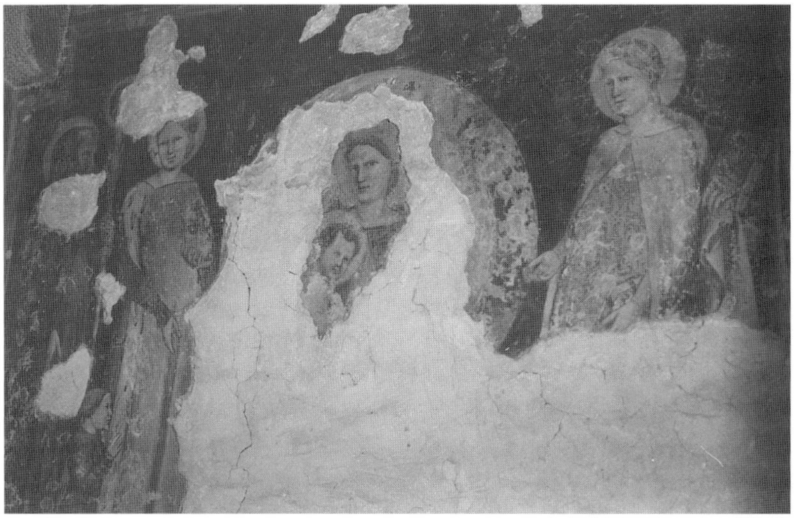

Fig. 81 Altichiero follower: *Madonna and Child with Saints and Donors* (detail). Verona, Castelvecchio.

decorated frame, with symbols of the Evangelists at the corners. The loss of the bottom right-hand corner of the fresco when a door was knocked through it has also, maddeningly, involved the loss of most of the large cartouche carrying a three-line inscription of which only the word *HOC* and part of the date survive. The extent of Altichiero's personal participation in the execution of this fresco is hard to determine, but that it is his, in the sense that he and/or his assistants executed it on the basis of his design, need not be doubted. It is a modest enough work compared with some of those we have already seen coming Altichiero's way, but we should not be dazzled by the qualities of the great fresco cycles into thinking that such commissions had no place in Altichiero's practice.

Another fresco with Altichieresque traits is located in the Castelvecchio, a large votive scene with an extension on the adjoining wall (fig. 81).[4] This, which was uncovered during the restoration work of 1924–6, is the only surviving figurative fresco in the Castelvecchio. It may have formed part of a much wider pictorial programme; a great deal of purely decorative painting survives on the walls of the principal apartments.[5] This type of work, geometric interlace with heraldic motifs, or fictive hanging fabrics of various kinds, is very like some of the surviving ornamental frescoes of the Carrarese Palace in Padua, and there are other examples, albeit heavily repainted, in parts of the Scaligeri Palace complex at S. Maria Antica.[6] This kind of decoration is reproduced several times by Altichiero – in the chamber of the *Council of King Ramiro* in S. Giacomo (a faded geometric pattern; pls. 66–8), and in the *Fall of the Idols* (alternating square panels and quatrefoils; pl. 101) and *Tortures of St Lucy* (a more delicately coloured diagonal pattern with elaborately punched and fretted geometrical motifs; pl. 113) in S. Giorgio.

[4] For this fresco see Sandberg-Vavalà, *La Pittura Veronese*, pp. 145–54 and Magagnato, *Da Altichiero a Pisanello*, p. 10.

[5] These are discussed by Frattaroli, 'Le Decorazioni', in Varanini, *Gli Scaligeri*, pp. 237–43.

[6] E.g. in the open space at the north-east end of the Piazza de'Signori, towards S. Maria Antica.

The votive fresco, *Madonna and Child with Saints and Donors* (the slippers of the right-hand donor are just visible), and two more saints and another donor on the adjacent wall, has the same sort of relationship to Altichiero's work as the Sezzana *Madonna* or the figure of St Catherine in Treviso discussed below (which is not to say they are by the same hand). The style is a simplified, rather bland, version of Altichiero's. The basic models for the Madonna and the female saints are his, but the modelling is less than forceful and the drawing of the saints' faces is slapdash and in places rather crude. The fresco is actually rather ingratiating, more so than the S. Zeno *Crucifixion*. But the Castelvecchio fresco lacks the weight of modelling which characterises the *Crucifixion* even in its poor state, and cannot be attributed to Altichiero himself. Given its location it is likely to have been a Scaligeri commission, though the precise identity of the three donors is unknown.[7]

Also housed in the Castelvecchio, but originally on the facade of S. Fermo Maggiore, are the remains of the fresco decoration from the tomb of CanGrande II's doctor, Aventino Fracastoro (pl. 121). Aventino died in 1368, but the tomb and its frescoes must be dated much later, to *c.* 1385, the date given in the epigraph inscribed below the tomb. The lunette fresco is in very poor condition, with a huge lacuna running right through the middle. It was suggested in early accounts[8] that the subject of this fresco was the Trinity, but the Coronation of the Virgin is a more plausible reading. The position of God the Father and the top of Christ's head suggests that it conformed to a version of the Coronation where the Virgin is kneeling, a type rather more common in Verona than elsewhere, already seen in Turone's SS Trinità polyptych (fig. 15), and used later by Martino da Verona in frescoes in S. Eufemia and S. Stefano (fig. 82). Not much can be gleaned from the badly abraded soffit frescoes, which have saints in polylobes with intersecting bands of Cosmatesque ornament. In general these do not particularly resemble Altichiero's border style – they are not at all like the soffit border of the Dotto tomb in Padua for instance. The legible part of the lunette fresco, with a large throne surrounded by musician angels, is more eloquent. The face of God the Father, even in its faded condition, is modelled with extreme refinement and delicacy, and has very clear affinities with Altichiero's style. The head may be compared with that of St George in the Cavalli fresco, with the younger of the two bearded men on the lower left side of the central bay of the S. Giacomo *Crucifixion*, with the face of Christ in the S. Giacomo *Resurrection*, and with many of the heads of S. Giorgio. The analogies are

7 The female donor of the side fresco appears to be a child, and the male donor of the main part a youth. The gender of the other donor in this part cannot be determined from the slippers alone, although the sliver of visible leg suggests a man's short tunic. Cansignorio della Scala had three 'naturali', two boys (Bartolomeo, b. *c.* 1360 and Antonio, b.1362) and a girl (Lucia), which fits the donor group apparently shown here. Any connections of this kind are highly speculative. Dating the fresco is difficult. The Castelvecchio was at least partly habitable in 1358. The fresco's affinities with Altichiero suggest that it must date from the mid 1360s at the earliest. It has little in common with the more extravagant styles of the late 1380s and 1390s, and a date of *c.* 1370–80 seems reasonable, although its general similarity to the fresco of the eponymous saint in S. Caterina in Treviso, discussed below (see n. 37), which must have been painted after 1388, allows for a later date.

8 See Varanini, *Gli Scaligeri*, pp. 545–7.

exact, and the intensity of expression in the Fracastoro God the Father is too great, too precisely typical of Altichiero himself, to allow for an attribution to a follower like Martino. Despite the difficulties involved in deciphering such a badly damaged painting, and despite the apparently distinctive design of the soffits, I am inclined to see this noble ruin as Altichiero's work. If it is not his, and the attribution must be regarded as tentative at best, he had a close follower much more talented than any we know by name and represented by no other surviving work.

Altichiero and his assistants have already shown their impatience with drying plaster in the *sinopie* of the Sala Grande soffits. Detachment of the Fracastoro *Coronation* in 1958 revealed a remarkable set of *sinopie* underneath the *intonaco* (pl. 121b), no fewer than four separate layers, only some of which have any iconographic connection with the fresco which overlay them. Those which can be connected confirm that the subject of the fresco was indeed the Coronation, for the gesture of Christ stretching out his arm in one of them is quite unmistakable, though, oddly, more redolent of the side-by-side version used by Altichiero in Padua than of the design eventually used. The other drawings are merely sketches, superior doodles, but they are of great interest, including a fairly well worked up profile of a bearded man, an expressive sketch of an older man's head, a rather bibulous looking putto or Christ-child, a lion's face, some vigorous figures engaged in some sort of struggle, either with each other or with some intractable piece of work, and studies of the artist's ultimate model, his own hand.

Altichiero nowhere aligns himself more with the painting of Verona than in his apparent concentration on fresco painting. The only exceptions to this so far discussed have been a handful of small drawings in manuscripts. There is, though, evidence that he painted panels, and in past discussions various panels have been, not always convincingly, advanced as examples of this. A Paduan document of 1382 records the commissioning of 'una anchona comperata da magistro Altichero [sic] per la Margareta, pagò Lariolo, lire X soldi XVI'.[9] Sartori suggests that 'Margareta' is probably Margherita di Scannuzzio Rossi, but a connection with the Lupi circle is as clearly maintained if she were Margherita di Corradino Lupi,[10] daughter (presumably) of the Corradino Lupi who assisted Caterina de'Francesi with the payments for S. Giacomo and wife of Ser Andrea de Bragacio, and, later, of Enrico de Alano of Treviso, who is documented in Padua throughout the later trecento, on one occasion in association with Bonifacio Lupi's heirs and descendants.[11] Sartori also published a document of April 1376 which showed that Bonifacio Lupi had paid for 'unius anchonae ab altari in ecclesia fratrum de riveria, seu Monte Oliveti, paduani districtus [i.e. Polverara]'.[12] Given the date and the identity of the patron this might have been by Altichiero, but there is no 'must' about it, as Sartori thought.

[9] First published by Coletti. See Sartori, 'Nota su Altichiero', p. 305.

[10] For Margherita Lupi see Gloria, *Monumenti*, nos. 1887, 1908, 2115.

[11] *Ibid.*, no. 1908.

[12] ASP Notarile, vol. 407, col. 58v, quoted in Sartori, 'Nota su Altichiero', p. 305.

Of the various extant panels attributed to Altichiero, some can be immediately dismissed. The *Crucifixion* (Milan, private collection) published by Arslan as an early work of Altichiero's, and by Pettenella, more circumspectly, as Veronese,[13] combines elements like the crenellated back wall which suggest the impact of Venetian tastes with a figure style very like that of Jacopo Avanzi – with the same cross intensity of facial expressions, receding hairlines, and exaggerated foreshortenings. This panel may show signs that its author has seen Altichiero's work, but it cannot be attributed to Altichiero himself at any period.

A smaller *Crucifixion* published by Mellini as 'Altichiero Giovane(?)' (Milan, Rasini Collection)[14] has Veronese traits, but the figure of Christ is much closer to Turone's type than to Altichiero's, though it is not inconceivable that a pre-Maso Altichiero might have been turning out work of this kind. There is no valid reason, though, to make any specific connection between him and this panel.

More plausible on at least one level is the *Madonna and Child* (Bergamo, Bossi-Hazon Collection) published by Zeri (as 'cerchia di').[15] The two figures are in a general Altichieresque mould, and the Child in particular has something of the qualities of Altichiero's various versions of the theme. But the expression of the Madonna is so wooden and the drawing so schematic that this panel cannot be brought any closer to Altichiero than is allowed for by Zeri's 'cerchia'.

Only two panels can be connected with Altichiero himself with any confidence, the Boi polyptych in the Castelvecchio in Verona, and a small Crucifixion triptych in the Virginia Museum of Fine Arts in Richmond, Virginia.

The polyptych (pl. 122), a *Madonna and Child with Four Saints and Two Donors*, comes from the chapel of the Zanardi family at Boi di Caprino, between Verona and Lake Garda. All the figures are recognisable Altichiero types. The face of the Madonna is constructed along lines similar to those of the Eremitani tondo (pl. 119), with eyebrows sharply outlined, curving in towards a long nose, and wide eyes with large irises. Sts James and Anthony Abbot can be compared with the whole range of bearded men in S. Giacomo and S. Giorgio. The quality of actual handling is variable, and it never rises to the standard of the finest figures in the Paduan frescoes or the Cavalli votive scene. The best painting, though – the Child, the sharply individualised donors – is still broadly comparable with much of the painting in the Paduan chapels. The Madonna's face is a little inert compared with that of the Eremitani tondo, though this is less evident in front of the panel than in some of the photographs which have been published. Her hands are rather mannered in conception, the proportions unconvincing (and this is an area where Altichiero is usually very persuasive). The articulation of St Christopher's body is poor, and the ill-proportioned and crudely painted Christ-child on his shoulder betrays studio intervention of a less than inspiring quality. Such mixtures of hands are entirely to be expected in such a context, and the Boi polyptych

[13] Arslan, 'Una Tavola di Altichiero', pp. 103–4, and Pettenella, *Altichiero*, pl. 17.

[14] Mellini, *Altichiero e Jacopo Avanzi*, fig. 313.

[15] Zeri, 'Un'Aggiunta', pp. 61–3. See also Lucco, '"Me Pinxit"', p. 264.

viewed as a whole is an impressive object, set in its richly crocketed frame. It is also, in a more nebulous sense, more or less what one would expect a medium-sized panel from Altichiero's workshop to look like. The hesitant attributions of early accounts must be partly due to the extensive repainting of the polyptych in the past, accretions which were removed in the restoration made in the 1950s. There seems no reason to doubt this polyptych's origins within Altichiero's workshop.

The Richmond triptych (pls. 124–7) must also be reassessed in the light of recent restoration. This has emphasised the fine quality of the painting, the delicate modulation of the modelling of Christ's body, and the singing quality of the colours. The chromatic range is wide, with three distinct kinds of blue, a rich scarlet for the male donor, a rather salmony pink for St John, and a dark green with red ornament for the female donor. This is all reminiscent of Altichiero's palette, and the stuff of the female donor's drapery is very similar to the background curtain in the Cavalli fresco. The figures, too, point to Altichiero's authorship. Christ, beautifully drawn, is of exactly the same type as that of the S. Giorgio *Crucifixion*, and St John registers grief by the same contraction of the eyebrows and forehead. St James, in a splendid bright-blue cloak, has the same monumental qualities as his equivalent on the Dotto tomb, for all the reduced scale.

The 1981 restoration revealed that the donor seen in old photographs and convincingly indicated by Giuliano Briganti as evidence of Altichiero's authorship[16] was painted over an earlier figure, of quite different aspect. This first donor also had a female companion, painted over when the new male donor was added. Her face, unlike that of her counterpart, was scraped off. Altichiero himself seems to have done these alterations, given the clear affinities of the new male donor with a whole series of comparable examples by him, and probably not very long after the original execution of the panel. The intriguing aspects of this are enhanced by the possibility that this little triptych may have been commissioned by the Wittelsbach rulers of Bavaria, a family with whom the Scaligeri had a long and close association.[17] The style of the Richmond panel is close to that of S. Giorgio and it may be dated to the mid 1380s.[18]

The question of Altichiero's workshop has already surfaced in various contexts, but it is particularly pertinent to some of the works discussed here and at the end of chapter 6 above. In any well-integrated workshop the qualitative discrepancies between the work of the master and that of his assistants tend to be minimised – and the modern distinction between autograph and shop is hardly appropriate to a discussion of the essentially co-operative activity of fresco painting. Even so, clear distinctions can be made. The *Funeral of St Lucy* in S. Giorgio (pl. 115) is a case in point. The whole left-hand side, with its several superb portraits, may be contrasted with the greater part of the right side and the crowd behind St Lucy's bier. The blandness of expression and the weak drawing of many of the heads in this area clearly betray the hand of an assistant working on the basis of stock workshop models. Comparable figures can be seen in the back-

[16] E.g. Briganti, 'Un Trittichetto di Altichiero', figs. 12 and 14[a]; Mellini, *Altichiero e Jacopo Avanzi*, fig. 294.

[17] See Riedmann, 'Gli Scaligeri e il Mondo Germanico', and Weigand, 'Gli Scaligeri dopo gli Scaligeri', in Varanini, *Gli Scaligeri*, pp. 25–33 and 91–6.

[18] See Richards, 'A Re-used Altarpiece by Altichiero'.

ground of the *Coronation* (pls. 88–91) and amongst the saints whose busts fill the large border dividing the oratory's walls from the vault. These relatively unimportant areas are just where one would expect to see signs of delegation. Where the figures are clearly liable to receive close attention, the painting is of a much more uniform high standard. The foregrounds of all the main frescoes in S. Giorgio were clearly painted either by Altichiero himself or by the very best assistants and a scene like *St Lucy Before Judge Pascasio* (pls. 109–10) is extraordinarily resistant to hand-spotting.

In the past the St Catherine cycle in S. Giorgio has been seen as the work of a weaker hand throughout.[19] There are signs of weaker painting in some of the background figures of the third scene, but that is of no great significance. Gilbert's attribution of the foreground sacrifice in the first scene (pl. 105) to the same kind of dazzling assistant as was responsible, in his view, for the virtuoso drawing of the monochrome *Triumph of Fame*[20] is unconvincing. The first St Catherine scene as a whole is perhaps the least successful composition of S. Giorgio, something which may, however, be substantially due to its appalling condition.[21] In any case the composition as such, even if entrusted to workshop execution, is still going to have been Altichiero's in all fundamentals, and such attempts to hive off parts of S. Giorgio in this way must be a consequence of the lingering and completely unjustified extension of the collaboration theory to these frescoes. It is precisely because it is so homogeneous that S. Giorgio serves as the touchstone, the basic comparative material, for consideration of Altichiero's art.

Any attempt to count, let alone name, the assistants at work in S. Giorgio or on the paintings discussed in this chapter strikes me as hazardous and probably futile. There are, all the same, reasons for thinking that painters like Martino or Jacopo da Verona had formative contact with Altichiero. In Jacopo's case the fact of his having worked under his own steam in Padua, and in a clearly post-Altichieresque vein (for which see below), does at least suggest that he came to Padua in Altichiero's shop and stayed to make his own career.[22] We cannot be absolutely certain of this, though, in the absence of any documentary record of an association of this kind between Jacopo and Altichiero.

Evidence of this kind does exist which suggests that Altichiero's nephew Antonio worked in his shop at some stage, and probably in Padua. In a document of April 1402 Antonio, 'nunc habitator Paduae', is referred to as 'Antonius pictor, nepos q.Alticherii de Verona'.[23] This style of nomenclature, using his uncle's name instead of that of his father Pietro, is most easily accounted for as a reflection of some professional identity with Altichiero which Antonio, for obvious commercial reasons, found it useful to advertise.[24] This, as well as Antonio's presence in Padua, where he is documented from 1392 to 1422, strongly suggests that he emerged from his prestigious uncle's workshop,

[19] This view of the St Catherine cycle goes back as far as Selvatico's description of the frescoes in 1869; see Selvatico, *Guida di Padova*, p. 26.

[20] Gilbert, 'Giotto in Milan', pp. 61–2.

[21] Mellini, *Altichiero e Jacopo Avanzi*, fig. 278, published a fifteenth-century drawing (Florence, Uffizi) which clarifies the design a little, though it is clear that the copyist has made changes of his own.

[22] For Jacopo see D'Arcais, 'Jacopo da Verona'.

[23] Sartori, 'La Cappella di S. Giacomo', pp. 277 and 325, no. 18.

[24] See Simon, 'Altichiero Versus Avanzo', p. 261.

trading on that pedigree in his career as an independent master. The family trade was passed on to a third generation at least in the shape of Antonio's son Cristoforo, documented as a painter in Padua in 1428.[25] Of Antonio's or Cristoforo's work we know nothing.

There is no particular reason to suppose, as Sartori does, that the painter Marco di Giovanni, a document of whose Altichiero witnessed in January 1383,[26] had any professional connection with him beyond that of men engaged in the same trade. Any painter from the same geographical area as Altichiero working in Padua in the years following Altichiero's work there, like Jacopo, or like Domenico di Antonio da Vicenza, whose wife was Veronese, and who took in 1394 a Veronese pupil (Matteo di Filippo),[27] may have had some connections with Altichiero, but in the absence of documentary proof such connections are entirely speculative. Painters of Veronese origin were comparatively rare in Padua, a city which imported a fair proportion of its talent.[28] Foreign artists in Padua tended to come from Venice or Bologna, with a scattering from various other cities. Apart from Altichiero and his relatives we can only point to Jacopo and to Matteo di Filippo as examples of Veronese painters in Padua (and Matteo was only an apprentice when his name was recorded). This contrasts with the dozen or so Venetian painters recorded as working in Padua between 1340 and 1405, or the ten from Bologna. The essentially limited qualities of Veronese painting before Altichiero's time are probably reflected in this preference for artists from the great cosmopolitan centres, each with a greater and more varied internal demand for painters' work.

A training in Altichiero's workshop must have left any young painter with one unmistakable legacy, manifested, as has already been mentioned, in the exuberant architectural backgrounds of even the most run-of-the-mill Madonnas painted on the walls of the Veneto and the Alto Adige after Altichiero's time. It is possible that within the workshop itself were found architectural specialists who devoted most of their time to this exacting business. The walls of S. Giorgio, much easier to examine than those of S. Giacomo, show clear traces of the care taken with these parts of the frescoes. Ruled guidance lines are everywhere evident, most visibly perhaps along the small arcade courses of the walls to left and right of *St George on the Wheel* (pl. 98). There are signs, too, of the use of pricked cartoons. The characteristic charcoal spots which indicate the use of these can still be seen here and there: along the right-hand 'crossing' pier of the basilica in *St George Baptising* (pl. 93), for instance.[29] The existence of extremely detailed drawings of the fictive buildings used by Altichiero is suggested by the existence in the cloister of S. Antonio in Polesine in Ferrara of a fresco fragment which comprises an exact replica of the upper part of this basilica, simplified only to the extent

25 Sartori, 'La Cappella di S. Giacomo', p. 325, 10 March 1428: 'Mag. Christophorus pictor, filius mag. Antonii pictoris de Verona, habitator Paduae'.

26 Sartori, 'Nota su Altichiero', pp. 324–5, no. XVII, discussed by Simon, 'Altichiero Versus Avanzo', p. 261, n.

27 Sartori, 'La Cappella di S. Giacomo', p. 328, no. 35.

28 For painters working in Padua in the trecento see *ibid.*, pp. 321–43, and Sartori, *Documenti*.

29 See Mellini, *Altichiero e Jacopo Avanzi*, fig. 198 and p. 70.

of having lost the red-and-white banding of the main and apsidal arches.[30] It is quite impossible to identify the subject of this fragment, but, unless S. Antonio also had a St George cycle, this design was probably adapted here to a quite different iconography. The fresco need not have been by Altichiero or his shop, but it seems most likely that it was painted by someone who had, or once had, access to Altichiero's designs in portable form.

The practical difficulties involved in combining the geometrical precision demanded by the extensive use of highly complex architectural settings of this kind with the layout of *giornate* must have been considerable, involving much careful planning, and it is remarkable that the frescoes of S. Giacomo and S. Giorgio are almost entirely free of obvious signs of these difficulties. *Giornate*, relatively easy to identify in S. Giorgio at any rate, tend to be bounded by one or more straight lines. Such a line can be seen running along the right-hand side of *St Lucy and the Bulls* (pl. 111), separating the lower elements of the balcony brackets from the window below and continuing to the left along the line of the crenellated wall-top leading to the gatehouse at the centre of the scene. The upper boundary of this *giornata* runs in a more customary loose curve through the sky above the right-hand pavilion, and this, with its complex staircase and balustrade, swallow-tail crenellations and delightful balcony, represents, like the Good Thief, one day's work.

It is clear that the inherent complexities were reduced as far as possible for the initial setting out of the architecture. A great deal of detail was left to be added later *a secco*, including many of the windows which are now so badly faded. The Lombard banding below the main cornice of the pavilion under discussion was added in this way, and it, like the foliage of the little balcony, is fast heading for invisibility.

Three painters whose names are both recorded and attached to extant paintings, and who worked in the area dominated by Altichiero towards the end of the trecento, can be put forward for consideration as direct products of his workshop. Of these the weakest is Battista da Vicenza, documented from 1404 to 1438, by which time he was already dead. If our knowledge of his work were restricted to the four little panels of Scenes from the Life of St Sylvester from a dismembered altarpiece in the Museo Civico in Vicenza,[31] then we might suppose him to be nothing more than one of many local artists adopting vaguely Altichieresque formulae. But the two *Madonna* panels in the same museum show him to be much closer to Altichiero himself. The gentle, large-eyed, rather square faces, with a little hint of fat under the chin, obviously derive from a type seen in the Eremitani tondo and elsewhere in Altichiero's work. These panels look exactly like little Altichiero *Madonnas* painted by a no more than capable assistant, which is just what Battista may have been.

We have met Martino da Verona before,[32] as the painter of the lunette fresco of Federigo Cavalli's tomb in S. Anastasia in Verona. This sumptuously coloured fresco

[30] See Ragghianti, *Pittura tra Giotto e Pisanello*, pl. 90.

[31] For Battista see Magagnato, *Da Altichiero a Pisanello*, pp. 25–6 and pl. XXIb. Battista's panels are reproduced and discussed in Ballarin, *Pinacoteca di Vicenza*, pp. 56–9.

[32] For Martino see Sandberg-Vavalà, *La Pittura Veronese*, chapter 13, and Cuppini, 'L'Arte Gotica', pp. 321–7.

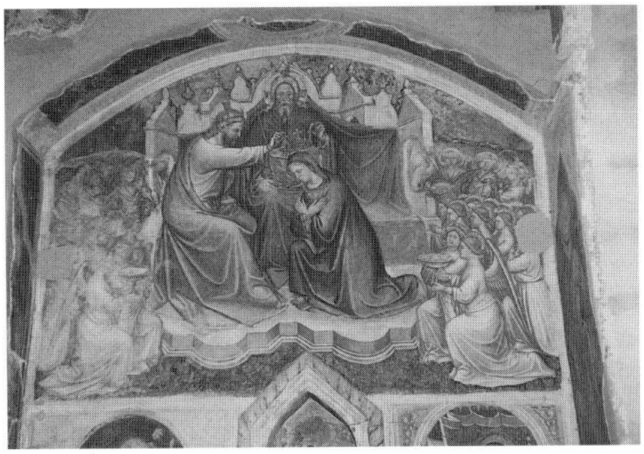

Fig. 82 Martino da Verona: *Coronation of the Virgin*. Verona, S. Stefano.

actually shows his style at its furthest from Altichiero, who is elsewhere clearly visible as the *fons et origo* of Martino's art. In early work like the *Miracle of S. Eligio* also once in the Cavalli Chapel,[33] or the Bevilacqua tomb *Madonna* (fig. 51) in the adjacent chapel, Altichiero's presence is strongly felt. It extends to the basic repertoire of Martino's architectural painting as well as to the vocabulary of his borders, both seen in the S. Stefano and S. Eufemia *Coronations,* with borders of a type seen in the Oratory of S. Giorgio and Altichieresque figures of God the Father. But here too are Martino's characteristically plump and friendly angels, beings much less exalted than Altichiero's, from whom they clearly derive. Throughout his career, which we can trace from the 1390s until his death some time before 1413, Martino systematically and cheerfully inflated Altichiero's compositions, thickening the architectural detail, coarsening the colour, and absorbing some of the more overtly ornamental tendencies of International Gothic. Never less than thoroughly professional, never at all profound, Martino's art enlivens the walls of Verona in a profusion which provokes feelings of envy in the student of Altichiero's Veronese career.

As has already been suggested, Jacopo da Verona can be connected with Altichiero on the basis of circumstantial as well as stylistic evidence. Jacopo's signed frescoes of 1397 in the Bovi Chapel, all that remains of the Church of S. Michele in Padua (and now known as the Oratory of S. Michele), display a remarkably ambitious approach to space and to architecture – his chief claim to attention, in fact. Jacopo's architectural settings are very clearly related to Altichiero's, as are his compositional habits and his figure style. The *Adoration of the Magi* is a variant of Altichiero's fresco in S. Giorgio, and the group of bystanders at the *Death of the Virgin*, probably portraits of members of the de'Bovi family, patrons of the chapel, is a rather inert version of a type of group seen in several different configurations in Altichiero's frescoes. Individual figures like the seated foreground figure in the *Death of the Virgin*[34] are so like some of the subordinate figures of S. Giorgio that the possibility that Jacopo was indeed one of the assistants on that commission comes to seem more and more plausible.

33 Varanini, *Gli Scaligeri*, pp. 387–8.

34 Lucco, '"Me Pinxit"', pl. 27a. Compare, e.g., the figures of the northern end of the S. Giorgio upper border.

Beyond the work of these masters a whole penumbra of Altichieresque painting spreads out, merging finally into the more ornately Gothic painting of the early quattrocento. In Padua Altichiero's influence preserved something of the solidity of style he himself inherited from Giotto. The major monument of this late Paduan Altichieresque manner is not a fresco cycle but a series of illustrations to a Paduan picture Bible now divided between London and Rovigo.[35] The painters of this fine manuscript, copiously inventive in the face of the considerable demands of such a book, draw on various sources. Several of Giusto de'Menabuoi's compositions surface in reduced versions here, but the dominant influence is Altichiero's, on the levels both of narrative technique and pictorial organisation. It is tempting to wonder what records of lost frescoes by Altichiero lie unrecognised in the pages of this Bible.

The weightier aspects of Altichiero's style had less impact in Verona, to judge from the considerable amount of late-trecento and early quattrocento painting which reflects his example, though there are exceptions to this rule. One of these is the fresco decoration of the tomb of Guidone da Montechiaro, facing the entrance to the Cavalli Chapel in S. Anastasia. The frescoes, of *c.* 1380, are in poor condition, but the compact and solid figures of the principal votive scene do have affinities with the styles characteristic of the Paduan response to Altichiero. The Madonna is virtually illegible but appears to be of a broadly Altichieresque type.

The other post-Altichiero frescoes of S. Anastasia tend towards a more attenuated version of the models on which they draw. The Pellegrini tomb, facing the Bevilacqua tomb (fig. 51) in the Pellegrini Chapel replaces the tubby saints of Martino's fresco with the rather self-conscious elegance of figures like the St John the Baptist. The tomb of Giovanni Salerni (d.1380) in his family's chapel, its architectural detail still richly polychromed, shows, to my eye, some affinities with the style of Jacopo da Verona (the tomb, of course, need not have been made as early as 1380), with the customary elaborate throne and a Roman imperial head *all'antica* on each outer flank of the arch.

Two partly ruined frescoes of the *Madonna and Child* in the choir of S. Maria della Scala mark the continued development of the architectural throne. In the better preserved of these the Madonna, still preserving the salient aspects of Altichiero's versions, and wearing a folded kerchief on her head, sits with a very solid child on a throne whose architectural trappings fill the entire pictorial field. Both of these frescoes can be related to one formerly in St Stephen's Cathedral in Vienna,[36] which looks like the work of a native Veronese rather than of a northern artist interpreting Italian style. The presence of such a fresco in Vienna may, like that of the Richmond triptych in Bavaria, be connected with the flight of the Scaligeri and, presumably, numbers of their functionaries to the north after 1387.

It is clear, though, that Altichiero's influence had already worked its way up the Adige

[35] Rovigo, Biblioteca dell'Accademia dei Concordi MS 212, fondo Silvestri, and British Museum MS Add. 15277; published by Mellini and Folena, *Bibbia Istoriata Padovana*.

[36] Pettenella, *Altichiero*, pl. 51. The fresco is now in the Kunsthistorisches Museum, Vienna.

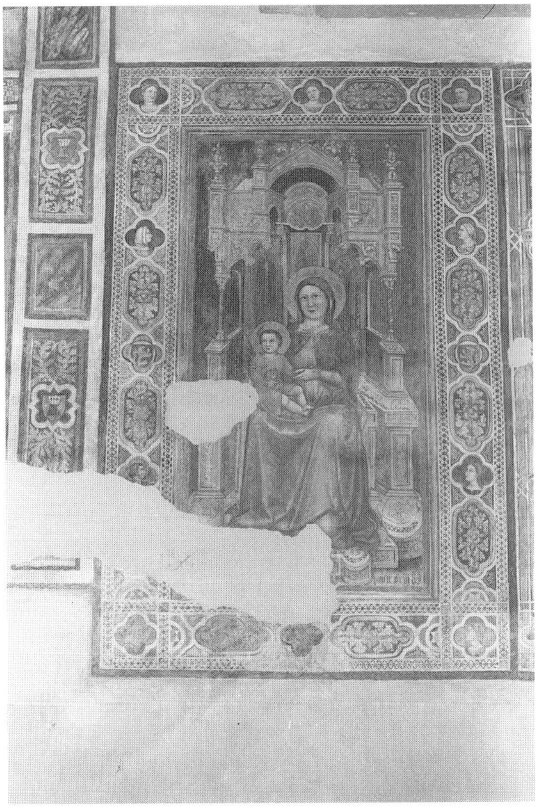

Fig. 83 Altichiero follower: Castelbarco *Madonna and Child.* Bolzano, S. Domenico.

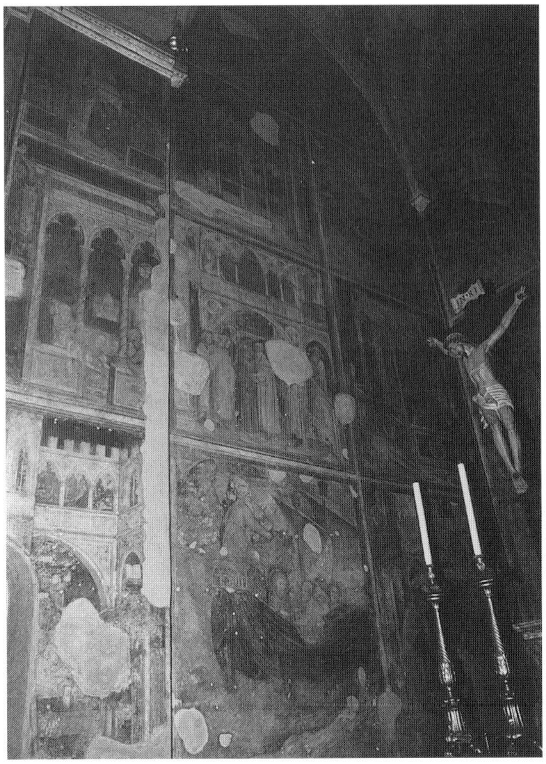

Fig. 84 Verona, S. Maria della Scala, Chapel of S. Girolamo. Frescoes by Giovanni Badile.

by itself. A dated fresco of 1378 in S. Domenico in Bolzano (fig. 83), commissioned by the Castelbarco family, whose native territory this is, is as clearly influenced by Altichiero as it is manifestly not by him or any member of his shop. This fresco, with a border containing medallions enclosing what seem to be portraits (a comparable border by Martino frames his paired scholar-saints on the S. Fermo pulpit; fig. 61), may be attributed to an artist from the Alto Adige in touch with contemporary developments around the lower reaches of the river. Another fresco in S. Domenico, of later date, the *Madonna and Child with Sts James and Anthony Abbot*, shows the response of an artist possibly even more northern in origin to the Veronese style.

In Verona itself Altichiero's influence proved highly durable. Reflections of his style surface in various forms during the early years of the quattrocento, and his is still clearly the dominant influence on the frescoes in the Chapel of S. Girolamo in S. Maria della Scala, painted by Giovanni Badile in the early 1440s (fig. 84). The architecture in these frescoes, three-bay boxes, upper loggias and all, looks directly back to the frescoes of S. Giorgio and S. Giacomo, across an intervening period of some sixty years, testimony either to the conservatism of Veronese painting or to the enduring influence of Altichiero, depending on one's point of view.

There are clear indications of Altichiero's art having made an impact well outside the areas in which he himself worked or which, like the Alto Adige, had traditional links with Veronese culture. Paduan interests in Treviso probably account for the Altichieresque flavour of a fresco of a standing St Catherine in the Church of S. Caterina there,[37] and a *Crucifixion* in S. Lucia,[38] both once attributed to Tomaso da Modena or his school. The *St Catherine* is painted in a version of Altichiero's style cognate with the more linear, less fully modelled, rather simplified style we have already seen in various contexts. The figures in the *Crucifixion*, which is less immediately attractive than the elegant saint, are stocky in a way which indicates the attempt of an artist much less gifted than Altichiero himself to take on board something of his sense of plasticity and weight. This fresco is close in style to a fictive altarpiece of the *Crucifixion* painted on the north wall of the Church of S. Nicolo in Padua. The Treviso fresco is rather closely modelled on Altichiero's in S. Giorgio (or another, lost, version of similar configuration), with the thieves' crosses set at an angle to Christ's and with the thieves themselves attached to the crosses in an identical manner, their arms wrapped round the cross bars.

Altichiero's influence can be felt further south, too. A fresco of the *Madonna of Humility* from a private house in Ferrara, now in the Pinacoteca and dated *c.* 1380, was very clearly painted in his shadow. A large lunette fresco of the *Madonna and Child with Sts John, John the Baptist, and a Donor Bishop* in the Rusconi Chapel in the crypt of Parma Cathedral, which can be dated to the early quattrocento, illustrates the extent to which Altichiero's influence was open to modernisation and adaptation to new stylistic contexts. The standing saints and musician angels have no affinities with Altichiero whatsoever, but they frame a Madonna whose face derives directly from Altichiero's slightly plump Eremitani format, seated on a gigantic throne of unmistakably Alticherian aspect.

The impact of Altichiero's architectural inventiveness was felt even further afield. The Brussels Initials Master lifted a number of Altichiero's most elaborate architectural backdrops for his illustrations to a series of manuscripts.[39] The *Annunciation* from the Hours of Charles le Noble (Cleveland Museum of Art) takes place in a building quite openly based on the central, three-bay, structure of the *Tortures of St Lucy* in S. Giorgio. There are several other examples of this direct borrowing, which leads one to wonder whether other instances of the Initials Master's work in which the architecture looks obviously Alticherian but which reflects no particular known example of his work may record the architectural settings of lost works. It is clear that the Initials Master had been both in S. Giorgio, from which he borrowed at least twice, and in S. Giacomo, from which he picked up the un-Altichieresque round wings of the second *St James* fresco.

[37] Reproduced in colour in Boccazzi, *Tommaso da Modena*, pl. XVI, and in monochrome in Gibbs, *Tomaso da Modena*, fig. 31a. The banner of St Mark held up by the saint flies over the little city. Treviso came under Venetian control in December 1388 after four years of Carrarese rule.

[38] Pettenella, *Altichiero*, pl. 22.

[39] Meiss, *French Painting in the Time of Jean de Berry: The Late XIV Century and the Patronage of the Duke*, pls. 745, 747, 771, 772 and 776, e.g.

S. Giorgio seems to have caught the eye of later painters too. The standing figure looking up at the cross in a Van Eyck circle *Crucifixion* (New York, Metropolitan Museum) may, as Châtelet suggests,[40] derive from the figure in the equivalent position in the S. Giorgio *Crucifixion*. Much more certain is the dependence on this same figure, indeed on the group in which it is located, of the foreground of Jean Fouquet's *Crucifixion* from the Hours of Etienne Chevalier.[41] The derivation is absolutely unmistakable. Fouquet is not known for certain to have come this way during his Italian travels, and he may have had access to Altichiero's work in the form of drawings, but his interest, which finds general expression throughout his later work, further fleshes out the scrappy indications of quattrocento enthusiasm for Altichiero given by the accounts and copies of the Sala Grande. The same can be said for the abundant, but invariably unspecific recollections of Altichiero's work in the drawings of Jacopo Bellini. Jacopo clearly made a profound study of the Paduan frescoes. He seems to have been attracted as much by the elaborate and sometimes fantastic qualities of Altichiero's architectural invention as by the mature and expansive organisation of the pictorial space in which Altichiero sets his narratives.

Nothing now surviving there suggests that Altichiero or any of his close followers ever worked in Mantua. It is quite reasonable, though, to assume that his work was known there, given the intense traffic between the Paduan and Mantuan Petrarch circles, between the Carrarese and Gonzaga courts, and perhaps also via Raimondino Lupi. We know, in any case, that at least one work of his existed in Mantua during the trecento. In April 1393 two Mantuan goldsmiths undertook to make a gilded silver crucifix on the basis of a design supplied by Altichiero ('secundum formam quam pinxit et dessignavit bonae memoriae magister Aldegherius magister de Verona') and in the possession of Bonamente Aliprandi, the Gonzaga treasurer ('deposita penes prudentem virum Bonamentem de Alliprandis generalem rectorem introytuum et expensarum magnifici domini Mantuae').[42] Bonamente's status obviously allows us to think that Altichiero's work was at least known at the Gonzaga court. The wording also gives us one more crucial piece of information. By the time this document was drawn up (10 April 1393) Altichiero – 'bonae memoriae' – was dead. Presumably he died in Verona, but where or when he was buried is not known.

40 Châtelet, *Van Eyck*, p. 32.

41 Reproduced in Sterling and Schaefer, *The Hours of Etienne Chevalier*, pl. 17.

42 Vattovani, 'Tomaso e Altichiero', pp. 273–4 and 275, n. The document is Mantua, Archivio Capitolare, Perg. b.16, no. 2250; 10 April 1393.

CATALOGUE

1. **PADUA, EREMITANI, SACRISTY**. *MADONNA AND CHILD*. DETACHED FRESCO, *C*.1381. (PL. 119)

DIMENSIONS Diameter of tondo *c*. 62 cm

PROVENANCE Probably from lunette fresco of tomb of Ilario Sanguinacci (d.1381) or another tomb in the same church.

CONDITION Considerable surface loss all over the Virgin's mantle and damage to the Child's head and neck. Surface generally subject to fine cracking of the plaster. The edge of the tondo is extremely ragged.

PRINCIPAL REFERENCES Bettini, *Giusto de'Menabuoi e l'Arte del Trecento*, p. 72. Toesca, *Il Trecento*, p. 790. Magagnato, *Da Altichiero a Pisanello*, pp. 13–14. Pettenella, *Altichiero*, p. 58. Mellini, *Altichiero e Jacopo Avanzi*, p. 56, Bettini and Puppi, *La Chiesa degli Eremitani*, p. 48. Grossato, *Da Giotto a Mantegna*, no. 50. Lucco, '"Me Pinxit"', pp. 264–5.

2. **PADUA. BASILICA DEL SANTO. CHAPEL OF S. GIACOMO** (1372–77). *LIFE AND MIRACLES OF ST.JAMES THE GREAT* (1–11). *ANNUNCIATION, PIETÀ, RESURRECTION, CRUCIFIXION, VOTIVE SCENE* (12–17). BORDER AND VAULT *SAINTS, PROPHETS*, ETC. (18–25). FRESCO, 1377–9. (PLS. 39–75)

DIMENSIONS The chapel measures *c*.16.5 m.×7.76 m. The plan is slightly rhomboid; both short walls are angled slightly towards the east. The height from the pavement to the crown of the vaults is 10.67 m. The arcade measures 2.7 m between columns. The large lunettes of the side walls (3 and 7) are 5.16 m wide×3.91 m high, including borders. The small lunettes (2, 4, 6 and 8) measure 4 m.×3.91 m. The east-wall lunette (1) measures 6.2 m.×3.91 m. The east-wall middle zone (9–11) measures 6.5 m×3.7 m and the *Crucifixion* 8.58 m×4.58 m as a whole.

CHRONOLOGY 1372, 12 Feb. Contract between Bonifacio Lupi and Andriolo de'Santi for construction of the Chapel of S. Giacomo and for the sculptures to be placed on the entrance wall.

1372, 20 Feb. Payments for work carried out on the new chapel begin.

1376, 20 March Andriolo and Giovanni de'Santi complete their work on the tombs in the chapel. They are paid 500 ducats.

1376, June Tomaso da Venezia paid for making a window in the sacristy.

1376, 19 Oct. Agreement between Bonifacio and the Franciscans of the Santo concerning the masses to be said in the chapel after his death and their funding. The architecture of the chapel is largely complete by this date ('in ipsa capella, quam sub titulo s.Iacobi Maioris extrui feci').

1377? Bonifacio refused permission to be buried in Florence Cathedral.
1377, March Payment for the demolition of the builders' scaffolding ('per fare abasare l'armamento de la capella') and for five mats for painting ('per store V per lo dipinctore').
1378, April Payment for scaffolding used for the painting of the heraldic helmets of the chapel ('per l'armadura per pingere lo cimiero').
1378, 3 May The provincial chapter of the Franciscans confirms the agreement of 19 Oct. 1376.
1379, May(?) Payment made to Altichiero for his work in the chapel ('Ancora dado al maestro Altichiero, per ogni raxon ch'aveva a fare cum messer Bonifacio cussì nel dipingere la capella de san Iacomo como per la sacrestia, como appare nel libro de la capella, ducati settecentononantadui ducati DCC.LXXXXII.').
1379, May(?) Payment to Rinaldino da Francia for the carved figures to be placed on the altar.
1384, 4 June Bonifacio and the Franciscans again confirm the agreement set out in the 1376 document.
1384, 29 Sept. New arrangements are agreed whereby masses will be said in the chapel during Bonifacio's lifetime. Lands owned by Bonifacio in the Eugenean Hills, to be endowed for the funding of these masses and handed over to the convent of the *Clarisse* at Arcella Nova, are specified, along with the precise sum of money (104 ducats) envisaged.
1385, 17 July Bonifacio makes a will specifying that he is to be buried in the chapel. His heir is to be his nephew Ugolotto Biancardo, or, if he is dead, Antonio di Guido Lupi and Raimondino di Antonio Lupi.
1386, 12 Feb. Urban VI grants 140 days' indulgence for any visit made to the chapel on the feast day of St James.
1389, 23 Jan. Date of inscription recording endowment arrangements (drawing V, E).
1389, 30 Aug. Confirmation of agreement of 29 Sept. 1384.
1390, 21 June Probable date of Bonifacio's death.
1391, 10? March (1390 Florentine style) Permission given in Florence for a service in memory of Bonifacio Lupi to be organised by the consuls of the Arte di Calimala.

CONDITION The frescoes are all (as of 1996/7) extremely dirty. The chromatic range is consequently quite markedly restricted compared with that of the much cleaner frescoes in S. Giorgio or the best parts of the Cavalli fresco. The characteristic tart apple-greens and light brick-pinks of Altichiero's palette need the extra enhancement of strong lighting and persuasive photography before they reveal themselves. Under normal viewing conditions the frescoes seem tonally subdued.

The current condition of the original paint surface is hard to assess given the film of dirt through which it must be viewed. Comparison of parts of the frescoes with older photographs suggests that paint has been lost within the last 100 years, or even more recently. The heraldic wolf on the red shield in the foreground of the *Battle of Clavigo*, for instance, has become noticeably more shadowy since the photograph published by Mellini was taken. Other parts of the *Battle* are rather hard to read and seem to have suffered extensive damage. Much of the heraldic detail has either faded or fallen off, and the crest of the king's helmet has become semi-transparent. The architecture of *Ramiro's Dream* and his *Council* has suffered and the wall patterns in the *Council* are badly faded.

The general condition of the west-wall frescoes is poor – the *Votive Fresco* is particularly bad, and illegible in places. Parts of it also seem to have been heavily repainted. The faces of the Virgin and the Child seem to have been partially erased, and the throne steps and lower part of Bonifacio's figure look very sketchy. The lower part of the *St James's Disciples Brought Before the King of Spain* has been completely repainted.

The lower part of the *Crucifixion*, especially the central bay, is disfigured by graffiti and badly abraded, and a number of the faces in the foreground of the left bay of the fresco are practically unreadable. The architecture of the left bay has lost considerable areas of paint and the right bay has several long cracks in the plaster. The recumbent lion in the fictive niche below the Rossi tomb, clearly visible in a nineteenth-century print of the chapel, is now a mere shadow. Several of the stall saints on the east wall are badly cracked and abraded, and those of the west wall almost wholly repainted.

The frescoes have been restored on several occasions. In 1661 they were stripped of their covering of dust and washed. In 1749 a major fire caused the lead covering of the Santo's domes, including the one directly above the chapel, to melt and run down into the church, causing widespread damage, and possibly accounted for the rather 'smoked' appearance of the frescoes. In 1772–3 Francesco Zannoni embarked on a major restoration campaign. The west wall of the chapel must, even then, have been in poor condition, for Zannoni's only addition, a St Christopher, was here. This no longer exists – Sartori suggests it was painted *a secco* – but it was presumably located to the right of the window, where there is now a fictive arch with thin painted mullions, added in 1857. The original condition of this part of the wall is unclear. The lower part has the endowment stone set into it, with a framework of fictive architecture which looks original (if restored). Nothing in the documents gives any clue, but the area above the stone is too large to have been left a blank, and there may have been something here to balance the votive fresco at the same level on the other side of the window. In 1857 the frescoes were again freed of dust by Giambattista Monici, who added the fictive arch on the wall. A detailed report on the condition of the *intonaco* throughout the chapel was made in 1895 by Antonio Bertolli and a restoration based on his recommendations was made in the same year by Antonio Bonetti. A further restoration was carried out in the 1920s. The pre-restoration photograph of the first St James scene published by Mellini shows a paint surface in very poor condition and obvious signs of intervention by earlier restorers. Only a thorough and scientific new campaign (which is currently near completion) would reveal how much more of the chapel is the work of the restorers, but some areas, such as parts of the west wall stall canopy saints and the window soffit *God the Father*, are obviously restorations.

INSCRIPTIONS All three inscriptions are carved on single stones let into the wall surface.
West wall
ANNO DOMINI.M.CCC.LXXVI.INDICIONE XIIII.
NOBILIS MILES ET MARCHIO SORANEAE DNS BONIFACIUS
DE LUPIS. FECIT.FIERI HANC CAPELLAM.AD HONOREM DEI EIUSQUE.
GLORIOSAE MATRIS VIRGINIS MARIAE ET BEATI IACOBI MAIORIS APOSTOLI.CUIUS
CAPELLAE ALTARE.CONSECRATUM EST.NOMINE IPSIUS INCLITI APOSTOLI
SUPER QUO.DE CONSENSU MINISTRI PROVINCIALIS. GUARDIANUS ET FRA-
TRES HUIUS ECCLESIAE QUI PRO TEMPORE FUERINT PROMISERUNT FACERE CE-
LEBRARI.PERPETUO SINGULIS DIEBUS TRES MISSAS. PRO ANIMA PRAEDICTI
MILITIS OMNIUMQUE DEFUNCTORUM SUORUM.ET PRO HIS QUIDEM FIR-
MITER OBSERVANDIS QUONIAM OMNIS LABOR OPTAT PRAEMIUM.
PRAEFATUS. DNS BONIFACIUS RELIQUIT FRATRIBUS PRAEDICTIS ANNUATIM
DIVERSIS TEMPORIBUS ANNI CENTUM ET QUADRAGINTA DUCATOS AURI.QUOS
DARE EISDEM TENENTUR SORORES MINORES DE ARCELLA NOVA
PADUAE ABSQUE ALIQUO EARUMDEM GRAVAMINE.UT EX TESTAMEN
TO ANTEDICTI MILITIS PLENISSIME CONTINETUR.
(The 1376 date inscribed here refers not to the placement of the stone or to any aspect of the chapel's construction as such, but to a document of 13 October 1376 in which Bonifacio set out the endowment arrangements for the chapel. The stone records Bonifacio's later, revised, plan, by which masses would be said during his lifetime rather than only after his death and it must have been inserted after 29 September 1384, the date of the document in which this revised plan is first mooted. The twelfth line of inscription contains a clearly visible recutting of the stone at the words 'et quadraginta', marking a late change in the actual sum, originally 104 ducats, involved.)

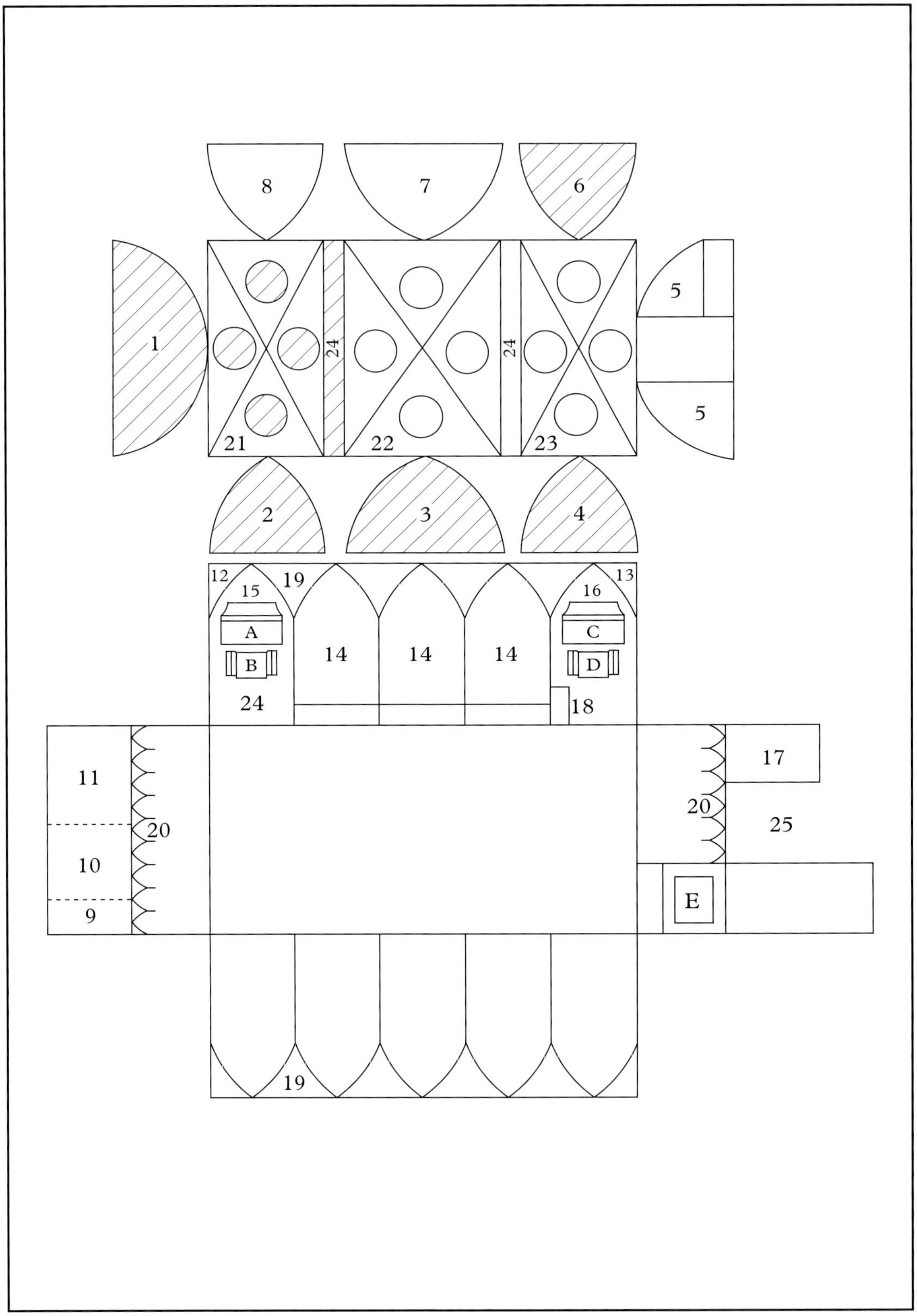

Drawing v Chapel of S.Giacomo. Plan of frescoes.

KEY
A Rossi tomb
B Inscription stone below Rossi tomb
C Tomb of Bonifacio Lupi
D Inscription stone below Lupi tomb
E Endowment stone

FRESCOES (shaded areas indicate frescoes here attributed to Jacopo Avanzi)

1 *Hermogenes Instructs his Disciple Filetus. Debate Between St James and Filetus. Hermogenes Summons Demons*
2 *Hermogenes Transported to St James by Demons. St James Baptises Hermogenes. Filetus Burns the Magic Books*
3 *St James, Led to his Execution, Heals a Paralytic. Execution of St James*
4 *The ship, Steered by an Angel, Carries the Body of St James to Spain. The Miraculous Burial of St James. Report of the Miracle to Queen Lupa*
5 *St James's Disciples Brought Before the King of Spain* (left) *The Disciples are Imprisoned* (right)
6 *The Disciples are Freed by an Angel. Collapse of a Bridge Beneath Their Pursuers. The Disciples Recalled to Compostella by the King of Spain*
7 *The Disciples Kill a Dragon with the Sign of the Cross. The Bulls Pulling the Body of St James Take it of Their Own Accord to Lupa's Palace*
8 *Hermogenes Baptises Lupa. She Rededicates her Palace as a Church*
9 *Ramiro's Dream*
10 *Ramiro Reveals his Dream in Council*
11 *The Battle of Clavigo*
12 *The Archangel Gabriel*
13 *The Annunciate Virgin*
14 *The Crucifixion*
15 *Pietà*
16 *Resurrection*
17 *Sts James and Catherine Present Bonifacio Lupi and Caterina dei Francesi to the Virgin and Child*
18 *Bonifacio Lupi in Franciscan Habit*
19 Spandrel roundels with half-length saints. South wall, left to right: *Sts Clare, Anthony of Padua, Francis, Louis*. North wall, left to right: *Sts Benedict, Giustina, Paul, John the Baptist, Mary Magdalen, Anthony Abbot*
20 Stall canopy busts of saints (east and west walls)
21 *Prophets*
22 *Evangelists*
23 *Doctors of the Church*
24 *Recumbent Lion*
25 *God the Father and Angels* (window soffit)

South wall, below Bonifacio Lupi's tomb
PRO DOLOR.HAC MILES IAM BELLO CLARUS ET ARMIS
IAM TERRA PELAGOQUE MICANS BONIFACIUS ATRA
.MOLLE IACET.QUEM PARMA TULIT.QUI MARCHIO VIXIT
SORANAE.GENTIS DECUS ET SUMMA LUPORUM
GLORIA.PRO LATIIS QUI QUONDAM PLURIMA GESSIT
PRAELIA DUCTOR HERIS ET SAEPE DECORA TRIUMPHIS.
HIC HIC CUIUS ERAT CONSULTA RESUMERE LAETUS
IMPERIALIS APEX.REGIQUE DOMESTICUS IDEM
ASTITIT UNGARICO DNO VIR GRATUS UTRIQUE
QUIDNI? CONSILIO FUIT HIC.PROBITAE.FIDEQUE
IUSTICIAQUE NITENS. SPERUM DEVOTUS. ET ALMAE
RELLIGIONIS AMANS.QUO NON PRAESTANTIOR ALTER
RECTA SEQUI.MAIORQUE SUI DILECTOR HONORIS.
AT QUID FATA VIRUM TANTI PROSTRASSE IUVABIT?
SIDERA MENS SCANDIT. GELIDUM LICET OSSA SEPULCRUM
STRINGAT.ET AETERNUM SUA VIVET FAMA PER AEVUM.
M.CCC.LXXXVIIII.DIE XXIII.
(Bonifacio's inscription was placed *in situ* before his death, and the date records the placement of the stone. There is abundant documentary proof of his continuing existence after the date given on the stone. The date on the tomb of Caterina dei Francesi, originally in S. Giacomo, 20 June 1405, must in a similar fashion record the insertion of the tomb slab, as Caterina was certainly alive after this date.)

South wall, below the Rossi tomb
QVATUOR HOC MARMOR PROCERUM TEGIT OSSA SEPULCRI
HECTORE QUIS POTIOR.QUIS NESTORE DOCTIOR ISTIC?
GUGLIELMINUS ERAT RUBEIS SATUS INCLITA PARMA
EDDIDIT HUNC ANIMOSA DUCEM CUM QUO GENITOS TRES
ARCHA TENET FELIX TANTI GENITURA PARENTIS.
ROLANDUS VIRTUTE ANIMI GENEROSUS IN OMNI
DOTE NITENS DEXTRE TREMOR HOSTIBUS AXIS AMICIS
ARDENS PARMIGENIS LAMPAS PIETATIS ASILLUM.
SUPRA HOMINEM CINCTUS TITULIS MARSILIUS ARMIS
STRENUUS IRRIGUUS LIBRATI CONSILII FONS.
SPES PATRIAE DOMUIQ . IUBAR PARME DECUS ALTUM.
QUID PETRE MUSA CANET DE TE NISI QUOD POLUS UNQUAM
NON FLUXIT PROBITATE PAREM.NAM DUX VAFER ALTER
SCIPIO MAGNANIMUS FUERAS. SUPER HIS ET LILIA RUBRA
QUOS PROCUL A PATRIA BUSTO HOC FORTUNA COEGIT
CARRIGENUM AFFINES COMMIXTO FEDERE TEDE
CORPORE FORMOSOS ANIMI VIRTUTE CORUSCOS.
IMPRIME ROMULEIS HORUM SUA GESTA TRIUMPHIS.
POSTERITAS LINGUIS RESONIS RECOLENDA PER EVUM.
UT LOCET A DEXTRIS DEUS HOS SUPPLEXQ . PRECARE.
OBIIT AUT. PFATUS DNS PETR PARV.ANTE ALIOS TRES PDCOS D.
M.CCC.XXXVII.AUGUS.VII

ATTRIBUTIONS The attributional history of the frescoes of S. Giacomo is highly complex, and the key issues are discussed in chapter 5 above. The following is a list of the chief attributional divisions published so far. Savonarola (*c.* 1440): all the frescoes by Jacopo Avanzi of Bologna. Michiel (1520–43): Altichiero and Avanzo of Padua, or Verona, or Bologna. Polidoro (1590): Giotto. Schubring (1898): lower zone by Altichiero, lunettes by a 'Maestro delle

Lunette'. Venturi (1907): lower zone by Altichiero, lunettes by Avanzo. Van Marle (1924): all frescoes by Altichiero, with the help of an assistant in the lunettes. Coletti (1931): Altichiero and, in the lunettes, a Tuscan painter (Cennino Cennini?). Toesca (1951): Altichiero, with a different hand at work in the lunettes, for him the author of the *Massacre of the Hebrews* at Mezzaratta. Sartori (1963 and 1966): all the frescoes by Altichiero. Mellini (1965): nos. 1, 2, 3, 4, 6, 21 and 24 by Jacopo Avanzi of Bologna, all the rest by Altichiero. Kruft (1966): lower zone by Altichiero and upper zone designed by him, but partly executed by another hand. Simon (1977): Altichiero throughout, with normal workshop assistance. D'Arcais (1984): lower zone by Altichiero, nos. 1, 2, 3, 4, 6, 21 and 24 by 'Avanzo'.

SIGNATURES Sartori published several photographs showing what he claimed to be signatures by Altichiero here and in S. Giorgio. Whatever the possible interpretations of the wording, the example in S. Giorgio is unmistakably lettering of some kind. Neither of the two signatures Sartori claimed for the *Battle of Clavigo* are so easily identifiable even as inscriptions of any kind. The longer 'signature', along the leading edge of the shield of the standing soldier in the centre of the scene, was transcribed by Sartori as ALTICHERIUS DEPINXIT HOC OPUS. He also claimed to find ALTICHERIUS on the cornice below the fresco, though the later of his two important papers on Altichiero finds him rather shyer of this second inscription. It would, indeed, be rather odd for an artist to put two signatures on the same fresco. It is, as Sartori admitted, impossible to read his two putative signatures under normal viewing conditions, but even with the benefit of his photographs it requires the eye of faith to see what Sartori made out 'con maggior difficoltà ma con sicurezza'. Mellini identified the marks on the edge of the shield as parts of a decorative border. The best that can be said for Sartori's plates is that two or three of the shield marks do at least resemble Gothic lettering. An old Alinari photograph of the *Battle* allows for a clearer look at the disputed area. The marks look more like letters than in Sartori's plates, but they still defy interpretation.

THE SACRISTY OF S. GIACOMO The 1379 payment to Altichiero establishes that as well as painting in the main chapel he had also worked in a sacristy associated with it ('per ogni raxon ch'aveva a fare . . . cussì dipingere la capella . . . como per la sacrestia'). A document of 1384 confirms the existence of this sacristy and that it specifically belongs to the Chapel of S. Giacomo, making arrangements for the maintenance and eventual repair of the chapel and the sacristy when necessary ('vel ad decorem vel ad necessitatem ipsius capellae vel eius secretiae'). A document of 1468 mentions 'una sagrestia in la capela', which Sartori interpreted as meaning adjacent to the chapel. Gonzati and Simon both identify the site of the present Chapel of the Cross, to the west of S. Giacomo, as that of the lost sacristy. The extant chapel only half fills the available space, and the evidence of the cloister wall at this point suggests that there was an older door in from the cloister, now filled in. A payment of 1376 reveals that the sacristy had a window, but, given the restricted site and the need to avoid any obstruction of the west window of the main chapel, the sacristy cannot have amounted to much more than an 'annexe', as Simon describes it. Sartori discusses, and dismisses, a suggestion that the sacristy originally communicated directly with the chapel, via a door located close to the window. This argument, emanating from Santo sources, was based on a perceived discrepancy between the stone colour of the two southern stall canopies of the west wall, meaning that they must have been added later when this door was filled in. The condition of the wall at this point actually allows no such reading of the evidence, and it is overwhelmingly likely that the priest's route from the sacristy to the chapel was via the south aisle of the basilica. Sartori suggests that the sacristy was 'in cattive condizioni' as early as 1468. The Chapel of the Cross was erected in 1624. The Sacristy was just possibly decorated with a *Last Supper* by Altichiero mentioned by Vasari, whose sources had by the time he was describing the Paduan frescoes led him into areas of total confusion, in connection with S. Giorgio ('dipinse . . . Aldigieri alcune storie di Santa Lucia ed un Cenacolo', *Le Vite*, vol. III, p. 634). There is nowhere for there to have been a fresco of this subject in S. Giorgio, but we know Altichiero at least did something for the S. Giacomo sacristy.

OTHER ALTERATIONS Apart from various routine restorations of the fabric and the loss of the sacristy, there have been several other alterations which have affected the chapel. Towards 1500 the present high cornice was added to the facade to bring the chapel more in line with Renaissance tastes. It must be assumed that the gables of S. Giacomo were originally decorated with crockets and finials in the normal manner, and that these were removed when the new cornice was constructed, the effect of which has been further to block the view of the upper parts of the transept. In 1503 the chapel was rededicated to S. Felice, whose shrine was placed in the chapel. The shrine was raised on a high podium, reached by steps, and the central bay of the *Crucifixion* was partially obscured. The altar was reduced to its present height in the 1960s. The chapel has lost the iron grille, mentioned by Polidoro (*Religiose Memorie*, p. 22), which originally separated it from the main body of the basilica, and it has also lost the impressive effigial slab of Caterina dei Francesi, which lay at the foot of her husband's tomb until it was removed to the adjacent cloister passage in 1773. The oval windows above the left and right bays of the *Crucifixion*, closed up when the cloister was rebuilt, were experimentally re-opened in the nineteenth century, but closed again when it was realised that a light source here made the *Crucifixion* very difficult to see.

PRINCIPAL REFERENCES Savonarola, *Libellus*, p. 44. Michiel, *Notizie*, pp. 5–6. Sartori, 'Nota su Altichiero'. Sartori, 'La Cappella di S. Giacomo'. Pettenella, *Altichiero*, pp. 39–42. Mellini, *Altichiero e Jacopo Avanzi*, pp. 41–53. Kruft, *Altichiero und Avanzo*, pp. 13–46. Simon, 'Altichiero Versus Avanzo', pp. 252–8. D'Arcais, 'San Giacomo', pp. 15–42. Edwards, 'The Chapel of S. Felice'. Benati, *Jacopo Avanzi*, pp. 92–108. Norman, *Siena, Florence and Padua*, vol.II, pp. 179–93.

3. **PADUA. ORATORY OF S. GIORGIO**. *SCENES FROM THE LIFE OF CHRIST. SCENES FROM THE LIVES OF STS GEORGE, CATHERINE AND LUCY*. FRESCO, 1379–84. (PLS. 76–116)

DIMENSIONS *Crucifixion*: *c.* 4.30 m × *c.* 3.82 m; outer scenes of lower side walls, *c.* 2.9 m × *c.* 2.37 m; inner scenes of lower side walls, *c.* 2.9 m. × *c.* 3.85 m; *Coronation* (lower edge), *c.* 6.5 m (all after Kruft, *Altichiero und Avanzo*, p. 75).

CHRONOLOGY 1377, Nov. Date of inscription on oratory facade.
1378, May 3. Confirmation of foundation of oratory and statement of endowment arrangements. The confirmation document (ASP Corona b.75, fo. 201v, in Sartori, 'Nota su Altichiero', pp. 307–8) reveals that the oratory has already been built: 'Cum dns Raimondinus extrui fecerit unam capellam sub vocabulo s.Georgii.'
1379, Nov. 30 Death of Raimondino Lupi.
1379, Dec. 1 Raimondino's executors, Bonifacio di Ugolotto Lupi, Antonio and Simone di Guido Lupi, confirm the endowment arrangements made by Raimondino previously. The document recording this (ASP Corona b.68 perg. 6718, in Sartori, 'Nota su Altichiero', pp. 308–9) reveals that Raimondino has already been buried in the oratory: 'considerantes praefatum d.Raimondinum fideli mente fundasse et construi fecisse unam capellam sub vocabulo s.Georgii, prope ecclesiam s.Antonii confessoris de Padua, et ipsum d.Raimondinum morte praeventum, in eadem capella sepultum, proposuisse infrascriptam possessionem suam relinquere, ut eius reditibus et proventibus continue posset divinus cultus in dicta capella celebrari'.
1384, May 30 Two documents (ASP Notarile, vol. 407, fos. 146v and 147v, in Sartori, 'Nota su Altichiero', pp. 305–7) are drawn up testifying that both Altichiero and Bonifacio Lupi agree that Altichiero's original contract with Raimondino Lupi has been satisfactorily carried out. Altichiero's document reveals that he had been contracted to paint Raimondino's tomb as well as the oratory itself.

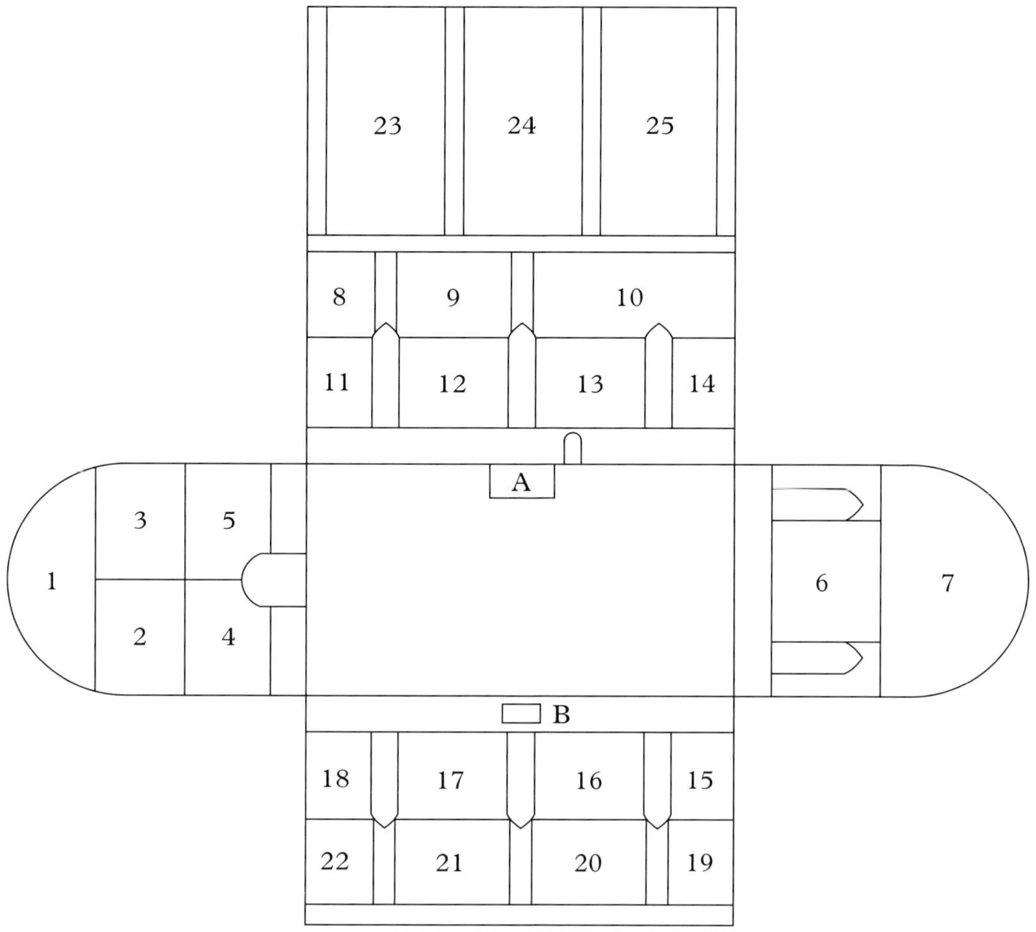

Drawing VI Oratory of S. Giorgio. Plan of frescoes.

KEY
A Present site of sarcophagus
B Inscription stone
1 *Annunciation*
2 *Nativity*
3 *Adoration of the Magi*
4 *Flight into Egypt*
5 *Presentation in the Temple*
6 *Crucifixion*
7 *Coronation of the Virgin*
8 *St George and the Dragon*
9 *St George Baptising King Sevio and his Court*
10 Votive fresco
11 *St George Condemned to Drink Poison*
12 *St George on the Wheel*
13 *Fall of the Idols*
14 *Execution of St George*
15 *St Catherine Refusing to Worship the Pagan Idols*
16 *St Catherine converting the Pagan Philosophers; Burning of the Philosophers*
17 *St Catherine on the Wheel*
18 *Execution of St Catherine*
19 *St Lucy Before Judge Pascasio*
20 *Miracle of St Lucy and the Bulls*
21 *St Lucy Burned at the Stake, Exposed Naked in a Brothel, Stabbed in the Neck*
22 *Last Communion and Funeral of St Lucy*
23 *Prophets*
24 *Doctors of the Church*
25 *Evangelists*

CONDITION (as of 1996/7) Variable. The frescoes are much cleaner than those of S. Giacomo and the chromatic range is consequently wider. One or two frescoes (no. 9, for example) are in good condition, though no part of the oratory has escaped surface damage and abrasion of various kinds. In addition, large areas have been badly affected by damp. The first two scenes of the St Catherine cycle (15 and 16) are the most damaged. Nearly half of no. 16 is illegible. The third and fourth scenes (17 and 18) are better, but the upper areas of both have suffered only slightly milder attacks of the same kind. The St Lucy frescoes on the same wall have suffered less, though no. 22 has lost a large area of *intonaco*. The St George cycle on the east wall is generally in better condition. The architecture of the fourth scene (11) has small areas of paint loss, and the lower left side of the sixth scene (13) has lost all its paint, leaving only shadows of the underdrawing visible. The entrance-wall frescoes are generally in a fair condition, though no. 4 has lost a huge area of plaster at the top and no. 2 a rather smaller area just above the lower border. The vault frescoes are extensively damaged. Four out of five figures apiece in the Prophets bay and the Doctors bay are lost. The four Evangelists survive, in poor condition, but the central cusped oval is blank. Large areas of the border framing the vault are damaged, though isolated figures are still in reasonable condition. The frescoes were whitewashed during the Napoleonic period and only uncovered by Ernest Förster in 1837. Metallic detail, on armour and weapons, etc., is tarnished or lost, and parts of the architectural backgrounds which were added *a secco* are badly faded. See, for example, the windows in no. 13 and in the upper left part of no. 21. The frescoes were restored in 1844, 1871, 1942 and recently by L.Tintori. A further restoration is nearing completion.

INSCRIPTIONS

On facade

ORATHORIUM.HOC.SUB.AUSPICIIS
BEATI.GEORGII.UBI.CHONDENTIS. EST
SEPULCRUM.PRO EIUS. PARENTUMQUE.AC.FRATRUM.ET.NEPOTUM
INDELENDA.MEMORIA.MILES.
EGREGIUS.RAIMONDINUS.DE.LU/
PIS. PARMENSIS. SORANEE.MARCHIO
EDIFECIT.ANO.DNI.M.CCC.LXX
VII.DE.MENSE.NOVEMBRIS.

On stone set into west wall

MARCHIO SORANIE MILES PIETATIS ASILLUM
HOC RAYMONDINUS MARMORE PACE CUBAT
IN BELLIS PUGIL INDOMITUS RECITANDA LUPOR
FAMA VIRENS ARMIS CONSCILIUMQ FUIT
GRISOPOLIS GAUDE TANTO CELEBERIMA NATO
CUIUS CU SUPERIS MENS SEDET ANTE DEUM
Q.D.RAY.OBIIT M CCC LXXIX XXX NOVEB.

THE TOMB S'erge con segnalata magnificenza l'altro (tomb) nel mezo dell'illustre luogo, essendosi prima fondata sopra un sodo piano, al quale s'ascende per tre gradi, nel mezo del quale è un'Arca di viva pietra, incassato a gran quadri di marmo africano, di lunghezza, larghezza ed altezza commune, sostenuto da quattro colonne, fermate sopra le schiene di quattro Lupi: e tutto questo è ricevuto nel mezo da sei colonne che d'altezza avanzano la maggior dell'Arca, talmente situate e ben poste, che tre in una, e tre nell'altra parte drizzandosi, lasciano tra sè uguali distanze d'ogni intorno, e danno commodo a due ordini di una volta, che cuopre quanto s'è detto; sopra la volta poi, tenendo la parte di mezo, ancor s'inalcia une gran Piramide, che d'intorno la bassezza sua lascia tanta larghezza, che vi si possono fermare dieci gran statue rappresentanti valorosi uomini armati, con insegne militari, e cimieri molto strani appresso de'moderni, oltre gli scolpiti Lupi e portati negli scudi, gl'intagli nelle pietre, le pitture ne'colori, et aggravamenti d'Argento e d'Oro; ciascheduno poi di quelle statue si ferma sopra un quadrotto di pietra a modo di Pedestallo et in ognuno a buone lettere è intagliato il nome del rappresentato nella statua; però comminciandosi da quella parte che riguarda l'Altare, e continuandosi in giro alla destra de quell'opera, si va leggendo:

Dominus Rolandinus egregius Miles Soraneae Marchio pater.
Domina Mathilda eius coniux, Marchionissa, mater.
Guido Marchio Soraneae, filius.
Bonifacius " "
Antonius " "
Montinus " "
Dominus Raimondinus " "
Dominus Fulgus Marchio Soraneae, Miles, nepus.
" Simon " " " "
" Antonius " " " "

Polidoro, *Le Religiose Memorie*, 1590

Polidoro's text is slightly self-contradictory, as Mathilda Lupi is unlikely to have been represented by the figure of an armed warrior, but there is no reason to doubt the overall accuracy of his description.

ATTRIBUTIONS The attributional history of the S. Giorgio frescoes was as complex as that of S. Giacomo until recently, when Altichiero's sole authorship came to be generally accepted after the publication of the documents proving his role and given the manifest stylistic homogeneity of the frescoes. The following are the chief attributions: Savonarola (*c.* 1440): Altichiero. Riccio (via Michiel): Altichiero ('solo'). Campagnola (via Michiel): Altichiero and Avanzo. Vasari (1568): Jacopo Avanzi, Altichiero and 'Sebeto'. Förster (1841): Avanzo. Gonzati (1852): Avanzo. Selvatico (1869): Altichiero, Avanzi, and, for the St Catherine scenes, a third painter inferior to either. Von Schlosser (1895): Altichiero. Schübring (1898): Altichiero and Avanzo. Van Marle (1924): Altichiero. Sandberg-Vavalà (1926): Altichiero. Coletti (1931): Avanzo. Bettini (1944 and 1960): Avanzo. Toesca (1950): Altichiero. Longhi (1958): Altichiero. Pettenella (1961): Altichiero and a 'collaboratore principale'. Pallucchini (1964): Altichiero. Sartori (1963 and 1966): Altichiero. Mellini (1965): Altichiero. Kruft (1966): Altichiero and Avanzo da Vicenza. Simon (1977): Altichiero. D'Arcais (1987): Altichiero.

SIGNATURE Much of the attributional confusion surrounding S. Giorgio was consequent on Förster's belief that part of the badly faded inscription on the frame below the *Funeral of St Lucy* (pls. 115–16, fig. 73) could be read as AVANTIUS VE, which he interpreted as AVANTIUS VERONENSIS. Selvatico came to subscribe to this reading despite having at first claimed to read IACOBUS. Over a century later Sartori claimed, in complete contrast, to read ALTICHERIUS, remarking that 'il resto è di lettura molto più difficile, quasi disperata' but suggesting that the signature continued Q.DOMINICI DE VERONA DEPINXIT. The inscription is extremely faint and in my view quite indecipherable. The very careful and logical examination of this question by Simon ('Altichiero Versus Avanzo', pp. 261–3) leads inexorably to the conclusion that 'the one thing there could not have been in S. Giorgio was Avanzo's signature'. The early and generally reliable sources, Savonarola and Riccio, both attribute the frescoes to Altichiero alone, which they could not have done had the signature – which is prominently displayed – been anything but Altichiero's, whose authorship is in any case proved by the 1384 completion documents.

PRINCIPAL REFERENCES Förster (trans. Selvatico), *S. Giorgio*. Gonzati, *S. Antonio*, vol. I, pp. 270ff., vol. II, pp. 78ff. Selvatico, *Guida di Padova*, pp. 22–8. Sandberg-Vavalà, *La Pittura Veronese*, pp. 162–76. Pettenella, *Altichiero*, pp. 43–9. Sartori, 'Nota su Altichiero', pp. 293–8. Mellini, *Altichiero e Jacopo Avanzi*, pp. 57–80. Kruft, *Altichiero und Avanzo*, pp. 65ff. Simon, 'Altichiero Versus Avanzo', pp. 258ff. D'Arcais, 'San Giorgio', pp. 43–62. Edwards, 'Altichiero as Architect'.

4. **PADUA. SALA DEI GIGANTI** (FORMER SALA VIRORUM ILLUSTRIUM). THIRTY-SIX FIGURES FROM PETRARCH'S *DE VIRIS ILLUSTRIBUS* (LOST). NARRATIVE SCENES (PRESUMED AND LOST). *PORTRAIT OF PETRARCH. PORTRAIT OF LOMBARDO DELLA SETA* (LOST). FRESCO, *C.* 1370–9. (PL. 33)

FRESCOES Subject in brackets indicates lost trecento fresco. Nos. 3–39 included on basis of order in the *De Viris Illustribus*. An asterisk indicates the inclusion of a portrait of the same figure in the sixteenth-century fresco scheme (which has fourty-four portraits to the presumed thirty-six-plus-two of the Sala Virorum Illustrium). The titles given here are the correct names of the men portrayed in the SVI frescoes. The trecento texts of the *DVI* in its different versions offer a number of variants, some simply wrong. It is more than likely, indeed, that some of these inaccurate names were painted below the frescoes. Even so it seems more helpful for the understanding of the scheme to identify the Illustrious Men correctly. Where the Petrarchan source is significantly at odds with the correct nomenclature, or where it adds to it in a way that might indicate the painted title, the fourteenth-century version is given in square brackets.

1 Portrait of Petrarch (extant, in sixteenth-century setting)*
2 (Portrait of Lombardo della Seta. Presumed from existence of repainted portrait facing Petrarch's and from Michiel's account.)*
3 (Romulus)*
4 (Numa Pompilius)*
5 (Tullus Hostilius)*
6 (Ancus Martius)*
7 (Marcus Junius Brutus)*
8 (Horatius Cocles)
9 (Titus Quinctius Cincinnatus)* [Lucius Quinctius . . . Paris, BN MS Lat. 6069F; Lucio Quinto . . . Darmstadt, Cod. 101]
10 (M.Furius Camillus)*
11 (Marcus Valerius Corvinus)* [Marco Valerio Corbo . . . Darmstadt, Cod. 101]
12 (T.Manlius Torquatus)*
13 (P.Decius Mus)
14 (L.Papirius Cursor)*
15 (Manius Curius Dentatus)* [Marcus Curius Dentatus . . . Paris, BN MS Lat. 6069F; Marco Curio . . . Darmstadt, Cod. 101]
16 (C.Fabricius Luscinus)* [Fabricius Lucilius . . . Paris, BN MS Lat. 6069F; Fabricius Lucius . . . Vat. Lat. 19861]
17 (Alexander)
18 (Pyrrhus)
19 (Hannibal)
20 (Q.Fabius Maximus Cunctator)*
21 (M.Claudius Marcellus)*
22 (C.Claudius Nero)*
23 (M.Livius Salinator)
24 (P.Cornelius Scipio Africanus)*
25 (M.Porcius Cato 'Censorius')*
26 (P.Cornelius Scipio Nasica)
27 (T.Quinctius Flaminius)*
28 (L.Cornelius Scipio Asiaticus)
29 (L.Aemilius Paullus Macedonicus)*
30 (Q.Caecilius Metellus Macedonicus)
31 (P.Cornelius Scipio Aemilianus Africanus)*
32 (C.Marius)*
33 (Cn.Pompeius)* [Pompeio Magno . . . Paris, BN MS Lat. 6069F]
34 (C.Julius Caesar)*

35 (Augustus)* [Divus Augustus Cesare Octavianus . . . Paris, BN MS Lat. 6069F]
36 (Vespasian)*
37 (Titus)*
38 (Trajan)* [Ulpius Trayanus . . . Paris, BN MS Lat. 6069F]

CONDITION All the frescoes of the Sala Virorum Illustrium were covered over by the new decoration of 1540 (by Domenico Campagnola and Stefano dell'Arzere) except for the portrait of Petrarch. The condition of this is poor, but legible. The range of colours is extremely restricted. The surface seems relatively stable.

PRINCIPAL REFERENCES Savonarola, *Libellus,* p. 49. Michiel, *Notizie,* p. 34. Schlosser, 'Ein Veronisches Bilderbuch', pp. 183–93. Mommsen, 'Sala Virorum Illustrium'. Wilkins, *Petrarch's Later Years,* pp. 295–302. Mellini, *Altichiero a Jacopo Avanzi,* pp. 94–8. Kruft, *Altichiero und Avanzo,* pp. 133–9. Gasparotto, 'Gli Ultimi Affreschi', pp. 34–5. Simon, 'Altichiero Versus Avanzo', pp. 266–71. Richards, 'Altichiero and Humanist Patronage'. Benati, *Jacopo Avanzi,* pp. 76–83.

5. **PARIS. BIBLIOTHEQUE NATIONALE**, MS LAT. 6069F: PETRARCH, *DE VIRIS ILLUSTRIBUS* (WITH ADDITIONAL MATERIAL BY LOMBARDO DELLA SETA, SCRIBE OF THIS MS). *PORTRAIT OF PETRARCH* (FO. AV). *TRIUMPH OF FAME* (FO.1R). PARCHMENT. MS COMPLETED 25 JANUARY 1379. (PL. 36)

DIMENSIONS OF MS 320 mm × 230 mm

PROVENANCE Padua, Francesco da Carrara until 1388. Pavia, GianGaleazzo Visconti from 1388. Pavia, Sforza Library. Chateau de Blois, Louis XII of France, from 1499.

CONDITION Good.

Principal REFERENCES Shorr, 'Triumph of Fame', pp. 103–4. Martellotti, *Petrarca,* pp. XV-XVII. Magagnato, *Da Altichiero a Pisanello,* p. 14. Pellegrin, 'Manuscrits de Pétrarque', pp. 373–4. Kruft, *Altichiero und Avanzo,* pp. 133–9. Mellini, *Altichiero e Jacopo Avanzi,* pp. 36–7. Gilbert, 'Giotto in Milan'. Simon, 'Altichiero Versus Avanzo', pp. 268–70. *Dix Siècles,* pp. 87–9 (no.73). Richards, 'Altichiero and Humanist Patronage', ch. 3.

6. **PARIS, BIBLIOTHEQUE NATIONALE**, MS LAT. 6069I: PETRARCH, *DE VIRIS ILLUSTRIBUS. TRIUMPH OF FAME* (FO.1R). PARCHMENT, *C.* 1380. (PL. 37)

DIMENSIONS OF MS 360 mm × 250 mm

PROVENANCE Padua, Francesco da Carrara until 1388. Pavia, GianGaleazzo Visconti from 1388. Pavia, Sforza Library. Chateau de Blois, Louis XII of France, from 1499.

CONDITION Coloured sky and vegetation added later. Some flaking of paint at top and around mandorla.

Principal REFERENCES Shorr, 'Triumph of Fame', pp. 103–4. Martellotti, *Petrarca,* pp. XXIV-XXVI. Magagnato, *Da Altichiero a Pisanello,* p. 14. Pellegrin, 'Manuscrits de Pétrarque', pp. 376–7. Mellini, *Altichiero e Jacopo Avanzi,* pp. 36–7. Kruft, *Altichiero und Avanzo,* pp. 133–9. Gilbert, 'Giotto in Milan'. Simon, 'Altichiero Versus Avanzo', pp. 268–70. *Dix Siècles,* p. 89 (no. 74). Richards, 'Altichiero and Humanist Patronage', ch. 3.

7. **PARIS, BIBLIOTHEQUE NATIONALE**, MS LAT. 6069G: PETRARCH, *COMPENDIUM* OF THE *DE VIRIS ILLUSTRIBUS* (WITH ADDITIONAL MATERIAL BY LOMBARDO DELLA SETA, SCRIBE OF THIS MS). *THE BULL OF PADUA PUSHING THE LION OF VENICE INTO THE SEA* (FO. AV). PARCHMENT. MS COMPLETED 9 DECEMBER 1380. (PL. 38)

DIMENSIONS OF MS 238 mm×174 mm

PROVENANCE Padua, Francesco da Carrara until 1388. Pavia, GianGaleazzo Visconti from 1388. Pavia, Sforza Library. Chateau de Blois, Louis XII of France, from 1499.

CONDITION Serious paint loss in some areas and general abrasion. Pricked for copying (see Simon, 'Altichiero Versus Avanzo', p. 268, n.).

PRINCIPAL REFERENCES Magagnato, *Da Altichiero a Pisanello,* p. 15. Pellegrin, 'Manuscrits de Pétrarque', pp. 374–5. Magagnato, *Arte e Civiltà,* pp. 86–8 and 109. Fiocco, 'La Rivincità', p. 285. Mellini, *Altichiero e Jacopo Avanzi,* p. 78. Kruft, *Altichiero und Avanzo,* pp. 138–9. Simon, 'Altichiero Versus Avanzo', p. 268. *Dix Siècles,* pp. 89–90 (no. 75). Richards, 'Altichiero and Humanist Patronage', ch. 3.

8. **RICHMOND, VIRGINIA. VIRGINIA MUSEUM OF FINE ARTS** (NO. 59.5). *CRUCIFIXION WITH STS JAMES, CATHERINE, ANTHONY ABBOT AND JEROME, AND TWO DONORS.* TEMPERA ON PANEL, *C.* 1385. (PLS. 124–7)

DIMENSIONS Central panel 32.4 cm×22.2 cm; wings each 31.1 cm×9.5 cm.

PROVENANCE Crown Prince Clemens (Wittelsbach) of Bavaria. Arthur and Margaret Glasgow Fund, from Newhouse Galleries, New York.

CONDITION Generally good. The triptych was cleaned and restored in 1981. The surface of the wings look to have been rubbed, with some loss of detail. The female donor was painted out and her face is lost. The male donor was painted over at some stage, probably not long after the painting was first completed and his drapery has lost some surface modelling. The drapery of the replacement donor was itself repainted at a later stage. The gold ground of the central panel is somewhat abraded. The frame was probably made in the same workshop as that of the Boi polyptych.

PRINCIPAL REFERENCES Briganti, 'Un Trittichetto di Altichiero', pp. 58–61. Mellini, *Altichiero e Jacopo Avanzi,* pp. 56–7. Kruft, *Altichiero und Avanzo,* pp. 142–3. Simon, 'Altichiero Versus Avanzo', p. 261, n. Richards, 'A Re-used Altarpiece'.

9. **VERONA, S. ANASTASIA, CAVALLI CHAPEL**. *THREE MEMBERS OF THE CAVALLI FAMILY PRESENTED TO THE VIRGIN AND CHILD BY STS GEORGE, MARTIN AND JAMES THE GREAT.* FRESCO, *C.* 1370. (PLS. 16–20)

DIMENSIONS *c.* 5.35 m×3.66 m.

CONDITION The lower right-hand corner was lost when the tomb of Federigo Cavalli was erected *c.* 1390, though it is clear from the comparative neatness of the break in Altichiero's *intonaco* that some care was taken to ensure the fresco suffered as little as possible. At the same time, or possibly later, the lower edge of Altichiero's plaster along the whole length of the fresco was cut, something covered over by the rather perfunctory lower border, visible in older photographs, which was removed during the 1968 restoration of the whole chapel. The general condition of the surviving portions is better than that of the lower-wall frescoes. The metalled surfaces of the armour worn by the donors and St George have been abraded and blackened, and most of the dark blue-green curtain with red motifs that hangs across the background arcade has been lost, some of it since the photographs published by Mellini were taken (e.g. the area round St George's legs). Much of the architectural detail in the upper part of the fresco is illegible, and the heraldic horses in the gables are in very poor condition. The vault above the south wall of the chapel seems to have leaked, resulting in the three white streaks which run down the left side of the fresco. The surface has suffered a number of minor scratches and abrasions.

PRINCIPAL REFERENCES Corso, 'La Cappella Cavalli'. Magagnato, *Arte e Civiltà,* pp. 75–6. Pettenella, *Altichiero,* pp. 52–5. Kruft, *Altichiero und Avanzo,* pp. 127–30. Mellini, *Altichiero e Jacopo Avanzi,* pp. 38–40. Cuppini, 'L'Arte Gotica', pp. 316–21.

10. **VERONA, CASTELVECCHIO**. *CORONATION OF THE VIRGIN*. FRESCO (DETACHED) AND FOUR LAYERS OF SINOPIE, *C.* 1385–90. ARCH BORDER, FOUR PROPHETS. (PL. 121)

DIMENSIONS Lunette 160 cm × 265 cm; border 425 cm × 84 cm

PROVENANCE Verona, S. Fermo Maggiore, tomb of Aventino Fracastoro. Aventino died in 1368, but a plaque below the sarcophagus records a later date

DOCTOR AVENTINUS MEDICA CLARIS SIMUSARTE
NATA FRECASTORE LUX GENEROSA TRIBUS
ASTRA POLI NOVIT NOVITQUE LATENCIA RERUM
EIUS IN HOC TUMULO CORPORIS OSSA IACENT
QUEM MERITIS QUISQUE DOCTAVIT SCALIGER HEROS
UTILE CONSILIUM CIVIBUS ET DOMINIS
SUB DECIES OCTO QUINIS CUM MILLE TRECENT
TIS IN MEDIO CHIRON MENSE NOVEMBRIS ER/
AT.

Wolters (*Scultura Veneziana Gotica*, p.207) suggests a date for the tomb itself closer to the date of Aventino's death, on the grounds of its 'rapporti stilistici con un gran numero di opere veneziane del terzo quarto del Trecento'.

CONDITION The lunette fresco, detached in 1958, has lost around half of its *intonaco*. The remaining sections are in poor condition, to the extent that past interpretations of the iconography have been as wide-ranging as the attributions (late Turone to early Stefano, via Altichiero and Martino). The version of the *Coronation* depicted here is one involving God the Father as well as Christ and the Virgin. What cannot be seen with any certainty is whether the Virgin is here crowned by Christ alone or by Father and Son together. As is pointed out in the full discussion in Varanini (*Gli Scaligeri*, p. 546), examples of both versions can be found amongst Martino's works in Veronese churches. Simeoni's attribution of this fresco to Martino himself is, however, not persuasive.

PRINCIPAL REFERENCES Simeoni, *Verona,* p. 243. Sandberg-Vavalà, *La Pittura Veronese,* p. 366. Magagnato, *Da Altichiero a Pisanello,* pp. 15–16. Wolters, *Scultura Veneziana Gotica,* p. 207. Varanini, *Gli Scaligeri,* pp. 545–7.

11. **VERONA, CASTELVECCHIO.** POLYPTYCH: *MADONNA AND CHILD WITH STS JAMES, ANTHONY ABBOT, JOHN, CHRISTOPHER AND TWO DONORS.* TEMPERA ON PANEL, *C.* 1385. (PLS. 122–3)

DIMENSIONS Central panel 95 cm×38.5 cm; side panels each 87 cm×23 cm

PROVENANCE Zanardi Chapel, Boi di Caprino

CONDITION There has been some paint loss on parts of the polyptych. This seems to have affected the right side of the panel more than the left. The draperies of Sts John and Christopher and of the female donor have lost considerable areas of surface modelling and colour. The gold ground has also been damaged in certain areas all over the panel, with creasing and cracking above St John and a missing area above St James. The central section has a long crack running through the Madonna's face. The outer elements of the frame have lost their forward mouldings, and the whole of the predella frame is missing. The polyptych, which had been heavily repainted (see Magagnato, *Da Altichiero a Pisanello*), was restored and cleaned for the 1958 exhibition in the Castelvecchio. The frame is very like that of Paolo Veneziano's S. Chiara polyptych of 1354–8 (Venice, Accademia, pol. no. 21) and a smaller altarpiece attributed to Guariento (Bergamo, private collection).

PRINCIPAL REFERENCES Sandberg-Vavalà, *La Pittura Veronese,* p. 263. Toesca, *Il Trecento,* p. 792. Magagnato, *Da Altichiero a Pisanello,* pp. 12–13 and 14. Zeri, 'Un'Aggiunta', pp. 62–3. Arslan, 'Una Tavola di Altichiero', p. 104. Pettenella, *Altichiero,* pp. 58–9. Mellini, *Altichiero e Jacopo Avanzi,* 1965 p. 82. Kruft, *Altichiero und Avanzo,* p. 143. Richards, 'A Re-used Altarpiece'.

12. **VERONA, LOGGIA OF CANSIGNORIO DELLA SCALA** (SALA GRANDE). (I) SCENES FROM THE *DE BELLO JUDAICO* OF FLAVIUS JOSEPHUS (LOST). (II) TWO *TRIUMPHS* (LOST). (III) *PORTRAITS OF MEMBERS OF THE DELLA SCALA FAMILY AND OTHER NOTABLES* (LOST). (IV). *BUSTS OF ROMAN EMPERORS,* FRESCO, *C.* 1364–70. (PLS. 1–15)

DIMENSIONS The upper-hall interior measures *c.* 38.2 m×*c.* 9.7 m in plan. The walls are *c.* 6.9 m high. The south-west wall, excluding the window, is *c.* 6.4 m wide. The surviving surface of the soffit border averages *c.* 70 cm in width.

FRESCOES (IV) Names in brackets denote a missing or largely destroyed head included on the evidence of the *Historia Imperialis* sequence. References to *HI* MS sources are all to Vat. Chigi I. vii. 259 unless otherwise specified.

SPANDRELS (CONJECTURAL) (1. Julius Caesar, 2. Augustus, 3. Tiberius, 4. Caligula, 5. Claudius, 6. Nero, 7. Galba, 8. Otho, 9. Vitellius, 10. Vespasian, 11. Titus, 12. Domitian)

SOFFITS 0 = south-east window; 1–11 = windows of north-east wall
0.1 (Nerva)
0.2 (Trajan)
0.3 (Antoninus Pius)
0.4 (Marcus Aurelius)
1.1 (Lucius Verus)
1.2 (Commodus)
1.3 (Pertinax)
1.4 (D.Julianus)

2.1 **Hadrian.** Illegible fragment of inscription at top. Identified by Mellini in 1959 but described by him in 1965 just as 'imperatore romano'. The features bear some resemblance to those of the coin portraits. *HI* inscription (Verona, Biblioteca Capitolare, cod.CCIV, fo.10r) HADRIANUS AUGUSTUS. Identical to the inscriptions on some coins (see Robertson, *Roman Imperial Coins*, vol. II, pp. xlixff. and p. liii). Restoration has left the face with less of the profile than was visible in the photographs published by Mellini in 1959 and 1965.
2.2 **Geta.** Inscription legible in 1959 as (left, faint) GET* (top) ANTONI* (right) G (Aug?). *HI* inscription (fo.3v) GETA ANTONINUS CAESAR P P M. Not based on a coin inscription. The inauthentic ANTONINUS of the *HI* is drawn from the *Historia Augusta*, whose text Giovanni follows closely in the first section of his account (compare with *SHA*, *Geta* II, 6). The *HI* portrait is probably based on early coin portraits of Geta, minted in Septimius Severus's time (see Robertson, *Roman Imperial Coins*, vol. III, pls. 22–3). Facial features of fresco heavily abraded. Identified by Mellini in 1965.
2.3 (Septimius Severus)
2.4 **Sabina.** Inscription legible in 1959 (barely decipherable in present condition) as (left) *ABINA (right) AVGVSTA. Identified by Mellini in 1959. *HI* inscription (Verona, Bibl. Cap. cod.CCIV, fo.10r) SABINA AUGUSTA – identical to the inscriptions on many coins (see Robertson, *Roman Imperial Coins*, vol. II, pp. lxixff.). The condition of this head is reasonable, though the nose and part of the mouth have been lost in the process of removing repainted areas.
3.1 **Caracalla.** Inscription legible in 1959 (visible but less easily read in present condition) as (left)******N (top) VS. ANT*N (i.e. Bassianus Marcus Antonius). Identified by Mellini in 1965 as 'Marco Antonio Bassiano'. *HI* inscription (fo. 4r) IMP BASSIANUS MARCUS ANTONINUS AUG. The name BASSIANUS occurs on no coins but is found both in the *Historia Augusta* (*SHA*, *Caracalla* I) and in Eutropius (*Breviarum*, bk.VIII, 20: 'M . . . Aurelius Antoninus Bassianus, idemque Caracalla' Giovanni refers to him as 'Caracalla' in his text, e.g. fo. 4r, col. 2 l. 9). Portrait almost certainly not copied from a coin (see discussion in chapter 2 above), and for the coinage, Robertson, *Roman Imperial Coins*, vol. III, pl. 24. Nos.74 and 77 have a similar treatment of the beard to the *HI* portrait. One of the best preserved of the series – only the dark infill and the inscription have been seriously damaged.
3.2 **Macrinus**. No inscription is or was legible on this fresco, but from its position, following Caracalla's portrait as in the *HI*, and resembling the *HI* drawing with its full cheek and jawline (fo. 4v), there is no reason to doubt that this is Macrinus.
3.3 (Diadumenianus)
3.4 (Elagabalus)
4.1 **Faustina Senior.** Inscription legible in 1959, largely illegible in present condition, as (left) DIVA FAV (right) STINA, Identified by Mellini in 1959. No surviving *HI* portrait (but the inscription DIVA FAVSTINA is found on coins). Fairly well preserved, except for paint losses down the profile and on the infill and inscription. The surrounding frame has also suffered some damage.
4.2 **Severus Alexander.** Inscription legible in 1959 as (left) IMP*** (top) ALE***. Identified by Mellini in 1959 as 'Antonio' and in 1965 as 'Severus Alexander'. *HI* portrait fo. 6. The fresco was in poor condition in 1959, with most of the facial detail lost.
4.3 **Maximinus.** Inscription legible in 1959 as (left) *XIMINV (top) PIV* (i.e., Maximinus Pius [Augustus Germanicus]). Identified by Mellini in 1965. *HI* (fo. 11r) inscription MAXIMINUS PIUS AUG GERM. Identical to inscriptions on some issues of coinage. *HI* portrait closely based on coins (see Robertson, *Roman Imperial Coins*, vol. III, pl. 52).
4.4 **Maximus.** Inscription legible in 1959, and partly in present condition, as (left) MAXIMINVS (top) AVG (right) CAESAR PP. Identified by Mellini in 1959 and 1965 as 'Massimino' and, erroneously, by Schmitt ('Zur Wiederbelebung', fig. 31) as 'Maximinus Thrax', Maximus's father and the subject of 4.3. The source for the incorrect *Maximinus* is the *HI* (fo. 10v), where the inscription is MAXIMINUS AUG CAESAR PP, which resembles the inscriptions on Maximus's coins no more than does the portrait drawing. Fairly well preserved, with some paint losses about the head.

5.1 **Gordian I.** Inscription legible in 1959 (partially in present condition) as (left) IMP*GORDIA (top) NVS ANT (right) ONINVS: IVS*. Identified by Mellini in 1959 as 'Gordiano' and 1965 as 'Gordiano Antonino', and, less vaguely but erroneously, by Schmitt ('Zur Wiederbelebung', fig. 38) as Gordian III. *HI* (fo. 12r) inscription IMP GORDIANUS ANTONINUS IUSTE AUG. Inscription not coin-based. The IUSTE of the *HI* is probably Giovanni's reflection of the praise of Gordian in the *Historia Augusta*. Giovanni's account is substantially based on the highly inaccurate and fanciful Gordian sections. Compare *HI* (fo. 12r, l. 41ff.) and *SHA, Gordiani Tres* III. The ANTONINUS of the *HI* is incorrect and should be ANTONIUS. The same mistake occurs in the *Historia Augusta*. The *HI* portrait, not coin-based, reflects the great age of Gordian I, recorded in the literary sources (Herodian, *History* VII, 5, 2), more than do the coins (which are perhaps partly based on the coinage of Maximinus; see Robertson, *Roman Imperial Coins*, vol. III, pl. 56). There is no doubt, from the evidence of the inscription as well as the fresco's place in the sequence, that this is a bust of Gordian I, not Gordian III as Schmitt thought. The anachronistic youthfulness of the portrait has little bearing on this.

5.2 (Gordian II)

5.3 **Pupienus.** Inscription legible in 1959 (illegible now) as (right) IENVS:AVG. The face, of which only the leading edge has survived restoration, is broadly in accordance with the coin portraits. Not identified by either Mellini or Schmitt. *HI* inscription (fo. 13r) IMP MAXIMUS PUPPIENUS AUG. Not coin-based. The whole left side of this quatrefoil has been lost, together with the back of the emperor's head. In addition, the area above the eyes is completely abraded. It can be argued (see chapter 2 above) that in this case Altichiero had access to coins not available to Giovanni.

5.4 **Balbinus.** Inscription legible as (left) CLODIVS (top) BALBINV (right) SAVGVSTVS. *HI* inscription (fo. 13r) CLODIUS BALBINUS AUGUSTUS. The source for the incorrect name by both Giovanni de Matoci and, following him, Altichiero is the *Historia Augusta* (*SHA, Gordiani Tres* X, 1 and XXII, 1). Quite well preserved, though the mouth has been lost.

6.1 **Gordian III**. No inscription was legible in 1959, but the appearance of the portrait, which had even in 1959 lost its profile, is still obviously that of a very young man, which is right for this emperor. Giovanni de Matoci's drawing (fo. 14r) has the same characteristic, as do many coin portraits.

6.2 **Philip I.** Inscription legible as (left) IMP.M.IVL.PHIL (top) LIPPVS. CA (right) ESAR.AVG. Misread by Mellini in 1959 and 1965 as 'Tullio Filippo'. *HI* inscription (fo. 15v) IMP M IUL PHILLIPUS CAESAR AUG. Reasonably close to inscriptions on some coin issues (e.g. IMP (CAES) M IUL PHILLIPUS AUG). The *HI* portrait is evidently based on a coin example with a radiate portrait bust (see Robertson, *Roman Imperial Coins*, vol. III, pl. 67. Altichiero's fresco has a laureate head). The fresco has suffered damage down the profile, and was evidently heavily repainted.

6.3 (Philip II)

6.4 (Decius)

7.1 (T.Gallus)

7.2 (Volusianus)

7.3 (Valerianus I)

7.4 (Valerianus II)

8.1 (Gallienus)

8.2 (Claudius Gothicus)

8.3 (Quintillus)

8.4 **Aurelian.** Inscription legible in 1959 (now illegible) as (left) *URELIAN** (top) AVG**T (right) VS.IMPR. Identified by Mellini in 1965 and by Schmitt. *HI* inscription (fo. 24v) AURELIANUS AUGUSTUS IMPR. The inscription has the same elements as those of some issues of coinage but not in the same order (e.g. IMP AURELIANUS AUG). Portrait probably based on coin (see Robertson, *Roman Imperial Coins*, vol. IV, pl. 31, nos. 17–28). The fresco portrait is almost illegible in its present condition (compare Mellini, *Altichiero e Jacopo Avanzi*, pl. 13).

9.1 **Tacitus**. Inscription legible as (left) IMP**M* (top) *ACIT** (right) *AVGVSTV*. Radiate, like coin portraits and facially similar. *HI* inscription (fo. 27r) IMP C M C TACITUS AUG. Inscription close to some coins (e.g. IMP C M CL TACITUS AUG). Portrait reasonably close to those on coins of Roman mint (cited inscription is from that mint. See Robertson, *Roman Imperial Coins*, vol. IV, pl. 36, no. 18, for example). Paint loss round eye and ear, but general features still legible.
9.2 (Florianus)
9.3 (Probus)
9.4 **Carus.** Inscription legible as (left) IMP CARVS (top) INVICTV* (right) AVGVSTVS. Identified by Mellini in 1959 and 1965. *HI* inscription (fo.29r) IMP CARUS INVICTUS AUG. Neither inscription nor portrait coin-based. Badly abraded, but general appearance still discernible.
10.1 (Carinus)
10.2 (Numerianus)
10.3 (Diocletian)
10.4 (Maximian)
11.1 (Constantius)
11.2 (Helena). A fresco of Helena is assumed on the basis of her inclusion in the sequence of *HI* portraits (fo. 37r).
11.3 (Galerius or M. Daia)
11.4 (Licinius)

GENERAL CONDITION Apart from the specific losses mentioned above, the border has suffered considerable overall damage and was heavily, though not, to judge from Mellini's 1959 photographs, insensitively, repainted. Whole areas of several arches had clearly lost all their original paint. In many instances the surrounding dark infill of the quatrefoils and the inscriptions (most of which had been touched up at least) have fared rather worse than the busts themselves.

PRINCIPAL REFERENCES Mellini, 'La "Sala Grande"'. Mellini, *Altichiero e Jacopo Avanzi,* pp. 25–37. Kruft, *Altichiero und Avanzo,* pp. 131–3. Cuppini, 'L'Arte Gotica', pp. 310–18. Schmitt, 'Zur Wiederbelebung'. Avesani, 'Preumanesimo Veronese', pp. 132ff.. Richards, 'Altichiero and Humanist Patronage', pp. 13–91 and 205–13. Brugnoli, '"Donna e Regina"', p. 221. Varanini, *Gli Scaligeri,* pp. 318–20. Benati, *Jacopo Avanzi,* pp. 83–92.

13. **VERONA. S. ZENO MAGGIORE**. *CRUCIFIXION AND FIVE SAINTS*. FRESCO, 1380s. (PL. 120)

DIMENSIONS *c.* 2.90 m × *c.* 2.60 m

CONDITION Generally poor. The face and drapery of the Virgin are badly abraded, and much of the surface modelling of the donor has been lost. The figure of Christ has lost a great deal of definition. There are a number of blank patches in the sky and one of the angels has been virtually erased. Parts of the border (lower left corner) are still in good condition. Areas of the fresco seem to have been touched up since the photograph published by Sandberg-Vavalà was taken. In her plate the fresco looks almost wholly ruined.

PRINCIPAL REFERENCES Simeoni, *San Zeno,* p. 77. Sandberg-Vavalà, *La Pittura Veronese,* pp. 190–2. Mellini, *Altichiero e Jacopo Avanzi,* pp. 81–4. Richards, 'A Re-used Altarpiece'.

BIBLIOGRAPHY

Acta Inedita: Charles IV, Innsbruck, 1891.

Adami, C. 'Per la Biografia di Giovanni Mansionario', *Italia Medioevale e Umanistica*, 26 (1982), pp. 347–63.

Allen, A. M. *A History of Verona,* London, 1910.

Alvarez, G. Bresciani. 'L'Architettura e l'Arredo della Cappella di S. Giacomo ora detta di S. Felice al Santo', *Il Santo*, 5 (1965), pp. 131–41.

'La Basilica del Santo nei Restauri e Ampliamenti dal Quattrocento al Tardo Barocco' in Lorenzoni, ed., *L'Edificio del Santo*, pp. 83–124.

Arcangeli, F. 'Affreschi Veronesi di Jacopino di Francesco', *Paragone*, 9 (1950), pp. 35–42.

Arnaldi, G. 'Il Primo Secolo dello Studio di Padova' in Folena, ed., *Storia della Cultura Veneta*, pp. 1–18.

Arslan, E. 'Una Tavola di Altichiero e un Affresco di Turone', *Commentarii*, 11 (1960), pp. 103–6.

Ashdown, C. H. *British and Continental Arms and Armour*, London, 1970.

Atiya, A. S. *The Crusade in the Later Middle Ages*, London, 1938.

Avena, A. 'Guglielmo da Pastrengo e gli Inizi dell'Umanesimo in Verona', *Atti Mem. Accad. Agr. Sc. Lett. Verona*, 4.6 (1907), pp. 229ff.

Avesani, R. 'Il Preumanesimo Veronese' in Folena, ed., *Storia della Cultura Veneta*, pp. 111–41.

Azarii, P. *Liber Gestorum in Lombardia* in *RIS*², vol. XVI.

Ballarin, A. *Pinacoteca di Vicenza*, Vicenza, 1982.

Barbieri, F. *Il Museo Civico di Vicenza: Dipinti e Scultore dal XIV al XV Secoli,* Venice, 1962.

Baron, H. *From Petrarch to Leonardo Bruni,* Chicago and London, 1968.

The Crisis of the Early Renaissance, Princeton, 1955.

Baxandall, M. *Giotto and the Orators,* Oxford, 1971 and 1986.

'Guarino, Pisanello and Manuel Chrysoloras', *Journal of the Warburg and Courtauld Institutes*, 28 (1965), pp. 183–204.

Bayley, C. C. 'Petrarch, Charles IV, and the "Renovatio Imperii"', *Speculum*, 17 (1942), pp. 323–41.

Benati, D. *Jacopo Avanzi nel Rinnovamento della Pittura Padana del Secondo '300,* Bologna, 1992.

Berenson, B. *Italian Painters of the Renaissance,* Oxford, 1907.

Bernardo, A. S. *Petrarch, Scipio and the Africa,* Baltimore, 1962.

Berrigan, J. R. 'Benzo d'Alessandria and the Cities of Northern Italy', *Studies in Mediaeval and Renaissance History*, 4 (1967), pp. 125–93.

Bertin, B. 'I Carraresi e la Fondazione di Cappelle Affrescate' in *I Dondi e la Padova dei Carraresi*, exh. cat., Padua, 1988.
Bertolini, V. 'Cansignorio e la Città Marmorina' in Varanini, ed., *Gli Scaligeri*, pp. 255–60.
Bettini, S. *Giusto de'Menabuoi e l'Arte del Trecento*, Padua, 1944.
Giusto de'Menabuoi nel Battistero del Duomo di Padova, Venice, 1960.
Bettini, S. and L. Puppi. *La Chiesa degli Eremitani di Padova*, Vicenza, 1970.
Biadego, G. 'Per la Storia della Cultura Veronese nel XIV Secolo: Antonio da Legnago e Rinaldo da Villafranca. Nuove Ricerche', *Atti Istit. Ven.*, 62.2 (1903–4), pp. 1049ff.
'Un Maestro di Grammatica Amico del Petrarca (Rinaldo Cavalchini da Villafranca)', *Atti Istit. Ven.*, 57.2 (1898–9), pp. 261ff.
Biancolini, G. B. *Cronica della Città di Verona descritta da Pier Zagata, colla Continuazione di Jacopo Rizzoni*, 2 vols., Verona, 1745–7.
Notizie Storiche delle Chiese di Verona, Verona, 1749–71.
Billanovich, Giuseppe. *Petrarca Letterato*, vol. I, *Lo Scrittoio del Petrarca*, Rome, 1947.
'I Primi Umanisti e l'Antichità Classica' in Bolger, ed., *Classical Influences*, pp. 57–66.
'Petrarch and the Textual Tradition of Livy', *Journal of the Warburg and Courtauld Institutes*, 14 (1951), pp. 137–208.
Billanovich, Giuseppe and E. Pellegrin, 'Una nuova Lettera di Lombardo della Seta e la prima Fortuna delle Opere del Petrarca' in C. Henderson, ed., *Classical, Mediaeval and Renaissance Studies in Honor of Berthold Louis Ullman*, Rome, 1964, vol. II, pp. 215–36.
Billanovich, Guido. 'Il Preumanesimo Padovano' in Folena, ed., *Storia della Cultura Veneta*, pp. 19–110.
Billanovich, M. C. Ganguzza. 'La Cappella della Madonna Mora e dell'Arca in un Nuovo Documento del XIV Secolo', *Il Santo*, 19 (1979), pp. 67–79.
Bishop, M. *Petrarch and his World*, London, 1964.
Bober, P. P. and R. O. Rubinstein, *Renaissance Artists and Antique Sculpture*, London and Oxford, 1986.
Boccazzi, F. Z. *Tommaso da Modena*, Milan, 1966.
Bolger, R. R., ed. *Classical Influences on European Culture, AD 500–1500*, Cambridge, 1971.
Bordin, B. 'I Frati del Santo e i Monasteri Femminili di Padova e del Veneto' in Poppi, ed., *Liturgia e Pietà*, pp. 419–64.
Borelli, G., ed.. *Chiese e Monasteri di Verona*, Verona, 1980.
Boskovits, M. *Pittura Fiorentina alla Vigilia del Rinascimento, 1370–1400*, Florence, 1975.
Briganti, G. 'Un Trittichetto di Altichiero', *Paragone*, 107 (1958), pp. 58–61.
Bronstein, L. *Altichiero. L'Artiste et son Œuvre*, Paris, 1932.
Brown, H. H. *Studies in the History of Venice*, London, 1907.
Bruère, R. T. 'Lucan and Petrarch's Africa', *Classical Philology*, 56 (1961).
Brugnoli, P. P. 'Donna e Regina de le Terre Italice': Realtà e Immagine di Verona Scaligera', in Varanini, ed. *Gli Scaligeri*, pp. 215–24.
Buddensieg, T. 'Gregory the Great, the Destroyer of Pagan Idols', *Journal of the Warburg and Courtauld Institutes*, 28 (1965), pp. 44–65.
Callman, E. *Apollonio di Giovanni*, Oxford, 1974.
Cappelletti, G. *La Basilica di S. Anastasia*, Verona, 1981.
Carli, E. *La Pittura Senese del Trecento*, Venice, 1981.
Carrara, M. *Gli Scaligeri*, Milan, 1966.
'Gli Scrittori Latini dell'Età Scaligera' in Cavallari *et al.*, *Verona*, pp. 5–78.

Cartolari, A. *Cenni sopra varie Famiglie Illustri di Verona,* Verona, 1855.

Cavallari, V., Gazzola, P., Scolari, A. *Verona e il suo Territorio*, vol. III, book 1, Verona, 1975; vol. III, book 2, Verona, 1969.

Cenci, C. 'Bonifacio Lupi di Soragna e i Frati Minori', *Archivium Franciscanum Historicum* (1964), pp. 90–109.

Cerri, F., ed. *Puccio Capanna*, exh. cat., Assisi, 1989.

Cessi, F. 'Monetazione e Medaglistica dei Carraresi' in Grossato, ed., *Da Giotto al Mantegna*, pp. 86–9.

Châtelet, A. *Van Eyck,* New York, 1980.

Chronicon Estense, in *RIS*², vol. XV.

Chronicon Parmense, ed. G. Bonazzi, in *RIS*², vol. IX.

Chronicon Veronense, see Paride da Cerea.

Cipolla, C. *Antiche Chronache Veronesi. Monumenti Storici Pubblicati dalla R. Deputazione Veneta di Storia Patria*, S. III, *Cronache e Diarii*, II, Venice, 1890.

Compendio della Storia Politica di Verona, Verona, 1889; reprinted Mantua, 1976.

Notizie intorno a Leonardo da Quinto Giudice e Letterato Veronese del Secolo XIV, Verona, 1885.

'Ricerche Storiche intorno alla Chiesa di Santa Anastasia in Verona', *L'Arte,* 17, pp. 181–97, pp. 396–414; (1914), pp. 91–106; 17 (1915), pp. 157–71; 19 (1916) pp. 115–24, pp. 234–40.

Cognasso, F. *I Visconti,* Milan, 1966.

Cole, B. *Agnolo Gaddi*, Oxford, 1977.

Coletti, L. 'Studi sulla Pittura del Trecento a Padova. Altichiero e Avanzo', *Rivista d'Arte* (1931).

L'Arte di Tomaso da Modena, 2nd edn, Venice, 1962–3

I Primitivi, Novara, 1947.

Conforto da Costoza. *Frammenti di Storia Vicentina (AA.1371–1387)* in *RIS*², vol. XIII, part 1.

Corna da Soncino, F. *Fioretto de le Antiche Croniche de Verona,* 1477; ed. G. P. Marchi, and p. Brugnoli, Verona, 1973.

Corso, G. 'La Cappella Cavalli in S. Anastasia Verona', *Pro Verona* (1910), no. 5, pp. 3–5; no. 6, pp. 10–11; no. 7, pp. 7–8.

Cortese, D. 'Il Petrarca e le Traslazioni di Sant'Antonio di Padova', *Il Santo,* 18 (1978), pp. 313–23.

Cosenza, M. E. *Francesco Petrarca and the Revolution of Cola di Rienzo,* Chicago, 1913.

Cox, E. L. *The Green Count of Savoy. Amadeus VI and Transalpine Savoy in the Fourteenth Century,* Princeton, 1967.

Cuenod. J. 'Les Apparitions de Saint Jacques et deux Fresques d'Altichiero', *Gazette des Beaux-Arts*, 52 (1910), pp. 293–315.

Cuppini, M. T. 'Alcune Pitture del Trecento a Verona', *Commentarii*, 11 (1960), pp. 237–43.

'L'Arte Gotica a Verona nei Secoli XIV-XV' in Cavallari *et al.*, *Verona e il suo Territorio*, vol. II, pp. 213–366.

'Pitture del Trecento a Verona', *Commentarii*, 12 (1961), pp. 75–83.

'Pitture del Trecento a Verona II', *Commentarii*, 12 (1961), pp. 241–4.

Dal Pozzo, B. *Le Vite de' Piu' Eccellenti Pittori, Scultori e Architetti Veronesi,* Verona, 1718.

D'Amico, R. and R. Grandi, eds. *Il Cantiere di San Petronio*, exh. cat., Bologna, 1987.

D'Arcais, F. *Guariento*, Venice, 1965.

'La Decorazione della Cappella di San Giacomo' in Semenzato, ed., *Pitture del Santo,* pp. 15–42.

'La Decorazione della Cappella di San Giorgio' in Semenzato, ed., *Pitture del Santo,* pp. 43–62.

'Jacopo da Verona e la Decorazione della Cappella Bovi in S. Michele a Padova', *Arte Veneta,* 27 (1973), pp. 9–24.
'La Pittura nelle Chiese e nei Monasteri di Verona' in Borelli, ed., *Chiese e Monasteri di Verona,* pp. 443–532.
'Presenza di Giotto al Santo' in Semenzato, ed., *Pitture del Santo,* pp. 3–13.
Delaney, B. L. 'Giusto de'Menabuoi in Lombardy', *Art Bulletin* (1976), pp. 19–35.
Dellwing, H. *Studien zur Baukunst der Bettelorden im Veneto*, Munich, 1970.
Dix Siècles d'Enluminure Italienne – VIe–XVIe Siècles, exh. cat., Paris, Bibliothèque Nationale, 1984.
Dizionario Biografico degli Italiani, Rome, 1960– .
Ederle, G. *Dizionario Cronologico Bio-Bibliografico dei Vescovi di Verona*, Verona, 1965.
Edwards, M. E. 'Altichiero as Architect', *Il Santo,* 29, fasc. 3 (1989), pp. 303–31.
'The Chapel of S. Felice in Padua as Gesamtkunstwerk', *Journal of the Society of Architectural Historians*, 47 (1985), pp. 160–76.
Encyclopaedia Judaica, 16 vols., Jerusalem, 1971.
Eutropius, *Breviarium Ab Urbe Condita*, ed. F. Ruehe, Leipzig, 1919.
Feldman, L. H. *Josephus and Modern Scholarship*, Berlin and New York, 1984.
Fernie, E. and P. Crossley, eds. *Medieval Architecture and its Intellectual Context – Studies in Honour of Peter Kidson*, London, 1990.
Filippini, F. and G. Zucchini. *Miniatori e Pittori a Bologna*, Florence, 1947.
Fiocco, G. 'La Rivincita di Altichiero', *Il Santo,* 3 (1963), pp. 283–9.
'"Storia e Storie" della Cappella di S. Giacomo al Santo', *Il Santo,* 6, (1966), pp. 261–6.
Folena, G., ed. *Storia della Cultura Veneta,* volume II, *Il Trecento*. Vicenza, 1976.
Folena, G. and G. L. Mellini. *Bibbia Istoriata della Fine del Trecento*, Venice, 1962.
Förster, E. *Die St Georgskapelle zu Padua*, Berlin, 1841.
I Dipinti nella Cappella di S. Giorgio, trans. P. Selvatico, Padua, 1846.
Foss, C. *Roman Historical Coins*, London, 1990.
Fox, J. *Roman Coins and How to Collect Them*, London, 1983.
Franzin, E., ed. *Padova e le sue Mura*, Padua, 1982.
Frattaroli, P. 'Le Decorazioni di interni in Castelvecchio' in Varanini, ed., *Gli Scaligeri*, pp. 237–43.
Gargan, L. *Cultura e Arte nel Veneto al Tempo di Petrarca*, Padua, 1978.
'Oliviero Forzetta e la Diffusione dei Testi Classici nel Veneto al Tempo di Petrarca' in Bolger, ed., *Classical Influences,* pp. 73–80.
'Il Preumanesimo a Vicenza, Treviso e Venezia' in Folena, ed., *Storia della Cultura Veneta,* pp. 142–70.
Garibotto, G. 'Un Amico del Petrarca (Gasparo Squaro dei Broaspini)', *Atti Mem. Accad. Agr. Sc. Lett. Verona*, 5.7 (1930), pp. 169ff.
Gasparotto, C. 'Gli Ultimi Affreschi venuti in Luce nella Reggia dei da Carrara e una Documentazione inedita sulla Camera di Camillo', *Atti e Memorie della Accademia Patavina di SS. LL. AA.,* 81 (1968/9), pp. 237–61.
'La Reggia dei da Carrara', *Atti e Memorie della Accademia Patavina di SS. LL. AA.,* 79 (1966/7), pp. 71–116.
Gatari, G. B. *Cronaca Carrarese* in *RIS*², vol. XVII, part I, ed. A. Medin and G. Tolomei, Città di Castello, 1911.
Gerola, G. 'I Cavalieri Tedeschi ed i loro Ritratti e Stemmi dei Secoli XIV–XV in San Giorgetto di Verona', *Madonna Verona,* 6 (1912), pp. 198–209.

'L'Effigie di Luigi il Grande d'Ungheria in un Affresco a Padova', *Turismo d'Italia*, 3.6 (1929), pp. 17–20.
'Questioni Storiche d'Arte Veronese', *Madonna Verona*, 2 (1908).
Gibbs, R. *L'Occhio di Tomaso*, Treviso, 1981.
Tomaso da Modena: Painting in Emilia and the March of Treviso, 1340–1380, Cambridge, 1989.
'The Brussels Initial Master. From Proto-Renaissance to Northern Renaissance and Back', *Apollo*, 134 (1991), pp. 317–21.
'A Group of Bolognese Painters Active in the Veneto', *Burlington Magazine*, 124 (1982), pp. 77–86.
'Images of Higher Education in Fourteenth-Century Bologna' in Fernie and Crossley, ed., *Medieval Architecture*, pp. 269–82.
'Recent Literature on Jacopo Avanzi', *Apollo* (December 1994), pp. 61–2.
'Two Families of Painters in Bologna in the Later Fourteenth Century', *Burlington Magazine*, 121 (1979), pp. 560–8.
Gilbert, C. 'The Fresco by Giotto in Milan', *Arte Lombarda*, 47/8 (1977), pp. 31–72.
Gloria, A. *Documenti in editi intorno al Petrarca con alcuni cenni della casa di lui in Arquà e della Reggia dei da Carrara in Padova (discorso tenuto per l'inaugurazione del Museo Petrarchescho di Arquà)*, Padua, 1878.
Monumenti dell'Università di Padova (1318–1405), Padua, 1888.
Gonzati, B. *La Basilica di S. Antonio di Padova*, 2 vols., Padua, 1852.
Gorini, G. 'Iconografia Monetale e Cultura Figurativa a Padova nei Secoli XIV e XV' in Grossato, ed., *Da Giotto al Mantegna*, pp. 81–5.
Grandi, R. *I Monumenti dei Dottori e la Scultura a Bologna, 1267–1348*, Bologna, 1982.
Grossato, L., ed. *Da Giotto al Mantegna*, exh. cat., Padua, Palazzo della Ragione, 1974.
Guarino Veronese. *Epistolario*, ed. R. Sabbadini, Venice, 1915.
Hartley, C. G. *The Story of Santiago de Compostella*, London, 1912.
Hauser, A. *The Social History of Art*, 4 vols., London, 1962.
Hay, D. *The Italian Renaissance in its Historical Background*, Cambridge, 1970.
Hekscher, W. S. 'Relics of Pagan Antiquity in Mediaeval Settings', *Journal of the Warburg and Courtauld Institutes*, 1 (1937–8), pp. 204ff.
Herlihy, D. 'Mapping Households in Medieval Italy', *Catholic Historical Review* (1972).
'The Population of Verona in the First Century of Venetian Rule' in D. Hale, ed., *Renaissance Venice*, London, 1973, pp. 91–120.
Herodian, *History*, ed. and trans. C. R. Whittaker, Loeb Classical Texts, London and Cambridge, Mass. 1969.
Hoch, A. 'The Antique Origins of an Emperor by Simone Martini', *Paragone*, 443 (January 1987), pp. 42–7.
Hudson, P. 'Il Palazzo Scaligero di S. Maria Antica', in Varanini, ed., *Gli Scaligeri*, pp. 225–35
Hyde, J. K. *Padua in the Age of Dante*, Manchester, 1966.
James, M. R. *The Apocryphal New Testament*, first edn, Oxford, 1924; reprinted 1960.
Jannaco, C. 'Donato Casentinese Volgarizzatore del Petrarca', *Studi Petrarcheschi*, 1 (1948), pp. 185–94.
Jorga, N. 'Philippe de Mezières et la Croisade au XIVe Siècle', *Bibliothèque de l'Ecole des Hautes Etudes*, 109/10 (1895).
Josephus, Flavius. *The Jewish War*, trans. and ed. G. A. Williamson, Harmondsworth, 1959; revised. edn 1981, by E. M. Smallwood.
Kaftal, G. *Iconography of the Saints in the Painting of North-East Italy*, Florence, 1978.

Keen, M. *Chivalry*, Yale, 1984.

Kent, J. P. C. 'Monumental Brasses – A New Classification of Military Effigies, *c.* 1360–*c.* 1485', *Journal of the British Archaeological Association*, 12 (1949).

Kohl, B. G. *Padua under the Carrara 1318–1405*, Baltimore & London 1998.

Kohl, B. G. 'Petrarch's Prefaces to *De Viris Illustribus*', *History and Theory*, 13 (1974), pp. 132–44.

Kohl, B. G. and R. G. Witt. *The Earthly Republic*, Manchester, 1978.

Krautheimer, R. *Lorenzo Ghiberti*, Princeton, 1956.

Rome. Profile of a City, 312–1308, Princeton, 1980.

Kruft, H. W. *Altichiero und Avanzo*, Bonn, 1966.

Larner, J. *Culture and Society in Italy, 1290–1420*, London, 1971.

Italy in the Age of Dante and Petrarch, London, 1980.

Lazzarini, L. 'La Cultura delle Signorie Venete e i Poeti di Corte' in Folena, ed., *Storia della Cultura Veneta*, vol. II, pp. 477–516.

Lenotti, T. *Verona nei suoi Antichi Rioni*, Verona, 1967.

Levi, E. *Francesco di Vannozzo e la Lirica nelle Corti Lombarde durante la seconda Metà del sec. XIV*, Florence, 1908.

Limentani, A. 'L'Epica in "Lengue de France": L'Entrée d'Espagne e Niccolo da Verona' in *Storia della Cultura Veneta – il Trecento*, Vicenza, 1976, pp. 338–68.

Livy. *Ab Urbe Condita*, trans. H. Betterson, B. Radice, and A. de Selincourt, 4 vols., Harmondsworth, 1960, 1965, 1976 and 1982.

Longhi, R. 'Due Pannelli del Seguito di Altichiero', *Paragone*, 107 (1958), pp. 64–5.

'Stefano Fiorentino', *Paragone* (January 1951), pp. 18–40.

Lorenzoni, G. 'Cenni per una Storia della Fondazione della Basilica alla Luce dei Documenti (con Ipotesi Interpretative)', in Lorenzoni, ed., *L'Edificio*, pp. 17–30.

ed. *L'Edificio del Santo di Padova*, Vicenza, 1981.

Lucco, M. '"Me Pinxit": Schede per un Catalogo del Museo Antoniano', *Il Santo*, 17 (1977), pp. 243–81

McHam, S. B. *The Chapel of St Anthony at the Santo and the Development of Venetian Renaissance Sculpture*, 1994.

Maffei, S. *Verona Illustrata*, Verona, 1731.

Magagnato, L. *Arte e Civiltà del Medioevo Veronese*, Turin, 1962.

ed. *Da Altichiero a Pisanello*, exh. cat., Verona, 1958.

Mandeville, J. *The Travels of Sir John Mandeville*, trans. and ed. C. W. R. D. Moseley, Harmondsworth, 1983.

Marangon, P. and C. Bellinati. 'La Basilica del Santo nei Documenti d'Archivio e Storico-Letterati dalle Origini al 1405' in Lorenzoni, ed., *L'Edificio*, pp. 187–228.

Marcianò, A. F. *Padova 1399*, Padua, 1980.

Mardersteig, G. 'I Ritratti del Petrarca e dei suoi Amici di Padova', *Italia Medioevale e Umanistica*, 17 (1974), pp. 251–80.

Martellotti, G., ed. *Petrarca – De Viris Illustribus*, Florence, 1962.

Matalon, S. and F. Mazzini. *Affreschi del Tre e Quattrocento in Lombardia*, Milan, 1958.

Matarosso, P. M., trans. and ed. *The Quest of the Holy Grail*, Harmondsworth, 1969, 1982.

Meiss, M. *French Painting in the Time of Jean de Berry: The Late XIV Century and the Patronage of the Duke*, 2nd edn, London, 1969.

'French and Italian Variations on an Early Fifteenth-century Theme: St Jerome in his Study', *Gazette des Beaux-Arts*, 62 (1963), pp. 147–70.

Mellini, G. L. *Altichiero e Jacopo Avanzi*, Milan, 1965.
Sculturi Veronesi del Trecento, Milan, 1971.
'Considerazioni su Probabile Rapporti tra Altichiero e Petrarca' in Grossato, ed., *Da Giotto a Mantegna*, pp. 51–4.
'Disegni di Altichiero e della sua Scuola', *Critica d'Arte,* 51 (1962), part 1, pp. 1–24.
'Disegni di Altichiero e della sua Scuola', *Critica d'Arte,* 53 (1962), part 2, pp. 9–19.
'La "Sala Grande" di Altichiero e Jacopo d'Avanzo', *Critica d'Arte,* 35 (1958), pp. 313–34.
Mellini, G. L. and G. Folena. *Bibbia Istoriata Padovana della Fine del Trecento*, Venice, 1962.
Michiel, M. A. *Notizie di Opere di Disegno,* ed. G. Frizzoni, Bologna, 1884.
Mommsen, T. E. *Petrarch's Testament,* Ithaca, 1957.
'Petrarch and the Decoration of the Sala Virorum Illustrium in Padua', *Art Bulletin,* 34 (1952), pp. 95–116.
'Petrarch and the Story of the Choice of Hercules', *Journal of the Warburg and Courtauld Institutes,* 16 (1953), pp. 178ff.
'Petrarch's Concept of the Dark Ages', *Speculum,* 17 (1942), pp. 226ff.
Montel, C. S. *Gli Affreschi Gotici Lombardi,* 2 vols., Milan, 1966.
Montobbio, L. *Splendore e Utopia nella Padova dei Carraresi*, Padua, 1988.
Moschetti, A. 'Due Antichi Ritratti di F. Petrarca', *Atti e Mem. R. Accad. SS. LL. AA. di Padova* (1928).
Moschini, G. *Dell'Origine e delle Vicende della Pittura in Padova*, Padua, 1826.
Nolhac, P. de. *Pétrarque et l'Humanisme*, Paris, 1907.
Norman, D., ed. *Siena, Florence and Padua: Art, Society and Religion, 1280–1400*, 2 vols., London, 1995.
Norwich, J. J. *A History of Venice*, Harmondsworth, 1983.
Offner, R. 'Four Panels, a Fresco, and a Problem', *Burlington Magazine,* 54 (1929), pp. 224–45.
Offner, R. and K. Steinweg. *A Corpus of Florentine Painting. The Fourteenth Century*, Section 4, vol. III, *Jacopo di Cione*, New York, 1965.
Orti-Manara, G. *Di Alcuni Antichi Veronesi Guerrieri che Fiorirono ai Tempi Scaligeri*, Verona, 1842.
Paatz, W. and E. *Die Kirchen von Florenz*, vol. I, Frankfurt, 1940.
Pallucchini, R. *La Pittura Veneziana del Trecento*, Venice and Rome, 1964.
Panofsky, E. *Renaissance and Renascences in Western Art,* Stockholm, 1960.
Panofsky, E. and F. Saxl. 'Classical Mythology in Medieval Art', *Metropolitan Museum Studies,* 4.2 (1933), pp. 228ff.
Paride da Cerea. *Chronicon Veronense. Adiecta et continuatio cuiusdam anonimi auctoris,* in *RIS*[1], cols. 617–59.
Pellegrin, E. 'Manuscrits de Pétrarque en France', *Italia Medioevale e Umanistica,* 4 (1961), pp. 373ff.
Perbellini, G. *Castelli Scaligeri,* Milan, 1982.
Pettenella, P. *Altichiero e la Pittura Veronese del Trecento*, Verona, 1961.
Pezzana, A. *Storia della Città di Parma*, vol. I, Parma, 1837.
Plant, M. 'Portraits and Politics in Padua: Altichiero's Frescoes in the S. Felice Chapel, S. Antonio', *Art Bulletin,* 63 (1981), pp. 406–25.
Poeschke, J. *Die Kirche San Francesco in Assisi und ihre Wandmalereien*, Munich, 1985.
Polidoro, V. *Le Religiose Memorie*, Venice, 1590.
Popham, A. E. and P. Pouncey, *Italian Drawings in the Department of Prints and Drawings in the British Museum. The Fourteenth and Fifteenth Centuries*, London, 1950.

Poppi, A., ed. *Liturgia, Pietà e Ministeri*, Vicenza, 1978.
Portenari, A. *Della Felicità di Padova*, Padua, 1623.
Ragghianti, C. L. *Pittura tra Giotto e Pisanello*, Ferrara, 1987.
Stefano da Ferrara, Florence, 1972.
Rasmo, N. *Affreschi Medievali Atesini*, Milan, 1971.
'Note sulla Pittura Giottesca Padovana nella Ragione Atesina' in Grossato, ed. *Da Giotto a Mantegna*, pp. 63–7.
Richards, J. C. 'Altichiero and Humanist Patronage at the Courts of Verona and Padua 1360–1390', Ph.D. thesis, University of Glasgow, 1988.
'A Re-used Altarpiece by Altichiero', *Apollo* (December 1995), pp. 48–54.
Riedmann, J. 'Gli Scaligeri e il Mondo Germanico', in Varanini, ed., *Gli Scaligeri*, pp. 25–33.
Rerum Italicarum Scriptores [*RIS*[1]], 25 vols., ed., L. A. Muratori, Milan, 1723–51.
Rerum Italicarum Scriptores [*RIS*[2]], ed. A. Medin and G. Tolomei, Citta di Castello, 1911.
Riva, F. 'Il Trecento Volgare' in Cavallari *et al.*, eds., *Verona,* vol. III, bk 2, pp. 85–185.
Robertson, A. S. *Roman Imperial Coins in the Hunter Coin Cabinet*, vol. I, Glasgow, 1962; vol. II, Glasgow, 1971; vol. III, Glasgow, 1977; vol. IV, Glasgow, 1978; vol. V, Glasgow, 1982.
Robey, D. 'P. P. Vergerio the Elder: Republicanism and Civic Values in the Work of an Early Humanist', *Past and Present,* 58 (1973).
Rossini, E. 'La Città e i suoi Problemi' in Cavallari *et al.*, eds., *Verona*, vol. III, bk 1, pp. 1–80.
'La Signoria Scaligera' in Cavallari *et al.*, eds., *Verona*, vol. III, bk 1, pp. 81–310.
'La Signoria Scaligera dopo CanGrande' in Cavallari *et al.*, eds., *Verona*, vol. III, bk 1, pp. 453–726.
'Il Territorio e i suoi Problemi', in Cavallari *et al.*, eds., *Verona*, vol. III, bk 1, pp. 349–449.
Rubin, P.L. *Giorgio Vasari: Art and History*, New Haven and London, 1995.
Rubinstein, N. 'Political Ideas in Sienese Art: the Frescoes by Ambrogio Lorenzetti and Taddeo di Bartolo in the Palazzo Pubblico', *Journal of the Warburg and Courtauld Institutes*, 21 (1958), pp. 179–207.
Sabbadini, R. *Giovanni da Ravenna*, Como, 1924.
Le Scoperte dei Codici Latini e Greci ne'Secoli XIV e XV, 2 vols., Florence, 1905 and 1914.
Salutati, C. *Epistolario*, ed. F. Novati, 4. vols., Rome, 1891–1911.
Salvatori, M. 'Costruzione della Basilica dall'Origine al Secolo XIV' in Lorenzoni, ed., *L'Edificio*, pp. 31–82.
Sambin, P. 'Libri del Petrarca presso suoi Discendenti', *Italia Medioevale e Umanistica,* 1 (1958), pp. 359–69.
Sancassani, G. 'Notizie Genealogiche degli Scaligeri di Verona: le Origini (1147–1277)' in Cavallari *et al.*, eds., *Verona*, vol. III, bk 1, pp. 312–43.
'Notizie Genealogiche degli Scaligeri di Verona: da Alberto I ad Antonio della Scala (1277–1387)' in Cavallari *et al.*, eds., *Verona*, vol. III, bk 1, pp. 728–59.
Sandberg-Vavalà, E. *La Pittura Veronese del Trecento e del Primo Quattrocento*, Verona, 1926.
Sandri, G. *I Palazzi Scaligeri di S. Maria Antica*, Verona, 1931.
Sanuto, M. *Itinerario per la Terraferma Veneziana,* 1483; Padua, 1847.
Saraina, T. *Le Historie e Fatti de'Veronesi*, Verona, 1649.
Sartori, A. *Documenti per la Storia dell'Arte a Padova*, Vicenza, 1976.
'La Cappella di S. Giacomo al Santo', *Il Santo,* 6 (1966), pp. 267–359.
'Nota su Altichiero', *Il Santo,* 3 (1963), pp. 291–326.
'Da San Giacomo a San Felice', *Il Santo,* 5 (1963), pp. 157–80.

Sartori, A. and H. Luisetto. *Archivio Sartori: Documenti di Storia e Arte Francescana*, Padua, 1983.

Savonarola, M. *Libellus,* in *RIS²*, vol. XXIV, 15, ed. A. Segarizzi, Città di Castello, 1902.

Scaralla, F. *Gli Alighieri di Verona*, Verona, 1965.

Scarpellini, P. 'Di Alcuni Pittori Giotteschi nella Città e nel Territorio di Assisi' in *Giotto e i Giotteschi in Assisi*, Rome, 1969, pp. 241–62.

Schiller, G. *The Iconography of Christian Art*, 2 vols., London, 1971.

Schlosser, J. von *L'Arte di Corte nel Secolo Decimoquarto*, trans. G. L. Mellini, Milan, 1965.

'Ein Veronisches Bilderbuch und die Hofische Kunst des XIV Jahrhunderts', *Jahrbuch d.k. Sammlungen d.a. Kaiserhauses* XVI, 1895.

Schmitt, A. 'Zur Wiederbelebung der Antike im Trecento', *Mitteilungen des Kunsthistorischen Instituts in Florenz*, 18 (1974), pp. 169–218.

Schubring, P. *Altichiero und seine Schule*, Leipzig, 1898.

Schumann, R. *Authority and the Commune, Parma, 833–1133*, Parma, 1973.

Scriptores Historia Augusta, ed. and trans. D. Magie, Loeb Classical Texts, London and Cambridge, Mass.: vol. I, 1921; vol. II, 1924; vol. III, 1932.

Seigel, J. E. 'Civic Humanism or Ciceronian Rhetoric? The Culture of Petrarch and Bruni', *Past and Present*, 34 (1966), pp. 3–48.

Selvatico, P. *Guida di Padova*, Padua, 1869.

Semenzato, C., ed. *La Cappella del Beato Luca e Giusto de'Menabuoi nella Basilica di Sant'Antonio*, Padua, 1988.

Giotto e i Giotteschi a Padova, Milan and Rome, 1988.

Le Pitture del Santo di Padova, Vicenza, 1984.

Shorr, D. 'Some Notes on the Iconography of Petrarch's Triumph of Fame', *Art Bulletin*, 20 (1938), pp. 100–7.

Simeoni, L. *La Basilica di S. Zeno in Verona*, Verona, 1909.

Verona. Guida Storica e Artistica della Città e Provincia, Verona, 1909.

'La Famiglia di Giovanni Mansionario Autore delle Historie Imperiales', *Atti Mem. Accad. Agr. Sc. Lett. Verona*, 4.4 (1903–4), pp. 65ff.

Simon, R. 'Altichiero Versus Avanzo', *Papers of the British School at Rome*, 45 (1977), pp. 252–71.

'Little and Large. Manuscript Reflections of Altichiero's Frescoes', *Apollo*, 134 (1991), pp. 299–300.

Simpson, W. 'A new Codex of Petrarch's "De Viris Illustribus"', *Italia Medioevale e Umanistica*, 3 (1960), pp. 267–70.

Smalley, B. 'Sallust in the Middle Ages' in Bolger, ed., *Classical Influences*, pp. 165–75.

Sottili, A. 'Codici del Petrarca nella Germania Occ.1', *Italia Medioevale e Umanistica*, 10 (1967), pp. 411–92.

Spiazzi, A. M., ed. *Giusto de'Menabuoi nel Battistero di Padova*, Trieste, 1989.

Sterling, C. and C. Schaefer *The Hours of Etienne Chevalier*, Jean Fouquet, London, 1972.

Storia Pistoresi, ed. S. A. Barbi, *RIS*, vol. XI.

Strong, D. E. *Roman Imperial Sculpture*, London, 1961.

Strong, E. *Roman Sculpture from Augustus to Constantine*, London, 1907.

Syme, R. *Ammianus and the Historia Augusta*, Oxford, 1968.

Emperors and Biography, Oxford, 1971.

Temple Leader, J. and G. Marcotti. *Sir John Hawkwood*, London, 1889.

Todini, F. and B. Zanardi, *La Pinacoteca Communale di Assisi*, Florence, 1980.

Toesca, P. *Il Trecento*, Turin, 1951.

Toynbee, J. M. C. *The Flavian Reliefs from the Palazzo della Cancelleria in Rome*, London and Oxford, 1957.

Ullman, B. L. *The Humanism of Coluccio Salutati*, Padua, 1963.

Van Marle, R. *The Development of the Italian Schools of Painting*, vol. IV, The Hague, 1924.

Varanini, G. M., ed. *Gli Scaligeri, 1277–1387*, exh. cat. Verona, 1988.

Vasari, G. *Le Vite*, ed. G. Milanesi, 9 vols, Florence, 1908.

Vattovani, F. S. '*Tomaso e Altichiero*' in *Tomaso da Modena e il suo Tempo*, Atti del Convegno Int. di Studi per il 6^0 Centenari della Morte, Treviso, 1980, pp. 271–6.

Venturi, A. *Storia dell'Arte Italiana*, 18 vols., Milan, 1901–40.

Verci, G. B. *Storia della Marca Trivigiana e Veronese*, 10 vols., Venice, 1786–91.

Villani, G. *Cronica*, Florence, 1823.

Villani, M. *Cronica*, Florence, 1825.

Volpe, C. *La Pittura Riminese del Trecento*, Milan, 1965.

Weigand, W. 'Gli Scaligeri dopo gli Scaligeri', in Varanini, ed., *Gli Scaligeri*, pp. 91–6.

Weiss, R. *The Dawn of Humanism in Italy*, London, 1947.

The Renaissance Discovery of Classical Antiquity, Oxford, 1969.

'Ausonius in the Fourteenth Century' in Bolger, ed., *Classical Influences*, pp. 67–72.

'La Cultura Preumanistica Veronese e Vicentina del Tempo di Dante' in *Dante e la Cultura Veneta*, Florence, 1966, pp. 265–72.

'The Study of Ancient Numismatics During the Renaissance (1313–1517)', *Numismatic Chronicle* (1968), pp. 177–87.

Wentzel, H. 'Italienische Siegelstempel und Siegel all'antica im 13. und 14. Jahrhundert', *Mitteilungen des Kunsthistorischen Instituts in Florenz*, 7 (1955), pp. 73ff.

'Mittelalterliche Gemmen in den Sammlungen Italiens', *Mitteilungen des Kunsthistorischen Instituts im Florenz*, 8 (1956), pp. 239ff.

'Portraits *à l'Antique* on French Mediaeval Gems and Seals', *Journal of the Warburg and Courtauld Institutes*, 16 (1953), pp. 342ff.

Whitfield, J. H. *Petrarch and the Renascence*, Oxford, 1943.

Wilkins, E. H. *Life of Petrarch*, Chicago, 1961.

Petrarch's Eight Years in Milan, Cambridge, Mass., 1958.

Petrarch's Later Years, Cambridge, Mass., 1959.

Studies in the Life and Works of Petrarch, Cambridge, Mass., 1955.

'Petrarch and Giacomo de' Rossi', *Speculum*, 25 (1950), pp. 374–8.

'Petrarch and Manno Donati', *Speculum*, 35 (1960), pp. 381–93.

Wolff, P. *The Awakening of Europe*, Harmondsworth, 1968 and 1985.

Wolters, W. *La Scultura Veneziana Gotica*, Venice, 1976.

Zeri, F. 'Altri due Scomparti Veronesi della Fine del '300', *Paragone*, 107 (1958), pp. 65–6.

'Un'Aggiunta alla Cerchia di Altichiero', *Paragone*, 107 (1958), pp. 61–3.

Zucchi, R. 'Ottonello Descalzi a la Fortuna del De Viris Illustribus', *Italia Medioevale a Umanistica*, 17 (1974), pp. 469–92.

INDEX

NB Surnames. No approach to trecento names satisfactorily combines modern expectations of fixed, transferable surnames with the less stable reality of fourteenth-century patterns. I have adhered as far as possible to common practice, or what I take to be common practice.

PLATES

All works of art are by Altichero unless otherwise stated.

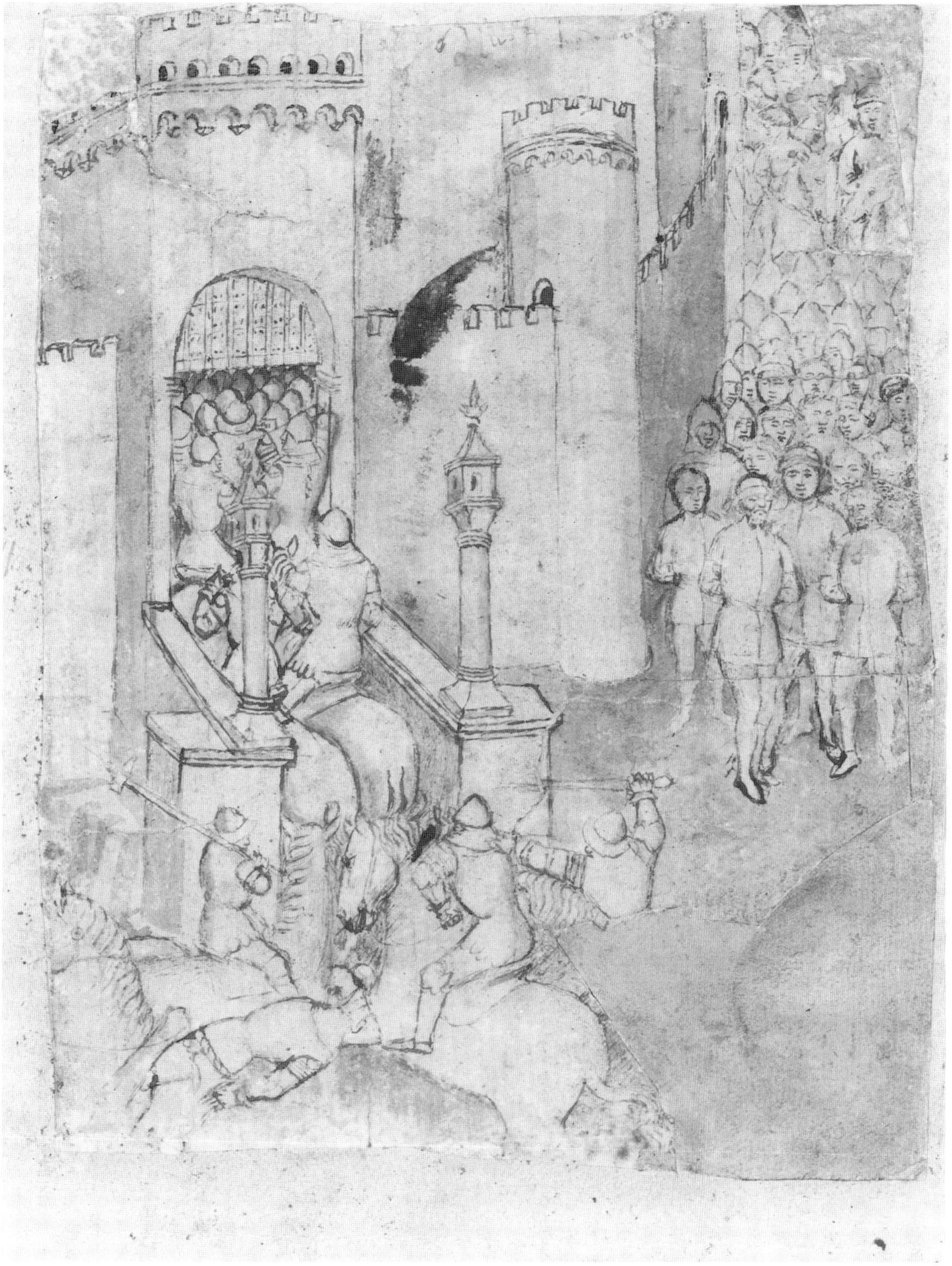

Plate I After Altichiero: *Entry of Troops into a City*. Private collection.

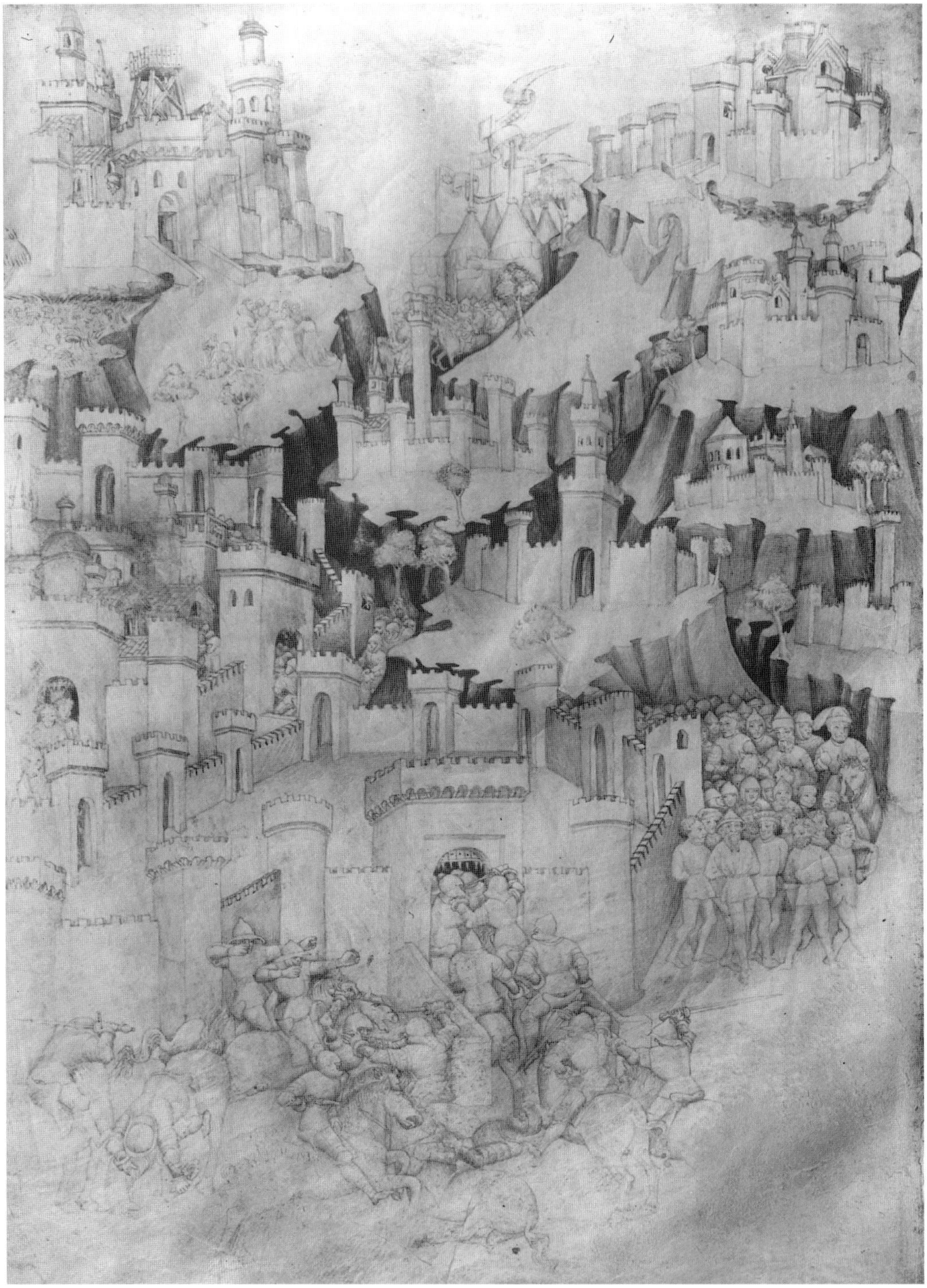

Plate 2 After Altichiero: *Entry of Troops into a City and Other Scenes*. Paris, Louvre.

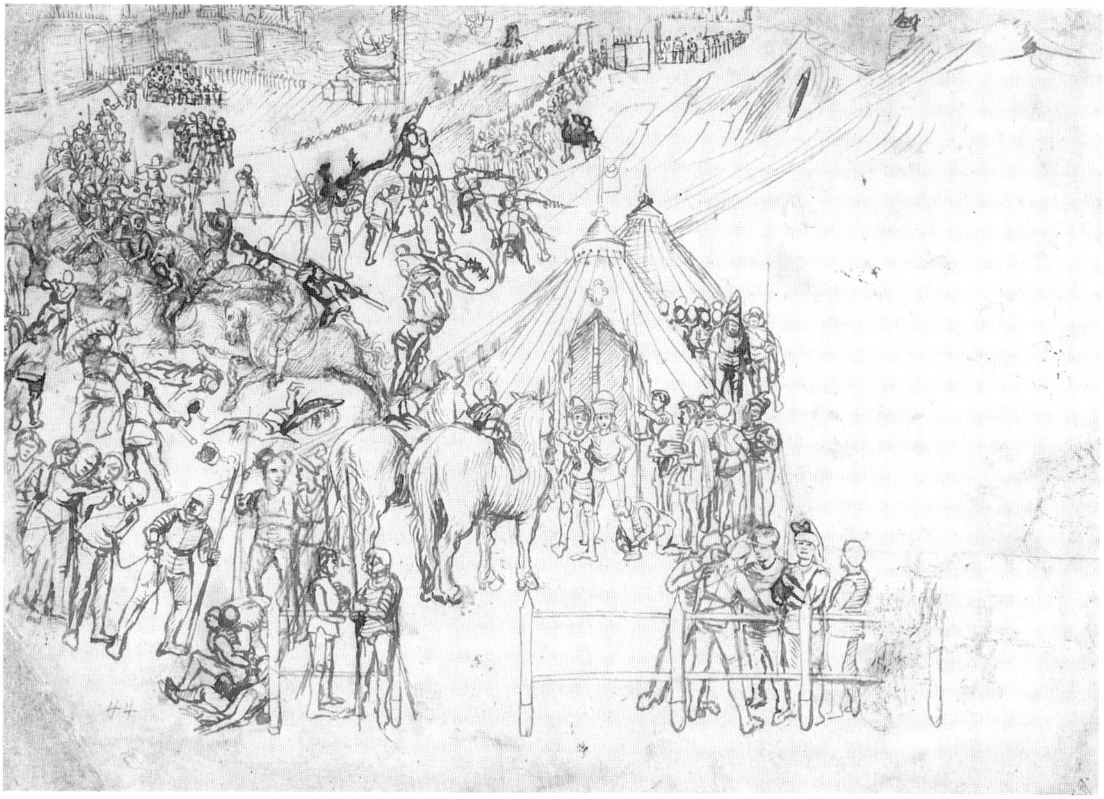

Plate 3 After Altichiero (?): *Camp Scene*. London, British Museum.

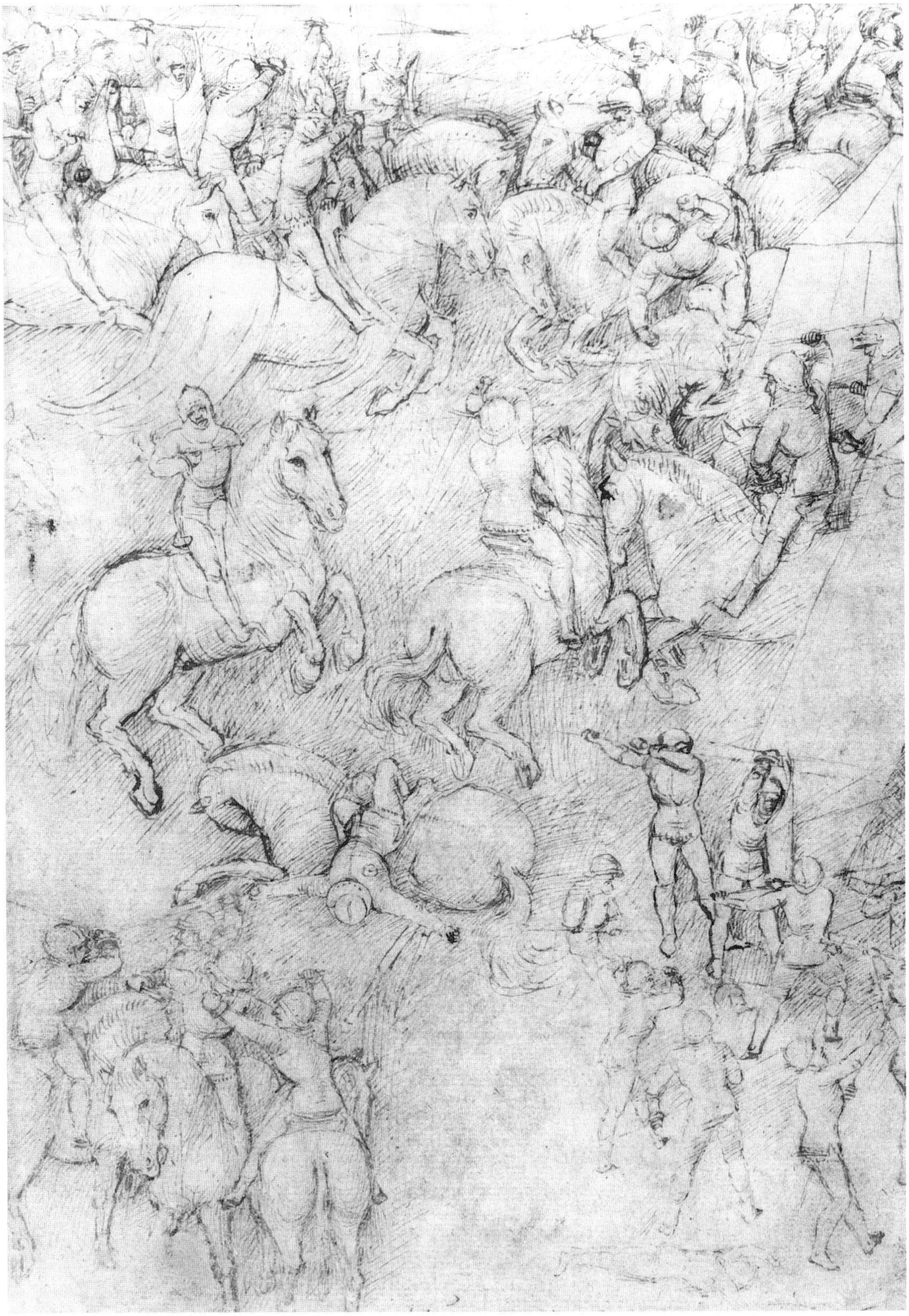

Plate 4 After Altichiero: *Battle Scene*. London, British Museum.

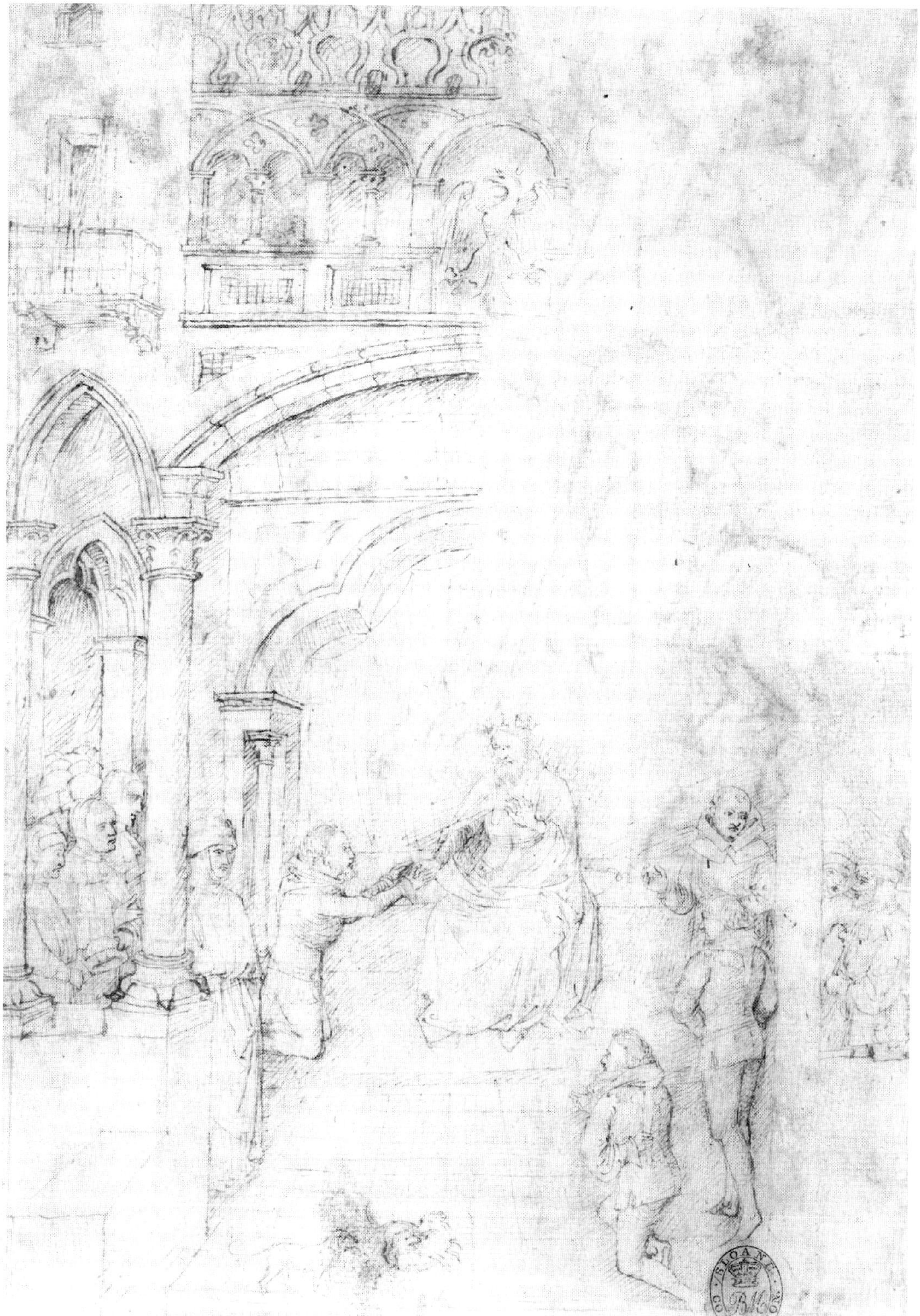

Plate 5 After Altichiero: *Court Scene*. London, British Museum.

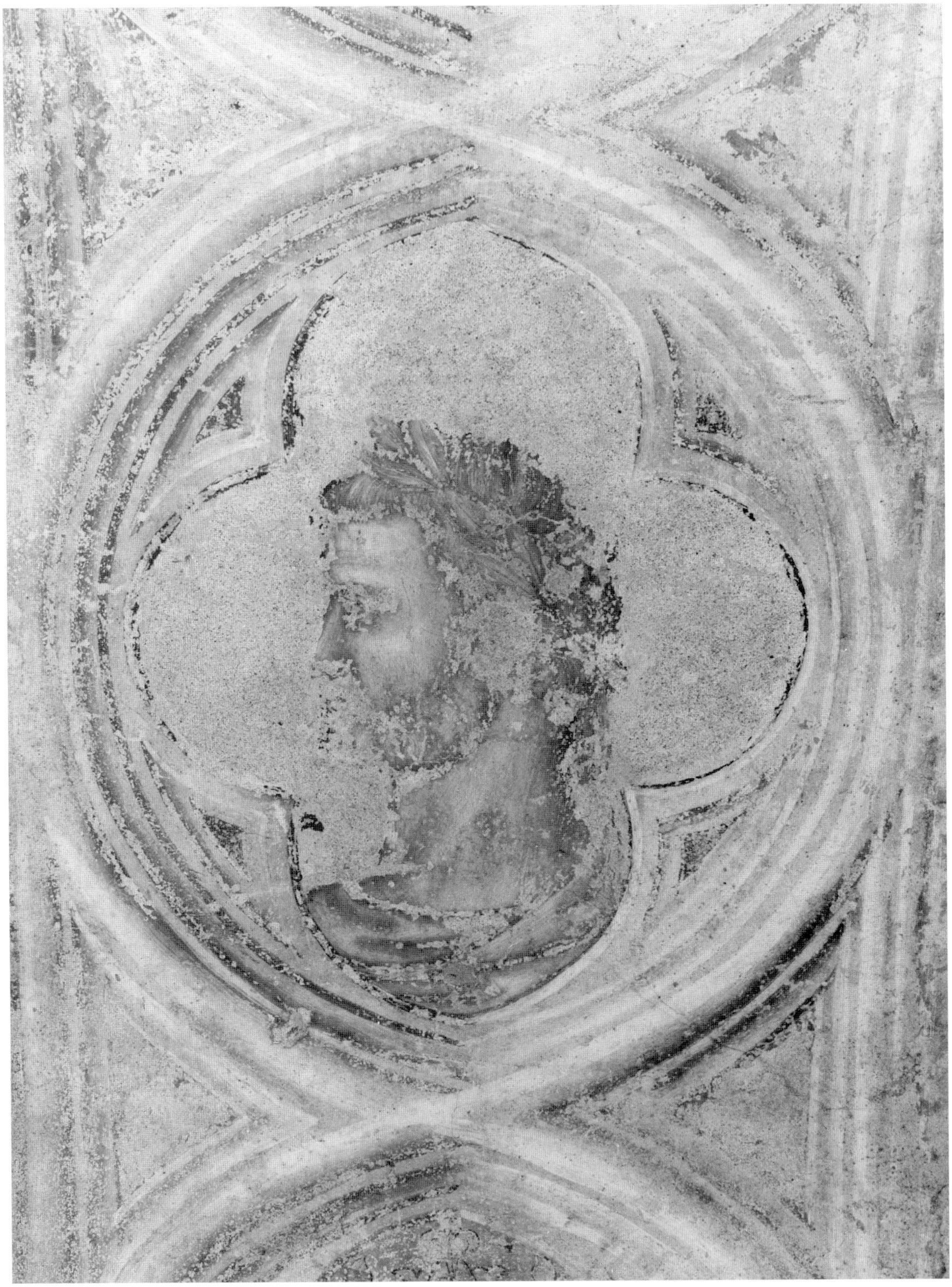

Plate 6 *Hadrian*. Verona, Castelvecchio.

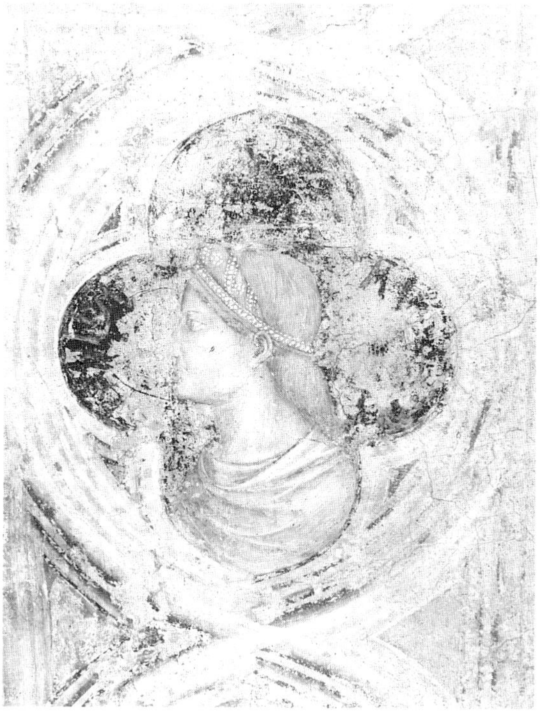

Plate 7 *Sabina*. Verona, Castelvecchio.

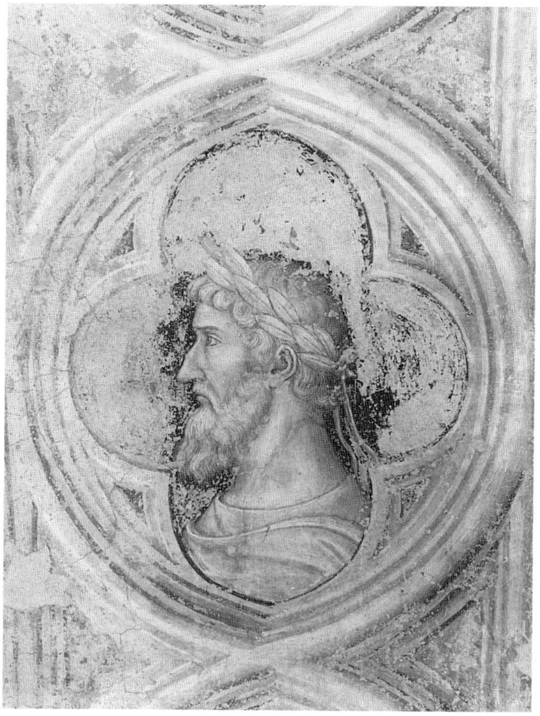

Plate 8 *Caracalla*. Verona, Castelvecchio.

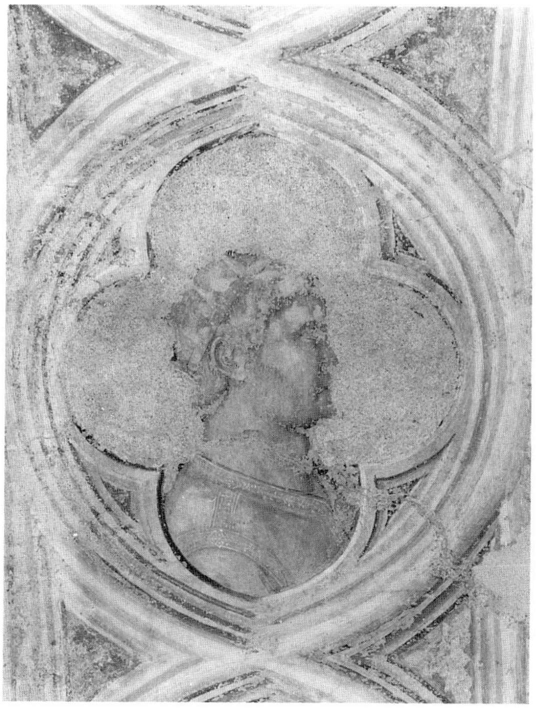

Plate 9 *Macrinus*. Verona, Castelvecchio.

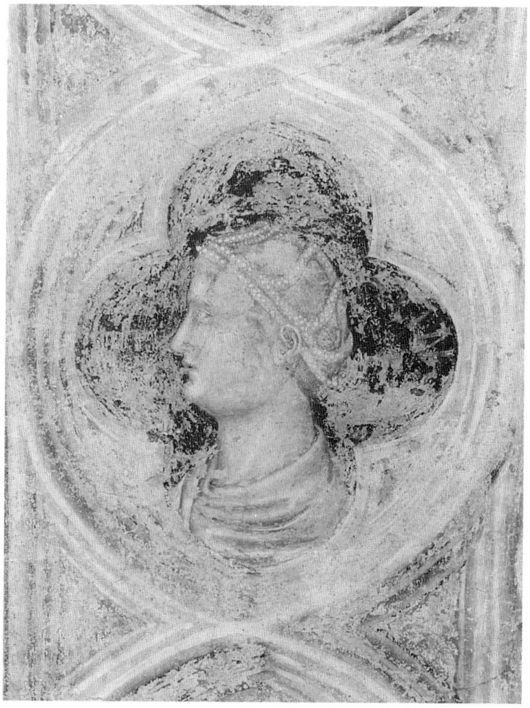

Plate 10 *Faustina*. Verona, Castelvecchio.

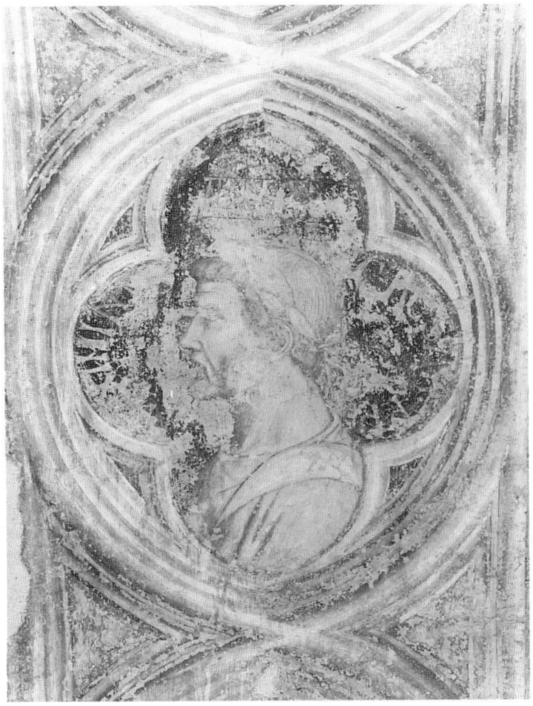

Plate 11 *Maximus Caesar*. Verona, Castelvecchio.

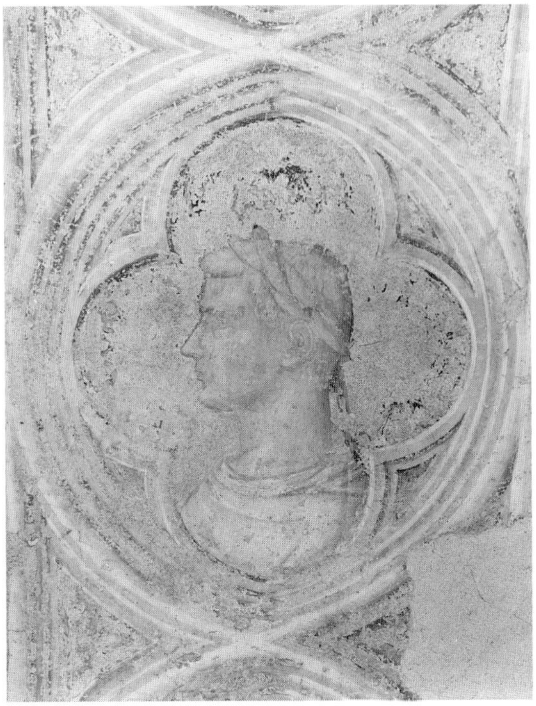

Plate 12 *Gordian I*. Verona, Castelvecchio.

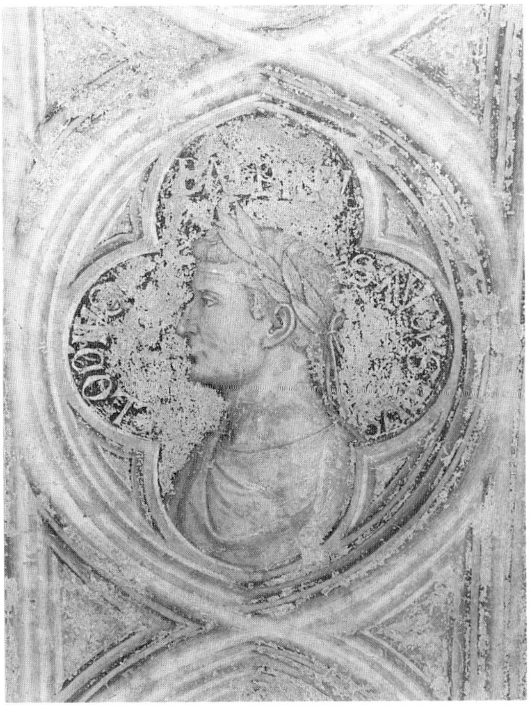

Plate 13 *Balbinus*. Verona, Castelvecchio.

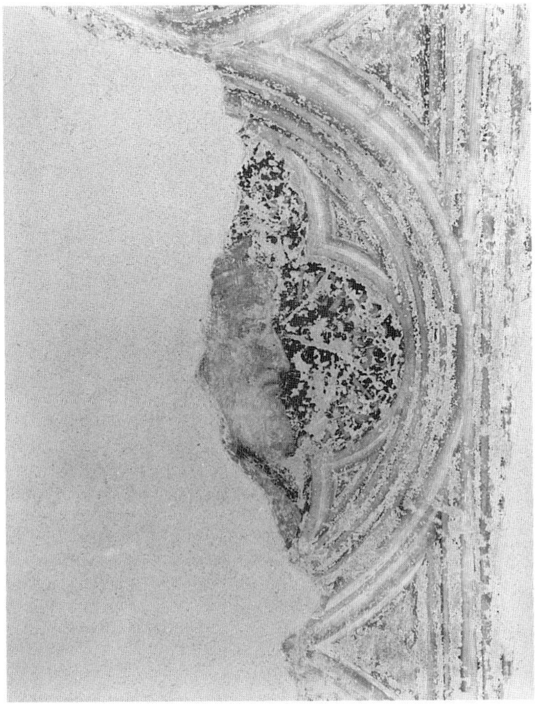

Plate 14 *Pupienus*. Verona, Castelvecchio.

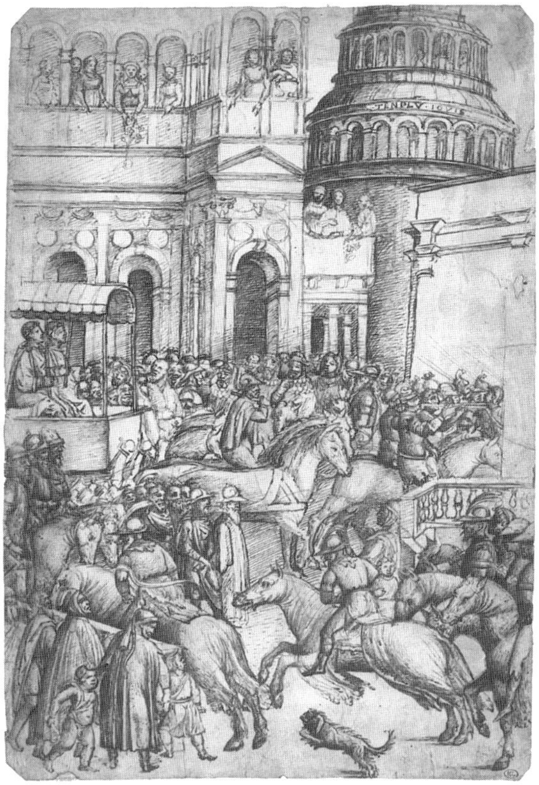

Plate 15 After Altichiero: *Triumph* [*?*] *of Titus and Vespasian*. Paris, Louvre.

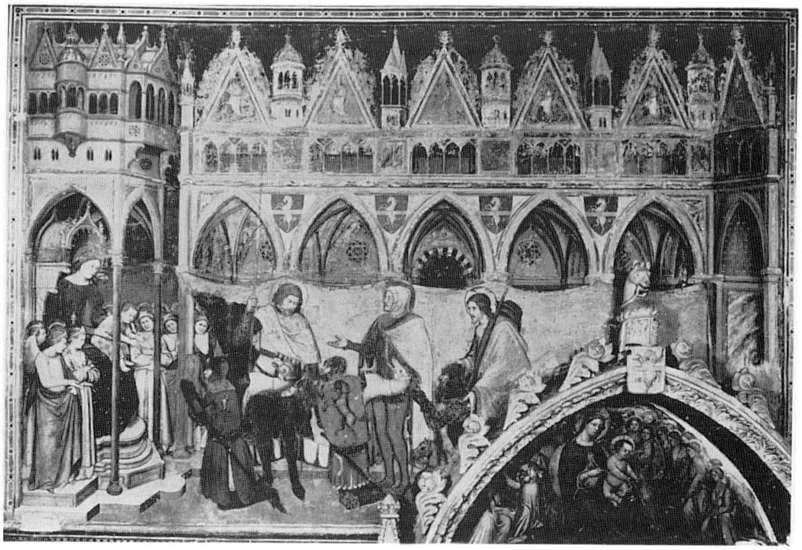

Plate 16 Cavalli votive fresco. Verona, S. Anastasia, Cavalli Chapel.

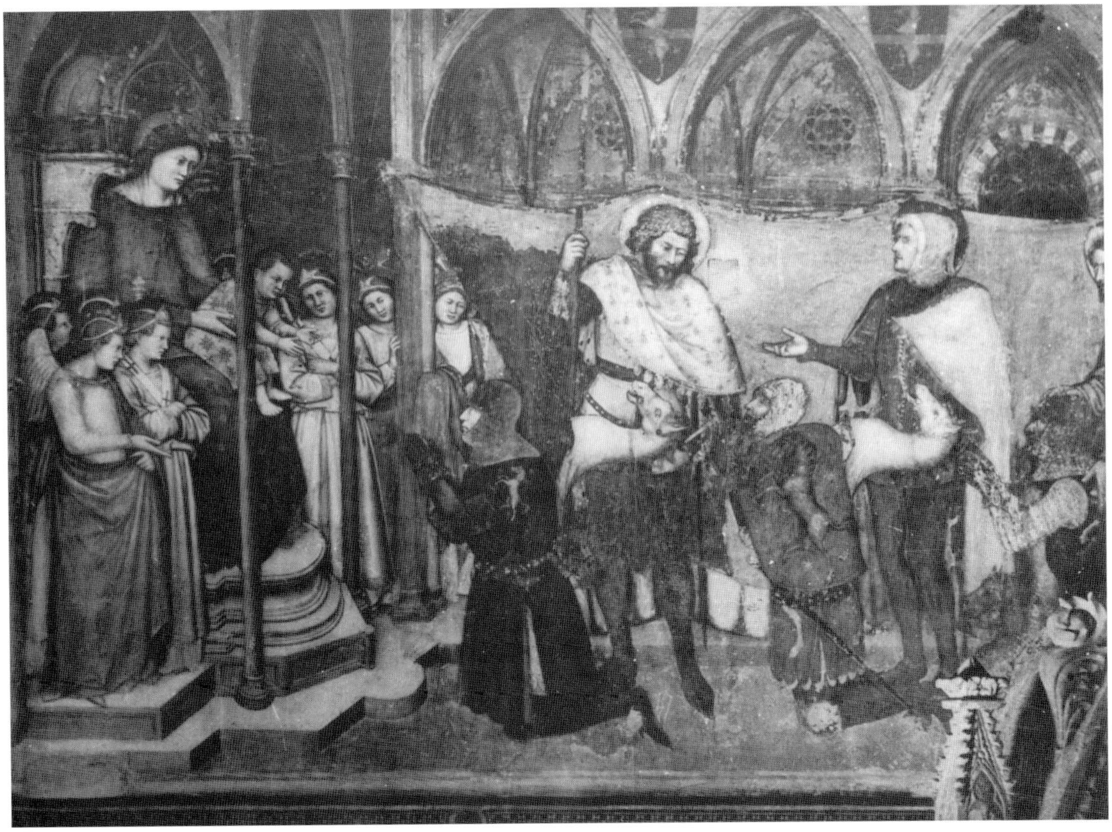

Plate 17 Cavalli votive fresco (detail). Verona, S. Anastasia, Cavalli Chapel.

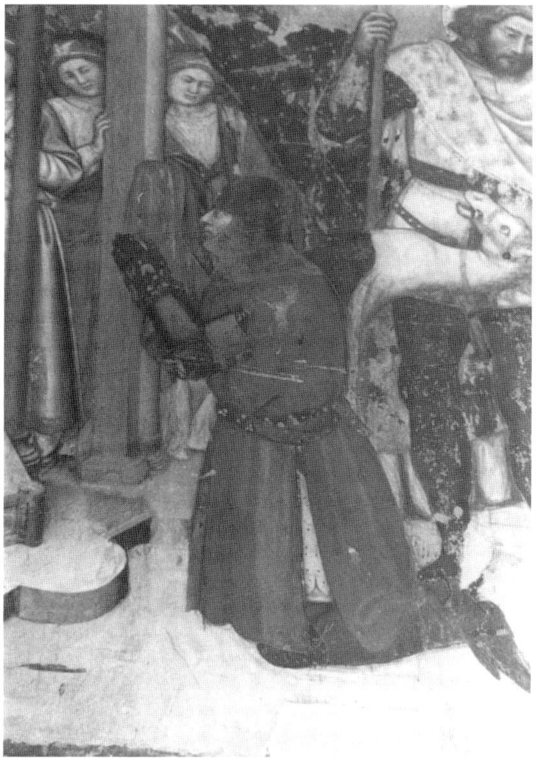

Plate 18 Cavalli votive fresco (detail).
Verona, S. Anastasia, Cavalli Chapel.

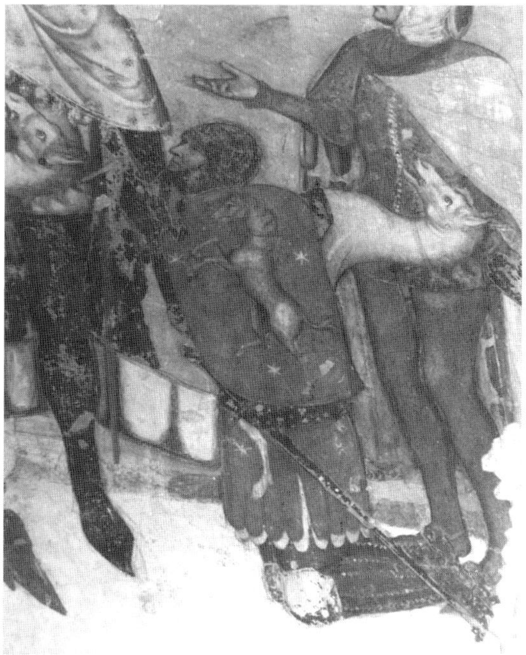

Plate 19 Cavalli votive fresco (detail).
Verona, S. Anastasia, Cavalli Chapel.

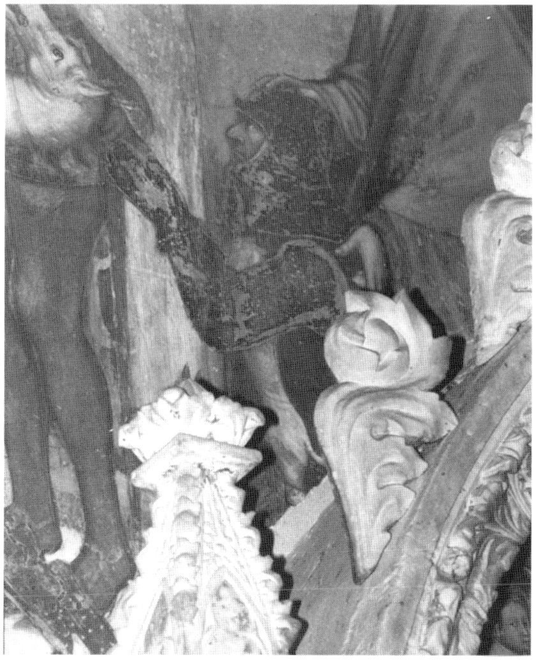

Plate 20 Cavalli votive fresco (detail).
Verona, S. Anastasia, Cavalli Chapel.

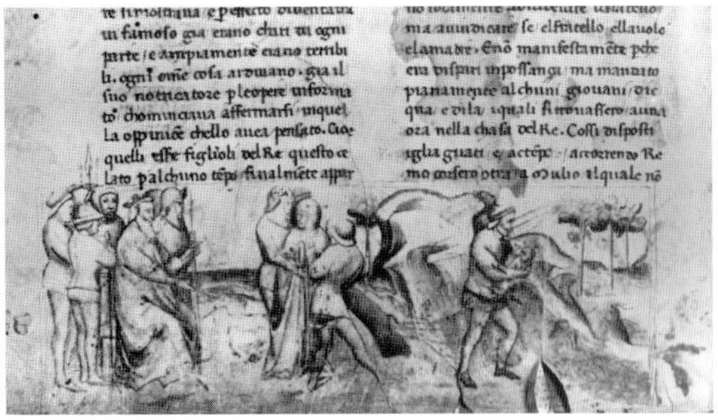

Plate 21a After Altichiero: *King Amulius, Rhea Silvia, Romulus and Remus Carried by a Soldier*. From Petrarch, *De Viris Illustribus,* Darmstadt, Hessische Landes-und-Hochschul-Bibliothek, cod. 101, fo. 2v.

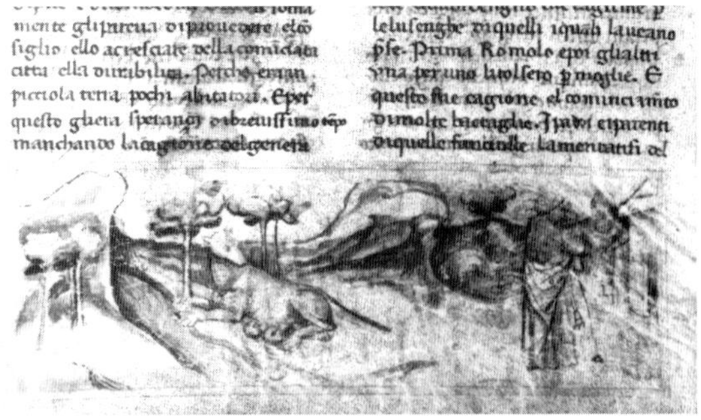

Plate 21b After Altichiero: *The Twins with the She-Wolf*; *The Twins with Ara Larentia*. From Petrarch, *De Viris Illustribus,* Darmstadt, Hessische Landes-und-Hochschul-Bibliothek, cod. 101, fo. 3r.

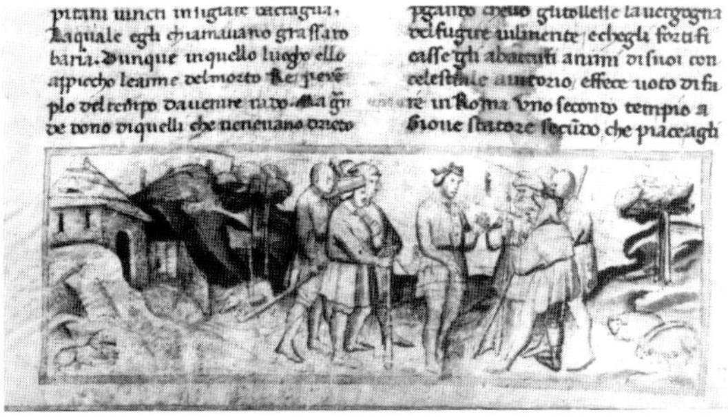

Plate 22a After Altichiero: *Romulus and the Farmers*. From Petrarch, *De Viris Illustribus,* Darmstadt, Hessische Landes-und-Hochschul-Bibliothek, cod. 101, fo. 3v.

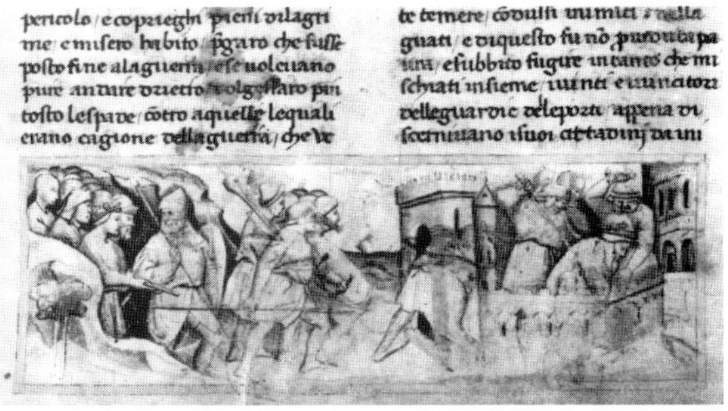

Plate 22b After Altichiero: *Romulus and Alba. The Death of Amulius.* From Petrarch, *De Viris Illustribus,* Darmstadt, Hessische Landes-und-Hochschul-Bibliothek, cod. 101, fo. 4r.

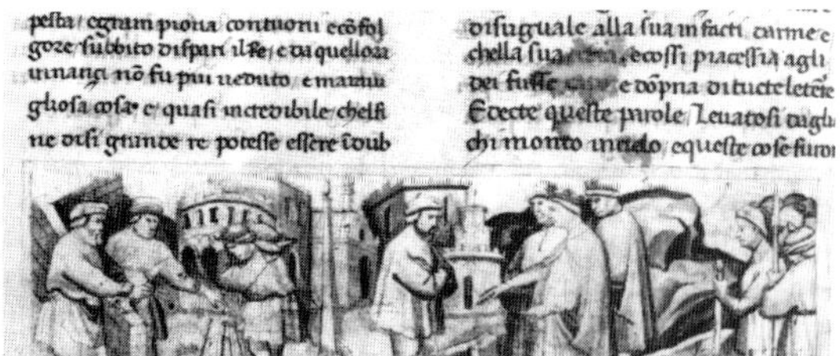

Plate 23a After Altichiero: *The Building of the Walls, Quarrel between Romulus and Remus.* From Petrarch, *De Viris Illustribus,* Darmstadt, Hessische Landes-und-Hochschul-Bibliothek, cod. 101, fo. 4v.

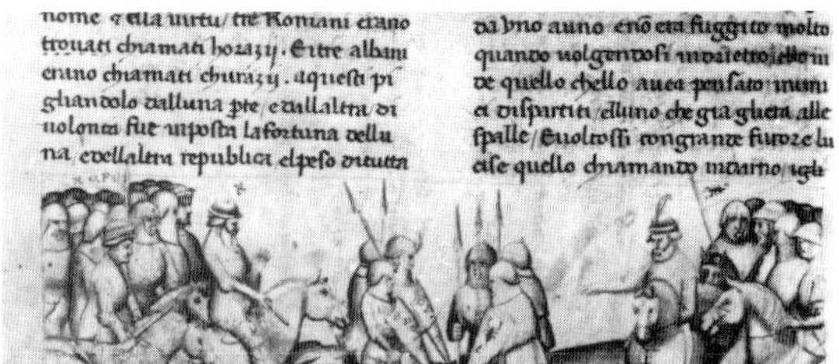

Plate 23b After Altichiero: *The Horatii and Curiatii Between the Roman and Alban Armies.* From Petrarch, *De Viris Illustribus,* Darmstadt, Hessische Landes-und-Hochschul-Bibliothek, cod. 101, fo. 6v.

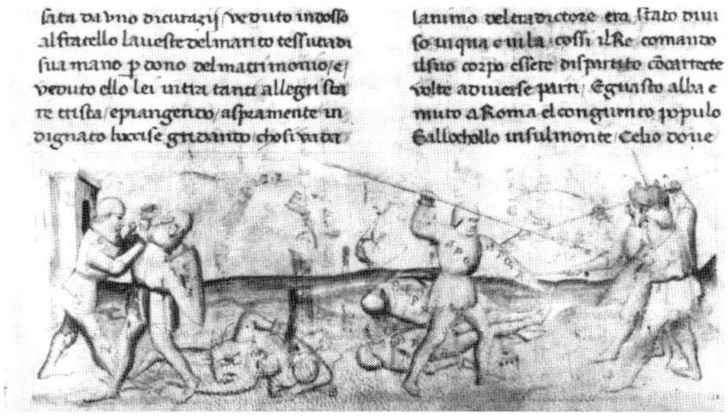

Plate 24a After Altichiero: *The Battle of the Horatii and Curiatii*. From Petrarch, *De Viris Illustribus,* Darmstadt, Hessische Landes-und-Hochschul-Bibliothek, cod. 101, fo. 7r.

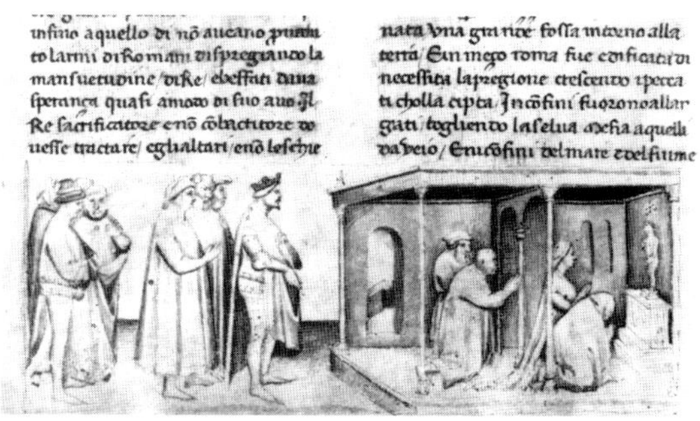

Plate 24b After Altichiero: *Ancus Martius and the Worship of Jupiter Feretrius*. From Petrarch, *De Viris Illustribus,* Darmstadt, Hessische Landes-und-Hochschul-Bibliothek, cod. 101, fo. 7v.

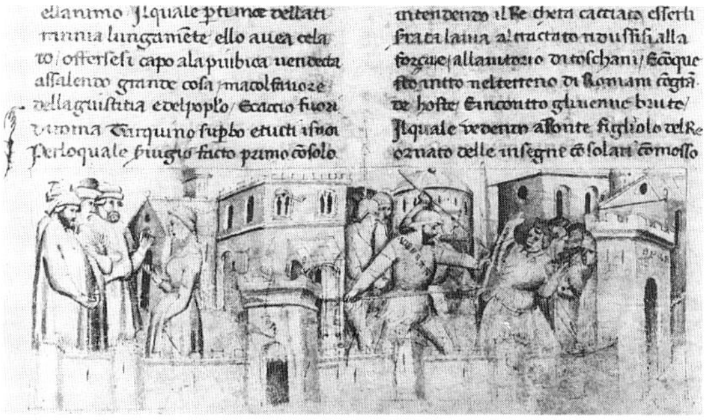

Plate 25a After Altichiero: *Lucretia and the Expulsion of Tarquin*. From Petrarch, *De Viris Illustribus,* Darmstadt, Hessische Landes-und-Hochschul-Bibliothek, cod. 101, fo. 8r.

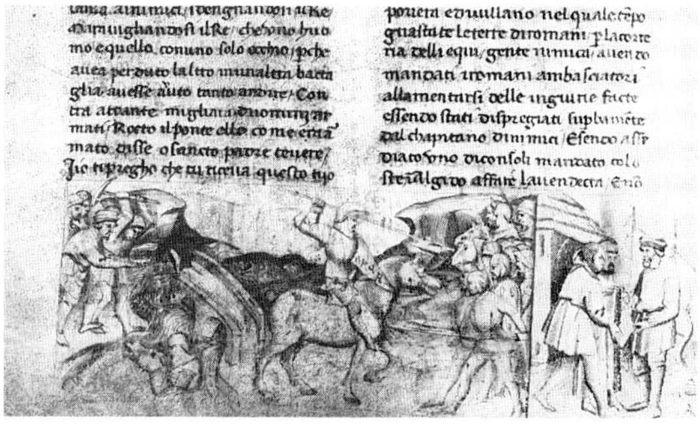

Plate 25b After Altichiero: *Horatius Cocles; The Recall of Cincinnatus*. From Petrarch, *De Viris Illustribus,* Darmstadt, Hessische Landes-und-Hochschul-Bibliothek, cod. 101, fo. 8v.

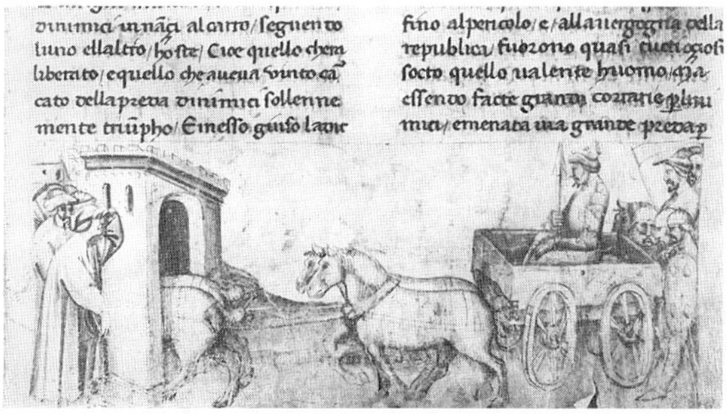

Plate 26a After Altichiero: *The Triumph of Camillus*. From Petrarch, *De Viris Illustribus,* Darmstadt, Hessische Landes-und-Hochschul-Bibliothek, cod. 101, fo. 9r.

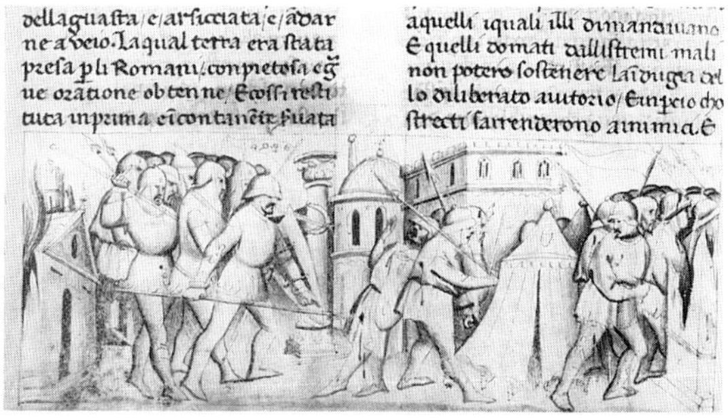

Plate 26b After Altichiero: *Camillus Expelling the Gauls from Rome*. From Petrarch, *De Viris Illustribus,* Darmstadt, Hessische Landes-und-Hochschul-Bibliothek, cod. 101, fo. 11r.

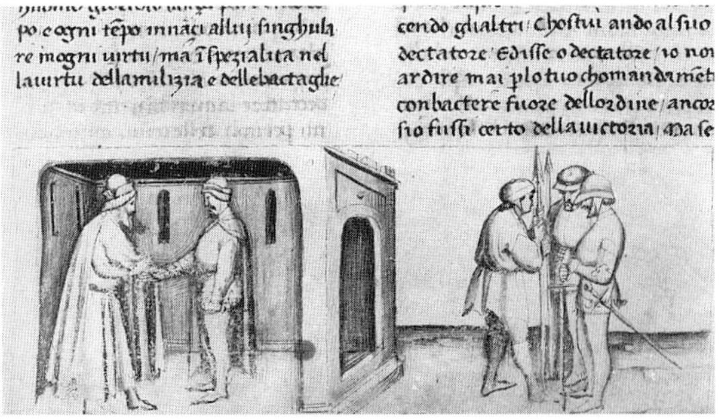

Plate 27a After Altichiero: *T. Manlius Torquatus Threatening Pomponius*. From Petrarch, *De Viris Illustribus,* Darmstadt, Hessische Landes-und-Hochschul-Bibliothek, cod. 101, fo. 14r.

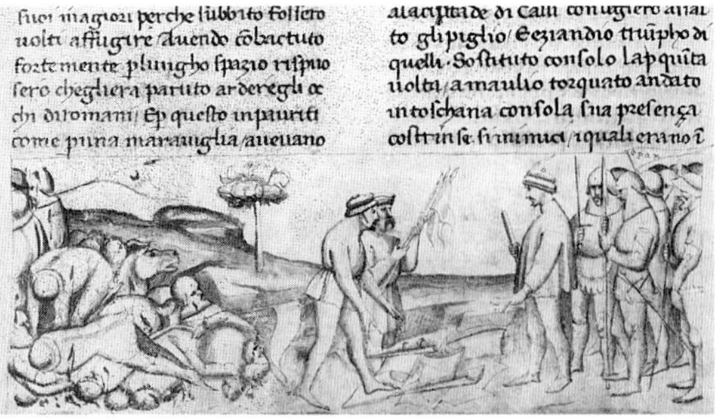

Plate 27b After Altichiero: *Valerius Corvinus Receiving the Samnites' Arms*. From Petrarch, *De Viris Illustribus,* Darmstadt, Hessische Landes-und-Hochschul-Bibliothek, cod. 101, fo. 15r.

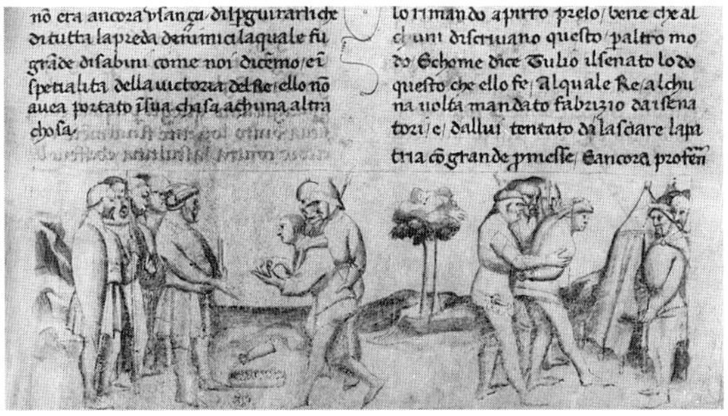

Plate 28a After Altichiero: *Fabricius and Pyrrhus's Slave; of the Slave*. From Petrarch, *De Viris Illustribus,* Darmstadt, Hessische Landes-und-Hochschul-Bibliothek, cod. 101, fo. 18r.

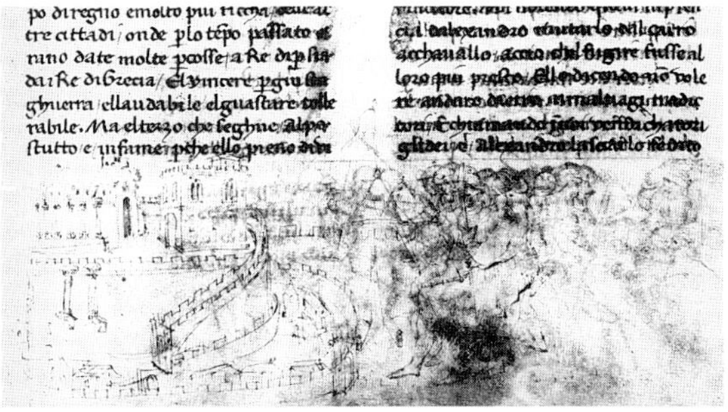

Plate 28b After Altichiero: *Alexander Besieging a City*. From Petrarch, *De Viris Illustribus,* Darmstadt, Hessische Landes-und-Hochschul-Bibliothek, cod. 101, fo. 19r.

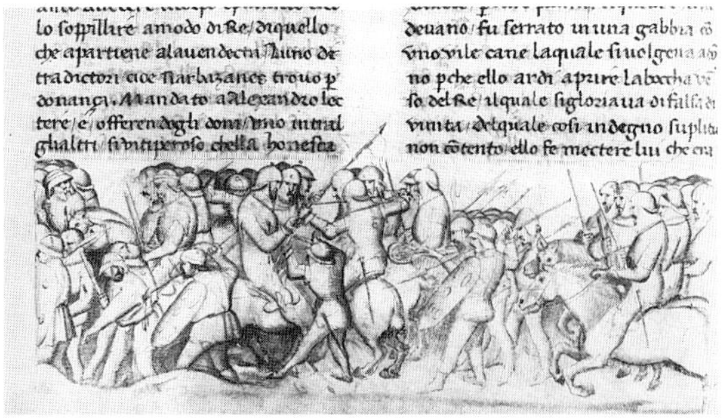

Plate 29a After Altichiero: *Battle Between the Armies of Darius and Alexander*. From Petrarch, *De Viris Illustribus,* Darmstadt, Hessische Landes-und-Hochschul-Bibliothek, cod. 101, fo. 19v.

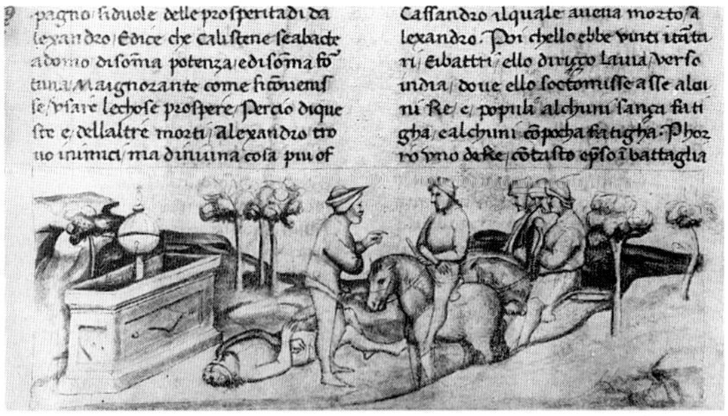

Plate 29b After Altichiero: *The Discovery of Darius's Body*. From Petrarch, *De Viris Illustribus,* Darmstadt, Hessische Landes-und-Hochschul-Bibliothek, cod.101, fo. 20r.

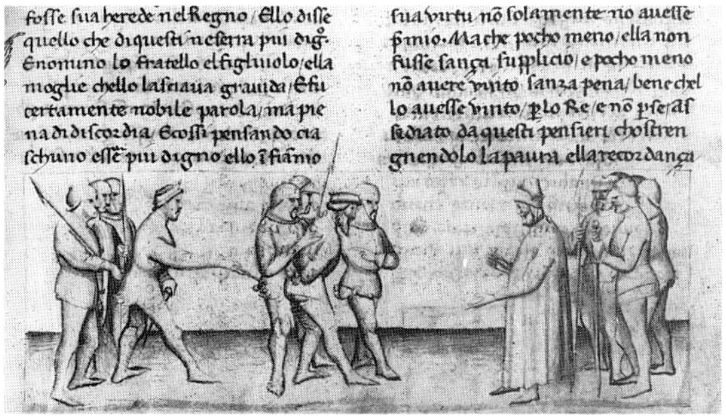

Plate 30a After Altichiero: *Alexander and a Prisoner*. From Petrarch, *De Viris Illustribus,* Darmstadt, Hessische Landes-und-Hochschul-Bibliothek, cod. 101, fo. 21r.

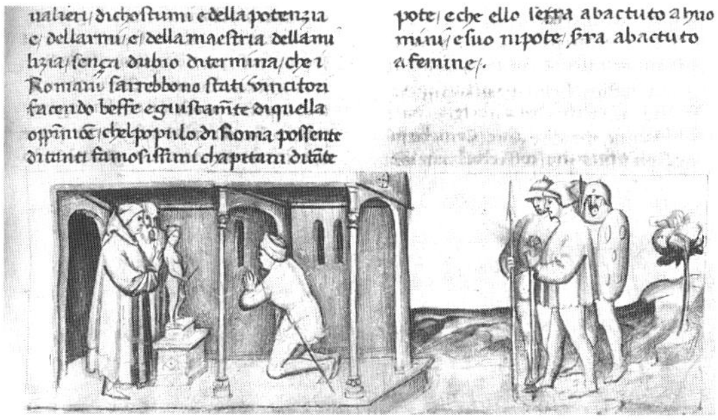

Plate 30b After Altichiero: *Alexander Worshipping a Goddess*. From Petrarch, *De Viris Illustribus,* Darmstadt, Hessische Landes-und-Hochschul-Bibliothek, cod. 101, fo. 22r.

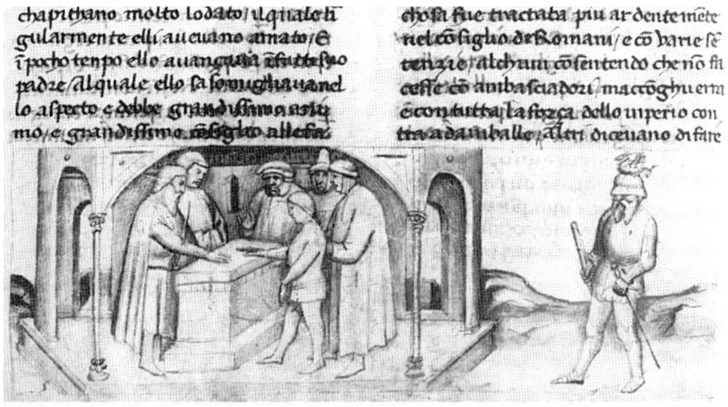

Plate 31a After Altichiero: *The Oath of Hannibal. Hamilcar*. From Petrarch, *De Viris Illustribus,* Darmstadt, Hessische Landes-und-Hochschul-Bibliothek, cod. 101, fo. 24v.

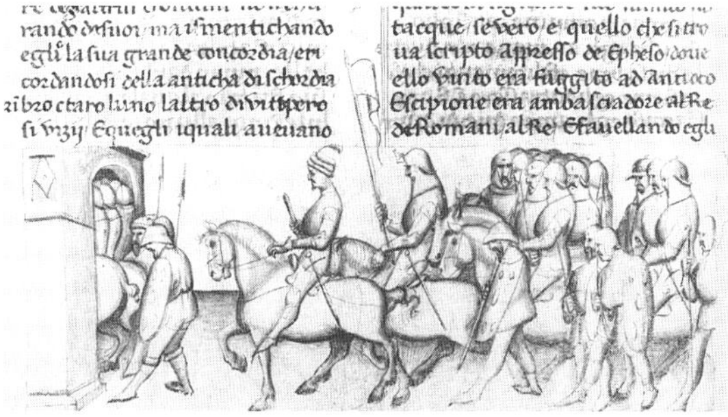

Plate 31b After Altichiero: *The Triumph of Claudius Nero and Livius Salinator*. From Petrarch, *De Viris Illustribus,* Darmstadt, Hessische Landes-und-Hochschul-Bibliothek, cod. 101, fo. 51v.

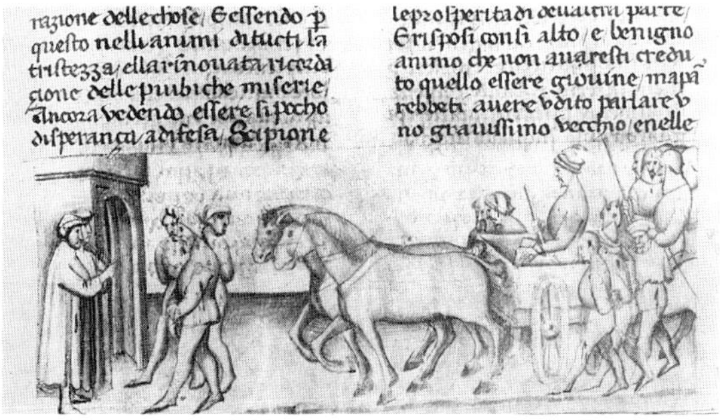

Plate 32a After Altichiero: *The Triumph of Scipio Africanus*. From Petrarch, *De Viris Illustribus,* Darmstadt, Hessische Landes-und-Hochschul-Bibliothek, cod. 101, fo. 53v.

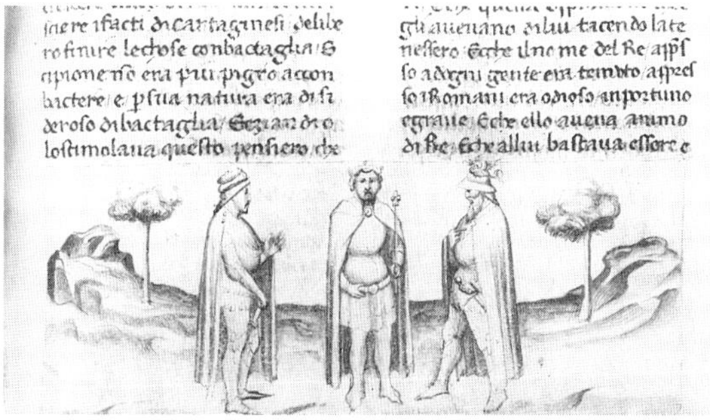

Plate 32b After Altichiero: *Scipio, Masinissa and Hannibal*. From Petrarch, *De Viris Illustribus,* Darmstadt, Hessische Landes-und-Hochschul-Bibliothek, cod. 101, fo. 54r.

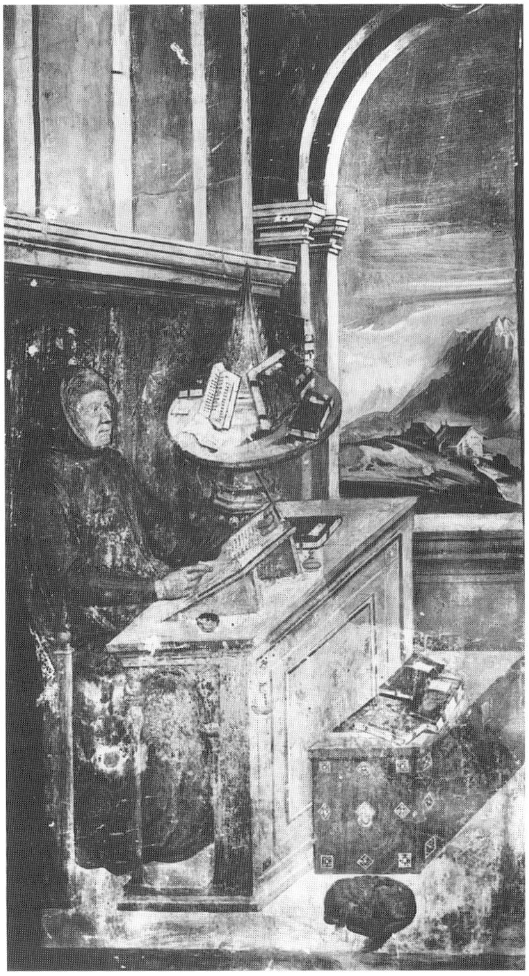

Plate 33 *Petrarch in his Study*. Padua, Sala dei Giganti.

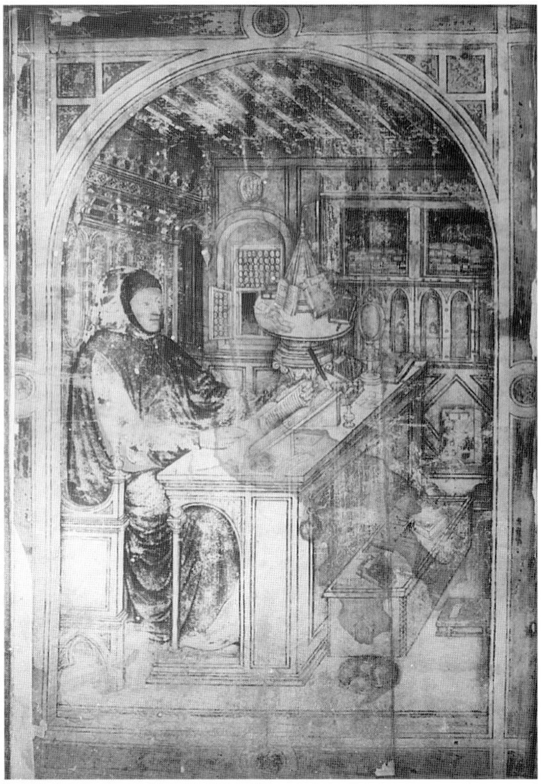

Plate 34 After Altichiero: *Petrarch in his Study*. Darmstadt, Hessische Landes-und-Hochschul-Bibliothek, cod. 101.

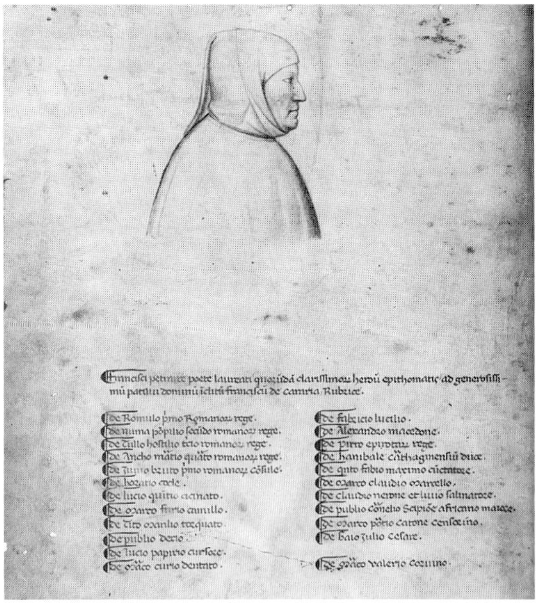

Plate 35 *Portrait of Petrarch*. Paris, Bibliothèque Nationale, MS Lat. 6069F.

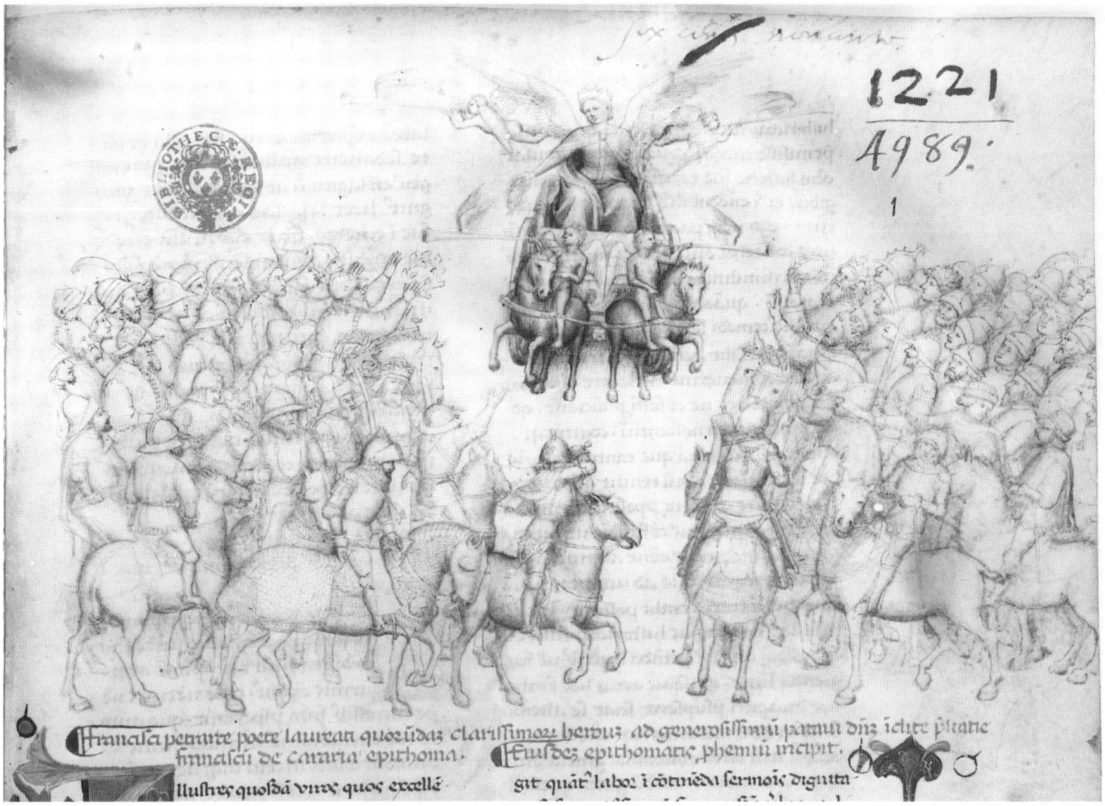

Plate 36 *Triumph of Fame*. Paris, Bibliothèque Nationale, MS Lat. 6069F.

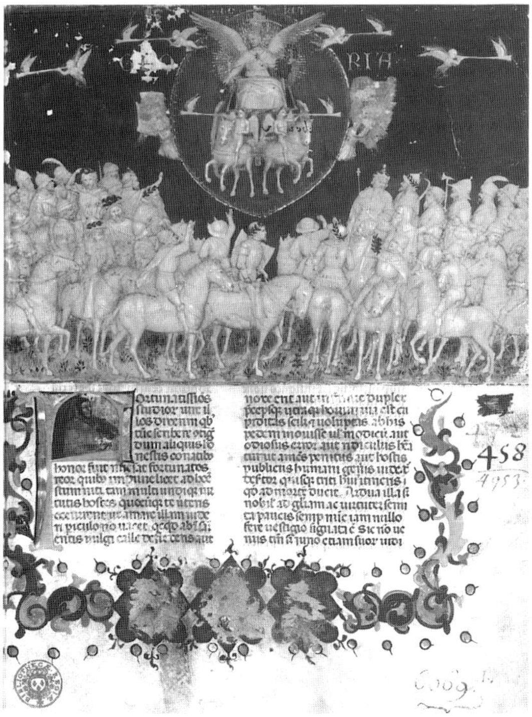

Plate 37 Altichiero Workshop: *Triumph of Fame*. Paris, Bibliothèque Nationale, MS Lat. 6069I.

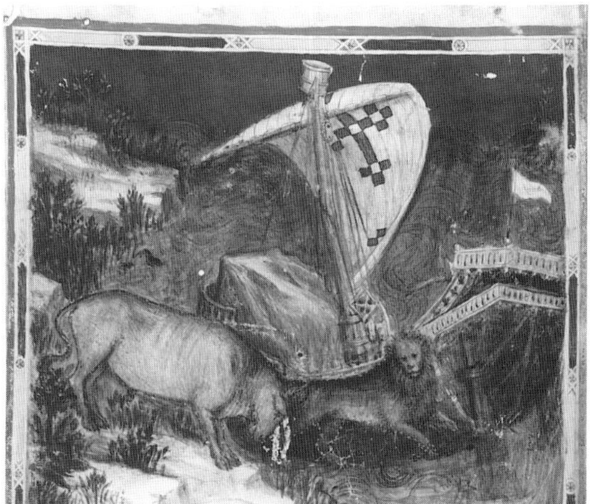

Plate 38 *The Bull of Padua Pushing the Lion of Venice into the Sea*. Paris, Bibliothèque Nationale MS Lat. 6069G.

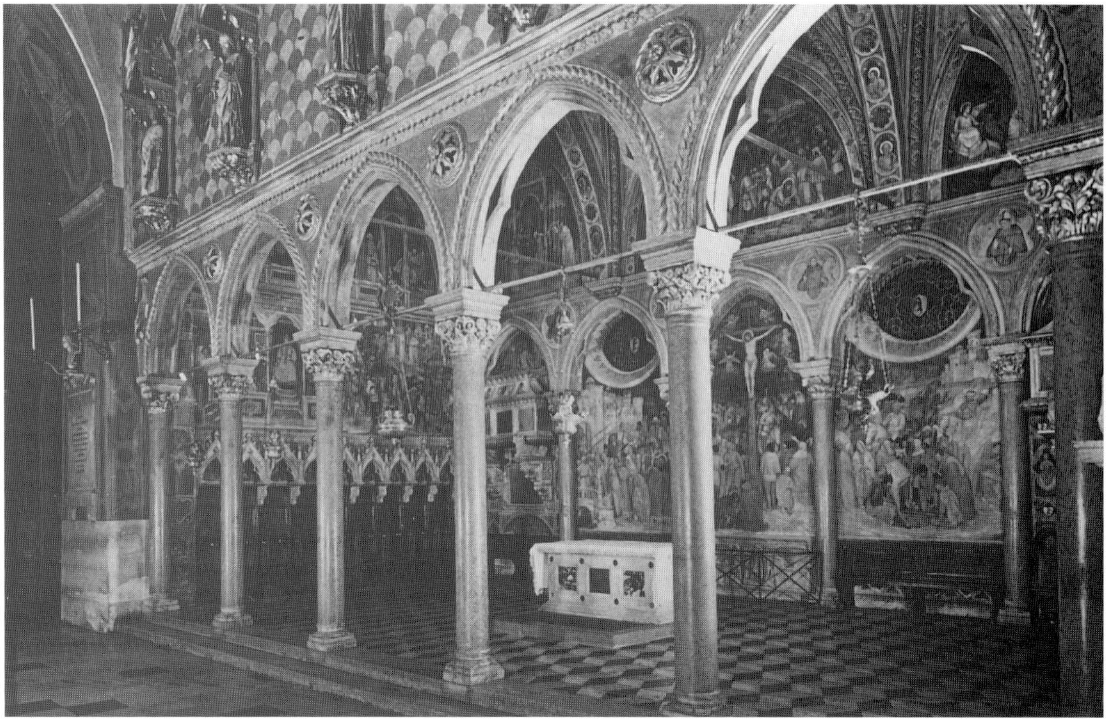

Plate 39 Padua, Il Santo, Chapel of S. Giacomo from the north-west.

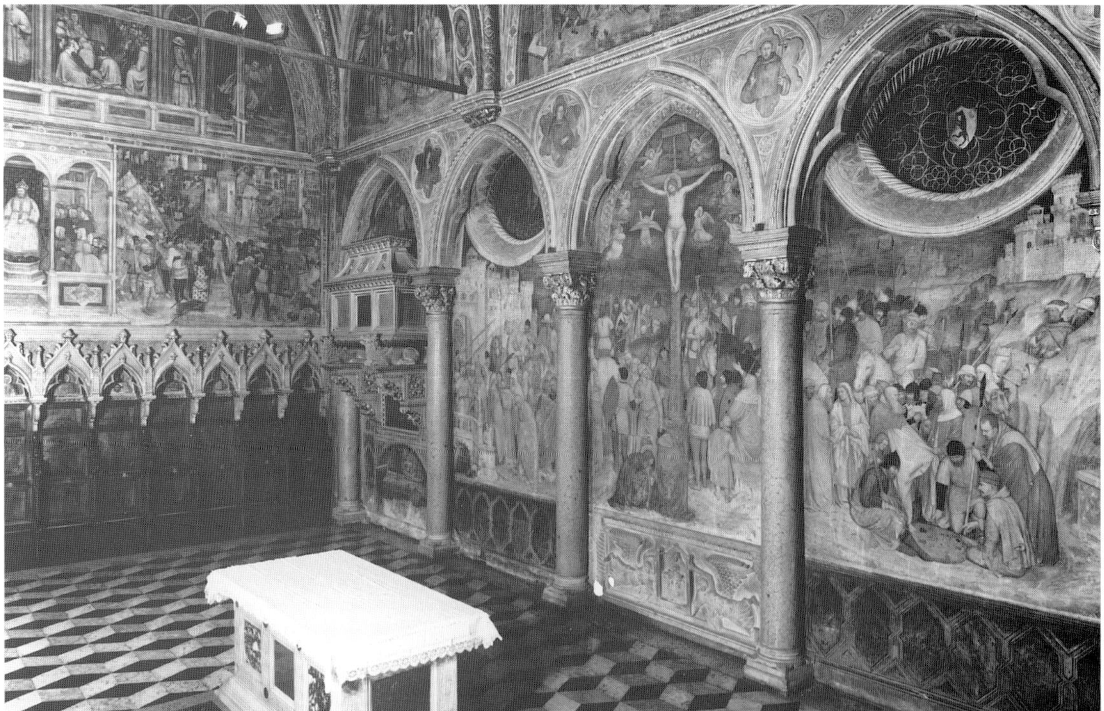

Plate 40 Padua, Il Santo, Chapel of S. Giacomo to south-east.

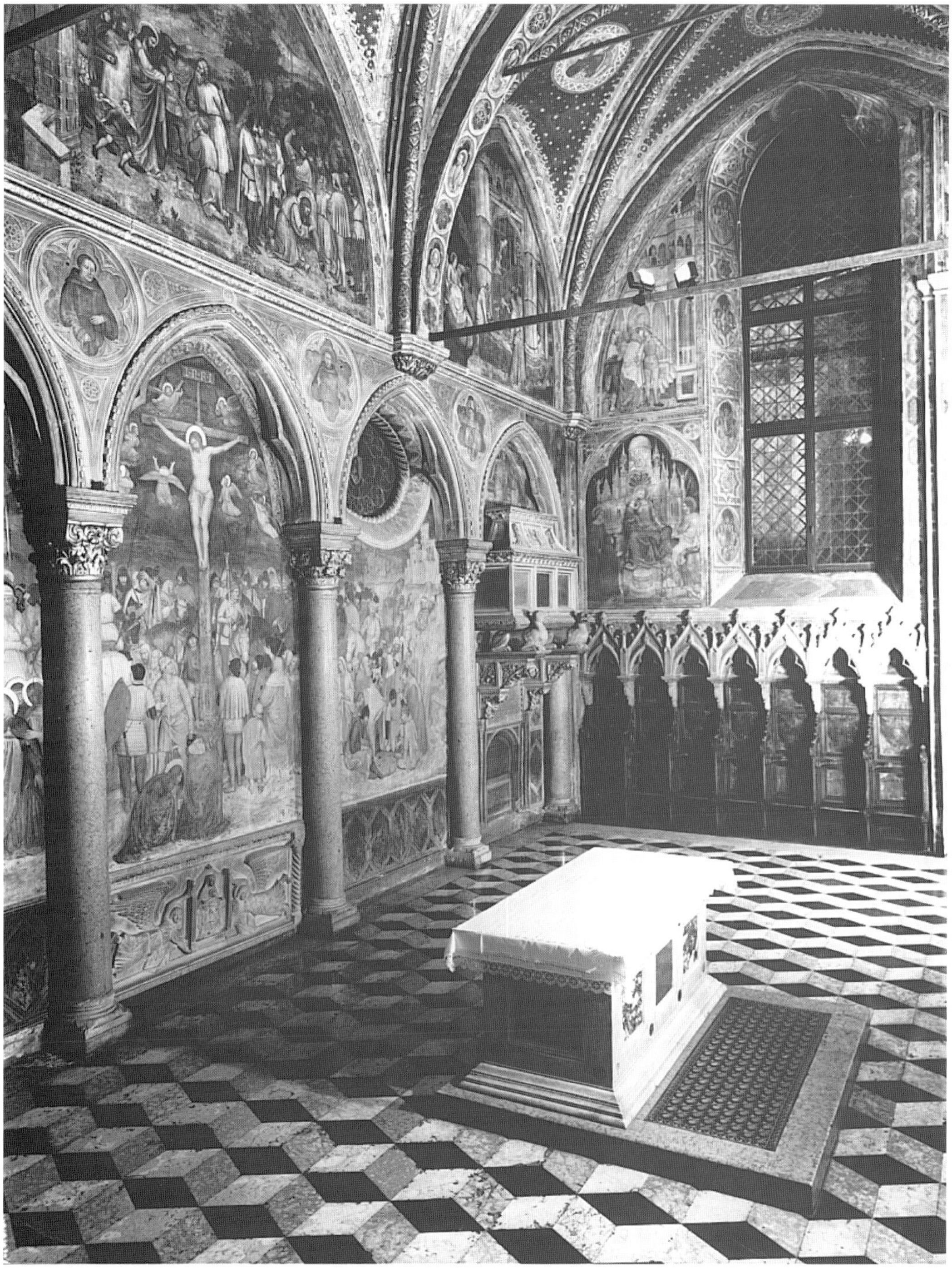

Plate 41 Padua, Il Santo, Chapel of S. Giacomo to south-west.

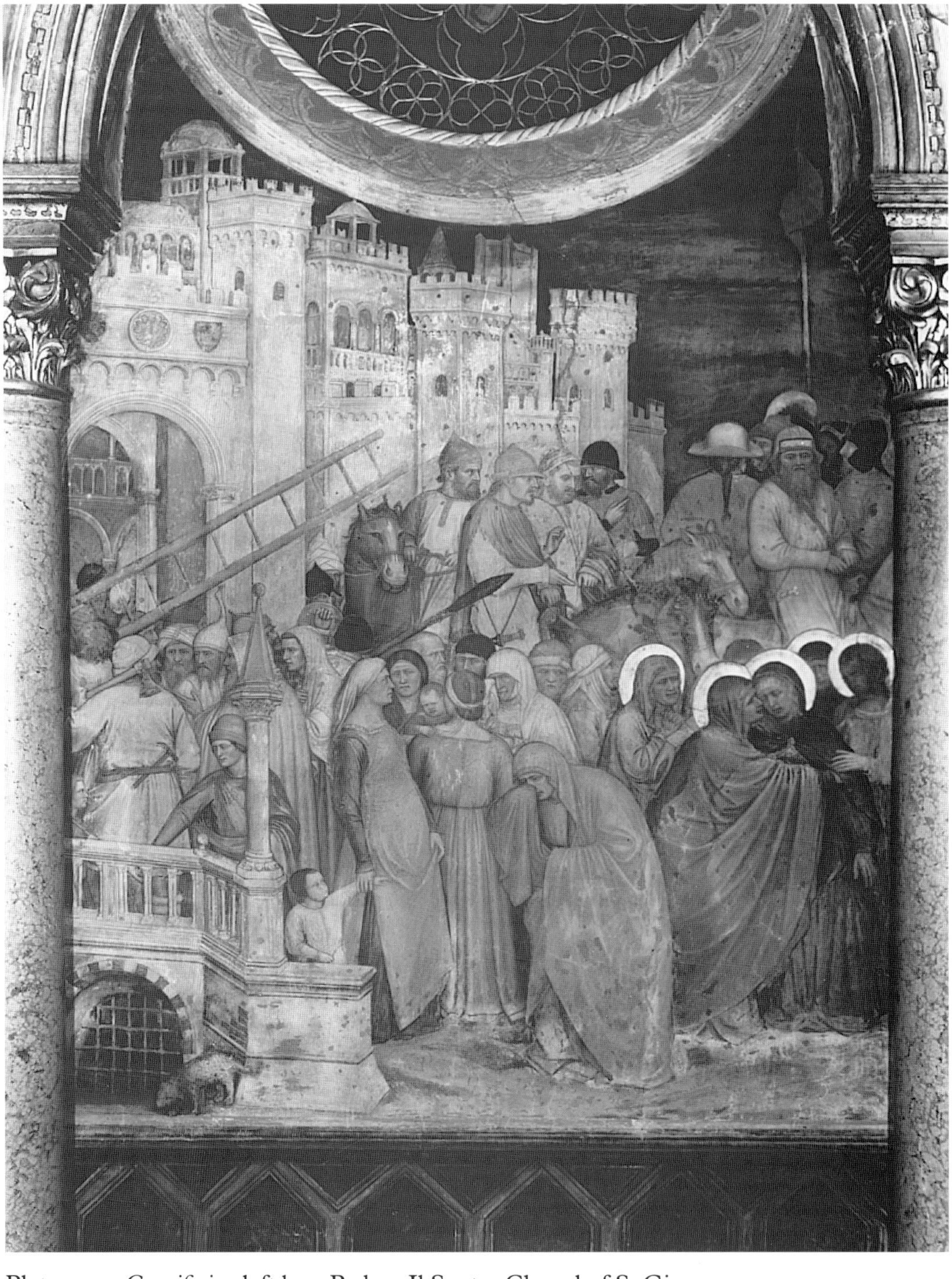

Plate 42 *Crucifixion* left bay. Padua, Il Santo, Chapel of S. Giacomo.

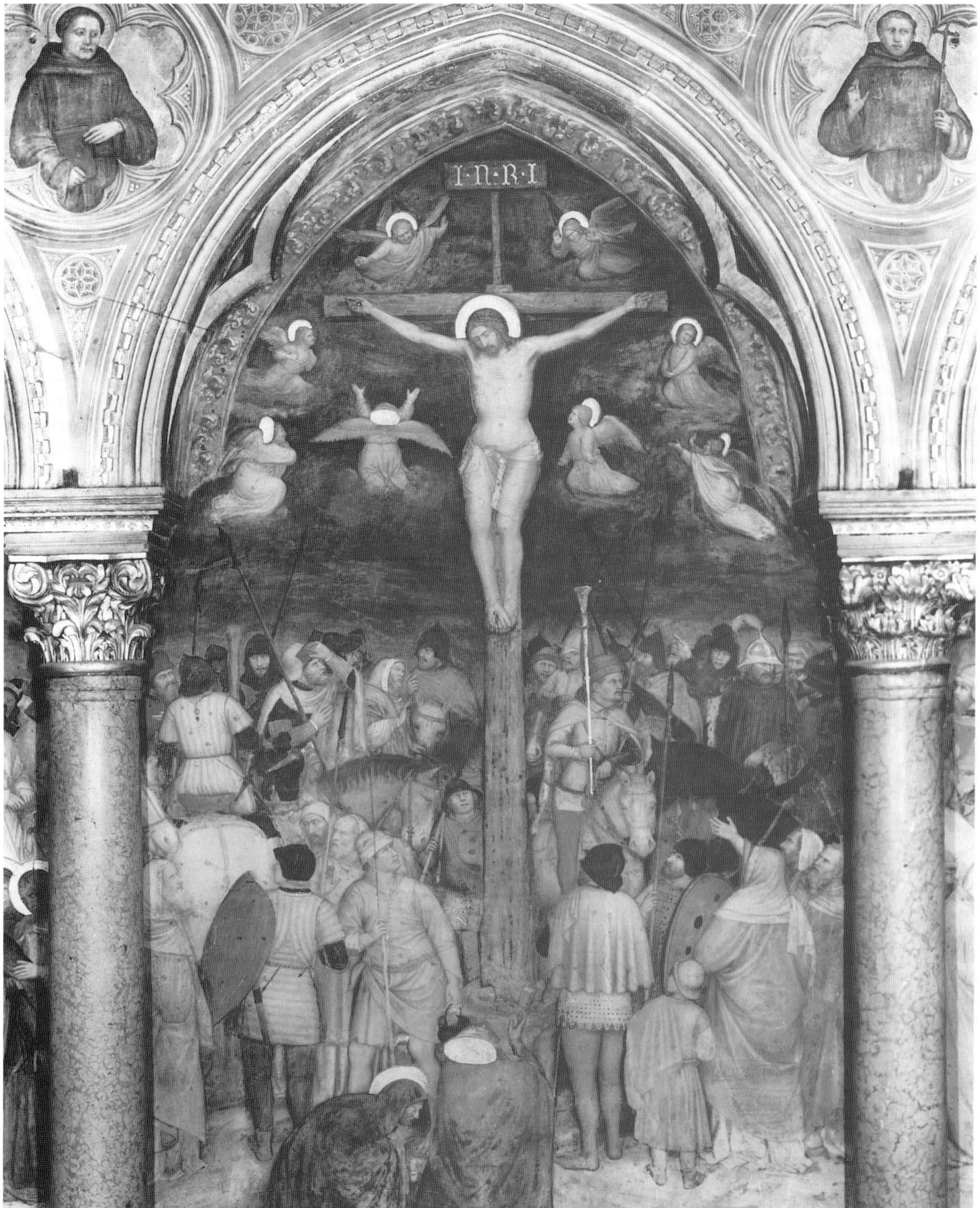

Plate 43 *Crucifixion* central bay. Padua, Il Santo, Chapel of S. Giacomo.

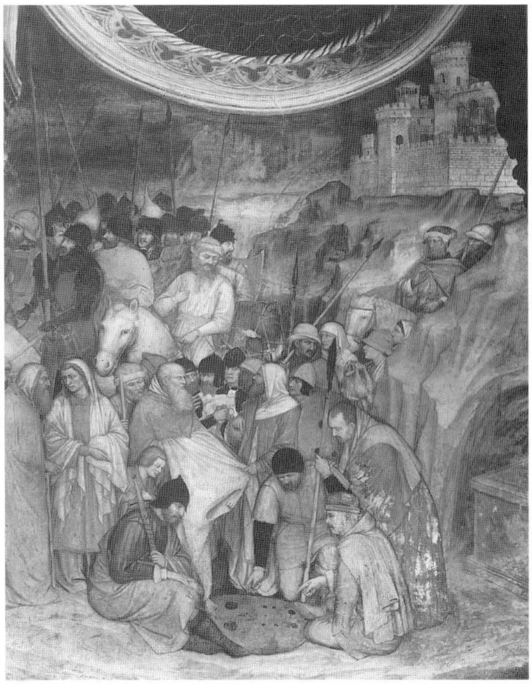

Plate 44 *Crucifixion* right bay. Padua, Il Santo, Chapel of S. Giacomo.

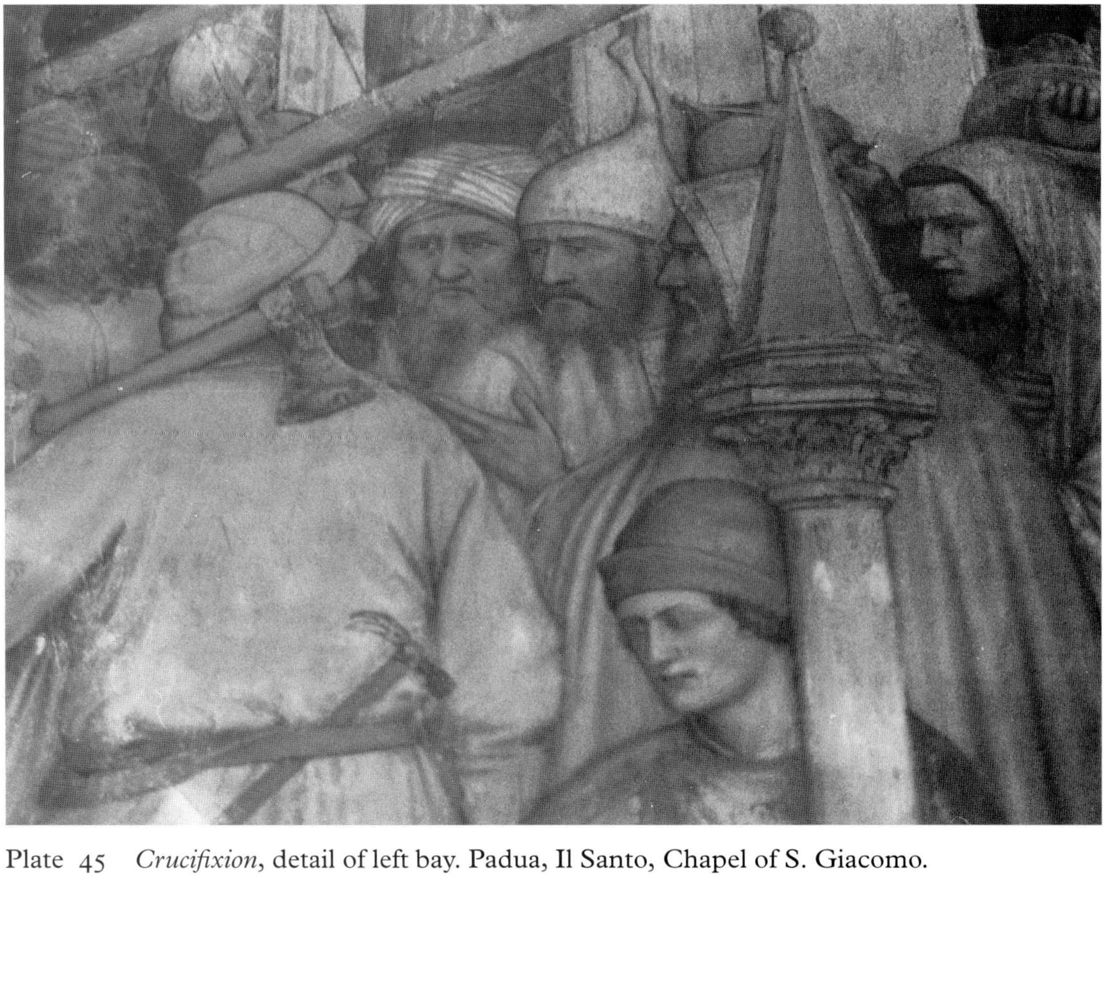

Plate 45 *Crucifixion*, detail of left bay. Padua, Il Santo, Chapel of S. Giacomo.

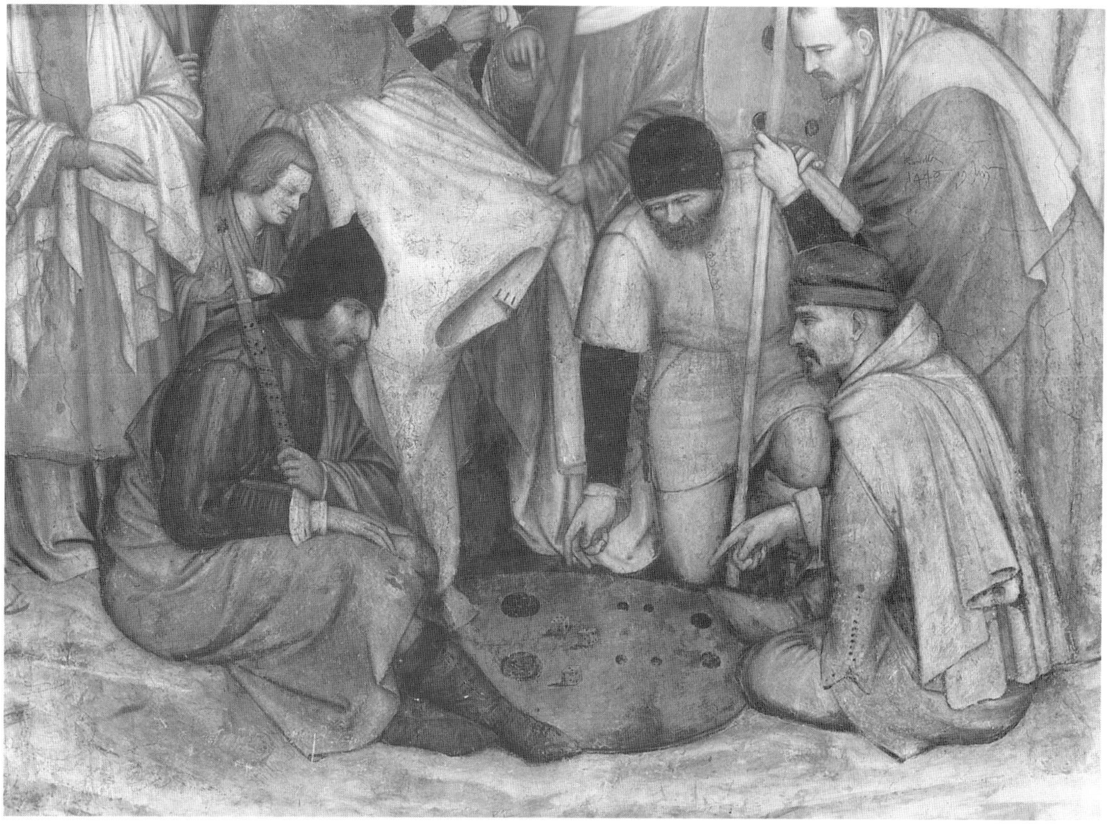

Plate 46 *Crucifixion*, detail of right bay. Padua, Il Santo, Chapel of S. Giacomo.

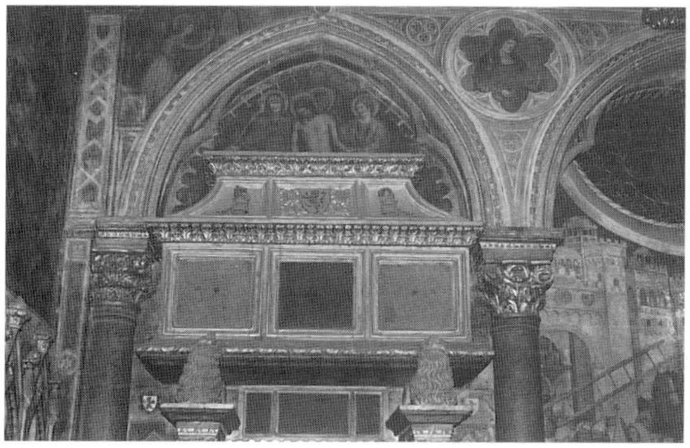

Plate 47 Padua, Il Santo, Chapel of S. Giacomo. Rossi tomb with *Pietà* and *Archangel Gabriel*.

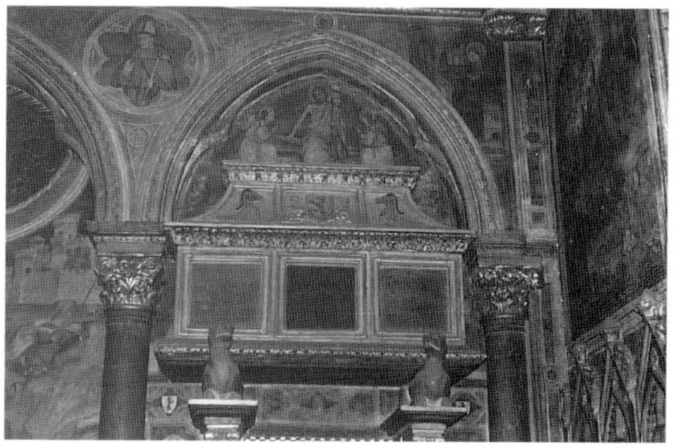

Plate 48 Padua, Il Santo, Chapel of S. Giacomo. Tomb of Bonifacio Lupi with *Resurrection* and *Virgin Annunciate*.

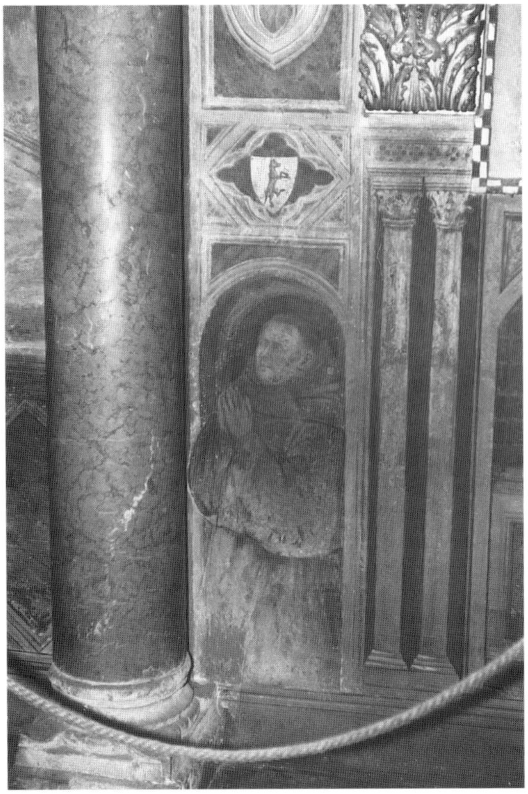

Plate 49 *Bonifacio Lupi [?] in Franciscan Habit*. Padua, Il Santo, Chapel of S. Giacomo.

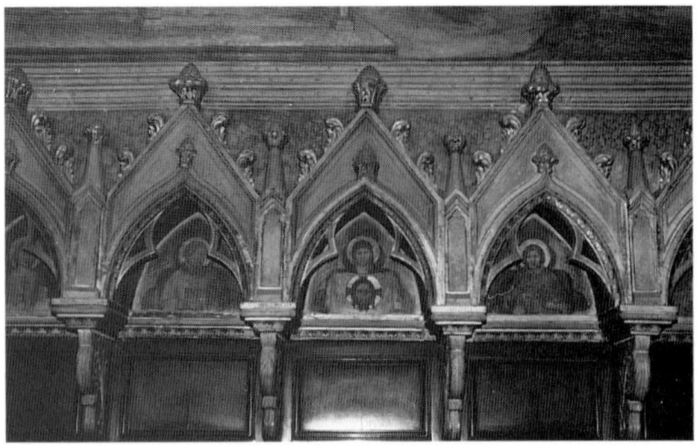

Plate 50a Padua, Il Santo, Chapel of S. Giacomo. Stall canopies and frescoes.

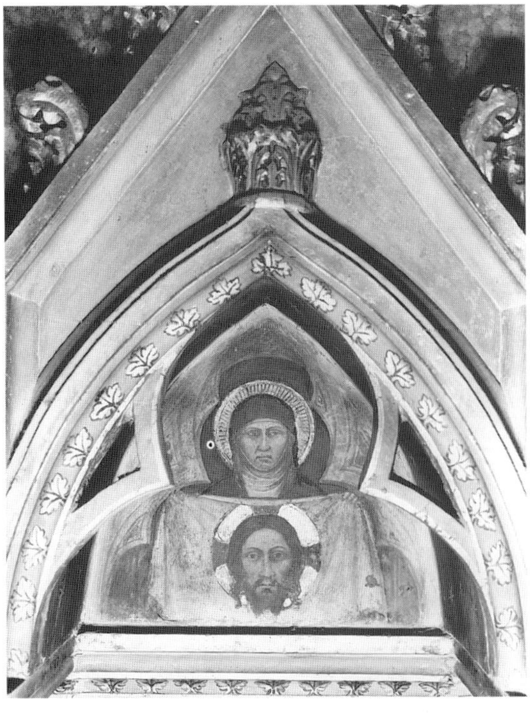

Plate 50b *St Veronica*. Padua, Il Santo, Chapel of S. Giacomo.

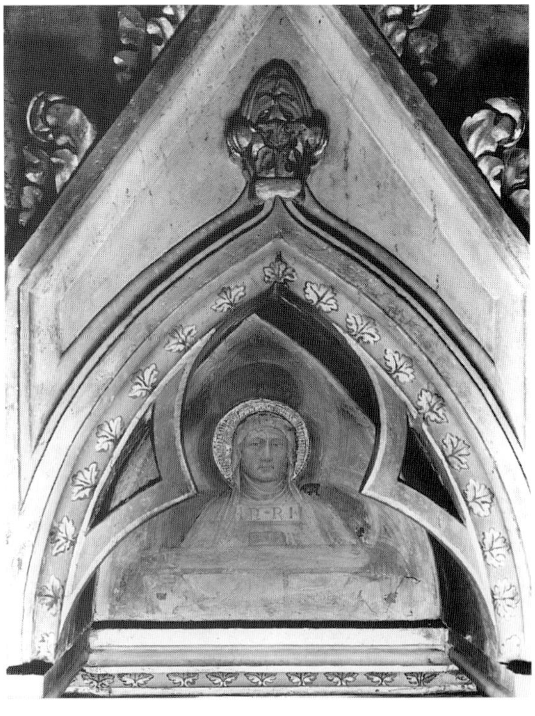

Plate 50c *St Helena*. Padua, Il Santo, Chapel of S. Giacomo.

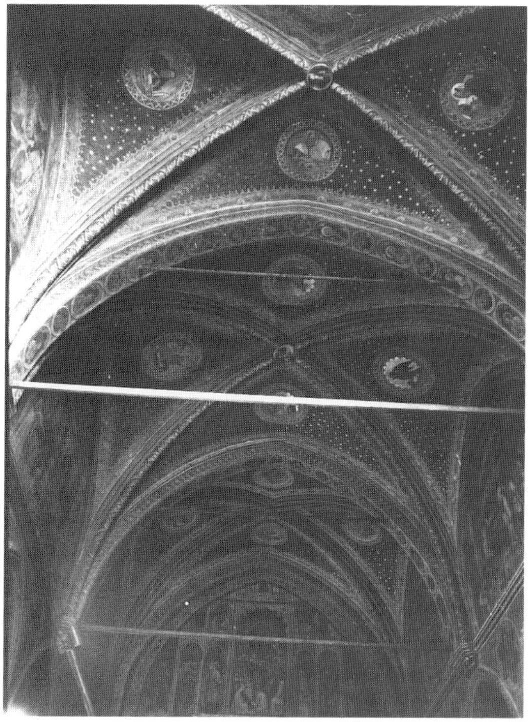

Plate 51a Padua, Il Santo, Chapel of S. Giacomo. Vaults.

Plate 51b Padua, Il Santo, Chapel of S. Giacomo. Vault decoration.

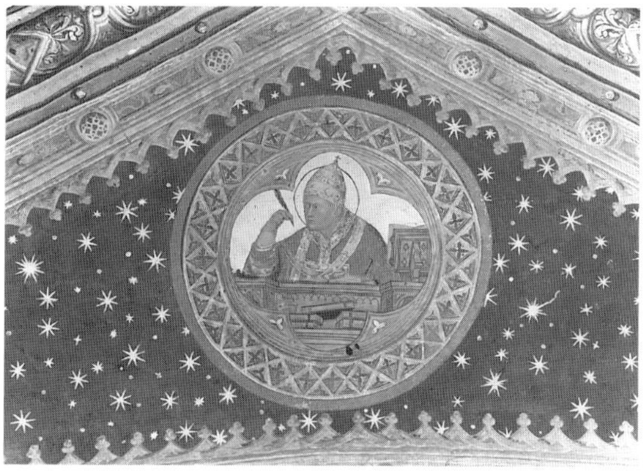

Plate 51c *St Gregory*. Padua, Il Santo, Chapel of S. Giacomo.

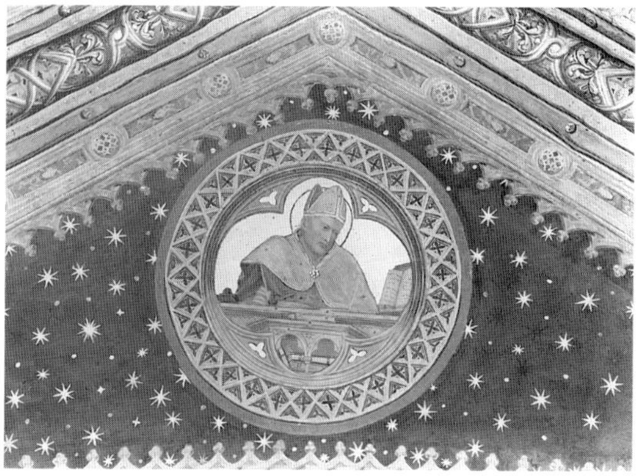

Plate 51d *St Ambrose*. Padua, Il Santo, Chapel of S. Giacomo.

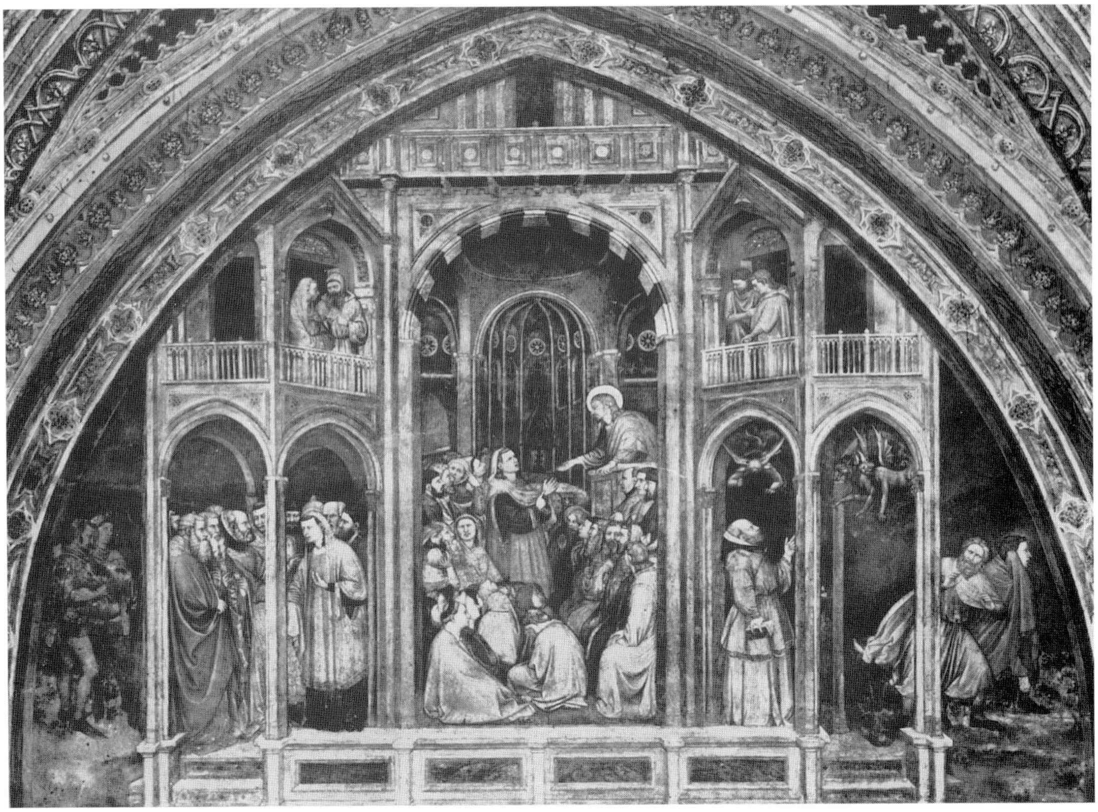

Plate 52 Jacopo Avanzi ([?] plinth of basilica by Altichiero): *Hermogenes Instructing Filetus; St James Disputing with Filetus; Hermogenes Summoning Demons*. Padua, Il Santo, Chapel of S. Giacomo.

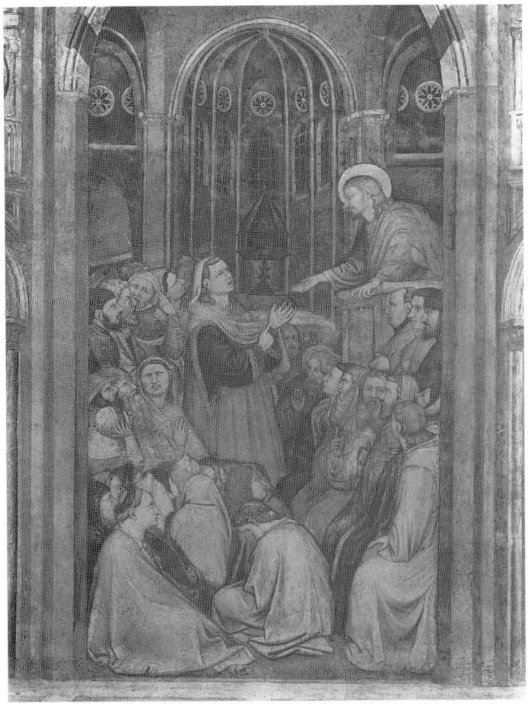

Plate 53 Jacopo Avanzi: *St James Disputing with Filetus*. Padua, Il Santo, Chapel of S. Giacomo.

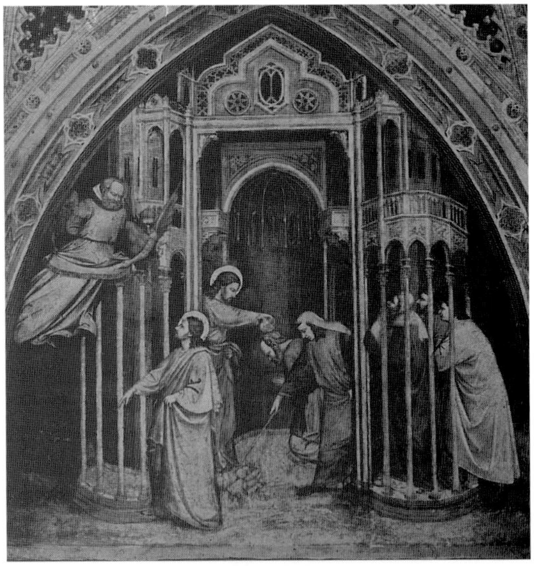

Plate 54 Jacopo Avanzi: *Hermogenes Transported by Demons; Baptism of Hermogenes and Burning of the Magic Books*. Padua, Il Santo, Chapel of S. Giacomo.

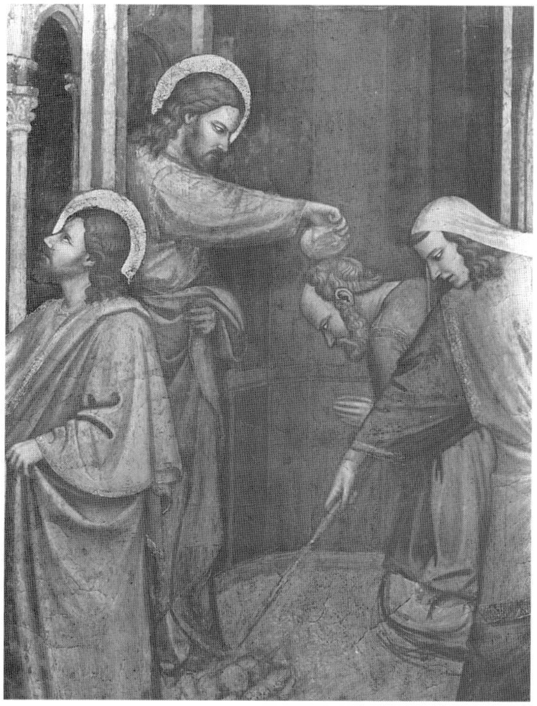

Plate 55 Jacopo Avanzi: *Baptism of Hermogenes and Burning of the Magic Books* (detail). Padua, Il Santo, Chapel of S. Giacomo.

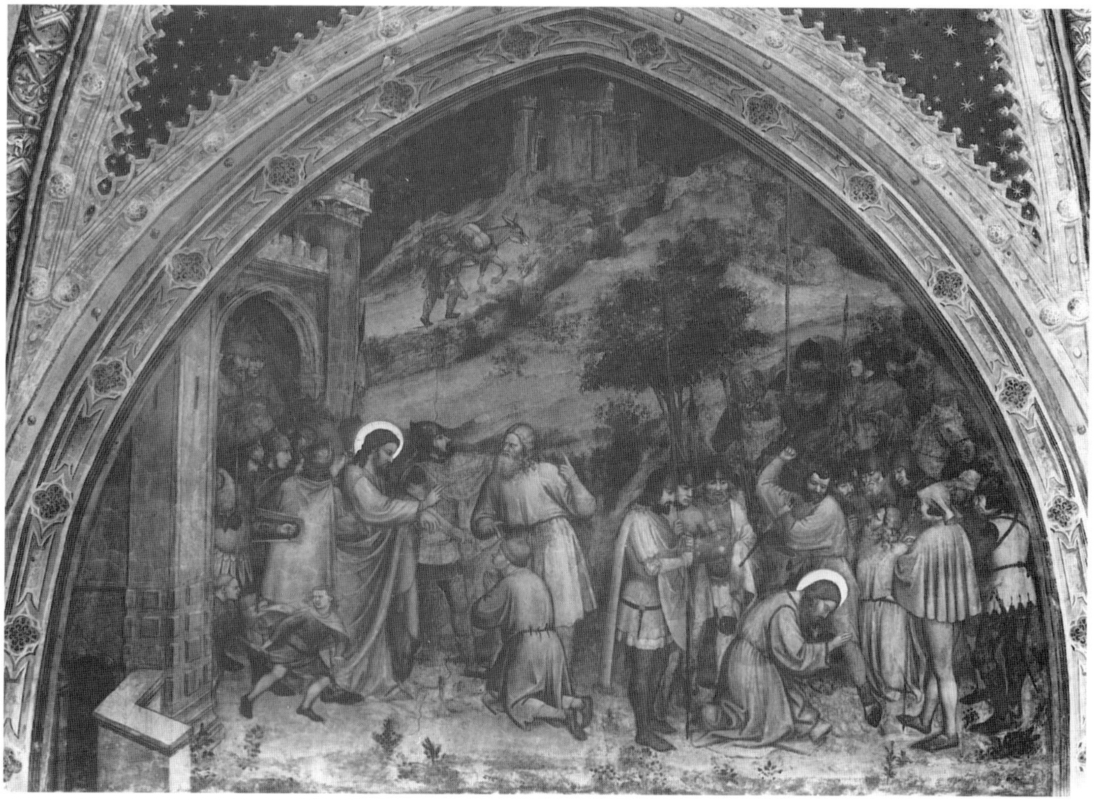

Plate 56 Jacopo Avanzi: *St James Healing the Sick; Execution of St James*. Padua, Il Santo, Chapel of S. Giacomo.

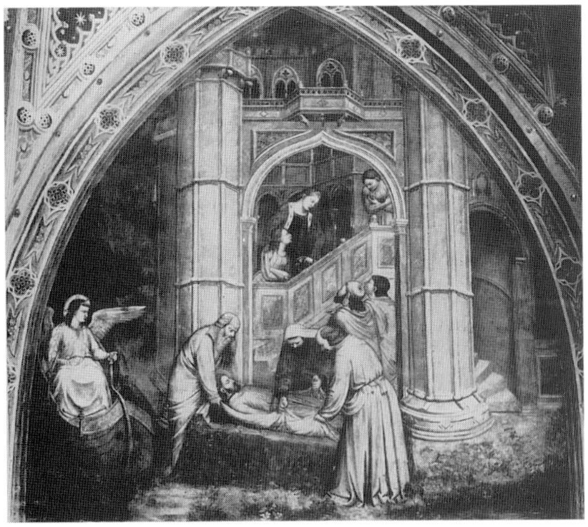

Plate 57 Jacopo Avanzi: *Miraculous Burial of St James; Queen Lupa Told of the Miracle.* Padua, Il Santo, Chapel of S. Giacomo.

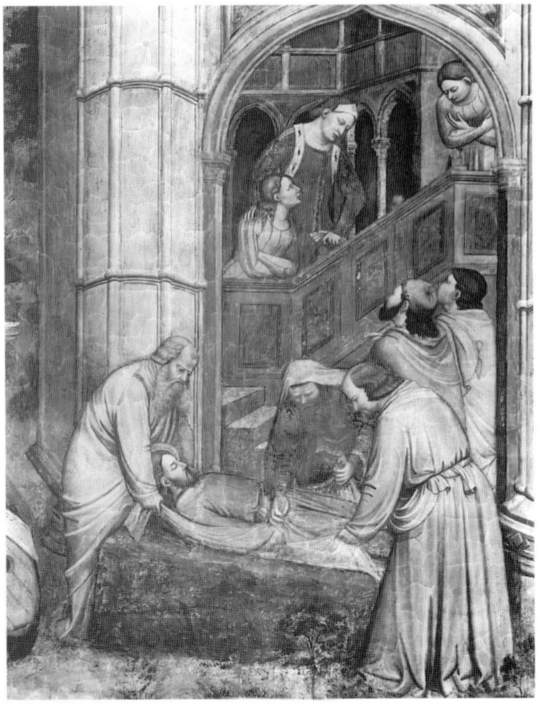

Plate 58 Jacopo Avanzi: *Miraculous Burial of St James* (detail). Padua, Il Santo, Chapel of S. Giacomo.

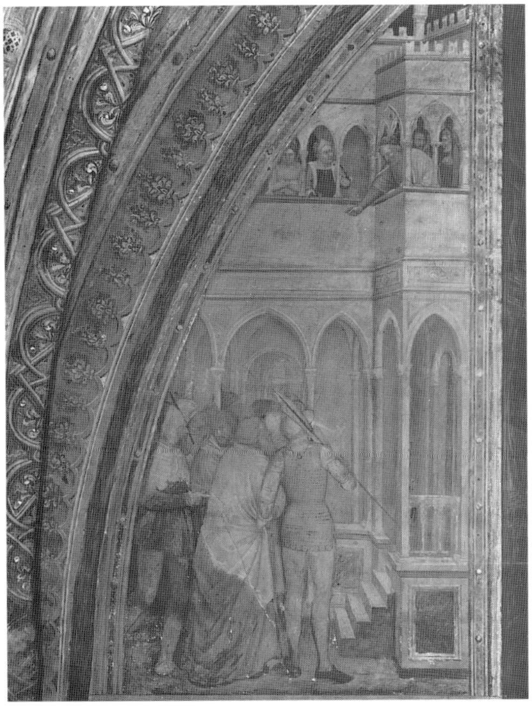

Plate 59 *St James's Disciples Taken Before the King of Spain.* Padua, Il Santo, Chapel of S. Giacomo.

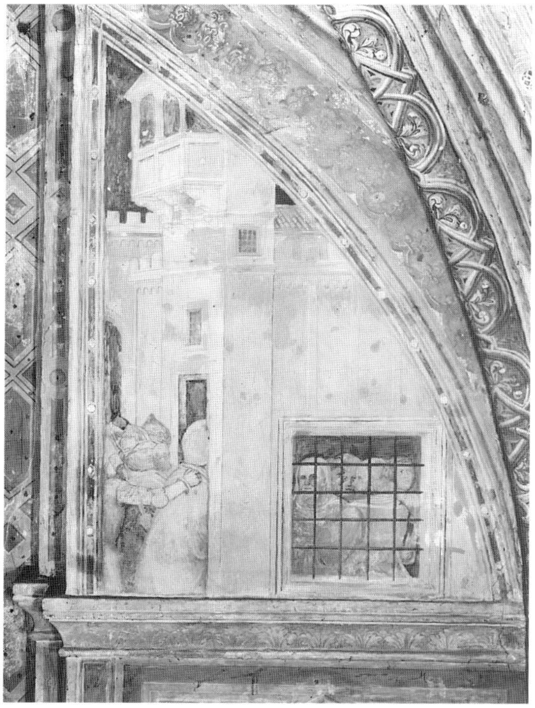

Plate 60 *Imprisonment of the Disciples*. Padua, Il Santo, Chapel of S. Giacomo.

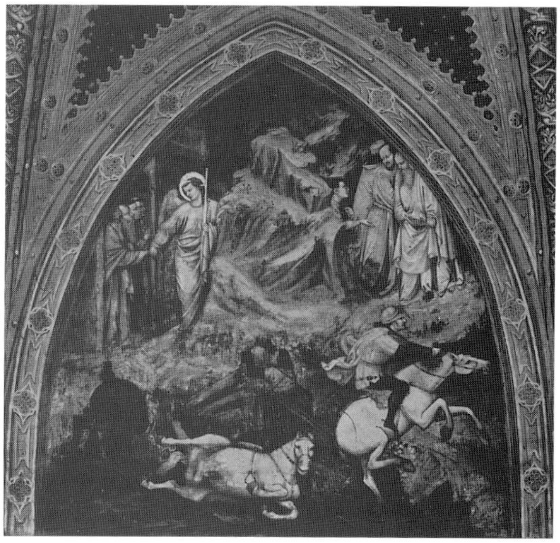

Plate 61 Jacopo Avanzi: *Escape of the Disciples and Their Recall to Compostella*. Padua, Il Santo, Chapel of S. Giacomo.

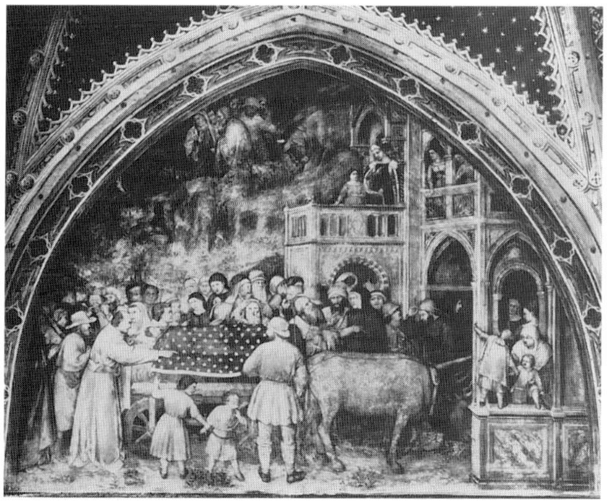

Plate 62 *Wild Bulls Take the Body of St James to Queen Lupa's Palace*. Padua, Il Santo, Chapel of S. Giacomo.

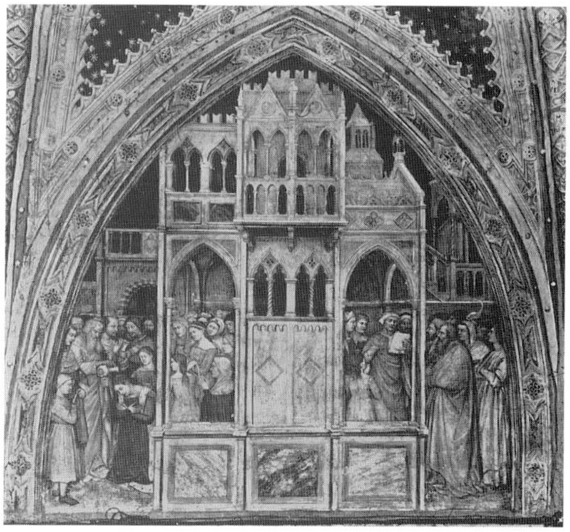

Plate 63 *Hermogenes Baptising Queen Lupa. Rededication of her Palace as a Church*. Padua, Il Santo, Chapel of S. Giacomo.

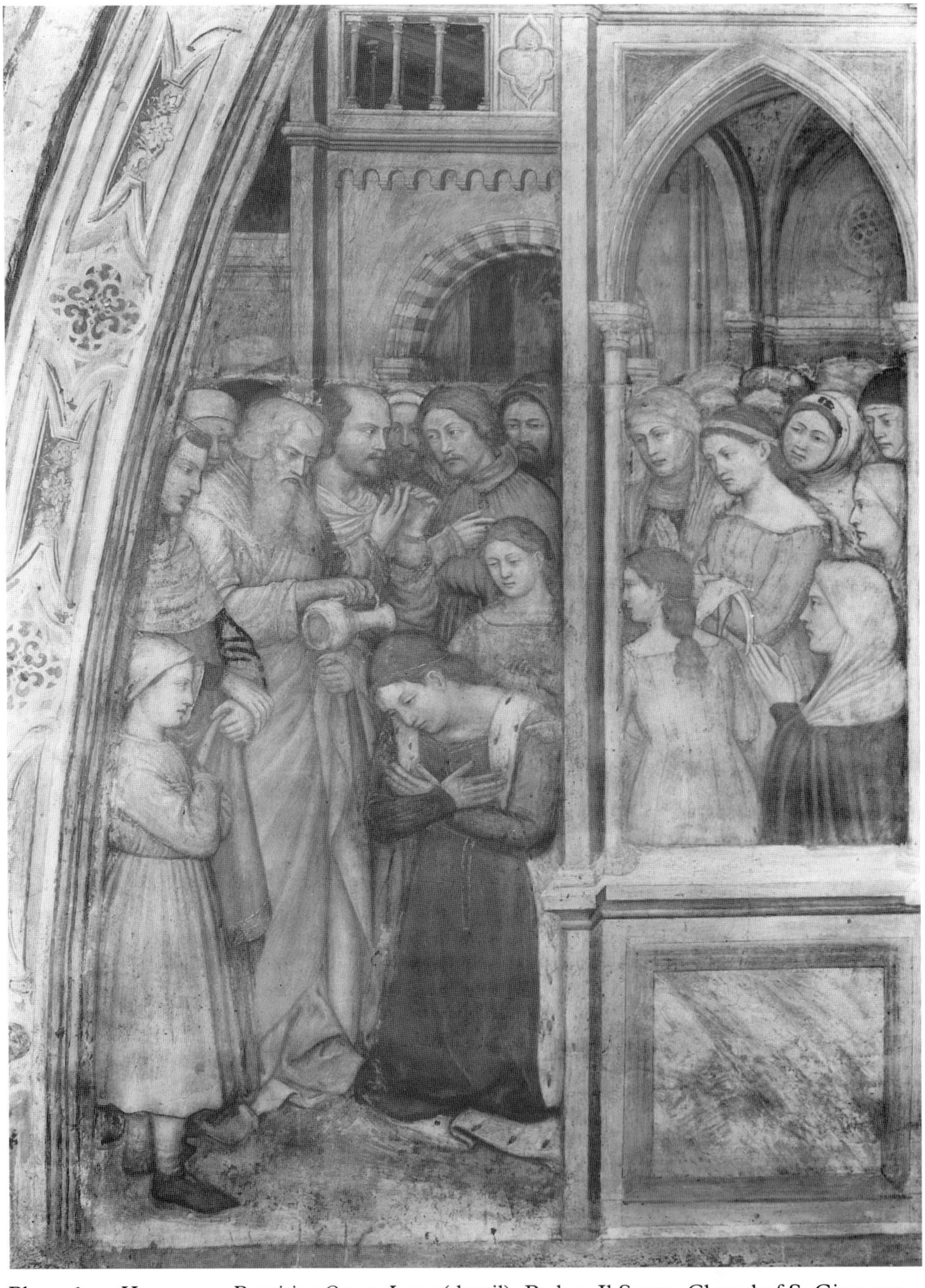

Plate 64 *Hermogenes Baptising Queen Lupa* (detail). Padua, Il Santo, Chapel of S. Giacomo.

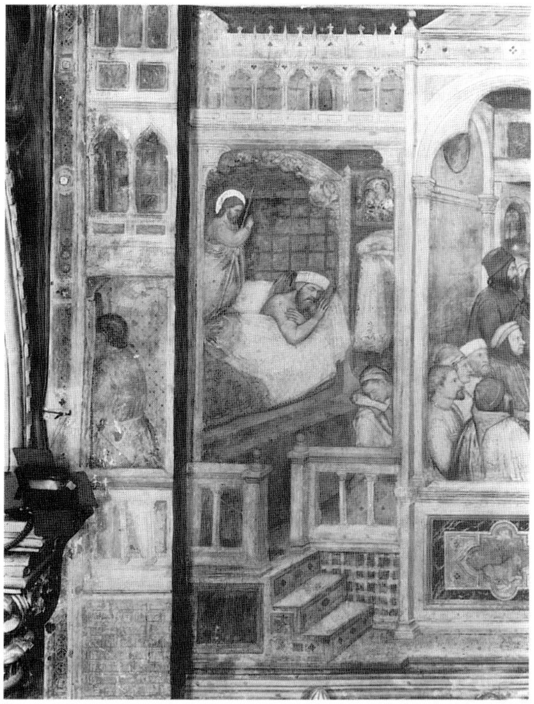

Plate 65 *King Ramiro's Dream*. Padua, Il Santo, Chapel of S. Giacomo.

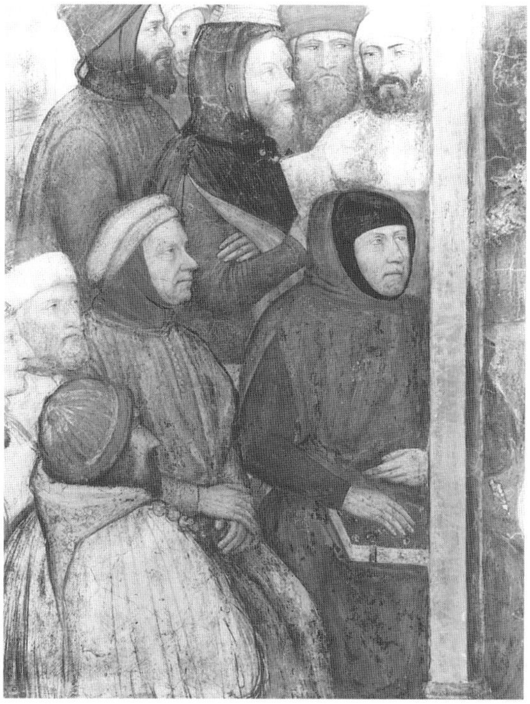

Plate 67 *Council of King Ramiro* (detail): Lombardo della Seta (centre left) and Petrarch (centre right). Padua, Il Santo, Chapel of S. Giacomo.

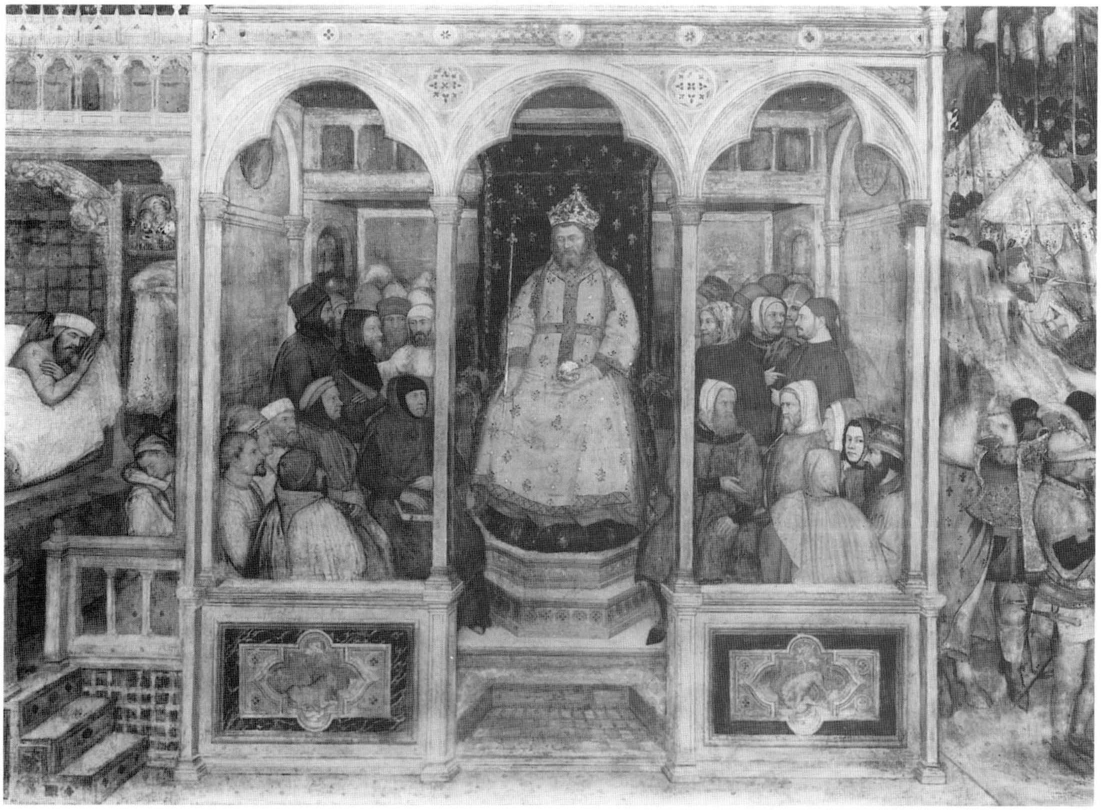

Plate 66 *Council of King Ramiro*. Padua, Il Santo, Chapel of S. Giacomo.

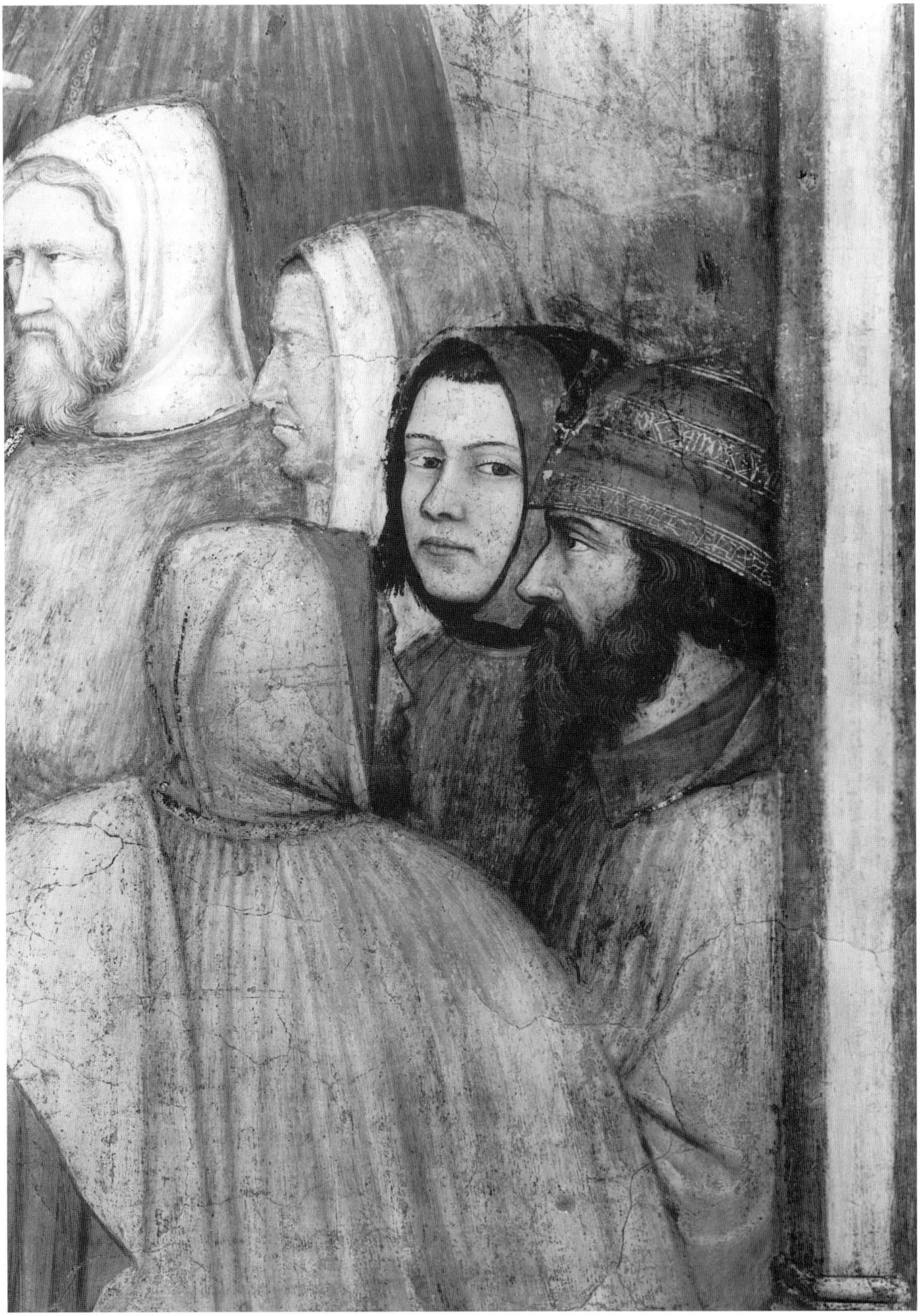

Plate 68 *Council of King Ramiro* (detail): Bonifacio Lupi and Caterina de'Francesi. Padua, Il Santo, Chapel of S. Giacomo.

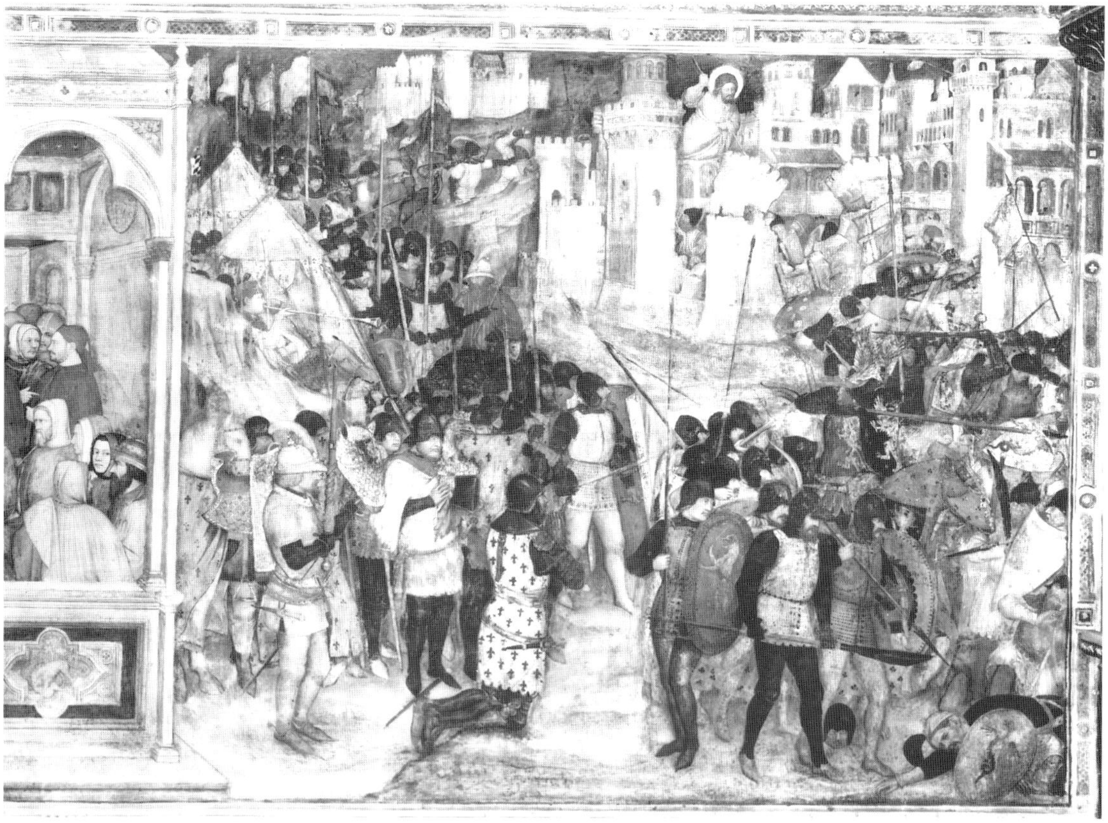

Plate 69 *Battle of Clavigo*. Padua, Il Santo, Chapel of S. Giacomo.

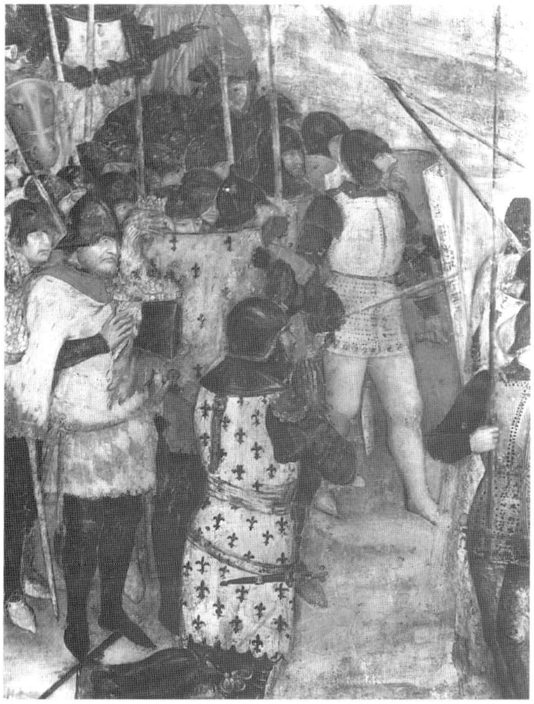

Plate 70 *Battle of Clavigo* (detail). Padua, Il Santo, Chapel of S. Giacomo.

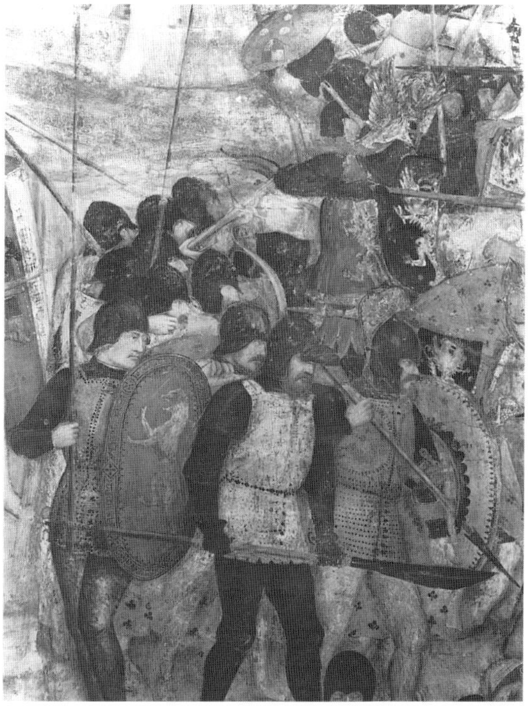

Plate 71 *Battle of Clavigo* (detail). Padua, Il Santo, Chapel of S. Giacomo.

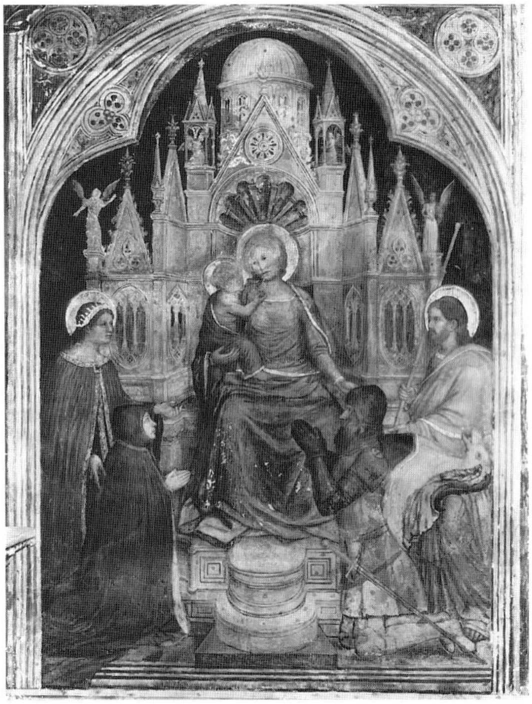

Plate 72 Votive fresco, Padua, Il Santo, Chapel of S. Giacomo.

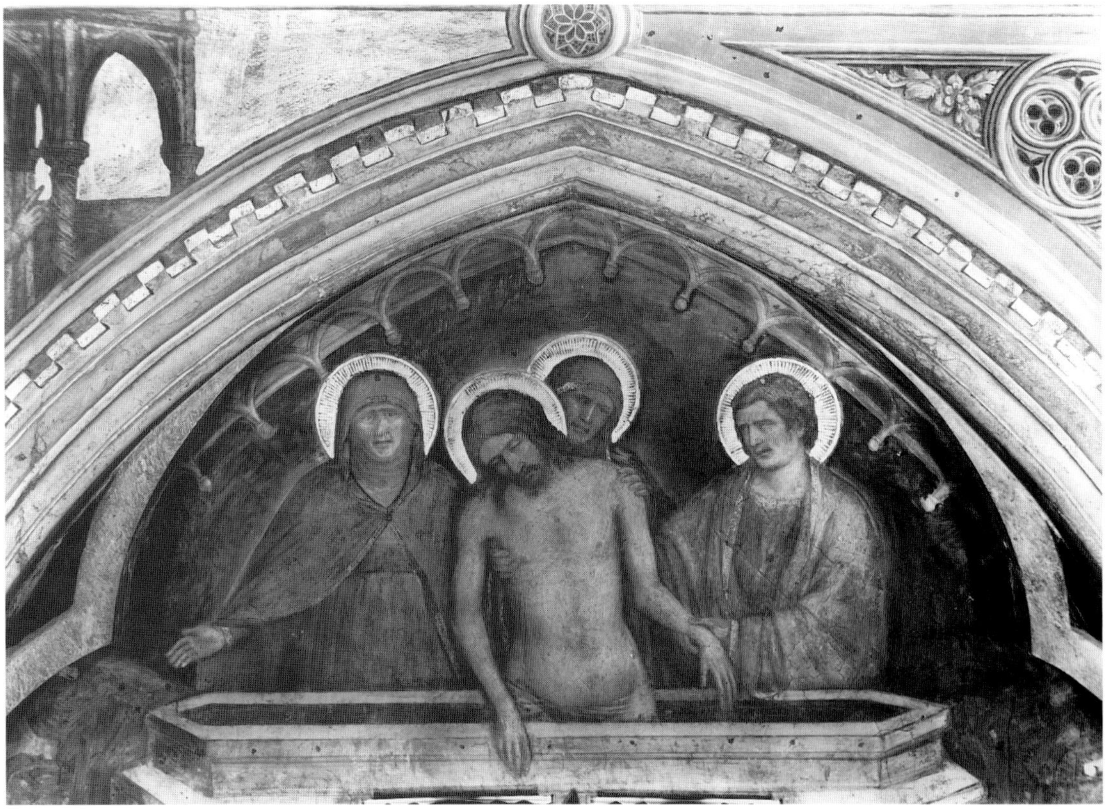

Plate 73 *Pietà*. Padua, Il Santo, Chapel of S. Giacomo.

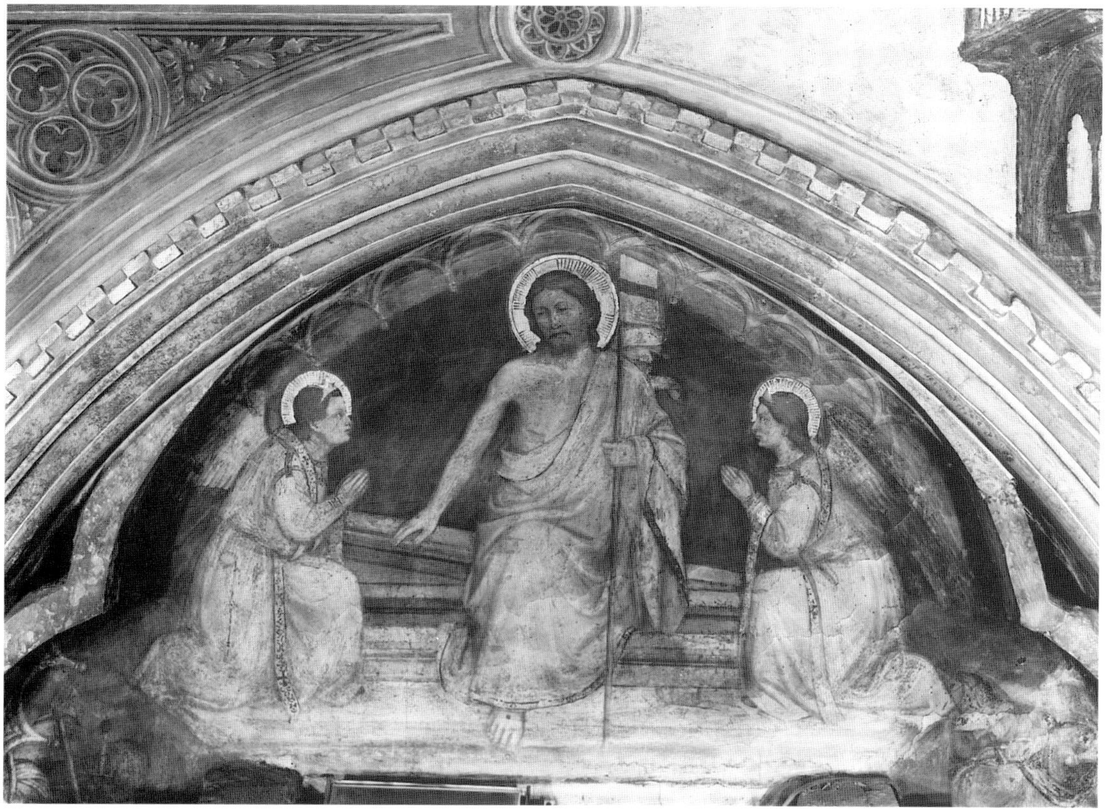

Plate 74 *Resurrection*. Padua, Il Santo, Chapel of S. Giacomo.

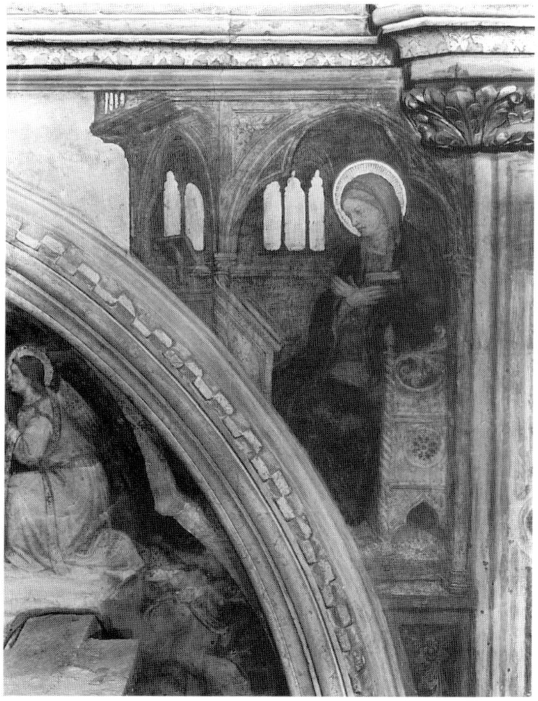

Plate 75 *Annunciate Virgin*. Padua, Il Santo, Chapel of S. Giacomo.

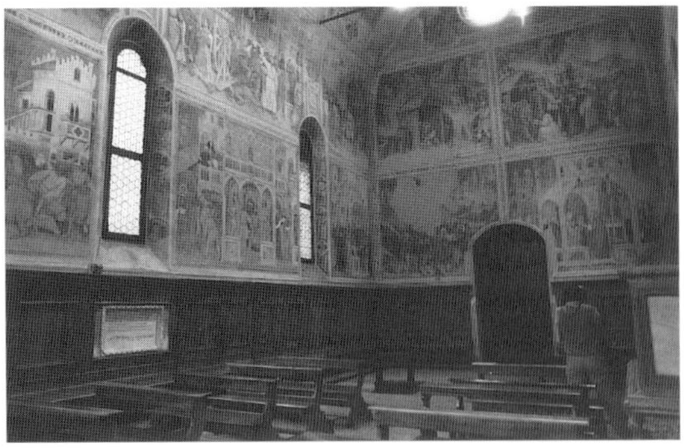

Plate 76a Padua, Oratory of S. Giorgio. Interior to north-west.

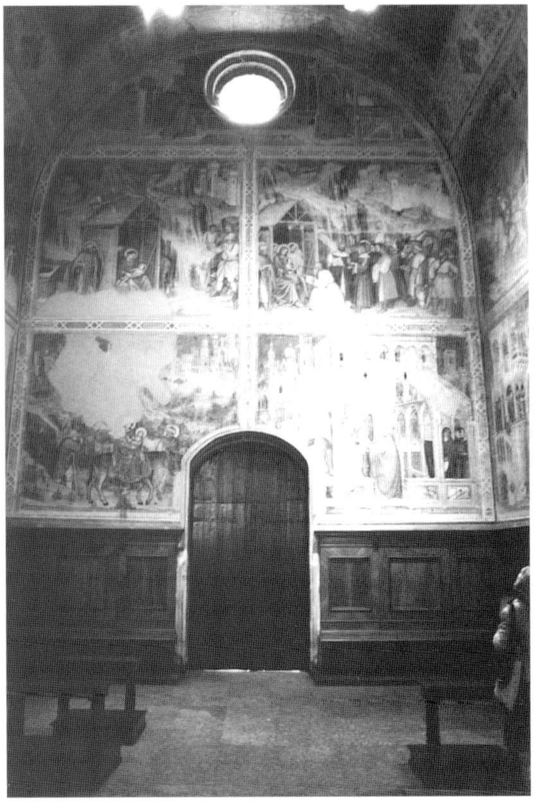

Plate 76b Padua, Oratory of S. Giorgio. Interior to north.

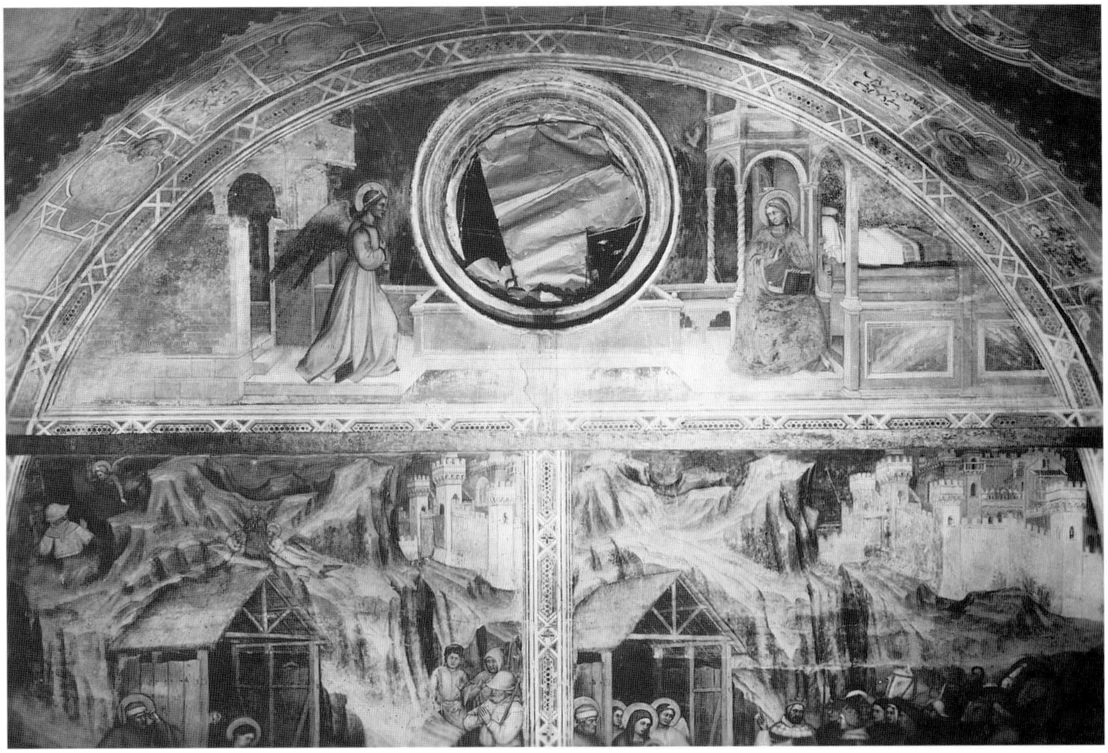

Plate 77 *Annunciation*. Padua, Oratory of S. Giorgio.

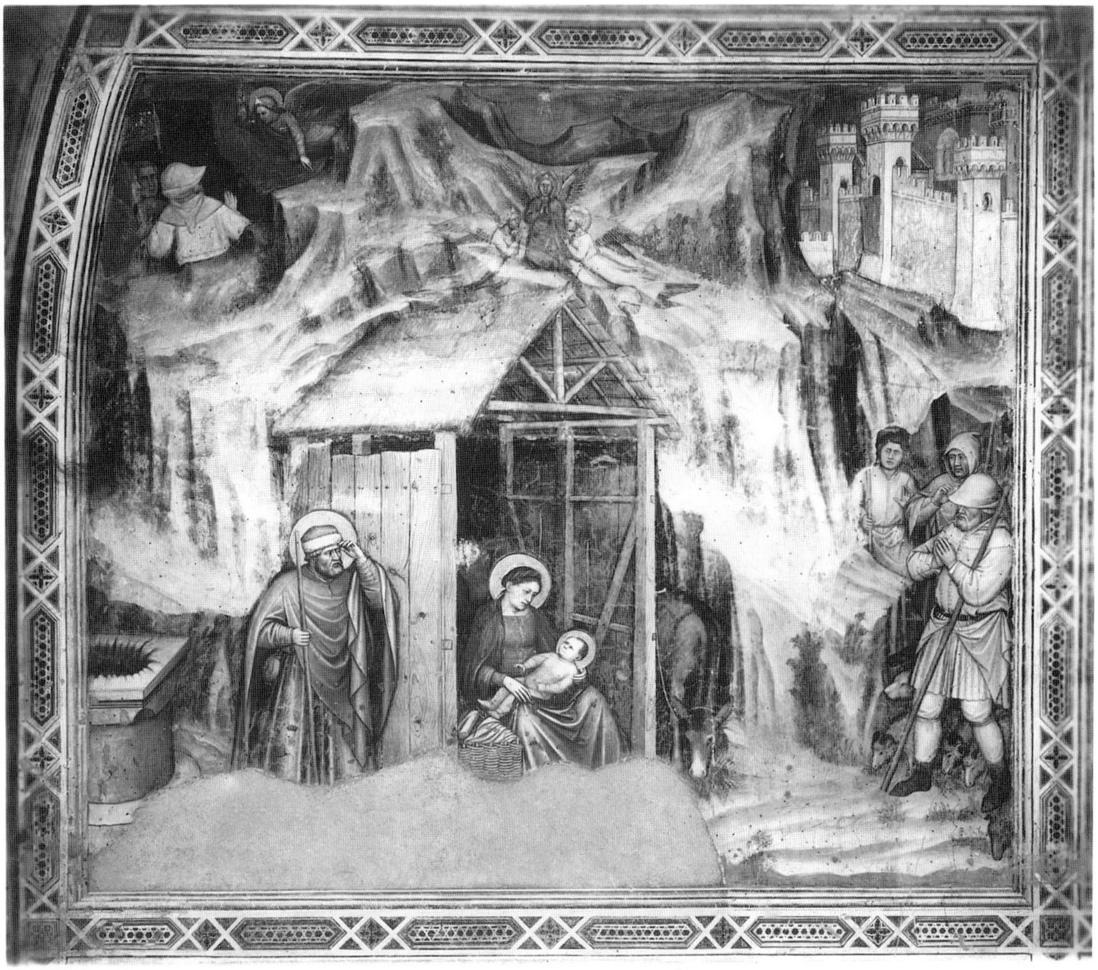

Plate 78 *Nativity*. Padua, Oratory of S. Giorgio.

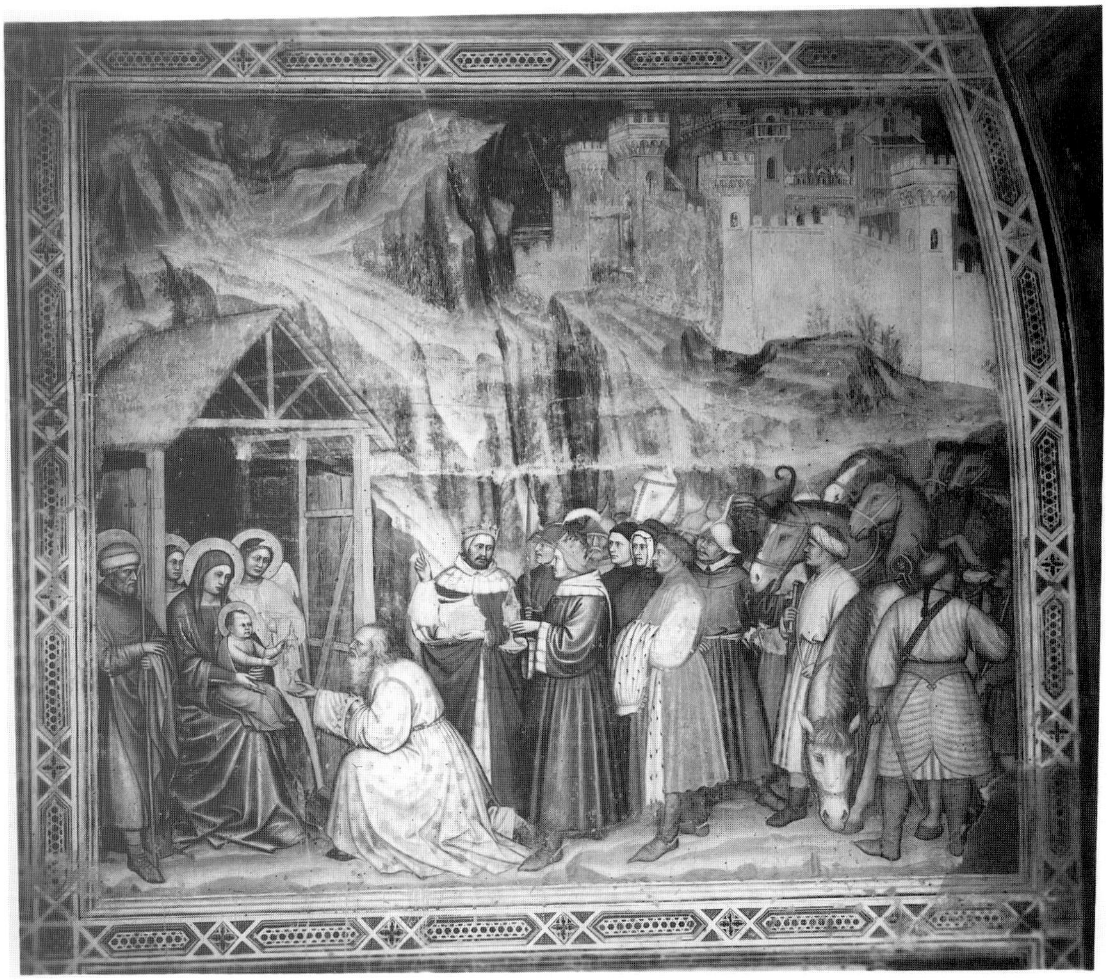

Plate 79 *Adoration of the Magi*. Padua, Oratory of S. Giorgio.

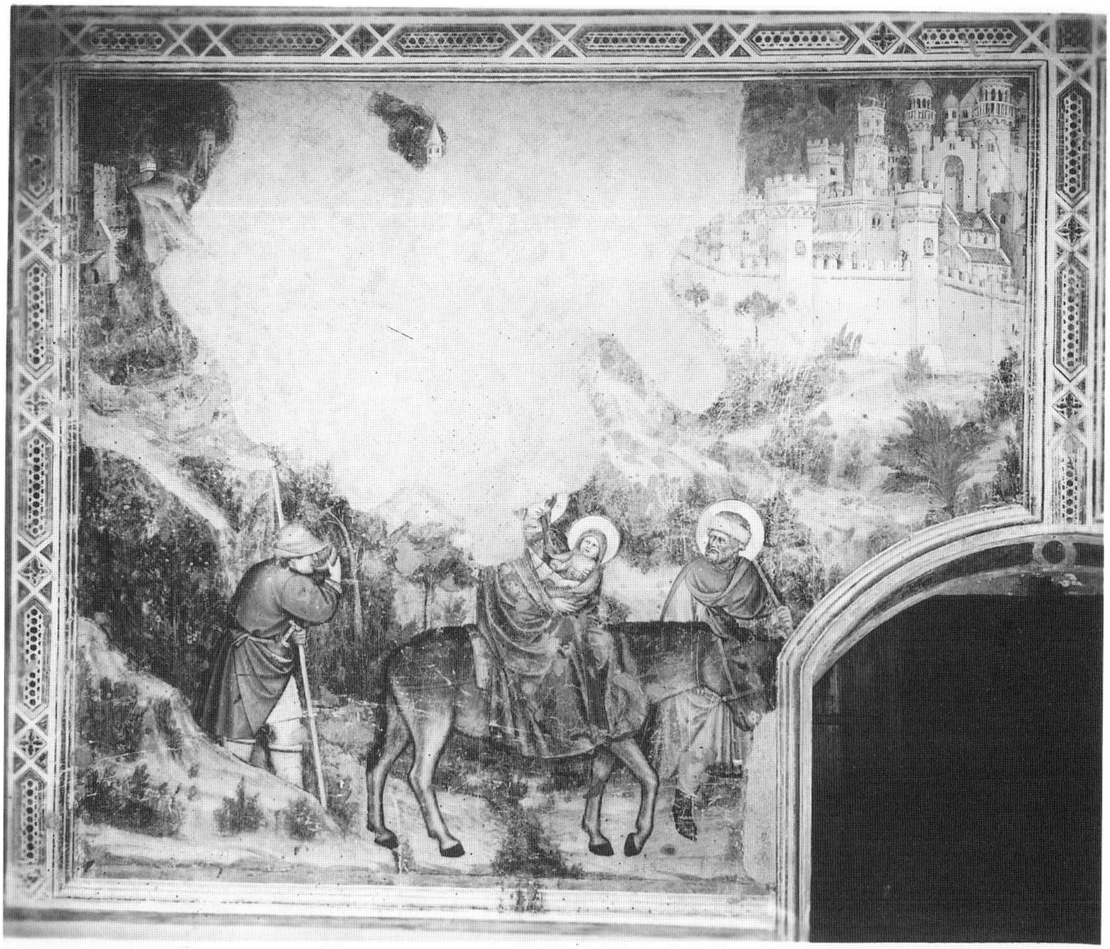

Plate 80 *Flight into Egypt*. Padua, Oratory of S. Giorgio.

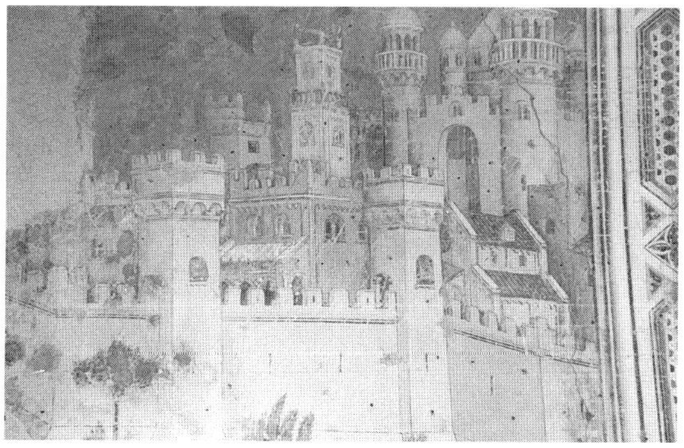

Plate 81 *Flight into Egypt* (detail). Padua, Oratory of S. Giorgio.

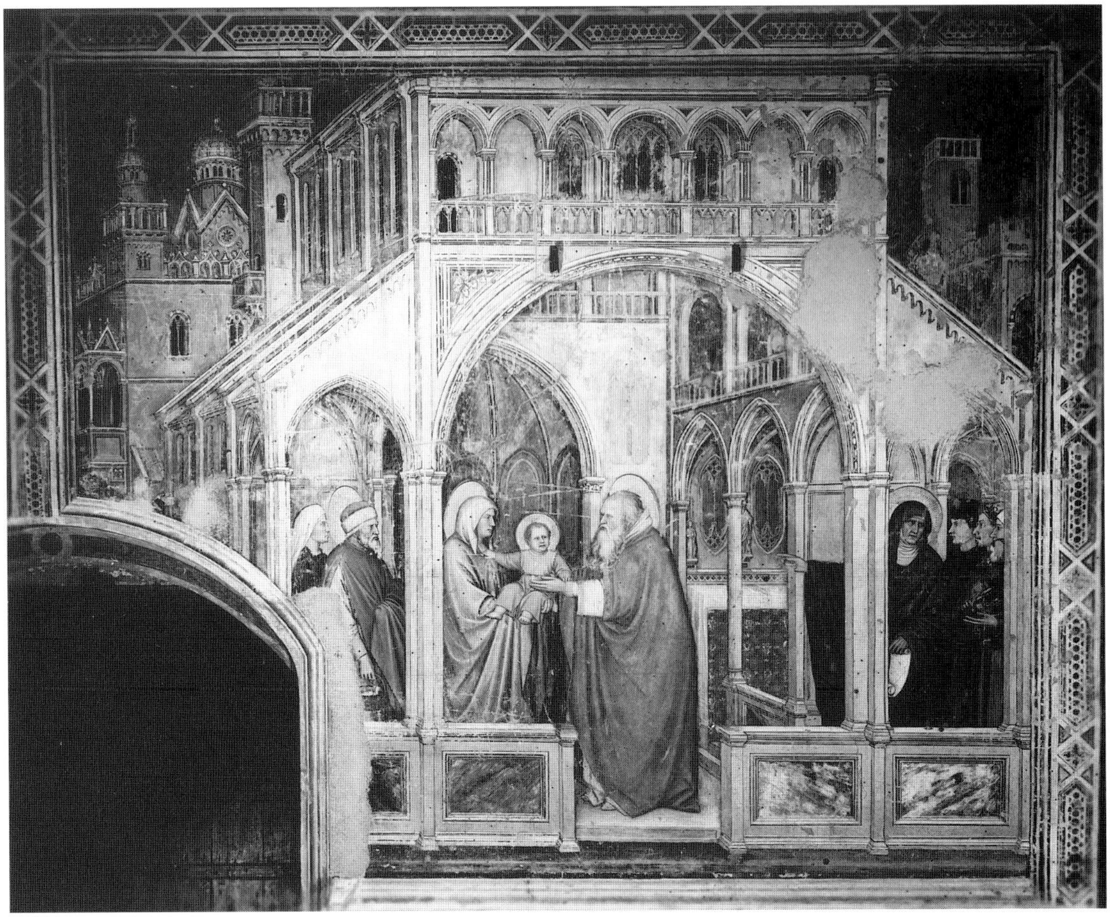

Plate 82 *Presentation in the Temple*. Padua, Oratory of S. Giorgio.

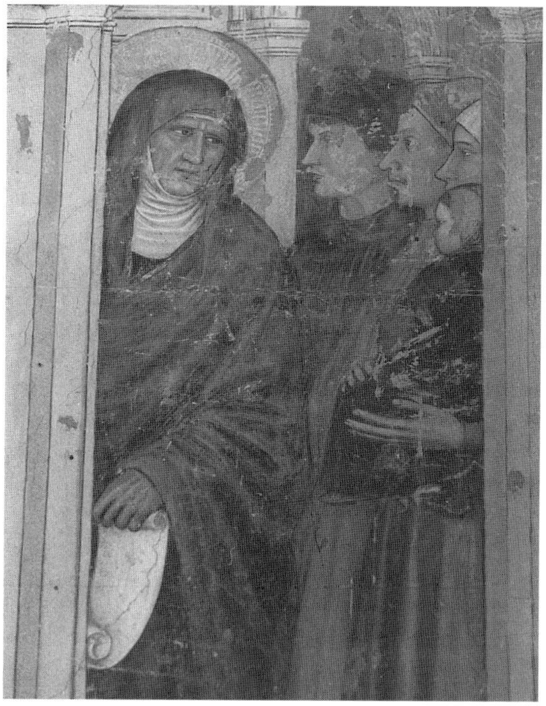

Plate 83 *Presentation in the Temple* (detail). Padua, Oratory of S. Giorgio.

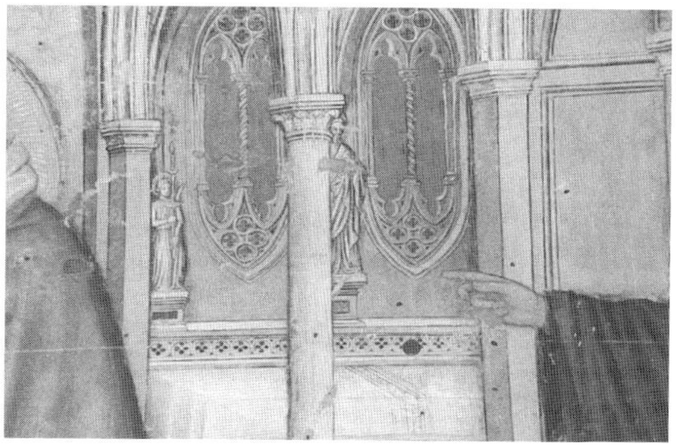

Plate 84 *Presentation in the Temple* (detail). Padua, Oratory of S. Giorgio.

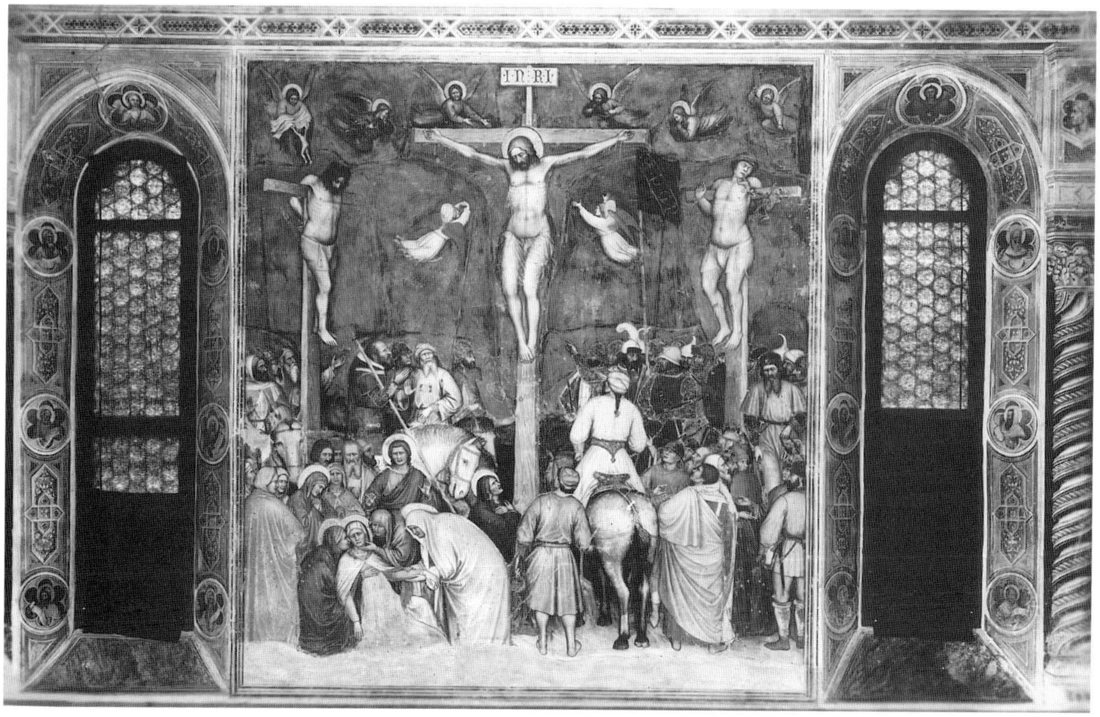

Plate 85 Padua, Oratory of S. Giorgio. Lower part of altar wall.

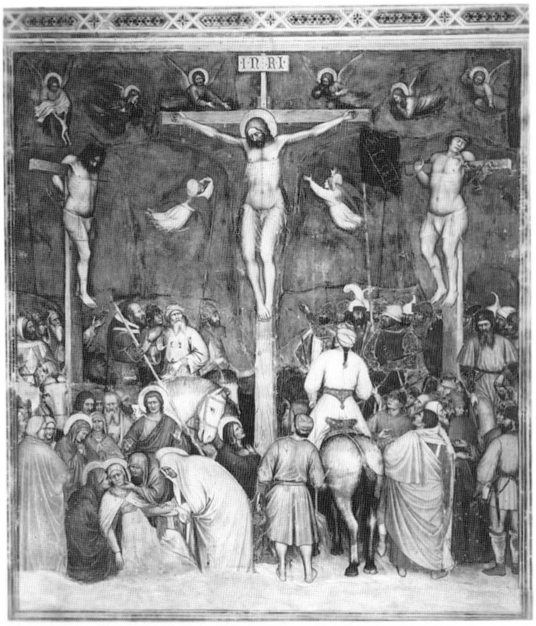

Plate 86 *Crucifixion*. Padua, Oratory of S. Giorgio.

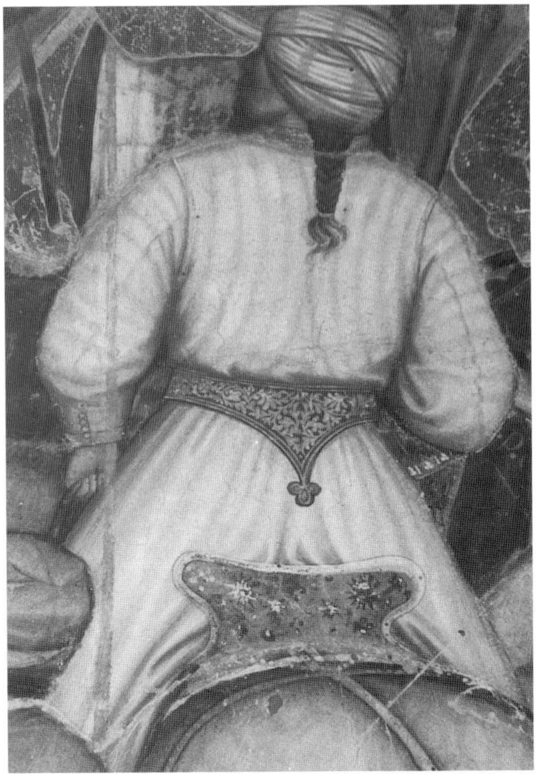

Plate 87 *Crucifixion* (detail). Padua, Oratory of S. Giorgio.

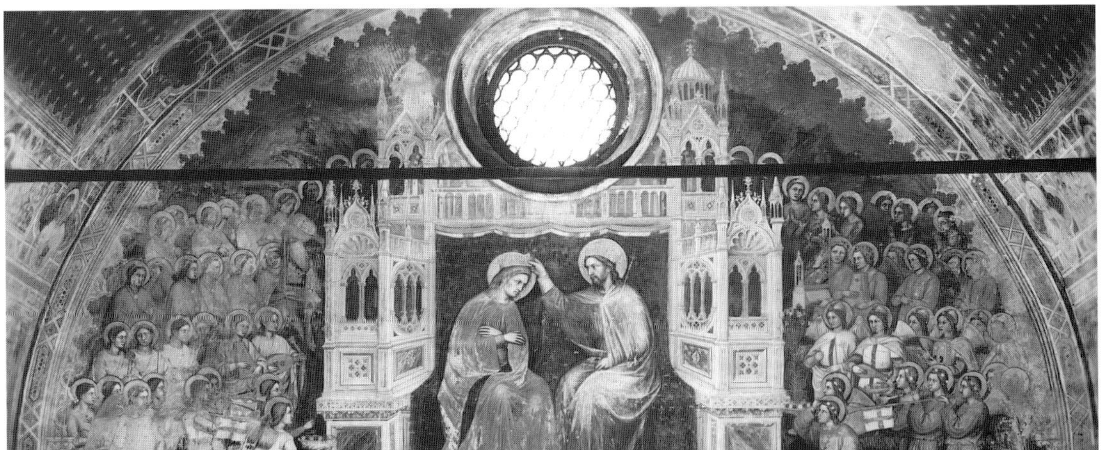

Plate 88 *Coronation of the Virgin*. Padua, Oratory of S. Giorgio.

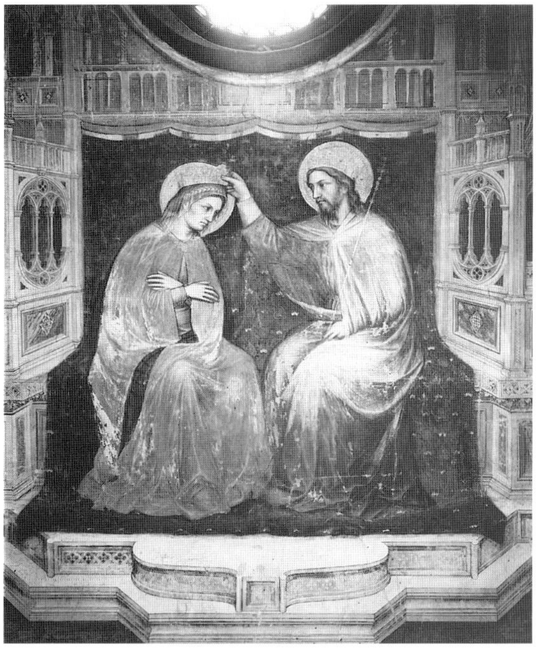

Plate 89 *Coronation of the Virgin* (detail). Padua, Oratory of S. Giorgio.

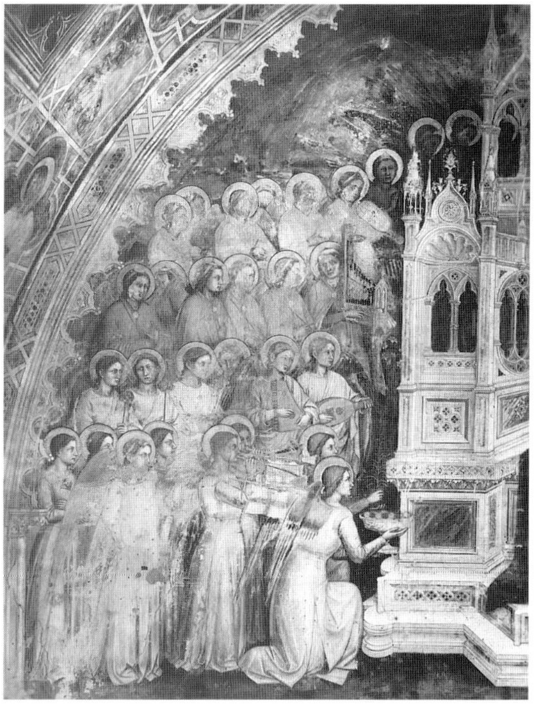

Plate 90 *Coronation of the Virgin* (detail). Padua, Oratory of S. Giorgio.

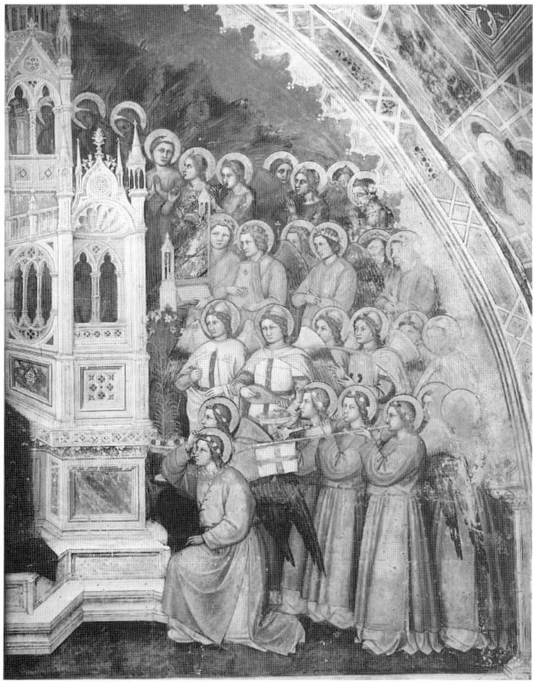

Plate 91 *Coronation of the Virgin* (detail). Padua, Oratory of S. Giorgio.

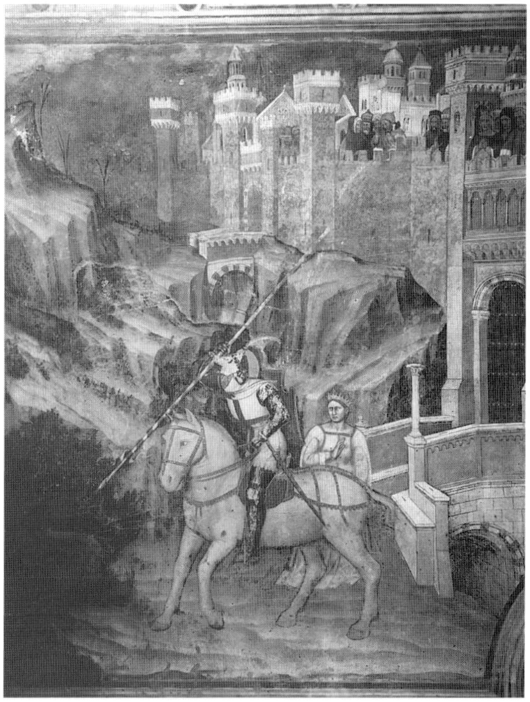

Plate 92 *St George and the Dragon*. Padua, Oratory of S. Giorgio.

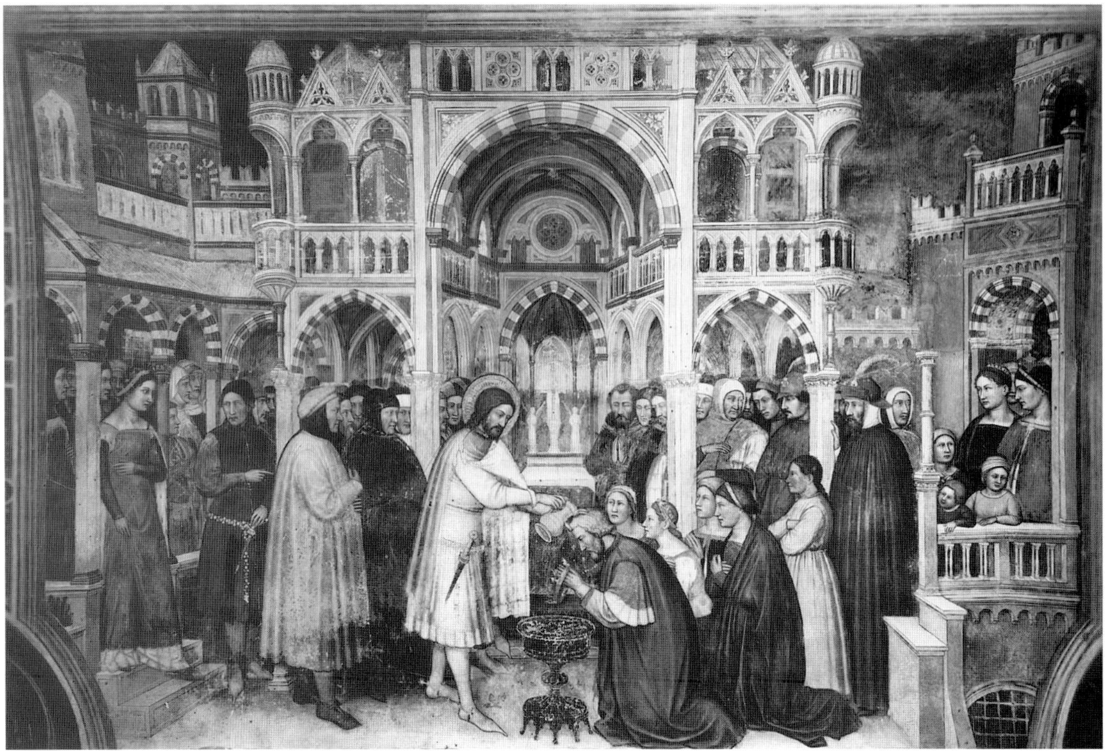

Plate 93 *St George Baptising King Sevio and his Court*. Padua, Oratory of S. Giorgio.

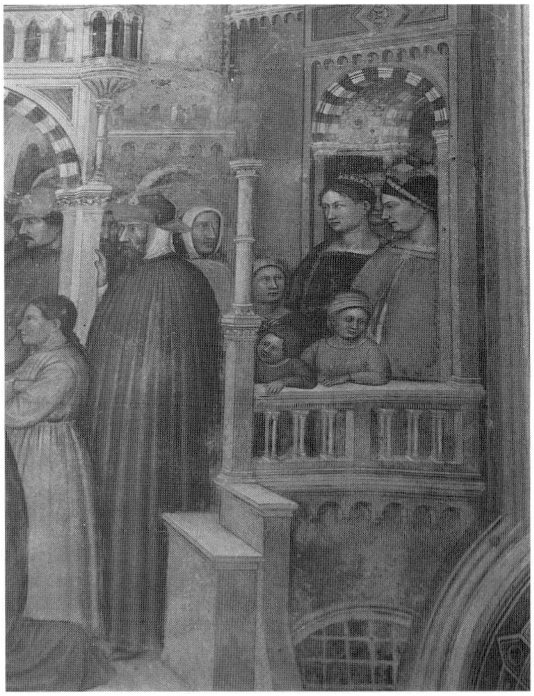

Plate 94 *St George Baptising King Sevio and his Court* (detail). Padua, Oratory of S. Giorgio.

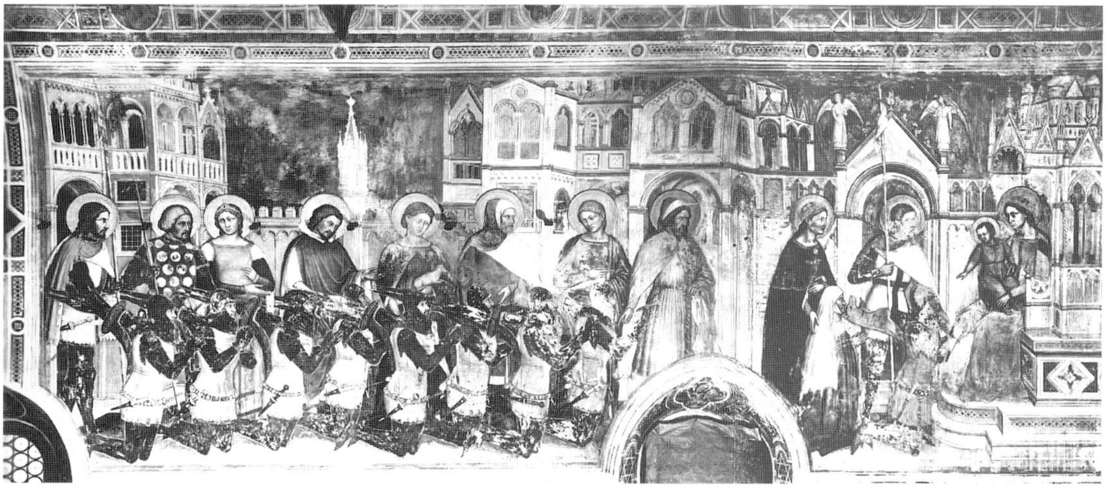

Plate 95 Votive fresco. Padua, Oratory of S. Giorgio.

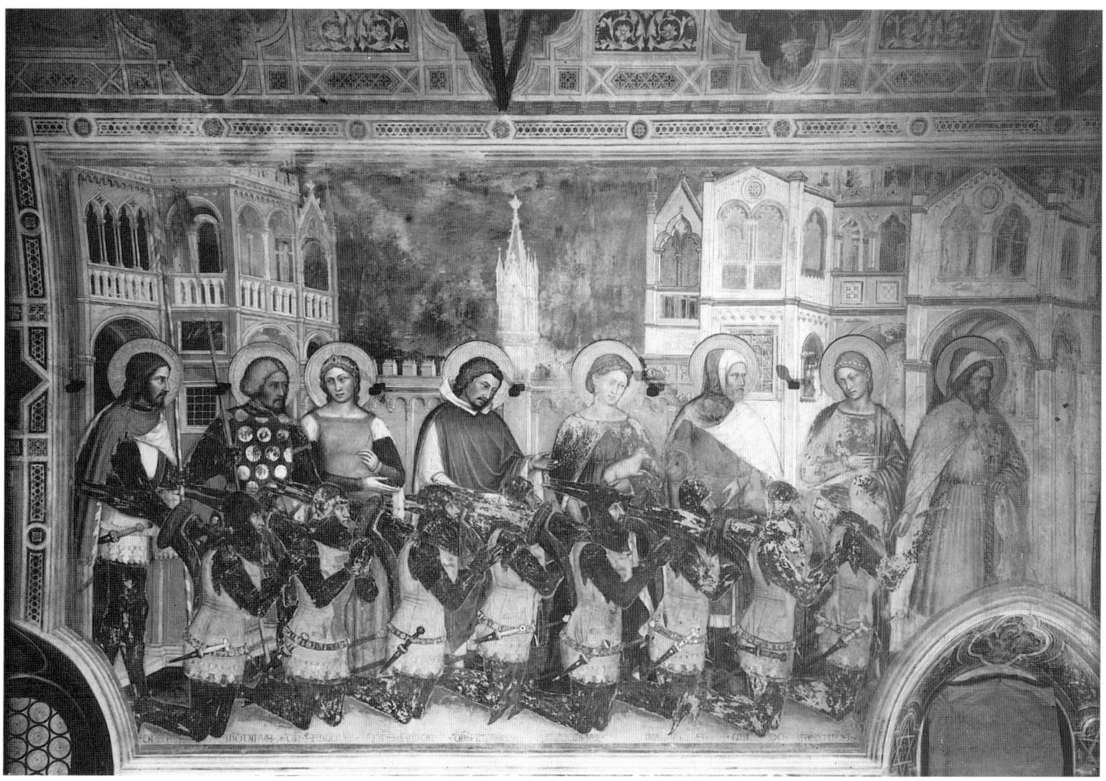

Plate 96 Votive fresco (detail). Padua, Oratory of S. Giorgio.

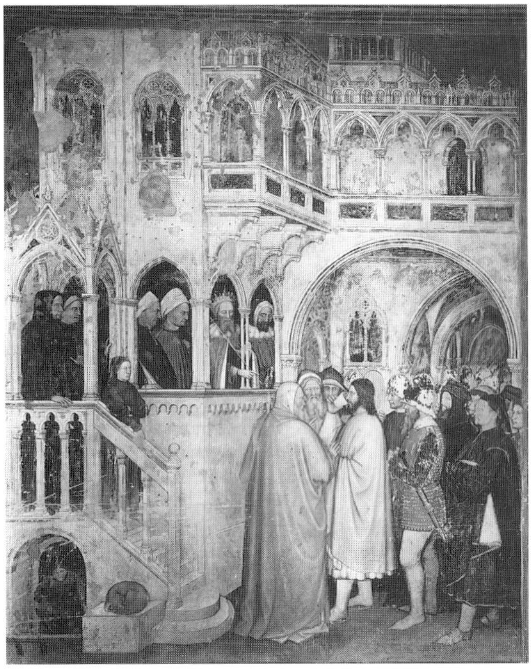

Plate 97 *St George Condemned to Drink Poison*. Padua, Oratory of S. Giorgio.

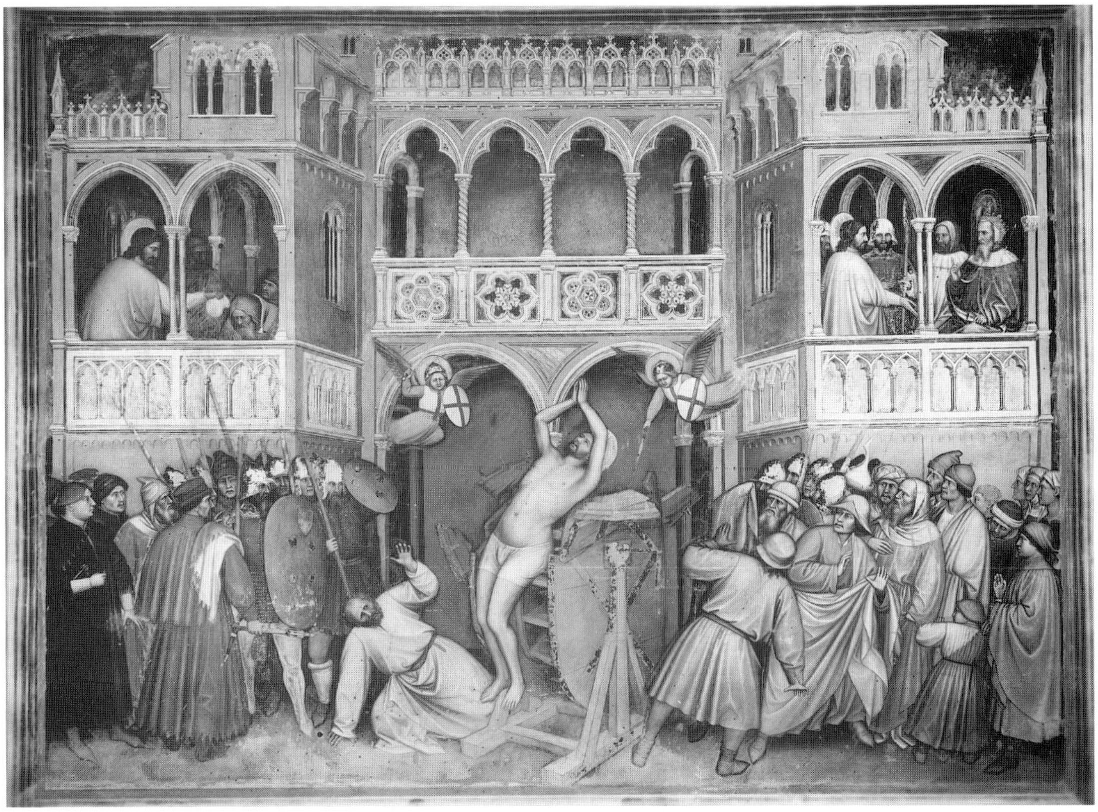

Plate 98 *St George on the Wheel*. Padua, Oratory of S. Giorgio.

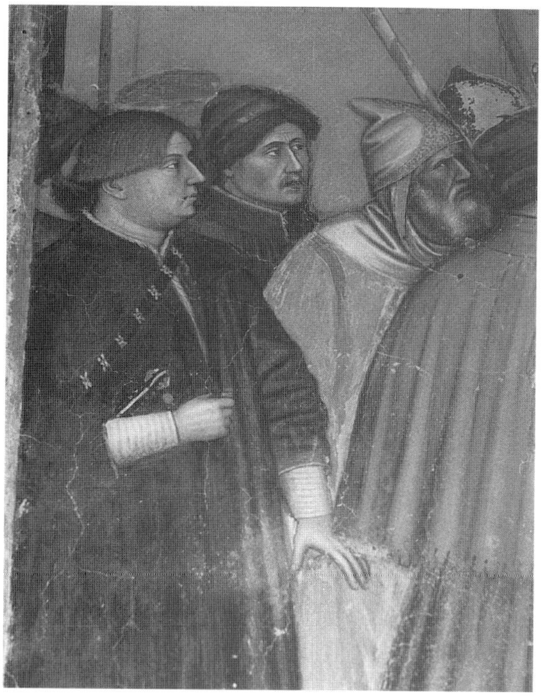

Plate 99 *St George on the Wheel* (detail). Padua, Oratory of S. Giorgio.

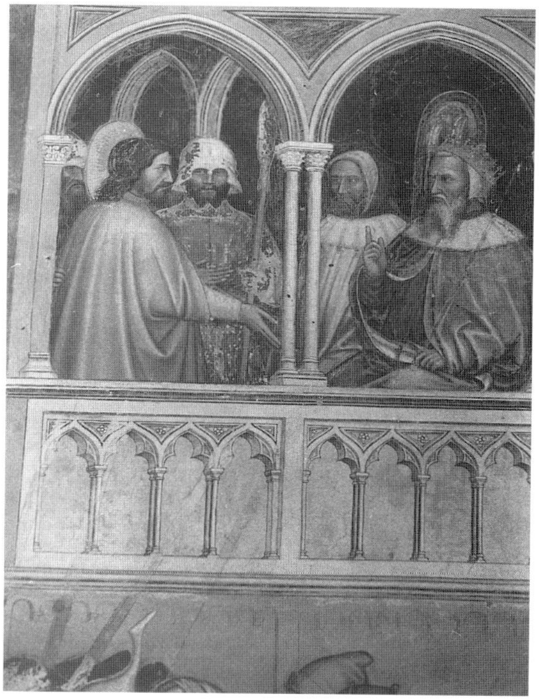

Plate 100 *St George on the Wheel* (detail). Padua, Oratory of S. Giorgio.

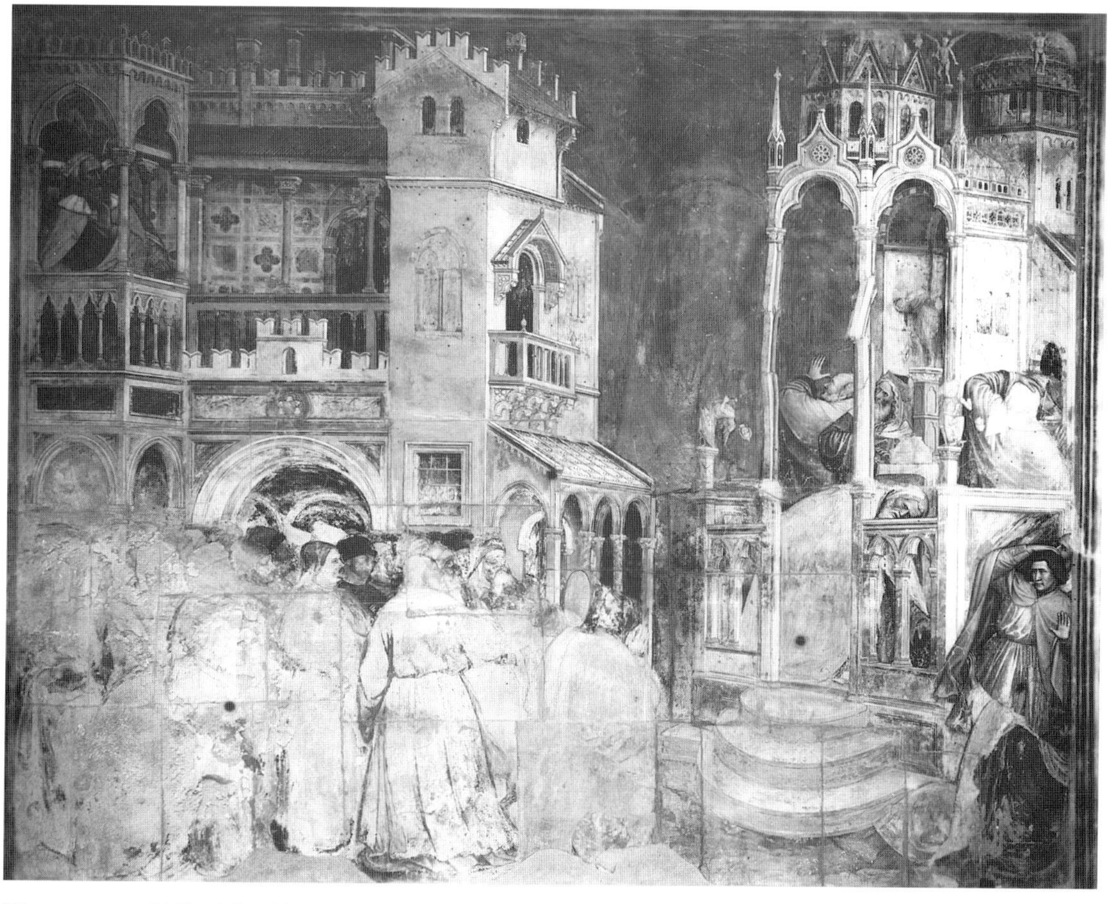

Plate 101 *Fall of the Idols*. Padua, Oratory of S. Giorgio.

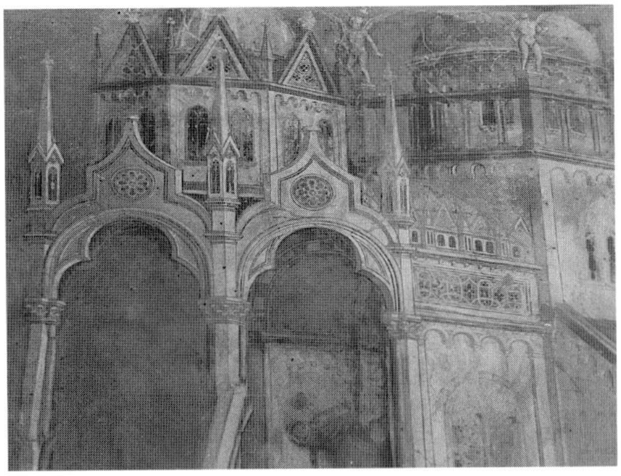

Plate 102 *Fall of the Idols* (detail). Padua, Oratory of S. Giorgio.

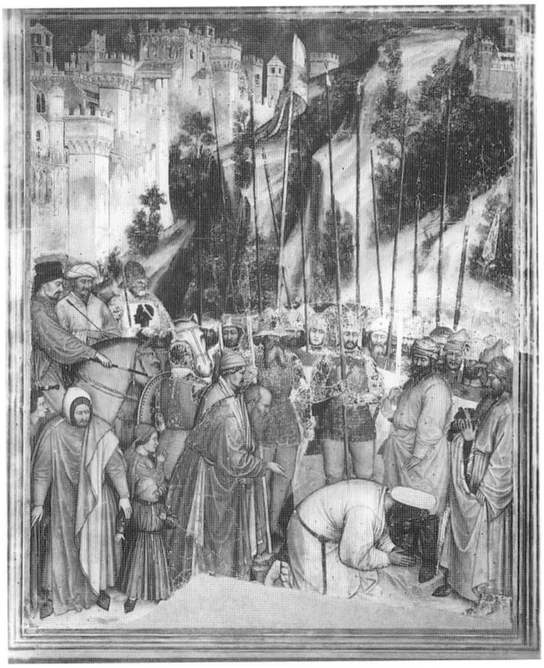

Plate 103 *Execution of St George*. Padua, Oratory of S. Giorgio.

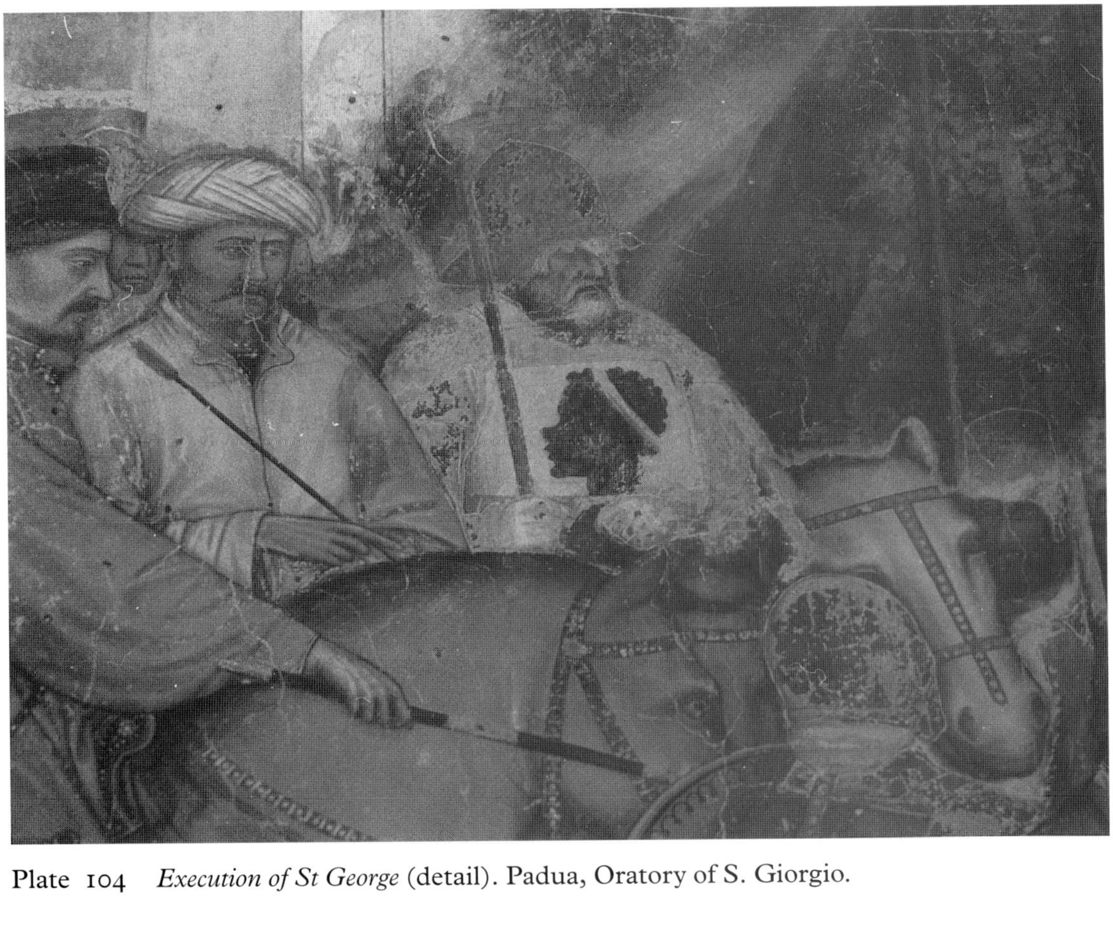

Plate 104 *Execution of St George* (detail). Padua, Oratory of S. Giorgio.

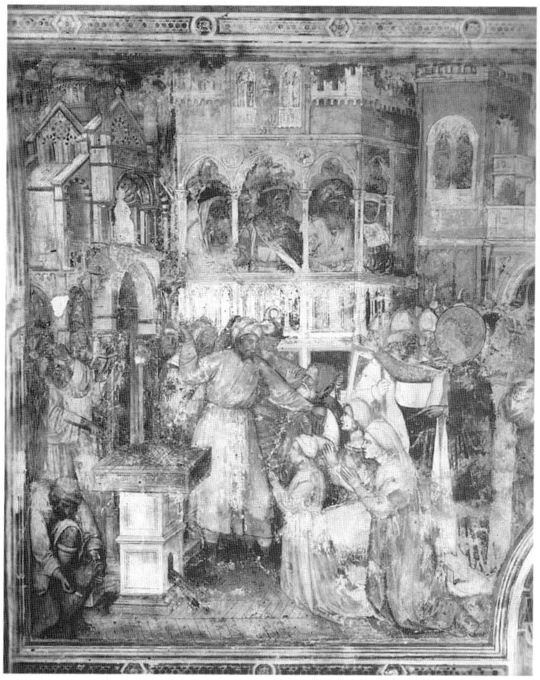

Plate 105 *St Catherine Refusing to Worship Pagan Idols*. Padua, Oratory of S. Giorgio.

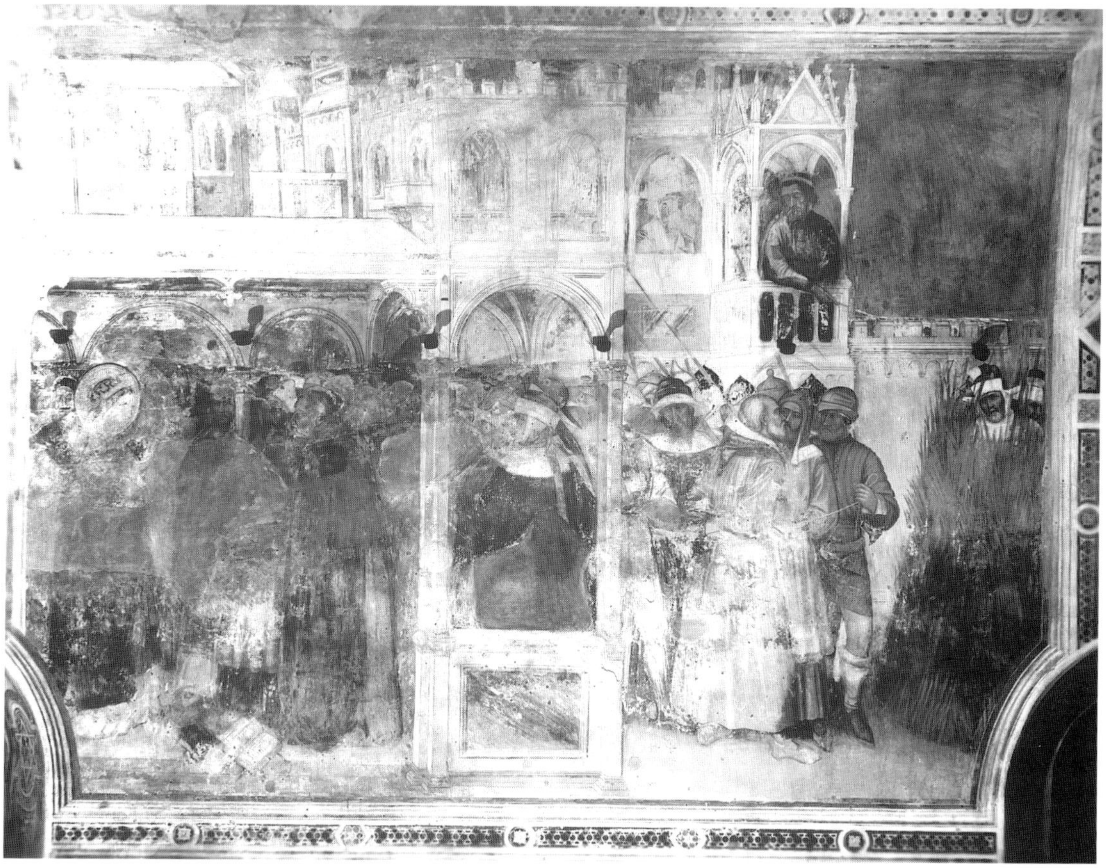

Plate 106 *St Catherine Converting the Pagan Philosophers; Burning of the Philosophers*. Padua, Oratory of S. Giorgio.

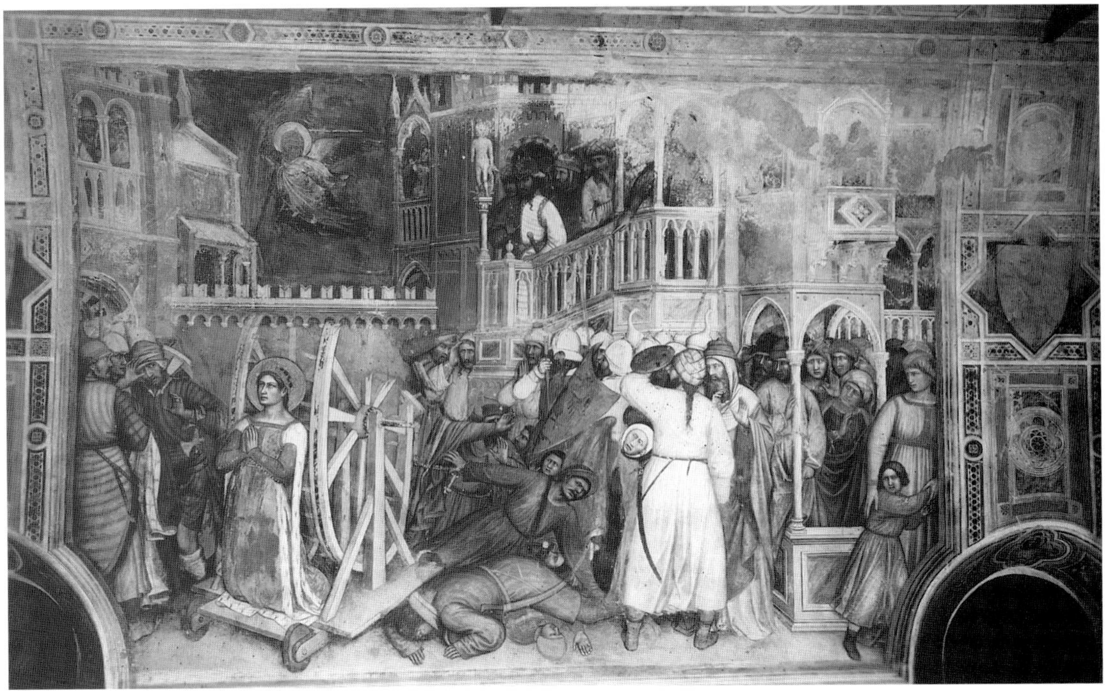

Plate 107 *St Catherine on the Wheel*. Padua, Oratory of S. Giorgio.

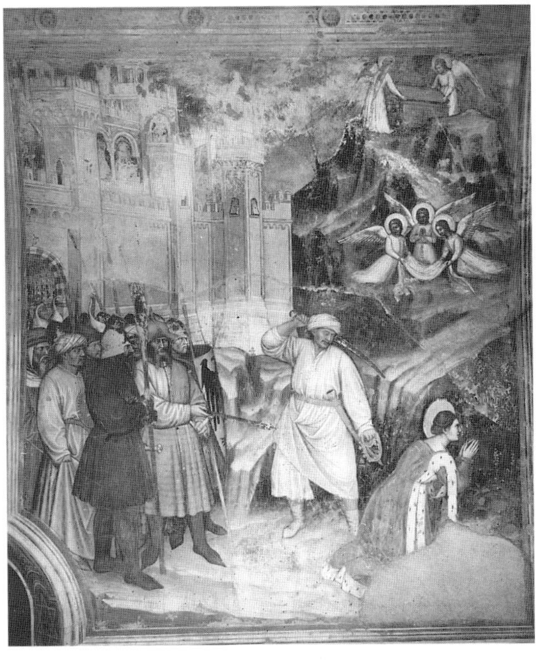

Plate 108 *Execution of St Catherine; Her Burial on Mt Sinai*. Padua, Oratory of S. Giorgio.

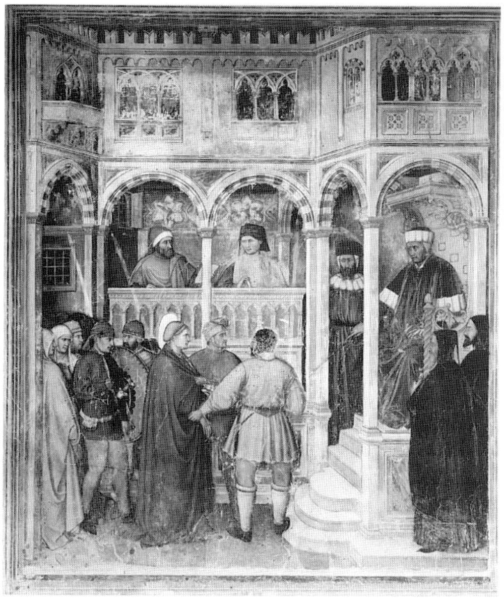

Plate 109 *St Lucy Before Judge Pascasio*. Padua, Oratory of S. Giorgio.

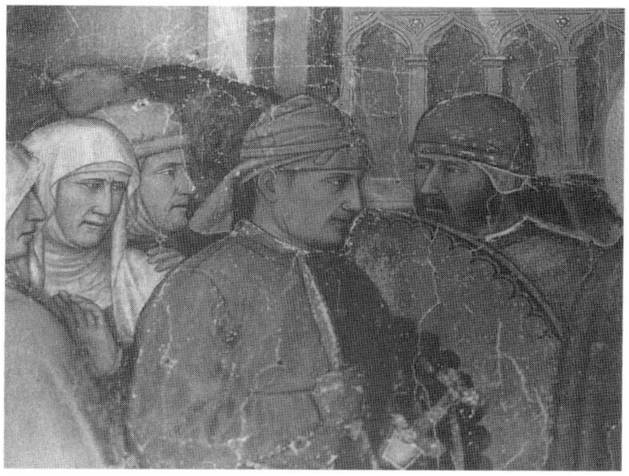

Plate 110 *St Lucy Before Judge Pascasio* (detail). Padua, Oratory of S. Giorgio.

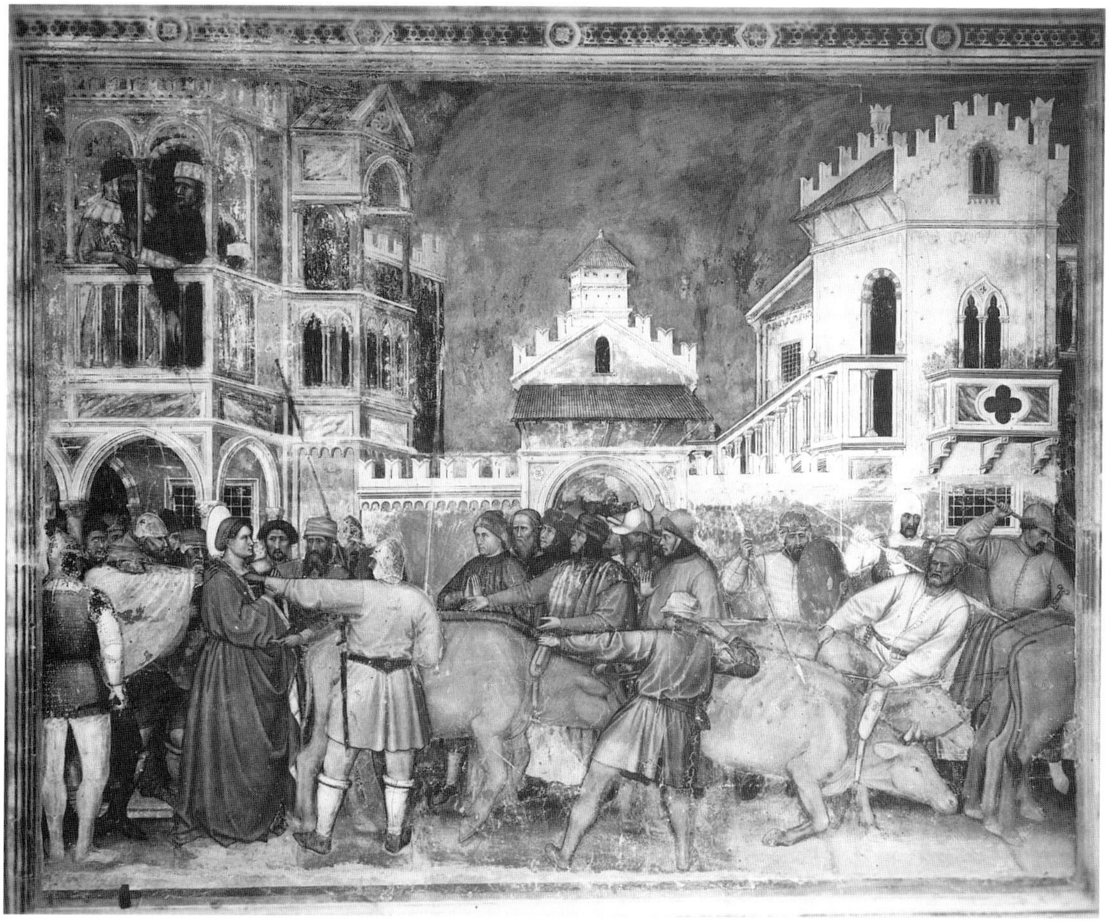

Plate 111 *Miracle of St Lucy and the Bulls*. Padua, Oratory of S. Giorgio.

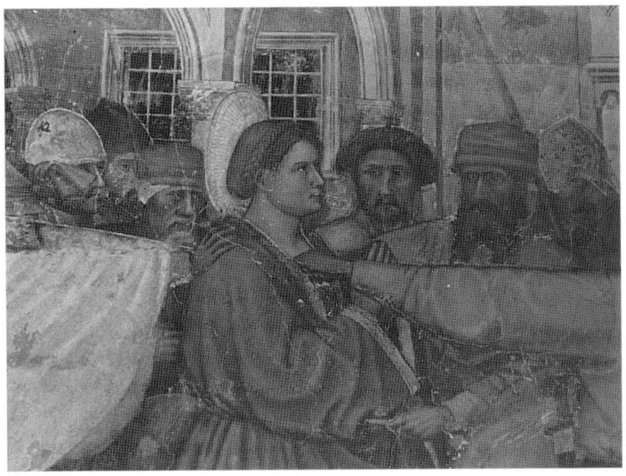

Plate 112 *Miracle of St Lucy and the Bulls* (detail). Padua, Oratory of S. Giorgio.

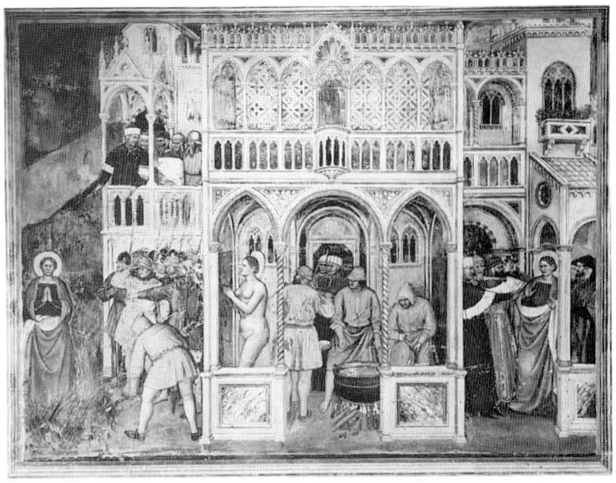

Plate 113 *Tortures of St Lucy*. Padua, Oratory of S. Giorgio.

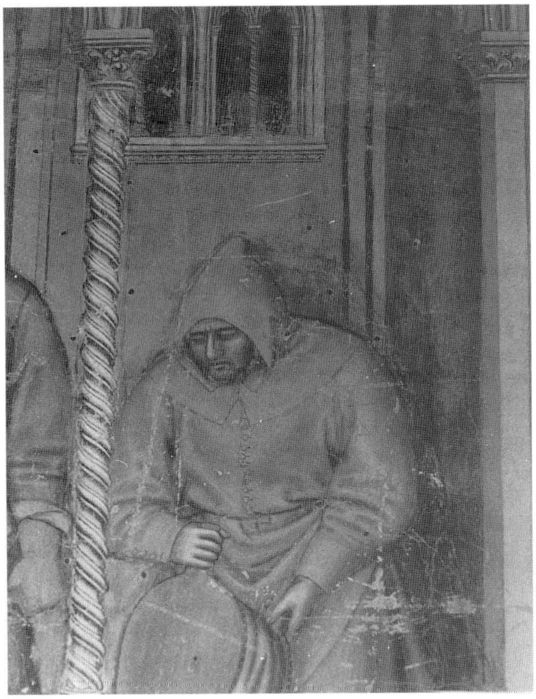

Plate 114 *Tortures of St Lucy* (detail). Padua, Oratory of S. Giorgio.

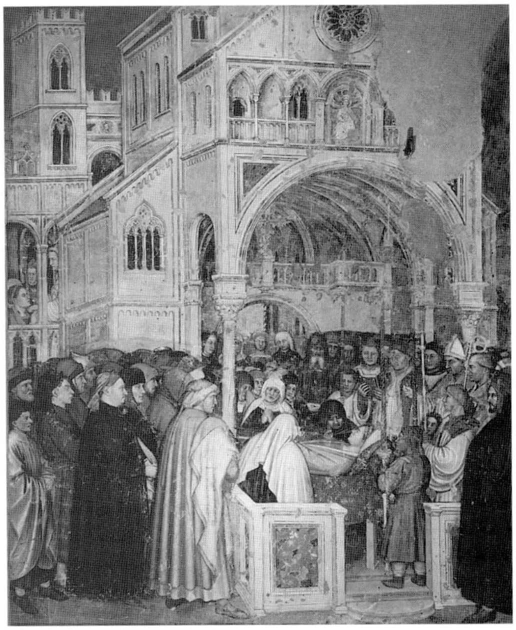

Plate 115 *Funeral of St Lucy*. Padua, Oratory of S. Giorgio.

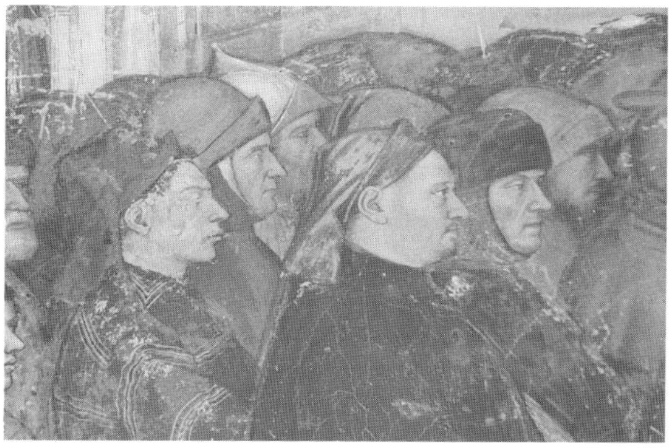

Plate 116 *Funeral of St Lucy* (detail). Padua, Oratory of S. Giorgio.

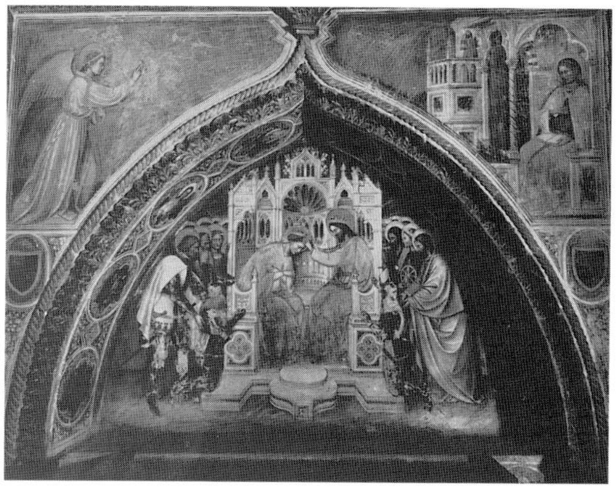

Plate 117 Dotto tomb frescoes (destroyed 1944). Formerly Padua, Eremitani.

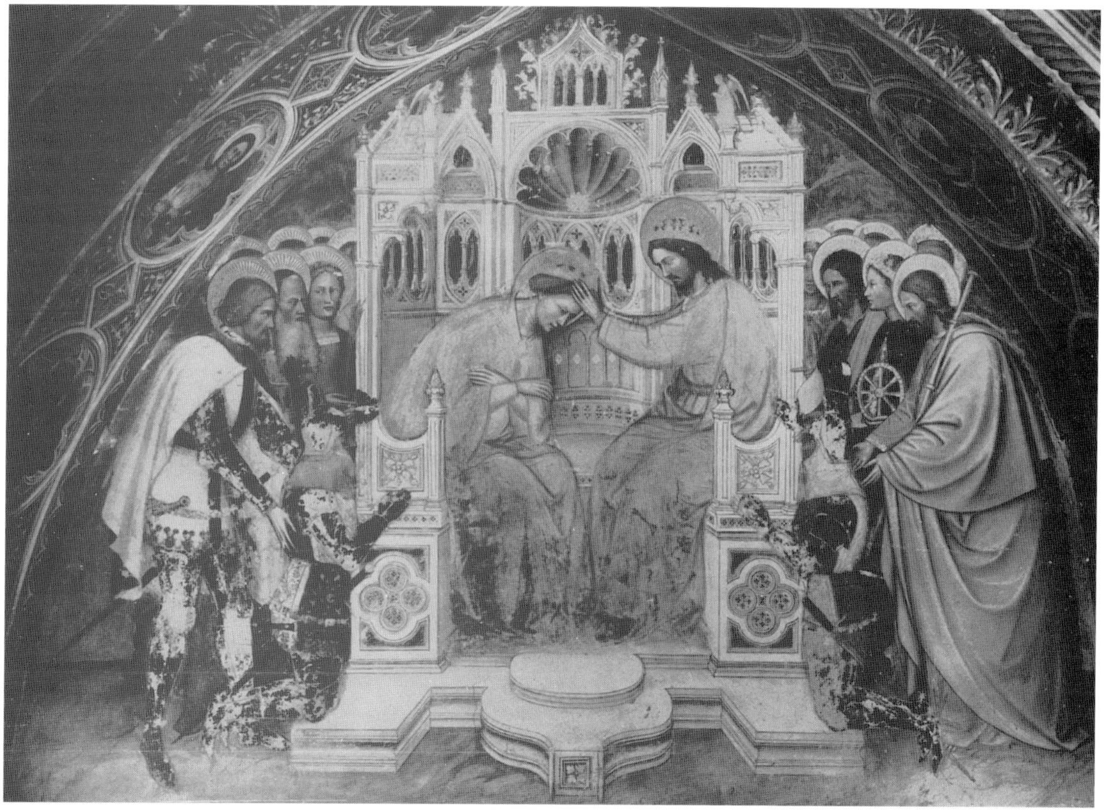

Plate 118 *Coronation of the Virgin* (destroyed 1944). Formerly Padua, Eremitani.

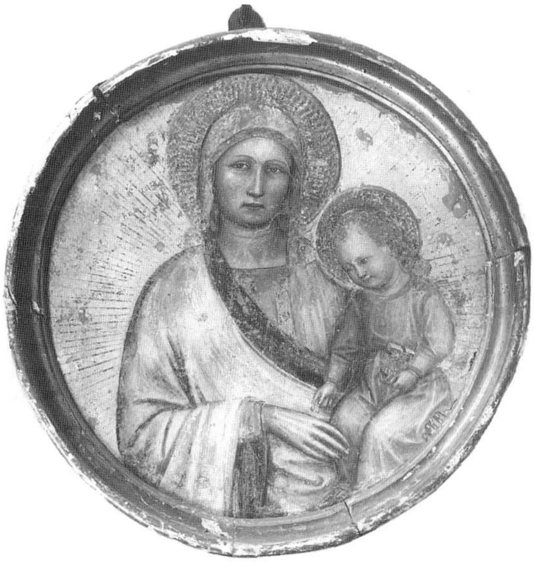

Plate 119 *Madonna and Child*. Padua, Eremitani.

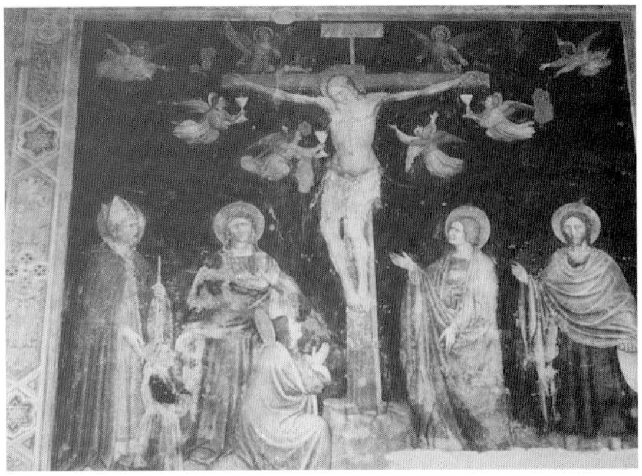

Plate 120a *Crucifixion*. Verona, S. Zeno Maggiore.

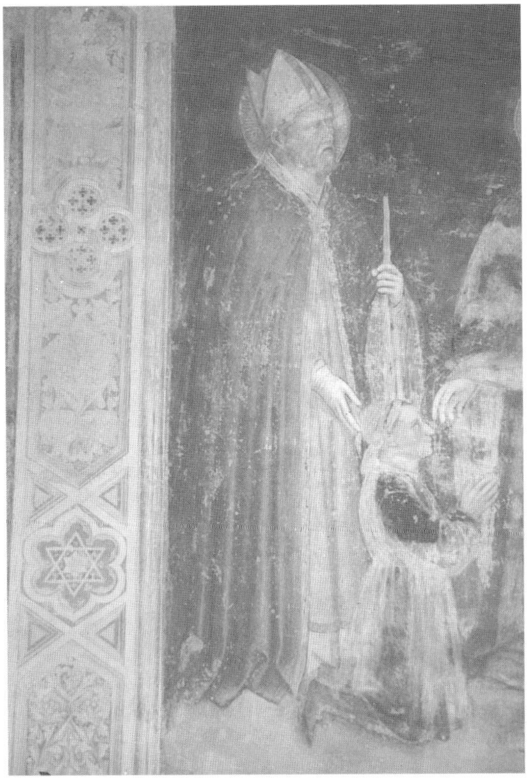

Plate 120b *Crucifixion* (detail). Verona, S. Zeno Maggiore.

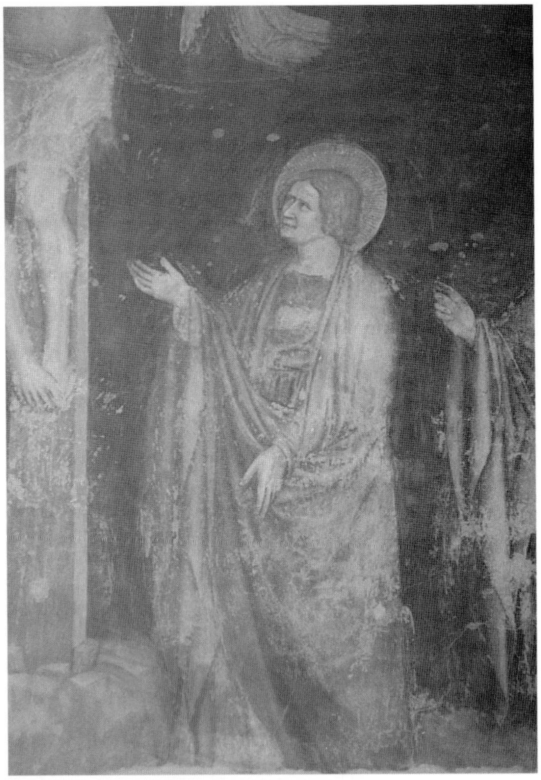

Plate 120c *Crucifixion* (detail). Verona, S. Zeno Maggiore.

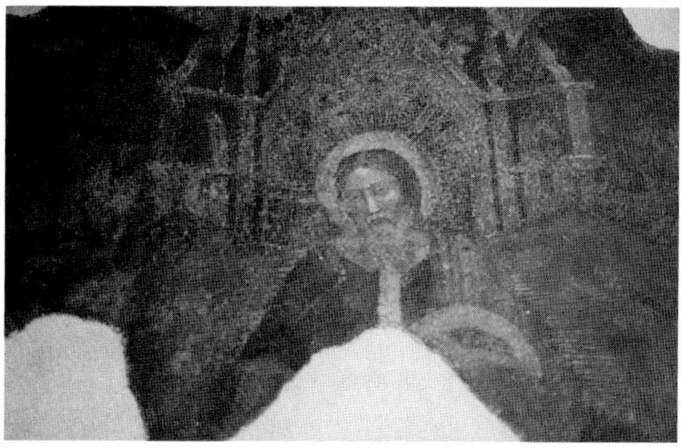

Plate 121a Fracastoro *Coronation of the Virgin* (detail). Verona, Castelvecchio.

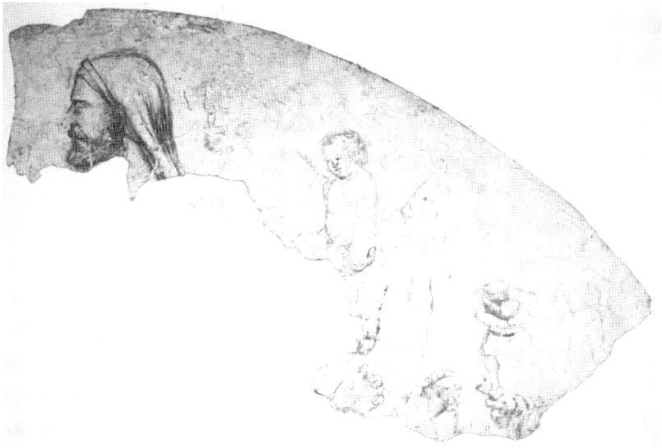

Plate 121b Sinopia of Fracastoro *Coronation*. Verona, Castelvecchio.

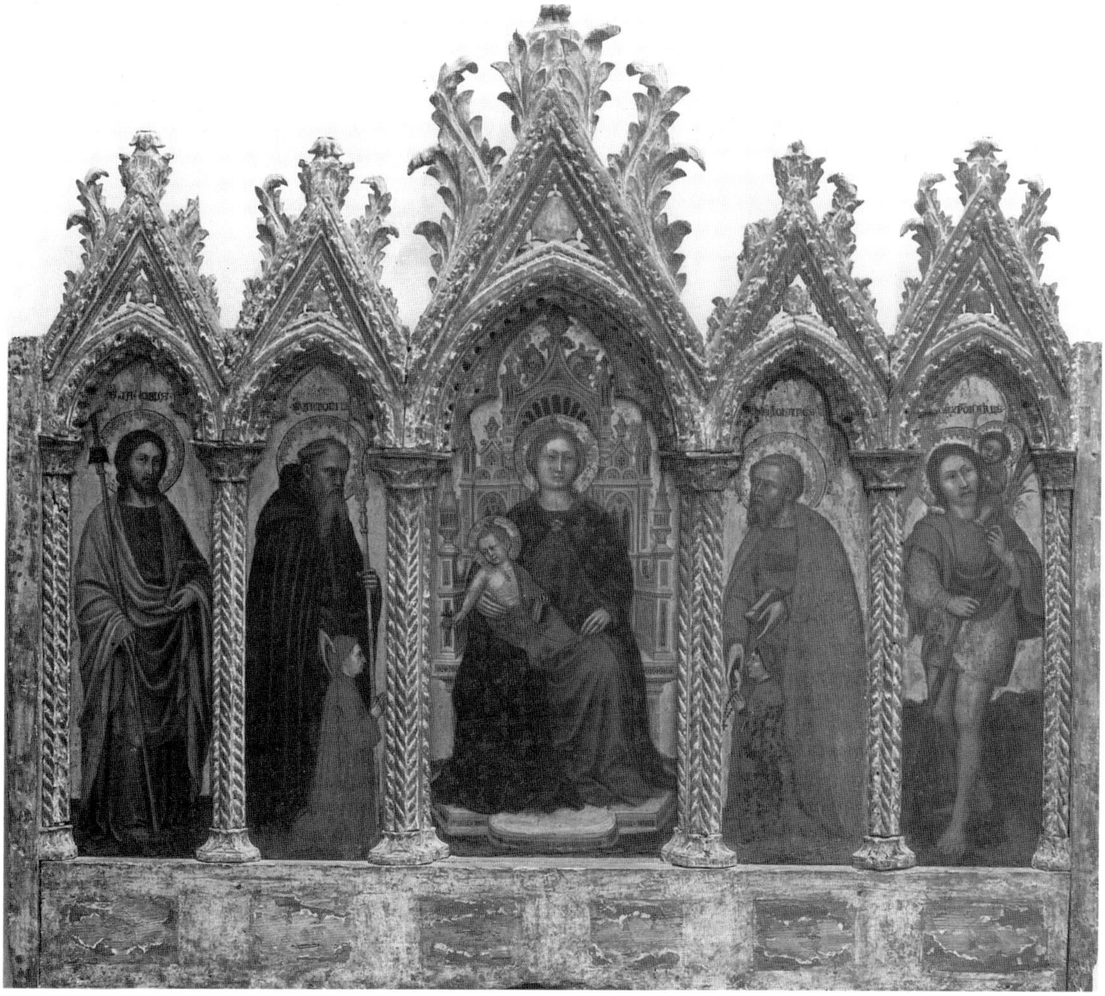

Plate 122 *Madonna and Child with Four Saints and Two Donors* (the Boi polyptych). Verona, Castelvecchio.

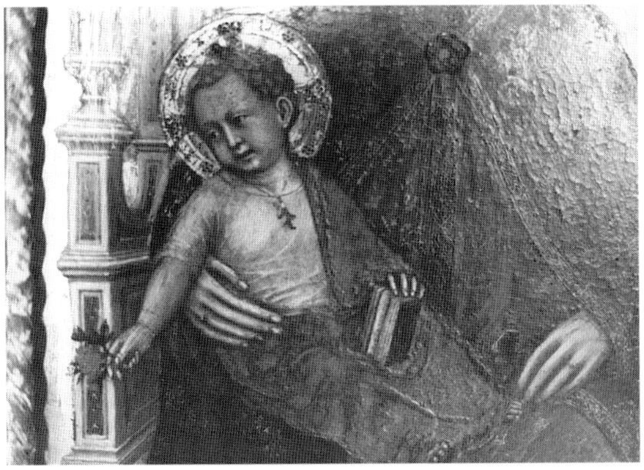

Plate 123a Boi polyptych (detail): *Christ*. Verona, Castelvecchio.

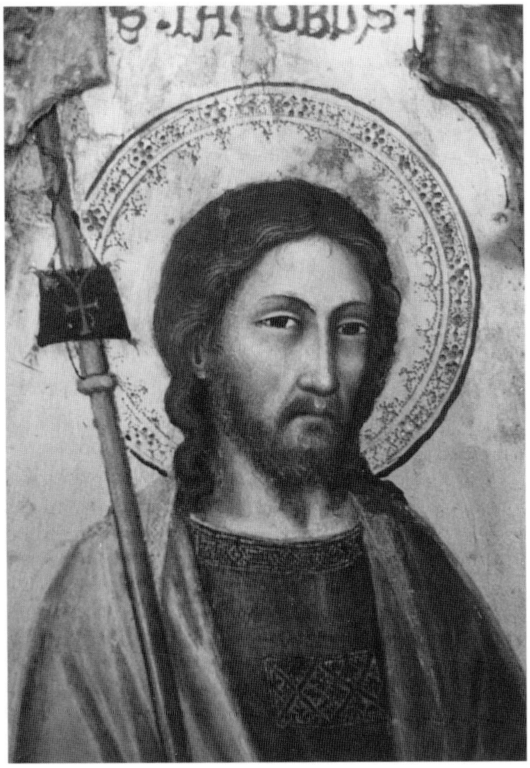

Plate 123b Boi polyptych (detail): *St James*. Verona, Castelvecchio.

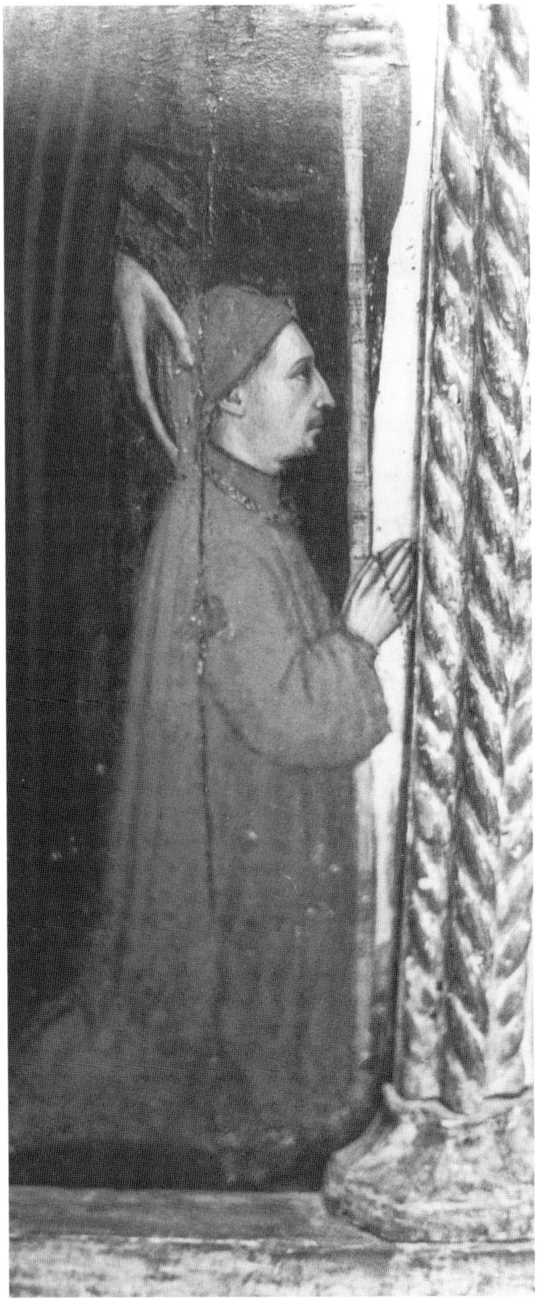

Plate 123c Boi polyptych (detail): *Male Donor*. Verona, Castelvecchio.

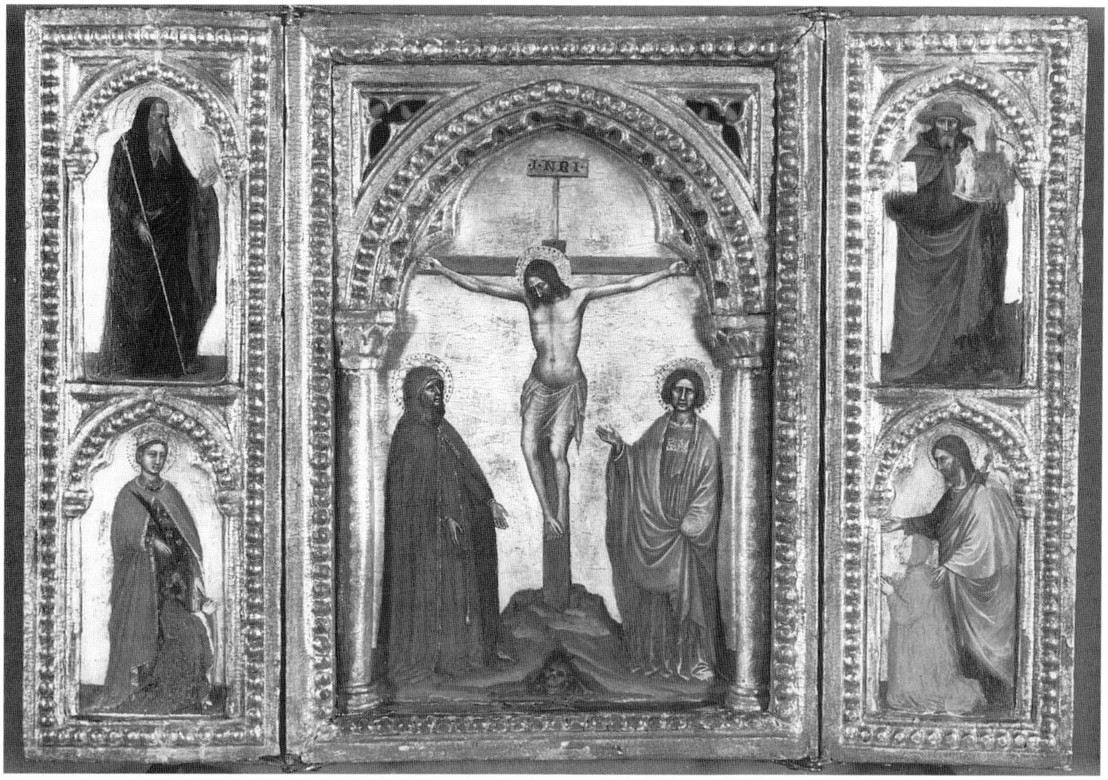

Plate 124 *Crucifixion* triptych. Virginia Museum of Fine Arts, Richmond, VA. The Arthur and Margaret Glasgow Fund.

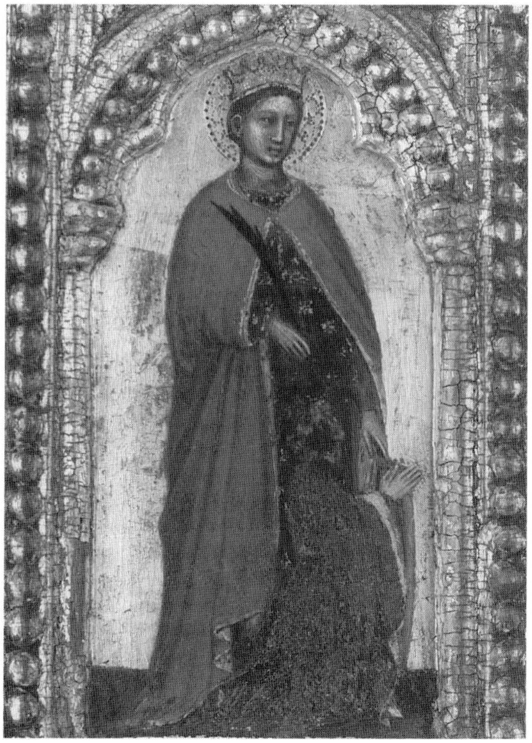

Plate 125 *Crucifixion* triptych (detail): *St Catherine and a Female Donor*. Virginia Museum of Fine Arts, Richmond, VA. The Arthur and Margaret Glasgow Fund.

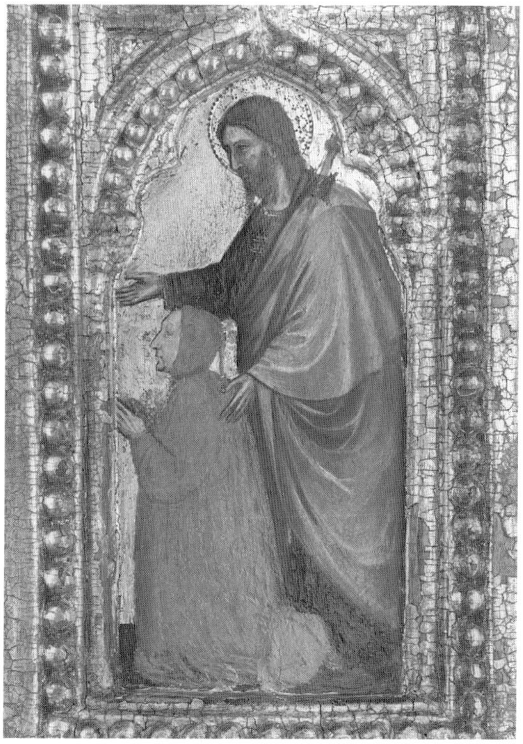

Plate 126 *Crucifixion* triptych (detail): *St James and a Male Donor*. Virginia Museum of Fine Arts, Richmond, VA. The Arthur and Margaret Glasgow Fund.

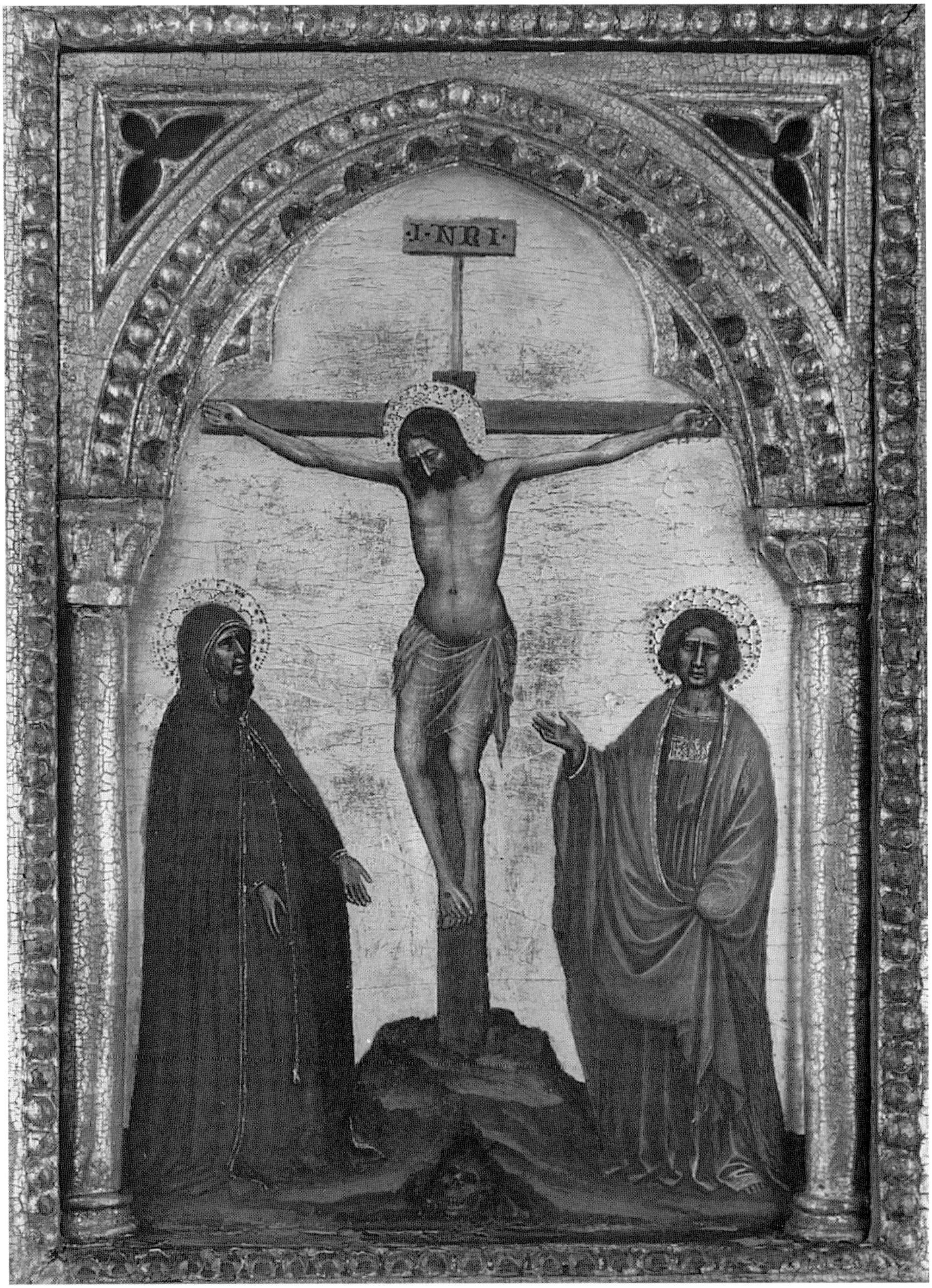

Plate 127 *Crucifixion* triptych (detail): *Crucifixion* Virginia Museum of Fine Arts, Richmond, VA. The Arthur and Margaret Glasgow Fund.